The Cambridge Handbook of the Changing Nature of Work

This handbook provides an overview of the research on the changing nature of work and workers by marshaling interdisciplinary research to summarize the empirical evidence and provide documentation of what has actually changed. Connections are explored between the changing nature of work and macro-level trends in technological change, income inequality, global labor markets, labor unions, organizational forms, and skill polarization, among others. This edited volume also reviews evidence for changes in workers, including generational change (or lack thereof), that has accumulated across domains. Based on documented changes in work and worker behavior, the handbook derives implications for a range of management functions, such as selection, performance management, leadership, workplace ethics, and employee wellbeing. This evaluation of the extent of changes and their impact gives guidance on what best practices should be put in place to harness these developments to achieve success.

BRIAN J. HOFFMAN is Professor and Chair of the Industrial-Organizational Psychology Program at the University of Georgia, USA, and Fellow of the Society for Industrial-Organizational Psychology.

MINDY K. SHOSS is Associate Professor of Psychology at the University of Central Florida, USA, and Honorary Fellow of Australian Catholic University, Australia.

LAUREN A. WEGMAN graduated from the University of Georgia, USA, where her research focus was the changing nature of work. She now works in the people analytics field.

The Cambridge Handbook of the Changing Nature of Work

Edited by

Brian J. Hoffman
University of Georgia

Mindy K. Shoss
University of Central Florida

Lauren A. Wegman
University of Georgia

CAMBRIDGE
UNIVERSITY PRESS

University Printing House, Cambridge CB2 8BS, United Kingdom

One Liberty Plaza, 20th Floor, New York, NY 10006, USA

477 Williamstown Road, Port Melbourne, VIC 3207, Australia

314–321, 3rd Floor, Plot 3, Splendor Forum, Jasola District Centre, New Delhi – 110025, India

79 Anson Road, #06–04/06, Singapore 079906

Cambridge University Press is part of the University of Cambridge.

It furthers the University's mission by disseminating knowledge in the pursuit of education, learning, and research at the highest international levels of excellence.

www.cambridge.org
Information on this title: www.cambridge.org/9781108417631
DOI: 10.1017/9781108278034

© Cambridge University Press 2020

This publication is in copyright. Subject to statutory exception and to the provisions of relevant collective licensing agreements, no reproduction of any part may take place without the written permission of Cambridge University Press.

First published 2020

A catalogue record for this publication is available from the British Library.

Library of Congress Cataloging-in-Publication Data
Names: Hoffman, Brian J., editor. | Shoss, Mindy K., 1986– editor. | Wegman, Lauren A., 1986– editor.
Title: The Cambridge handbook of the changing nature of work / Edited by Brian J. Hoffman, University of Georgia, Mindy K. Shoss, University of Central Florida, Lauren A. Wegman, University of Georgia.
Other titles: Handbook of the changing nature of work
Description: United Kingdom ; New York, NY : Cambridge University Press, 2020. | Series: Cambridge handbooks in psychology | Includes bibliographical references and index.
Identifiers: LCCN 2019038884 (print) | LCCN 2019038885 (ebook) | ISBN 9781108417631 (hardback) | ISBN 9781108405539 (paperback) | ISBN 9781108278034 (epub)
Subjects: LCSH: Work–Social aspects. | Quality of work life. | Employees–Technological innovations on.
Classification: LCC HD6955 .C27 2020 (print) | LCC HD6955 (ebook) | DDC 331–dc23
LC record available at https://lccn.loc.gov/2019038884
LC ebook record available at https://lccn.loc.gov/2019038885

ISBN 978-1-108-41763-1 Hardback
ISBN 978-1-108-40553-9 Paperback

Cambridge University Press has no responsibility for the persistence or accuracy of URLs for external or third-party internet websites referred to in this publication and does not guarantee that any content on such websites is, or will remain, accurate or appropriate.

Contents

List of Figures	*page* viii
List of Tables	ix
List of Contributors	x

Part I Introduction to the Changing Nature of Work

1 The Changing Nature of Work and Workers: An Introduction
   BRIAN J. HOFFMAN, MINDY K. SHOSS, AND LAUREN A. WEGMAN   3

2 Inappropriate Inferences from Generational Research
   DAVID P. COSTANZA, LISA M. FINKELSTEIN,
   RUTH A. IMOSE, AND DANIEL M. RAVID   20

3 What Has Changed and What Has Not?
   KEVIN R. MURPHY AND WARREN TIERNEY   42

Part II What Has Changed?

4 Changes in Technology
   JEROD WHITE, TARA BEHREND, AND IAN SIDERITS   69

5 The Changing Nature of Work: A Global Perspective
   CHRISTOPHER CLOTT   101

6 Changes in Occupations, Jobs, and Skill Polarization
   ARTHUR SAKAMOTO, CHANGHWAN KIM, AND CHRISTOPHER
   R. TAMBORINI   133

7 Changes in the Legal Landscape
   CHESTER HANVEY AND KAYO SADY   154

8 The Rise and Decline of Organized Labor in the United States: American Unions from Truman to Trump
   RAYMOND L. HOGLER   173

9 Changes in Organizational Income Inequality: The Causes and Consequences
   LIXIN JIANG   192

10 Work and Employment in Fluid Organizational Forms
   JÖRG SYDOW AND MARKUS HELFEN   214

11 Changes in Worker Demographics
   SHANNON CHENG, ABBY CORRINGTON, EDEN KING, AND
   LINNEA NG   237

12 Generational Changes in Personality, Values, and Abilities
   JORGE LUMBRERAS AND W. KEITH CAMPBELL   261

13 Changes in Work Behavior Patterns
   SARA JANSEN PERRY, EMILY M. DAVID, AND LARS U. JOHNSON   274

Part III Implications for Talent Management and Impact on Employees

14 Implications of the Changing Nature of Work for Selection
   BRIAN D. LYONS, ALEXANDER ALONSO, ROBERT H. MOORMAN,
   AND ASHLEY MILLER   297

15 Implications of the Changing Nature of Work for Recruitment and Retention
   WAYNE F. CASCIO   318

16 Performance Management and the Changing Nature of Work
   DEIDRA J. SCHLEICHER AND HEIDI M. BAUMANN   340

17 Implications of the Changing Nature of Work for Training
   TIFFANY M. BISBEY, ALLISON TRAYLOR, AND EDUARDO SALAS   364

18 Leader Behaviors and the Changing Nature of Work
   JOHN W. MICHEL AND GARY YUKL   383

19 The Changing Nature of Teams: Recommendations for Managing Twenty-First-Century Teamwork
   JUSTIN M. JONES, GOURI MOHAN, HAYLEY M. TRAINER, AND
   DOROTHY R. CARTER   406

20 Managing Employees across the Working Lifespan
   CORT W. RUDOLPH AND HANNES ZACHER   425

21 Implications of the Changing Nature of Work for Employee Attitudes and Work Perceptions
   LAUREN A. WEGMAN AND BRIAN J. HOFFMAN   446

22	Implications of the Changing Nature of Work for the Interface between Work and Nonwork Roles JEFFREY H. GREENHAUS AND GERARD A. CALLALAN	467
23	Implications of the Changing Nature of Work for Employee Health and Safety ROBERT R. SINCLAIR, JOHN MORGAN, AND ELYSSA JOHNSON	489
24	The Dark Side of Workplace Technology: Cyber-Related Counterproductive Work Behavior, Workplace Mistreatment, and Violation of Workplace Ethics DAVID J. HOWARD AND PAUL E. SPECTOR	509
25	Implications of the Changing Nature of Work for the Employee–Organization Relationship MINDY K. SHOSS, ROBERT EISENBERGER, JUSEOB LEE, BLAINE A. LEWIS, DUSTIN MANEETHAI, XUEQI WEN, JIA YU, AND JIMMY ZHENG	532
26	The Future of Work MURIEL CLAUSON	555
27	Sustainability as a Driver of Organizational Change LORI FOSTER AND TELMA VIALE	583
	Index	619

Figures

1.1	Conceptual model of the changing nature of work	*page* 11
3.1	Proportion of US working population employed in agriculture	47
3.2	Proportion of nonfarm workforce who are union members	48
8.1	Union membership density percentage: 1950–2010	178
11.1	Changing gender demographics in the workforce: 1976–2016	238
11.2	Changing race and ethnicity demographics in the workforce: 1976–2016	240
11.3	Changing age demographics in the workforce: 1976–2016	242
23.1	Linking the organization of work to occupational health outcomes	492
25.1	Perceived job insecurity over time from responses to: "My job is secure."	542
25.2	Perceived job insecurity over time from responses to: "Do you worry about the possibility of losing your job?"	542

Tables

2.1	Summary of inferences, with exemplars, identified from the generations literature	page 25
3.1	Proportion of occupations in which specific abilities and skills are rated as important	53
3.2	Proportion of occupations in which specific work styles are rated as important	54
4.1	Technology characteristics and industry examples	73
6.1	Percentage employment of labor force in one-digit occupational categories by year	135
6.2	Percentage employment of the labor force in the quintile categorization of occupation by year and gender	137
6.3	Percentage employment in the quintile categorization of equivalized household income by year based on the 1980 quintile thresholds	138
6.4	Percentage employment in the quintile categorization of occupation by year and educational level	140
6.5	Percentage employment in the quintile categorization of occupation by year and race/ethnicity	143
6.6	Change in three-digit occupation over three years in the survey of income and program participation	145
6.7	Changes in earnings and occupation over three years in the survey of income and program participation	146
6.8	Changes in earnings and occupation over three years in the survey of income and program participation	148
6.9A	Descriptive statistics	153
6.9B	Educational attainment by year and gender	153
10.1	Characteristics of bureaucratic and post-bureaucratic organizations	218
12.1	Age, period and cohorts effects and generational differences	262
14.1	Nine competencies that address the changing nature of work	300
17.1	Nine best-practices for training effectiveness	368
17.2	Summary of training implications	376
18.1	Examples of leadership behaviors that are becoming more important	398
19.1	The changing nature of teamwork: recommendations for management	407
25.1	Key changes in employment practices since the 1970s	535
26.1	Potential for automation: summary of studies	566
27.1	The United Nations Sustainable Development Goals	586
27.2	Corporate action on the SDGs: examples from the transportation sector	593

Contributors

ALEXANDER ALONSO, Society for Human Resource Management, USA
HEIDI M. BAUMANN, Bradley University, USA
TARA BEHREND, The George Washington University, USA
TIFFANY M. BISBEY, Rice University, USA
GERARD A. CALLANAN, West Chester University, USA
W. KEITH CAMPBELL, The University of Georgia, USA
DOROTHY R. CARTER, The University of Georgia, USA
WAYNE F. CASCIO, University of Colorado Denver, USA
SHANNON CHENG, Rice University, USA
MURIEL CLAUSON, The University of Georgia, USA
CHRISTOPHER CLOTT, State University of New York, Maritime College, USA
ABBY CORRINGTON, Rice University, USA
DAVID P. COSTANZA, The George Washington University, USA
EMILY M. DAVID, China Europe International Business School (CEIBS), China
ROBERT EISENBERGER, University of Houston, USA
LISA M. FINKELSTEIN, Northern Illinois University, USA
LORI FOSTER, North Carolina State University, USA, and University of Cape Town, South Africa
JEFFREY H. GREENHAUS, Drexel University, USA
CHESTER HANVEY, Berkeley Research Group, LLC., USA
MARKUS HELFEN, University of Innsbruck, Austria
BRIAN J. HOFFMAN, The University of Georgia, USA
RAYMOND L. HOGLER, Colorado State University, USA
DAVID J. HOWARD, University of South Florida, USA

RUTH A. IMOSE, Northern Illinois University, USA

LIXIN JIANG, University of Auckland, New Zealand

ELYSSA JOHNSON, Clemson University, USA

LARS U. JOHNSON, Wayne State University, USA

JUSTIN M. JONES, The University of Georgia, USA

CHANGHWAN KIM, University of Kansas, USA

EDEN KING, Rice University, USA

JUSEOB LEE, University of Central Florida, USA

BLAINE A. LEWIS, University of Houston, USA

JORGE LUMBRERAS, The University of Georgia, USA

BRIAN D. LYONS, Elon University, USA

DUSTIN MANEETHAI, University of Houston, USA

JOHN W. MICHEL, Loyola University Maryland, USA

ASHLEY MILLER, Society for Human Resource Management, USA

GOURI MOHAN, Ivey Business School, Canada

ROBERT H. MOORMAN, Elon University, USA

JOHN MORGAN, Clemson University, USA

KEVIN R. MURPHY, University of Limerick, Ireland

LINNEA NG, Rice University, USA

SARA JANSEN PERRY, Baylor University, USA

DANIEL M. RAVID, The George Washington University, USA

CORT W. RUDOLPH, Saint Louis University, USA

KAYO SADY, DCI Consulting Group, Inc. , USA

ARTHUR SAKAMOTO, Texas A&M University, USA

EDUARDO SALAS, Rice University, USA

DEIDRA J. SCHLEICHER, Iowa State University, USA

MINDY K. SHOSS, University of Central Florida, USA

IAN SIDERITS, The George Washington University, USA

ROBERT R. SINCLAIR, Clemson University, USA

PAUL E. SPECTOR, University of South Florida, USA

JÖRG SYDOW, Freie Universität Berlin, Germany

CHRISTOPHER R. TAMBORINI, University of Maryland, College Park & US Social Security Administration, USA

WARREN TIERNEY, University of Limerick, Ireland

HAYLEY M. TRAINER, The University of Georgia, USA

ALLISON TRAYLOR, Rice University, USA

TELMA VIALE, KennedyFitch, USA

LAUREN A. WEGMAN, University of Georgia, USA

XUEQI (CECILIA) WEN, University of Houston, USA

JEROD WHITE, The George Washington University, USA

JIA YU, Louisiana State University Shreveport, USA

GARY YUKL, Louisiana State University Shreveport, USA

HANNES ZACHER, Leipzig University, Germany

JIMMY ZHENG, University of Central Florida, USA

PART I

Introduction to the Changing Nature of Work

1 The Changing Nature of Work and Workers

An Introduction

Brian J. Hoffman, Mindy K. Shoss, and Lauren A. Wegman

The changing nature of work and workers is a topic that has excited substantial interest and discussion across academic disciplines, organizations, and the popular press. To the degree that statements and proposals "due to the changing nature of work/workers" are supported and therefore, the nature of work/workers has changed, then the approaches commonly used by organizations for attracting, retaining, and rewarding talent must also change in order to maintain a competitive advantage. Similarly, to the extent that work has changed, workers will need to adapt to a workplace that requires different skills, is differently organized, and where the assumptions of the past may no longer hold. This chapter introduces the topic of the changing nature of work and workers, describes common methods used to analyze change, offers a conceptual model of the changing nature of work, and summarizes the major themes that are covered in this handbook.

Introduction

The changing nature of work has been the subject of considerable discussion among scholars, the popular press, and organizations. A perusal of the popular press reveals frequent discussion of the changing demography of the workforce, generational differences at work, increasing levels of income inequality, and technological changes that some argue will fundamentally change the landscape of work. Likewise, scholars from a variety of disciplines, such as economics, sociology, management, and industrial–organizational (IO) psychology, have sought to understand how work and workers have changed and the implications of the changes for their various disciplines. Finally, organizations, their leaders, and employees have navigated these changes and sought ways to better prepare themselves to meet the demands of the modern world of work.

To be sure, the workplace has undertaken significant changes over the centuries, ranging from shifts from agrarian-focused economies to industrialization and shifts to manufacturing, knowledge and service economies. Indeed, it may be reasonably argued that the nature of work is constantly evolving (Murphy & Tierney, Chapter 3, this volume). Yet, many have observed that recent and potentially upcoming changes differ from evolutionary change commonly associated with the changing nature of work (Clauson, Chapter 26, this volume). Rapid advances in technology and a more connected world in particular have already changed workplaces and are frequently proposed to result in more profound changes in the years to come (White, Behrend, & Siderits, Chapter 4, this volume). Indeed, these changes have led some of the world's leaders to express concern about the future of work. For instance, Bill Gates has argued that "Twenty years from now, labor demand for lots of skill sets will be substantially lower. I don't think people have that in their mental model" (Bort, 2014). Additionally, in his farewell address as president of the United States, Barrack Obama noted, "The next wave of economic dislocations won't come from overseas. It will come from the relentless pace of automation that makes a lot of good, middle-class jobs obsolete" (Miller, 2017). He further described how changes in work can have a pervasive impact on social values, with the "world upended by economic, cultural and technological change."

In 1999, the National Academy of Sciences issued a call for interdisciplinary research on the future of work. The scholarly community has responded by seeking to analyze the changing nature of work and its implications. Economists have focused their attention on changes in the occupations, critical skills, and wages (Acemoglu & Autor, 2011). Sociologists have focused more heavily on changes in the nature of occupations, shifts in the nature of employment relationships, and the growth of precarious work (Kalleberg, 2009; Sakamoto, Kim, & Tamborini, Chapter 6). Finally, management research has focused on the way that organizational structures and processes have changed in response to environment changes (Barley, Bechky, & Milliken, 2017). This handbook seeks to bring together insights from these diverse disciplines to inform I-O psychology research and practice.

Much I-O research, like research and practice in adjacent fields, has used the changing nature of work as rationale to study a variety of phenomena, such as organizational commitment in light of perceived increases in job and organizational hopping, extra-role performance behaviors in light of the perceived increasing fluidity of work roles, and work–life conflict in light of the increasing hours worked per household. In addition, I-O psychology research has focused much attention on demographic and generational changes in workforce composition (Costanza & Finklestein, 2015). Clearly, I-O psychologists believe that changes in the workplace have key implications for modern employees and organizations.

In fact, in considering the trajectory of I-O psychology as a field, changes in the nature of work and workers are at least partly responsible for the growth of the discipline. For instance, in the 1950s and 1960s the United States was grappling with the Civil Rights Movement. In response, the federal government passed the Civil Rights Act of 1964, which, among other things prohibited employment decisions being made on the basis of sex, color, race, religion, and nation of origin. Over the course of the next decade, I-O psychology saw rapid growth, both in terms of the number of practicing I-O psychologists as well as the number of I-O psychology doctoral programs. In particular, organizations increasingly sought the expertise of I-O psychologists to ensure that the methods used to hire and promote employees were valid and legally defensible.

More recently, I-O psychology has seen another stage of rapid growth. In 2014, the US Bureau of Labor Statistics listed I-O psychology as the fastest-growing profession in the United States, and the Department of Labor has listed I-O psychology as a hot job. Why the growing demand? We believe that a key reason that organizations are increasingly seeking out this expertise is to meet the demands of the changing nature of work. Although organizations have long made the claim that "Our people are our most important resource," the past few decades have seen this platitude become increasingly true. As the economy has shifted from manufacturing and service to more professional or knowledge-based, employees contribute an increasing portion to a firm's competitive advantage. In addition, as the workforce demands more educated employees who also have more soft skills, there is now a premium on employee talent. Finally, as employees have become more mobile, organizations are now competing with one another over relatively scarce talent. In short, organizations must increasingly find ways to recruit, select, motivate, and retain talented employees in order to maintain their competitive advantage. In this economic environment, the expertise of I-O psychologists and management researchers is vital.

We hasten to note that the interplay between I-O psychologists and the changing nature of work is not new. In 1995, Howard published the edited volume *The changing nature of work*. This highly influential volume summarized major changes in the world or work, with a specific focus on those changes expected to impact I-O psychology. However, 1995 was a long time ago and much has changed in the past quarter century. For instance, in the mid-1990s, only 0.3% of the world's population had Internet access, compared to nearly 60% today. Indeed, 42% of the US population had never heard of the Internet (Fox & Rainie, 2014)! Only around 30% of households in the United States owned a cell phone in 1995, compared to 95% of adults in the United States today. While an obvious change, of course, technology is not the only significant change. The way that employees prepare for retirement and the benefits that organizations offer have also changed drastically. In 1998, around 59% of *Fortune* 500 companies offered newly hired salaried employees some form of pension plan, compared to only 16% today (McFarland, 2018). In addition, a Gallup survey estimated that in the mid-1990s the average US employee retired at age 57 compared to 61 today (Brown, 2013). And, although still only 5% of *Fortune* 500 companies have a female chief executive officer (CEO), before 1995 only three women had ever headed a *Fortune* 500 company. Since 1995, 57 women have headed a *Fortune* 500 company, an exponential increase over earlier years (Yost, 2018). In light of change in the nature of work over the past quarter century, it is time to update Howard's impactful work. This handbook seeks to expand and update Howard (1995) by summarizing the changing nature of work for the modern generation of organizational scientists.

Scope of this Handbook

Heraclitus said that "the only thing that is constant is change." The same can be said for the world of work. Over time, the nature of work has constantly evolved. In order to make this handbook as manageable and relevant as possible, we have constrained the scope in several ways. First, the chapters focus on changes that have occurred over the past 50 years or so, with a primary emphasis on changes that have occurred over the past 30 years. Although it is certainly interesting and informative to consider changes that have occurred over a longer period, more recent changes are more relevant to understanding how knowledge and practices currently used in the management field should also change. That is, the economies of the world's economic leaders are certainly very different from the agrarian economy that typified past centuries. However, a comparison to the recent past is more relevant to understanding how the organization and management of modern organizations and their employees should and has changed.

Next, we chose to focus on changes that would have implications for topics and processes associated with management and I-O psychology. That is, we were interested in changes in the work environment, workers, and work itself that influence the strategies used to manage employees. Certainly, changes in the legal landscape such as copyright and intellectual property law have influenced the way that organizations do businesses. But such changes are less likely to influence what employees do on a day-to-day basis and the associated management processes and strategies. Accordingly, such changes are not our primary focus. Instead, we chose to focus on changes that are expected to influence the ways (a) that organizations recruit, select, organize, compensate, motivate, and otherwise manage their employees and (b) that employees manage their relationships with their work organization and their careers.

In terms of the coverage and discussion of changes, the chapters tend to focus on average changes. This is an important caveat. Clearly, it is unlikely that any observed change will be felt the same way across all occupations or workers that comprise the economy. That is, just because on average, workers are more diverse or jobs are more complex, this does not mean that these changes will function similarly across all jobs in the economy. Instead, it is likely that key changes have a differential influence on different sectors, occupations, and industries. Nevertheless, a clear understanding of average changes is of value to researchers and practitioners. A clear understanding of the average changes of the broader economy gives a picture of the broader milieu in which work is done. In addition, it alerts management researchers to key features that are more likely to be at play in any given context. Finally, understanding mean changes is useful in directing attention to contexts that require increased research attention, given their prevalence in the workplace.

Next, the majority of the book focuses on data from industrialized countries. This decision was made out of necessity: which is to say that the majority of the available data on changes in the nature of work stems from industrialized countries. In addition, many of the changes that have been examined or discussed in the management literature pertain to the effects of advanced economies (e.g., changes in organizational structures to meet global demands). This is in no way intended to imply that changes in industrializing countries are less important. To the contrary, industrializing countries will provide an excellent lens through which to directly examine changes in work. We hope researchers will take advantage of this opportunity to collect data and develop theory so that we can better understand how changes in the nature of work impact more and less advanced economies.

Finally, we attempted, as much as possible, to start with a foundation of empirically supported changes. That is, there has been much written about how modern work and workers are different from years gone by. However, much of this lacks empirical support. For instance, it has been alternatively argued among popular press commentators that that millennial employees desire more explicit direction from their supervisors (Reshwan, 2015) and that this same group of employees primarily desire more autonomy (Notter, 2018). Likewise, it has been argued that modern workers are both disengaged (Mann & Harter, 2016) and overengaged (Seppala & Moeller, 2018). As with answering any complex question, answers to these do not come easily. But when possible, chapter authors attempted to leverage empirical data to support the changes we describe. However, in some cases this simply is not possible given existing research, particularly when discussing implications of changes. For instance, although we may well find evidence that, on average, jobs are more complex, or the workforce is more diverse, it is often necessary to extrapolate what the implications might be of this increasing complexity and diversity in terms of the recommended best practices and management strategies. Thus, although a primary value of this handbook will be to summarize available empirical literature in terms of changes, an equally important contribution will be to focus attention on needed areas of research.

Methods of Analyzing Change

As the reader may infer from the preceding discussion on challenges accompanying empirical analysis of the changing nature of work and workers, providing empirical analysis of change over time can be a challenging endeavor. There are a few reasons for this difficulty. Foremost is the availability of data. Specifically, in order to examine how work and workers have changed, data dating back a number of years must be obtained. That is, if we want to know whether levels of job satisfaction have increased, on average, relative to the 1970s, then we must have year-over-year job satisfaction data using a measure of satisfaction consistently since the 1970s. In addition, we must have a sample that we can use to compare the version from the 1970s to the present measure that is reasonably similar in order to ensure that sample differences are not the cause of any observed differences in satisfaction.

Clearly, it would not even be possible to examine more recently defined constructs, such as engagement.

One approach to providing such comparisons is sample matching. In this method, a historic sample is identified in which a construct of interest is measured during a timeframe of interest. For comparison, a modern-day sample is taken matching the historic sample characteristics (e.g., industry, tenure, demographics, location) and using the same measure, items, and scaling. Matching the sample characteristics is an attempt to ensure that any observed differences are attributable to differences in the focal constructs over time and not differences in characteristics of the sample. Once both samples are collected, a simple mean comparison is conducted to determine whether the mean level of the focal variable has changed over time. Smola & Sutton (2002) used this approach to compare generational differences in work values between a sample from a study published in 1974 and the sample they collected in 1999. The primary criticisms of this method concern the potential for a lack of representativeness. Consequently, researchers must be deliberate in collecting the new sample, as observed differences could be due to differences in the samples, rather than differences in the constructs of interest. In addition, a comparison based on two individual samples will typically lack the statistical power to develop strong, generalizable inferences of changes.

Next, researchers have used repeated cross-sectional data to examine changes. In a repeated cross-sectional design, different samples of respondents respond to the same items over multiple years. While this can be accomplished when researchers use their own samples that they have collected over time, more commonly researchers leverage existing large-scale databases such as the General Social Survey (GSS) and the Monitoring the Future survey. The key weaknesses with this approach are that it is contingent on the availability of a sample that dates back an extended period of time and measures the variables of interest with the same items. That is, many of the variables that might be of interest simply are not available in a repeated cross-sectional database. Thus, the researcher is limited by what was measured decades ago and, just as important, *how* it was measured decades ago. For instance, many of the large national databases such as the GSS use a single item to measure focal constructs. Consequently, researchers must often sacrifice the analysis of scale reliability and (grudgingly) accept the use of single item scales. Although this practice is often resisted by management and I-O psychology researchers, unfortunately it is not possible to leverage these databases unless one is willing to conduct analyses on single item scales. In addition, with large and nationally representative samples, other fields such as sociology and political science have a long history of forming inferences based on single item scales, leading to somewhat of a limit to what we think we know. Despite these limitations, we believe that repeated cross-sectional designs are arguably the best available method to examine time-based changes, as the researcher has access to the primary data, the sample sizes are usually quite large, and in many cases the samples from existing databases such as the GSS are nationally representative.

In addition, one can conduct more advanced analyses than with afforded sample matching and cross-temporal meta-analysis.

Specifically, the repeated cross-sectional data allow for the use of the hierarchical Age–Period–Cohort (APC) model (Yang & Land, 2006). This model partitions variance into effects associated with respondents' age, effects associated with respondents' birth cohort, and effects associated with the time period. This partitioning of variance allows for much clearer interpretation of the nature and source of any observed changes (Yang & Land, 2006). Age effects are physiological or developmental changes that occur due to the physiological aging process and are evident in cross-sections of people who are of a certain age, regardless of the time period or generation. For instance, as workers get older, the type of rewards they value may shift away from extrinsic rewards and toward more altruistic rewards. In contrast, cohort effects (or generational effects) reflect common experiences of individuals who undergo similar macrosocial influences throughout their early lives that have a formative impact on their personality, values, beliefs, or other stable characteristics. For instance, individuals who grew up during the Great Depression might be more frugal with their money or have less trust of financial institutions throughout the rest of their lives. Finally, period effects occur when specific events or broad social and historical differences impact people living at a given time, regardless of the person's age or their generation. For example, as women have increasingly taken more professional work roles and the hours worked per household have increased, it is possible that the mean level of work–life balance has dropped across all age groups and generations. A key limitation of the APC model is that data are often not available that would provide the ability to run this model. For instance, one needs data in which the same question is asked over multiple years over a relatively long period of time and in which the intervals are equally spaced (the same time period between each measurement occasion). Clearly, this limits the ability to use the APC model.

A third approach that involves relying on past research to develop inferences is cross-temporal meta-analysis (CTMA; Twenge & Campbell, 2001). Whereas traditional meta-analysis focuses on aggregating effect sizes in order to obtain a summary of the magnitude of association between two variables, CTMA instead focuses on mean levels of the variables of interest. By collecting the means for a focal variable and examining the association between the study-level means and the year the data were collected, it is possible to estimate the degree of change in the focal variable over time. For instance, if the means reported in primary studies have gotten larger in recent years, this would suggest that the prevalence of the focal variable has increased. Recently, Wegman, Hoffman, Carter, Twenge, & Guenole (2018) used CTMA to investigate changes in the core job characteristics and showed that autonomy and skill variety had increased (see also Eisenberger, Rockstuhl, Shoss, Wen, & Dulebohn, 2019, for a CTMA examining changes in the employee–organization relationship). CTMA is a valuable tool to examine change, as it does not require the availability of primary data going back a number of years as do repeated cross-sectional designs. In addition, as a meta-analytic procedure, CTMA is a more powerful approach than sample matching, because it summarizes mean levels of a variable across the available literature. On the other hand, like other meta-analysis, CTMA is limited by the available literature. For instance, if a given variable has become less commonly examined in recent years, it would be difficult to conduct a meaningful CTMA on the variable. Similarly, if the commonly used measurement scales to measure a focal construct have changed substantially over the years, it is difficult to determine if changes reflect changes in the construct or changes in the measurement. Finally, CTMA does not allow for a clear determination of whether any observed changes are a function of generation or period effects.

Until now, the methods reviewed have emphasized average changes in the characteristics of work and workers. In other words, typically studies using single sample comparisons, CTMA, and repeated cross-sectional designs focus on the mean level of some characteristic of interest, such as worker values or the core job characteristics. However, another way to view changes in work and workers and a critical next step for researchers is the analysis of changes in the nature of relationships between substantive variables over time (Johns, 2006). In this type of analysis, time becomes a surrogate for associated changes in the context. For instance, if work characteristics have become more interdependent over time, then it might be reasonable to hypothesize that interpersonal skills will, on average, be more important determinants of effective performance in recent years. Knowledge of whether commonly studied variables have grown more (or less) important based on their association with key outcomes can provide critical information regarding where organizations should focus scarce resources. Unfortunately, in many cases it will not be possible to directly examine year as a moderator of substantive relationships, such as when existing data are insufficient to support moderated meta-analysis. In such instances, it might be possible to focus on key contextual characteristics that have been previously isolated as increasingly prevalent in the modern workplace instead of year. For instance, meta-analysis might focus on analyzing the influence of interdependence, occupational diversity, or knowledge work on substantive relationships.

In summary, there are multiple analytic tools, data structures, and data sources to facilitate the analysis of the changing nature of work. However, it is also true that providing firm empirical analysis of the changing nature of work poses many challenges to the researcher. Probably the biggest challenge is the availability of data. Although there are datasets available, many of these operationalize key constructs using a single item. Similarly, although cross-temporal meta-analysis provides useful information on construct-level change, there are also important limitations in terms of the ability to make inferences regarding the source of effects. Together, given the challenges in finding data coupled with the importance of understanding how changes can impact organizational functioning, it is important that the research community be receptive to studies that attempt to understand the changing nature of work. In other words, if we want to study and better understand the way the world of work has changed and the implications of these changes, we must also be prepared to accept certain limitations inherent to research in this area (e.g., single item scales or difficulty isolating the source of effects). It is our view that some information on how work has changed, even if it is imperfect, is better than no information at all.

Structure of this Book

Figure 1.1 depicts a conceptual model of the changing nature of work that serves as the overarching structure for this handbook. In the first section of the book, we lay the foundation for these discussions. Following these

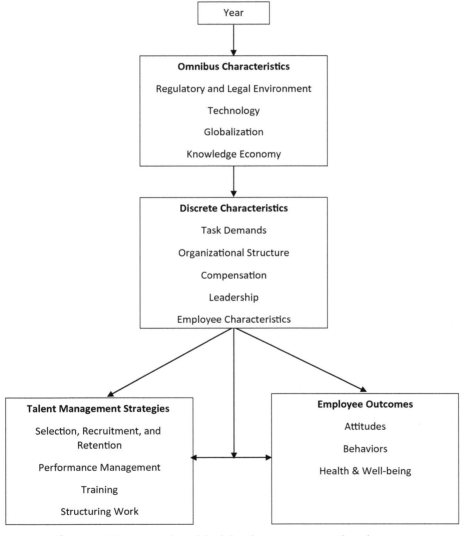

Figure 1.1 *Conceptual model of the changing nature of work.*

introductory chapters, the next two parts discuss the primary features of the conceptual model. In our conceptual model, time is viewed as the focal antecedent of the changing nature of work. The central assumption is that as time has progressed, the world has changed in important ways. In essence, time is treated as a surrogate for a variety of environmental characteristics that form the context of the world of work during a given time period. As time has progressed, broad macroeconomic environmental characteristics have also changed. These broad features are referred to as the omnibus context (Johns, 2006). For instance, globalization, changes in the legal landscape, and shifts in the occupational make-up of the economy are all omnibus characteristics that are thought to have changed over the years. Then, these omnibus characteristics are proposed to influence the characteristics of the more immediate work environment, labeled discrete context (Johns, 2006). Discrete context includes aspects of a workers' immediate work environment such as financial incentives, the type of tasks completed, and the nature of the social interactions. As an important note, we include employee characteristics as an element of discrete context. We do so in the spirit of Schneider's (1987) Attraction–Selection–Attrition model which proposes that the context of a given work environment is heavily influenced by the characteristics of the employees. In this way, we view changes in the demographics, personality, or values of employees as a potentially salient feature of the work environment.

The third and final section of the book describes how changes in discrete and omnibus context are expected to have a direct effect on both organizational strategies for managing talent and employee attitudes, behaviors, and well-being. Conceptually, our assumption here is that, as time has passed and the context has changed, organizational strategies have needed to change with the times in order to most effectively manage talent. As organizations have adapted their strategies to meet changing operational realities, these changes have likely directly influenced employee outcomes, such as their behaviors, health, and well-being. We also expect reverse causality to operate in this model, such that, as employee outcomes have changed along with the context, this has driven organizations to change their talent management strategies. Finally, this model includes a moderating path between discrete environmental characteristics to the relationship between talent management strategies and employee outcomes. This moderating effect is meant to signify that, as time has passed and the context has changed, the effectiveness of various talent management strategies has also changed.

We acknowledge that the boundaries of the organizing framework presented here are semi-permeable. It is likely that a given type of variable, such as leadership, will fall within a multiple of the broader categories. For instance, although leadership is conceptualized in the model as an element of discrete context, leadership can also be viewed as an employee outcome, as we would expect both discrete context and talent management strategies to have a direct effect on the context. In addition, there is likely reverse causation in multiple elements of the model, such that employee outcomes and talent management strategies will shape the discrete context, in addition to being shaped by the discrete context. Thus, our framework offers more of a way of thinking about the changing nature of work than a prescriptive model.

Having outlined the basic structure of this handbook, we now briefly describe each section.

Part I: Introduction. In this chapter, we have sought to set the stage for the discussion of the changing nature of work and workers. We have presented a conceptual model that guides the book and described the methodological approaches and challenges to examining the changing nature of work and workers. The next two chapters of the introduction are intended to help set realistic expectations in terms of what we can and cannot conclude as it pertains to the changing nature of work and workers. In Chapter 2, Costanza, Finkelstein, Imose, and Ravid caution against misattributing sources of changes in worker characteristics to generational differences (as opposed to age-related effects) and especially against the possibility for age-related discrimination that can occur when attempting to apply the findings of generational research. Next, Murphy and Tierney (Chapter 3) argue that changes in the world of work tend to be evolutionary rather than revolutionary and emphasize that changes have not impacted all industries and indeed countries similarly. In doing so, they urge the reader to avoid the temptation to overgeneralize evidence for changes in work.

Part II: What Has Changed? The chapters in this part describe available evidence in terms of what has changed in the world of work. As discussed above, given that there is more easily available evidence for changes in the omnibus context (e.g., social indicators, economic trends), most of the chapters focus on documenting these relatively broad changes. However, where possible, chapters are also devoted to evidence of change in discrete context.

The first three chapters of Part II describe some of the more significant omnibus changes that are referenced when discussing the changing nature of work: technology, globalization, and occupational changes. Technology is arguably the primary driver of a host of the changes that have occurred in the world of work. In Chapter 4, White, Behrend, and Sidertis describe how technology has advanced over time and describe eight characteristics of modern technology. White et al. then offer an insightful strength–weakness–opportunity–threat analysis of technological changes for modern work and workers. The next two chapters describe two key implications of rapidly advancing technology. In Chapter 5, Clott offers an analysis of the impact of changes brought about by globalization. He addresses several issues surrounding the globalized workforce, including global and local talent clusters, labor mobility, access for women, and country-specific efforts to build skilled workforces in technology and financial sectors. In Chapter 6, Sakamoto, Kim, and Tamborini describe how changes in technology have yielded changes in occupational make-up of the economy and skill polarization. As we will see, these changes in occupations have critical implications for the type of jobs available, the skills needed for success, and what workers do on a day-to day-basis.

The next three chapters in Part II describe changes associated with organizations and organizational functioning, including: changes in the legal landscape, changes in income and income inequality, and changes in organizational structure. These chapters are largely focused on the United States. Although we would have liked to include corresponding chapters from different cultures and in different countries, a full accounting of cross-cultural differences in changes in employment laws and income inequality could fill multiple handbooks. We hope that future work can focus on analyzing cross-cultural differences in changes to organizations. In Chapter 7, Hanvey and Sady describe changes in the legal landscape. This chapter expands the field's traditional emphasis on employment discrimination to include a discussion of modern issues facing society, such as legal challenges associated with employee social media use and the legal implications of a growing number of contract workers. In Chapter 8, Hogler discusses the decline of organized labor in the United States in terms of the legislative and political environment that has precipitated these declines as well as the resulting impact on employee compensation systems and the employee–organization relationship. Next, Jiang summarizes the evidence for a phenomenon that has received much attention in recent years: the growing levels of wage stagnation and income inequality (Chapter 9). She then offers a more micro perspective on this broader social issue by discussing firm-level discrepancies between top management and employee pay. Finally, Sydow and Helfen (Chapter 10) focus on the ways in which organizations structure work has changed over time, from functional approaches to more fluid, matrix-type structures.

In the final group of chapters in Part II, the authors describe changes associated with workers. In Chapter 11, Cheng, Corrington, King, and Ng describe demographic shifts in the workforce, emphasizing the clear trends of a workforce that is quickly diversifying. Next, Lumbreras and Campbell (Chapter 12) discuss generational shifts in worker personality and values. This chapter summarizes the growing literature on generational differences and emphasizes the ways in which changes in employee characteristics have important implications for the climate of modern organizations. In Chapter 13, Perry, David, and Johnson describe changes in work behavior patterns. As technology has advanced and the economy has shifted to a bifurcated economy comprised of service jobs on one end and more complex knowledge work on the other, the way that employees enact the process of work has changed. Ranging from workforce participation to the number of hours spent at work, changes in worker behavior patterns are pivotal to understanding the milieu of modern work.

Part III: Implications for Talent Management and Impact on Employees. In concert, these shifts in the macroeconomic context, organizational structure and operational realities, and employee characteristics and behaviors have yielded a growing recognition that organizations must change the way they do business in order to compete for talent and maintain a competitive advantage. Moreover, they suggest meaningful implications for employees' day-to-day work experiences and how they react to these experiences. The chapters included in the third and final part describe the implications of the previously discussed changes in omnibus and discrete context for organizations' talent management strategies and employee attitudes, behaviors, and well-being. Where relevant, the authors summarize evidence for changes in context and then go on to describe how changes in context have necessitated that organizations change their strategies in order to more effectively manage their talent.

The first group of chapters in Part III describes ongoing and recommended changes to several key talent management functions based on changes in the nature of work and workers. In Chapter 14, Lyons, Alonzo, Moorman, and Miller describe the implications for personnel selection, focusing on how changes in context have changed critical knowledge, skills, and abilities, required for effective performance, the types of constructs assessed, and in some cases the approach and methods used in personnel selection settings. As organizations find themselves competing over scarce talent and along with evidence that a handful of elite performers tend to provide a disproportionate contribution to organizational effectiveness (O'Boyle & Aguinis, 2012), it is increasingly apparent that an organization's ability to recruit and retain talent will distinguish successful organizations. In Chapter 15, Cascio describes how approaches to recruit and retain talent differ in the modern world of work. The next two chapters focus on getting the most out of employees once an organization has recruited and selected its workforce. In Chapter 16, Schleicher and Baumann discuss the emergence of the concept of performance management as a contrast to traditional performance appraisal. This chapter presents a meso-level model of the performance management process and describes why the shift to performance management is necessary in the modern world of work. Then, Bisbey, Traylor, and Salas (Chapter 17) discuss how the world of work has impacted training. This chapter focuses on differences in the content of training as well as differences in the model of presentation of formal training programs. Then, Chapter 18 by Michel and Yukl applies the classic contingency theories of leadership in a novel way: to understand how changes in context might necessitate changes in commonly prescribed leader behaviors relative to what was expected in earlier research. Finally, in Chapter 19, Jones, Mohan, Trainer, and Carter describe changes associated with the ways that organizations structure modern work. Their chapter describes the increasing use of teams, with a focus on recent increases in multiteam systems, multifunctional teams, and teams composed of geographically dispersed individuals. There is currently substantial variation in terms of the age of the workforce in the United States. Given evidence for the impact of age on work values and attitudes, simultaneously managing employees of such diverse age range poses unique challenges for organizations. In Chapter 20, Rudolph and Zacher discuss these challenges and outline strategies that organizations can use to manage an age-diverse workforce.

The next set of chapters in Part III revolve around what might be considered employee outcome variables. These are variables that are thought to be impacted by both the discrete context and firm talent management strategies.

The central assumption here is that as time has progressed and the world of work has changed, both changes in context and talent management strategies have impacted the experiences, attitudes, and behaviors of employees. In our view, understanding the psychological experience of modern work is critical in directing the attention of researchers and organizations to the needs of modern employees. Further, if employees are increasingly viewed as a source of competitive advantage in the modern economy, then understanding how the typical employee experience has changed is essential to maximize organizational functioning.

In Chapter 21, Wegman and Hoffman describe changes in employee attitudes and engagement and the implications of these changes for maintaining a motivated and satisfied workforce. As the number of dual income families has increased and women have increasingly taken full-time work and professional jobs, managing the demands of work and non-work domains has become a fixture when discussing challenges facing modern employees. Greenhaus and Callanan (Chapter 22) discuss the modern challenge of striking a balance between work and non-work. Expanding some of these issues, Chapter 23 by Sinclair, Morgan, and Johnson describes the toll that modern work can take on employee health and how organizations can respond to reinforce a healthy workplace. In Chapter 24, Howard and Spector consider how employees may use technology to enact dysfunctional organizational and interpersonal behaviors, especially when experiencing stressful workplace conditions. On a related note, some have argued that increased employee mobility and the decline of labor unions and pension plans have yielded a fundamental shift in the relationship between employees and their organization. Shoss, Eisenberger, and colleagues (Chapter 25) evaluate the reasons behind these claims and the implications of the proposed shift in the nature of the employment relationship.

The final set of chapters take a broader view on the changing nature of work. Having outlined existing evidence for changes and the implications of changes, Clauson (Chapter 26) next describes how work might look in the future. Finally, in Chapter 27, Foster and Viale discuss an ongoing shift in the perspective of many organizations that many commentators expect to increasingly define the future: the shift toward social responsibility and sustainability. They describe the potential benefits of this shift in mentality for addressing several societal challenges described by the United Nations' 2030 Agenda for Sustainable Development.

The Importance of Understanding Change

In closing, we would like to offer a brief commentary on why it is critical to understand changes in work and workers. The hallmarks of psychological research are to describe, predict, understand, and apply/intervene. We believe that the analysis of the changing nature of work is in line with these goals of psychological research and essential to our mission to enhance organizational and individual well-being.

In terms of description, it is first necessary to describe how the workplace and workers have changed over time. And in fact, the vast majority of management research on the changing nature of work has focused on the overarching goal of description. For instance, studies on changes in worker values, workforce demography, the occupational makeup of the economy, and levels of compensation over time have all sought to better describe the milieu of modern work. This research is a critical first step to understanding the ways that the context in which organizations operate has changed. In doing so, this could reveal critical factors that require research from scholars and intervention from organizations and government.

The next commonly stated goal of psychology is to predict human behaviors, thoughts, and feelings. Here again, a better understanding of the changing nature of work can be instrumental to more accurately predicting employee behaviors at, attitudes toward, and reactions to their work. In other words, to the extent that the micro and macro context surrounding employees has changed, then it seems likely that employee behaviors as well as employee reactions to their work will have changed. For instance, if, on average, work has become more team-based, then greater coordination and interpersonally oriented behaviors will be an increasingly important aspect of success. A recognition of changes in the environment and the influence they have on employees can help organizational leaders more actively anticipate demands on employee behavior or employee reactions to their work environment. Similarly, educational institutions and policy makers can use this information to develop curriculum to ensure that the workforce is ready to meet economic challenges.

Next, the goal of understanding is relevant to the changing nature of work so that organizations and policy makers can implement the most effective response to changes. First, clearly documenting the boundary conditions to changes in work and workers can help determine when a certain strategy is likely to be particularly important. For example, if increases in hours worked per week are only being seen in certain segments of the economy, then occupational health and related public policy interventions can be better targeted to where they are needed. Similarly, understanding the explanatory mechanisms underlying change is critical to implementing effective interventions. For instance, whether observed changes in employee characteristics and perceptions are due to age, period, or cohort effects has critical implications for the appropriate response to changes. If changes in employee values are due to worker age then organizations should emphasize different types of incentives to younger and older employees in the recruitment process. On the other hand, if changes in employee values are due to generations, then the strategies used to incentivize and recruit younger employees in the 1970s would be less effective for younger employees today. Thus, the best-practice recommendations found in management textbooks should change, as should employee recruitment strategies. Finally, if changes in values are due to time periods, then this would suggest that some change has affected the average employee, regardless of their generation and regardless of their age. Accordingly, this would suggest that organizations should change the types of incentives they offer to all employees, not just employees from a certain generation. Although merely one example, it is clear that understanding the source of changes is critical to understanding the appropriate response to observed changes.

Finally, by marshaling research that seeks to describe changes in the nature of work, predict the impact of changes on employee behaviors and attitudes, and understand the locus and boundary conditions of changes, it will be possible to design interventions to help organizations more effectively respond to changes. A key theme in the chapters that follow is that various aspects of work and workers have changed. These changes are wide reaching and include factors such as changes in: the occupations that make up the economy, the demographic makeup of the workforce, the skills required for employees and organizations to be effective, and the impact of work on employee health and well-being. As described in Part III of this handbook, these changes have critical implications for many aspects of how organizations manage their talent. Consequently, rigorous research that seeks to describe, predict, and understand the changing nature of work and workers is critical to informing needed changes in talent management strategies and practices.

In sum, we believe that a clearer understanding of changes in work and workers is critical to I-O psychology research and practice, organizations, and more generally, society. This belief rests on the central idea that as the world changes, individuals and organizations must adapt to effectively meet current challenges. Accordingly, it is our sincere hope that this handbook will help employees and organizations alike to better navigate an ever changing world of work. Furthermore, we hope this work will serve as a springboard for future research on the important topic of the changing nature of work and its implications for work and workers.

References

Acemoglu, D., & Autor, D. (2011). Skills, tasks and technologies: Implications for employment and earnings. In *Handbook of labor economics* (Vol. 4, pp. 1043–1171). North Holland: Elsevier.

Barley, S. R., Bechky, B. A., & Milliken, F. J. (2017). The changing nature of work: Careers, identities, and work lives in the 21st century. *Academy of Management Annals, 3*, 111–115.

Bort, J. (2014). Bill Gates: People don't realize how many jobs will soon be replaced by software bots. *Business Insider*. www.businessinsider.com/bill-gates-bots-are-taking-away-jobs-2014-3

Brown, A. (2013). In U.S. average retirement age up to 61. Retrieved from www.news.gallup.com

Costanza, D. P., & Finkelstein, L. M. (2015). Generationally based differences in the workplace: Is there a there there? *Industrial and Organizational Psychology, 8*, 308–323.

Eisenberger, R., Rockstuhl, T., Shoss, M.K., Wen, X., & Dulebohn, J. (2019). Is the employee–organization relationship dying or thriving? A temporal meta-analysis. *Journal of Applied Psychology, 104*(8), 1036–1057.

Fox, S., & Rainie, L. (2014, February 27). The web at 25 in the US. *Pew Research Center Report.* Retrieved from www.pewinternet.org/2014/02/27/the-web-at-25-in-the-u-s/

Howard, A. E. (1995). *The changing nature of work.* San Francisco, CA: Jossey-Bass.

Johns, G. (2006). The essential impact of context on organizational behavior. *Academy of Management Review, 31,* 386–408.

Kalleberg, A. L. (2009). Precarious work, insecure workers: Employment relations in transition. *American Sociological Review, 74,* 1–22.

Mann, A., & Harter, J. (2016). The worldwide employee engagement crisis. *Gallup Business Journal,* January 7.

McFarland, B. (2018). Retirement offerings in the 21st century: A retrospective. *Insider, 28*(2). Retrieved from www.willistowerswatson.com/en-US/Insights/2018/02/evolution-of-retirement-plans-in-fortune-500-companies

Miller. C. C. (2017). A darker theme in Obama's farewell: Automation can divide us. *New York Times.* www.nytimes.com/2017/01/12/upshot/in-obamas-farewell-a-warning-on-automations-perils.html

Notter, J. (2018). Motivating millennials (and everyone else for that matter). Retrieved from www.forbes.com/sites/forbescoachescouncil/2018/03/14/motivating-millennials-and-everyone-else-for-that-matter/#7a42db5b57c1

O'Boyle Jr., E., & Aguinis, H. (2012). The best and the rest: Revisiting the norm of normality of individual performance. *Personnel Psychology, 65,* 79–119.

Reshwan, R. (2015). Four tips for managing millennial employees. Retrieved October 11, 2015, from https://money.usnews.com/money

Schneider, B. (1987). The people make the place. *Personnel Psychology, 40,* 437–453.

Seppala, E., & Moeller, J. (2018). One in five employees is highly engaged and at risk of burnout. *Harvard Business Review,* May 16.

Smola, K. W., & Sutton, C. D. (2002). Generational differences: Revisiting generational work values for the new millennium. *Journal of Organizational Behavior, 23,* 363–382.

Twenge, J. M., & Campbell, W. K. (2001). Age and birth cohort differences in self-esteem: A cross-temporal meta-analysis. *Personality and Social Psychology Review, 5,* 321–344.

Wegman, L. A., Hoffman, B. J., Carter, N. T., Twenge, J. M., & Guenole, N. (2018). Placing job characteristics in context: Cross-temporal meta-analysis of changes in job characteristics since 1975. *Journal of Management, 44,* 352–386.

Yang, Y., & Land, K. C. (2006). A mixed models approach to the age-period-cohort analysis of repeated cross-section surveys, with an application to data on trends in verbal test scores. *Sociological Methodology, 36,* 75–97.

Yost, K. (2018). Female CEO's of Fortune 500 Companies. Retrieved October 10, 2018, from http://kdmengineering.com/female-ceos-fortune-500-companies/

2 Inappropriate Inferences from Generational Research

David P. Costanza, Lisa M. Finkelstein, Ruth A. Imose, and Daniel M. Ravid

Academic research, popular press articles, books, and practitioner reports on generations and generational differences continue to proliferate despite inconsistent empirical evidence for their existence and lingering questions about the theoretical foundations that underpin the reasons for any such differences. While some researchers report finding generational differences (Becton, Walker, & Jones-Farmer, 2014; Twenge, Campbell, Hoffman, & Lance, 2010; Twenge, Konrath, Foster, Campbell, & Bushman, 2008) or discuss organizational interventions to deal with them (Espinoza, & Ukleja, 2016; Zemke, Raines, & Filipczak, 2013), others have raised questions about the body of research, including questions about theoretical assumptions (Parry & Urwin, 2011; Rudolph & Zacher, 2017), methodological and analytical challenges (Costanza, Darrow, Yost, & Severt, 2017; Parry & Urwin, 2017), and the appropriateness of the inferences researchers and practitioners may draw from this literature (Costanza, Badger, Fraser, Severt, & Gade, 2012; Costanza & Finkelstein, 2015; Macky, Gardner, & Forsyth, 2008; Rudolph, Rauvola, & Zacher, 2017; Zabel, Biermeier-Hanson, Early, & Shepard, 2017).

While many of the theoretical, analytical, and methodological issues have been quite thoroughly discussed previously (see Costanza & Finkelstein, 2015; 2017), one area in the literature that has received far less attention is whether the inferences suggested by research that has found generational differences in the workplace are appropriate. That is, when researchers find a difference and attribute it to generations, what are the implications of those findings and are the inferences managers and organizations draw from those implications appropriate? To date, there has been no review, accounting, or critical analysis of the common and generalizable inferences from research in this area. In particular, if one is going to make conclusions about generational differences in the workplace and recommendations on how organizations and managers should deal with such differences, it is important to understand what the research showing such differences is suggesting and to critically examine these inferences.

Generational differences are certainly an area where practice and the pop press far outpace the research. Various surveys of, and stories for, practitioners, HR managers, and researchers identify generations and generational differences as key issues facing organizations despite the mixed empirical and theoretical evidence. For example, the Society for Industrial and Organizational Psychology (SIOP) annually publishes a list of "Top 10 Workforce Trends" and the

2015, 2016, and 2017 lists (SIOP.org) all explicitly mention generations, generational differences, and the changing nature of the workforce.

Other academic organizations such as the American Psychological Association (APA) and practitioner-oriented groups such as the Society for Human Resources Management (SHRM) have published member surveys, newsletter articles, and cited links to newspaper and web stories about generations, generational differences, and generational comparisons in the workplace and often, importantly, what organizations should do about them. Clearly, organizations, their members, and their representative professional organizations seem to think generations are important, particularly in terms of their impact on HR systems, talent acquisition and management, and organizational development.

The idea of studying generational differences at all, and specifically in the workplace, is a fairly recent phenomenon. While the idea of generations as an identifiable and measurable phenomenon has been around since the 1950s and 1960s (e.g., Mannheim, 1952; Ryder, 1965), the recent explosion of interest in generations probably finds its origins with the publication of books by Strauss and Howe (1991) and Howe and Strauss (2000) on generations in general and Millennials in particular. After their 2000 book on Millennials, there was a steady increase in pop-press, practitioner, and, later on, academic articles on generations, generational differences, and implications for the modern workplace.

In 2012, Costanza and colleagues published a meta-analysis on the generational differences in common workplace outcomes (Costanza et al., 2012). Although they reported that a Google search of "generational differences in the workplace" yielded over 18 million hits, their academic literature search found only 20 articles that met the criteria for inclusion in a quantitative meta-analysis, thus reinforcing that the phenomenon was primarily practice driven and that the science was well behind. While the number of research-based articles has increased in the interim, many have noted since then (Costanza et al., 2017; Costanza & Finkelstein, 2017: Rudolph, 2015; Rudolph & Zacher, 2017) that most of these efforts face the same problems and limitations as the literature did in 2012. In essence, while the number of practice and pop-press pieces and the number of organizations feeling like they have to do something about generational differences continue to increase, the research supporting the existence of such differences and what managers and organizations should do about such differences continues to lag behind, and what is there is equivocal at best.

It is important to stress that a skepticism regarding generational differences and the resultant associated recommendations for the workplace is not intended to imply a disregard for the multitude of changes that occur – at widely differing rates – when workers age and the associated best practices for maximizing a healthy and productive aging workforce. Indeed, many disciplines including industrial–organizational (I-O) psychology, gerontology, human factors, and HR management among others have amassed research documenting the physical, cognitive, emotional, and social changes that occur intra-individually for workers over the course of their lifespan (Czaja & Sharit, 2009; Finkelstein, Truxillo, Fraccaroli, & Kanfer, 2015).

Moreover, these personal changes occur in a dynamic context reflecting the changes in the nature of work, the workplace, and in our society documented throughout this volume. Recommendations for HR practices, including those that consider adaptations for the changing skills, strengths, and needs that may accompany age (e.g., deLange, Kooij, & van der Heijden, 2015; Kooij, Jansen, Dikkers, & deLange, 2014), as well as age-inclusive HR practices that promote age-friendly work climates (e.g., Boehm, Kunze, & Bruch, 2014), are important developments. That said, such practices are not the same as those inferences drawn from the generational differences research discussed in this chapter; in the remainder of this chapter, we provide examples of those inferences and caution the reader to a host of problems that could result from following their prescriptions.

Accordingly, the purpose of the present effort was to review the recent generations literature, including academic and practitioner pieces, identify common inferences, and offer a critical review of the appropriateness of each of the inferences. Below, we review the findings from this effort and then discuss the inferences in depth as they relate to the changing nature of work. We conclude by giving our thoughts about what all this means for research and practice on generations literature as well as for the changing nature of work.

Literature Search for Generational Inferences

In order to identify a common set of generalized inferences that could be deduced from recent generations literature, we conducted a search for any academic studies or practitioner articles written in the last 10 years that discussed or made recommendations pertaining to generations in the workplace. We excluded pop-press pieces and books, the former of which are far too numerous to code and the latter of which are often based on the primary articles on which we focused. Articles were coded for information such as year published, whether the article was a research study or not, whether the article included data, what methods of data collection were used, what methods of analyses were used, the main inferences, whether the authors of the article noted caveats to these inferences, and if so what the caveats were.

It is worth noting that for the purposes of this effort, we defined an inference as a direct statement by the authors about what should or should not be done based on what the research or article found. For example, a research effort may have found that members of one generation differed from members of another generation on satisfaction with job benefits. The authors then stated that organizations should tailor their benefits and compensation plans to maximize satisfaction across generations. The inference is that organizations should change their plans because different generations expect different benefits.

Prior to the full literature search, two rounds of pilot coding were conducted. In the first pilot round, two of the authors individually coded four exemplar generations articles for inferences and then all four authors met to discuss the results. Where differences existed, such as whether information qualified as a conclusion or an inference, the four authors discussed until consensus was attained. The second pilot round proceeded in the same way, with four new generations articles coded by the same two authors and then all four authors discussing until consensus was achieved. It is important to note that our objective was not to generate data for a quantitative analysis of every single inference, no matter how often it appeared, but rather to conduct a comprehensive qualitative analysis and reduction of extant inferences and themes that were present in recent generations literature.

After the two rounds of pilot coding were completed, the full literature search was conducted. For this, we looked at the past 10+ years (beginning of 2007 through the middle of 2017 when coding started), dividing them such that one author was responsible for searching and coding articles published in 2007–2011 while the other author simultaneously did the same for articles published in 2012–2017. The literature searches were primarily conducted using Google Scholar with results cross-checked using PsychINFO, ABI-Inform, and Sociological Abstracts. This cross-check was to ensure a thorough review of the generations literature and identification of articles for inclusion, and the additional databases yielded very few additional articles in any given year. The keyword search terms used included *generations, generational differences, generational comparisons, traditionals/silents, baby boomers, generation X, millennials, generation Z, greatest generation, digital natives, generation Y, and iGen,* and articles that focused in some way on work and the workplace were identified. If in doubt as to whether an article was relevant, the searchers erred on the side of inclusion.

From this search, approximately 550 articles published from 2007 to the middle of 2017 were identified that had been written about generations and generational differences in the context of work or the workplace. Coding proceeded such that the methods, analysis, inferences, and caveats were recorded for approximately the first 15–20 articles found in each year or until the inferences began to repeat. When no new inferences were found in a year, indicating conceptual saturation, coders began to skip articles, scanning every other article and then every fifth article in the data set. In the case that a new inference was found during the skip coding, coders went back to coding each article to see whether the inference was the beginning of a trend or was anomalous.

In the end, inferences, methods, analysis, and caveats were coded for approximately 300 of the 550 articles identified. Next, the two authors responsible for the coding independently identified what they thought were the most common and primary inferences in this literature. These two authors then discussed their conclusions and compiled a combined list of generalized inferences as well as a set of other implications, findings, trends, and observations based on their review.

Following this, the other two authors independently reviewed the coding sheets for the 300 articles and generated their own lists of generalized inferences and other issues. These two authors then met and discussed their list of inferences as well as the first two authors' lists. From this, we identified a common set of four main inferences that could be drawn from the generations literature as well as a set of four additional implications and trends. Each of the four inferences had 110 or more mentions, meaning they appeared in at least 20% of the articles we found. A summary of the results can be found in Table 2.1.[1]

Challenging the Inferences

Having identified the four most common inferences, we now turn to the question of determining whether these inferences are appropriate. We see four key issues that could be used to address, challenge, or debunk the major inferences of generational research. Of course, these issues are interrelated to a certain extent, so we present them in an order in which organizations might consider when thinking about generations in the workplace and any changes or interventions they might implement as a result.

The first issue is whether making employment decisions based on generational differences is *legal*. Generation category membership is determined entirely by age, and treating people in the workplace differently because of their age, under many circumstances, is illegal under the Age Discrimination in Employment Act. The second issue is the extent to which any action based on these inferences would be valid. That is, are the inferences about generational differences the result of sound and appropriate *methodological and statistical approaches*? Are the conclusions appropriate or are they not warranted given the data, methods, and statistics used?

The third issue is whether acting on generational differences is a *good business practice*. That is, would the inference stated or implied by findings regarding generational differences help an organization to be more strategic, effective, or competitive? Would doing so enhance the profitability, reputation, or efficiency of the organization? The final issue is whether the inference is *grounded in theoretical reasoning*. Do we have compelling theoretical justification for how and why generational groupings would produce meaningful psychological and behavioral differences?

Although each of these issues likely applies to all or most of the four inferences we identified from our review of the literature, in the sections below we apply a different one to each of the key inferences. This allows us to go into some detail regarding each point and issue while avoiding redundancy.

Customized HR Policies: Legal Lens

One common inference in the literature is that human resources policies and practices should be customized to meet the unique needs of each generation. For example, organizations may need to develop and implement different strategies

---

[1] A full list of all articles in our database is available from the publisher upon request.

Table 2.1 Summary of inferences, with examplars, identified from the generations literature

Inference	Notes	Exemplar articles	Method & statistics used	Generational focus	Inference type
Customized HR Policies Human resource policies and practices should be customized to meet the differing needs of the generations. For example, organizations need different strategies to attract (recruit) and retain different generations.	Less than a handful of experimental designs; although a mix of generations studied, about 40% studied one generation in isolation	Dencker, Joshi, & Martocchio (2008)	Theoretical paper	Silents, Baby Boomers, Gen X, Gen Y	Tempered
		Twenge, Campbell, Hoffman, & Lance (2010)	Empirical, time-lagged; CTMA	Baby Boomers, Gen X, Gen Y	Tempered
		Allen, R. S., Allen, D. E., Karl, & White (2015)	Empirical, cross-sectional; ANOVA	Baby Boomers, Gen X, Gen Y	Tempered
		Giambatista et al. (2017)	Literature review	Gen Y	Tempered
Leading Generations Differently Different generations need different types of leadership in order to motivate them. For example, organizations and managers should adjust their leadership approach; customize to meet different generational needs.	Though those included here all tempered, significant majority of conclusions were blanketed	Sessa et al. (2007)	Empirical, cross-sectional; MANOVA	Silents, Baby Boomers, Gen X, Gen Y	Tempered
		De Hauw & De Vos (2010)	Empirical, cross-sectional; ANOVA	Gen Y	Tempered
		Lyons & Kuron (2014)	Conceptual framework development	Silents, Baby Boomers, Gen X, Gen Y	Tempered
		Cates, Cojanu, & Pettine (2013)	Empirical, cross-sectional; ANOVA	Silents, Baby Boomers, Gen X, Gen Y	Tempered

Table 2.1 (cont.)

Inference	Notes	Exemplar articles	Method & statistics used	Generational focus	Inference type
Generational Differences and Conflict *Generational differences cause inter-generational conflicts at work. Generations will clash because of their different values, expectations, and motivations.*		Gursoy, Maier, & Chi (2008)	Empirical, cross-sectional; ANOVA	Baby Boomers, Gen X, Gen Y	Blanketed
		Mhatre & Conger (2011)	Literature review	Gen X, Gen Y	Blanketed
		Hendricks & Cope (2013)	Literature review	Veterans, Baby Boomers, Gen X, Gen Y	Blanketed
		Williams (2016)	Empirical, cross-sectional; regression	Silents, Baby Boomers, Gen X	Tempered
Capitalize on Generational Strengths and Learn from Other Generations *Organizations should work to identify generational differences and capture unique group characteristics of their workforce for competitive advantage.*	Predominantly examining Millennials; most studies non-empirical	Ballone (2007)	Practitioner	Silents, Baby Boomers, Gen X, Gen Y	Blanketed
		Salahuddin (2010)	Qualitative; cross-sectional	Silents, Baby Boomers, Gen X, Gen Y	Blanketed
		Rajput, Marwah, Balli, & Gupta (2013)	Empirical, cross-sectional; ANOVA	Baby Boomers, Gen X, Gen Y	Tempered
		Baran (2014)	Empirical, cross-sectional; descriptives	Silents, Baby Boomers, Gen X, Gen Y	Blanketed

Notes: Because of the number of articles, we used examples rather than a comprehensive listing. **Generational focus** refers to the generational cohort descriptors the researchers used that were the focus of their discussion or investigation. **Inference type** (tempered or blanketed) refers to whether the conclusions and recommendations offered are cautioned (i.e., tempered) for any reason (e.g., methodological limitations of the work in question).
Statistics: CTMA, cross-temporal meta-analysis; ANOVA, analysis of variance; MANOVA, multivariate analysis of variance.

to recruit (Lindquist, 2008), motivate (Baldonado, 2013), or succession plan for (Crumpacker & Crumpacker, 2007) members of different generations. The idea that cuts across these examples is that members of each generation have some common set of characteristics (e.g., values, motivators, preferences), that differentiate them from members of other generations, and an HR approach that serves members of one generation well might cause problems for another. As Costanza and Finkelstein (2015) suggested, an organization might offer specific types of feedback or compensation to members of particular generations based on stereotypical characteristics only to discover that a number of members of a specific generation do not share those common characteristics.

From a legal standpoint, treating individuals differently based on group characteristics is inherently problematic. The Civil Rights Act of 1964, Title VII, the Age Discrimination in Employment Act (1967), the Americans with Disabilities Act (1991), and others all make treating groups differently on the basis of a variety of characteristics illegal. Under these laws, discriminating based on color, race, sex, religion, national origin, disability and, most relevantly age, is prohibited. While there is no "Generational Membership Protection Act," in terms of age, those over the age of 40 are generally protected, a cutoff that covers almost everyone in the workforce born before 1977 (i.e., all the Silents and Boomers and many Gen Xers). As such, any employment-related decisions such as selection, compensation, or promotion that rely on generational stereotypes could well be challenged if the decisions were made, or were perceived to be made, based on the employee's age. We should also consider the possibility that some organizations might use the lack of protections for generations to make ageist decisions under the guise of customizing HR policies, creating a new realm of legal problems. Regardless of the reasons for employment-related decisions based on perceived generational differences, organizations could find themselves in legal jeopardy if they cannot provide a valid reason for such decisions.

Beyond the legal jeopardy, from a practical standpoint, tailoring HR policies and practices to generations also creates logistical and implementation challenges for organizations. Many organizations already have parallel HR systems, say one for hourly workers and one for salaried managers. Imagine the complexity of an HR system for a large employer, with union and non-union members, hourly and salaried employees, working in multiple locations, domestically and internationally (each of which may have its own policies, regulations, and laws), and now trying to customize those plans to meet the supposedly varying needs of workers from differing generations. The cost, complexity, and difficulty of doing so make the head spin and the return on investment of doing so would be hard to justify given the limited validity of the research demonstrating generational differences. Instead of customizing HR policies and practices based on such differences, organizations could use information about their overall workforce and its characteristics to train recruiters, develop and refine policies, and offer customizable benefit packages that appeal to a broad range of employees, regardless of generation. Again, the focus is on all employees and their needs and not just those of a particular generation.

Given this, that the inference about customizing HR policies and practices based on generational membership was so prevalent is concerning. An organization or manager reviewing this literature, or being told about it by a consultant, might readily conclude that certain groups do or do not respond to a certain type of benefit, pay, motivational strategy, or leadership style. The implication for organizations relying on this inference could easily lead to decrements in performance, motivation, effectiveness, and long-term success as HR policies get modified and administered to people for whom they do not apply or are not desired. Deciding to customize HR policies and practices therefore not only creates legal problems but also might result in vast swaths of employees being "given" benefits that they do not want or being rewarded in ways that do not motivate them. In essence, by trying to better serve the generations, an organization could easily end up serving none of them well and simultaneously increase the chance that the organization gets sued for discrimination. That is certainly a lose–lose proposition.

Generational Differences and Conflict: Methods/Statistics Lens

Another common inference is that generational differences cause intergenerational conflicts at work. A number of papers suggested that members of different generations in the workplace will clash because of their differing values (Fogg, 2009), goals (Kelly, Elizabeth, Bharat, & Jitendra, 2016), and attitudes (Gursoy, Maier, & Chi, 2008) and also that organizations should consider various training and intervention strategies to help minimize any such conflicts (Schofield & Honoré, 2009; Zhu, Yang, & Bai, 2016). The general idea is that members of different generations vary so much on their values, attitudes, and goals that conflict is inevitable. However, this inference is one that is based on methods and statistics that do not necessarily support the idea that generational differences cause conflicts.

In terms of the various methods and analytical techniques that have been used in generations research, Costanza and his colleagues (2012, 2015, 2017) have gone into great detail explicating the limits of the empirical approaches as well as the statistical challenges of separating out age, period, and cohort effects. In their 2017 piece (Costanza et al., 2017), they discussed the strengths and limitations of three approaches: between-group comparisons using cross-sectional data, cross-temporal meta-analysis using time-lagged panels, and cross-classified hierarchical linear modeling using time-lagged panels. They used the three techniques on two large data sets and reported how the results varied depending on the technique used. Results showed that each method produced slightly different results and that none of them was able to fully capture differences attributable to generations. Others have also criticized cross-sectional designs (Rudolph, 2015; Twenge, 2010) and cross-temporal meta-analysis (Rudolph & Zacher, 2017), and the limitations of anecdotal reports and case studies are well-established.

In fact, many of the articles we found that addressed inter-generational clashes and conflicts were based on cross-sectional studies, anecdotal reports, and journalistic writing, raising questions about whether the generational groups are actually different or in conflict at all. Given the methodological and statistical limitations of the research showing intergenerational conflict, it is appropriate to question the validity of this inference. Further, this criticism applies to most of the inferences we came across as many of the pieces claiming generational differences were based on research designs and using data that inherently cannot separate out generational effects from alternate explanations.

Despite these limitations, models of conflict do suggest that when there is a large goal differential among or between parties, conflict is more likely (Lewicki, Weiss, & Lewin, 1992; Pondy, 1967; Van de Vliert & De Dreu, 1994), so there is some basis in theory and research supporting this inference. For example, the classic systems model of conflict (Pondy, 1967) assumes that the fundamental source of conflict within a goal-oriented system is differences in goals or goal ordering among subunits within that system. Hence, there may be some basis to the claims of conflict among workers, but whether that conflict is related to, attributable to, or caused by generational membership is questionable.

As with the other inferences, we are not arguing that people of different ages do not vary in terms of goals, values, and attitudes or that conflicts among older and younger workers do not exist. Indeed, as people age they often experience somewhat predictable shifts in personality and affect (Lachman & James, 1997), work and life goals (Warr, 2001), and work motivations (Inceoglu, Segers, & Bartram, 2012). In addition, older workers may differ from younger workers in personal and functional experience, job tenure, and within-organization networks and influence. All of these differences exist completely independent of any specific generation into which a person was born, and any of them may lead to work conflict between younger and older workers.

That said, the inference that this conflict among older and younger workers exists *because* they are from different generations, rather than any of these or other more theoretically and methodologically defensible factors, is not appropriate. The methods and the statistics do not support this inference of group differences. Despite this, as in other areas in I-O psychology, organizational behavior, and human resources, there is a danger in finding group differences, assigning those characteristics to all the members of that group, and then attributing conflict to the fact that the individuals come from those groups. Instead, we should be focusing on the underlying causes of the conflict, why the specific parties involved actually have different values, and how to ameliorate those conflicts using established practices and interventions.

Leading Generations Differently: Business Practice Lens

A third inference in the literature is that generations should each be led differently and leaders who ignore the generation of followers do so at their own peril. Some of the specific aspects of leadership that have either been investigated empirically, or more often considered in conceptual papers and reflection essays, include the appropriate motivational tactics and incentives to be used (e.g., Acar, 2014), the types of job characteristics that should be factored into work design (e.g., Hernaus & Pološki Vokic, 2014), and the manner in which feedback is delivered (e.g., Anderson, Buchko, & Buchko, 2016), among others. The inference is that to keep up, have a competitive advantage, and make sure you are getting the most from your workers, leadership strategies stratified by generational groups are a modern-day imperative.

Taking a business strategy approach for this inference one could ask: Is it an urgent and unqualified strategy that leaders need to lead generations differently? Or, perhaps are there any nuggets of reasonable advice in here being buried under sweeping generalizations that can put blinders on leaders about meaningful differences?

The general argument behind this inference is that the differences in values and preferences that have been uncovered at the generational level are strong enough to make an investment in training leaders to handle their various generational members differently worthwhile (Berkup, 2014; Chou, 2012; Festing & Schäfer, 2014, Sessa, Kabacoff, Deal, & Brown, 2007). Generational membership, then, can provide a shortcut to determine a team member's values, desires, and motivations, and tapping into those things that make people tick will help increase productivity and engagement. Research typically has examined self-reported values rankings and attitude endorsements and then suggests how leaders appealing to these factors should improve worker behavior; however, the actual connection to improved behavior is rarely tested or its absence offered up by researchers as a recognized limitation of the research.

The idea of regular environmental scanning to consider the individual needs and preferences of one's team members and tailoring leadership styles to suit what resonates with individuals (within the bounds, of course, of standard fair treatment practices) makes good business sense as does understanding that those may change over the course of time and with various organizational contexts (Costanza & Finkelstein, 2015). Taking a more transformational approach to leadership, with its emphasis on individual consideration and empowerment of followers, rather than a rigid bureaucratic approach, may also pay dividends for all employees, (Green, 2008; Thompson & Gregory, 2012), not just for serving the unique needs of Millennials as is often suggested.

Conversely, relying on average group differences in reported values or leadership trait preferences, which have been found in some studies (though not consistently), and treating large groups of people the same (though different from other large groups of people) is likely to be perceived as unfair and as looking like a lazy herding of people into a stereotype. This could also cause some within-team friction among members in multi-generational teams who can see that they receive different feedback strategies or incentives depending on their generational group. The business case for investing in training managers to adapt their leadership style by generation is hard to make (Becton et al., 2014) and can backfire.

But is there any helpful advice here within this inference at all? Considering generation as one potential influence, along with life stage, socio-economic status, gender, ethnic diversity, personality, experience, etc., that contributes to making each employee unique, gauging the types of people on one's team, and figuring out strategic ways to use this profile information to manage each member that is both fair to all but brings out the best in them – that is good practice (Costanza & Finkelstein, 2015; Guillot-Soulez & Soulez, 2014). Some of the articles we saw took a caveated stance of sorts, expressing caution for relying only on generational differences as a guide for a leadership approach but still expressing enough confidence in generational findings to endorse some catering to generational values (e.g., Greenwood, Gibson, & Murphy, 2008; Sessa et al., 2007). We agree with the generational differences supporters that one size does not fit all but we do not believe that research supports that the "sizes" should be Millennials, Gen X, and Baby Boomer.

Capitalize on Generational Strengths and Learn from Other Generations: Theoretical Lens

This final inference offers a somewhat more positive tone on generational differences than the others. The suggestion here is that generations have distinctly different qualities and preferences that define them, each with important strengths that together work to increase the effectiveness of organization. In other words, organizations need everyone and can learn from each group's best qualities. Thus, it is important that generations are given opportunities to meaningfully interact for cross-generational respect and to facilitate intergenerational learning. This seems to be the latest manifestation of the shift in the general diversity literature over time from "managing diversity" to "embracing diversity and inclusion" – both out of fairness and business savvy (Thomas, 2005). At first blush this advice certainly sounds promising and we will argue that there is some value in its premise, but not for the reasons typically given. Although this inference could be viewed critically through a number of lenses, we are choosing to highlight here the theoretical problems with this suggestion.

In past writings, we (Costanza & Finkelstein, 2015, 2017) have lamented the lack of theory in the generations literature as a fundamental problem for this research. In response to our work, we have received pushback on this point (e.g., Parry & Urwin, 2017; Perry, Golom, & McCarthy, 2015), with researchers citing Mannheim's classic work (Mannheim, 1952) as an overarching theoretical framework for generations. Admittedly we should have more clearly acknowledged that there have been theoretical attempts, with Mannheim's the most oft cited (though others exist; see Rudolph & Zacher, 2017, for a thorough review) to explain why birth cohorts should be defined by the historical events occurring while they are at particular stages of development. However, we see two problems with these approaches that led to our assertion.

First, these theories generally do not explain the *processes* by which individual members of generations, as defined by particular generational cutoffs, absorb and process historical or cultural events and transfer these into shared values and attitudes. Second, it is even less clear why the variety of attitudes and personality differences that supposedly define the different generations would all be affected by these common events in the same way. Although one could argue that we may be holding a nascent and thus far largely descriptive area of research to perhaps too high of a standard by demanding a strong theoretical grounding, we believe that good science should include asking questions of why a proposed phenomenon is happening. Indeed, if the "why" question is ignored or misinterpreted, it could have negative ramifications for attempts at workplace intervention for the reasons noted above.

Promisingly, a new theoretical take on the meaning and potential influence of generations has recently been articulated by Rudolph and Zacher (2017). Theirs is an encouraging advancement and provides an overarching theoretical approach that also offers guidelines for the development of more precise theory-driven tests of developmental differences at work and their effects. We encourage readers to review their work in detail, but, in brief, they adopt a lifespan development approach, stressing that an individual's trajectory for development over time will be influenced by many factors – biological, social, and others. This view acknowledges that historical and sociocultural events are part of the context within which an individual develops and that can impact their trajectory (aligning it with common approach to generations) but makes no claims about collective experiences nor shared reactions to those experiences. Moreover, Rudolph and Zacher (2017) explain that many types of cohorts can develop that are more likely to directly influence individuals in a more meaningful way than a birth period-based cohort. For example, there are shared personal life events (e.g., having children) that may bond people together and localized organizational events (e.g., plant closures) that create meaningful history-based cohorts.

Finkelstein (2012) presented some supportive qualitative interview data that illustrate these concepts. For example, when asked whether generations were a meaningful concept in her organization, one interviewee stated that she believed that people in her organization tended to group more around life stage/event. She had a baby later in life and gravitated toward the shared experiences of women, much younger than her, with newborns. She saw those employees as her meaningful cohort. Another participant in a different organization said that they had what might look to others like a generation gap in his organization, but it was actually based on a division between those who had worked for the company – a major airline – before or after a buyout. This was the key localized historical touchstone that affected people's viewpoints and approaches to the organization.

What does all this mean for the inference regarding learning from generational differences? The theoretical problems arise at a few levels. First, the multitude of supposed strengths in terms of approaches and motivations and personalities do not have a clear explanation in any kind of pure generational theory. Although some cross-sectional mean differences in values or motives appear in the literature, the question is why. What explains those group differences and if there is a basis for them, isn't a generational breakdown too rough of a heuristic to make? Long-standing research in I-O and management supports the consideration of *individual* differences. Someone following the advice to set up situations (trainings, project groups, mentoring relationships, etc.) where the generations can learn each other's strengths and appreciate one another's novel perspectives and choose representatives from different generations with suppositions of their strengths and qualities based on supposed differences and group characteristics assigned to individuals may find people insulted by those assumptions about the qualities they do or do not have.

If we apply the lifespan development perspective to this inference, we can think about the unique experiences that people have had over the course of time and encourage people to share their individual learnings and stories – both where they come from and how they have developed. The notion of learning from one another's strengths and appreciating them is good advice; the idea of dividing people up by generation to administer the particular wisdom of an entire generation is not.

We and others have also acknowledged that even if generational differences do not exist or have minimal evidence, many people believe that they do and this belief is likely reinforced by the media's catchy headlines and clickbait stories. For example, Lester, Standifer, Shultz, and Windsor (2012) directly compared the actual endorsement of various work-relevant values across generations to the beliefs that generational members had about the values of other generations, finding that the suppositions about other generations were stronger than actual differences and in some cases were actually wrong. Another reason, then, that creating chances for members of different generations to work together could be valuable is to bring to life the differences among members within one generation who shared the same historical influences but were shaped differently by them.

Two people may share nostalgic memories for their favorite TV shows of youth and laugh at the silly clothes they each wore to the prom, but how they have reacted to shared historical events may depend on their own filters through which they absorbed these influences – biological, sociocultural, familial, etc. By the same token, these types of interactions could uncover some commonalities across members of different generations who share similarities, be they personality, ethnic background, musical preference, and so on. Note that theory and research from social psychology regarding contact across cultures or other diverse groups stresses that these situations only allow for reduction of stereotypes and building of goodwill under certain circumstances. For example, people from different groups should not feel forced to connect, should feel a sense of equal status within the group, and should have the opportunity to interact in ways to build positive affect (Baron, Byrne, & Branscombe, 2009).

Other Observations from the Generations Literature

Beyond the broad inferences discussed above, we identified a second set of observations, trends, and issues that were present in many of the articles reviewed. We review these in turn followed by some thoughts about their implications. The first observation is that there is an increasing number of academics and researchers who are writing that there is little support for differences among generations and who are offering substantive cautions against using tailored interventions or practices based on supposed differences (e.g., Deal, Altman, & Rosenberg, 2010; Kowske, Rasch, & Wiley, 2010; McHenry & Ash, 2013; Zabel et al., 2017). While we have written a number of articles and research projects addressing the problems with research and practice on generational differences, we certainly are not alone in offering this perspective.

There also is a related trend of researchers calling for a new framework for what generations are, what we should do with them, and why what is out there supporting generational differences is not justified. It is encouraging that more and more researchers and practitioners are calling for caution when considering generational differences and asking for better, more appropriate models for understanding what causes people to change over time, why, and how those changes are manifested (Costanza et al., 2017; Parry & Urwin, 2017; Rudolph & Zacher, 2017).

Despite a multitude of pop-press articles, books, and practitioner pieces, some authored by academics, the evidence continues to point to something possibly being there (to paraphrase Costanza & Finkelstein [2015]) with generations but it is still not clear what it is. Even some of the most ardent proponents of generational differences are acknowledging that the lines between generations are not as clear or defined as once thought (Campbell, Twenge, & Campbell, 2017) and that generations may be proxies for broader cultural changes (Twenge, 2017). More researchers and practitioners questioning the findings and their implications, and looking for alternate explanations is, we think, a good thing.

Second, we found a number of studies (approximately 15 percent) that used Asian, Greek, or multicultural samples. This raises the question of whether the specific events people experience that create generation differences are culturally or geographically constrained. Some recent work (Akhavan Sarraf, Abzari, Isfahani, & Fathi, 2016) has suggested that generations do vary by culture, country, and geography. Thus, if a significant percentage of the generations literature relies on generations that are not defined by the country or culture where the organization is located, any inferences and implications could be mildly to wildly inaccurate if they were developed in one country or culture but are applied to others.

The third observation is a somewhat depressing one: almost every quantitative study of generations is still using a cross-sectional design and ANOVA frameworks for investigating possible generational differences. As many have pointed out (e.g., Costanza et al., 2012, 2017; Parry & Urwin, 2017; Twenge, 2010; Twenge, Carter, & Campbell, 2017) cross-sectional designs with ANOVA cannot separate out age and cohort effects, meaning that the studies using this approach that do find "generational differences" may actually just be finding age-based differences.

There are some studies that have used cross-temporal meta-analysis (most of these have been conducted by one group of researchers) and even fewer that have used cross-classified hierarchical linear modeling, but both of these approaches are limited in the extent to which they can appropriately partition age, period, and cohort effects (see Costanza et al., 2017, for a full discussion of these issues). We did come across articles that used other methods and approaches, including interviews and focus groups as well as non-data driven investigations, thought pieces, and anecdotal stories, but these types of efforts are also quite limited in their ability to identify generalizable principles.

Overall, as noted above, the statistical and methodological limitations of the generations literature are the same as they were five years ago and, in essence, continue to be intractable so long as the age, period, cohort conceptualization of generations predominates. This points to the need for new frameworks and we second the recommendations of Lyons and Schweitzer (2016), Rudolph (2015), and Rudolph and Zacher (2017), among others, who are calling for new ways of conceptualizing whatever generations are.

The final trend that we noticed is that the focus of the literature seems to change over time, with the emphasis being on whatever the "hot" generation is at that time. The earliest generations research on possible workplace differences was more focused on Baby Boomers and Gen Xers, with later shifts toward Xers and eventually Millennials. Accordingly, given that the bulk of the pieces were published as Millennials were entering the workforce, most of them focused to some extent on Millennials as the new, not understood group of entering workers.

More recently, we are starting to see pop-press pieces, books, and practice pieces focused on the next up-and-coming generation, variously termed post-Millennials, Gen Z, and other marketing-oriented names. This is not surprising given that, regardless of what the "new" generation is, it is less well known, less understood, and more mysterious to organizations and managers and hence worthy of study, investigation, and, unfortunately, stereotyping, misrepresentations, and misunderstandings.

Conclusions

Our review of the generations literature and search for common inferences was both enlightening and somewhat disheartening. Given that evidence of generational differences to this point is largely unsupported from a theoretical standpoint (Rudolph & Zacher, 2017) and flawed from a methodological standpoint (Costanza et al., 2017), literature that implies that organizations should use generational characteristics and differences to develop and guide new organizational training and change interventions and HRM policy is misguided at best and misleading at worst. Further, beyond the inherent limitations that come with treating people a certain way based on stereotypes, generational or otherwise, doing so in the workplace also raises organizational questions of ethics, justice, and legality (Costanza & Finkelstein, 2015).

Nonetheless, it is clear to us after reading this literature as well as other work on changes in organizations, environments, and workers, the generations literature may help shed some light on the changing nature of work. Some may expect that our critique of the generations literature and its related inferences indicates that we and others similarly aligned have our heads in the sand and are blind to important work-related changes occurring over time. This is hardly the case. Nor do we align with those who suggest that rather than organizations changing to accommodate the new generation, we should communicate with the new generation early to realign their expectations to match with the reality of the workplace (e.g., Weresh, 2009).

Our position, instead, is that within and across any given historical time period(s), environments, organizations, work, and workers change. The geopolitical, economic, and technological environments are always in flux, and changes do not always occur in a gradual or easily predictable way. Indeed, certain important events in time (as emphasized in the more classical generations work) may spark, halt, or redirect changes in more dramatic and memorable ways. These trigger-events, along with the more gradual changes in laws, markets, and even natural disasters, affect organizational policies and strategies. They affect the type of work that needs to be done to keep an economy thriving and the processes for getting that work done in an efficient and healthy way. Finally, they affect workers, although the precise way that workers change over time may be influenced by their age and stage of development at the time.

For example, young people may be educated under certain policies and with techniques that impact their skills, comfort with, and expectations for certain teaching approaches. People educated formally at an earlier time (though likely not at a precise generational cut point) may not have shared those experiences and could have different reactions. However, a host of other individual differences that we have discussed throughout this chapter also likely impact how workers react to any period-based changes at any point in their career.

In other words, while everyone should recognize that workers do change over time, assuming that these changes are purely generational is far too simplistic. It is also trivializing for people to say that if the changes are occurring and newer workers are indeed different than older ones, whether it is generational, cultural, or periodic may not make a difference. *Why* workers, work, and organizations are changing is extremely important. Yes, workers from all "generations" are changing with time and in response to important events and doing so at a pace and with outcomes that may vary notably across people. Our challenge is not to advocate for changes in organizational environments to fit the influx of a large group of people who have been defined by generalized characteristics; it is more complex than that. Instead, our challenge is to understand the multiple and varied set of factors that might spark changes in the organization, in work, and in workers, and to use this insight to help organizations remain flexible and adaptable as they strive to maximize the efficiency and health of their workforce.

References

Acar, A. B. (2014). Do intrinsic and extrinsic motivation factors differ for Generation X and Generation Y? *International Journal of Business and Social Science, 5,* 12–20.

Akhavan Sarraf, A. R., Abzari, M., Nasr Isfahani, A., & Fathi, S. (2016). The impact of generational groups on organizational behavior in Iran. *Human Systems Management, 35*(3), 175–183.

Allen, R. S., Allen, D. E., Karl, K., & White, C. S. (2015). Are millennials really an entitled generation? An investigation into generational equity sensitivity differences. *Journal of Business Diversity, 15*(2), 14–26.

Anderson, E., Buchko, A. A., & Buchko, K. J. (2016). Giving negative feedback to Millennials. *Management Research Review, 39,* 692–705.

Baldonado, A. M. (2013). Motivating generation Y and virtual teams. *Open Journal of Business and Management, 1*(2), 39–44.

Ballone, C. (2007). Consulting your clients to leverage the multi-generational workforce. *Journal of Practical Consulting, 2*(1), 9–15.

Baran, M. (2014). Mutual mentoring as a tool for managing employees of different generations in the enterprise. *Journal of Positive Management, 5*(2), 20–29.

Baron, R. A., Byrne, D. R., & Branscombe, N. R. (2009). *Social Psychology* (12th ed.). New York, NY: Pearson.

Becton, J. B., Walker, H. J., & Jones-Farmer, A. (2014). Generational differences in workplace behavior. *Journal of Applied Social Psychology, 44*(3), 175–189.

Berkup, S. B. (2014). Working with Generations X and Y in Generation Z period: Management of different generations in business life. *Mediterranean Journal of Social Sciences, 5,* 218–229.

Boehm, S. A., Kunze, F., & Bruch, H. (2014). Spotlight on age-diversity climate: The impact of age-inclusive HR practices on firm-level outcomes. *Personnel Psychology, 67*(3), 667–704.

Campbell, S. M., Twenge, J. M., & Campbell, W. K. (2017). Fuzzy but useful constructs: Making sense of the differences between generations. *Work, Aging and Retirement, 3*(2), 130–139.

Cates, S. V., Cojanu, K. A., & Pettine, S. (2013). Can you lead effectively? An analysis of the leadership styles of four generations of American employees. *International Review of Management and Business Research, 2*(4), 1025–1041.

Chou, S. Y. (2012). Millennials in the workplace: A conceptual analysis of Millennials' leadership and followership styles. *International Journal of Human Resource Studies, 2,* 71–83.

Costanza, D. P., Badger, J. M., Fraser, R. L., Severt, J. B., & Gade, P. A. (2012). Generational differences in work-related attitudes: A meta-analysis. *Journal of Business and Psychology, 27*(4), 375–394.

Costanza, D. P., Darrow, J. B., Yost, A. B., & Severt, J. B. (2017). A review of analytical methods used to study generational differences: Strengths and limitations. *Work, Aging and Retirement, 3*(2), 149–165.

Costanza, D. P., & Finkelstein, L. M. (2015). Generationally based differences in the workplace: Is there a there there? *Industrial and Organizational Psychology, 8*(3), 308–323.

Costanza, D. P., & Finkelstein, L. M. (2017). Generations, age, and the space between: Introduction to the special issue. *Work, Aging and Retirement, 3*(2), 109–112. doi: 10.1093/workar/wax003.

Crumpacker, M., & Crumpacker, J. M. (2007). Succession planning and generational stereotypes: Should HR consider age-based values and attitudes a relevant factor or a passing fad? *Public Personnel Management, 36*(4), 349–369.

Czaja, S. J., & Sharit, J. (2009). *Aging and work: issues and implications in a changing landscape.* Baltimore, MD: Johns Hopkins University Press.

Deal, J. J., Altman, D. G., & Rogelberg, S. G. (2010). Millennials at work: What we know and what we need to do (if anything). *Journal of Business and Psychology, 25*, 191–199.

De Hauw, S., & De Vos, A. (2010). Millennials' career perspective and psychological contract expectations: does the recession lead to lowered expectations? *Journal of Business and Psychology, 25*(2), 293–302.

de Lange, A. H., Kooij, D. T. A. M., & van der Heijen, B. I. J. M. (2015). Human resource management and sustainability at work across the lifespan: An integrative perspective. In L. Finkelstein, D. Truxillo, F. Fraccaroli, and R. Kanfer (Eds.), *Facing the challenges of a multi-age workforce: A use-inspired approach* (pp. 50–79). New York, NY: Routledge.

Dencker, J. C., Joshi, A., & Martocchio, J. J. (2008). Towards a theoretical framework linking generational memories to workplace attitudes and behaviors. *Human Resource Management Review, 18*(3), 180–187.

Espinoza, C., & Ukleja, M. (2016). *Managing the Millennials: Discover the core competencies for managing today's workforce.* Chichester: John Wiley & Sons.

Festing, M., & Schäfer, L. (2014). Generational challenges to talent management: A framework for talent retention based on the psychological-contract perspective. *Journal of World Business, 49*(2), 262–271.

Finkelstein, L. M. (2012). Aging and work: Linking our work to practitioner needs. Paper presented at the International Federation of Scholarly Associations of Management, Limerick, Ireland. June.

Finkelstein, L. M., Truxillo, D. M., Fraccaroli, F., & Kanfer, R. (2015). An introduction to facing the challenges of a multi-age workforce: A use-inspired approach. In L. Finkelstein, D. Truxillo, F. Fraccaroli, and R. Kanfer (Eds.), *Facing the challenges of a multi-age workforce: A use-inspired approach* (pp. 3–22). New York, NY: Routledge.

Fogg, P. (2009). When generations collide. *Education Digest, 74*(6), 25–30.

Giambatista, R. C., Hoover, J. D., & Tribble, L. (2017). Millennials, learning, and development: Managing complexity avoidance and narcissism. *Psychologist-Manager Journal, 20*(3), 176–193.

Green, D. (2008). Knowledge management for a postmodern workforce: Rethinking leadership styles in the public sector. *Journal of Strategic Leadership, 1*, 16–24.

Greenwood, R. A., Gibson, J. W., & Murphy Jr, E. F. (2008). An investigation of generational values in the workplace: Divergence, convergence, and implications for leadership. *International Leadership Journal, 20*, 57–76.

Guillot-Soulez, C., & Soulez, S. (2014). On the heterogeneity of Generation Y job preferences. *Employee Relations, 36*, 319–332.

Gursoy, D., Maier, T. A., & Chi, C. G. (2008). Generational differences: An examination of work values and generational gaps in the hospitality workforce. *International Journal of Hospitality Management, 27*(3), 448–458.

Hendricks, J. M., & Cope, V. C. (2013). Generational diversity: What nurse managers need to know. *Journal of Advanced Nursing, 69*(3), 717–725.

Hernaus, T., & Pološki Vokic, N. (2014). Work design for different generational cohorts: Determining common and idiosyncratic job characteristics. *Journal of Organizational Change Management, 27*, 615–641.

Howe, N., & Strauss, W. (2000). *Millennials rising: The next great generation.* New York, NY: Vintage.

Inceoglu, I., Segers, J., & Bartram, D. (2012). Age-related differences in work motivation. *Journal of Occupational and Organizational Psychology, 85*(2), 300–329.

Kelly, C., Elizabeth, F., Bharat, M., & Jitendra, M. (2016). Generation gaps: Changes in the workplace due to differing generational values. *Advances in Management, 9*(5), 1–8.

Kooij, D. T. A. M., Jansen, P. G. W., Dikkers, J. S. E., & de Lange, A. H. (2014). Managing aging workers: A mixed methods study on bundles of HR practices for aging workers. *International Journal of Human Resource Management, 25*, 2192–2212.

Kowske, B. J., Rasch, R., & Wiley, J. (2010). Millennials' (lack of) attitude problem: An empirical examination of generational effects on work attitudes. *Journal of Business and Psychology, 25*, 265–279.

Lachman, M. E., & James, J. B. (Eds.) (1997). *Multiple paths of midlife development.* Chicago, IL: University of Chicago Press.

Lester, S. W., Standifer, R. L., Schultz, N. J., & Windsor, J. M. (2012). Actual versus perceived generational differences at work: An empirical examination. *Journal of Leadership & Organizational Studies, 19*, 341–354.

Lewicki, R. J., Weiss, S. E., & Lewin, D. (1992). Models of conflict, negotiation and third-party intervention: A review and synthesis. *Journal of organizational behavior, 13*(3), 209–252.

Lindquist, T. M. (2008). Recruiting the millennium generation: The new CPA. *CPA Journal, 78*(8), 56.

Lyons, S., & Kuron, L. (2014). Generational differences in the workplace: A review of the evidence and directions for future research. *Journal of Organizational Behavior, 35*(S1), S139–S157.

Lyons, S. T., & Schweitzer, L. (2016). A qualitative exploration of generational identity: Making sense of young and old in the context of today's workplace. *Work, Aging and Retirement, 3*(2), 209–224.

Macky, K., Gardner, D., & Forsyth, S. (2008). Generational differences at work: Introduction and overview. *Journal of Managerial Psychology, 23*(8), 857–861.

Mannheim, K. (1952). The problem of generations. In K. Mannheim (Ed.), *Essays on the sociology of knowledge* (pp. 276–322). London: Routledge.

Mhatre, K. H., & Conger, J. A. (2011). Bridging the gap between Gen X and Gen Y. *Journal of Leadership Studies, 5*(3), 72–76.

McHenry, W. K., & Ash, S. R. (2013). Knowledge management and collaboration: Generation X vs. Generation Y. *International Journal of Business and Social Science, 4*, 78–87.

Parry, E., & Urwin, P. (2011). Generational differences in work values: A review of theory and evidence. *International Journal of Management Reviews, 13*(1), 79–96.

Parry, E., & Urwin, P. (2017). The evidence base for generational differences: Where do we go from here? *Work, Aging and Retirement, 3*(2), 140–148.

Perry, E. L., Golom, F. D., & McCarthy, J. A. (2015). Generational differences: Let's not throw the baby boomer out with the bathwater. *Industrial and Organizational Psychology: Perspectives of Science and Practice, 8*, 376–382.

Pondy, L. R. (1967). Organizational conflict: Concepts and models. *Administrative Science Quarterly*, 296–320.

Rajput, N., Marwah, P., Balli, R., & Gupta, M. (2013). Managing multigenerational workforce: Challenge for millennium managers. *International Journal of Marketing and Technology, 3*(2), 132–149.

Rudolph, C. W. (2015). A note on the folly of cross-sectional operationalizations of generations. *Industrial and Organizational Psychology, 8*, 362–366. doi: 10.1017/iop.2015.50.

Rudolph, C. W., Rauvola, R. S., & Zacher, H. (2017). Leadership and generations at work: A critical review. *Leadership Quarterly, 29*(1), 44–57.

Rudolph, C. W., & Zacher, H. (2017). Considering generations from a lifespan developmental perspective. *Work, Aging and Retirement, 3*(2), 113–129.

Ryder, N. (1965). The cohort as a concept in the study of social change. *American Sociological Review, 30*(6), 843–861.

Salahuddin, M. M. (2010). Generational differences impact on leadership style and organizational success. *Journal of Diversity Management, 5*(2), 1–6.

Schofield, C. P., & Honoré, S. (2009). Generation Y and learning. *Ashridge Journal*, Winter, 26–32.

Sessa, V. I., Kabacoff, R. I., Deal, J., & Brown, H. (2007). Generational differences in leader values and leadership behaviors. *Psychologist-Manager Journal, 10*, 47–74.

Strauss, W., & Howe, N. (1991). *Generations: The history of America's future, 1584 to 2069.* New York, NY: William Morrow & Co.

Thomas, K. M. (2005). *Diversity dynamics in the workplace.* Belmont, CA: Wadsworth Publishing.

Thompson, C., & Gregory, J. B. (2012). Managing Millennials: A framework for improving attraction, motivation, and retention. *Psychologist-Manager Journal, 15*(4), 237–246.

Twenge, J. M. (2010). A review of the empirical evidence on generational differences in work attitudes. *Journal of Business and Psychology, 25*(2), 201–210.

Twenge, J. M. (2017). The real truth about generational differences: Millennials are not a myth. Get over it. *Psychology Today Blog.* May 12.

Twenge, J. M., Campbell, S. M., Hoffman, B. J., & Lance, C. E. (2010). Generational differences in work values: Leisure and extrinsic values increasing, social and intrinsic values decreasing. *Journal of Management, 36*(5), 1117–1142.

Twenge, J. M., Carter, N. T., & Campbell, W. K. (2017). Age, time period, and birth cohort differences in self-esteem: Reexamining a cohort-sequential longitudinal study. *Journal of Personality and Social Psychology, 112*(5), e9–e17.

Twenge, J. M., Konrath, S., Foster, J. D., Keith Campbell, W., & Bushman, B. J. (2008). Egos inflating over time: A cross-temporal meta-analysis of the Narcissistic Personality Inventory. *Journal of Personality, 76*(4), 875–902.

Van de Vliert, E., & De Dreu, C. K. (1994). Optimizing performance by conflict stimulation. *International Journal of Conflict Management, 5*(3), 211–222.

Warr, P. (2001). Age and work behavior: Physical attributes, cognitive abilities, knowledge, personality traits, and motives. *International Review of Industrial and Organizational Psychology, 16*, 1–36.

Weresh, M. H. (2009). I'll start walking your way, you start walking mine: Sociological perspectives on professional identity development and influence of generational differences. *SCL Review, 61*, 337–392.

Williams, M. (2016). Being trusted: How team generational age diversity promotes and undermines trust in cross-boundary relationships. *Journal of Organizational Behavior, 37*(3), 346–373.

Zabel, K. L., Biermeier-Hanson, B. J., Baltes, B. B., Early, B. J., & Shepard, A. (2017). Generational differences in work ethic: Fact or fiction? *Journal of Business and Psychology, 32*, 301–315.

Zemke, R., Raines, C., & Filipczak, B. (2013). *Generations at work: Managing the clash of Boomers, Gen Xers, and Gen Yers in the workplace.* New York, NY: American Management Association.

Zhu, Y., Yang, H., & Bai, G. (2016). Effect of superior–subordinate intergenerational conflict on job performance of new generation employees. *Social Behavior and Personality, 44*(9), 1499–1514.

3 What Has Changed and What Has Not?

Kevin R. Murphy and Warren Tierney

There is a great deal of interest in the changing nature of work, and this interest is to some extent justified. There have been important and meaningful changes in the way many jobs are performed, in the types of jobs that are or are not available, and in the relationships between workers and their work environments. In the last 30–35 years, there have been a number of important and impactful changes to the way work is performed and the types of work that are available.

There is a wide-ranging literature dealing with changes in the nature of work (e.g., Burke & Ng, 2006; Howard, 1995; NASEM, 2017; National Research Council, 1999; Zuboff, 1988), and this literature has documented a large number of changes. In the business press, claims about the scope, rapidity and importance of these changes are frequently made (e.g., Dudowsky, 2014; Kokakowski, 2017; Schwartz, Collins, Stockton, Wagner, & Walsh, 2017). Different papers highlight different specific changes, but the general message of this literature is that the nature of work has changed substantially in recent years and that these changes have been relatively sudden, sharp and widespread. The principal themes of this literature are that there have been substantial and fairly sudden changes in: (1) jobs – it is often claimed that jobs are becoming increasingly complex; (2) the workforce – in many nations, the workforce is becoming older and more culturally diverse, and there are increasing instances of gaps between the skills workers possess and those jobs require; (3) employment relationships – many papers comment on the growth of numerous alternatives to the traditional norm of long-term full-time employment with the same employer, with a great deal of attention given to the "gig economy," (4) organizations – organizations are simultaneously becoming more complex (e.g., vertical integration, multinational organizations) and less hierarchical in structure; and (5) interactions with others in the organization – the rise of quicker communication, virtual information sharing, telecommuting, cross-national collaboration, etc. is thought to be changing the way people interact in organizations.

We believe that important changes are occurring in all five areas, but we also believe that the widespread belief that the nature of work is changing, and that these changes are rapid, relatively recent, and widespread is an oversimplification. The goal of this chapter is to consider changes in these five areas in the context of broader historical trends in the workplace and to examine factors that: (1) make these changes seem more sudden and sharp than they actually are and (2) limit the influence of these five changes on the nature of work as it is experienced by employees. We will make three main arguments. First, we will argue that the notion that changes in the nature of work are a relatively recent phenomenon (as evidenced by the large literature describing the changing nature of work that has emerged since the 1980s) is not consistent with the historical record. Second, we will argue that some changes look large mainly because we are comparing the present state of work with a misleading benchmark – i.e., the brief period between 1940 and the 1980s when the American economy was unusually stable, strong, and dominant. Compared to that "golden age," things do look quite different, but this comparison is not necessarily a useful one. Third, changes have occurred in many parts of the world economy, but there are also many parts of this economy where change has been and is likely to remain minimal. It is important to realize that the factors that have led to this widespread belief that the world of work is rapidly changing have had little or no impact on large sectors of the workforce.

We should highlight that several major reports have sounded cautionary notes about the belief that the nature of work is undergoing sudden and widespread changes. For example, a report by the National Academies of Sciences, Engineering, and Medicine (NASEM, 2017) describes the growth of computer technology, particularly in the area of artificial intelligence, which has the potential to significantly expand the range of jobs in which automation is replacing human workers. However, this report also notes that some widely discussed changes in the nature of work (e.g., on-demand work, working as an independent contractor rather than as an employee) still affect only a small slice of the workforce. The World Bank Development Report (2019) notes that change is more rapid and extensive in the advanced economies, but there that there are still large parts of the world and the workforce where changes in the nature of work are minimal. We hope to add to this literature by encouraging researchers to think more critically about claims regarding the changing nature of work. Large changes are occurring, but they are best understood in the context of the continuing evolution of work and the workplace.

We start by summarizing the major changes that have occurred in recent years and that continue to occur. In the later sections of this chapter, we will: (1) consider these changes in the context of broader patterns of historical change, (2) consider factors that make recent changes seem larger than they are, and (3) consider limits to the scope of these changes.

Changes in Jobs

Many jobs are becoming more complex. Repetitive, low-skilled work is becoming less frequent and less important (Autor et al., 2003; Cascio, 1995); although a good deal of routine work is being offshored to low-wage countries and is not disappearing altogether (e.g., Autor, Katz, & Kearney, 2006; Baumgarten, Geishecker, & Görg, 2010; Becker et al., 2013). Conversely, higher-level occupations are expanding, both in the United States and around the world (Acemoglu & Autor, 2011; Autor & Dorn, 2013). In an environment that features changing technologies, organizations, and workplaces, complex problem solving and organizational learning have become increasingly critical for occupational and organizational success (Bontis, Crossan, & Hulland, 2002; Neubert, Mainert, Kretzschmar, & Greiff, 2015). In particular, jobs at all levels are increasingly likely to demand higher-order thinking skills to plan, actively explore, execute, and monitor one's work tasks (Autor, Levy, & Murnane, 2003; Cascio, 1995; Neubert, Mainert, Kretzschmar, & Greiff, 2015). Complex problem solving (CPS) is an important representative of these higher-order thinking skills that are considered critical for success (National Research Council, 2012; OECD, 2013a), in large part because they are characterized by an increasing amount of dynamic, interactive, and nonroutine tasks and a decreasing amount of well-defined organizational practices and routines (e.g., Middleton, 2002).

Many jobs are being displaced because of technology. This is most obvious in manufacturing, where the number of person hours required to produce many goods has declined dramatically in recent years, especially in manufacturing environments where automation and robotics has replaced manual work with work done by machines[1] (Coco, 2016; National Research Council, 1999; see, however, Andes & Muro, 2015). The combination of increasing cognitive demands for jobs and the decrease in high-paying jobs that do not require higher levels of education and cognitive ability has contributed substantially to decreasing opportunities for employees who once could count on good jobs in manufacturing and in other arenas where the cognitive demands of work were not excessive, but do not possess the abilities, cognitive skills, education, and training to compete in a modern economy.

One change that appears to be more recent is the increase in job crafting, a process in which individual employees modify their jobs, crafting them to match their interests and abilities (Wrzesniewski & Dutton, 2001). Even here, it is likely that employee-initiated changes in jobs, to the extent that they are growing, are doing so at a gradual rate and that job crafting is not a new feature of the workplace, simply one that had not received a great deal of attention prior to Wrzesniewski and Dutton's (2001) paper.

Burke and Ng (2006) note that while the work performed in many jobs is becoming increasingly complex, some jobs require *less* skill than in the past because so many cognitively demanding tasks have moved from human operators to computerized systems. They cite examples such as use of AutoCAD in designing and building houses, MS Project in managing projects, and GPS and navigation systems in flying an aircraft; arguably these types of technologies deskill only a small number of jobs. The development of computerized systems for tracking and managing inventories, deliveries, and material handling impacts a far larger number of jobs, and as these systems become easier to learn and use, the skill sets

---

[1] This same report notes that automation has also displaced many jobs in banking and in other types of office work.

required for jobs performed in warehouses, distribution centers, delivery services, baggage handlers and the like are expected to become progressively narrower. It is true that these jobs will now require incumbents to interact with computers and related electronic devices, but these devices will also remove the need for judgment, memory, spatial skills, product knowledge, and the like from many of these jobs.

Changes in Work Interactions

The shift from manufacturing work to service-based employment has signaled the change from manual labor to more cognitive-based interdependent group work. In the current work environment one of the most important attributes of an employee is his/her ability to be adept at social interactions (Wegman et al., 2018). The method of how workers interact has changed substantially, with information technology (IT) applications allowing tasks to be completed in non-collocated work arrangements. As a consequence of this ability to transcend time and space, who we interact with has also changed. Another important ability at modern work is the employee's ability to work with people from an array of cultural backgrounds.

How We Work

Historically, one of the axioms of how work was undertaken was that workers must be collocated, but since the introduction of IT into the workplace, this assumption has been dispelled. Virtually located teams that work via electronic media to unite and achieve a set of shared goals have become more common (Bell & Kozlowski, 2002). In 2000 it was suggested that less than 50% of companies used virtual teams; by 2012 it was estimated 66% of multinational companies used virtual teams (Gilson, Maynard, Jones Young, Vartiainen, & Hakonen, 2015), while 80% of organizations surveyed projected that number would continue growing (Perry, 2008). As a result, the modern employee working in a large multinational company is increasingly likely to be working in virtual teams.

This transition from primarily collocated work to global virtual teams has brought about some advantages, as well as disadvantages. Some of the most pertinent advantages are that it is possible to form a team of experts dispersed throughout space and time (see Chapter 19 in this volume). This reduces the time and cost associated with travelling, it allows the team to function across a 24-hour workday, and it allows for companies to offer staffing flexibility to meet market demands (Kirkman, Gibson, & Kim, 2012). Still, there are some challenges associated with managing and working in global virtual teams: for instance, group interactions are much more complicated because the traditional cues used to understand one another are obscured, and virtual teams have been found to have lower levels of team cohesion, trust, social control, and commitment to team goals (Hoch & Kozlowski, 2014). Although these qualities are undoubtedly undesirable for virtual teams, this work arrangement is still in its infancy, and it is likely, in particular as society becomes more integrated through IT and IT itself becomes more adept, that virtual teams will become more effective.

Who We Work With

Since the 1950s, economic ideals, such as deregulation and free movement of labor, have become prominent features of the world economy. This has led to the proliferation of the globalized economy; as a result, organizations are increasingly diverse, multicultural environments (Javidan, Dorfman, De Luque, & House, 2006). This means that in the modern workplace, managing and leveraging cultural differences are an intricate component of the workplace. Research on cultural workways has identified an array of mental models that members from different backgrounds use to engage within workplace relationships (Levine, Harrington, & Uhlmann, in press). For instance, *guanxi*, the most prominent relational norm of Chinese organizations, where dense networks of personal relationships guide business relations (Sanchez-Burks & Lee, 2007), or *simpatía*, a relationship style in Latin cultures where social harmony is emphasized (Markus & Lin, 1999), represent types of cultural relationship management which are consistent with more collectivistic values. Alternative relationship approaches such as the Protestant Relational Ideology, the belief that relational and affective concerns should not be considered at work (Sanchez-Burks & Lee, 2007), are more typical of an individualistic view of the world. As a consequence of all these different ways that different cultures approach work, it is necessary for the modern employee to be very aware of cultural difference, in order to successfully negotiate the workplace. It is no longer possible to take a one-size-fits-all approach when it comes to work relationships, managing others and team interactions.

Putting These Changes into Perspective

The changes described in previous chapters and above seem substantial, but this may simply be a matter of perspective. First, most examinations of the changing nature of work focus on a narrow time perspective; broader historical reviews suggest that the workplace has been going through a steady period of change that goes back to before the US Civil War. In this sense, a chapter on the "Changing Nature of Work" might have been just as appropriate and timely in the 1890s as it was in the 1990s and beyond. Second, our perceptions of the extent and importance of the changes documented in this book are strongly influenced by the fact that they are often viewed in comparison to a faulty standard – the so-called "Golden Age" of employment in the United States – that brief and unrepresentative interval when full employment at a good wage for a lifetime with the same employer was the norm.

Change is the Norm, Not the Exception

Consider one of the most fundamental shifts in US employment over the last 150 years: the dramatic shift in the proportion of the US workforce engaged in agriculture. As Figure 3.1 shows, in 1950, more than 11% of the US working population

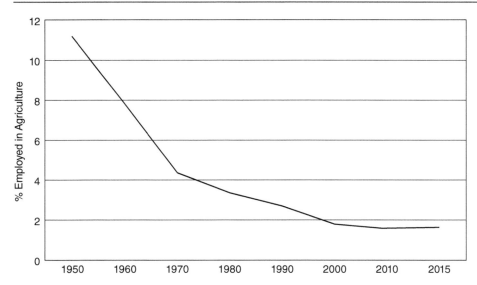

Figure 3.1 *Proportion of US working population employed in agriculture.*

was employed in agriculture[2]. By 1970, this figure was approximately 4.4%, and by 2000 it was below 2%. The shift away from agriculture as a major employer is even more stark if a longer historical perspective is taken. In 1870, over 50% of the US workforce was employed in agriculture (Lebergott, 1966). This represents a truly seismic shift, one that makes the current set of workplace changes seem small in comparison. We are certainly experiencing changes in the current economy, but in comparison to changes of this sort, they do not seem so fundamental.

The label "post-industrial economy" suggests a major shift in the nature of work, in particular a shift from manufacturing and production to services. This shift has indeed taken place. In 1950, approximately 40% of the nonfarm workforce was employed in manufacturing or the production of goods and about the same proportion was engaged in providing government services and other service-related industries (Lee & Mather, 2008). By 2005, manufacturing and the production of goods employed about 18% of the nonfarm workforce, and service-related occupations (including government service) employed almost two-thirds of the nonfarm workforce. However, these changes are neither recent nor sudden. For example, approximately 30% of the US nonfarm workforce was employed in manufacturing in 1960. This figure declined by approximately 5% every 10 years between 1960 and 2000, showing a near-linear rate of decline over this 40-year period.

Similarly, there have been striking changes in the composition of the US workforce over the last 50 years, but these changes are often quite gradual and slow. For example, the proportion of women in the workforce increased from approximately 40% in 1970 to approximately 60% in 2000, but this is not a recent shift, but rather a continuation of a trend more than a century old (in 1900, only

---

[2] Figure 3.1 was constructed using figures from the US Bureau of Labor Statistics (www.bls.gov/cps/cpsaat01.pdf).

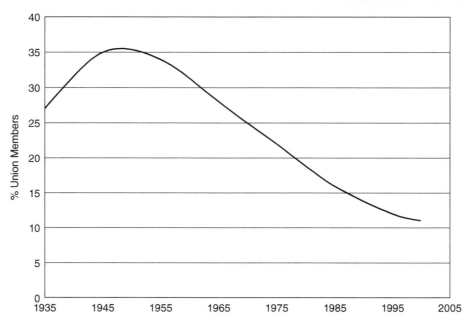

Figure 3.2 *Proportion of nonfarm workforce who are union members.*

19% of women were in the workforce or seeking work; Lee & Mather, 2008). There has been a good deal of recent discussion of the decreased power and membership of unions (e.g., Hogler, 2015), but as Figure 3.2 shows, decreases seen over the last 20–30 years are part of a much longer trend, in which union membership peaked in the 1940s and has been steadily declining for almost 70 years.[3]

In part because of the relative strength of unions at the time, the 1940s and 1950s provided low-skilled employees with unique opportunities to earn relatively high wages, especially in manufacturing and transportation (Hogler, 2015). However, the shift from assembly lines in which low-skilled employees performed simple and repetitive work for high pay to the current manufacturing environment where fewer workers perform more complex work is hardly a recent one. As early as the 1970s, Swedish auto manufacturers were relying on autonomous work teams rather than assembly lines to manufacture cars (Lohr, 1987). Although the track record of team-based manufacturing has sometimes been spotty, many of the concepts pioneered by Volvo and similar manufacturers spread to other sectors of the Swedish economy (Greenwood & Randle, 2007) and to Japan by the 1970s and 1980s.

Finally, the belief that changes in jobs and in the workplace are creating unparalleled challenges and disruption in the nature of work and in the ability to find meaningful and remunerative work for large sections of the workforce is hardly new. Similar views were widespread in the 1930s (World Bank, 2016), and these concerns can most certainly be traced back to the beginnings of the

---

[3] Figure 3.2 is based on figures from Mayer (2004).

Industrial Revolution (Sale, 1995), if not earlier (Frey & Osborne, 2013). Donkin (2010), in his massive history of work, details the changes in the meaning and nature of work over millennia; in describing the nature of work, he aptly quotes Hercalitus' dictum from 2,500 years ago that "nothing is permanent but change." Current changes in the nature of work are being driven by a number of forces, most notably technology, but this type of change is hardly unique to the current generation.

Within the last 100 years, the US economy *has* experienced a fairly sudden technological change that created widespread changes in the nature of work – i.e., the replacement of the horse by the automobile. For example, in 1900, there were over 20 million working horses in the United States, and industries that depended on horses (e.g., horse breeding, horse drivers, carriage making, waste disposal) were both major employers and were a highly visible part of daily life. Nikiforuk (2013) notes that in 1900 a businessman in any major American city would see more horses and interact with more horses than a cowboy in Texas or Wyoming. Horse-drawn transportation created a host of ancillary industries (e.g., facilities to stable, feed, shoe and clean up after horses) that employed large numbers of workers, virtually all of whom had to find work in other industries within a few decades.[4] Scholars who now bemoan the loss of manufacturing jobs could have said much the same thing in the 1920s and 1930s about the loss of jobs among saddle makers, horse breeders and, most important, the army of workers needed to clear horse manure from the streets.

In the United States, much of the discussion of the changing nature of work has focused on topics such as automation and computerization, but if one takes a global perspective, the challenges to providing meaningful and remunerative work to sectors of the workforce that are not highly skilled are quite different. In many parts of the world, the principal challenge to providing good employment to workers with a wide range of knowledge, skills and abilities is not that computers and robots are taking jobs, but rather that a combination of a shortage of capital, informal employment, forced labor, human trafficking and child labor are constricting the availability of decent work for entire generations (International Labor Office, 2016). American workers are broadly concerned with being replaced by machines, but in much of the world, the threat to employees is that you will be replaced by slaves and by coerced labor, and the solution is more likely to be to build and support the rule of law than to devise retraining programs.

A Faulty Mirror: Why Recent Changes Seem So Substantial

There have been important and meaningful changes in the nature of work in the last 30–35 years. On the other hand, there are reasons to believe that discussions of the changing nature of work are sometimes overblown. The way "work" has been

---

[4] It is worth noting that even in this case, the transition from one technology to another was not as swift or as widespread as might have been imagined. The transition from horse to automobile in the US was not complete into the middle of the twentieth century. Freihofer's, a major bakery in New York, continued to use horse-drawn wagons to deliver their wares to customers' homes as late as 1962.

conceptualized and understood in the United States (and because of the disproportionate global influence of US culture, in much of the rest of the world) in the twentieth and twenty-first centuries has been substantially shaped by a set of historical anomalies. In particular, the perspective from which we currently evaluate the changing nature of work is arguably a distorted one that uses a very unrepresentative part of our history as a starting point, and that will necessarily lead to the impression that we are in a period of wrenching and unprecedented change.

During the period roughly from the late 1940s through the 1980s, the United States had a dominant position in the world economy and a relatively stable economy characterized by: (1) a large and strong middle class, (2) relatively easy access to the middle class for workers with low to moderate skill levels, (3) a workforce that was relatively homogeneous, (4) patterns of long-term, if not lifetime employment with the same organization, (5) high wages for full-time work in a predictable and favorable labor market, and (6) little effective economic competition from other nations. This type of economy, labor market, and set of opportunities became accepted as normal, and as this anomalous pattern started to break down, books and articles dealing with the changing nature of work became increasingly common. For example, Howard's (1995) book *The Changing Nature of Work* examined the implications of shifts toward a "post-industrial" economy for understanding the nature of work. The National Research Council's (1999) study of the changing nature of work examined how changes in the workforce, the workplace and work itself influence efforts to develop adequate taxonomies of work and occupations. Zuboff (1988) explored the ways in which a shift toward information-based work was likely to change both the skills that would be required of workers and the relationships between management and employees.

A theme of much of the scholarship describing the changing nature of work is that the model of employment that was accepted as normal in the 1940s through 1980s no longer holds. For example, Cappelli (2000) describes a "New Deal at Work," starting with the observation "Most observers of the corporate world believe that the traditional relationship between employer and employee is gone" (p. 1193). The implications of these changes continue to play an important part in understanding many aspects of current society, ranging from politics[5] to educational policy.[6]

The change from the "normal" of the period of approximately 1945–1980 is the subject of a great deal of discussion and concern, but there are good reasons to believe that much of this discussion is misguided. First, the "normal" that has been accepted as a starting point for evaluating the changing nature of work is far from normal. Considered from a broader historical perspective, the period 1945–1980 is

---

[5] It can be argued that nostalgia for the economy of 1945–1980 was a substantial factor in the election of Donald Trump as president of the United States.

[6] For example, both the National Research Council (2012) and the Organization for Economic Cooperation and Development (2013a, 2013b) have identified the development of higher levels of complex problem-solving skills as a critical challenge for education and training systems around the world.

a highly unusual one, and the fact this state of affairs did not last forever is not something that requires explanation. Second, the idea that the nature of work has changed since the 1980s applies more strongly to some parts of the economy than to others. That is, the changes in the workplace that have been the focus of over 20 years of research on the changing nature of work have in fact often been localized, and in the grand scheme of things, relatively unimportant.

What Is Changing and What Is Not?

The current set of changes in the US workplace can be thought of in terms of three principal dimensions: (1) changes in jobs and in the ways these jobs are performed, (2) changes in the relationship with organizations (e.g., nonstandard employment, part-time, contingent work), and (3) changes in the workforce (e.g., changes in employment patterns for women and members of racial and ethnic minority groups). We will focus here on the first two sets of changes, because these have a direct bearing on the argument that the nature of work and the work relationship is changing. The changing workforce creates both opportunities and challenges to organizations, and it introduces competition that has historically not been present for lower-skilled employees who once had ready access to good jobs and good pay. However, changes in the workforce do not always have a direct impact on the nature of work itself.[7]

Understanding Where Changes in Jobs Are Most and Least Likely

One way to test the hypothesis that the world of work is changing is to look for changes in patterns of employment. At least in the short to medium term, the data do not support the idea that there are widespread changes in the world of work. For example, if you look at US data over the last 15–17 years, the overall trend is for considerable stability, with a few notable exceptions. The Bureau of Labor Statistics (2017) examined the percentage of the US workforce working in over 20 different sectors of the US economy (e.g., architecture and engineering, computer and mathematical occupations, healthcare, management occupations, personal care and service occupations) in 1999, 2002, 2007, 2012, and 2016. With the exception of food preparation and related occupations (where the proportion of the workforce has increased slightly over time) and production operations (here the proportion of the workforce has decreased slightly over time), there have been very few changes in the distribution of the workforce across occupations. Over this entire period, there was remarkable stability in overall employment patterns, with the bulk of the US workforce employed in office and administrative support, sales, food preparation and serving, education and training, business and financial services and

---

[7] Some changes, including increasing immigration (legal and illegal), might lead to an increase in the number of employees with low skill levels, especially language skills.

production (Bureau of Labor Statistics, 2017). There have been nontrivial declines in production and noteworthy increases in both food preparation and service and business and financial services, but the main message of this analysis is one of broad stability.

Analyzing Jobs and Occupations to Assess Exposure to Change

IT represents one of the fastest drivers of change in current occupations (Pissarides, 2000). A combination of automation, Internet, and social media devices has substantially changed some jobs (e.g., agricultural workers), and has virtually eliminated others (e.g., typist), but has had only minimal effects in other jobs (e.g., therapists) (World Bank Development Report, 2016). Many of the jobs most susceptible to automation are characterized as highly routine and requiring limited judgment. Frey and Osborne (2013) outline three job characteristics that pose substantial barriers to computerization and automation: (1) job tasks that involve complex perception and manipulation, (2) creative intelligence tasks, and (3) tasks that require social intelligence. In a sense, these job characteristics reflect the relative simplicity of modern IT; given the pace of progress in this field it is likely that in the future artificial intelligence will enable the automation of many non-routine and highly complex tasks. However, for the moment, at least, the probability of an occupation becoming redundant as a result of automation can be best understood as a function of the task characteristics (Frey & Osborne, 2013).

There are several methods of estimating the vulnerability of jobs to automation. Frey and Osborne (2013) used O*NET to identify occupations that are relatively low risk for automation, on the basis of job requirements that involved high levels of detailed perception and manipulation, creative intelligence or social intelligence. They concluded that 47% of US employees were in occupations, particularly in the areas of sales, office, and administrative support and some service occupations, that were highly susceptible to computerization. Arntz, Gregory and Zierahn (2016) used reports of tasks individuals performed in their jobs to carry out a comparable analysis, first regressing task characteristics on Frey and Osborne's (2013) estimates of automation risks, then using these regression equations to generalize prior results to an international sample of individuals participating in the Programme for the International Assessment of Adult Competencies. They concluded that while large number of individuals in the population they studied (employees in 21 countries within the OECD) are in *occupations* that are susceptible to computerization and automation, a much smaller number (i.e., 9%) are in *jobs* that have a substantial probability of being easily replaced by machines.[8] They note that even if a particular occupation might be at risk of being replaced by machines, the people who hold jobs within these occupations often carry out key job tasks that involve social interactions or creative effort. The

---

[8] Here, a job is described as susceptible to automation if the probability that key job tasks could readily be automated is 0.70 or higher.

Table 3.1 *Proportion of occupations in which specific abilities and skills are rated as important*

Abilities	Important	Very Important or Higher
Oral comprehension	96.8	45.0
Oral expression	94.7	41.1
Written expression	82.4	17.1
Fluency of ideas[9]	50.6	1.1
Originality	44.3	1.1
Inductive reasoning	84.0	17.8
Deductive reasoning	90.8	21.0
Category flexibility[10]	78.1	1.1
Speech clarity	87.6	11.6
Skills		
Active listening	92.3	27.3
Writing	64.6	10.4
Speaking	89,6	25.6
Complex problem solving	70.8	5.6
Coordination	74.6	2.8
Critical thinking	89.8	21.7
Judgment and decision making	77.0	5.7
Time management	73.0	1.2
Social perceptiveness	64.1	7.2
Complex problem solving[11]	70.8	5.6

vulnerability of jobs to being replaced by automation varies considerably across countries, with higher levels of vulnerability in less developed economies (World Bank, 2016).[12]

To get a better insight into the trends discussed by Arntz et al. (2016) and Frey and Osborne (2013), we examined the O*NET database to determine the proportion of occupations in which several abilities or skills that might be difficult to replace with automation are rated as important.[13] Our results are presented in Table 3.1; the figures in this table suggest that in a very large proportion of occupations there are abilities or skills that are rated as at least moderately important (i.e., at or above the scale midpoint), and quite a few in which they are rated as very important or higher, that might be difficult to replace with automation. There is a critical caveat – i.e., that computers and

---

[9] The ability to come up with a number of ideas about a topic (the *number* of ideas is important, *not* their quality, correctness, or creativity).
[10] The ability to generate or use different sets of rules for combining or grouping things in different ways.
[11] Identifying complex problems and reviewing related information to develop and evaluate options and implement solutions.
[12] However, in many of these countries, the limited availability of capital hinders the growth of automation.
[13] The ability and skills ratings databases each include 966 separate occupations.

Table 3.2 *Proportion of occupations in which specific work styles are rated as important*

	Important	Very Important or Higher
Leadership	90.6	26.9
Concern for others	93.6	33.2
Social orientation	76.9	17.7
Self-control	99.7	50.8
Stress tolerance	98.7	98.7
Integrity	99.6	77.7

machines are constantly evolving, and it is possible that abilities like oral expression, fluency of ideas, written expression or originality might be captured by emerging technologies. Similarly, while there are some skills (e.g., active listening, persuasiveness, negotiation) that may be hard to capture with technology today, it is unlikely that these skills will never be adequately captured by automated devices (Cascio & Montealegre, 2016). Nevertheless, it is clear that a large proportion of occupations still require abilities and skills that are at least somewhat resistant to automation.

We performed a similar analysis of ratings of work styles; the results of this analysis are shown in Table 3.2. Stress tolerance, integrity, and a number of socially oriented work styles are rated as important in most occupations, and some of these are rated as very important in large numbers of occupations. Again, we do not claim that all of these work styles are completely resistant to automation, but these types of activities will certainly be difficult to replace with robots or computers in the near future.

Barriers to Automation

Although the idea of automation is appealing for employers, there still remains an array of barriers in place that prevent the implementation of these technological innovations. First, technology is subject to the same social norms as any other social invention; as a result economic, legal and social hurdles hinder the introduction of technology. For instance, jobs that require an intimacy between both parties, such as negotiations between companies, will still be best suited to humans. Therefore, "some human services will probably continue to command a premium compared to robotically produced ones" (Pratt, 2015, p. 58). Moreover, ethical concerns also slow the introduction of technology; for instance, how will a self-driving car decide between crashing into a car or a truck? Second, automation creates new jobs through the demand for new technologies and the increased competitiveness of companies that exploit their current processes to deliver a more efficient product. Third, even when technologies are introduced, employees can switch job task, rather than becoming completely redundant. In addition, it is difficult for automation to capture the tacit knowledge of an organization due to the unpredictability of complex job tasks, as well as the intricacy of the social dimensions at work. For instance, although it may be possible through machine learning to identify the worker who possesses high network brokerage, it will be extremely difficult for a robot to appeal to this person's interests. Thus, non-routine jobs which require high emotional intelligence and intense human interactions will still hold a premium.

Finally, the likelihood of widespread automation is likely to vary as a function of the size and the pool of resources available to an organization. The Small Business Administration (2016) estimates that (1) over 99% of all the businesses in the United States are classified as small businesses – i.e., businesses that employ fewer than 500 people, (2) roughly half of the American workforce is employed by a small business, (3) roughly one-third of the American workforce work in a business that employs fewer than 100 people, and (4) 17% of the workforce work in businesses that employ fewer than 20 people. Some small businesses are able to take advantage of progress in technology, and this trend is likely to accelerate as once-expensive technologies (e.g., manufacturing robots) become smaller and more affordable (Cascio & Monteleagre, 2016). Nevertheless, many small businesses are likely to lack the combination of capital and expertise needed to transform the work their employees perform.

Automation Both Creates and Destroys Jobs

Even though automation is a challenge facing modern workers, the Internet has created a multitude of sectors where employees can work. This is primarily due to the fact that the Internet allows workers and entrepreneurs to circumvent many of the barriers to entry that previously only large organizations could afford. For instance, social media facilitates instantaneous communication across the world, in the modern-day society anyone with an Internet connection can create their own channel on YouTube; some YouTube performers make millions each year (Berg, 2017). People provide reviews about brands, services and/or products. As a reaction to these reviews, companies sponsor these channels to have their products reviewed or endorsed. This creates a revenue stream for the channel (Johansson, 2016). This new digital marketplace is more dynamic and targeted towards the end user, as service providers can instantly create content that consumers can access from an array of devices (Mangold & Faulds, 2009).

In sum, there are jobs which are made redundant through automation, but other jobs are also facilitated through IT, while in the future it seems that jobs which are more social will possess a premium. Nevertheless, there is a steady trend emerging: computers are increasingly competing with human labor in a variety of cognitive tasks (Brynjolfsson & McAfee, 2011).

Changes in the Relationships between Employers and Employees

In charting the changing nature of the relationships between employers and employees, Wartzman (2017) describes "the end of loyalty" – i.e., the idea that the reciprocal bonds between employers and employees that characterized the golden age of employment in America (particularly the postwar boom of the late 1940s and 1950s) have frayed. It is often argued that the employer–employee relationship has deteriorated from a partnership-oriented relationship (Wartzman, 2017) to a relationship in which employees are dehumanized and commoditized. Indeed, one of the criticisms of the concept of human capital is that it tends to reduce workers to a bundle of interchangeable resources that can be made available to employers (Tan, 2014).

The frayed bonds between employers and employees are manifested in a number of ways, but three are most frequently cited. First, several authors have suggested that employment has become less secure, contrasting a model of long-term attachment with a single employer that was more common during the "golden age" with a more precarious set of links today (Farber, 2008; Hanauer & Rolf, 2015). Second, there is widespread concern that employees have failed to reap the benefits they deserve: while productivity and corporate profits have risen sharply for several decades, wages have been relatively flat, except at the very top of organizations (Bivens, Gould, Mishel, & Shierholz, 2014; Gould, 2016; see, however, Pessoa & Van Reenan, 2013).

Finally, there is widespread concern over the apparent growth in forms of employment that are undependable and that are insufficient to support employees and their families. For example, a substantial number of employees work in jobs that are temporary (i.e., jobs with a predetermined termination date, such as the end of the project); approximately 11% of all jobs in OECD countries and 14% of all jobs in the European Union are classified as temporary.[14] A substantial number of employees, whether in permanent or temporary jobs, work part-time. In the United States, approximately 21% of the workforce are part-time employees; in the OECD, approximately 16% of the workforce is employed part-time.[15] A growing numbers of individuals provide services directly to customers through the so-called gig economy, where traditional employer–employee relationships have been replaced by a model in which there may be an organization (e.g., Uber, Lyft, Deliveroo) that helps to connect individual customers with individual service providers without necessarily acting as an employer.

The Gig Economy and Related Forms of Employment

A trend that has received tremendous attention in the business press is the gig economy, in which individuals provide on-demand services to customers (Lowry, 2017; Strauss, 2017a, 2017b). This form of work poses important legal challenges in determining who is or is not an employee (Aguinis & Lawal, 2013;

---

[14] The Organisation for Economic Co-operation and Development is a group of 35 nations with advanced or developing economies. OECD and European Union figures for temporary jobs are from https://data.oecd.org/emp/temporary-employment.htm#indicator-chart_

[15] US part-time employment rate: www.bls.gov/cps/cpsaat20.pdf; OECD rate: https://data.oecd.org/emp/part-time-employment-rate.htm

Cunningham-Parameter, 2016; Levy, 2016), particularly when these individuals appear to be employed by larger entities, but the primary concern in many analyses of this form of employment is the low and undependable pay it often provides.

The gig economy primarily occurs in two forms, "crowdwork" and "work on-demand via apps" (Cardon & Casilli, 2015). "Crowdwork" refers to virtual platforms, such as Amazon Mechanical Turk, where an online marketplace offers the chance for workers to complete ad hoc tasks. On the other hand, "Work on-demand via apps" is another online marketplace, such as Uber; however in this instance, the worker is available to complete more traditional tasks, such as transport, etc. (Aloisi, 2015). Estimates around the amount of people employed by the gig economy vary; for instance, there are claims that over a third of the US workforce is part of the gig economy (CNN, 2017). However, there is evidence that these claims are likely to be inflated. For instance, the same person could engage in an array of gigs for an array of companies at the same time, and this often leads to double-counting of the same individual when calculating the size of the gig economy (Singer, 2014).

Although there are differing views on the extent to which people engage with the gig economy, one thing is certain: ad hoc jobs which were once contracted work, or likely occurred on the black market, are now more formalized in an official space where people can legally engage with the gig economy. Nevertheless, a series of recent cases and decisions (e.g., Green, 2015; Employment Law – National Labor Relations Board, 2016) suggests that the federal government is placing the classification of people who might reasonably be assumed to be employees as independent contractors under increasing scrutiny.

O'Sullivan and colleagues have examined the growing prevalence of "zero hours contracts," in which individuals are contractually obligated to make themselves available to perform work for an employer, but are not guaranteed any hours of work, as well as variants that provide workers with little assurance of receiving work, while being under various levels of obligations to provide their services to employers when requested (O'Sullivan et al., 2017, 2015). They note that the prevalence of this type of work arrangement varies extensively across different sectors of the economy and across nations. Large proportions of the workforce in the countries they studied have work contracts that produce some level of uncertainty in work relationships. For example, about a third of the workforce in Ireland report regular changes in their work schedule, sometimes with minimal notice. However, they also note that employees whose contracts do not guarantee them particular amounts of work often end up working fairly regular schedules, and that there can be large discrepancies between hours as guaranteed in one's contract and hours worked.

Contractor Relationships and Third-Party Employment

The US Department of Labor is engaged in a wide-ranging effort to identify and rectify the misclassification of employees as independent contractors

(Dubé, 2015); in 2015, their investigations resulted in over $74 million in back wages to over 100,000 employees. Under common law, the most important factor determining whether or not an individual is an employee is the employer's control over the work (e.g., how the work is performed, hours, breaks), but under the Fair Labor Standards Act, a broader array of factors are relevant. The Department of Labor has issued detailed guidance in making a determination whether an individual is in fact an employee or an independent contractor (US Department of Labor, 2015).

Wears and Fisher (2012) note that the increasing reliance on staffing firms and temporary employment agencies by organizations to fill positions creates a triangular relationship between the individual worker, the staffing firm and the organization in which the worker performs his or her job. The use of third-party firms to help staff contingent positions is not new; relationships of this sort have been documented since the 1800s. However, this type of employment relationship is becoming increasingly common (Davis-Blake & Broschak, 2009).

As Wears and Fisher (2012) note, in triangular reemployment relationships, neither state nor federal law provides a completely clear answer to the question of which organization (the staffing firm or the organization that contracts for these employees) is responsible for protecting the legal rights of workers (e.g., rights to overtime, protection against sexual harassment). They suggest that one key factor is who controls the manner and means by which products are created or services are offered and it is possible that either the staffing agency, the contracting organization, or both (under the joint employment doctrine) might be considered as employers. There is a growing literature examining the nature and implications of such triangular employment relationships (Coyle-Shapiro, Morrow, & Kessler, 2006; Fisher, Wasserman, Wolf, & Wears, 2008; Liden, Wayne, Kraimer, & Sparrowe, 2003; Malos, Haynes, & Bowal, 2003; Mitlacher, 2005; Nesheim, Olsen, & Kalleberg, 2007).

Are Some Changes More Apparent Than Real?

There is little doubt that large numbers of workers are employed in jobs where the pay is low, working hours are variable, and the bonds between employers and employees are not particularly strong. What is less clear is whether these facts provide a meaningful indication of the changing nature of the relationship between employers and employees. For example, while it is true that part-time work is widespread in the US economy, only a small proportion of part-time work exists because of employers' inability or unwillingness to offer full-time employment. In the United States, over 80% of part-time workers are employed part-time rather than full-time because of non-economic reasons, ranging from childcare and family demands, being in school or in training to being retired or in poor health.[16]

---

[16] www.bls.gov/cps/cpsaat20.pdf

Similarly, it is often claimed that larger proportions of the workforce depend on the gig economy or other unstable forms of work, but there are good reasons to believe that these claims are greatly overstated. For example, a detailed analysis of US tax records suggests that at most 12% of all tax filers in the United States are self-employed (Jackson, Looney, & Ramnath, 2017). This figure includes a large number of fairly traditional sole proprietorships (e.g., accounts, medical professionals, consultants) who operate their own businesses in ways that have not changed substantially over the years, leaving only a small portion of the population of tax filers available for full-time work in the modern gig economy. Sherman (2017) suggests that in 2014, less than 1% of the workforce were exclusively "gig workers," although larger numbers of individuals have a mix of employment income and gig income.

In theory, one stark difference between the "golden age" and the current work environment is a shift from long-term (if not lifetime) employment with a single organization to careers in which moving from organization to organization is common and sometimes necessary (Bidwell, 2013; Farber, 2008). While there are some reasons to believe that shifting jobs and employers is more common in the current economy than in the economy of the 1940s–1980s, the data do not support the idea that workers are moving between jobs or organizations more frequently now than in the past. Hyatt and Spetzler (2016) have shown that there has actually been a shift toward slightly longer-tenure jobs since 2000, although trends are confounded by changes in workforce demographics (older workers show less job mobility). Bidwell (2013) examined data over a slightly longer period (1979–2008), and his analysis suggested at least some decline in tenure. However, none of the available data suggest that there has been a large and meaningful change in job or organizational tenure across the board. Copeland (2012) summarizes the major trends in job tenure, noting that "The data on employee tenure – the amount of time an individual has been with his or her current employer – show that career jobs *never* existed for most workers and have continued not to exist for most workers. These tenure results indicate that, historically, most workers have repeatedly changed jobs during their working careers, and all evidence suggests that they will continue to do so in the future (p. 13, emphasis added).

Three Conclusions about the Changing World of Work

Our review leads to three important conclusions. First, the world of work is changing, but the current set of changes are not necessarily any more jarring or impactful than previous changes. The US economy and the US workforce has been exposed to a number of important changes over time, and the current set of changes that automation and precarious work arrangements have bought about are small in comparison with the shift from agriculture to industrial production or the shift from horse-drawn to motorized transport. The world of work is always changing, and while each change creates new and pressing challenges, it is not clear that the current set of challenges is in any way unique.

Second, perspective matters. If the US labor market during the brief period between 1940 and 1980 is taken as a starting point, the current world of work will look bleak indeed. However, there were many non-sustainable factors that both contributed to a short golden age of employment in the United States, such as the virtual destruction of most economic competitors in the Second World War, and this period cannot be treated as a normal state we should expect or strive for.

Third, the changes that have received the most attention in the last 25 years (changes in employment and methods of work linked to technology, changes in careers and job tenure) are far from uniform. There are large sectors of the labor market that are largely insulated from many of these changes, because of the nature of the organizations that employ them (e.g., a large proportion of the workforce is employed in small businesses), or the nature of the jobs themselves (e.g., large numbers of jobs still require skills and activities that are difficult to replace with technology). There are entire sectors of the economy, such as the military, police, fire and protective services, where changes have been small and where the outlook for major changes in the future seems unlikely. Thus, it should not be assumed that changes impact all occupations, and research should be focused on determining which occupations are most affected, and attention directed there, rather than over-generalizing to the entire economy.

In sum, the world of work is changing, but it has been changing over the last 150 years, and the current round of changes are not necessarily more substantial or disruptive than previous changes. These changes can create a number of challenges to both employees and managers, especially changes related to how we work and who we work with, but reports of these changes must be taken with a grain of salt. A large proportion of the workforce is employed in jobs or in settings that are largely insulated from many of these changes, because of the nature of the work (e.g., jobs require activities that are not easily automated) or the nature of the organization (e.g., employment in small firms that have limited access to or need for many emerging technologies). Work in many settings is becoming more complex, and in many ways, this is likely to be the most disruptive change. In the 1930s, workers who were displaced from saddle manufacturing might find the adjustment to other sorts of manufacturing relatively easy. Workers who once had access to well-paying jobs that required minimal levels of cognitive skills and knowledge may find it difficult to adjust to the emerging demands of the workplace. Nevertheless, when you read about how the world of work is changing, we believe it is important to appreciate that much of what you read is presented without adequate attention to the broader context, in which change is a fairly constant but a far from uniform process.

Finally, although the purpose of this chapter is to argue that the rhetoric on the changing nature of work is sometimes overblown, it is important to recognize that there are sectors of the economy where changes *have* been substantial and quick. This volume discusses a wide range of changes and only some of these are directly addressed in this chapter. It is also important to recognize that there are other sectors of the economy that are poised for quick change once a handful of obstacles (e.g., barriers to automation) come down, and it is likely that in some sectors of the economy, the type of change that has been hyped since the mid-1990s *will* come. Our long history of meaningful changes in technology and in the organization of work suggests that these changes will be wrenching for some workers, but also suggests a degree of resilience and adaptability that is likely to mitigate the negative disruptions change can often trigger.

References

Acemoglu, D., & Autor, D. (2011). Skill, tasks and technologies: Implications for employment earnings. In O. Ashenfelter & D. Card (Eds.), *The handbook of labor economics, Vol. 4b* (pp. 1043–1171). Amsterdam: Elsevier.

Aguinis, H., & Lawal, S.O. (2013). eLancing: A review and research agenda for bridging the science–practice gap. *Human Resource Management Review*, 23, 6–17.

Aloisi, A. (2015). Commoditized workers: Case study research on labor law issues arising from a set of on-demand/gig economy platforms. *Comparative Labor Law and Policy Journal*, 37, 653–690.

Andes, S., & Muro, M. (2015, April 29). Don't blame robots for the loss of manufacturing jobs. *Brookings Advanced Industries Series*. Retrieved from www.brookings.edu/blog/the-avenue/2015/04/29/dont-blame-the-robots-for-lost-manufacturing-jobs/

Arntz, M., Gregory, T., & Zierahn, U. (2016). The risk of automation for jobs in OECD countries: a comparative analysis. *OECD Social, Employment and Migration Working Papers*, No. 189. Paris: OECD Publishing.

Autor, D. H., & Dorn, D. (2013). The growth of low-skill service jobs and the polarization of the US labor market. *American Economic Review*, 103, 1553–1597.

Autor, D. H., Katz, L. F., & Kearney, M. S. (2006). The polarization of the US labor market. *American Economic Review*, 96, 189–194.

Autor, D. H., Levy, F., & Murnane, R. J. (2003). The skill content of recent technological change: An empirical exploration. *Quarterly Journal of Economics*, 118, 1279–1333.

Baumgarten, D., Geishecker, I., & Görg, H. (2010). Offshoring, tasks, and the skill–wage pattern. *CEGE Discussion Paper*, 98. doi: 10.2139/ssrn.1574784

Becker, S. O., Ekholm, K., & Muendler, M. A. (2013). Offshoring and the onshore composition of tasks and skills. *Journal of International Economics*, 90, 91–106.

Bell, B. S., & Kozlowski, S. W. (2002). A typology of virtual teams: Implications for effective leadership. *Group and Organization Management*, 27, 14–49.

Berg, M. (2017). The highest-paid YouTube stars 2017: Gamer DanTDM takes the crown with $16.5 million. Retrieved from www.forbes.com/sites/maddieberg/2017/12/07/

Bidwell, M. J. (2013). What happened to long-term employment: The role of worker power and environmental turbulence in explaining declines in worker tenure. *Organizational Science*, 24, 1061–1082.

Bivens, J., Gould, E., Mishel, L., & Shierholz, H. (2014). Raising America's pay: Why it's our central policy challenge. *Briefing Paper* #378. Washington, DC: Economic Policy Institute.

Bontis, N., Crossan, M. M., & Hulland, J. (2002). Managing an organizational learning system by aligning stocks and flows. *Journal of Management Studies*, *39*, 437–469.

Brynjolfsson, E., and McAfee, A. (2011). *Race against the machine: How the digital revolution is accelerating innovation, driving productivity, and irreversibly transforming employment and the economy.* Lexington, MA: Digital Frontier Press.

Bureau of Labor Statistics. (2017). Washington (DC): USDOL Bureau of Labor Statistics. Occupational employment statistics. Retrieved September 12, 2017, from www.bls.gov/oes/tables.htm.

Burke, R. J., & Ng, E. (2006). The changing nature of work and organizations: Implications for human resource management. *Human Management Resource Review*, *16*, 86–94.

Cappelli, P. (2000). The New Deal at work. *Chicago-Kent Law Review*, *76*, 1169–1193.

Cardon, D., & Casilli, A. A. (2015). *Qu'est-ce que le digital labor?* Paris: Institut National de l'Audiovisual.

Cascio, W. F., (1995). Whither industrial and organizational psychology in a changing world of work? *American Psychologist*, *50*, 928–939.

Cascio, W. F. & Montealegre, R. (2016). How technology is changing work and organizations. *Annual Review of Organizational Psychology and Organizational Behavior*, *3*, 349–375.

CNN. (2017). Intuit: Gig economy now accounts for 34% of US workforce. Retrieved October 16, 2017, from http://money.cnn.com/2017/05/24/news/economy/gig-economy-intuit/index.html

Coco, F. (2016). Most US manufacturing jobs lost to technology, not trade. *Financial Times*. December 2. www.ft.com/content/dec677c0-b7e6-11e6-ba85-95d1533d9a62

Copeland, C. (2012). Employee tenure trends, 1983–2012. *Employee Benefits Research Institute Notes*, *33*(12), 1–13.

Coyle-Shapiro, J. A., Morrow, P. C., & Kessler, I. (2006). Serving two organizations: Exploring the employment relationship of contracted employees. *Human Resource Management*, *45*, 561–583.

Cunningham-Parameter, K. (2016). From Amazon to Uber: Defining employment in the modern economy. *Boston University Law Review*, *96*, 1673–1728.

Davis-Blake, A., & Broschak, J. P. (2009). Outsourcing and the changing nature of work. *Annual Review of Sociology*, *35*, 321–340.

Donkin, R. (2010). *The history of work.* New York, NY: Macmillan.

Dubé, L. E. (2015). Misclassification remains major issue for attorneys and the Labor Department. *HR Focus*, *92*, 1–3.

Dudowsky, J. (2014). Changing nature of work in the 21st century. https://research-methodology.net/changing-nature-of-work-in-the-21st-century/

Employment law – National Labor Relations Board (2016). NLRB classifies canvassers as employees, not independent contractors. *Harvard Law Review*, *129*, 2039–2046.

Farber, H. S. (2008). Employment insecurity: The decline of worker–firm attachment in the United States. *CEPS Working Paper* No. 172. Princeton, NJ: Center for Economic Policy Studies.

Fisher, S. L., Wasserman, M. E., Wolf, P. P., & Wears, K. H. (2008). Human resource issues in outsourcing: Integrating research and practice. *Human Resource Management*, *47*, 501–523.

Frey, C. B., & Obsorne, M. A. (2013). The future of employment: How susceptible are jobs to computerization? *Technological Forecasting and Social Change, 114*, 254–280.

Gilson, L. L., Maynard, M. T., Jones Young, N. C., Vartiainen, M., & Hakonen, M. (2015). Virtual teams research: 10 years, 10 themes, and 10 opportunities. *Journal of Management, 41*(5), 1313–1337.

Gould, E. (2016). Wage inequality continues its 35-year rise in 2015. *Briefing Paper* #421. Washington, DC: Economic Policy Institute.

Green, M. Z. (2015). The NLRB as an überagency for the evolving workplace. *Emory Law Journal, 64*, 1621–1646.

Greenwood, I., & Randle, H. (2007). Team work, restructuring and skills in the UK and Sweden. *European Journal of Industrial Relations, 13*, 361–377.

Hanauer, N., & Rolf, D. (2015). Shared security and shared growth. *Democracy*, No 37. https://democracyjournal.org/magazine/37/shared-security-shared-growth/

Hoch, J. E., & Kozlowski, S. W. (2014). Leading virtual teams: Hierarchical leadership, structural supports, and shared team leadership. *Journal of Applied Psychology, 99*(3), 390–403.

Hogler, R. (2015). *The end of American labor unions: The right-to-work movement and the erosion of collective bargaining*. Santa Barbara, CA: ABC-CLIO.

Howard, A. (Ed.) (1995). *The changing nature of work*. San Francisco, CA: Jossey-Bass.

Hyatt, H. R., & Spetzler, J. R. (2016). The shifting job tenure distribution. *Discussion Paper* No. 9776. Bonn: Institute for the Study of Labor.

International Labor Office. (2016). *World employment and social outlook: Trends 2016*. Geneva: ILO.

Jackson, E., Looney, A., & Ramnath, S. (2017). The rise of alternative work arrangements: Evidence and implications for tax filing and benefit coverage. *Office of Tax Analysis Working Paper* 114. www.treasury.gov/resource-center/tax-policy/tax analysis/Documents/WP-114.pdf

Javidan, M., Dorfman, P. W., De Luque, M. S., & House, R. J. (2006). In the eye of the beholder: Cross cultural lessons in leadership from project GLOBE. *The Academy of Management Perspectives, 20*, 67–90.

Johansson, A. (2016). Here's how you can actually make money with YouTube. Retrieved September 3, 2017, fromwww.entrepreneur.com/article/280966.

Kirkman, B. L., Gibson, C. B., & Kim, K. (2012). Across borders and technologies: Advancements in virtual teams research. In I. S. Kozlowski (Ed.), *The Oxford handbook of organizational psychology, Vol. 2* (pp. 789–858). New York, NY: Oxford University Press.

Kokakowski, N. (2017, August 1). Google pouring $50 million into 'changing nature of work'. https://insights.dice.com/2017/08/01/google-50-million-changing-nature-work/

Lebergott, S. (1966). Labor force and employment: 1800–1960. In D. S. Brady (Ed.), *Employment and productivity on the United States after 1800* (pp. 117–204). Cambridge, MA: National Bureau of Economic Research.

Lee, M. A., & Mather, M. (2008). US labor force trends. *Population Bulletin, 63*, 1–16.

Levine, B. R., Harrington, J. R., & Uhlmann, E. L. (in press). Culture and work. Chapter to appear in D. Cohen and S. Kitayama, *The handbook of cross-cultural psychology* (2nd ed.). New York, NY: Guilford Press.

Levy, R. (2016). Impact of the gig economy on legal classification of health care workers. *Journal of Health Care Compliance, 18*, 45–46.

Liden, R. C., Wayne, S. J., Kraimer, M. L., & Sparrowe, R. T. (2003). The dual commitments of contingent workers: An examination of contingents' commitments to the agency and the organization. *Journal of Organizational Behavior, 24*, 609–625.

Lohr, S. (1987). Making cars the Volvo way. *New York Times*, June 23. www.nytimes.com/1987/06/23/business/making-cars-the-volvo-way.html?pagewanted=all&mcubz=0

Lowry, A. (2017). What the gig economy looks like worldwide. *The Atlantic*. www.theatlantic.com/business/archive/2017/04/gig-economy-global/522954/

Malos, S., Haynes, P., & Bowal, P. (2003). A contingency approach to the employment relationship: form, function, and effectiveness implications. *Employee Responsibilities and Rights Journal, 15*, 149–167.

Mangold, W. G., & Faulds, D. J. (2009). Social media: The new hybrid element of the promotion mix. *Business Horizons, 52*, 357–365.

Markus, H. R., & Lin, L. R. (1999). Conflictways: Cultural diversity in the meanings and practices of conflict. In D. A. Prentice and D. R. Miller (Eds.), *Cultural divides: Understanding and overcoming group conflict* (pp. 302–333). New York, NY: Russell Sage.

Mayer, G. (2004). *Union membership trends in the United States*. Washington, DC: Congressional Research Service.

Middleton, H. (2002). Complex problem solving in a workplace setting. *International Journal of Educational Research, 37*, 67–84.

Mitlacher, L. (2005). Temporary agency work, the changing employment relationship and its impact on human resource management. *Management Revue, 16*, 370–388.

National Academies of Sciences, Engineering, and Medicine (NASEM) (2017). *Information technology and the US workforce: Where are we and where do we go from here?* Washington, DC: The National Academies Press.

National Research Council (1999). *The changing nature of work: Implications for occupational analysis*. Washington, DC: The National Academies Press.

National Research Council (2012). *Education for life and work: Developing transferable knowledge and skills in the 21st century*. Washington, DC: The National Academies Press.

Nesheim, T., Olsen, K. M., & Kalleberg, A. L. (2007). Externalizing the core firms' use of employment intermediaries in the information and communication technology industries. *Human Resource Management, 46*, 247–264.

Neubert, J. C., Mainert, J., Kretzschmar, A., & Greiff, S. (2015). The assessment of 21st century skills in industrial and organizational psychology: Complex and collaborative problem solving. *Industrial and Organizational Psychology: Perspectives on Science and Practice, 8*, 1–31.

Nikiforuk, A. (2013). The big shift last time: From horse dung to car smog. https://thetyee.ca/News/2013/03/06/Horse-Dung-Big-Shift/

OECD. (2013a). *OECD skills outlook 2013: First results from the survey of adult skills*. Paris: OECD Publishing.

OECD. (2013b). *PISA 2012 assessment and analytical framework*. Paris: OECD Publishing.

O'Sullivan, M., Turner, T., Lavelle, J., MacMahon, J., Ryan, L., Murphy, C., Gunnigle, P., & O'Brien, M. (2017). The role of the state in shaping zero hours work in an atypical liberal market economy. *Economic and Industrial Democracy*, November. doi: 10.1177/0143831X17735181

O'Sullivan, M., Turner, T., MacMahon, J., Ryan, L., Lavelle, J., Murphy, C., O'Brien, M., & Gunnigle, P. (2015). *A study on the prevalence of zero hours contracts among Irish employers and their impact on employees*. Limerick: Kemmy Business School, University of Limerick.

Perry, B. (2008). Virtual teams now a reality: Two out of three companies say they will rely more on virtual teams in the future. www.pr.com/press-release/103409.

Pessoa, J. P., & Van Reenan, J. (2013). Wage growth and productivity growth: The myth and reality of 'decoupling'. *CEP Discussion Paper* No. 146. London: Center for Economic Progress, London School of Economics.

Pissarides, C. A. (2000). *Equilibrium unemployment theory*. Cambridge, MA: MIT Press.

Pratt, G. A. (2015), Is a Cambrian explosion coming for robotics? *Journal of Economic Perspectives*, *29*(3), 51–60.

Sale, K. (1995). *Rebels against the future: The Luddites and their war against the industrial revolution: Lessons for the computer age*. New York, NY: Basic Books.

Sanchez-Burks, J., & Lee, F. (2007). Cultural psychology of workways. *Handbook of Cultural Psychology*, *1*, 346–369.

Schwartz, J., Collins, L., Stockton, H., Wagner, D., & Walsh, B. (2017). The future of work: The augmented workforce. www2.deloitte.com/insights/us/en/focus/human-capital-trends/2017/future-workforce-changing-nature-of-work.html

Sherman, E. (2017). New count of gig economy says old employment has nothing to worry about. www.inc.com/erik-sherman/the-real-size-of-the-gig-economy-is-smaller-than-you-may-think.html

Singer, N. (2014). In the sharing economy, workers find both freedom and uncertainty. *New York Times*. August 16. www.nytimes.com/2014/08/17/technology/in-the-sharing-economy-workersfind-both-freedom-and-uncertainty.html?_r=0.

Small Business Administration. (2016). Small business profile. Retrieved September 26, 2017, from www.sba.gov/sites/default/files/advocacy/United_States.pdf

Strauss, K. (2017a). 10 great "gig economy" jobs for 2017. *Forbes*. www.forbes.com/sites/karstenstrauss/2017/03/08/10-great-gig-economy-jobs-for-2017/#6db97d4e25c9

Strauss, K. (2017b). What's driving the gig economy? *Forbes*. www.forbes.com/sites/karstenstrauss/2017/02/21/what-is-driving-the-gig-economy/#297a77b653c3

Tan, E. (2014). Human capital theory: A holistic criticism. *Review of Educational Research*, *84*, 311–345.

US Department of Labor. (2015). Administrator's Interpretation No. 2015-1. www.dol.gov/whd/workers/Misclassification/AI-2015_1.pdf

Wartzman, R. (2017). *The end of loyalty: The rise and fall of good jobs in America*. New York, NY: Public Affairs.

Wears, K. H., & Fisher, S. L. (2012). Who is the employer in the triangular employment relationship? Sorting through the definitional confusion. *Employee Responsibilities and Rights Journal*, *24*, 159–176.

Wegman, L. A., Hoffman, B. J., Carter, N. T., Twenge, J. M., & Guenole, N. (2018). Placing job characteristics in context: cross-temporal meta-analysis of changes in job characteristics since 1975. *Journal of Management, 44*(1), 352–386.

World Bank Development Report. (2016). *Digital dividends.* Washington, DC: International Bank for Reconstruction and Development / The World Bank.

World Bank Development Report. (2019). *The changing nature of work.* Working draft, April 20, 2018. Washington, DC: International Bank for Reconstruction and Development / The World Bank.

Wrzesniewski, A., & Dutton, J. E. (2001). Crafting a job: Revisioning employees as active crafters of their work. *Academy of Management Review,* 26, 179–201.

Zuboff, S. (1988). *In the age of the smart machine: The future of work and power.* New York, NY: Basic Books.

PART II

What Has Changed?

4 Changes in Technology

Jerod White, Tara Behrend, and Ian Siderits

This chapter accomplishes three primary goals. First, we review the history of technologies that have been influential in the world of work, from the abacus to innovations of present day. We then identify eight characteristics that describe modern technologies: power, portability, usability, networking, encryption, ubiquity, immersion, and predictiveness. Finally, we present a SWOT analysis that identifies the implications of these characteristics for the future of work. In doing so, we demonstrate that although technological change is a constant, so too is humans' ability to adapt to change.

Introduction

In 1952, science fiction author Kurt Vonnegut envisioned an automated workforce of the near future in his novel, *Player piano*. A player piano, which is a self-playing instrument, operates on pre-programmed music recorded onto perforated paper. In the novel, engineers build machines that can complete tasks more efficiently than factory workers can. A small group of managers supervise these engineers, and soon all other men are left without jobs. In essence, the economy becomes a player piano, operating on pre-programmed machines. Most citizens acquiesce to living out meaningless lives as they watch technology seize their contributions to society. The fears captured by this novel were also reflected in some economic thinking of that time: workers were rapidly being displaced from the agricultural and manufacturing industries, leading prominent economists to consider the possibility of widespread unemployment and an oversupply of labor (Simon, 1965). Our relationship with technology has always been one of both fear and hope, whether the topic is automation replacing jobs, or text communication killing the art of conversation, or videogames seducing us away from nature. The workplace has been the focal point of many of these discussions, not surprisingly given the economic and psychological importance of work. In this chapter, we define workplace technology, review its history, discuss its current trends, and forecast its influence on the future of work.

The Evolution of Workplace Technology: 3000 BCE to 2010 CE

Since the invention of the abacus in 3000 BCE Babylonia, the work of humans has been supported by new and evolving technologies (Information technology timeline, 2003). We define **workplace technology** as any tool developed from scientific knowledge that is used to perform work. Technology continually shapes the nature of work as we search for ways to complete tasks more efficiently and effectively. Importantly, new tools do not uniformly change work; their influence depends on a variety of technology characteristics. The abacus was best characterized by its usability because it provided an easy-to-operate tool to workers whose tasks involved counting. However, some pieces of technology were characterized by more than their usability. By the 1700s, for example, Oliver Evans' creation of the continuous production line allowed for mass production in the manufacturing industry (Ginzberg, 1982). Workers could finally use a tool to complete some of their tedious job tasks, such as moving objects from one location to another. The continuous production line was easy to use by some accounts, but it is better characterized by its ability to complete tasks independently. Such tools, termed predictive technologies, influence work differently than user-friendly technologies by completing, rather than assisting in, the execution of workers' tasks.

The 1800s were characterized by a spike in computational technologies with inventions such as the arithmometer (i.e., the first mass-produced calculator) and the mechanical computer (Bunch & Hellemans, 1993). These early inventions introduced the concept of computing power, a technology characteristic that describes a machine's ability to store and process information. Concurrently, the discoveries of wireless communication by Nikola Tesla and the radio signal by Guglielmo Marconi introduced another technology characteristic: networking (Bunch & Hellemans, 1993; McNeil, 1990). Digital forms of communication were imperfect at this time, but they made possible the eventual interactions of workers separated by vast geographic distances.

Workplace technologies continued to advance during the first half of the 1900s. By the 1930s, the Telex messaging network – which started as a way to distribute military messages – became a powerful worldwide network of both official and commercial text messaging (McNeil, 1990). The 1940s contained several technology milestones: Isaac Asimov coined the term "robot" to describe new autonomous tools (Ralston, Reilly, & Hemmendinger, 2000), the first operational Colossus computer at Bletchley Park broke the complex Lorenz ciphers used by the Nazis in World War II (McNeil, 1990), and the USSR launched the first artificial satellite (Zakon, 2018). Despite emphasizing different technological characteristics, each of these milestones set precedence for the development of subsequent workplace tools.

The 1950s was a critical time for computing power, with the introduction of the first commercially produced computers (i.e., the ERA1101; Moreau, 1984), magnetic drum memory (Ceruzzi, 1998), the FORTRAN programming language for numeric computation (McNeil, 1990), and even the now-basic concept of hyperlinks (Bercik & Bond, 1996). Although these advancements were absent from traditional workplaces at the time, they began to change employee perceptions of the computer as a useful workplace tool.

Soon after, new technologies spurred further improvement of the networking and capabilities of existing tools. The Compatible Time-Sharing System (CTSS), an early inter-user operating system, included basic messaging features that resembled today's email tools (Bunch & Hellemans, 1993). In addition to the CTSS, the 1960s saw the creation of robotic arms (Devol, 1966) and the first mobile robot with enough artificial intelligence to navigate on its own through a set of rooms (Moravec, 1988). At this point, predictive technologies were equipped to perform tasks that were much more complex than those prescribed by Evans' early production lines.

Computational power tremendously improved throughout the 1970s in the form of semiconductor memory, ROM chips, floppy disks, and the C programming language (Bunch & Hellemans, 1993; Ceruzzi, 1998; Deitel & Deitel, 2007; Zakon, 2018). Simultaneously, networking advancements occurred with the advent of email, Ethernet, and modern mobile networks (Zakon, 2018). The momentum of this decade continued into the 1980s with the first mass-produced portable computer, the first mass Web, LAN operating systems, CD-ROMs, Microsoft Word, the Apple Macintosh, flash memory, and C++ programming (Bunch & Hellemans, 1993; Ceruzzi, 1998; Deitel & Deitel, 2007; McNeil, 1990; Zakon, 2018). Computing power advanced so much by this point that a machine was able to defeat a professional chess player (Bunch & Hellemans, 1993). Perhaps more so than any prior decade, the 1980s introduced technologies that could be characterized by their decreasing physical size. This trend toward portability enabled many traditional workers – not just advanced programmers – to fit computers in their workplaces alongside other tools such as printers and telephones. As a result, the Internet had grown to over 100,000 host machines by the end of the decade (Zakon, 2018).

Given the growing number of users on the Internet, the 1990s introduced technologies that improved the security of existing networked tools. Tim Berners-Lee brought the World Wide Web into existence at the very outset of the 1990s, and this invention was followed closely by public-key encryption programs to ensure authentication in the digital exchange of information (Zakon, 2018). Along with encryption, computer power and networking advancements continued in the 1990s with Java 1.0, JavaScript, and Wi-Fi short-range radio networking (Ceruzzi, 1998; Goodman & Morrison, 2007). Notably, the technological boom of the 1990s marked the true beginning of the average office worker using the Internet to complete basic job tasks.

The early 2000s followed the portability and power trends of workers' cellphones, from the first camera phone through advanced Internet-enabled smartphones. Similarly, computer memory has improved drastically in the twenty-first century with portable limited capacity USB flash drives and powerful multi-terabyte external hard-drives. The vast majority of tools developed in the 2000s possessed networking capabilities, allowing for professional information sharing on websites such as LinkedIn and Dropbox (Zakon, 2018). At present, computers are everywhere: From workers' desks to their pockets, today's technologies enable workers to perform a diverse range of tasks.

The Progression of Workplace Technology

For centuries, workplace technologies have exhibited several distinct characteristics. To understand the current state of workplace technology, we identify eight characteristics that describe the ways that our tools have evolved over time: namely, that they have become more powerful, portable, usable, networked, encrypted, ubiquitous, immersive, and predictive. A few of these characteristics (i.e., ubiquity and immersion) represent relatively new changes to workplace technology, while others represent ongoing changes that have unfolded for centuries. These characteristics are not mutually exclusive, and many of the illustrative examples capture more than one characteristic. To explain the technology used in every industry is beyond the scope of this chapter, but we highlight the education, healthcare, and military sectors to demonstrate each characteristic, explained in Table 4.1.

Powerful

As illustrated through the evolution of workplace technologies, computing power has increased exponentially since the 1800s. In 1965, Intel co-founder Gordon Moore observed that the number of transistors (i.e., tiny switches triggered by electrical signals) on a microchip doubled every two years since their invention. This observation is now referred to as Moore's Law, which essentially describes the exponential trend for our computing devices to become twice as powerful every 18–24 months (1965). The earliest transistors were big enough to be picked up by hand, but today's versions are microscopically small. As such, the trend toward more powerful devices largely results from improvements in computing hardware. We identify two work-related implications of these hardware improvements: robust data storage and superior information processing.

Increased computing power allows workers to store and access immense amounts of rich information. Consider the US healthcare alliance network, Premier, which must store information on thousands of discharged patients. Premier has amassed an enormous, comprehensive database of patient, financial, and supply chain data. Using these robust information sources to guide their decision-making processes, Premier doctors have reduced healthcare spending by approximately $7 billion and saved an estimated 29,000 lives (IBM, 2013). Compared to physical file drawer storage methods that healthcare professionals once used, computer storage methods more comprehensively and conveniently compile information.

Table 4.1 Technology characteristics and industry examples

	Education	Healthcare	Military
Powerful *Computing devices store and process large amounts of data, enabling users to complete complex tasks quickly.*	Analyzing large amounts of student data to evaluate teachers' performance (Means, Gallagher, & Padilla, 2008)	Compiling comprehensive lists of patient, financial, and supply chain data to make treatment plans (Wang, Kung, & Byrd, 2018)	Saving mission area maps, video imagery, and other classified data on flash memory devices to make combat decisions ("Rugged cards," 2001)
Portable *Physically smaller devices are created without losses in computing power.*	Providing teachers with live feedback using small earbuds (Behrend, Gloss, & Thompson, 2013)	Locating patients' veins with a small, lightweight device that displays a real-time vein map (AccuVein, 2012)	Replacing bulky robot operating control units with mobile phone controllers (Yagoda & Hill, 2011)
Usable *Customized devices and operating systems reduce user barriers and make technology accessible to many people.*	Presenting customized multimedia content on large, easy-to-use interactive whiteboards (Marzano, 2009)	Attaching a stabilization tool to scalpels to maintain a steady grip during operations (Song, Gehlbach, & Kang, 2012)	Accessing customized military weather apps quickly using seamless smartphone interfaces (Sauter, 2011)
Networked *Devices are connected, often wirelessly, allowing users to quickly and easily share information with one another.*	Increasing collaboration between teachers and students with online open-source learning systems ("Moodle," n.d.)	Collectively diagnosing difficult cases by soliciting input from other doctors across the globe ("Sermo," n.d.)	Receiving critical mission information from soldiers thousands of miles away using wideband tactical radios ("Tactical Communications," n.d.)
Encrypted *Networked devices protect users from the misuse of shared information by digitally encoding files.*	Ensuring test-taker honesty via webcam during Internet-based assessments (Karim, Kaminsky, & Behrend, 2014)	Acquiring patients' health data quickly in emergency situations by initiating a secure break-glass access control system (Yang, Liu, & Deng, 2017)	Sending false GPS signals to mislead adversaries; developing detectors of such deceptive signals (Psiaki, Humphreys, & Stauffer, 2016)

Table 4.1 (cont.)

	Education	Healthcare	Military
Ubiquitous *Devices are used everywhere, allowing for rich, multifaceted information to be collected and stored.*	Monitoring erratic school bus movements to evaluate driver performance ("Using the Internet of Things," 2017)	Attaching electronic tags to nurses to monitor their interactions with patients (Boulos & Berry, 2012)	Using rugged radios specially designed to operate in high-altitude environments ("Tactical Communications," n.d.)
Immersive *Devices and software fully engage users in activities for which sources of sensory stimulation are delivered.*	Interacting with diverse student avatars using virtual reality software (Bousfield, Dieker, Hughes, & Hynes, 2016)	Playing simulation games to learn pathogens and antibiotics needed to diagnose and treat patients ("Microbe Invader," n.d.)	Exposing soldiers to the physiological effects of parachute jumps in a safe virtual environment (Bollermann, Osborn, & Hughan, 2017)
Predictive *Devices make decisions and act independently using the systematic combination of digital information.*	Evaluating students' short answer responses with automatic grading systems (Mohler & Mihalcea, 2009)	Setting diabetic patients' personalized diet and exercise goals using computer-generated suggestions (Stein, 2017)	Using autonomous robots to monitor adversaries and carry objects from one location to another (Ningombam, Singh, & Chanu, 2018)

Regarding the computer's capacity to process information, many researchers have questioned how long Moore's Law will hold true (e.g., Kish, 2002; Waldrop, 2016). One reoccurring and regularly disputed concern is that, given the laws of physics, transistors can only become so small before processing power reaches a standstill. In the early 1900s, for example, statisticians believed conducting any form of complex analysis using the processors found within early calculators and computers seemed highly unlikely, if not impossible. In the decades since, however, processing advancements have allowed users to conduct the most complex of statistical tests in seconds using analysis software such as SAS and R. Broadly speaking, storing and processing large amounts of information on computers enables workers to use technology in ways that would otherwise be impossible sans power advancements. As producers continue to make hardware changes that improve the power of their devices, they simultaneously make technological tools that adhere to the remaining seven trends.

Portable

In addition to computing power, Moore's Law also explains the trend of workplace technologies becoming physically smaller. This miniaturization of technology is demonstrated in comparing today's small tablet devices to early computers that occupied as much as 1,800 square feet ("ENIAC," 2003). Without significant losses in power, many of today's workplace technologies can easily be transported by workers from one location to another.

Portable devices can easily be carried in one hand and enable workers to communicate with others in novel ways. Whereas early communication technologies such as telephones were bound to wired locations, today's wireless devices allow workers to multitask and communicate on-the-go. In 2011, the Bill and Melinda Gates Foundation funded earbuds to provide new Teach for America trainees with developmental feedback (Behrend, Gloss, & Thompson, 2013). Participating teachers wore the earbuds and received live in-ear feedback from a private coach as they taught their lessons. These portable earbuds enabled teachers to alter their instructional material in real time. Perhaps more importantly, the earbud coaching served as a goal-setting intervention that provided new and inexperienced teachers with the timely feedback needed to become effective educators.

Small tablet and smartphone devices have an added convenience over traditional computers due to their increased portability. For example, tablets also serve a practical purpose in the military, where soldiers can use them to control robotic devices in battlefield environments. Traditional operator control units (OCUs) resemble bulky personal laptops, but researchers recently developed controlling systems that are optimized for portable Android mobile phones (Yagoda & Hill, 2011). Preliminary evidence suggests that the mobile units perform as well as the traditional OCUs, all while freeing a soldier's hand to allow for greater flexibility in combat.

The miniaturization of technology allows employees to use wearable devices in the workplace. The most common wearable device, the smartwatch, enables workers to track their physical activity, access the Internet, and communicate with others, all from their wrists. A 2015 Salesforce report suggests that 76 percent of organizations report improvements in employee performance after introducing smartwatches in their workplace. One explanation for these improvements is that, unlike smartphones, smartwatches are less distracting because they only provide information at a glance. A second explanation – and one that is discussed at greater length later in this chapter – is that employers monitor the data collected from these devices to make employees safer and more productive on the job (Khakurel, Poysa, & Porras, 2016). The latter explanation supports a recent patent from Amazon that seeks to track its warehouse workers' gestures with digital wristbands. The employees will be trained to interact appropriately with their work environment by receiving haptic feedback alerts when they make errors (Yeginsu, 2018). As other wearable devices such as smart glasses (e.g., Google Glass) enter the workplace, employees may eventually opt out from using their more cumbersome devices.

Usable

Workplace technology is developed to meet organizational and societal needs, but new tools cannot satisfy these needs if workers struggle to use them. **Usability** is defined as "the extent to which a product can be used by specified users to achieve specified effectiveness, efficiency, and satisfaction in a specified context of use" (ISO, 1998, p. 2). User-friendliness remains a central focus in human–computer interaction research because it represents a relative, rather than absolute, technological feature. To maximize productivity and efficiency, employers implement technology that assists workers in completing organizational tasks. The primary challenge in developing usable technologies is that perceptions of usability for the same tool will differ across workers and organizational contexts (Newman & Taylor, 1999). For example, experienced workers may find a novel computer software harder to use than newly hired workers who have no experience with the pre-existing software. As such, researchers strive to develop workforce technologies that are usable across a variety of populations and contexts.

To illustrate the recent trend toward user-friendliness, we describe two types of usable technology: personalized tools and assistive equipment. When workers can tailor a technological tool to enhance their completion of organizational tasks, that tool is said to be personalizable. When workers use a technological tool to enable them to complete tasks for which they were previously incapable, that tool is said to be assistive. Both forms – personalizable and assistive – typically make tools easy to use and increase workers' effectiveness, efficiency, or satisfaction.

In the education industry, the interactive whiteboard represents a personalizable tool that is revolutionizing the way that teachers across disciplines instruct their students. Throughout the twenty-first century, many teachers have used interactive whiteboards as a replacement for traditional blackboards (Marzano, 2009). While the hardware of these whiteboards is mostly consistent across classrooms, software options vary greatly. For example, math teachers can use the whiteboards to draw figures using interactive geometry software, while history teachers use the same technological tool to interact with maps of the world. Teachers can now easily instruct students from their fingertips by clicking, writing, and drawing directly on the content they wish to share, with minimal need for supplementary teaching tools such as blackboards.

Assistive tools can also be categorized as usable forms of technology. In occupational settings, **assistive equipment** is any tool that enables a disadvantaged worker to sufficiently complete job-related tasks. It is generally developed to help those with disabilities complete essential tasks, whether those be activities of daily living or job-related responsibilities (Mittler, 2007). One occupation-specific example of assistive technology is the Smart Micromanipulation Aided Robotic-surgical Tool (SMART). Using near-infrared lasers, the SMART is a hand-held device that surgeons can attach to scalpels to determine when and how much their hands shake while performing operations. This tool is categorized as user-friendly because its computer automatically compensates for slight hand tremors by moving the scalpel in the opposite direction, all without disrupting the surgeon's concentration (Song, Gehlbach, & Kang, 2012).

Assistive tools exist in other industries as well, and each of them improves disabled employees' work experiences. The Americans with Disabilities Act of 1990 prohibits worker discrimination on the basis of disability, requiring employers to provide disabled applicants with reasonable accommodations that enable them to perform on the job. In occupations that require driving, for example, affordable assistive technologies such as spinner knobs exist so that individuals with hand impairments can safely steer a vehicle using only one hand (Mross, 1971). As researchers continue to study usability in human–technology interactions, both able and disabled workers enjoy enriched employment opportunities.

Networked

Since the late 1960s, the computer no longer represents a standalone device. A **network** allows users to share resources by connecting computers with cables or wirelessly with radio waves. The primary goal of establishing networks is to enable a single computer to access more information and computing power than it could as a standalone device. Some common workplace uses for networking include facilitating communication, sharing hardware devices such as printers, and delivering files or software. The Internet is the largest computer network in the world, and there are many other types of smaller networks such as personal area networks (PANs), home area networks (HANs), and campus networks (Comer & Droms, 2003). Each of these smaller networks allows select individuals (e.g., those in the same household or university) to store and share resources with one another.

Networks have altered employees' perceptions of the traditional workplace. Recent statistics suggest that 22 percent of employees did some or all of their work at home in 2016 ("On days," 2016).

One clear benefit of using interconnected technologies at work is the ability to **crowdsource**, or solicit input from a large number of people while completing a task or project.

In the healthcare industry, physicians use both small and large networks to gather inputs from their expert peers. For example, Sermo is the largest social network for doctors, connecting over 800,000 verified and licensed physicians worldwide. Sermo users can anonymously ask fellow doctors real-life medical questions, allowing them to make informed decisions before treating their patients. Other medical networks are more specialized, such as Incision Academy which allows a few hundred surgeons to share their techniques with other surgeons across the globe.

In addition to peer communication, professionals also use networks to communicate with external stakeholders. Doctors often use technology to communicate with patients, sometimes even in place of traditional in-clinic visits (Greenhalgh et al., 2016). Referred to as telemedicine, virtual consultations were endorsed by nearly three-fourths of large employers in 2016 (National Business Group on Health, 2015). Telemedicine meetings serve as an attractive alternative to in-person medical visits to mediate scheduling conflicts. Medical professionals such as primary care physicians will surely continue to see a greater reliance on networks for communication as patients demand these convenient forms of consultation.

Similarly, educators use networks to communicate with students as a result of increases in online education enrollment. A 2016 report from the Babson Survey Research Group demonstrates that the number of students taking at least one online course has consistently grown by close to 4 percent for each of the past several years (Allen & Seaman, 2016). As a consequence of this growing trend, educators must shift from preparing in-class lectures and PowerPoint presentations to preparing video and audio recordings that can be shared and accessed online at any time. Indeed, many full- and part-time faculty members now teach strictly online classes at a variety of accredited online programs across the country.

Even in traditional face-to-face classrooms, teachers use networks by implementing complementary open-source learning systems. **Open source** refers to software that is freely available and may be shared or modified by any network member (Lakhani & von Hippel, 2003). For example, the learning management system Moodle is licensed under a general public license and allows teachers to develop customizable online learning modules. By developing online learning activities, assessments, and discussion forums, these systems allow teachers to share content and engage with their students at any time and from any location. Open source systems are also useful for professionals working in learning contexts outside of the classroom. For example, government and business professionals use the learning system Blackboard to build training programs, conduct web conferences, and create progress reports for their employees. By modifying publicly available software, educators and business professionals alike develop curricula that they can use to engage others in valuable learning opportunities.

Encrypted

Because technology is increasingly networked, researchers and practitioners are taking greater initiative to protect their digital tools from attack, damage, and unauthorized access. The primary goal for employers is to ensure that their networks are secure, but security itself does not yet represent a present-day technology trend. Full security would entail a network or technology that is completely resistant to any form of threat such as malware, phishing, or ransomware, which is unlikely given increasing technological interconnectivity. In an attempt to promote security, workplace networks are increasingly **encrypted**, or converted into codes, to prevent hackers from accessing them.

Encryption remains an important technology consideration for virtually every industry in today's workforce. Hackers often target financial firms due to the potential for monetary gains, as noted by a recent growth in the number, size, and sophistication of recent attacks on US finance organizations. Aside from monetary losses, financial organizations cite disruptions of operations, poorer-quality production, damage to physical property, and even harm to human life as additional consequences of cyber attacks on digital labor (PwC, 2017). Frequently, employers simply want to protect information, whether it concerns the organization, its employees, or its customers. In what is now regarded as the biggest data breach of the twenty-first century, Yahoo compromised the real names, dates of birth, telephone numbers, and email addresses of all 3 billion of its user accounts in September 2016, causing a decrease in the company's 2017 sale price (Perlroth, 2017).

While scholastic information may seem less sought-after than financial information, administrators in the education sector must be just as prepared for potential security violations. In 2013, 14 current and former foreign college students in the United States were found guilty of using test-taking proxies for admissions tests such as the SAT and for English-proficiency exams such as the TOEFL (Tyre, 2016). Today's teachers are concerned about security breaches in digitally administered exams, as fraudulent test-taking behaviors do not accurately represent their instructional efforts. Recent experimental research demonstrates that webcams can be used to verify test-takers' identities during Internet-based tests (Karim, Kaminsky, & Behrend, 2014). Some of today's test administration companies also use biometric checks that compare a candidate's fingerprint to the fingerprints of millions of other test-takers (e.g., Prometric, 2009). Particularly for teachers administering high-stakes tests (e.g., licensure exams) using computers or the Internet, encryption represents a vital concern to ensure that test scores reflect the educators' ability to teach others.

Encryption also plays a critical role for doctors who must store and access patients' medical information. A recent trend in the healthcare industry is for doctors to consult with patients via digital networks (e.g., Skype video calls). While virtual consultations, or virtual hospitals like iCliniq, are convenient for both parties, they raise important privacy concerns regarding who has access to information shared online. The integrity of iCliniq's doctors and psychiatrists rests at least partially on iCliniq's ability to hold to their website's promise of preserving confidentiality. Interconnected devices may pose a challenge this confidentiality; indeed, one study demonstrates that nearly a third of patients have privacy concerns with their doctors posting their visitation notes online for subsequent access (Vodicka et al., 2013).

Doctors practicing in person must also remain mindful of potential security concerns. Today's medical professionals typically store and aggregate patients' health information in the cloud, meaning that this data must be properly encrypted to protect patients' privacy. However, doctors may sometimes need to override encryptions to quickly access a patient's data in emergency situations. Recently, researchers have proposed two separate access systems for medical responders to view patients' records: one secure mechanism to be used in normal situations, and another "break glass" mechanism that can be initiated by authorized professionals in emergent situations (Yang, Liu, & Deng, 2017). By making these situational distinctions, doctors balance patients' privacy concerns with their duty to respond quickly in dire situations.

Organizations must anticipate the actions of potential hackers to promote security. This can be achieved through cryptography, the act of storing and sharing data so that only intended users can access it. At the same time, criminals likely anticipate that organizations have utilized a certain degree of encryption in their networks. This is seen in military contexts, where troopers can send false GPS signals to mislead adversaries to specific locations. Today's researchers are acutely aware of this "theory of mind" phenomenon in the military and are developing detectors of deceptive combat signals (Psiaki, Humphreys, & Stauffer, 2016). Given a general lack of full security across most industries in the workforce, developing similar detectors of security threats in traditional workplaces remains a critical technology goal for today's employers.

Ubiquitous

As digital tools become increasingly portable, more workers are constantly surrounded by technology. Technology is pervasive throughout the workplace, and employers recognize its potential for collecting rich, multifaceted information. **Electronic performance monitoring** (EPM) describes the use of technology to observe, record, and analyze employee behaviors. Common forms of EPM include surveillance cameras, computer monitoring, Internet monitoring, radio-frequency identification (RFID) access badges, and GPS trackers (American Management Association, 2007). Approximately 80 percent of organizations monitor employees in some way, and this number is expected to increase as technology follows its current trends (Ribitzky, 2007). Computer monitoring limits employers to collecting data for computer-related tasks, while smartphone monitoring expands the employer's data collection to include the GPS activity of an employee. In many ways, the ubiquitous digital tools used in today's workforce serve as an invisible eye that oversees each employee's behavior (Bhave, 2014).

The amount of data collected by technology – regardless of whether or not it is used for performance management purposes – has skyrocketed in recent years. **Big data** refers to extremely large data sets that are often so complex that traditional statistical processing programs are inadequate to process them. Employees at Uber, the smartphone-based taxi service, have been directly impacted by their organization's use of big data. Combining historical data on passenger ride requests with GPS-based traffic conditions, the Uber app determines not only when and where a driver should be driving but also how much they will be paid for their services (i.e., surge pricing). In addition, Uber also collects GPS, gyroscope, and accelerometer data from drivers' smartphones to provide them with recommendations to improve their routing, steering, and braking habits (Beinstein & Sumers, 2016). Some researchers have questioned the ethics of collecting endless amounts of data on employee behavior (Karim, Willford, & Behrend, 2015), but Uber maintains that it does so only to maximize the customer experience.

While GPS devices can accurately track employees who work outdoors, they show less accuracy for locating employees in more confined, indoor locations. As such, real-time locating systems (RTLS) have been developed for indoor workplaces and are used frequently in the healthcare industry (Boulos & Berry, 2012). A typical RTLS includes a small ID badge or tag attached to a nurse or doctor which transmits a unique location ID that can be traced back to a specific room or floor in a hospital. Many tags are often equipped with call buttons that identify and direct the nearest nurse to a specific location in emergency situations. Some systems even track how much time a nurse has spent by a given patient's bedside or cubicle. Such data can inform performance evaluations and even provide defensible data in cases of suspected neglect where a patient unexpectedly becomes ill or dies. Unlike traditional security cameras, the RTLS tracks the workers throughout their entire shifts. Above all, the RTLS sends two strong messages to medical professionals: assisting patients is their primary responsibility, and engaging in job-irrelevant activities while at work will not go unnoticed.

Despite their ubiquity, not all technologies are used for performance management purposes. In addition to portability, workplace technology is also ubiquitous as a result of sheer product innovation. The **Internet of Things** refers to the growing abundance of everyday objects with networked computing devices embedded inside of them (Ashton, 2009). For example, traditional office items such as printers, which once represented wired or standalone devices, now have Internet capabilities that wirelessly connect them to other devices such as computers and smartphones. Even office lightbulbs and thermostats are becoming "smarter," now with connectivity abilities that recognize workers' schedules and make adjustments when employees are out of the office (e.g., see Phillips's hue lightbulbs and Google's Nest thermostat).

The Internet of Things serves a practical purpose for many workers employed in the education industry. Consider employees working within schools who experience safety improvements as a result of ubiquitous computing technologies. In addition to surveillance cameras placed throughout schools and near exits, some schools use sensor-embedded devices that permit students and staff to enter the building (Selinger, Sepulveda, & Buchan, 2013). Threats to worker safety unfortunately exist beyond the education industry, so ubiquitous technologies will continually shape the workforce as we create safer work environments for employees.

Finally, workplace technologies are becoming pervasive due to fundamental improvements in product design. Using technology in extreme conditions (e.g., in severe heat) was once impossible for workers, but many of today's digital tools withstand such environmental pressures. For example, soldiers now have access to a variety of tactical radios specially designed for communication in novel environments, such as at high altitudes ("Tactical Communications," n. d.). Similarly, rugged tablet devices enable field service engineers and other traveling workers to bring their computing devices with them without worrying about potential damages from weather conditions or accidental drops. As our digital tools continue to become more portable, commonplace, and enduring, we will continue to see fewer and fewer work contexts untouched by technology.

Immersive

Today's technologies enable users to mentally travel across time and space from the comfort of their home or workplace. **Immersion** is defined as the full cognitive engagement of users in activities for which technology delivers sensory information (Blascovich, Loomis, Beall, Swinth, Hoyt, & Bailenson, 2002). While early media such as videos are slightly immersive in that they stimulate users' imaginations, today's technologies are truly engaging and often blur the lines between reality and computer simulation. Immersive technologies can engage any of the five human senses, but workplace technologies typically deliver visual, auditory, or tactile sensory information. We identify two closely related sub-elements of immersive technologies demonstrated by today's workplace technologies: gamification and virtual reality.

Immersive technologies show vast potential for improving employee training and development programs. In the workplace, **gamification** refers to the application of gaming principles in professional, nongame contexts (Deterding, Dixon, Khaled, & Nacke, 2013). By implementing games in the training process, employers aim to transform employees from passive recipients of job information to active learners and organizational contributors.

Current empirical research supports the claim that technology users learn new information while playing games. Landers and Callan (2011) demonstrated that students are not only more motivated to complete tests when they are offered virtual badges, but they also learn more than they do with traditional study methods. Additional research suggests that specific elements of games, such as leaderboards, motivate users to learn and become high performers (Landers, Bauer, & Callan, 2017). Although much of the research on learning and gamification has involved student participants, employees exhibit many of the same cognitive learning processes while playing training games.

To better understand how immersive technologies fully engage workers, Morris and colleagues (2013) identified three cognitive mechanisms that operate both when medics play training games and when they engage in scientific thinking. First, a motivational mechanism stems from trainees' feedback orientations and determines how much energy they will expend on either the game or a job task. Consider competitive doctors, whose desire to outperform others serves as a strong motivator to perform well both in medical videogames and on the job. Second, games elicit several cognitive mechanisms that utilize trainees' reasoning and problem-solving skills. Trainees playing the simulation game *Microbe Invader*, for example, must diagnose virtual patients in realistic situations. Making successful diagnoses, however, requires that the trainees learn about a variety of pathogens and antibiotics. Trainees initiate the third mechanism, metacognition, when they reflect on their current performance and make appropriate adjustments. Much like the scientific process of generating, testing, and revising hypotheses, medical games provide trainees with instructional feedback for behavioral adjustments in real time. Digital games create low-stakes learning environments that still engage workers and prepare them for high-stakes situations. By incorporating motivational and cognitive learning mechanisms, this framework illustrates both the appeal and utility of using games for training today's workers.

Similarly, some teachers use simulation games as part of their training programs. In contrast to traditional student teacher training, which is a time-intensive and costly process that often results in inconsistent feedback, gaming simulation training programs are consistent across trainees and provide each user with reliable, personalized performance data. The classroom simulation game *simSchool* immerses teachers-in-training in a virtual classroom full of cartoon students with varying interests, demographics, and personality characteristics (Knezek, Fisser, Gibson, Christensen, & Tyler-Wood, 2012). Teachers interact with the students by selecting from a variety of predetermined dialogues in a point-and-click style, and these selections are scored after about 10 minutes of gameplay to provide trainees with performance evaluations. Simulation games provide a quick and convenient alternative for fostering employee learning compared to in-person training programs.

One clear disadvantage of point-and-click simulation games is a lack of psychological fidelity for the user. Equally as useful for training but perhaps more immersive than videogames, **virtual reality** (VR) is a computer-generated simulation for which users can interact with environments in seemingly real or physical ways (Steuer, 1992). VR headsets such as the HTC Vive and the Oculus

Rift immerse users in digital environments with seamless visuals that deliver up to 90 image frames per second. Coupled with spatial audio that emulates sounds from different angles, properly designed VR environments can truly immerse employees in lifelike work situations.

While VR technology has long been marketed as a commercial entertainment device, it has clear implications for training in most jobs requiring physical activity or interpersonal interactions with others. In education, recent programs such as *TeachLivE*™ have expanded on the premise of *simSchool* to provide trainees with a more realistic and interactive virtual classroom environment (Bousfield, Dieker, Hughes, & Hynes, 2016). In healthcare, current research on medical virtual reality simulations demonstrates that the skills surgical residents learn during virtual trainings successfully transfer to the operating room environment (Seymour et al., 2002). In the military, VR increases combatants' awareness of novel environments. For example, VR simulations exist to get soldiers accustomed to the disorienting feeling of exiting an aircraft during a parachute jump in a safe environment (Bollermann, Osborn, & Hughan, 2017).

Virtual reality also represents a form of assistive equipment that benefits disabled workers. Individuals with autistic spectrum disorder (ASD) are consistently underrepresented in the US workforce (Taylor & Seltzer, 2011), and this partially results from the social anxiety that individuals with ASD have regarding job interviews (Maddox & White, 2015). In a randomized controlled trial, Smith and colleagues (2014) found that individuals with ASD showed greatest performance improvements in live job interview role-plays when they received virtual interview training beforehand. By experiencing the social dynamics of a job interview in a low-stakes environment, participants subsequently felt more comfortable in the live interviews. Most participants found the VR software easy and enjoyable to use, offering encouraging evidence that immersive technologies are improving the employment opportunities for those with disabilities.

Predictive

While employees once used technologies to assist them in completing certain projects, many of today's digital tools complete tasks with little or no human input. Behind most of these "smart" technologies are a series of basic mathematical operations. An **algorithm** is a set of rules that a computer follows to engage in problem-solving and other decision-making operations. As algorithms have become more common in the field of computer science, the subfield of artificial intelligence has gained popularity. **Artificial intelligence** (AI) refers to the development of computer systems that perform tasks otherwise requiring human intelligence (Russell & Norvig, 2016). In regard to Vonnegut's dystopian predictions of an automated workforce, AI is perhaps the most relevant technology characteristic.

AI directly influences the types of tasks that workers, like teachers, complete. Scantron technologies have long been used to grade multiple choice questions, and now artificially intelligent tools show potential in grading short-responses and essays. While not a perfectly accurate tool, automatic grading systems appear to provide scores that are often comparable to those provided by teachers (Burrows, Gurevych, & Stein, 2015; Mohler & Mihalcea, 2009). Automated grading systems reduce time and costs associated with evaluating large numbers of written responses, while overcoming manual grading errors such as those associated with order effects, fatigue, and bias (Haley et al., 2007). As this form of AI improves, the job of teacher may no longer emphasize the manual grading of student writing.

AI also performs interpersonal tasks associated with a given occupation. In addition to its role in grading, AI technology has engaged in online conversations with students. Using technologies from IBM's Watson platform, university professor Ashok Goel created a virtual teaching assistant that interacted with students in an online forum alongside eight human teaching assistants (TAs). Goel revealed the bot's identity after the students completed their final exams, much to the surprise of those who were planning to nominate the bot as an outstanding TA in the course's end-of-semester feedback report (Lipko, 2016). Similar to its influence on manual grading, AI shows clear potential in altering the ways that teachers interact with students.

Doctors' duties also change as a result of AI. Even with the assistance of networked technologies and the crowdsourcing of expert opinions, doctors still struggle to make treatment decisions in some life-or-death cases. To provide additional guidance in such situations, IBM launched Watson for Oncology, an AI bot that analyzes structured and unstructured clinical notes to provide doctors with treatment pathway suggestions for cancer patients ("IBM Watson Health," n.d.). Although the bot does not officially make the doctor's decisions, it does serve as an additional information source that medics can consider in particularly ambiguous situations. This technology is just as useful for lower-stakes medical situations, like an algorithm that can create a personalized diet and exercise goals for patients with diabetes (Stein, 2017). While AI advancements have not replaced medical experts' opinions, they may eventually shift doctors' duties away from generating diagnoses to verifying those produced by computers.

Just as the Internet of Things explains the connectedness of everyday objects, AI explains how objects become "smarter," or more predictive. A prime example of this predictive trend is the military robot, which once represented a remote-controlled device reliant on human inputs for operation. Today's military robots are largely autonomous, allowing soldiers to focus on other tasks while the devices complete their assigned duties. GPS-guided autonomous robots now exist, capable of not only following optimal paths between locations but also using robotic arms to deliver objects (Ningombam, Singh, & Chanu, 2018).

An everyday object shaped by AI is the car, representing a technology change that has immense potential to alter jobs involving driving. Companies like

Google have developed cars that create and maintain internal maps of their surroundings, ultimately allowing them to travel without a human behind the wheel ("Waymo," n.d.). Various algorithms ensure that the self-driving car appropriately accelerates, brakes, and steers itself, all while avoiding road obstacles. Today's AI-enabled cars are only partially autonomous, meaning that they still require human intervention in cases where the cars encounter uncertain obstacles. Similar to the unique knowledge of doctors, the motor skills of today's taxi, bus, and Uber drivers have not yet (?) been matched by current AI technologies.

SWOT Analysis of Workplace Technology

Strengths, Weaknesses, Opportunities, and Threats (SWOT) analyses are used to provide practitioners with factors that could impact the success of a new trend. As demonstrated, each of the eight technology characteristics has consistently advanced over time. Keeping in mind the trajectories of these characteristics, we next evaluate the potential influence of our digital tools on the success of the workforce by conducting a SWOT analysis on workplace technology.

Strength #1: Doing More with Less

Employees across industries rely on fewer pieces of technology than they did in the past as a result of increases in computing power. Teachers no longer need to transport large overhead projectors and televisions to their classrooms, and doctors rarely carry more than one or two networked gadgets to their consultations with patients. Before a technology can replace multiple existing tools, however, workers must be willing to use it. Originally proposed by Davis (1989), the Technology Acceptance Model (TAM) describes a user's approval or disapproval of a technological innovation. The two indicators of the TAM are perceived ease-of-use (PEOU) and perceived usefulness (PU). Characteristics such as portability and usability likely contribute to a worker's PEOU. For example, many portable technologies (e.g., smartwatches and earbuds) go unnoticed while being used because they work so seamlessly (Potosky, 2008). Likewise, characteristics such as power and predictiveness yield PU by providing workers with the necessary programs and information to complete complex projects. Ducey and Coovert (2016) applied the TAM in the healthcare industry to understand doctors' acceptance of tablet computers. Beyond the device's physical capabilities, individual and organizational factors determined whether doctors would accept the tablets as workplace tools. Although predicting technology acceptance is often difficult, today's new digital tools share structural similarities with the TAM's indicators, providing evidence that today's workers are both willing and able to accomplish more while using less.

Strength #2: Promoting Diversity and Equal Employment Opportunities

The networking characteristic of evolving workplace technologies can alleviate many diversity issues in the workplace. Particularly in the area of employee selection, networked technologies enable employers to communicate with diverse applicant pools despite differences in geographic regions. Title VII of the Civil Rights Act of 1964 prohibits the discrimination of employees due to race, color, religion, sex and national origin, and today's technology-mediated communication programs (e.g., Skype) help to ensure that none of these groups are overlooked due to job-irrelevant reasons such as travel expenses. Technology also promotes diversity among current employees by allowing colleagues of international organizations to collaborate despite differences in cultural values or time zones (Boudreau, Loch, Robey, & Straud, 1998).

As discussed, today's technologies also assist those with physical and psychological disabilities. While some forms of technology (e.g., VR) help disabled workers prepare for future employment, other forms (e.g., assistive equipment) enable current workers to perform sufficiently. The Americans with Disabilities Act (ADA) of 1990 protects disabled applicants and employees, and technology is changing the way that this law is enforced. Under the ADA, employers must provide reasonable accommodations – changes to a position or a workplace – that enable disabled workers to perform their jobs. With the advent of inexpensive assistive technologies, more and more disabled workers are, by law, afforded these accommodations.

Strength #3: Promoting Workplace Safety

Many technologies are developed to keep employees safe at work. Perhaps the most obvious way that technology improves safety is through the development of assistive and protective equipment. For example, researchers have developed power-assist suits that prevent industrial workers from putting undue stress and strain on their bodies after using heavy tools for long periods of time (Konishi, Wariishi, Tanibayashi, Kanchiku, & Fujimoto, 2015). Safety equipment also exists for traditional workplaces: the Wrist-Aid, for example, is a small device that alleviates symptoms of carpal tunnel syndrome for those doing copious amounts of typing.

In addition to equipment designed for safety, other forms of technology provide rich data that inform safety procedures within workplaces. Some electronic performance-monitoring practices such as those at Amazon's warehouses identify errors employees make that put themselves or their coworkers at risk and provide immediate feedback to prevent the errors from reoccurring (Yeginsu, 2018). Given the ubiquity of today's computing technologies, even everyday objects such as school buses are collecting information that can potentially save lives.

Weakness #1: Maintaining Technologies

On January 14, 1990, a single line of faulty software code rendered AT&T's phone lines dead, leaving thousands of employees without a means of communication (Burke, 1995). Technology failures restrict the usability of workplace technologies and incur serious performance and profit losses for organizations. Today's workers rely on technology to complete many of their essential tasks. Most employees using software to analyze data, for example, would not be able to compute the same statistical tests by hand. In the case that software failures occur, the average worker may not know how to troubleshoot the issue. According to a 2007 survey from the Pew Research Center's Internet & American Life project, 38 percent of technology users rely on help from tech support services when encountering issues with a device. In cases where these services are slow to respond, worker productivity may reach a standstill. To sustain employee productivity, organizations must invest in resources that can both minimize the number of technology malfunctions and resolve those that do arise.

Weakness #2: Distracting Employees

Even properly functioning technologies have the potential to hinder employee productivity. Cyberloafing, or accessing the Internet at work for personal use, remains a serious concern for many organizations. While some forms of EPM prevent cyberloafing activities on company-owned devices, most employees keep personal smartphones or wearables nearby during the workday. In fact, one survey found that 64 percent of employees use non-work websites *every day* at work (Henshell, 2013). Current research is inconclusive regarding the effects of cyberloafing on employee productivity. One lab study found that students who spent 10 minutes surfing the web before working on a boring task were 16 percent more productive than those who spent their break engaging in nonweb activities (Lim & Chen, 2012). While some claim that cyberloafing reduces stress, boredom, and fatigue (Eastin, Glynn, & Griffiths, 2007), others still consider the act a counterproductive work behavior (Jia, Jia, & Karau 2013). Although additional research is needed to understand the moderators of this relationship, networked devices do appear to at least temporarily distract workers on the job.

Weakness #3: Depersonalizing the Workplace

Because many tasks require the use of technology, employees often feel obligated to stay connected to their digital networks throughout the working day, meaning some employees lack in-person socialization. This is especially concerning for the 22 percent of employees who reported spending some time working remotely in 2016 ("On days," 2016). Prior research demonstrates that remote workers, despite outperforming their in-office peers, are half as likely to receive promotions (Bloom, Liang, Roberts, & Ying, 2015). One argument for this disparity is that unlike in-office workers who frequently see their managers in person, remote workers do not build strong personal connections with their superiors. As workers continue to use technologies to perform daily tasks, employers must recognize that face-to-face interactions foster relationships among colleagues that allow for a strong organizational culture.

Opportunity #1: Going Green with Workplace Technology

On current trends, workplace technologies show great potential for improving the environment. According to the US Environmental Protection Agency, industry commercial energy use accounts for over 20 percent of total US greenhouse gas emissions ("Sources of Greenhouse Gas Emissions," 2016). Workplace technologies help decrease these emissions by using alternative work practices that eliminate the need for travel. Using networked tools to complete virtual work or conduct remote job interviews, employers reduce rush-hour traffic, an occurrence that poses serious environmental threats (Behrend & Thompson, 2013).

The Internet of Things and artificial intelligence are also supporting sustainable initiatives by changing the ways that workers use everyday objects. Objects such as printers, lighting systems, and air conditioners with networking and predictive capabilities can automatically reduce their energy consumptions when not needed by employees. Even more, electronic performance-monitoring practices show potential for promoting a greener workforce. One monitoring system, for example, tracked individual workers' paper consumption on the job and provided them with regular feedback (Medland, 2010). While employees did not respond uniformly to the feedback, the system represents yet another purpose for implementing EPM: to protect the environment.

Opportunity #2: Becoming One with Nanotechnology

Now that workers roam their offices with small computers on their wrists, researchers are left asking one question: How much smaller can our computers get? Nanotechnology scientists strive to create technology from the atom- and molecule-level up, and their work is already utilized in the workplace. In the healthcare industry, for example, doctors can now prescribe their patients pill-sized computers as an alternative to conducting a colonoscopy ("Medtronic," n.d.). Similarly, employees at a Wisconsin technology company recently agreed to have rice-sized microchips installed into their hands so that they could gain entry to their workplace with a simple wave (Astor, 2017). As this trend toward miniaturization continues, workplace technologies may shift from peripheral labor tools to permanent worker attachments.

In a review of technology mediums used within personnel selection, Potosky (2008) introduced several attributes that describe our digital tools. Regarding nanotechnologies, the transparency attribute explains how permanent worker attachments could make our future workforce more successful. A transparent technology is described as one that users do not notice while interacting with others in the workplace. While peripheral tools such as smartphones can create public distractions and are prone to loss or theft, nanotechnology attachments are more privatized and fixed. Nanotechnologies assist workers in completing job-relevant tasks, as permanent worker attachments represent a reliable, easy-to-access workplace tool.

Opportunity #3: Collaborating with Robots

Artificial intelligence leads us closer to a world where humans and robots work collaboratively on projects. Referred to as **narrow AI**, current predictive technologies are built to precisely perform specific tasks. Much like we might hire an employee for having a particular college major, we can "hire" robots for possessing specific capabilities. For example, a narrow AI GPS feature enables Uber drivers to navigate through busy city streets more efficiently than the drivers would without such assistance. Current research demonstrates that narrow AI may be well suited for repetitive physical tasks, while humans are better suited for social management and creative tasks (Frey & Osborne, 2017). In understanding narrow AI's capabilities, employers can build teams that utilize robots' and humans' strengths.

Ray Kurzweil, director of engineering at Google, anticipates a thriving workforce involving AI. Noting that technological advancements always come with inherent risks, optimists such as Kurzweil view AI as they would any other workplace technology. Just as today's workers use computers, smartphones, and the Internet to do their jobs, workers of the future should rely on AI to complete tasks more effectively. Optimists of AI tend to focus on its assistive capacity in the workplace rather than its potential to steal workers' jobs. While optimists do recognize that AI will make certain jobs obsolete, they see its benefits as outweighing its risks. Kurzweil, who is known for putting forth accurate technology predictions, foresees the creation of a human-level AI by 2029 (Kurzweil, 2014).

Some futurists also anticipate peaceful collaborations with robots due to our inability to create **general AI**, or consciously aware technology capable of performing all intellectual tasks exhibited by humans. Kevin Kelly, executive editor of *Wired* magazine, doubts that creating a superhuman AI is even possible. Viewing human intelligence as a complex multidimensional trait, Kelly argues that our narrow forms of AI are not actually smarter than us, but just *different* than us. Because human intelligence is a very specific form of intelligence resulting from millions of years of evolution, futurists like Kelly consider general AI a futile research effort, and in some cases, a myth (Kelly, 2017). From this perspective, we can collaborate with robots to the extent that we continue building them to complete specified tasks.

Threat #1: Risking Human Safety

Workplace technologies may make our future workforce more successful, but there are a number of threats that could prevent such success. One critical concern is the risk associated with adopting new forms of technology. In March 2018, an experimental autonomous Uber vehicle struck and killed a bicyclist. The self-driving car, which included perceptive, predictive, and responsive modules, failed to accurately perceive the biker as she crossed a four-lane road. Identifying the woman as an "unknown object," the car predicted that she would stay out of its path, so it maintained its speed (Madrigal, 2018). Incidents such as this bring to light an ethical question for the future workplace technology: Can we trust autonomous devices to do our jobs? According to the Society for Industrial and Organizational Psychology (SIOP), automation ranks fourth on its current list of top ten workplace trends (2018), a sign that researchers must monitor this growing trend. While AI improves upon humans' biased decision making, it still makes decisions at least partially influenced by the biases of the humans who design it. Scientists are keenly aware of this and question whether the programmers, the end-users, or the device itself should be held accountable for costly AI mistakes (Bostrom & Yudkowsky, 2014). While many wish to blame the programmers, identifying the specific individuals at fault and determining the severity of their punishments remains a challenging task for stakeholders.

Although our evolving workplace technologies promote safety, they do not guarantee it. This is especially true for the encryption of technology, as hackers still breach thoroughly coded networks. Private employee information such as Social Security numbers, birth dates, and biometric records is stored within HR databases, and insufficient encryption could easily result in cases of identity theft from both within and outside of the organization (Nagele-Piazza, 2017). Employers are typically held responsible in these cases, but victims are still prone to severe financial and criminal charges in the process, not to mention potential threats to their physical safety.

Threat #2: Ending Moore's Law

A second threat concerns the longevity of Moore's Law. Since its inception in 1965, Moore's Law has accurately predicted our advancements in computing power and size. In recent years, however, headlines such as "Moore's Law is Dead" have surfaced within the computer science industry (Simonite, 2016). While past doubters have been proven wrong, today's scientists, more than ever before, are struggling to keep up with the doubling power trend while working with infinitely small transistors. While nanotechnology represents an opportunity for the future of workplace technology, researchers may need to invest in innovative alternatives (e.g., quantum computing) to sustain our advancements in workplace computing in the long run.

Threat #3: Obscuring Work–Life Balance

Technology poses a threat to employees' work–life balance in two conflicting, yet equally worrisome ways. First is the possibility that work will consume employees' lives. Already, nearly one-fourth of employed individuals report spending at least some of their time working from home ("On days," 2016). This trend blurs the line between work life and home life, making employees feel obligated to complete projects at locations and times that would otherwise be reserved for leisure or familial activities. Employees in a constantly connected workforce may find themselves replacing their nine-to-five schedules with intermittent work throughout the day. These new schedules may cause workers to feel stressed or burnt out, meaning technology poses a serious threat to employee satisfaction and productivity.

Conversely, technology may rob employees of their work, as there still remains the possibility for general AI. In this case, technology would no longer be viewed as a workplace tool that *assists* labor practices, but rather a functioning employee that *completes* labor practices. According to research from the Oxford Martin School, 47 percent of total US employees are at risk of losing their job to today's narrow AIs (Frey & Osborne, 2017). In a future with functioning general AI, the possibility of a fully automated workforce would increase.

Elon Musk, CEO of SpaceX and Tesla, believes that general AI technologies can be created, and he fears that they would behave unethically. Musk considers AI – even when produced with good intentions – to be more dangerous than nuclear weapons. Noting AI's capacity to outrace human management efforts during production, alarmists like Musk are wary to develop conscious technologies. In 2015, Musk founded OpenAI, a nonprofit research organization dedicated to building safe AI that contributes to humankind in positive ways (Browne, 2018).

Tim O'Reilly, founder of O'Reilly Media, also recognizes the potential for AI to act unethically, but he does not believe that we should fear AI. Instead, he believes that the primary ethical concern rests with the humans who create AI. O'Reilly recognizes that today's narrow AIs – such as the advanced algorithms behind Google and Facebook – already understand human behavior to a great extent. Often, it is the programming decisions behind these AIs – not the AI itself – that wreak havoc for humans. Realists such as O'Reilly apply this same rationale to the workforce. If we choose to build AI from algorithms that emphasize efficiency over any sort of employee satisfaction, we could very well see a fully automated workforce. However, we can develop AIs that behave similarly to existing workplace technologies, eliminating outdated jobs while introducing new ones for humans (O'Reilly, 2017).

Looking Ahead by Looking Back

Throughout history, employees have continuously feared that adopting new workplace technologies will bring about consequences; yet, such fears have rarely, if ever, been actualized. At the close of the 1990s, for example, workers worried that their computers were ill-equipped to process the formatting changes associated with the final digits of dates in the 2000s (e.g., 1900 and 2000 would be indiscernible). Organizations worried that computer programs with insufficient power would no longer accurately process date-released information. However, workers' fear proved to be overstated in relation to the research efforts undertaken in the years prior (e.g., Jones, 1997) and no massive computer failures occurred at the turn of the century.

In addition to computing power concerns, workers since the 1990s have also feared the consequences of using networked and immersive technologies. With networked technologies, workers fear that our tools keep us from communicating with one another in natural, face-to-face settings. While depersonalization does represent a weakness of networked technologies, globalization simultaneously represents a strength. In reality, today's technologies have connected employees in ways unimaginable a few decades ago. With regard to immersive technologies, human resource professionals and managers have doubted that employees will be able to transfer the knowledge, skills, and attitudes they acquire while playing games to their actual workplace (Alexander, Brunye, Sidman, & Weil, 2005). These concerns stem from the artificiality of environments found in games and VR: How could employees become better performers on the job without having any training experience on site? Even so, research has clearly demonstrated that trainees are still able to apply their virtual experiences to natural settings (Alexander, Brunye, Sidman, & Weil, 2005; Seymour et al., 2002).

At present, the predictive characteristic of workplace technologies is most worrisome due to its potential to automate occupations. Although some automation has occurred, workers must keep in mind that technology eliminates specific occupations, but not work in general (Autor, 2015). During the Industrial Revolution, for example, some citizens of Britain and Ireland worked professionally as knocker-ups. The primary duty of a knocker-up was to rouse sleeping clients by tapping on their windows or doors with a heavy stick. This job existed until as late as 1970, when alarm clocks became more reliable and user-friendly (Peek, 2016). While the alarm clock made the knocker-up occupation irrelevant, it did not eliminate our desire to wake up at a certain time each day. To efficiently meet this consumer need, knocker-ups were quickly replaced with different kinds of workers, such as clockmakers and factory workers.

A more recent occupation in the process of obsolescence is the video store clerk. At its peak in 2004, Blockbuster employed thousands of clerks in their over 9,000 video rental shops. Shortly after, online streaming services and automated movie kiosks completely altered the way that customers consumed video content. The occupation of video store clerk is now on the verge of extinction with fewer than ten Blockbuster locations remaining in the United States (Schmidt, 2017). Importantly, several new jobs emerged at various skill levels in the absence of video store clerks. For example, field-service representatives manually stock movies in Redbox kiosks, and video engineers ensure high-quality streaming experiences for Netflix users.

When Vonnegut wrote *Player piano* over 60 years ago, offices did not have personal computers. At the time, many of the technologies envisioned in the novel seemed unbelievable – how could inanimate objects possibly take away a society's livelihood? Even though many of our current technologies transcend those mentioned in the novel, we are still far from a fully automated workforce. Each of the eight technology characteristics discussed shows potential for improving future employees' productivity on the job, yet concerns about automation, depersonalization, and safety still exist. In recognizing that technology changes are typically accompanied by exaggerated fears, we anticipate that future workplace tools will continue to change, but not eliminate, the work of humans. Only time will truly tell whether Vonnegut's automated workforce becomes a reality, and in the meantime, we close with an aphorism from the novel: "It isn't knowledge that's making trouble, but the uses it's put to."

Acknowledgements

We would like to acknowledge our WAVE Lab members – Lili Greenstein, Daniel Ravid, David Tomczak, and Sarah Zarsky – for their collaboration in developing the eight technology characteristics discussed in this chapter.

References

AccuVein. (2012). AccuVein AV400 user manual: A health professional's guide for use and operation of the AccuVein AV400. *AccuVein*. Retrieved June 15, 2018, from www.accuvein.com

Alexander, A. L., Brunyé, T., Sidman, J., & Weil, S. A. (2005). From gaming to training: A review of studies on fidelity, immersion, presence, and buy-in and their effects on transfer in pc-based simulations and games. *DARWARS Training Impact Group, 5*, 1–14.

Allen, I. E., & Seaman, J. (2016). Online Report Card: Tracking Online Education in the United States. *Babson Survey Research Group*.

American Management Association (2007). Electronic monitoring and surveillance survey. *AMA/ePolicy Institute Research*. Retrieved from www.amanet.org/training/articles/the-latest-on-workplace-monitoring-and-surveillance.aspx

Ashton, K. (2009). That 'internet of things' thing. *RFID Journal, 22*(7), 97–114.

Astor, M. (2017). Microchip implants for employees? One company says yes. *New York Times*. July 25. www.nytimes.com/2017/07/25/technology/microchips-wisconsin-company- employees.html?mcubz=3

Autor, D. (2015). Why are there still so many jobs? The history and future of workplace automation. *Journal of Economic Perspectives, 29*(3), 3–30.

Behrend, T. S., Gloss, A. E., & Thompson, L. F. (2013). Global development through the psychology of workplace technology. In M. D. Coovert & L. F. Thompson (Eds.), *The psychology of workplace technology* (pp. 261–283). New York, NY: Taylor & Francis.

Behrend, T. S., & Thompson, L. F. (2013). Combining I-O psychology and technology for an environmentally sustainable world. In A. H. Huffman & S. R. Klein (Eds.), *Green organizations: Driving change with I-O psychology* (pp. 300–322). New York, NY: Routledge.

Beinstein, A., & Sumers, T. (2016, June 29). How Uber engineering increases safe driving with telematics. Retrieved from https://eng.uber.com/telematics/

Bercik, B., & Bond, J. (1996). *Inside JavaScript*. Indianapolis, IN: New Riders Publishing.

Bhave, D. P. (2014). The invisible eye? Electronic performance monitoring and employee job performance. *Personnel Psychology, 67*(3), 605–635.

Blascovich, J., Loomis, J., Beall, A. C., Swinth, K. R., Hoyt, C. L., & Bailenson, J. N. (2002). Immersive virtual environment technology as a methodological tool for social psychology. *Psychological Inquiry, 13*(2), 103–124.

Bloom, N., Liang, J., Roberts, J., & Ying, Z. J. (2015). Does working from home work? Evidence from a Chinese experiment. *Quarterly Journal of Economics, 130*(1), 165–218.

Bollermann, B., Osborn, L., & Hughan, R. (2017). *U.S. Patent Application No. 15/618,064*.

Bostrom, N., & Yudkowsky, E. (2014). The ethics of artificial intelligence. In K. Frankish & W. Ramsey (Eds.), *The Cambridge handbook of artificial intelligence* (pp. 316–334). Cambridge, UK: Cambridge University Press.

Boudreau, M. C., Loch, K. D., Robey, D., & Straud, D. (1998). Going global: Using information technology to advance the competitiveness of the virtual transnational organization. *The Academy of Management Executive, 12*(4), 120–128.

Boulos, M. N. K., & Berry, G. (2012). Real-time locating systems (RTLS) in healthcare: A condensed primer. *International Journal of Health Geographics, 11*(1), 25–32.

Bousfield, T., Dieker, L., Hughes, C. E., & Hynes, M. (Eds.) (2016). *Proceedings from TeachLivE 2016: 4th International TLE TeachLivE Conference: Virtual Human Performance*. Orlando, FL: University of Central Florida.

Browne, R. (2018, April 6). Elon Musk warns A.I. could create an 'immortal dictator from which we can never escape.' *CNBC*. Retrieved from www.cnbc.com/2018/04/06/elon-musk-warns-ai-could-create-immortal-dictator-in-documentary.html

Bunch, B., & Hellemans, A. (1993). *The timetables of technology: A chronology of the most important people and events in the history of technology*. New York, NY: Simon & Schuster.

Burke, D. (1995). All circuits are busy now: The 1990 AT&T long distance network collapse. *California Polytechnic State University*. Retrieved June 15, 2018, from http://users.csc.calpoly.edu/~jdalbey/SWE/Papers/att_collapse

Burrows, S., Gurevych, I., & Stein, B. (2015). The eras and trends of automatic short answer grading. *International Journal of Artificial Intelligence in Education, 25*(1), 60–117.

Ceruzzi, P. (1998). In I. Cohen & W. Aspray (Eds.), *A history of modern computing*. Cambridge, MA: The MIT Press.

Comer, D. E., & Droms, R. E. (2003). *Computer networks and internets*. Upper Saddle River, NJ: Prentice Hall, Inc.

Davis, F. D. (1989). Perceived usefulness, perceived ease of use, and user acceptance of information technology. *MIS Quarterly, 13*, 319–340.

Deitel, P., & Deitel, H. (2007). *Java: How to program* (7th ed.). Upper Saddle River, NJ: Pearson Prentice Hall.

Deterding, S., Khaled, R., Nacke L. E., & Dixon, D. (2011). Gamification: Toward a definition. *CHI 2011 Gamification Workshop Proceedings*, Vancouver, 12–15.

Devol, G. C. (1966). *U.S. Patent No. 3,283,918*. Washington, DC: US Patent and Trademark Office.

Ducey, A. J., & Coovert, M. D. (2016). Predicting tablet computer use: An extended Technology Acceptance Model for physicians. *Health Policy and Technology*, 5(3), 268–284.

Eastin, M.S., Glynn, C. J., & Griffiths, R. P. (2007). Psychology of communication technology use in the workplace. *Cyberpsychology and Behavior, 10*, 436–443

ENIAC (Electronic Numerical Integrator and Computer) (2003). *McGraw-Hill Dictionary of Scientific & Technical Terms, 6E*. http://encyclopedia2.thefreedictionary.com/ENIAC

Frey, C. B., & Osborne, M. A. (2017). The future of employment: how susceptible are jobs to computerisation? *Technological Forecasting and Social Change, 114*, 254–280.

Ginzberg, E. (1982). The mechanization of work. *Scientific American, 247*(3), 66–75.

Goodman, D., & Morrison, M. (2007). *JavaScript bible* (6th ed.). Indianapolis, IN: Wiley Publishing.

Greenhalgh, T., Vijayaraghavan, S., Wherton, J., Shaw, S., Byrne, E., Campbell-Richards, D., Bhattacharya, S., Hanson, P., Ramoutar, S., Gutteridge, C., Hodkinson, I., Collard, A., & Morris, J. (2016). Virtual online consultations: advantages and limitations (VOCAL) study. *BMJ Open, 6*(1).

Haley, D.T., Thomas, P., Roeck, A.D., & Petre, M. (2007). Measuring improvement in latent semantic analysis-based marking systems: Using a computer to mark questions about HTML. In S. Mann & Simon (Eds.), *Proceedings of the 9th Australasian Conference on Computing Education, Volume 66 of ACE* (pp. 35–42). Ballarat: Australian Computer Society.

Henshell, J. (2013, January 14). Cyberloafing, BYOD, and the ethics of using technology devices at work. Retrieved from www.digitalethics.org/essays/cyberloafing-byod- and-ethics-using-technology-devices-work

IBM. (2013). *Data-driven healthcare organizations use big data analytics for big gains* [White paper]. Somers, NY: IBM Corporation.

"IBM Watson Health." (n.d.). Retrieved from www.ibm.com/watson/health/oncology-and-genomics/

"iCliniq." (n.d.). Retrieved from www.icliniq.com/p/aboutus

Information technology timeline. (2003). *IETE Journal of Education, 44*(1), 21–22.

ISO (International Standards Organization) (1998). Ergonomic requirements for office work with visual display terminal. Part II: Guidance on usability (ISO 9241-11:1998).

Jia, H., Jia, R., & Karau, S. (2013). Cyberloafing and personality: The impact of the Big Five traits and workplace situational factors. *Journal of Leadership and Organizational Studies, 20*(3), 358–365.

Jones, C. (1997). *The year 2000 software problem: Quantifying the costs and assessing the consequences.* New York, NY: ACM Press/Addison-Wesley Publishing Co.

Karim, M. N., Kaminsky, S. E., & Behrend, T. S. (2014). Cheating, reactions, and performance in remotely proctored testing: An exploratory experimental study. *Journal of Business and Psychology, 29*(4), 555–572.

Karim, M. N., Willford, J. C., & Behrend, T. S. (2015). Big data, little individual: Considering the human side of big data. *Industrial and Organizational Psychology, 8*(4), 527–533.

Kelly, K. (2017). The myth of a superhuman AI. *Wired*. Retrieved from www.wired.com/2017/04/the-myth-of-a-superhuman-ai/

Khakurel, J., Pöysä, S., & Porras, J. (2016, November). The use of wearable devices in the workplace: A systematic literature review. In *International Conference on Smart Objects and Technologies for Social Good* (pp. 284–294). Cham: Springer.

Kish, L. B. (2002). End of Moore's law: thermal (noise) death of integration in micro and nano electronics. *Physics Letters A, 305*(3–4), 144–149.

Knezek, G., Fisser, P., Gibson, D., Christensen, R., & Tyler-Wood, T. (2012). SimSchool: Research outcomes from simulated classrooms. In *Proceedings of the Society for Information Technology & Teacher Education International Conference 2012*. Chesapeake, VA: American Association for the Advancement of Computing in Education.

Konishi, M., Wariishi, T., Tanibayashi, H., Kanchiku, H., & Fujimoto, H. (2015). *U.S. Patent Application No. D781430*

Kurzweil, R. (2014). Don't fear artificial intelligence. *TIME*. Retrieved from http://time.com/3641921/dont-fear-artificial-intelligence/

Lakhani, K. R., & von Hippel, E. (2003). How open source software works: "Free" user-to-user assistance. *Research Policy, 32*(6), 923–943.

Landers, R. N., Bauer, K. N., & Callan, R. C. (2017). Gamification of task performance with leaderboards: A goal setting experiment. *Computers in Human Behavior, 71*, 508–515.

Landers, R. N., & Callan, R. C. (2011). Casual social games as serious games: The psychology of gamification in undergraduate education and employee training. In M. Ma & A. Oikonomou (Eds.), *Serious games and edutainment applications* (pp. 399–423). London: Springer.

Lim, V. K., & Chen, D. J. (2012). Cyberloafing at the workplace: gain or drain on work? *Behaviour and Information Technology, 31*(4), 343–353.

Lipko, H. (2016, November 10). Meet Jill Watson: Georgia Tech's first AI teaching assistant. Retrieved from https://pe.gatech.edu/blog/meet-jill-watson-georgia-techs-first-ai- teaching-assistant

Maddox, B. B., & White, S. W. (2015). Comorbid social anxiety disorder in adults with autism spectrum disorder. *Journal of Autism and Developmental Disorders, 45*(12), 3949–3960.

Madrigal, A. C. (2018, May 24). Uber's self-driving car didn't malfunction, it was just bad. *The Atlantic*. Retrieved from www.theatlantic.com/technology/archive/2018/05/ubers- self-driving-car-didnt-malfunction-it-was-just-bad/561185/

Marzano, R. J. (2009). Teaching with interactive whiteboards. *Educational Leadership, 67*(3), 80–82.

McNeil, I. (1990). *An encyclopedia of the history of technology*. New York, NY: Routledge.

Means, B., Gallagher, L., & Padilla, C. (2008). *Teachers' use of student data systems to improve instruction: 2005 to 2007*. Washington, DC: US Department of Education.

Medland, R. (2010, November). Curbing paper wastage using flavoured feedback. In *Proceedings of the 22nd Conference of the Computer–Human Interaction*

Special Interest Group of Australia on Computer–Human Interaction (pp. 224–227). New York, NY: ACM Press.

"Medtronic." (n.d.) Retrieved from www.medtronic.com/us-en/index.html

"Microbe Invader." (n.d.). Retrieved from www.microbeinvader.com/

Mittler, J. (2007). Assistive technology and IDEA. In C. Warger (Ed.), *Technology integration: Providing access to the curriculum for students with disabilities*. Arlington, VA: Technology and Media Division (TAM).

Mohler, M., & Mihalcea, R. (2009, March). Text-to-text semantic similarity for automatic short answer grading. In *Proceedings of the 12th Conference of the European Chapter of the Association for Computational Linguistics* (pp. 567–575). Association for Computational Linguistics, Athens, Greece.

"Moodle." (n.d.) Retrieved from https://moodle.org/

Moravec, H. (1988). *Mind children: The future of robot and human intelligence*. Cambridge, MA: Harvard University Press.

Moreau, R. (1984). In I. Cohen & W. Aspray (Eds.), *The computer comes of age* (J. Howlett Trans.). (English ed.). Cambridge, MA: The MIT Press.

Morris, B., Croker, S., Zimmerman, C., Gill, D., & Romig, C. (2013). Gaming science: The "gamification" of scientific thinking. *Frontiers in Psychology, 4*(607), 1–16.

Mross, C. P. (1971). *U.S. Patent No. 3,554,052*. Washington, DC: US Patent and Trademark Office.

Nagele-Piazza, L. (2017, November 2017). Employers may be liable for worker identity theft. Retrieved from www.shrm.org/resourcesandtools/legal-and-compliance/state-and- local-updates/pages/employers-may-be-liable-for-worker-identity-theft.aspx

National Business Group on Health. (2015). *Large employers' health plan design survey: Reducing costs while looking to the future* [Press Conference]. Washington, DC: National Business Group on Health.

Newman, W. M., & Taylor, A. S. (1999, September). Towards a methodology employing critical parameters to deliver performance improvements in interactive systems. *INTERACT, 99*, 605–612.

Ningombam, D., Singh, A., & Chanu, K. T. (2018). Multipurpose GPS guided autonomous mobile robot. In K. Saeed, N. Chaki., B. Pati, S. Bakshi & D. Mohapatra (Eds.), *Progress in advanced computing and intelligent engineering*. Advances in Intelligent Systems and Computing, 564 (pp. 361–372). Singapore: Springer.

"On days they worked, 22 percent of employed did some or all of their work at home in 2016." *The Economics Daily*. Retrieved from www.bls.gov/opub/ted/2017/on-days-they-worked-22-percent-of-employed-did-some-or-all-of-their-work-at-home-in- 2016.htm

O'Reilly, T. (2017). Using AI to create new jobs. *O'Reilly*. Retrieved from www.oreilly.com/ideas/using-ai-to-create-new-jobs

Peek, S. (2016, March 27). Knocker uppers: Waking up the workers in industrial Britain. *BBC*. Retrieved from www.bbc.com/news/uk-england-35840393

Perlroth, N. (2017, October 3). All 3 billion Yahoo accounts were affected by 2013 attack. *New York Times*. Retrieved from www.nytimes.com/2017/10/03/technology/yahoo-hack-3-billion-users.html

Potosky, D. (2008). A conceptual framework for the role of the administration medium in the personnel assessment process. *The Academy of Management Review, 33*(3), 629–648.

Prometric. (2009). *Biometric-enabled check-in.* Retrieved June 15, 2018, from www.prometric.com/en-us/clients/documents/20090928Biometrics4pager.pdf

Psiaki, M. L., Humphreys, T. E., & Stauffer, B. (2016). Attackers can spoof navigation signals without our knowledge. Here's how to fight back GPS lies. *IEEE Spectrum, 53*(8), 26–53.

PwC. (2017, October 26). *Global State of Information Security Survey 2018* [Newsbrief]. Vietnam: PwC.

Ralston A., Reilly E., & Hemmendinger D. (2000). *Encyclopedia of computer science.* (4th ed.). New York, NY: Nature Publishing Group.

Ribitzky, R. (2007). Active monitoring of employees rises to 78%. *ABC News.* Retrieved from http://abcnews.go.com/Business/story?id=88319&page=1

"Rugged Cards Store Critical Mission Data Flash Replaces Other Storage Technologies in Military Applications." (2001, October 16). Retrieved from www.targa systems.com/press/pr2910.htm

Russell, S. J., & Norvig, P. (2016). *Artificial intelligence: A modern approach.* Malaysia: Pearson Education Limited.

"Salesforce research shows success with wearables motivates 86 percent of adopters to increase spending on enterprise wearables initiatives." (2015, April 22). Retrieved from https://investor.salesforce.com/about-us/investor/investor-news/investor-news- details/2015/

Sauter, D. (2011). *Android smartphone relevance to military weather applications* (No. ARL- TR-5793). White Sands Missile Range, NM: Army Research Lab.

Schmidt, S. (2017, April 26). Blockbuster has survived in the most curious of places – Alaska. *Washington Post.* Retrieved from www.washingtonpost.com/news/morning- mix/wp/2017/04/26/

Selinger, M., Sepulveda, A., & Buchan, J. (2013). *Education and the Internet of everything.* San Jose, CA: Cisco Systems, Inc.

"Sermo: Talk Real Medicine." (n.d.) Retrieved from www.sermo.com/

Seymour, N. E., Gallagher, A. G., Roman, S. A., O'Brien, M. K., Bansal, V. K., Andersen, D. K., & Satava, R. M. (2002). Virtual reality training improves operating room performance: results of a randomized, double-blinded study. *Annals of Surgery, 236*(4), 458–463.

Simon, H. (1965). *The shape of automation for men and management.* New York, NY: Harper and Row.

Simonite, T. (2016, May 13). Moore's Law is dead. Now what? *Technology Review.* Retrieved from www.technologyreview.com/s/601441/moores-law-is-dead-now-what/

"SIOP Announces Top 10 Workplace Trends for 2018." (2018, January 25). Retrieved from www.siop.org/article_view.aspx?article=1766

Smith, M. J., Ginger, E. J., Wright, K., Wright, M. A., Taylor, J. L., Humm, L. B., ... & Fleming, M. F. (2014). Virtual reality job interview training in adults with autism spectrum disorder. *Journal of Autism and Developmental Disorders, 44*(10), 2450–2463.

Song, C., Gehlbach, P. L., & Kang, J. U. (2012). Active tremor cancellation by a "smart" handheld vitreoretinal microsurgical tool using swept source optical coherence tomography. *Optics Express, 20*(21), 23414–23421.

"Sources of Greenhouse Gas Emissions." (2016). Retrieved from www.epa.gov/ghgemis sions/sources-greenhouse-gas-emissions

Stein, N. (2017). The future of population health management: Artificial intelligence as a cost-effective behavior change and chronic disease prevention and management solution. *MOJ Public Health*, 6(5), 00188.

Steuer, J. (1992). Defining virtual reality: Dimensions determining telepresence. *Journal of Communication*, 42(4), 73–93.

"Tactical Communications." (n.d.) Retrieved from www.harris.com/what-we-do/tactical- communications

Taylor, J. L., & Seltzer, M. M. (2011). Employment and post-secondary educational activities for young adults with autism spectrum disorders during the transition to adulthood. *Journal of Autism and Developmental Disorders*, 41(5), 566–574.

Tyre, P. (2016, March 21). How sophisticated test scams from China making their way into the US. *The Atlantic*. Retrieved from www.theatlantic.com/education/archive/2016/03/how-sophisticated-test-scams- from-china-are-making-their-way-into-the-us/474474/

"Using the Internet of Things to Boost School Safety." (2017, October 27). Retrieved from www.ipctech.com/using-the-internet-of-things-to-boost-school-safety

Vodicka, E., Mejilla, R., Leveille, S. G., Ralston, J. D., Darer, J. D., Delbanco, T., Walker, J., & Elmore, J. G. (2013). Online access to doctors' notes: patient concerns about privacy. *Journal of Medical Internet Research*, 15(9), e208.

Vonnegut, K. (1952). *Player piano*. New York, NY: Delacorte Press.

Waldrop, M. M. (2016, February 9). The chips are down for Moore's Law. *Nature*. Retrieved from www.nature.com/news/the-chips-are-down-for-moore-s-law-1.19338

Wang, Y., Kung, L., & Byrd, T. A. (2018). Big data analytics: Understanding its capabilities and potential benefits for healthcare organizations. *Technological Forecasting and Social Change*, 126, 3–13.

"Waymo." (n.d.). Retrieved from www.google.com/selfdrivingcar/

"Wrist-Aid." (n.d.). Retrieved from www.wrist-aid.com/

Yagoda, R. E., & Hill, S. G. (2011). *Using mobile devices for robotic controllers: Examples and some initial concepts for experimentation* (No. ARL-TN-436). Aberdeen Proving Ground, MD: Army Research Lab.

Yang, Y., Liu, X., & Deng, R. H. (2017). Lightweight break-glass access control system for healthcare internet-of-things. *IEEE Transactions on Industrial Informatics*, 14(8), 3610–3617.

Yeginsu, C. (2018, February 1). If workers slack off, the wristband will know (And Amazon has a patent for it.). *New York Times*. Retrieved from www.nytimes.com/2018/02/01/technology/amazon-wristband-tracking- privacy.html

Zakon, R. H. (2018). Hobbes' Internet Timeline 25 – the definitive ARPAnet & Internet history. Retrieved June 15, 2018, from www.zakon.org/robert/internet/timeline/

5 The Changing Nature of Work
A Global Perspective

Christopher Clott

> *Two vectors shape the world – technology and globalization. The first helps determine human preferences; the second, economic realities. Regardless of how much preferences evolve and diverge, they also gradually converge and form markets where economies of scale lead to reduction of costs and prices.*
> Theodore Levitt, "The Globalization of Markets,"
> *Harvard Business Review*, 1983

It has been nearly 35 years since the publication of Levitt's seminal work that first used the term "globalization." In that time, the world and the very nature of work have been transformed through technology and globalization; but the enormous gains to mankind in productivity and prosperity have been distributed very unevenly across the world landscape. A major by-product of these twin vectors has been the growth of a global workforce comprised of low-wage workers at one end of the spectrum clustered around areas of manufacturing, and increasingly higher-wage, and talented "knowledge workers," a term first used by the management theorist Peter Drucker (1959) to define individuals involved in business services on the other end. Recent research suggests knowledge workers with specific skills are being supplanted by "learning workers" with skills to learn and adapt to changing workplace environments (Manuti, et al., 2015).

The desires and aspirations of the world's most dynamic talent to live and work in particular world locations, combined with many countries' and cities' substantial investments to attract these workers, are now factored heavily into the choice of where to locate operations (Sanz, 2009). As organizations have globalized and become more reliant on technology, critical functions performed within them require sophisticated talent with global acumen, multicultural fluency, technological literacy, entrepreneurial skills, and the ability to manage in increasingly de-layered, disaggregated organizations across the globe (Briscoe, Schuler, & Claus, 2009). The growth and maturation of artificial intelligence (AI) has also accelerated a movement toward finding, retaining and rewarding individuals skilled in the manipulation of data regardless of their geographic location. This suggests the need for a much more fluid system for the movement of factors of production (land, labor, capital, management, information innovation, etc.) during a period of rapid change in the workplace environment.

What makes a location creative and attractive while another languishes? Researchers have tried to identify the key ingredients that enable talented people to thrive in particular environments (Saxenian, 2006; Weiner, 2016). Technology and globalization have given rise to innovative "superstar" cities and regions worldwide where breakthrough technologies and cutting edge organizations are developed (Lanvin, 2017). Ambitious and talented individuals mix and merge together into a new kind of society of knowledge workers; but also one increasingly detached from older less desirable locations – often within the same country (Florida, 2017). Recently, this has led to tension between "have" and "have not" cluster locations, resulting in major political upheaval and popular uprisings within the developed world where globalization is blamed for the rise of income inequality. Major coastal cities such as New York City and San Francisco in the United States attract talent and concentrations of high value-added industries at the expense of older, primarily inland locations such as St. Louis (MO) and Memphis (TN). Predictable evolutionary change has given way to disruptive, asymmetric change in the areas of technology, globalization, and work structure that is much more difficult to plan for (Dahl, 2017).

This chapter will look at recent research on the globalized workforce with an effort to understand the development, recruitment, and training of talent to implement strategic or technological innovation. Research considering global talent management, human resource management and organizational behavior as it relates to global work, artificial intelligence, and growing restrictions on the free flow of global work will be examined. Will we continue to see further extension of the globalized workforce influenced and in some cases determined by multinational enterprises that has been ongoing over the last three decades? Or will we enter a new era of privileged access to markets based less on workplace location and talent than on specific citizenship, ethnicity, religion, or other non-work factors (Strange, 1996)?

World Commerce: Production and Services

For hundreds of years the centers of world commerce were situated on the basis of geography: safe harbors for waterborne transportation and power for energy; later – air, rail, and truck/car access, and convenience to key markets have been prominent reasons for location of major cities (Ellison & Glaeser, 1999). Commerce required an adequate workforce to manufacture goods and supply services that grew where there was geographic access, adequate infrastructure and abundant labor. As globalization increased in the mid-1990s due to technological developments such as the Internet, growing liberalization of markets, and the spread of commerce to large developing countries such as China, firms from developed countries were encouraged to pursue low-cost labor alternatives offshore (Clott, 2004; Kehal & Singh 2006). Global outsourcing of manufacturing and services grew exponentially in the first decade of the 2000s, with new factories and information technology (IT) centers that were built, owned, and operated by large global firms in low-cost countries. Small and mid-size firms followed this exodus with their own locations, and sophisticated third-party operators grew to connect multiple suppliers to customers under contracts that made geographic location flexible and less relevant to the company hiring the services. The advent of "blockchain" contracts connecting the supply chain has the potential for substantially changing the design of this network in the future.

In the offshore manufacturing environment, mass producing shoes, for example, had much to do with automating tasks and building a disciplined workforce to produce product efficiently at the lowest wages permissible. Employees would presumably be attracted to the offshore manufacturing location by the promise of paid work with few other alternatives, i.e. monopsony of the workplace. Locating a manufacturing firm on the basis of particular individual skills and talents was not expected or desired. One simply needed a pool of compliant individuals who could be taught basic manufacturing skills usually at company expense. Aspects of production in the making of textiles, for example, have followed this basic pattern to the present. Locations have changed as formerly low-cost countries or areas have evolved to higher-value (and higher-wage) regions. Global manufacturers adjusted by locating to new low-wage locations or spinning off the manufacturing to third-party suppliers, and these decisions are now going beyond merely cost considerations to include supply chain and political considerations (Ellram, Tate, & Peterson, 2013; Rivoli, 2005).

In the area of business services, a supply of low-cost workers similar to the manufacturing environment continued to be the way many firms perceived the world services economy from the 1980s to the first decade of the 2000s (Laudicina, Gott, & Peterson, 2014; Lewin, Massini, & Peeters, 2009; Mankiw & Swagel, 2006). Public institutions provided the bulk of the sophisticated training, with only the details specific to the firm covered by the company. In the early days of offshoring, mainly done by IT firms, high-tech jobs went to locations such as India where skilled workers could be had for wages much lower than those in the United States and Europe (Clott, 2004). Global offshoring of back office operations scaled up to outsourcing through third-party operators, with non-core operations increasingly done by vendors' familiar with specific product needs. Global companies followed different paths; some providing all of their proprietary information to outsourcing partners, while others attempted to retain key aspects of their business in-house. The perception was that outsourcing of low-skill service work would be performed by low-wage individuals in offshore locations while high-skill, high-value work would continue to be primarily located in developed countries. This thesis overlooked changes in the clustering of talent in certain locations, particularly for the global services economy, and how this contributed to speed and innovation as well as competitive success (Saxenian, 2006). The need for analytical talent with the necessary skill sets to create value through the capture, analysis, and exchange of large amounts of data suggests that location choices for firms must be driven by educational attainment, IT infrastructure, language skills, security, intellectual property guarantees and cultural adaptability far more than cost considerations (Florida, 2017; Oshri, Kotlarsky, & Willcocks, 2009). Some research suggests that in the United States alone, the economy will have a shortage of 140–190,000 people with analytical expertise, as well as a shortfall of another 1.5 million managers and analysts with the skills to understand and make decisions (Ransbotham, Kiron, & Prentice, 2015). As the developed economies grow, there will also be a shortage of workers in business services to do unskilled, low-paying work that cannot be entirely automated. This may create "centers of labor" to which immigrants and disadvantaged individuals might locate if given the opportunity to do so (Scott, 2006).

Location Choice and Knowledge Clusters

A plethora of academic and consulting-driven research has focused in the 2000s upon where to access pools of talent at locations across the globe (Hales, Pena, Peterson, & Dessibourg-Freer, 2016; Lanvin & Evans, 2017; Tarique & Schuler, 2010). As technology has reduced the need for physical infrastructure, time and distance have ceased to be all-important in location choice. The new imperative is to find and retain capable individuals in particular fields who can interact easily in this environment. While different factors are weighed depending upon value considerations related to human capital and talent competitiveness, there are certain essential criteria such as the factors listed below that have influenced research in this area over the previous 20 years. These factors may also tend to favor the established knowledge clusters and to mitigate the establishment of new clusters (Chatterji, Glaeser, & Kerr, 2013).

1. Access to a skilled and educated workforce with networking and cooperation possibilities
2. Proximity to world-class universities and research institutions
3. An attractive quality of life including factors such as climate, cultural environment, safety, and easy access to health and education
4. Access to venture capital
5. Reasonable costs of doing business
6. An established technology presence
7. Available bandwidth for IT and adequate infrastructure
8. A favorable business climate and regulatory environment
9. The presence of suppliers and partners, particularly in industry clusters
10. Availability of community incentives such as tax abatements and lower costs of living (Dutta, Lanvin, & Wunch-Vincent, 2015).

Countries and Cities

Rankings of countries and cities have been performed for transparency, skill sets, business development, sustainability, political stability, etc. for many years (Bhambal & Vasistha, 2007; Globalsherpa.org, 2017). Educational testing in such areas as the annual PISA (The Program for International Student Assessment), administered by the Organisation for Economic Co-operation and Development (OECD) and used to measure educational attainment in math, science and reading skills, has been conducted since 2000 in member and nonmember countries. In the 2000s, new varieties of indexes were created by consulting firms and governing bodies such as the European Commission to rank countries on their relative merits related to human capital and talent competitiveness. Country-specific strengths in "soft skills" were ranked alongside items such as "business environment" in statistical models to provide reliable and valid measures of weighted variables (Saisana, Becker, & Dominguez-Torreiro, 2017). Whether or not these measures are influenced by large multinational enterprises with an affinity for certain areas of the world is a fair question. To date, there has been little academic research on the efficacy of country rankings and whether or not the measures are statistically coherent and balanced in their understanding of differences in world cultures and larger issues impacting locations, such as climate change (Apaza, 2009).

As effectiveness measures have been refined, the rankings of specific "world cities" that compare progress on development, sustainability, quality of life, globalization and innovation have been added as a basis of comparison. Similar to what is done for countries, global rankings of cities and regions attempt to look at global talent hubs that attract skilled and creative workers from all parts of the world. Specific advantages related to geography, culture, cost and quality of living, safety, innovation, etc. are measured in statistical formulas to determine a city's global reach. The "connectivity" of a city is considered by some researchers to be the key aspect of world economic activity (e.g., Hales, King, & Pena, 2010; Jakobsen, 2017; Mercer Co., 2019; OECD, 2017). Examples of globally connected cities as measured by use of digital media and air flight connections would be Paris, Berlin, Los Angeles, London, and New York City (Gottlieb Duttweiler Institute, 2017).

There is no monopoly on intellect despite the imbalance of opportunities for development. The diffusion of knowledge throughout the world has increased dramatically in the last two decades, in part due to higher levels of global literacy in emerging countries. In the knowledge-intensive services environment, firms must seek out and recruit numerous skilled individuals throughout the world due to the growing demand for knowledge workers with the right kinds of skill sets to fill positions throughout their organizations. This will intensify as falling birthrates and an aging workforce in the developed world shift the focus to the recruitment of young talent in the world's emerging markets (DeLong & Vijayaraghavan, 2003; Guthridge et al. 2008). The global skills shortage suggests that firms must now also consider the location of their operations not only on the basis of proximity to customers or low-cost labor but also on where the skilled talent is located (Collings & Mellahi, 2009; Dossani & Kenney, 2004). As the labor content of products continues to decline, it is no longer sensible to allocate administrative cost by the amount of labor hours a product requires. Employees will be able to work from anywhere in the world or wherever their skills are needed rather than remaining with one company, so locations that reduce living costs or contribute to quality of life, for example, can arise as new clusters for scarce talent. Pressure will grow for cities to create livable spaces, recreational options, and other hospitality factors to retain talent (Lanvin, 2017).

While cost factors are still a key consideration in sourcing decisions for firms trying to access global talent, it is apparent that skill-intensive work involving ever greater analysis and judgment in emerging economies will require compensation at similar pay scales to that done by compatriots and colleagues in more highly developed economies. If immigration policies become more restrictive, thus reducing labor mobility, issues of pay disparities among workers across different countries will grow in importance. A mathematician based in Hungary for example would justifiably expect to be paid a salary commensurate with a mathematician based in the United States if performing the same work (with possible societal consequences as talented individuals separate themselves from others in their home countries on the basis of income). Pay disparities, particularly with regard to gender, are longstanding and becoming more widely publicized (Economist, 2017). Thus it becomes no longer a discussion about locating operations solely on cost issues but around where and how a firm can find potential young talent to implement strategic or technological innovation (Hill, 2006). An important caveat here is whether or not education and training is comparable within various countries (e.g., engineering education) as well as accessibility of skilled workers to firms with the need to hire them. In a world where the majority of global services are available online in the cloud, this alters the constraints of geography that previously allowed only a few skilled individuals to obtain privileged access to markets (Blinder, 2005; Bryan & Fraser, 1999). Massive open online courses (MOOCs) of the sort offered by consortiums. such as Udacity and Coursera, of highly ranked global universities have also opened up knowledge to a growing worldwide audience (Pelster, Johnson, Stempel, & van der Vyer, 2017). Individuals throughout the world can now have access to higher education, with some platforms offering fully accredited degrees (Liyangunawardena, Adams, & Williams, 2014). The proliferation of communication technology is also diminishing the proportion of employees who work from a central company location. (Schmit, 2014). Remote work, particularly in the developing world, enables companies to access a deeper pool of available educated labor. However, the technology-dependent outsourcing teams that now permeate major companies throw up wholly new and complex managerial challenges of communication and cultural differences while avoiding potential discord and conflict (Clott, 2007).

It is critical to note that any discussion of talent competitiveness cannot disregard the threats and risks to the free flow of information and people throughout the world. Efforts have been made by particular countries to place impediments to global workplaces including curbs on information transparency, such as those instituted by some countries to block particular Internet accessibility, as well as the installation of stricter limits on immigration and travel between countries, imposed to combat terrorism and preserve jobs for domestic workers. Cybersecurity concerns about "hacked" information and illegal transactions will constitute a threat to the globalized work environment for some time to come. The advent of open source blockchain distributed ledgers with payment in bitcoins may reduce data hacking in the future, but technical and legal safeguards are still being worked out (Wright & DeFilippi, 2015). Additional research in this area has examined security risks in financial services (Cobb, 2003), intellectual property rights (Roy & Sivakumar, 2012) and risks of offshoring services (Ahmed, Capretz, Maqsoud, & Raza, 2014), among others.

The US Knowledge Base

The United States has been a major beneficiary of a flood of skilled and talented foreign-born science and engineering graduates migrating to the country to study or work over the last 40 years. By attracting scientists and engineers born and trained abroad, the country maintained the growth of the labor force without an attendant increase in the training of native US citizens to these fields (National Science Board, 2016). This emigration fueled the development of Silicon Valley in California and a host of other regions in the country, starting in the 1980s, that attracted high-technology economic development. Research has shown that as much as 40 percent of the entrepreneurial economic growth of the United States over the last two decades was due to the skilled émigré labor base (Lowell & Gerova, 2004). The lack of a clear federal US immigration policy may impact the level of migration and begin to reduce the attractiveness of the nation for talented workers (Florida, 2004; Shacher, 2006). At this writing, more than 4 million people are waiting in line to be granted legal status as permanent US residents. The H1B visas allocated to skilled workers are capped at 85,000 despite much pressure by firms and congressional members to enlarge this number and equal pressure to limit the number to 50,000 or less (Grassley, 2017).

The United States remains a base for entrepreneurship due to longstanding connections between universities and industry, but despite the creation of high-tech "incubators" in major cities there has been a long-term decline in start-up businesses (Bureau of Labor Statistics, 2016). Some research suggests that larger technology firms such as Google, Facebook, Microsoft, Amazon, etc. in the California 'Silicon Valley' and Pacific Northwest have become more entrepreneurial in their business models and have purchased promising start-up operations around the world. This fosters the continuing debate as to whether knowledge-intensive talent is better served by specific industrial policies adopted by many countries to guide capital competition, or by a more organic form of development guided by large firms (Li et al., 2016).

The tremendous breadth and depth of US higher education institutions was, until very recently, unmatched by any other nation, thus providing a magnet for the best and brightest minds in the world to study, live, and work with like-minded individuals. Approximately 40 percent of Ph.D. scientists working in the United States were born abroad and over half of the current Ph.D.s in the hard sciences are being attained by foreign students (Matthews, 2007). Research suggests that upwards of 80 percent of immigrant high-tech entrepreneurs operate in the 25 largest US metropolitan areas (The Kauffman Index, 2017). A drastic tightening in immigration policies in the aftermath of the 9/11 terrorist attacks in 2001, and continuing to this writing, has made it more difficult to enter the country, thus dispersing global talent elsewhere (Mahroum, 2002; Yigitcanlar, 2009). Among nations that benefited from tighter US policies were Canada and Australia, both English-speaking with a substantial multicultural influence. The presence of large numbers of skilled immigrants has also redefined cities such as Toronto, Vancouver, Melbourne, and Perth. Other world locations that have wooed the global talent base have included Singapore; Dubai and Abu Dhabi in the United Arab Emirates; New Zealand, Sweden, Ireland, and France (Manning, Massini, & Lewin, 2008; Shachar, 2006). While the United States will continue to remain an attractive destination for world talent in spite of the tighter restrictions, it is no longer the only destination (Goodall, 2008). It remains to be seen how recent anti-immigrant policies in the United States may impact global talent migration.

A substantial upgrade in foreign educational systems over the past decade has cut into the longstanding leadership of US universities in educational attainment. There is a realization that skills and talents can now be developed in many other nations (e.g., Singapore, Malaysia, China, Australia, and Canada) that match or surpass US research universities (Labi, 2008). To expand their brand name and global reach, many US research universities and a substantial number of other degree-granting institutions ranging from community colleges to small liberal arts colleges have developed programs overseas in an effort to attract talented (and wealthier) foreign students (Lewin, 2008).

Within the US government, there is widespread acknowledgment of the pressing need to have more of the young future American workforce educated in particular skills, notably "STEM" disciplines involving science, technology, engineering, and mathematics. In August 2007, the "America Competes Act" was passed in Congress and signed into law as a means of strengthening the US scientific and engineering communities. Subsequently, the law was superseded by the "American Innovation and Competitiveness Act" of 2010 and 2016. The Act provides federal funds to encourage US citizens to study and teach mathematics and science, along with supporting research into emerging technologies. While the Act addresses the need to strengthen the math and science curriculum for American students in the primary grades, it has done little to address the present shortage of high skilled, educated workers and access to higher education for large numbers of individuals.

Three trends of particular concern have been identified related to the American workforce: 1. "an increasingly ill-prepared domestic workforce; 2. a steadily depleting stock of high skilled and educated foreigners; and 3. an aging population" (James, 2005). US high school seniors have ranked at or near the bottom in comparable math and science scores worldwide despite more federal government attention and funding. The controversial "No Child Left Behind Act" of 2001 for elementary and secondary schools that required more testing and assessment of basic skills was widely criticized and ultimately replaced by the "Every Student Succeeds Act" in 2015, turning much of the program back to individual US states. Evidence suggests that American universities are not graduating enough scientists, engineers, designers and others whose economic function is to create new ideas, technology, and creative content (Florida, 2004). The foreign nationals who previously filled this void are finding opportunities abroad as bureaucratic barriers, particularly to obtaining visas, keep them out of the United States (James, 2005). These trends have been noted and discussed by researchers and policy makers in numerous government and academic studies (e.g., National Science Board, 2004, 2016; Shacher, 2006). What remains less understood by the general US public is where and why global firms competing in world markets locate significant portions of their revenue-producing operations on the basis of where available talent can be found. To date, government-sponsored job retraining programs to match job needs with skills acquired have been confusing and poorly executed (Graham, 2017). This may lead to further economic stratification in the United States that will negatively impact the ability of the country as a whole to lift its productive output.

Talent Clusters: Organic and Specific

Once skilled talent is located and a base of operations is established, it attracts additional complementary talent that seeks opportunities of the same type in knowledge clusters (Porter, 1990, 2008). "Talent clusters" that have grown more or less organically in the United States, such as the Silicon Valley area near San Francisco/San Jose, Route 128 near Cambridge/Boston and Research Triangle near Chapel Hill, North Carolina, were spawned in the United States from the abundance of university research institutes nearby (Khanna, 2016). They became "centers of innovation" that attracted firms requiring a concentration of intellectual expertise. Many nations, cities and states have attempted to create their own talent clusters by providing tax incentives and available land to start-up firms in particular areas. China has established research centers near Beijing, Shanghai, and Shenzhen while India is developing new centers outside of the main concentration around Bangalore and Hyderabad. Singapore, Germany, and Canada among others are spending hundreds of millions on research parks that will bring established and entrepreneurial firms to their shores. IBM, for example, has moved 60 percent of its workforce to specific cities in India and China, while Microsoft has established two of its most recent research and development campuses outside of Bangalore and Beijing to take advantage of the presence of promising computer science graduates at nearby universities. In the United States the city of Atlanta became the US headquarters city for Wipro Technologies, the Indian outsourcing firm.

India is the acknowledged center of global services outsourcing, but is by no means the only area where services outsourcing has developed. Specific nations and locales such as university centers in Eastern Europe, Asia, and Latin America have emerged as key outsourcing destinations in this decade (Laudicina, Gott, & Peterson, 2014). The ability to send complex and strategic work offshore to these locations for collaboration across country borders was heretofore considered too costly and unorganized to be actively considered. As organizational design and practice more thoroughly integrates emerging talent clusters, this becomes more acceptable. Firms that rely on specific talents and expertise to perform necessary work can now look at "global zones of competency" where talent can be easily accessed for a particular frame of identified work. These zones have much to do with the knowledge innovation within a specific service or industry segment, IT or financial services for example, and where it is considered to reside. Accessing the zones of competency becomes ever more important as new developments drive continued profitability. Firms that do not have access to the best minds will be constantly behind the curve in delivering solutions to demanding customers.

The global talent pool must not only be available and accessible to firms. There needs to also be a "scalability of talent" to meet evolving organizational needs. Scalability indicates an ability to handle growing complexity in the work performed as more demands are added and expertise grows such that these individuals can have a larger role in the company. The scalability of talent also necessitates a way to teach highly talented but inexperienced individuals how to acquire more imagination and creativity in seeing how a specific application they perform can be applied to a larger underlying business model within the firm. The key for firms seeking talent is to zero in on particular individual core competencies that can be developed within the confines of the organization and utilized to add value to their offerings. The winning companies of the future are those most adept at leveraging global talent to transform themselves and their industries. Thus a premium is placed on gaining specific talent competencies.

As suggested earlier, the world's most innovative locations are in large urban hubs that attract talented workers. Much research has been devoted to where "millennial" workers comfortable with technology want to reside. Walkable, mixed-use neighborhoods, factory and warehouse lofts, and proximity to downtown office buildings have "gentrified" close-in neighborhoods within global cities and displaced former light industry firms and working-class individuals (Florida, 2017). Firms have followed this talent, and attempt to create ecosystems for digital nomads that offer a low cost of living combined with connectivity, quality of life, and educational opportunities. Global workers who are reluctant or unable to relocate due to familial, cultural, or cost of living considerations can now interact with headquarters locations through social media work collaboration platforms such as Slack, Collokia, Kaltura, Asana, LeanKit, and others. Thus the use of technology to assist people with daily living activities can also help foster the development of new clusters in small countries or less developed regions that have the ability to attract talent (Calestous, 2012).

Global Niches and Knowledge Centers

Numerous countries that have watched the growth of India as a destination point for the new economy are attempting to fashion cadres of talented people with expertise to attract global corporations. Nations that can gain a niche in the global delivery environment hope to jump-start their own economies if they can become known as centers for particular knowledge-based industries. Brazil, Argentina, and Chile have all secured outsourcing of IT, software development, and call centers with European firms with which they share cultural links, as well as with US and Indian firms anxious to establish diverse networks of sourcing locations. The Dominican Republic in the Caribbean has sought to become a financial services back office center by touting its proximity to the New York and London financial markets and favorable tax laws. In Africa, the Republic of South Africa and the island of Mauritius aspire to become major service economy hubs by emphasizing their human capital that is "qualified, skilled, flexible and ready to learn" to enable these nations to become knowledge-based economies. In the northeast Chinese province of Manchuria, linguistic and cultural knowledge have enabled this region to become the back office of Japan just as the Baltic nation of Estonia has become an offshore point for Finland and a model for the rest of the world of what a digital society may look like (Walt, 2017). The island of Malta in the Mediterranean is developing a "SmartCity" knowledge-based cluster that draws on the success that the city of Dubai in the United Arab Emirates has had in attracting a critical mass of knowledge-based industries that are a haven for talent. All of these developments have in common the desire to leverage common attractions: nearby university research capabilities, a talent pool developed by other established firms drawn to the area, and any other possible competitive advantage, be it an agreeable climate or ease of travel to build a talent cluster (Wessner & Wolff, 2012).

A problem for countries and cities seeking to develop their global niches is recent trends in the speed of technology development that have redefined the competitive landscape for global organizations. Industry sectors are blurring the distinction between different sectors of work. The immense field of logistics, for example, is being dramatically altered by disparate technologies such as autonomous vehicles and blockchain processing. Investments in fixed assets by countries seeking to become new talent centers come with the caveat that industry rationalization can render the location where a task is actually performed virtually meaningless. Geography remains relevant, but industry positions can change very quickly due to opportunities across business sectors. The new emphasis on flexibility and resiliency has made firms think about having more than one location that can do quite similar work. This is a hedge against one location suddenly becoming untenable due to a natural or political disaster. It also allows work to be shifted to where the total landed cost of the output is lower. Locations' economics and currency fluctuations may also play a role. Understanding emerging ecosystems in new business sectors assumes paramount importance when skilled talent can come from different locations

(Oxford Economics, 2012). Allowing skilled talent to mix and match through online and onsite forums with the freedom to integrate new ideas as business models are reinvented can be a way to retain and grow the base of opportunities. Surprisingly, many companies have yet to develop effective talent strategies to attract new tech data workers (Anonymous, 2015).

Difficulties in Building Talent Clusters, Job Hopping, and the Movement of Talent

Knowledge clusters are highly desirable to all nations and regions as they bring together skilled individuals, innovations that can be prominently advertised, and substantial outside investment into the locales where they are created (Mongkhonvanit, 2014). The problem with developing strategic knowledge clusters around promising talent pools is that they are often quite shallow or nonexistent thus requiring an inflow of talent from elsewhere. In Eastern Europe for example, the talent base is highly fragmented. The many small countries in this region with unique languages, cultural differences and confusing legal systems make it difficult to have scalability and flexibility. Outside of the European Union (EU) countries there is no common labor market and highly restricted labor mobility. Large numbers of skilled individuals from Eastern Europe have emigrated to the West forcing firms to increase wages substantially in their home countries or risk operating at less than optimal levels. Other nations face similar predicaments. India is attempting to spread its knowledge economy outside of congested Bangalore and Mumbai to "tier two" cities that are less intensively developed. Investment in new areas such as the state of Kerala, however, must compete with the emigration of Indian talent that has tended to migrate to the Arab Gulf countries, the United States, and elsewhere to work, rather than stay in the region. China has problems with a talent base that is wide but not particularly deep in software development and other key innovative areas. Countries also find that it is one thing to commit to large-scale investment in a geographic area and quite another to sustain and attract the creative individuals needed to move it forward. Lee Kwan Yu, the former prime minister of Singapore, has recognized this dilemma as one of attracting well-educated younger people who wish to surf the Internet, travel without constraint, lead non-traditional personal lives, choose their own work schedules, and otherwise live in an open, not closed, society. "If we are not connected to this modern world, we are dead. We'll go back to the fishing village we once were" (Mydans & Arnold, 2007).

A dwindling youth population in developed economies with restrictive immigration policies is causing skills shortages in particular fields. Some of these shortages are being filled by older workers, more women in the workforce and cross-border migration, but there is a growing reluctance of workers to relocate to global locations they are unfamiliar with (Levitz, 2017). Demographic as well as cultural diversity will continue to define the global workforce as companies seek to fill shortages, gain market efficiencies, and acquire strategic assets. Older workers provide experience, but they also pose challenges for organizations, including providing healthcare for a population that will experience four-and-a-half-times as many disabilities as younger workers. This is compounded in a global workforce that combines differing management and work styles based on individual cultures. The challenge is to identify the right job roles, incentives, and retraining opportunities for each worker while avoiding age-discrimination practices.

Within the booming new economies of global-sourcing nations and particularly within the sought-after talent clusters, job switching is looked upon as a way for individuals to fast-track their careers. A shortage of key individuals with the "right" skill sets has meant that firms are paying out ever larger incentives to retain the top people they need and looking to poach key individuals from competitors. Such skill sets change over time; for example, enterprise resource planning (ERP) skills are less in demand than data analytics skills at present. Few companies can command the loyalty of young workers to stay if they are offered a more interesting and/or remunerative opportunity with another firm. Young talent is often impatient talent; they are uninterested in moving up the career ladder as employees might have done a generation ago. Moving to another job offers a means of gaining additional compensation or career incentives. In the supercharged financial services and consulting markets for example, this has meant large signing bonuses and career tracks that must be carefully tended to by firms to ensure that ambitious individuals are given added duties. Few global companies however have created a sophisticated global workforce strategy that can plan for growth and track key individuals that must be retained (Lazarova & Cerdin, 2007). It can take eight to ten years to train and develop individuals that can take on complex project management and consultant roles within firms. This shows the need for new forms of communication and leadership by senior management to ensure talent needs are addressed before individuals move elsewhere. A different set of capabilities will be required by global managers to assess these needs than has hitherto been the case.

What is also often ignored by senior managers (but not future-minded city and economic development planners) is the desire for talented individuals to have a life outside of the job while being at the center of the action. This had enabled London in the early 2000s, with its soft attractions of agreeable living and cosmopolitan atmosphere, to become a destination of choice for ambitious professionals in global financial services. Within India, Bangalore emerged as the destination of choice despite its infrastructure difficulties, thanks to the number of young talented people who can communicate and socialize with each other in an open atmosphere. Other cities such as Dubai and Singapore have attempted to address this need for more agreeable work surroundings as well as paying top wages in their quest to entice foreign talent (Dore, 2006).

Access for Women

A crucial resource for firms in the race to develop global talent is the ability to access, retain, and promote talented women for leadership roles. Women comprise 50 percent of the world's population but hold little of the world's wealth and have a tiny presence within the senior management of firms, corporate boards, and other decision-making bodies. Longstanding cultural barriers to educational opportunities are being removed in both developed and emerging countries with respect to the attainment of primary and advanced degrees by females, with attendant increases in higher education degrees. But the lack of equalization of pay and promotion for women in global companies remains stubbornly present despite much research and worldwide attention paid to this dilemma (World Bank, 2012). Career visibility and opportunity for women are often wrapped around traditional ideas of family caregiving and precedent given to the husbands' career aspirations. With an eye toward women leaving the workforce for extended periods and the assumption that they will stop working, females are often tracked into the "softer" roles of the global business firm rather than areas such as engineering (King, Botsford, & Hebl, 2010). Within the global services environment, women are taking on a greater degree of mid-manager roles but barriers to entry at higher levels, "C-levels," of management within global organizations remain difficult to overcome (Barsh & Lee, 2012). Multinational corporations, particularly American and European, have led the way in empowering female managers due to their ability to offer work solutions customized for women seeking to bear children, spend time raising them and still have international career opportunities. The need to empower skilled women for global service positions is a necessity as the dearth of qualified younger workers becomes a central issue for organizations (Cheng, Dohrmann, Kerlin, Law, & Ramaswamy, 2018). Achieving senior management status within male-only corporate cultures will change only when governments and companies address social pressures for women to stop working after marriage. Non-traditional work platforms are one possible solution, as is the requirement in some European firms that 50 percent of board members need to be women (Committee on Science, Engineering and Public Policy, 2007; National Science Board, 2016; Schiessl, 2008).

Cultural and organizational barriers to the advancement of women in the knowledge-intensive globalized workplace are increasingly visible, in large part due to litigation by aggrieved parties and a spotlight placed on norms and practices that harass and discourage women (Bennett, 2017; Langone, 2018). Loss of talent, loss of investment, and costly settlements, in addition to negative publicity, have fueled a reappraisal of the need for women to have a critical role in the growth and success of global firms. The number of women with access to education, financing, and mentorship opportunities has grown, albeit slowly, in many countries worldwide. Firms within the European Union in particular have made efforts to accelerate this process. Female entrepreneurs searching for a place to launch companies are increasingly drawn to major continental European cities such as Paris where funding and governmental encouragement are propelling new business opportunities (Feinstein, 2017). In developing countries, technology that can simplify crucial tasks such as gathering water and cooking fuel can free up more time for women to gain education and develop potential to earn money for their family and community. The Gates

Foundation among others has committed resources to unlocking the economic chains that have often discouraged talented women from otherwise entering the global workforce (Gates Foundation, 2016; Kristof & WuDunn, 2017).

Artificial Intelligence

Human activity in the global workplace will be redefined by advancements in artificial intelligence (AI) and other technologies that can "learn" complex decision making. AI will most certainly replace people doing repetitive work (truck driving, clerical tasks, etc.) but will not have widespread adoption in developed economies that have only recently generated a sizeable middle class, particularly in Asia. Significant job redefinition and transformation due to AI will not exist solely within developed economies or in low-wage occupations (Chui, Manyika, & Miremadi, 2015). Strategic and operational decisions within companies that have long relied on specific individual judgments and cultural prejudices could engender an entirely different managerial focus with the widespread adoption of AI throughout the world. This has the potential to completely transform numerous large knowledge-intensive industries such as law, financial services, engineering, accounting, and insurance. The adoption of AI will be determined in large part on the sheer economics of when, where, and how much to invest, with an eye on the speed and direction of adoption in business sectors. The nation of China in particular has an ambitious plan to lead the world in AI by 2030 (Lee, 2017).

While AI may render many workplace positions superfluous it may also free individuals for creative tasks in new organizations that flock together in "virtual watercoolers" that are online or at worktables and workstations in cafes, delis, and other non-traditional settings. Creative talent that can be harnessed in these gathering spaces will change the definition of work from labor in physical work environments to communication defined more by networks connected by platforms such as social media. This assumes that barriers to entry into these organic networks can be reduced for more of the world's population than is currently the case. What the nature of global work becomes to the extent that automation limits work or restricts wages that drive increased prosperity will be key issues that need to be addressed in coming years. Perhaps some "friction" will need to be built into the overall world of work to enable individuals to have a meaningful human existence (Brand, 1999).

Where Are the Skilled Knowledge Workers?

Talent attraction is the foundation of everything else we do
George Yeo, Singapore minister of trade and industry

Higher education centers of knowledge and proximity to commercial markets that could utilize the skills developed have long been theorized as places where knowledge workers would be congregated (Porter, 1990; Reich, 1991). The end of the Cold War, the globalization of higher education, and advanced technology enabling knowledge workers to gain access to the workplace from all corners of the world, has meant a dispersion of work based upon expertise as well as cost. From trading in global financial derivatives in Paris by graduates of the prestigious Ecole National d'Administration, to advanced nanotechnology applications by graduates of Massachusetts Institute of Technology (MIT) and the Indian Institute of Technology–Bombay, there is now a widespread ability for highly skilled individuals, wherever they are located, to be involved in global service networks. As service networks grow and expand, they are drawn to the cities and countries that provide the best advantages, convenience, and attractiveness for talented people (Zachary, 2000). As previously addressed, numerous rankings of top emerging outsourcing cities and countries have been introduced and refined as firms seek to locate in places where there is a degree of political stability, business catalysts, financial stability, skills, infrastructure and quality of life (Kearney, 2007; Sethi & Gott, 2017). The skill sets below are examined for where individual global talent is located.

Mathematics

Mathematics and mathematics application have always been important aspects of individual business success. In the world of databases and algorithms that underpin most transactions in a virtual environment, a strong knowledge of mathematics has become more essential to a skilled workforce (Read, 2007). It is beyond the scope of this work to ascertain whether or not certain ethnic or national groups are intrinsically predisposed to excel in mathematics or the hard sciences. Multiple research studies exist that suggest that differences in the teaching and study of mathematics may have more to do with variations in math skills than ethnic make-up, gender, race, etc. (LaTurner, 2002). A talent pool for this critical competency exists in all countries but is particularly notable in several areas of the world:

Asia: Within Asia, strong mathematics skills, as evidenced by comparative tests, exist in Korea, Japan, Taiwan, Singapore, Malaysia, Hong Kong, and major cities in China (Shanghai, Beijing, Jiangsu and Guangdong). Nations in the Pacific Rim have utilized this skill set in their workforce to attract numerous multinational corporations as well as establishing favored "national champion firms," e.g. Samsung in South Korea, over a 40-year span of time.

Greater economic opportunities and more diversified economies in the countries noted above have meant that firms look particularly at the emerging economies of India, Vietnam, and China as designated points for global sourcing locations where a strong grounding in mathematics is desired. These nations have long emphasized a strong theoretical grounding that is highly exam-driven. National standards of textbook content and teacher preparation as well as a core curriculum that emphasizes mathematics skills provide students with a strong grounding in the subject. While China has the more developed infrastructure to utilize the mathematics talent, there are several IT and financial services firms, particularly in and around Hanoi and Ho Chi Minh City, that have established Vietnam as a base of operations (Bradsher, 2004). The Chinese focus on the theoretical aspects of mathematics has emerged as a significant core competency that has spurred much interest by the government in further development of high-technology development zones where resources will be concentrated to support technological development. Indian mathematical skills have historically been a comparative advantage that showed up in the number of physicians, academics, and skilled engineers working around the world as part of the greater Indian diaspora and more recently in global service firms seeking to locate firms in the country to take advantage of these skills. A strong work ethic, parental pressure, practical training in family-owned small businesses, and a highly competitive process for admittance to top-tier national institutions have been suggested as some of the reasons for Indian mathematical skills (Cheney, Ruzzi, & Muralidharan, 2005).

Eastern Europe: In Eastern Europe, long years of Soviet rule emphasized the hard sciences in university training for use in manufacturing and production. As a result, Russia, Romania, Hungary, Poland, Ukraine, Belarus, and the Czech Republic, with strong traditions in both mathematics and the hard sciences, are often considered to be the best locations to find individuals with the requisite mathematics skills. The nation of Hungary in particular is noted by the marketplace for individuals with strong foundations in mathematics and theoretical physics, while Russia has a talent pool of over 4.7 million students, 50 percent of whom are majoring in science, complex math, and computer sciences (Gordon, 2009). The cities of Moscow, Krakow, Budapest, Prague, and Bratislava, each with a major university presence, have become key beneficiaries of situational locations for locating research centers that can avail themselves of the mathematics talent nearby.

Western Europe: Switzerland, Finland, and Estonia are highly regarded locations for skilled individuals possessing mathematical skills. The primary grades for all three countries are oriented toward mathematics, the natural sciences, and technical knowledge. (Finland placed number five in the world in sciences in the OECD Test of 2015.) The school systems are set up such that one is not likely to advance to the higher education system without a proficiency in mathematics. Teaching is theoretical, with an emphasis on understanding the underlying model of the theorem rather than the more pragmatic, empirical orientation of the US system. The result has been a stream of graduates who perform well in certain fields such as computer science and econometric modeling.

Information Technology

Hand in hand with mathematics grounding is finding the individuals with essential computer sciences skills. Skilled coders and programmers reside throughout Eastern Europe, with particular concentrations in Russia, Poland,

Czech Republic, Hungary, Romania, Ukraine, and the Baltic republics of Lithuania, Latvia and Estonia. Further out, the capital city of Chisinau in Moldova has emerged as an IT hub due to several universities within the city. Within India, the cities of Bangalore, Delhi (Gurgaon and Greater Noida area), Hyderabad and Mumbai (Bombay) are acknowledged hubs of IT outsourcing, in large part due to the supply of nearby university talent. Numerous "tier two" cities in India for information technology include Chennai, Pune, and Kolkata among others that are "centers of excellence" specific to particular IT or business processes.

In China, Beijing and Shanghai have concentrations of IT workers, with Shenzhen growing in importance. China graduates over 200,000 engineers each year but relatively few computer science engineers from top tier programs such as Fudan University in Shanghai. According to an estimate by the Chinese Education Research Network, there are currently 50 million science and engineering students in China. The majority of these graduates are from universities with substandard facilities. The return of large numbers of US-trained and educated computer scientists to Taiwan in the last decade created many new start-up firms that began in Taiwan but have increasingly been based in the Shanghai region of China to take advantage of the presence of technically skilled university graduates (Saxenian, 2006). Korea has also seen the return of many trained computer scientists in the last five years (Lazonick, 2007).

Due to the many immigrant professionals from India, Taiwan, and China, the "Silicon Valley" area near San Jose, California still remains the preeminent center for IT services and continues to have the largest pool of experienced computer scientists, software engineers, and systems architects. The rising cost of doing business and living in the area and the shortage of immigrant talent, particularly from Asia, may remove the concentration of experienced engineers and providers that have underpinned the Valley for many years. Silicon Valley remains an essential place for face-to-face communication and "deal making" but may lose much of its critical mass of talent if present trends continue. Other areas of the United States that have significant IT talent concentrations are Incline Village, Nevada near Lake Tahoe; Austin and Dallas, Texas; the Seattle–Portland area; the Research Triangle in North Carolina (Raleigh, Durham, and Chapel Hill); and Route 128 outside of Boston. In addition, there are concentrations of talented IT professionals in Chicago, San Diego, Philadelphia, Pittsburgh, the Washington DC area, Salt Lake City, Atlanta, Minneapolis–St. Paul; Albuquerque, New Mexico; Boise, Idaho; and Boulder, Colorado. The premier US institutions for information technology – Carnegie Mellon, MIT, University of California–Berkeley, and Stanford – remain magnets for talented individuals in advanced computational sciences. These institutions are also extending their world reach through overseas campuses (Lewin, 2008).

Many nations and localities have sought the designation of the "next Silicon Valley." The "high-tech" designation typically suggests an environmentally friendly location, a positive and vibrant business climate, an educated workforce, strong educational facilities, venture capital availability and a communications infrastructure. Tech centers are home to telecommunications firms, information technology, computer software and hardware, electronics, and newer industries such as biotechnology. Among the areas most commonly associated with information technology in addition to those mentioned above are the following:

Europe: Virtually every European nation has a high-tech designated area and in some cases more than one. The following list of locations is by no means exhaustive:

Ireland's *Silicon Bog* has had a sustained technology presence since the early 1990s in the Dublin area with many major multinational firms.

In the United Kingdom, the town of Reading near London is known as the *Silicon Corridor* containing high-tech firms, while an area near Cambridge is known as *Silicon Fen*. *Silicon Glen* is an area stretching from Glasgow to Edinburgh.

In Finland, the municipality of *Kempele* has become a base for high-tech businesses utilizing the skilled individual talent available in this country.

In the Netherlands and Belgium exists the *Silicon Polder* between the Netherlands and Flanders.

France has the *Sophia Antipolis* technology park outside of Nice and *Nancy-Beaubois* near Nancy in the north.

Germany has the city of *Stuttgart* that in addition to the automotive industry is now an IT base.

Spain has the *Malaga* area, while Italy sees promise with a technology park in *Sardinia*.

The Americas: Canada has "*Silicon Valley North*" in the Ottawa area and a growing technology presence in Vancouver, and Saskatoon.

Brazil hosts the *Campinas* technology park near São Paulo, and the *Curitiba* area.

Costa Rica has a high-tech presence in the *San José* area.

Asia: Outside of China and India, there are a number of technology areas that have been spawned through infrastructure investment to become areas of growth and development.

Japan has the *Bit Valley* Technology strip in the Shibuya suburb of Tokyo that is known for its cluster of high-tech and Internet companies.

Taiwan has developed a substantial technology area in the *Hsinchu-Hsien*.

Penang in Malaysia has developed a strategic plan to promote a skill-intensive, technology-intensive, and high value-added set of industries through the building of a research and development infrastructure with a qualified workforce.

In Hong Kong, the *Wanchai* district has become a destination for IT firms.

Singapore has become a major worldwide technology center that continues to develop its infrastructure in IT.

Engineering

Engineering services represent a highly specialized series of distinct skill sets that are dependent upon the type of industry involved. Conflicting definitions of what an engineer is and how they are educated complicate efforts to find the right talent pools. A Duke University study argued that there are two main groups of engineering graduates: dynamic and transactional. Dynamic engineers have good team skills, work across borders, have strong interpersonal skills, and are sought after for their innovation abilities. Transactional engineers possess engineering fundamentals but are largely confined to rote and repetitive tasks in the workplace. These positions are the most subject to offshore outsourcing to reduce costs (Wadhwa & Gereffi, 2005). The study suggests that transactional engineers constitute large numbers of the Chinese and Indian graduates but a growing subset of foreign dynamic engineers with high language proficiencies and proximity to commercial centers will compete with US-based engineers for future offshore engineering jobs.

Engineering talent is widely distributed around the world and concentrated around particular production centers and/or major technical universities. A number of competing engineering schools in an area create a critical mass of individuals for development of a knowledge cluster. Global sourcing decisions in the engineering areas must take into account not only where the market growth will be, but also where the skilled engineering talent is located. For high-technology and telecommunications work involving computers, communications, electrical electromechanical systems and software, the top locations are Krakow, Poland; Shenzhen, China; Taipei, Taiwan; Bangalore, India; and Peta Tikva, Israel. For automotive engineering the top cities for talent are New Delhi, India; Rayong, Thailand; and São Benard do Campo SP, Brazil. For utility engineering, mechanical engineering, and machine design they are Dukovany, Czech Republic; Singapore; and Suez, Egypt. Industrial construction engineering destinations are Beijing, China; Chennai, India; and Samutprakarn, Thailand. Finally, aerospace engineering talent is in Moscow; Nanchang, China; and Pretoria, South Africa; while naval engineering is associated with Guangzhou, China; Oslo, Norway; and Ulsan, South Korea.

The high consumption of engineering services throughout the world is a function of growing demand for particular sectors that have the scalability to meet demand. Demand for engineering talent in emerging market countries plays an important role in expansion. Firms are looking for access to a high-quality talent pool that can grow engineering capacity and increase productivity.

English Language Skills

Talent often cannot converse in English.
Interview by author

Having the English language, the "business language" in much of the world, as one of the primary languages for communication has enabled several countries in addition to India to be considered ideal sourcing destinations. This has been particularly true regarding the location of call support centers. Call centers are established by firms to interact with customers in providing help, sales support, and a multitude of other services and were first set up offshore in Caribbean nations such as Barbados and Jamaica as well as the Republic of Ireland in the 1990s to take advantage of a large literate underemployed population with requisite English language skills. Call centers are often considered as the bottom of the global outsourcing food chain and have had difficulty retaining experienced workers if other higher end positions are available. Many firms provide little training, with high turnover of employees expected, while some firms have rigorous training requirements. Staffed often by young people just out of school, call center jobs have been considered a means of earning money while working in a clean office setting (Freeman, 2000). The British Commonwealth nations, and countries or territories with economic, political, historic, and strategic ties to the United States, are often considered to have an advantage in becoming a key sourcing location due to cultural and linguistic ties. Service firms that rely on English communication have tended to cluster within these nations. In many cases, poor or nonexistent English language skills have denied otherwise technically gifted talent the means to communicate in a global business environment.

While India is often associated in the popular Western mind with call centers for the United States and United Kingdom, call center growth has moved to other global locations including "reshoring" to the United States. The Philippines has emerged as a favored destination due to the "neutral" English spoken within the nation. The Philippines' social, political and educational systems are patterned after the United States, with "American English" taught to young Filipinos, so their English is more attuned to the American ear; whereas the English spoken in India is closer to British English (Greenlees, 2006). Some disadvantages of the Philippines are that it has a smaller pool of skilled employees, a less attractive time zone for Western businesses and deteriorating English proficiency which may affect its future ability to handle back-office work (Kyodo, 2006; Valanju, 2005). The Caribbean nations have also traditionally served as major call center points, and spent heavily in the 1990s and early 2000s to improve their telecommunications infrastructure (Metters, Metters, Pullman, & Walton, 2006).

Many countries all over the world with large, literate, underemployed populations whose competitive skills can be easily accessed by modern telecommunications have increased emphasis on learning to read and speak nominal English to become favored destination points, and part of the global economy. However, although countries require English language acquisition as part of their educational curriculum, it is often difficult for trained engineers to communicate in English with sufficient proficiency that anyone outside their specific field can understand or interpret what they say in a meaningful way. This hampers their ability to collaborate on projects with team members from multiple countries. Similarly, much of the native US population is not sufficiently proficient in higher-level English language communication skills to be considered qualified for knowledge-intensive positions in major cities.

Multilingual Skills

Literacy in several languages is a skill found in certain areas of the world more than others due to the need for proficiency and educational training that often requires mastery in multiple languages. In the majority of countries, children are taught to read and write in one language. Truly multilingual countries are few: Switzerland and Luxembourg in Western Europe, and India with sixteen regional spoken languages spoken in the country along with Hindi and English. The ability of technically skilled Eastern Europeans who can speak English, French, German, Russian, and local ethnic languages provides a value-added component to the area for global services sourcing (Tagliabue, 2007).

Unlike manufacturing, service knowledge work is greatly aided by physically speaking the same language. Recently, the trend has been to try to access multilingual talent that can converse in English and Spanish for example. Call centers have been located in Mexico for this purpose while Argentina and the Dominican Republic are attempting to do the same (Whelan, 2006).

English-speaking offshoring nations such as India have created intensive language schools in an effort to tap into the fast-growing Japanese market. They compete with firms based in Manchuria with a legacy of Japanese language. A value-added component for emerging outsourcing cities in Latin America is their geographical proximity, quality education and bilingual skills. Among cities that are seeing some investment due to bilingual skills are: Bogotá, Colombia; Brasilia and Curitiba, Brazil; Montevideo, Uruguay; Guatemala City, Guatemala; Managua, Nicaragua; San José, Costa Rica; Panama City, Panama; and Juarez and Monterrey, Mexico.

Financial Services

The nature of highly globalized financial services with little physical product and transactions that can be done by a third party, along with multiple competitive pressures to improve profit margins, has made offshore outsourcing an increasingly appealing strategic option for firms. While overall statistics are inexact, thousands of financial services positions were moved from the United States and United Kingdom during the period from 2000 to 2015. The process has slowed as offshore outsourcing matures and new technology platforms appear. In addition to back-office work, firms are moving a broader range of functions to lower-cost locations. These include higher-value functions in areas such as financial modeling, analysis, research, regulatory reporting, tax preparation and basic accounting, and mortgage processing. Some observers suggest up to 50 percent of the functions of financial services firms could be moved to lower-cost locations.

Among the most desirable global sourcing operations, financial services firms have established locations throughout the world to take advantage of certain time zones close to major world financial centers within the 24-hour marketplace that also enable ease of travel. Eastern Europe has emerged as the destination of choice for higher-end financial services analyses due to its proximity to major continental financial centers and London, still the key global financial capital. The supply of talent skilled in mathematics, engineering, and computer sciences and the maturity of financial knowledge over a 25-year period since the end of Communism in these countries have made these locations desirable and often more attractive than India. Competition between Eastern European nations and still chronic underemployment issues throughout the region have kept talent costs low up to this time, but increasing demand may create shortages. Some analysts look at the talent base in Russia as the short-term answer to talent shortages occurring in India and other parts of the world.

Global Financial Centers

London

Location, historical links with the majority of capital markets, an unobtrusive regulatory environment, and the availability of skilled personnel have all been important reasons why the City of London became and remains the world's preeminent financial center at this time. While being one of the most expensive cities in the world to live in, its cosmopolitan status and relatively open emigration policies made the city a magnet for skilled international talent. In this environment, financial services are constructed, bought, and sold for a global rather than a domestic market. The City of London was, and still is at this writing, a "cluster" in the knowledge economy just as Silicon Valley has been in the information economy. Virtually every financial services firm in the world has a London presence. A large proportion of these key employees are NRIs (non-resident Indians) from the large Indian population residing in the United Kingdom and the Indian diaspora that has existed for decades throughout the British Commonwealth. The openness and flexibility of the British labor market also attracted many French, Hungarian, Polish, and Islamic émigrés with the requisite financial skills.

The political earthquake known as Brexit, the shorthand version of the referendum passed in June of 2016 for withdrawal of the United Kingdom from the European Union has possibly changed the future calculus for London as a global financial center and its global talent. Negotiations with the European Union have focused on immigration into the British Isles that will most likely be far more restrictive than that of the EU countries. Financial firms are studying alternative locations within the EU, with Dublin, a favored back-office location due to its proximity to London, as a staging point, with Paris, Frankfurt, Amsterdam, Madrid, and Berlin potentially supplanting London as the major European financial center. What this would do to the worldwide connections offered by London is difficult to foresee at this writing (Stewart, 2016). While a mass exodus of financial services firms with massive investment in London real estate is unlikely, onerous conditions placed on immigration and work permission for EU workers and others by the central British government could lead to an outflow of skilled financial workers that the rest of the world covets.

New York City

New York remains a major international financial center given the size and importance of the US market, and historically "Wall Street" has been a destination point for worldwide talent. As mentioned with London, more restrictive immigration policies by the US government may impact New York in terms of its relative prominence. It remains second to London at this time in global financial importance. There is much interest and speculation as to whether the global economy will require a third global financial center somewhere in Asia. Tokyo was considered the third major financial center in the 1980s and 90s, but due to a closed and shallow financial system and a lack of cosmopolitan status has become less important as a global financial center in the last decade. Much speculation has centered on Shanghai due to the size of the Chinese economy, although Hong Kong and Singapore would seem to have the more developed regulatory infrastructure and skilled talent base at this time. An Asian center may well be established, but there is not yet a truly global financial presence to compete with London or New York as a third center. This may change dramatically in the next few years if Brexit terms require the movement of many financial firms to an EU city. Many executives in China and India believe the lack of global financial status is due to antiquated regulations and lack of financial transparency in their respective countries (McKinsey Global Institute, 2017). Among other possible cities in Asia hoping to be considered as financial service centers are Dubai and Mumbai. Both would provide ideal locations from a time zone standpoint but are still lacking the depth of financial talent necessary for the critical mass of firms to locate. In all of these cases the "tier one" individuals with requisite skill sets must be retained as they move up the value chain within firms. Keeping people challenged and interested within the highly competitive financial services environment becomes an important aspect of strategic management.

Biotechnology/Nanotechnology

Among the newest areas of global sourcing is the biotechnology, biomedical, and nanotechnology sector. For years these industries, and the research institutes that provide the crucial technological developments, have existed only in the United States and Europe. The capital-intensive, knowledge-intensive and research orientation of these new, often patented technologies has greatly limited where the firms in this field are congregated. The nature of the industry may prevent the same type of rapid clustering that took place in the IT industry where software was able to be moved quickly to worldwide locations. Global clusters may grow more slowly as a result in the short term, but advancements in the field may change the playing field.

As with other high-technology industries, the United States is still where the dominant talent clusters are located, particularly near the San Francisco Bay and Cambridge–Boston areas where major research universities are located and skilled talent still seeks to be. Sourcing in this area has been limited to firms who can structure the technical skills required and find the talent base for multinational firms. The most highly prized talent, however, derives from Asia, and the nations of China, India, and Singapore among others are seeking to create biotech/nanotech industry environments through major government investments that will attract and keep talent that would otherwise emigrate. Whether these "purpose built" research centers can attract a critical mass of talent as has been the case in information technology is still open to question. A global shift in scientific research and development investment to Asian nations may take many years, and other world areas where research talent exists, such as Eastern Europe, Israel, and Brazil, could change dynamics through their own growth strategies. The overall growth of research training centers in emerging countries will provide firms with many more places to access talent in coming years.

Conclusion

A bitter and divisive US presidential election in 2016 ushered in a major about-face for the United States in its stance on borders, immigration, and technology advancement. It is far too soon to see just how new governmental policies may affect the migration of global talent to the country. There is much discussion in US policy circles of potential immigration policies that would favor high-skilled workers but would be far more restrictive on the numbers of individuals allowed into the country. In addition, partisan politics have made major technology companies into battlegrounds of thought and political persuasion. Ethnicity issues, religious issues, and cultural issues of all types have become a part of the equation for global companies operating in the United States and the skilled talent that they employ. A reordering of the US status in the world and a decline of the nation-state paradigm as a driver of global economic development is perhaps long overdue but comes with significant ramifications. Were China to pick up the mantle as the new globalized economy a very different world view of global talent may emerge.

The quest for the ever elusive world talent pool may force firms and governments to address longstanding infrastructure issues within countries and be more tolerant of skilled individuals' desires to live in environments where they feel comfortable. But a reckoning of "have-not" locations that have not thrived in the pursuit of global talent with those who have could create ever greater chasms of wealth and opportunity that threaten the very essence of capitalism itself. Research that looks not only at global city "success stories" but the failure of some locations to develop fully within the global knowledge economy needs to be performed. The longstanding success of the United States in welcoming and retaining talent from all over the world has lately been put to the test. Nations in Eastern Europe, Russia, and China will need to have agreeable, safe and vibrant places for their talent to thrive if they hope to achieve the same levels of economic growth. This will require some major changes in attitudes and political direction from leaders who often exhibit little understanding of the dynamics driving the interconnected world economy.

Acknowledgements

The author wishes to thank Bruce Hartman, Deborah Burke and James Drogan who contributed their expertise to this piece.

References

Ahmed, F., Capretz, L., Maqsoud, A., & Raza, A. (2014). Analysis of risks faced by information technology offshore outsourcing providers. *Electrical and Computer Engineering Publications* paper no. 68. http://ir.lib.uwo.ca/cgi/viewcontent.cgi?article=1103&context=electricalpub

Anonymous. (2015). The talent dividend. *MIT Sloan Management Review* Research Report, Spring.

Apaza, C. (2009). Measuring governance and corruption through the worldwide governance indicators: Critiques, responses, and ongoing scholarly discussion. *Political Science & Politics, 42*(1), 139–143.

Barsh, J., and Lee, Y. (2012). Unlocking the full potential of women at work. *McKinsey & Company/Wall Street Journal* – mbamujeres.com

Bennett, J. (2017). Ellen Pao is not done fighting. *New York Times*, September 8.

Bhambal, J., & Vasistha, A. (2007). Top 50 emerging outsourcing cities. *Global Services/Tholons*, September 26.

Blinder, A. (2005). Fear of offshoring. *CEPS Working Paper* no. 119, Princeton University Center for Economic Policy Studies, December.

Bradsher, K. (2004). Outsourcing finds Vietnam. *New York Times*, September 30.

Brand, S. (1999). *Clock of the long now: Time and responsibility: The ideas behind the world's slowest computer*. New York, NY: Simon & Schuster.

Briscoe, D., Schuler, R., & Claus, E. (2009). *International human resource management* (3rd ed.). London, UK: Routledge.

Bryan, L. L., & Fraser, J. N. (1999, September 22). Getting to global. *The McKinsey Quarterly*. Retrieved from www.questia.com/library/journal/1G1-59427150/getting-to-global

Bureau of Labor Statistics (2016, April 28). Entrepreneurship and the US economy. Retrieved from www.bls.gov/bdm/entrepreneurship/entrepreneurship.htm

Calestous, L. (2012). Innovation clusters in the global economy: The welfare technology region in Denmark. *Harvard Business Review Case Study*. https://hbr.org/product/innovation-clusters-in-the-global-economy-the-welfare-technology-region-in-denmark/HKS722-PDF-ENG

Chatterji, A., Glaeser, E., & Kerr, W. (2013). Clusters of entrepreneurship and innovation. *NBER Working Paper* no. 19013. May. www.nber.org/papers/w19013

Cheney, G., Ruzzi, B., Muralidharan, K. (2005, November). A profile of the Indian education system. Paper prepared for the New Commission on the Skills of the American Workforce. National Center on Education and the Economy. www.ugc.ac.in/mrp/paper/MRP-MAJOR-EDUC-2013-25066-PAPER.pdf

Cheng, W.-L., Dohrmann, T., Kerlin, M., Law, J., & Ramaswamy, S. (2018, July). Creating an effective workforce system for the new economy. *McKinsey*. www.mckinsey.com/industries/public-sector/our-insights/creating-an-effective-workforce-system-for-the-new-economy

Chui, M., Manyika, J., & Miremadi, M. (2015). Four fundamentals of workplace automation. *McKinsey Quarterly*, November. www.mckinsey.com/business-functions/digital-mckinsey/our-insights/four-fundamentals-of-workplace-automation

Clott, C. (2004). Perspectives on global outsourcing and the changing nature of work. *Business and Society Review*, *109*(2), 153–170.

Clott, C. (2007). An uncertain future: A preliminary study of offshore outsourcing from the manager's perspective. *Management Research News*, *30*(7), 476–494. https://doi.org/10.1108/01409170710759702

Cobb, S. (2003). Offshore financial services and the Internet: Creating confidence in the use of cyberspace? *Growth and Change*, *34*(2), 244–259.

Collings, D., & Mellahi, K. (2009). Strategic talent management: A review and research agenda. *Human Resource Management Review*, *19*, 304–313.

Committee on Science, Engineering, and Public Policy (2007). *Beyond bias and barriers: Fulfilling the potential of women in academic science and engineering*. Washington, DC: National Academies Press.

Dahl, J. (2017). Mission impossible: The new age of ambiguity starring the CEO. *Korn Ferry Briefings Magazine*, 32.

DeLong, T., & Vijayaraghavan, V. (2003). Let's hear it for B players. *Harvard Business Review*, *81*(6), 96–101.

Dore, L. (2006). The challenges of outsourcing: Can Dubai's vision become a reality? *Khaleej Times*. www.khaleejtimes.com/businesses/

Dossani, R., & Kenney, M. (2004). Offshoring: Determinants of the location and value of services. *Sloan Workshop Series in Industry Studies, Stanford University*, August 13.

Drucker, P. (1959). *The landmarks of tomorrow* New York, NY: Harper and Row.

Dutta, S., Lanvin, B., & Wunch-Vincent, S. (2015). The global innovation index 2015. World Intellectual Property Organization. www.wipo.int/edocs/pubdocs/en/wipo_gii_2015.pdf

Economist. (2017). The gender pay gap. *The Economist*, July, 10. www.economist.com/international/2017/10/07/the-gender-pay-gap

Ellison, G., & Glaeser, E. (1999). The geographic concentration of industry: Does natural advantage explain agglomeration? *American Economic Review*, *89*(2), 311–316.

Ellram, L., Tate, W., & Petersen, K. (2013). Offshoring and reshoring: An update on the manufacturing location decision. *Journal of Supply Chain Management*, *49*, 14–22.

Feinstein, L. (2017). French girls are reinventing the tech scene in Paris. *Harpers Bazaar*. www.harpersbazaar.com/culture/a10302219/french-girls-rising-in-tech/

Florida, R. (2004). America's looming creativity crisis. *Harvard Business Review*, October.
Florida, R. (2017). Why America's richest cities keep getting richer. *The Atlantic*, April. www.theatlantic.com/business/archive/2017/04/richard-florida-winner-take-all-new-urban-crisis/522630/
Freeman, C. (2000). *High tech and high heels in the global economy*. Durham, NC: Duke University Press.
Gates Foundation. (2016). The Bill & Melinda Gates Foundation announces $80 million commitment to close gender data gaps and accelerate progress for women. www.gatesfoundation.org/Media-Center/Speeches/2017/06/Melinda-Gates-Unlocking-the-Potential-of-Women-and-Girls
Globalsherpa.org. (2017). World rankings for countries and cities. http://globalsherpa.org/world-rankings
Goodall, H. (2008). More foreign science and engineering grad students flock to US, new survey finds. *The Chronicle of Higher Education*, 30 January.
Gordon, E. (2009). *Winning the global talent showdown*. San Francisco, CA: Berrett-Koehler Publishers.
Gottlieb Duttweiler Institute. (2017). Global city index 2017: The most connected cities. www.globalinfluence.world/en/global-city-index-2017-connected-cities/
Graham, R. (2017). The retraining paradox. *New York Times*, February 23, 2017.
Grassley, C. (2017). S. 180 H-1B and L-1 Visa Reform Act of 2017. *US Senate*. www.congress.gov/bill/115th-congress/senate-bill/180
Greenlees, D. (2006). Philippine call center business booms. *International Herald Tribune*, November 20.
Guthridge, M., Komm, A., & Lawson, E. (2008). Making talent a strategic priority. *The McKinsey Quarterly*, January, 48–59.
Hales, M., King, S., & Pena, A. (2010). The urban elite. *AT Kearney Global Cities Index* 2010. www.atkearney.com/documents/10192/efd4176a-09dd-4ed4-b030-9d94ecc17e8b
Hales, M., Pena, A., Peterson, E., & Dessibourg-Freer, N. (2016). Global cities 2016. www.atkearney.com/documents/10192/8178456/Global+Cities+2016.pdf/8139cd44-c760-4a93-ad7d-11c5d347451a
Hill, A. (2006). A theory of evolution for outsourcers. *Financial Times*, 26 June. www.khaleejtimes.com/DisplayArticle.asp?xfile=data/business/2006/January/business_January178.xml&section=business&col
Jakobsen, E. (2017). The leading maritime capitals of the world. www.menon.no/wp-content/uploads/The-Leading-Maritime-Capitals-of-the-World-2017.pdf
James, J. (2005). *Losing the competitive advantage?: The challenge for science and technology in the United States*. Washington, DC: American Electronics Association.
The Kauffman Index. (2017). Startup activity: National trends. *The Ewing Marion Kauffman Foundation*. www.kauffman.org/kauffman-index/reporting//-/media/kauffman_org/kauffman-index/print-reports/startup-index/2017/
Kearney, A. T. (2007). Offshoring for long-term advantage. *Global Services Location Index* 2007.
Kehal, H., & Singh, V. P. (2006). *Outsourcing and offshoring in the 21st century: A socio-economic perspective*. Hershey, PA: Idea Group Publishing,.
Khanna, P. (2016). A new map for America. *New York Times*, April 15. www.nytimes.com/2016/04/17/opinion/sunday/a-new-map-for-america.html?...

King, E., Botsford, W., & Hebl, M. (2010). Benevolent sexism at work: Gender differences in the distribution of challenging developmental experiences. *Journal of Management*, April. http://journals.sagepub.com/doi/abs/10.1177/0149206310365902

Kristof, N., & WuDunn, S. (2017). Half the sky: Turning oppression into opportunity for women worldwide. www.halftheskymovement.org/pages/book

Kyodo News Service. (2006). English proficiency declining in Philippines: survey. 19 April.

Labi, A. (2008). US faces emerging rivals in foreign student market, study finds. *The Chronicle of Higher Education*, January 31.

Langone, A. (2018). #MeToo and time's up founders explain the difference between the 2 movements – And how they're alike. *Time*, March 8. http://time.com/5189945/whats-the-difference-between-the-metoo-and-times-up-movements/

Lanvin, B. (2017). Benchmarking cities as key players on the global talent scene. *The Global Talent Competitiveness Index* 2017. 99–113.

Lanvin, B., & Evans, P. (2017). Global talent competitiveness index. *INSEAD/Adecco Group/Human Capital Leadership Institute*.

LaTurner, R. J. (2002). Teachers' academic preparation and commitment to teach math and science. *Teaching and Teacher Education*, 18 (6), 653–63.

Laudicina, P., Gott, J., & Peterson, E. (2014). A wealth of choices: From anywhere on earth to no location at all. *A.T. Kearney Global Services Location Index*.

Lazarova, M. B., & Cerdin, J. L. (2007). Revisiting repatriation concerns: Organizational support versus career and contextual influences. *Journal of International Business Studies*, 38(3), 404–429.

Lazonick, W. (2007). Foreign direct investment, transactional migration, and indigenous innovation in the globalization of high-tech labor. Presentation at the International Forum of Comparative Political Economy of Globalization, February.

Lee, A. (2017). China scours the globe for talent to transform into world leader in artificial intelligence. *South China Morning Post*, November 4. www.scmp.com/tech/innovation/article/2118276/artificial-intelligence-and-big-data-will-be-growth-drivers-chinas

Levitt, T. (1983). The globalization of markets. *Harvard Business Review*, May, 92–102.

Levitz, J. (2017). The new corporate recruitment pool: Workers in dead-end jobs. *Wall Street Journal*, September 10.

Lewin, T. (2008). US universities rush to set up outposts abroad. *New York Times*, February 10.

Lewin, A. Y., Massini, S., & Peeters, C. (2009). Why are companies offshoring innovation? The emerging global race for talent. *Journal of International Business Studies*, 40(6), 901–925.

Li, M., Goetz, S. J, Partridge, M., & Fleming, D. A. (2016). Location determinants of high-growth firms. *Entrepreneurship & Regional Development: An International Journal*, 28(1/2), 97–125. doi: 10.1080/08985626.2015.1109003

Liyangunawardena, T., Adams, A., & Williams, S. (2014). MOOCs: A systematic study of the published literature 2008–2012. *Distance Education in China*, 3, 5–16.

Lowell, L., & Gerova, S. (2004). *Diasporas and economic development: state of knowledge*. Washington, DC: World Bank.

Mahroum, S. (2002). US Science and the fear of a backlash: The possible fall out of September 11th on the immigration of scientists and engineers to the US. *Globalization and World Cities Study Group and Network, Research Bulletin* 79, March 15.

Mankiw, G. N., & Swagel, P. (2006). The politics and economics of offshore outsourcing. *Harvard Institute of Economic Research Discussion Paper* no. 21120, July.

Manning, S., Massini, S., & Lewin, A. (2008). A dynamic perspective on next-generation offshoring: The global sourcing of science and engineering talent. *Academy of Management Perspectives* 22(3), 35–54.

Manuti, A., Pastore, S., Scardigno, M., & Morciano, D. (2015). Formal and informal learning in the workplace: A research review. *International Journal of Training and Development*, February. https://doi.org/10.1111/ijtd.12044

Matthews, C. (2007). Foreign science and engineering presence in US institutions and the labor force. *US Bureau of Labor Statistics*, June 21.

McKinsey Global Institute. (2017). The new dynamics of financial globalization. *The McKinsey Quarterly*, August.

Mercer Co. (2019). Global Talent Trends 2019. www.mercer.com/our-thinking/career/global-talent-hr-trends.html#contactForm

Metters, R., Metters, K., Pullman, M., & Walton, S. (2006). *Successful service operations management* (2nd ed.). Mason, OH: Thomson South-Western.

Mongkhonvanit, J. (2014). *Coopetition for regional competitiveness: The role of academe in knowledge-based industrial clustering.* Singapore: Springer.

Mydans, S., & Arnold, W. (2007). Lee Kuan Yew, founder of Singapore, changing with times. *International Herald Tribune*, August.

National Science Board. (2004). An emerging and critical problem of the science and engineering labor force. A Companion to Science and Engineering Indicators. January.

National Science Board. (2016). Science and engineering indicators. *National Science Foundation*. www.nsf.gov/statistics/2016/nsb20161/uploads/1/nsb20161.pdf

Nielsen, S., & Huse, M. (2010). The contribution of women on boards of directors: Going beyond the surface. *Corporate Governance: An International Review*, 18(2), 136–148.

OECD (Organisation for European Co-operation and Development). (2017). *Entrepreneurship at a glance.* Paris, France: OECD Publishing.

Oshri, I., Kotlarsky, J., & Willcocks, L. (2009). *The handbook of global outsourcing and offshoring.* London, UK: Palgrave Macmillan.

Oxford Economics. (2012). Global talent 2021: How the new geography of talent will transform human resource strategies. *Oxford Economics*, Oxford, UK. Retrieved from www.oxfordeconomics.com/Media/Default/Thought%20 Leadership/global-talent-2021.pdf

Pelster, B., Johnson, D., Stempel, J., & van der Vyver, B. (2017). *Careers and learning: Real time, all the time 2017 human capital trends.* New York, NY: Deloitte University Press. https://dupress.deloitte.com/dup-us-en/focus/human-capital-trends/2017/learning-in-the-digital-age.html

Porter, M. (1990). *The competitive advantage of nations.* New York, NY: Free Press.

Porter, M. (2008). The five competitive forces that shape strategy. *Harvard Business Review*, January.

Ransbotham, S., Kiron, D., & Kirk, P. (2015). Minding the analytics gap. *MIT Sloan Management Review*, Spring.
Read, M. (2007). Investment guru: Math skills critical to competitiveness. *Oakland Tribune*. May 19.
Reich, R. (1991). *The work of nations: Preparing ourselves for 21st century capitalism.* New York, NY: Vintage Books.
Rivoli, P. (2005). *Travels of a t-shirt in the global economy: An economist examines the markets, power, and politics of world trade.* New York, NY: Wiley.
Roy, S., & Sivakumar, K. (2012). Global outsourcing relationships and innovation: A conceptual framework and research propositions. *Journal of Product Innovation Management, 29*(4), 513–530. doi: 10.1111/j.1540-5885.2012.00922.
Saisana, M., Becker, W., & Dominguez-Torreiro, M. (2017). *JRC statistical audit of the global talent competitiveness index 2017.* Brussels, Belgium: European Commission Joint Research Centre.
Sanz, L. (2009). The knowledge economy. *Media Planet*, December. https://projects.ncsu.edu/econdev/documents/MediaPlanet.pdf
Saxenian, A. (2006). *The new Argonauts: Regional advantage in a global economy.* Cambridge, MA: Harvard University Press.
Schiessl, M. (2008). Microsoft reaps the rewards of female managers. *Der Spiegel*. February 8.
Schmit, M. (2014). Evolution of work and the worker. SHRM Foundation, *Economist Intelligence Unit* www.shrm.org/foundation/ourwork/initiatives/preparing-for-future-hr-trends/PublishingImages/Pages/
Scott, A. J. (2006). Creative cities: Conceptual issues and policy questions. *Journal of Urban Affairs, 28*(1), 1–17.
Sethi, A., & Gott, J. (2017). 2017 A.T. Kearney Global Services Location Index: The widening impact of automation. *A.T. Kearney.* www.atkearney.com/documents/20152/799350/The+widening+Impact+of+Automation.pdf/95d8d519-e2b0-0e4f-994d-15e8716b339e
Shachar, A. (2006). The race for talent: highly skilled migrants and competitive immigration regimes. 81 *New York University Law Review* 148, March 21.
Stewart, J. (2016). After Brexit, finding a new London for the financial world to call home. *New York Times*. June 30. www.nytimes.com/2016/07/01/business/after-brexit-finding-a-new-london-for-the-financial-world-to-call-home.html?mcubz=1
Strange, S. (1996). *The retreat of the state: The diffusion of power in the world economy.* Cambridge, UK: Cambridge University Press.
Tagliabue, J. (2007). Eastern Europe: a center for outsourcing. *The Hindu*, April 20.
Tarique, I., & Schuler, R. (2010). Global talent management: Literature review, integrative framework, and suggestions for further research. *Journal of World Business, 45,* 122–133.
Valanju, S. (2005). Site unseen. *Financial Management*, July/August, 16–20.
Wadhwa, V., & Gereffi, G. (2005). Framing the engineering outsourcing debate. 12 December.
Walt, V. (2017). Welcome to tomorrow land. *Fortune*, May, 60–67.
Weiner, E. (2016). *The geography of genius: A search for the world's most creative places from ancient Athens to Silicon Valley.* New York, NY: Simon & Schuster.

Wessner, C. W., & Wolff, A. W. (Eds.). (2012). Rising to the challenge: U.S. innovation policy for the global economy. Washington, DC: The National Academies Press.

Whelan, C. (2006). Is Buenos Aires the next Bangalore? www.argentina-canada.net/NewsUpdate.htm

World Bank. (2012). World Development Report – Gender equality and development. Washington, DC: World Bank.

Wright, A., & DeFillippi, P. (2015). Decentralized blockchain technology and the rise of lex cryptographia. *SSRN Electronic Journal*. https://papers.ssrn.com/sol3/papers.cfm?abstract_id=2580664

Yigitcanlar, T. (2009). Planning for knowledge-based urban development: Global perspectives. *Journal of Knowledge Management, 13*(5), 228–242.

Zachary, G. P. (2000). People who need people. *Wall Street Journal*, September 25.

6 Changes in Occupations, Jobs, and Skill Polarization

Arthur Sakamoto, ChangHwan Kim, and Christopher R. Tamborini

Introduction

Inequality in the United States continues to increase in terms of earnings and household income (Semega, Fontenot, & Kollar, 2017). As is well known, this trend began several decades ago (Piketty, 2014; Semega, Fontenot, & Kollar, 2017). Compared to other developed nations, inequality in the United States is generally regarded as being among the highest (Brandolini & Smeeding, 2009). Inequality has become so high that it may be exacerbating social problems (Wilkinson & Pickett, 2009; Stiglitz, 2015).

In part due to such concerns, researchers have sought to understand the sources of rising inequality. One potential source that has often been suggested is change in the job structure (Autor, 2014). If the distribution of jobs is becoming more unequal in regard to their typical skill levels and wages, then that trend might be an underlying cause of increasing income inequality. Some research has argued that the job structure is becoming more bifurcated and that this polarization is leading to a more unequal distribution of wages (Autor, Katz, & Kearney, 2006). In the following, we further investigate this issue.

Prior Literature

Rising inequality associated with the distribution of jobs is not a new concern. This theme is evident in the nineteenth-century writings of Karl Marx who believed that "proletarianization" was endemic to capitalism and would generate such extreme inequality that revolution was inevitable. In research on economic development, Kuznets (1955) argued that during the initial stage of industrialization, a high level of income inequality was generated by the shift in the job structure from those based on traditional production methods to those based on modern technologies. During the 1960s and 1970s, dual labor market theory posited that income inequality was generated by "dead-end jobs" which lacked job training and promotion opportunities (Reich, Gordon, & Edwards, 1973).

Discussions about rising polarization in the twenty-first century also focus on the evolution of technology and the organization of jobs. The influential work of Autor, Levy, and Murnane (2003) and Autor, Katz, and Kearney (2006) proposed models in which automation and related computerized technologies are replacing jobs that are characterized by well-defined, routine activities which do not require complex analytical skills, personalized service, or immediate environmental adaptability. That is, in the contemporary labor market, computerized technologies have become so sophisticated that they can now effectively replace many mid-level jobs (e.g., bank teller, bookkeeper, machine operator, sales and ticket agents, telephone operator) at lower costs to employers. The essential message of the polarization argument is that market competition is leading firms to "hollow out" (Autor, Katz, & Kearney, 2006, p. 193) their job distributions by replacing repetitive, predictable, mid-level job tasks with more cost-efficient automation.

Evidence for some decline in the proportion of middle-level occupations in the job structure is clearly evident since the 1980s through the first decade of the twenty-first century (Autor, Katz, & Kearney, 2006; Acemoglu & Autor, 2011; Autor, 2014). In the following, we provide a research update using more recent data. We further illuminate this phenomenon of job polarization by considering it more directly in connection with related issues involving household income inequality, educational attainment, and occupational change over the work career .

Empirical Analyses

In order to investigate these issues further, we analyze nationally representative data from the public-use samples of the US Census from 1980, 1990, and 2000 and the American Community Survey from 2001 through 2015. First, Table 6.1 shows the trend in employment by standard one-digit occupational codes. As of 2015, over half of the labor force was employed in Managers and Professionals (31.9%) or in Sales and Administrative Support (23.9%). About 3% were employed in Technicians and around 2% were employed in Farming, Forestry and Fishing (the latter figures are not much different from their employment levels in 1980). However, by 2015, employment in Services had grown to 16.7% while traditional blue-collar work had been reduced to little more than one in five jobs (9% in Precision, Production, Craft and Repair, and 12.2% in Operators, Fabricators and Laborers). The decline in traditional blue-collar work is evident in that it accounted for about one in three jobs as late as 1980 as shown in Table 6.1.

These trends seem consistent with the polarization view because employment declined from 1980 to 2015 in what might be seen as middle-level occupational categories including Sales and Administrative Support; Precision, Production, Craft and Repair; and Operators, Fabricators, and Laborers. Conversely, employment rose over this time period in occupations that are more likely to be non-routine and higher-skilled (i.e., Managers and Professionals; and Technicians) or non-routine and lower-skilled or otherwise requiring immediate environmental adaptability (i.e., Services).

Because the standard one-digit occupational codes are rather heterogeneous in terms of mean earnings and skill levels, Table 6.2 shows a more precise

Table 6.1 Percentage employment of labor force in one-digit occupational categories by year

Year	Managers and Professionals	Technicians	Sales, Admin Support	Services	Farming, Forestry, and Fishing	Precision Production, Craft and Repair	Operators, Fabricators, and Laborers	Total
1980	22.9	3.3	26.9	12.0	2.5	13.4	19.1	100.0
1990	26.8	3.8	28.0	12.5	2.2	11.5	15.2	100.0
2000	29.1	3.8	26.9	13.4	2.1	11.2	13.6	100.0
2001	28.8	3.8	26.8	14.0	2.1	11.0	13.6	100.0
2002	28.8	3.8	26.8	14.3	2.2	11.0	13.1	100.0
2003	29.1	3.8	26.5	14.7	2.2	10.9	12.8	100.0
2004	29.1	3.7	26.4	14.9	2.3	10.9	12.7	100.0
2005	29.2	3.7	26.2	14.9	2.2	10.9	13.0	100.0
2006	29.0	3.6	26.1	15.2	2.3	10.8	13.0	100.0
2007	29.7	3.6	25.8	15.3	2.3	10.5	12.8	100.0
2008	30.0	3.7	25.7	15.7	2.2	10.2	12.5	100.0
2009	30.2	3.7	25.5	16.3	2.3	9.9	12.1	100.0
2010	30.4	3.7	25.4	16.6	2.4	9.6	12.0	100.0
2011	30.5	3.7	25.1	17.0	2.4	9.4	12.0	100.0
2012	30.6	3.7	24.9	17.0	2.4	9.3	12.1	100.0
2013	31.0	3.7	24.6	17.1	2.4	9.1	12.1	100.0
2014	31.5	3.9	24.0	17.0	2.3	9.0	12.2	100.0
2015	31.9	3.9	23.9	16.7	2.3	9.0	12.2	100.0

Notes: Data are from IPUMS (Integrated Public Use Microdata Series) 1980, IPUMS 1990, IPUMS 2000 and American Community Survey 2001–2015. Samples are limited to persons aged 18 to 64 who have positive annual earnings.

description of the trend in polarization. Following the practice of Autor, Katz, and Kearney (2006), three-digit occupations were ordered in terms of their mean wage in 1980 (after adjusting for inflation). We then divided the three-digit occupations into five ordered wage quintiles (lowest quintile, second quintile, third quintile, fourth quintile, and highest quintile). Employment in these quintiles of occupations was ascertained for each year of data. The occupational categorization is not altered over time even though the mean hourly wage of some occupations changes over the years.

The results in Table 6.2 show that, for the total labor force, the percentage employment is approximately 20% in each quintile in 1980, with slight differences due to methodological issues (relating to rounding errors and the application of sample survey weights). By 2015, the percentage employed in the lowest quintile increased to 24.5% and the percentage employed in the highest quintile increased to 23.5%. Concomitantly over this time period from 1980 to 2015, employment in the third quintile declined to 18.4%. These changes are consistent with the polarization view.

Regarding the latest years, however, we note that the polarization trend has not been so evident since 2011 when employment in the lowest quintile reached its height at 25.3% and employment in the third quintile reached its lowest percentage at 18.0%. That is, employment in 2015 does not appear to be more clearly polarized than in 2011. The only change that is evident between these years is an approximately 1 percentage point increase in the highest quintile. It is too soon to conclude that polarization "has run its course," but the trend over the past five years does not show an obvious continuing pattern towards increasing polarization.

Other noteworthy findings from Table 6.2 relate to gender differences. The trend in occupational downgrading, we find, has been much more evident for men than for women. Among men, employment in the lowest quintile increased markedly from 10.7% in 1980 to 16.9% in 2015. The employment of men declined in the middle three quintiles over that time period while male employment in the highest quintile increased by less than 1 percentage point.

This change for men contrasts with that for women, among whom much of the trend was quite the opposite: employment in the lowest quintile changed by less than 1 percentage point while employment in the highest quintile increased sharply from 10.8% to 17.7%. Whereas women had been most concentrated in the lowest occupations in 1980, by 2015 women had substantially increased their employment in the upper two quintiles while their employment in the lowest two quintiles notably declined. So, while most men were experiencing occupational downgrading from 1980 to 2015, many women were experiencing occupational upgrading.

For exploratory purposes, Table 6.3 shows the quintile distribution of equivalized household incomes based on the quintile thresholds from 1980. Equivalized household income refers to total household income divided by the square root of the household size. This standardization controls for varying household sizes over time and accounts for economies of scale in consumption

Table 6.2 *Percentage employment of the labor force in the quintile categorization of occupation by year and gender*

Year	Total Lowest	Q2	Q3	Q4	Highest	Sum	Male Lowest	Q2	Q3	Q4	Highest	Sum	Female Lowest	Q2	Q3	Q4	Highest	Sum
1980	20.3	20.6	19.4	18.8	21.0	100.0	10.7	16.2	23.0	21.7	28.4	100.0	33.4	26.5	14.4	14.9	10.8	100.0
1990	19.2	19.0	20.9	19.1	21.8	100.0	11.4	15.3	24.8	20.9	27.6	100.0	28.7	23.3	16.2	17.0	14.8	100.0
2000	21.6	16.8	18.8	19.8	23.0	100.0	14.0	14.0	22.0	20.7	29.4	100.0	30.3	20.1	15.1	18.8	15.7	100.0
2001	21.8	16.8	18.9	19.3	23.1	100.0	14.1	14.1	22.1	20.4	29.4	100.0	30.7	20.0	15.3	18.1	15.9	100.0
2002	22.0	16.6	18.9	19.6	22.9	100.0	14.4	14.0	22.0	20.6	29.0	100.0	30.8	19.6	15.3	18.5	15.8	100.0
2003	22.5	16.5	18.7	19.5	22.7	100.0	14.9	14.0	22.0	20.4	28.8	100.0	31.4	19.5	15.0	18.6	15.7	100.0
2004	22.7	16.4	18.7	19.5	22.6	100.0	15.0	14.1	21.8	20.5	28.6	100.0	31.6	19.2	15.1	18.4	15.8	100.0
2005	22.6	16.4	19.0	19.5	22.5	100.0	14.8	14.0	22.4	20.4	28.4	100.0	31.6	19.1	15.1	18.5	15.6	100.0
2006	23.1	16.4	18.9	19.4	22.2	100.0	15.2	14.2	22.4	20.3	28.0	100.0	32.2	18.9	14.9	18.4	15.6	100.0
2007	23.1	16.2	18.8	19.5	22.6	100.0	15.3	14.0	22.2	20.2	28.3	100.0	31.9	18.7	14.8	18.6	16.0	100.0
2008	23.4	16.0	18.6	19.4	22.6	100.0	15.6	14.0	22.0	20.0	28.4	100.0	32.3	18.3	14.7	18.7	16.1	100.0
2009	24.0	16.1	18.3	19.0	22.6	100.0	16.3	14.2	21.7	19.6	28.2	100.0	32.7	18.2	14.6	18.3	16.3	100.0
2010	24.9	16.0	18.1	18.7	22.4	100.0	17.1	14.3	21.4	19.2	27.9	100.0	33.3	17.8	14.3	18.2	16.3	100.0
2011	25.3	15.9	18.0	18.5	22.3	100.0	17.5	14.5	21.3	18.9	27.8	100.0	33.8	17.4	14.3	18.1	16.3	100.0
2012	25.2	15.7	18.2	18.5	22.4	100.0	17.5	14.4	21.6	18.7	27.8	100.0	33.9	17.2	14.5	18.2	16.3	100.0
2013	25.2	15.6	18.2	18.3	22.7	100.0	17.6	14.4	21.5	18.4	28.1	100.0	33.7	16.9	14.5	18.1	16.8	100.0
2014	24.8	15.4	18.4	18.3	23.1	100.0	17.2	14.6	21.7	18.4	28.2	100.0	33.2	16.4	14.7	18.3	17.4	100.0
2015	24.5	15.2	18.4	18.3	23.5	100.0	16.9	14.3	21.8	18.2	28.9	100.0	32.9	16.2	14.8	18.4	17.7	100.0
(2015–1980)	(4.2)	(−5.4)	(−0.9)	(−0.5)	(2.6)		(6.2)	(−1.9)	(−1.2)	(−3.5)	(0.5)		(−0.5)	(−10.3)	(0.4)	(−3.5)	(−6.9)	
(2015–2000)	(2.9)	(−1.6)	(−0.3)	(−1.5)	(0.5)		(2.9)	(0.3)	(−0.2)	(−2.5)	(−0.5)		(2.6)	(−3.8)	(−0.3)	(−0.3)	(1.9)	

Notes: Data are from IPUMS 1980, IPUMS 1990, IPUMS 2000 and American Community Survey 2001–2015. Samples are limited to persons aged 18–64 who have positive annual earnings. The quintile categorization is based on the ordering of the mean hourly wage of three-digit occupations in 1980 adjusted for inflation.

Table 6.3 *Percentage employment in the quintile categorization of equivalized household income by year based on the 1980 quintile thresholds*

Year	Lowest	Q2	Q3	Q4	Highest	Sum	Mean Equivalized Income (2015 Constant $)
1980	19.8	19.8	19.8	19.8	20.8	100.0	47,052
1990	20.4	17.4	18.0	18.4	25.8	100.0	52,227
2000	20.0	16.5	16.3	17.8	29.4	100.0	57,751
2001	21.4	16.8	16.5	17.6	27.8	100.0	55,993
2002	22.0	16.5	16.6	17.2	27.7	100.0	55,418
2003	22.3	16.3	16.4	17.0	28.0	100.0	55,094
2004	22.6	16.3	16.1	17.2	27.8	100.0	55,713
2005	22.7	16.3	15.7	17.3	28.1	100.0	55,950
2006	22.2	15.6	15.7	17.4	29.1	100.0	56,375
2007	21.8	16.0	15.7	16.8	29.7	100.0	57,393
2008	22.2	15.7	15.4	17.0	29.8	100.0	57,441
2009	24.3	16.2	15.5	16.2	27.8	100.0	54,602
2010	25.4	16.0	15.2	15.8	27.6	100.0	53,880
2011	25.6	16.0	15.0	16.2	27.3	100.0	53,953
2012	25.8	16.0	15.3	15.7	27.2	100.0	53,750
2013	25.6	16.3	14.9	15.6	27.5	100.0	54,451
2014	25.4	16.2	14.7	15.8	27.9	100.0	54,860
2015	24.5	16.3	14.5	16.2	28.6	100.0	56,125
(2015–1980)	(4.6)	(−3.5)	(−5.3)	(−3.6)	(7.8)		
(2015–2000)	(4.4)	(−0.2)	(−1.8)	(−1.6)	(−0.8)		

Notes: Family income is adjusted to constant 2015 dollars by CPI-U (https://cps.ipums.org/cps/cpi99.shtml). Samples are limited to persons who have positive personal earnings and positive family income. Equivalized income is computed as total family income divided by the square root of household size.

(due to the use of the square root). The quintile thresholds are defined in terms of absolute dollars as observed in 1980 (after controlling for inflation) and are held constant across the years. The purpose of Table 6.3 is to assess the extent of quintile polarization in equivalized household incomes rather than in occupations.

The trend for the total labor force in Table 6.2 may be compared with the trend for equivalized household income in Table 6.3. In comparison to the total labor force in Table 6.2, household income in Table 6.3 seems more polarized. The household income distribution seems somewhat more "hollowed out" because its third and fourth quintiles for household income are smaller than for occupation. On the other hand, the highest quintile for household income is much larger than for occupation (i.e., 28.6% versus 23.5%, respectively). These comparisons show that the polarization of equivalized household income (which is more directly indicative of economic wellbeing) is greater than the polarization of the occupational structure.

The greater polarization of household income likely stems from the abovementioned gender differential (i.e., occupational downgrading among men but occupational upgrading for women) combined with increased "assortative mating" (Kim & Sakamoto, 2017). In other words, the correlation between the incomes of spouses has increased over this time period which exacerbates the polarization of earnings associated with the "hollowed out" occupational structure. Furthermore, the trend towards a continued increase in the polarization of household income seems more evident for the most recent years in Table 6.3 than is the case for occupations in Table 6.2. These findings suggest that polarization may be perceived or may "feel" somewhat greater to the individual on a household basis than is actually occurring in the occupational structure per se. The pattern is related in part to employment trends among married women and changing patterns in the relationship between work and family among women.

Further exploratory analyses are shown in Table 6.4 which breaks down the trend by educational level. As is well known, education has a large positive effect on obtaining higher occupational status (e.g., Fischer & Hout, 2006). What has been less commonly considered, however, is the significance of the relative aspect of educational attainment (Thurow, 1975). As the average level of educational attainment has risen notably in recent decades (Fischer & Hout, 2006), the relative ranking of one's educational level may be becoming more important in regard to its occupational returns (Sakamoto, Kim, & Woo 2012; Bills, 2016; Di Statsio, Bol, & Van de Werfhorst, 2016). In our analysis, occupation is measured in terms of an explicitly ordinal outcome (i.e., in terms of quintiles of the ranking of occupational mean wages as observed in 1980) so the relative aspect seems more apparent in our findings.

For example, in the case of workers without a high school degree (LTHS), Table 6.4 shows that they have experienced a dramatic decline in occupational returns when measured in terms of quintiles. Whereas 15.4% of LTHS workers were in the highest quintile in 1980, the corresponding figure had dwindled to 6.4% in 2015. While high-occupation LTHS workers have become uncommon, the percentage employed in the lowest quintile substantially increased from 24.9% in 1980 to 41.3% in 2015. Table 6.4 shows that high school graduates (i.e., HSG refers to workers without any college experience) have also experienced sharp declines in occupational returns although not quite as dramatic as for LTHS workers. Workers with some college (i.e., SC) had a similar notable drop in occupational returns over this time period as well (about the same as the decline for HSG workers).

For workers with a bachelor's degree (i.e., BA), Table 6.4 shows some significant increase in employment in the lowest quintile between 1980 and 2015 (i.e., from 8.0% to 12.7%). Only a small decline of about 1 percentage point, however, is evident for the highest quintile. For the most part, the results in Table 6.4 indicate that the occupational return to a BA degree has remained more stable over this time period in contrast to persons without a BA degree.

Table 6.4 *Percentage employment in the quintile categorization of occupation by year and educational level*

	Lowest	Q2	Q3	Q4	Highest	Sum
(A) LTHS						
1980	24.9	20.8	20.5	18.4	15.4	100.0
1990	26.2	22.5	22.0	17.3	12.1	100.0
2000	37.0	21.4	21.5	13.0	7.2	100.0
2005	37.8	20.2	21.8	13.6	6.6	100.0
2010	42.0	19.8	20.7	11.6	5.9	100.0
2015	41.3	19.4	21.3	11.7	6.4	100.0
(2015–1980)	(16.4)	(−1.5)	(0.8)	(−6.7)	(−9.0)	
(2015–2000)	(4.3)	(−2.0)	(−0.2)	(−1.3)	(−0.8)	
(B) HSG						
1980	22.4	25.4	21.3	15.5	15.4	100.0
1990	23.4	24.3	23.7	14.9	13.7	100.0
2000	26.8	22.6	22.4	15.4	12.7	100.0
2005	28.7	22.0	22.5	14.8	12.0	100.0
2010	31.4	21.6	21.6	13.7	11.8	100.0
2015	32.0	21.2	22.3	12.8	11.7	100.0
(2015–1980)	(9.6)	(−4.1)	(1.0)	(−2.7)	(−3.7)	
(2015–2000)	(5.2)	(−1.3)	(−0.1)	(−2.7)	(−1.0)	
(C) SC						
1980	20.0	22.4	19.9	17.9	19.9	100.0
1990	19.7	20.8	22.6	16.6	20.3	100.0
2000	22.3	19.1	19.6	19.4	19.7	100.0
2005	24.1	18.9	19.9	18.8	18.4	100.0
2010	28.4	18.9	19.2	16.9	16.6	100.0
2015	28.9	18.1	20.0	16.2	16.8	100.0
(2015–1980)	(9.0)	(−4.3)	(0.1)	(−1.7)	(−3.0)	
(2015–2000)	(6.6)	(−1.0)	(0.4)	(−3.2)	(−2.9)	
(D) BA						
1980	8.0	8.8	15.6	30.1	37.5	100.0
1990	7.3	8.1	18.1	29.2	37.3	100.0
2000	9.8	7.7	16.1	28.7	37.8	100.0
2005	11.1	8.3	16.8	27.7	36.1	100.0
2010	12.7	8.8	16.4	26.9	35.2	100.0
2015	12.7	8.4	16.6	25.9	36.5	100.0
(2015–1980)	(4.6)	(−0.4)	(1.0)	(−4.2)	(−1.0)	
(2015–2000)	(2.9)	(0.7)	(0.5)	(−2.8)	(−1.3)	
(E) Grad						
1980	5.7	3.6	6.2	25.6	58.9	100.0
1990	5.0	4.3	7.4	28.5	54.9	100.0
2000	5.7	3.7	7.1	26.3	57.3	100.0
2005	5.5	3.9	7.6	26.3	56.8	100.0
2010	5.6	4.2	7.3	27.0	55.8	100.0
2015	5.6	4.3	7.8	26.4	55.9	100.0
(2015–1980)	(−0.1)	(0.7)	(1.7)	(0.8)	(−3.0)	
(2015–2000)	(−0.0)	(0.6)	(0.7)	(0.1)	(−1.4)	

Notes: Data are from IPUMS and American Community Survey. Samples are limited to persons aged 18–64 who have positive annual earnings. The occupational quintiles are the same as in Table 6.2.

Among workers with a graduate degree (i.e., GRAD), Table 6.4 indicates essentially no change in employment at the lower end and only a small decline in the highest quintile from 58.9% in 1980 to 55.9% in 2015. The main pattern is still evident for GRAD workers in that the majority continue to be employed in the highest quintile of occupations. The percentage employment of GRAD workers in the other quintiles has been fairly consistent over the period.

Overall, these findings suggest the critical demarcation associated with having at least a bachelor's degree. For workers without it, lower-level occupational employment has become increasingly common. For BA workers, by contrast, occupational downgrading has been mostly averted while employment in the highest-level occupations continues to be the norm for GRAD workers. These findings seem consistent with Fischer and Hout's (2006: 247) summary of education and inequality during twentieth-century America which concludes by stating that "the division between the less- and more-educated grew and emerged as a powerful determinant of life chances and lifestyles."

This generic assessment and our findings should be viewed in the context of rising average levels of education attainment overall. As shown in Appendix Table 6.9A, the percentage of the labor force that was LTHS dropped from 28.8% in 1980 to 9.2% in 2015 while the percentage HSG declined significantly as well from 35.8% to 21.9%. The percentage SC almost doubled from 19.6% in 1980 to 36.8% in 2015. Workers with a BA degree also substantially increased over this time period. Thus, educational attainment greatly improved from 1980 to 2015.

For this reason, LTHS and HSD workers in 2015 have declined significantly in terms of their relative standing in the distribution of education. That is, in comparison to 1980, contemporary LTHS and HSD workers have much lower levels of relative educational attainment. Their declining relative occupational attainment in the twenty-first-century labor market (i.e., in terms of quintiles) corresponds with their declining relative position in the distribution of education.

Additional statistics on the distribution of educational attainment by year and gender are shown in Appendix Table 6.9B. The increase in educational attainment has been more pronounced among women. Whereas men in 1980 were more likely than women to have a bachelor's or graduate degree, by 2015 the reverse has become true. In 2015, 30.7% of men have at least a bachelor's degree (i.e., 20.0% for BA and 10.7% for GRAD in Appendix Table 6.9B) whereas for women the corresponding figure is 35.6% (i.e., 22.7% for BA and 12.9% for GRAD in Appendix Table 6.9B). At the other end of the distribution, only 6.9% of women do not have a high school degree in comparison to 10.8% among men.

The gender differential in educational attainment is likely part of the source of the notable occupational upgrading for women discussed in Table 6.2. At the same time, the increased percentages of women with bachelor's and graduate degrees is also probably associated with the increased polarization of household income and assortative mating mentioned earlier in regard to

Table 6.3. To the extent that relative educational attainment is important to relative occupational attainment (i.e., in terms of this categorization of quintiles), and to the extent that labor market queuing accounts for the association between education and occupation (Thurow, 1975), then the increasing educational attainment of female workers might also partly account for the high level of occupational downgrading experienced by male workers without a college degree.

In general, the foregoing results indicate that workers without a bachelor's degree have mostly experienced the occupational downgrading that is associated with the rising polarization of the job structure. By contrast, most workers with at least a college degree (though not all of them) have been able to maintain their employment in the highest two occupational quintiles. The average level of educational attainment in the distribution has notably increased over the past few decades with fewer workers lacking a high school, but rising polarization in the occupational structure (and especially in the distribution of household income) has occurred despite the lack of any significant polarization of educational attainment.

Racial/ethnic differentials are shown in Table 6.5. Whites are the largest group and for them the polarization trend is more clearly evident from 1980 to 2015 as employment increased in the lowest and highest quintiles while it decreased in the middle quintile. In the case of African Americans, growth in the highest quintile was also notable, increasing from 11.0% in 1980 to 15.01% in 2015. While a slight increase in employment in the lowest quintile occurred for African Americans, occupational upgrading over this time period seems to be more the dominant pattern. They experienced little change in employment in the middle and fourth quintiles and a significant decline in the second quintile.

Occupational upgrading is most prominent among Asians, for whom employment in each of the lower four quintiles declined. It was replaced by a marked increase in employment in the highest quintile from 24.2% in 1980 to 36.5% in 2015. The higher level of educational attainment among Asians is likely associated with this latter trend (Sakamoto, Goyette, & Kim, 2009). Indeed, Asians have the largest employment of any group (including Whites) in the highest quintile of occupations throughout this entire time period.

In the case of Hispanics, little change in employment in the highest three quintiles occurred over this time period. Table 6.5 shows that employment declined significantly in the second quintile while it increased by 6 percentage points in the lowest quintile (from 28.1% in 1980 to 34.1% in 2015). Rather than increased polarization as in the case for Whites or occupational upgrading as in the case for Blacks and Asians, occupational downgrading seems to be more descriptive of the trend for Hispanics.

The context for this latter result, however, is the particularly large increase in the size of the Hispanic population over this period. Fueled by both immigration and high fertility (Flores, 2017), the Hispanic labor force

Table 6.5 *Percentage employment in the quintile categorization of occupation by year and racelethnicity*

	Lowest	Q2	Q3	Q4	Highest	Sum
(A) Whites						
1980	18.5	19.7	19.6	19.6	22.7	100.0
1990	17.0	18.0	21.2	20.1	23.8	100.0
2000	19.0	15.8	18.7	21.1	25.4	100.0
2005	19.3	15.4	18.9	21.0	25.3	100.0
2010	21.0	15.1	18.0	20.6	25.4	100.0
2015	20.5	14.1	18.3	20.3	26.9	100.0
(2015–1980)	(2.0)	(−5.6)	(−1.2)	(0.7)	(4.1)	
(2015–2000)	(1.5)	(−1.7)	(−0.4)	(−0.8)	(1.5)	
(B) Blacks						
1980	29.7	25.8	18.6	15.0	11.0	100.0
1990	27.6	23.8	19.7	15.9	13.0	100.0
2000	28.5	21.7	18.7	17.0	14.2	100.0
2005	30.2	21.1	18.7	16.1	13.9	100.0
2010	31.6	20.5	17.6	15.6	14.7	100.0
2015	31.4	20.0	18.2	15.4	15.1	100.0
(2015–1980)	(1.7)	(−5.8)	(−0.4)	(0.4)	(4.1)	
(2015–2000)	(3.0)	(−1.7)	(−0.5)	(−1.6)	(0.9)	
(C) Hispanics						
1980	28.1	25.1	19.5	14.9	12.4	100.0
1990	28.5	23.4	21.3	14.5	12.4	100.0
2000	31.1	20.0	20.6	15.5	12.8	100.0
2005	31.9	18.7	21.2	16.1	12.1	100.0
2010	35.5	17.9	20.0	14.6	12.0	100.0
2015	34.1	17.3	20.8	14.6	13.2	100.0
(2015–1980)	(6.0)	(−7.8)	(1.3)	(−0.3)	(0.7)	
(2015–2000)	(3.0)	(−2.7)	(0.2)	(−0.9)	(0.4)	
(D) Asian Americans						
1980	26.3	18.1	14.6	16.8	24.2	100.0
1990	23.9	16.9	17.1	16.2	26.0	100.0
2000	23.7	13.9	14.8	15.1	32.5	100.0
2005	24.5	12.6	14.5	15.1	33.4	100.0
2010	25.7	12.3	13.8	14.8	33.4	100.0
2015	24.3	11.4	13.7	14.1	36.5	100.0
(2015–1980)	(−1.9)	(−6.8)	(−0.9)	(−2.8)	(12.3)	
(2015–2000)	(0.6)	(−2.5)	(−1.0)	(−1.0)	(4.0)	
(E) Other Races						
1980	24.0	22.5	18.5	19.7	15.3	100.0
1990	24.3	22.0	20.7	18.8	14.3	100.0
2000	26.3	18.1	18.6	18.1	18.9	100.0
2005	27.1	17.5	18.4	18.7	18.4	100.0
2010	29.1	17.2	17.1	17.1	19.5	100.0
2015	28.5	15.9	17.7	16.7	21.1	100.0
(2015–1980)	(4.5)	(−6.5)	(−0.8)	(−3.0)	(5.8)	
(2015–2000)	(2.2)	(−2.1)	(−0.8)	(−1.4)	(2.2)	

Notes: Data are from IPUMS and American Community Survey. Samples are limited to persons aged 18 to 64 who have positive annual earnings. The occupational quintiles are the same as in Table 6.2.

dramatically expanded from 5.4% in 1980 to 16.6% in 2015 as shown in Appendix Table 6.9A. The significant rise of Hispanics in the lowest quintile (as shown in Table 6.5) probably does not reflect so much the loss of middle-level jobs as the influx of Hispanic immigrants and the entry of younger Hispanics in the labor force directly into those lower-level occupations.

Although a smaller demographic group, Asians also have significant population growth. Asians increased from 1.6% of the labor force in 1980 to 5.7% in 2015 as is evident in Appendix Table 6.9A. Having a lower fertility rate than Hispanics, growth in the Asian labor force is somewhat more directly associated with immigration trends. An additional contrast with Hispanics is that Asian immigrants tend to be more highly educated and second-generation Asians are known for their high levels of educational attainment (Sakamoto, Goyette, & Kim, 2009). As noted above, the employment of Asians in the highest quintile rose over this time period, but this increase likely does not so much derive from the occupational upgrading of continuously employed Asian workers as from the employment of new immigrants and younger workers directly into those occupations due to their higher levels of educational attainment.

Additional Analysis: Longitudinal Patterns of Occupation Change

To explore the issue of occupational change from the point of view of the careers of individual workers in the context of polarization, we investigated three panels (1996, 2004, 2008) of nationally representative longitudinal data from the Survey of Income and Program Participation (SIPP). The SIPP collects data every four months (referred to as a wave) for the span of the panel, ranging from around two and a half to four years. To track individuals for three years, the analysis uses data from wave 1 and wave 12 in the noted SIPP panels. A key feature of these data is that we can follow the same individuals over a three-year period in each period, allowing us to examine the extent that workers change occupations over the course of several years of the career and its relationship with their earnings. This type of analysis cannot be done using cross-sectional reports.

Our analytic sample is limited to men and women who were aged 25–54 in the first wave of each panel, responded to waves 1 and 12, and had positive earnings. We examine several outcomes over the three-year interval, namely occupation (three-digit) and earnings. SIPP longitudinal weights are applied throughout this analysis.

Table 6.6 shows that over three years of a worker's life, occupational change at the three-digit was quite common in the periods examined (42.7% in the 1996 panel, 36.7% in the 2004 panel, and 26.1% in the 2008 panel). The trends in Table 6.6 for women are similar. Note that the observed downward trend probably reflects macroeconomic conditions during the periods of the panels:

Table 6.6 *Change in three-digit occupation over three years in the survey of income and program participation*

	1996 Panel	2004 Panel	2008 Panel
Men	42.7%	36.7%	26.1%
Women	43.7%	39.0%	26.4%

Notes: Samples are limited to persons who have positive earnings and a job in both wave 1 and wave 12.

the latter half of the 1990s was a period of economic boom whereas a major recession began in 2008. Nonetheless, Table 6.6 shows that some occupational change remains common among workers even after just three years of employment.

Table 6.7 provides some description of how occupational change relates to changes in earnings. In general, for both men and women, median gains in monthly earnings after three years of employment declined across the three panels, perhaps due to the weakening macroeconomic environment during the 2008 panel. Also reflecting this environment, Table 6.7 further shows that for both men and women who changed occupations as well as for those who did not, a monthly earnings gain of at least 5% after three years of employment was the modal pattern in the 1996 panel, but monthly earnings decline of at least 5% became the modal pattern in the 2008 panel. By the time of the 2008 panel, the median gain in monthly earnings for men over the three follow-up years was actually −2.0% (i.e., a decline of 2% in 2011 relative to median monthly earnings in 2008). Given that the 2008 panel spans the Great Recession, we again see that individual work careers are clearly impinged by the macroeconomic context.

Nonetheless, the data show that many workers also experienced gains in real earnings over the three-year observation window. Even amid the major recession of 2008, earnings increased by at least 5% among 39.7% of men who changed their occupations and 45.1% of women who changed their occupations. Among those who did not change their occupation after three years in the 2008 panel, earnings still increased by at least 5% among 34.4% of men and 37.8% of women. These patterns suggest that rising inequality is tenacious as some workers manage to garner higher earnings despite the lowered overall earnings and the increased economic constraints of many firms in a seriously contracting economic period. That is, in the twenty-first-century American labor market, workforce "churning" is characterized by many firms hiring and firing at the same time (Cappelli, 2001: 218).

In general, the findings in Tables 6.6 and 6.7 suggest that occupational change seems fairly common in workers' careers especially when the economy is growing and other jobs are being created which promote career mobility and the potential for higher earnings. While occupational changes

Table 6.7 *Changes in earnings and occupation over three years in the survey of income and program participation*

	1996 Panel	2004 Panel	2008 Panel
I. Men			
(1) Total			
- Median monthly earnings in wave 1	3,822	4,177	4,011
- Median monthly earnings in wave 12	4,264	4,350	3,929
- % change	11.6	4.1	−2.0
(2) Those who have the same occupation			
- Median monthly earnings in wave 1	4,283	4,512	4,513
- Median monthly earnings in wave 12	4,562	4,610	4,382
% change	9.1	1.2	−3.3
- Earnings down −5% or more (%)	32.6	40.7	47.2
- Earnings stay within ±5% range (%)	11.7	17.0	18.3
- Earnings up +5% or more (%)	55.7	42.3	34.4
(3) Those who changed occupation			
- Median monthly earnings in wave 1	3,622	4,011	3,809
- Median monthly earnings in wave 12	4,121	4,450	3,609
- % change	13.8	10.9	−5.3
- Earnings down −5% or more (%)	32.5	33.3	48.4
- Earnings stay within ±5% range (%)	8.6	15.2	11.9
- Earnings up +5% or more (%)	58.9	51.5	39.7
II. Women			
(1) Total			
- Median monthly earnings in wave 1	2,587	2,843	2,969
- Median monthly earnings in wave 12	2,950	2,969	3,008
- % change	14.0	4.4	1.3
(2) Those who have the same occupation			
- Median monthly earnings in wave 1	2,868	3,079	3,207
- Median monthly earnings in wave 12	3,212	3,243	3,215
- % change	12.0	5.3	0.2
- Earnings down −5% or more (%)	29.4	37.6	43.7
- Earnings stay within ±5% range (%)	10.8	16.1	18.5
- Earnings up +5% or more (%)	59.9	46.2	37.8
(3) Those who changed occupation			
- Median monthly earnings in wave 1	2,294	2,507	2,399
- Median monthly earnings in wave 12	2,675	2,664	2,268
- % change	16.6	6.3	−5.5
- Earnings down −5% or more (%)	31.7	34.8	45.1
- Earnings stay within ±5% range (%)	8.1	12.2	9.8
- Earnings up +5% or more (%)	60.1	53.0	45.1

Notes: Samples are limited to those who have positive earnings and a job in both wave 1 and wave 2.

are often associated with earnings increases, sometimes occupational changes are associated with earnings decreases, especially during periods of macroeconomic contraction. Furthermore, significant earnings growth can occur even without occupation changes. These results show that the relationship between earnings and occupation is not clearly defined and is likely mediated by other factors (Kim & Sakamoto, 2008; Sakamoto & Wang, 2017).

Table 6.8 provides additional statistics about changes in occupation and earnings. In contrast to Table 6.7, the findings in Table 6.8 indicate patterns of workers' own earnings relative to the earnings distribution in terms of three broad categories: (a) low (i.e., below half of the median), (b) middle (above half of the median but less than 150% of the median), and (c) high (150% or more of the median). The polarization of earnings is evident to the extent that workers become more concentrated in the low and high categories over the three-year follow-up period. The same three panels of the SIPP data are again used to assess changes in individual workers' careers after three years.

The results for men (see top portion of Table 6.8) indicate a slight increase in earnings polarization over this time period. We find that 59.6% of the sample of workers had earnings in the middle category in wave 1 in 1996 while this figure declined slightly to 57.2% in wave 1 in 2008. On the other hand, for women overall, earnings polarization in 2008 does not appear to be significantly greater than in 1996.

Regarding the relationship between occupational change and polarization, Table 6.8 shows that among men who changed their occupations between waves 1 and 12 in the 2008 panel, 25.6% were in the low earnings category and 21.1% were in the high earnings category. Among men who did not change their occupations over the same period, 13.7% were in the low earnings category and 28.6% were in the high earnings category. Furthermore, the proportion in the low category was greater among occupation changers after the occupational change (22.6–25.6%). Occupational changing therefore seems to be more associated with being in the low earnings category whereas occupational staying is more associated with being in the high earnings category. This pattern seems also largely consistent to 1996 and 2004 although in those years before the recession there was less earnings polarization and fewer men in the low earnings category.

Among women, Table 6.8 suggests that occupational change is also more associated with being in the low earnings category. Among women who changed their occupations from wave 1 to 12 in 2008, 28.2% were in the low earnings category and only 17.9% were in the high earnings category. Among women who did not change their occupations, 14.7% were in the low earnings category and 28.8% were in the high earnings category in wave 12 in 2008. These findings suggest that a useful avenue of future work would explore how job changes and occupational changes mediate patterns of polarization in the labor market.

Table 6.8 Changes in earnings and occupation over three years in the survey of income and program participation

	SIPP 1996 Wave 1	SIPP 1996 Wave 12	Change	SIPP 2004 Wave 1	SIPP 2004 Wave 12	Change	SIPP 2008 Wave 1	SIPP 2008 Wave 12	Change
I. Men									
Total									
% below half median	15.6	13.9	−1.7	14.7	14.3	−0.4	16.6	17.1	0.4
% between 50% and 150% of median	59.6	62.7	3.1	59.7	61.0	1.3	57.2	56.5	−0.7
% 1.5 times above median	24.8	23.4	−1.4	25.7	24.7	−1.0	26.1	26.4	0.3
Occupational Changer									
% below half median	21.1	17.6	−3.6	19.4	17.8	−1.6	22.6	25.6	3.0
% between 50% and 150% of median	58.9	62.4	3.5	59.3	57.4	−1.9	55.5	53.3	−2.2
% 1.5 times above median	19.9	20.0	0.1	21.3	24.8	3.5	21.9	21.1	−0.8
Occupational Stayer									
% below half median	11.5	11.2	−0.3	11.9	12.2	0.3	14.3	13.7	−0.6
% between 50% and 150% of median	60.0	62.8	2.8	59.9	63.2	3.3	57.9	57.8	−0.2
% 1.5 times above median	28.5	26.0	−2.5	28.2	24.6	−3.6	27.8	28.6	0.8
II. Women									
Total									
% below half median	18.3	16.0	−2.2	17.5	16.1	−1.4	18.8	18.3	−0.5
% between 50% and 150% of median	55.3	59.1	3.8	54.6	56.3	1.7	53.8	55.8	2.0
% 1.5 times above median	26.5	24.9	−1.6	27.9	27.6	−0.3	27.4	25.9	−1.5
Occupational Changer									
% below half median	23.5	19.7	−3.8	21.7	19.1	−2.6	26.6	28.2	1.6
% between 50% and 150% of median	54.9	59.7	4.8	56.1	57.9	1.8	54.2	53.9	−0.3
% 1.5 times above median	21.6	20.5	−1.1	22.2	23.0	0.8	19.2	17.9	−1.3
Occupational Stayer									
% below half median	14.2	13.2	−1.0	14.9	14.2	−0.7	16.0	14.7	−1.3
% between 50% and 150% of median	55.6	58.6	3.0	53.6	55.3	1.7	53.6	56.5	2.9
% 1.5 times above median	30.2	28.3	−1.9	31.5	30.5	−1.0	30.4	28.8	−1.6

Notes: Samples are limited to those who have positive earnings and a job in both wave 1 and wave 12.

Discussion and Conclusions

As has been often noted, especially by economists, the job structure has become more polarized in recent decades in the United States. Automation and related computerized technologies replaced many jobs which are characterized by well-defined, routine activities that do not require complex analytical skills, personalized service, or immediate environmental adaptability. We have used data from nationally representative samples of the labor force to further investigate this phenomenon. Our results largely confirm prior research that has found evidence for this trend. The occupational structure has indeed become more polarized since 1980 and that trend continued through the first decade of the twenty-first century.

Using more recent data up through 2015, we have ascertained that 2011 is the year when employment in the lowest quintile of occupations reached a maximum while employment in the third quintile reached a minimum. Since that time, however, job polarization does not appear to have increased. A pattern tilting towards a little more occupational upgrading has occurred since 2011. Our most recent data are for 2015 which is not a long time after 2011 so no strong conclusion may be drawn. Nonetheless, our findings suggest that the trend towards increased polarization is not currently ongoing.

Our analysis has also revealed that the overall trend towards polarization occurred as the product of two contrary patterns that differ by gender. For men, occupational downgrading was extensive while for women occupational upgrading was widespread. The latter two trends when combined with assortative mating (i.e., wealthier women marrying wealthier men) have resulted in a distribution of equivalized household income that is more unequal and polarized than the occupational structure. The popular perception of polarization may thus be somewhat greater than the actual bifurcation of the job structure due to a sort of "multiplier" effect generated by assortative mating. Indeed, equivalized household income has become slightly more unequal since 2011 whereas the occupational structure has not.

Another relevant trend during the last few decades is that educational attainment has risen considerably. The proportion of the labor force without a high school degree is now less than one in ten while more than two out of three workers have at least some college (i.e., post-secondary) education. Rising college completion has been greater for women than for men, which in part accounts for the pronounced occupational upgrading among women.

It is difficult to argue, however, that the distribution of educational attainment has become more polarized. In 1980 almost two out of three workers had no college or post-secondary education. By 2015, the corresponding figure declined by more than half (i.e., 30.8%). While persons with a bachelor's or graduate degree have increased since 1980, that increase has not been as large as the decline at the lower end of the educational distribution. Accordingly, across the five educational levels (i.e., LTHS, HSG, SC, BA, GRAD), the index of dissimilarity relative to a uniform distribution is greater for 1980 than for 2015.

In other words, rather than becoming more polarized, the distribution of education in the labor force has become more symmetric and unimodal (almost resembling a bell-curved or normal distribution).

We are rather skeptical of the view that the occupational structure is strongly related to the educational skills of the labor force, because the polarization of the job structure occurred while the educational distribution of workers was becoming less polarized. As the supply of lower-skilled workers declined, the percentage of workers in lower-skilled jobs nevertheless increased. Over the course of 35 years, the occupational distribution became less like a bell-curved distribution while the educational distribution became more like one. These patterns presumably emanate from the major intervening roles of capital investment, automation and globalization that mediate the relationship between the educational distribution and the job structure in the US labor market.

In this process, workers with only a high school degree or less became predominantly concentrated in the lowest two occupational quintiles in contrast to their distribution in 1980. Workers with some post-secondary schooling but no bachelor's degree also experienced a decline in their occupational standing over this period. On the other hand, workers with a graduate degree and most workers with a bachelor's degree were able to maintain their employment in the upper two quintiles of the job structure and were thus not substantially disadvantaged by polarization. Having a bachelor's degree seems to be the demarcation point for which the occupational downgrading associated with polarization begins. In fact, our findings imply that nearly two-thirds of workers in the upper two quintiles of the occupational structure have at least a bachelor's degree in 2015 in contrast to about one-third in 1980.

These trends could be interpreted as indicating the growing importance of relative educational attainment in the twenty-first-century labor market (Thurow, 1975; Bills, 2016). Depending upon relative (or "positional" [Di Stasio, Bol, & Van de Werfhorst, 2016]) educational attainment, workers get allocated to a higher level of occupational attainment. As lower-level occupations become more prominent due to automation hollowing out the job distribution by eliminating many middle-level occupations, workers with lower relative educational attainment become employed in lower-level jobs even though these workers have a higher absolute level of educational attainment compared to workers who held those same jobs decades ago. This emphasis on relative educational attainment recognizes the important roles that firms and capital technology play in mediating the relationship between workers' education levels and the occupational structure.

Regarding racial differentials, relative educational differentials also likely play a major role. Asians have the highest level of educational attainment and are the most likely to be employed in the highest quintile of the occupational distribution. Hispanics have the lowest level of educational attainment and have the lowest levels of occupational employment. In recent decades as the percentage of African Americans with college degrees has increased, employment in the highest occupational quintile has risen as well.

Workers' careers obviously extend over a period of years of course and cannot be fully depicted in terms of cross-sectional snapshots. When we therefore investigated longitudinal data, the results show that changes in earnings are often related to occupational changes. While both earnings gains as well as earnings declines may occur when workers change their occupations, earnings declines appear to be somewhat more common especially in recessionary years.

Nonetheless, we would emphasize that our findings indicate that the relationship between occupational change and earnings is only modest. Some occupational changes result in positive earnings gains even during recessionary years. Furthermore, even during recessionary years, occupational stayers can have positive earnings gains and remain in the upper portion of the earnings distribution over time. So, while quite important, the occupational structure does not have a deterministic influence on the earnings distribution overall (Kim & Sakamoto, 2008). In addition, as we have already discussed, the income of other family members constitutes an additional layering buffer between the occupational structure and the actual economic wellbeing of individuals.

In conclusion, we concur that concerns about job polarization are real and well founded. The occupational structure has indeed become more bifurcated in recent decades and that is undoubtedly an unequalizing force for the distribution of earnings. The rising sophistication of automated technologies may quite possibly continue in the future and may possibly further reduce employment in other relatively well-paying jobs. Public policy makers need to be concerned about the extent to which increasing educational attainment at the lower end of the distribution can effectively counter the growth of lower-skilled jobs.

On a more positive note, the trend towards polarization may be tapering off. Firms and workers may be adjusting better now to find other sorts of valued jobs that are beyond the economic reach of current capital technologies. The job distribution is not identical to the earnings distribution, and the incomes of other family members may sometimes compensate for the lowered earnings associated with lesser-skilled jobs. We hope that efficacious public policy measures may be developed to ameliorate the more negative consequences of job polarization.

References

Acemoglu, D., & Autor, D. (2011). Skills, tasks and technologies: implications for employment and earnings. In O. Ashenfelter & D. Card (Eds.), *Handbook of labor economics* (pp. 1043–1171). North Holland: Elsevier.

Autor, D. H. (2014). Skills, education, and the rise of earnings inequality among the other 99 percent. *Science, 344*(6186), 843–851.

Autor, D. H., Katz, L. F., & Kearney, M. S. (2006). The polarization of the US labor market. *American Economic Review, 96*(2), 189–194.

Autor, D. H., Levy, F., & Murnane, R. J. (2003). The skill content of recent technological change: an empirical exploration. *Quarterly Journal of Economics, 118*(4), 1279–1333.

Bills, D. B. (2016). Congested credentials: the material and positional economies of schooling. *Research in Social Stratification and Mobility, 43*, 65–70.

Brandolini, A., & Smeeding, T. M. (2009). Income inequality in richer and OECD countries. In W. Salverda, B. Noland, & T. M. Smeeding (Eds.), *The Oxford handbook of economic inequality* (pp.71–100). New York, NY: Oxford University Press.

Cappelli, P. (2001). Assessing the decline of internal labor markets. In I. Berg & A. Kalleberg (Eds.), *Sourcebook on labor markets: Evolving structures and processes* (pp. 207–245). New York, NY: Kluwer Plenum Publishers.

Di Stasio, V., Bol, T., & Van de Werfhorst, H. G., (2016). What makes education positional? Institutions, over-education and the competition for jobs. *Research in Social Stratification and Mobility, 43*, 53–63.

Fischer, C. S., & Hout, M. (2006). *Century of difference: How America changed in the last one hundred years*. New York, NY: Russell Sage Foundation.

Flores, A. (2017). *How the US Hispanic population is changing*. Washington, DC: Pew Research Center. Retrieved from www.pewresearch.org/fact-tank/2017/09/18/how-the-u-s-hispanic-population-is-changing/

Kim, C. H., & Sakamoto, A. (2008). The rise of intra-occupational wage inequality in the United States, 1983 to 2002. *American Sociological Review, 73*, 129–157.

Kim, C. H., & Sakamoto, A. (2017). Women's progress for men's gain? Gender-specific changes in the return to education as measured by family standard of living, 1990 to 2009–2011. *Demography, 54*(5), 1743–1772.

Kuznets, S. (1955). Economic growth and income inequality. *American Economic Review, 45*(1), 1–28.

Piketty, T. (2014). *Capital in the 21st century*. Cambridge, MA: Harvard University Press.

Reich, M., Gordon, D. M., & Edwards, R. C. (1973). A theory of labor market segmentation. *American Economic Review, 63*(2), 359–365.

Sakamoto, A., Goyette, K. A., & Kim, C. H. (2009). The socioeconomic attainments of Asian Americans. *Annual Review of Sociology, 35*, 255–276.

Sakamoto, A., Kim, C. H., & Woo, H. (2012). An empirical test of alternative theories of educational stratification. *Education Research International, 2012*, 1–11.

Sakamoto, A., & Wang, S. X. (2017). Occupational and organizational effects on wages among college-educated workers in 2003 and 2010. *Social Currents, 4*(2), 175–195.

Semega, J. L., Fontenot, K. R., & Kollar, M. A. (2017). Income and poverty in the United States: 2016. *Current Population Report* no. P60–259. Washington, DC: US Government Printing Office.

Stiglitz, J. E. (2015). Inequality in America: A policy agenda for a stronger future. *The ANNALS of the American Academy of Political and Social Science, 657*, 8–20.

Thurow, L. C. (1975). *Generating inequality*. New York, NY: Basic Books.

Wilkinson, R. G., & Pickett, K. E. (2009). Income inequality and social dysfunction. *Annual Review of Sociology, 35*, 493–511.

Appendix

Appendix Table 6.9A *Descriptive statistics*

	1980	1990	2000	2015	Change (2015–1980)
Gender (%)					
- Male	57.9	54.6	52.5	52.0	−5.9
- Female	42.1	45.5	47.5	48.0	+5.9
Race/ethnicity (%)					
- Whites	82.3	78.4	71.8	63.3	−19.0
- Blacks	9.8	10.1	10.9	11.8	+2.0
- Hispanics	5.4	7.9	11.2	16.6	+11.2
- Asians	1.6	2.8	3.8	5.7	+4.1
- Other races	0.6	0.7	2.4	2.7	+2.1
Education (%)					
- Less than high school	28.8	23.1	14.4	9.2	−19.6
- High school graduate	35.8	30.3	27.4	21.9	−13.9
- Some college	19.6	23.1	32.3	36.8	+17.2
- Bachelor's degree	10.0	15.4	16.9	20.7	+10.7
- Graduate degree	5.7	8.1	9.0	11.4	+5.7

Notes: Data are from IPUMS and American Community Survey. Samples are limited to persons aged 18 to 64 who have positive annual earnings.

Appendix Table 6.9B *Educational attainment by year and gender*

	LTHS	HSG	SC	BA	Grad	Sum
Total						
1980	28.8	35.8	19.6	10.0	5.7	100.0
1990	23.1	30.3	23.1	15.4	8.1	100.0
2000	12.9	27.1	32.6	17.8	9.6	100.0
2005	11.3	28.7	31.1	18.8	10.2	100.0
2010	9.9	22.8	36.6	19.9	10.8	100.0
2015	8.9	21.9	36.2	21.3	11.8	100.0
Men						
1980	30.8	33.2	18.5	10.5	7.1	100.0
1990	24.3	29.3	21.9	15.6	8.9	100.0
2000	14.9	27.6	30.1	17.5	10.0	100.0
2005	13.4	29.8	28.7	18.1	10.1	100.0
2010	12.0	24.3	34.4	19.0	10.3	100.0
2015	10.8	24.0	34.6	20.0	10.7	100.0
Women						
1980	26.1	39.4	21.2	9.4	3.9	100.0
1990	21.8	31.6	24.5	15.2	7.0	100.0
2000	10.6	26.6	35.4	18.2	9.2	100.0
2005	8.9	27.4	33.9	19.6	10.3	100.0
2010	7.6	21.1	39.0	20.9	11.4	100.0
2015	6.9	19.6	37.9	22.7	12.9	100.0

Notes: Data are from IPUMS 1980, IPUMS 1990, IPUMS 2000 and American Community Survey. Samples are limited to persons aged 18 to 64 who have positive annual earnings.

7 Changes in the Legal Landscape

Chester Hanvey and Kayo Sady

Introduction

As outlined in this volume, the changing nature of work offers both opportunities and challenges for organizations. Among those challenges are issues related to maintaining compliance with labor and employment legal obligations. As work, and the workforce, changes, traditional strategies for maintaining compliance may no longer meet organizational needs and legal requirements.

For over half a century, social scientists have been applying scientific principles to measure compliance with employment laws, to advise organizations and serve as expert witnesses in litigation. Both of our consulting practices have focused on addressing a variety of issues in the context of litigation, and through that work we have observed a variety of changes to legal issues commonly addressed by organizations. In this chapter, we highlight several areas in which the changing nature of work, the workforce, and the legal landscape may pose legal challenges for organizations going forward. We focus on four primary areas: (1) the classification of workers as "employees" versus "independent contractors," (2) the occurrence of off-the-clock work, (3) pay equity, and (4) applications of big data for solving human capital problems.

In the following section, we provide a brief background on the relevant legal standards, after which we address each of the four topic areas. We also note that we offer our understanding of legal standards based on our consulting and expert witness work in these areas. However, we are not attorneys so the information presented below should not be considered legal advice. The information below is intended to provide readers a broad overview of complex legal topics. However, context always matters when dealing these issues, and consulting a labor and employment attorney is often necessary to fully understand these issues.

Legal Landscape

Social scientists are frequently called upon to apply research methods expertise to answer questions related to legal compliance in organizations. The specific organizational policies or practices that are under scrutiny may vary widely, but industrial–organizational (I-O) psychologists working in this arena are typically focusing on two compliance areas: (1) wage and hour laws, and/or (2) equal employment opportunity (EEO) or, alternatively, anti-discrimination laws. Wage and hour laws provide a variety of protections to employees related to their wages and work hours. EEO laws protect applicants and employees from discrimination on the basis of protected class membership, including race, sex, national origin, age, disability and several other defined protected classes. We summarize the general legal framework in these two areas, although more thorough treatments can be found in Hanvey (2018)[1] and Gutman, Koppes, & Vodanovich (2010).[2]

Wage and Hour Law

Within the United States, employees are provided a variety of legal protections related to the wages they are paid and the hours they may work. These are known as "wage and hour" laws. At the federal level, wage and hour protections are primarily based on the Fair Labor Standards Act (FLSA) of 1938, along with associated regulations, promulgated by the US Department of Labor (DOL). The FLSA and accompanying DOL regulations include four basic requirements for employers: (1) establishes the minimum hourly wage that employees must be paid (29 U.S.C. § 206; US Department of Labor, n.d.a), (2) requires overtime for all hours worked in excess of 40 hours per workweek (29 U.S.C. § 207), (3) forbids "oppressive child labor" (29 U.S.C. § 212; 29 C.F.R. § 570; US Department of Labor, 2013), and (4) requires employers to maintain specific employment records related to wages and hours (29 U.S.C. § 212; 29 C.F.R. § 570; US Department of Labor, 2013). Within these basic employee protections are a variety of specific requirements that have encountered substantial legal scrutiny. I-O methods are commonly used to provide evidence to help resolve many of these disputes. For example, job analysis methods are often useful for helping to determine which employees are "exempt" from the requirement to pay overtime. When employees perform work that is not paid, the employer may be in danger of violating minimum wage or overtime requirements. I-O methods are often used to measure the frequency and duration of activities performed before clock-in or after clock-out to help resolve these allegations. In addition, disputes may arise over whether workers meet the legal definition of an "employee" of the organization or some other non-employee classification of worker such as an independent contractor. I-O methods are often useful in measuring several aspects of these classifications, which are described in more detail in a later section.

We should also note that in addition to federal wage and hour protections, many states have their own versions of wage and hour laws, which may offer additional employee protections beyond those in the FLSA. When federal and state laws differ, the more restrictive and employee-friendly law controls, thus

---

[1] Hanvey (2018) provides a more detailed review of wage and hour laws and methods and analyses used to address these issues.
[2] Gutman et al. (2010) provides a more detailed review of EEO laws and relevant court cases.

requiring employers to be compliant with wage and hour requirements within all states in which they have employees, which may require different human resources policies within the same organization, depending on the state in which the employee works. State laws may set more restrictive thresholds for protections than the FLSA, like higher minimum wages, or may provide additional requirements that are not covered by the FLSA, such as meal and rest breaks.

Allegations of wage and hour violations may be initiated by the Department of Labor or by private plaintiff attorneys. The vast majority of the high-profile wage and hour cases are brought as class or collective actions, in which one or more named plaintiffs seek to represent a group of current or former employees who have common claims or are "similarly situated." Before these cases can proceed to trial, the class or collective action must first be "certified" by the court, based on whether the claims of the group are similar enough to be resolved on a classwide basis. If the class or collective action is certified, legal exposure for organizations increases substantially as these actions may include tens of thousands of current or former employees. As a result, it is not uncommon for settlements or judgments to exceed tens of millions of dollars (see, e.g., Seyfarth Shaw, 2018). This creates a significant financial motivation for organizations to ensure compliance with wage and hour laws.

EEO Law

In 1964, President Lyndon B. Johnson signed the Civil Rights Act[3] (CRA) into law. Title VII of that Act prohibits any employment practice that discriminates against individuals based on their race, sex, national origin, color, or religion. Employment practices covered include the terms, conditions, privileges of employment, and compensation. Thus, Title VII claims may involve allegations of discrimination in hiring, firing, promotion, compensation, or other meaningful employment outcomes.

Title VII cases may involve a single individual alleging illegal discrimination or a *class* of individuals alleging illegal discrimination. Cases in which a sole individual alleges that s/he is the victim of a negative employment outcome because of her/his protected class status (race, sex, national origin, color, or religion) are known as d*isparate treatment* cases. These cases involve allegations that an employer *intentionally* discriminated against an employee. Cases of such intentional discrimination that affect an entire group of individuals with the same protected class subgroup status (e.g., a group of women, a group of Black/African Americans) are known as *disparate treatment – pattern or practice* cases. Alternatively, if a facially neutral process (such as a pre-employment test) produces differential outcomes depending on protected class subgroup status, the case is known as a *disparate impact* (aka *adverse impact*) case.

---

[3] The full text of the Civil Rights Act of 1964 is available online at www.eeoc.gov/laws/statutes/titlevii.cfm

In classwide allegations of discrimination, statistical techniques are applied to evaluate the statistical and practical significance of protected class subgroup differences in employment outcomes. For the interested reader, there are several comprehensive resources that describe the techniques and their proper application (Cohen, Aamodt, & Dunleavy, 2010; Morris & Dunleavy, 2016).

In addition to protections afforded the five protected classes specified by the CRA (1964), applicants and employees aged 40 or older are protected (Age Discrimination in Employment Act 1967), as are applicants and employees with disabilities (Americans with Disabilities Act 1990). Further, specific to protections related to compensation, the Equal Pay Act (EPA 1963) prohibits discrimination in pay on the basis of sex. A discussion of the differences between Title VII of the CRA (1964) and EPA (1963) compensation protections and legal standards can be found in other published works (Sady, Aamodt, & Cohen, 2015).

Finally, protections for employees based on sexual orientation and gender identity are found primarily in state legislation. While the EEOC accepts claims of sexual orientation or gender identity discrimination based on Title VII protections against discrimination based on sex, federal protection (in the private sector) from discrimination based on those characteristics does not formally exist. At the time that this chapter was being written, however, 26 states and the District of Columbia provided protection against employment discrimination based on sexual orientation and gender identity; one additional state protected against discrimination based on sexual orientation only.[4]

There are three federal agencies that enforce Title VII: Equal Employment Opportunity Commission (EEOC), Office of Federal Contracts Compliance Programs (OFCCP), and Department of Justice's (DOJ) Civil Right Division. EEOC enforcement is based on complaints brought against employers by employees, whereas OFCCP enforcement is based on the results of compliance audits to which federal contractors are subject. In rare cases, the Department of Justice may become involved in Title VII cases. Title VII lawsuits may also be levied against employers by private plaintiff's attorneys, with no government agency involved.

As with wage and hour cases, employment discrimination cases can pose significant costs to organizations, directly (legal fees and financial remedies) and indirectly (public relations and damage to brand). Thus, most organizations are incentivized to comply with applicable non-discrimination laws.

Employee or Independent Contractor?

In the modern workplace, a variety of more complex variations to the traditional employee–employer relationship have emerged. The "traditional" relationship between a full-time employee and a single employer is increasingly being supplanted by a variety of alternative work arrangements that reflect new

---

[4] More specific information can be found at www.hrc.org/state-maps/employment

and innovative staffing models. The emergence of the new models is reflected by the "gig economy" and other forms of "on demand," "contingent," or other temporary workers. Under these staffing models, workers provide a service on a temporary or "gig" basis and may perform services for multiple organizations concurrently. At many organizations, these workers are classified as independent contractors, rather than employees. Research has found that this form of work is a growing trend. For example, the number of independent contractors in the workforce has increased substantially over the past 20 years (Hathaway & Muro, 2016; US Government Accountability Office, 2016), and in 2015, between 5% and 33% of all US workers were considered "contingent workers" depending on how contingent worker is defined (US Government Accountability Office, 2015).

Implications for Workers and Organizations

In order for FLSA protections to apply to a worker, he or she must be an "employee" of the employer. In contrast, independent contractors are self-employed and therefore not employees of the organization for which they provide services. This has important consequences, as non-employee workers, such as independent contractors,[5] are not entitled to FLSA protections including minimum wage, overtime pay, and meal or rest breaks.[6] In addition, non-employee workers do not receive certain benefits such as family and medical leave and unemployment compensation insurance. The classification of workers as non-employees also has a financial impact on federal and state governments because the tax, unemployment insurance, and workers' compensation contributions are lower for non-employees than employees (US Department of Labor, n.d.b).

Some employers have financial incentives for classifying workers as independent contractors rather than employees. By doing so, they decrease their tax burden, reduce payroll costs, maximize staffing flexibility, and minimize costs associated with workers' tools and equipment. On the other hand, they may sacrifice control over the work that is performed by these workers, which can impact product quality. Further, their legal risk may increase if the classification is challenged.

Although some independent contractors pursue litigation to achieve employee status, many are highly satisfied with their independent contractor status (Manyika, Lund, Bughin, Robinson, Mischke, & Mahajan, 2016). Some workers believe the freedom and flexibility offered by an independent contractor relationship outweighs the benefits offered by employment status. Regardless of worker preference, the classification of workers must comply with the legal standards, which are summarized in the following section.

---

[5] Though the majority of attention in this chapter is paid to independent contractors, there are several other forms of non-employee relationships that have faced legal scrutiny, including: interns, trainees, and minor league and collegiate athletes.
[6] Meal and rest break requirements vary by state. See US Department of Labor (2017a, 2017b) for state-specific requirements.

Legal Standards for Employee Classification

In recent years, classification of workers as independent contractors has come under increased challenge from government enforcement agencies and private party plaintiffs. Many of the most well-known companies in the gig economy such as Uber, Lyft, Postmates, and Amazon Prime Now have faced litigation in this matter (Leberstein, 2012). The DOL has described the misclassification of employees as independent contractors as "one of the most serious problems facing affected workers, employers and the entire economy" (US Department of Labor, n.d.b). As a result, the Wage and Hour Division within the DOL has increased enforcement efforts to reduce misclassification of employees as independent contractors (US Department of Labor, n.d.b).

Under the FLSA, the term "employ" has been defined broadly as "suffer or permit to work," meaning that the employer directs the work or allows the work to take place. The DOL uses a multi-factor "economic realities test" that assesses whether a worker is truly in business for himself or herself or is economically dependent on the employer (i.e., independent contractor vs. employee).

One of the reasons that compliance with independent contractor classification is particularly challenging is that the specific factors to consider differ between government agencies, the courts, and even specific organizations when litigated. In addition to the DOL, other federal agencies, such as the Internal Revenue Service, along with some state agencies, like the California Employment Development Department, have published separate guidance on how to determine whether a worker is an employee or an independent contractor. In addition, each year state and federal courts issue decisions in independent contractor misclassification cases. These decisions shape the way the law is interpreted and applied. As an illustration of the lack of consistent criteria, the DOL Fact Sheet states that "there is no single rule or test for determining whether an individual is an independent contractor or an employee for purposes of the FLSA" (US Department of Labor, 2014). In addition, many states have alternative tests for independent contractors, which may be based on statute, agency interpretations, or court decisions. A recent example is the application of a three-factor "ABC Test" in states such as California, Massachusetts, and New Jersey.[7]

Compiling a list of all relevant criteria can be complex and often benefits from consultation with legal counsel. The interested reader should refer to Hanvey (2018) for a more detailed review of relevant factors cited by various publications.

---

[7] The three factors specified by the California Supreme Court in *Dynamex Operations West, Inc. v. Superior Court* are: (a) Is the worker free from the control and direction of the hiring entity in the performance of the work, both under the contract for the performance of the work and in fact? (b) Does the worker perform work that is outside the usual course of the hiring entity's business? (c) Is the worker customarily engaged in an independently established trade, occupation, or business of the same nature as the work performed for the hiring entity?

Methods for Measuring Employment Status

When studying independent contractor classification, it is necessary to consider which of the relevant factors can reliably be measured. Typically, the factor most amenable to measurement using methods from I-O psychology (or related disciplines) is the degree to which the organization "controls" the work performed by the worker, a factor which is typically considered relevant by all agencies and courts. When measuring control, it is important to develop a thorough understanding of the organization as control may look different depending on the industry, organization, or individual worker.

There are two groups of data collection approaches that are useful for measuring control: observational approaches and self-report approaches. Observations involve trained job analysts directly observing and systematically documenting workers' activities. Observations in this context are typically done in person because a live observer can move with the worker, hear conversations, collect contextual information about the work environment, and gather detailed information about the worker's activities such as what she/he is reading, who she/he is interacting with, and the nature of those interactions. Through observation, the amount of time interacting with company representatives, for example, can be precisely calculated along with the nature of those interactions (e.g., receiving instructions or sharing information). These data are often considered relevant aspects of control.

Self-report approaches may be in the form of verbal structured interviews or written/online surveys. Both involve workers, supervisors, or company representatives self-reporting various aspects of the worker's environment. This may include items such as: who determines the work schedule, who provides equipment, whether the worker works for other companies, whether the worker possesses specialized training, whether certain activities are prohibited by the organization, how decisions are made, or organizational policies.

Each data collection approach offers unique information and can be used to supplement or verify the accuracy of data collected using other methods. These data are often useful in helping organizational decision makers or the court make an informed determination about the proper classification of workers.

Despite the available published guidance and strategies for measuring relevant factors, many organizations continue to encounter substantial uncertainty surrounding whether staffing models that involved independent contractors are legally compliant. The legal uncertainty is likely to persist as the changing nature of work leads to new forms of work and additional variations of the employment relationship. To the extent possible, organizations should consider the legal risks associated with misclassification of independent contractors when making a decision whether to implement, or continue using, these staffing models.

Off-the-Clock Work

A second wage and hour issue that has become increasingly frequent in recent years involves allegations that employees were not paid for all time worked. The hours worked by non-exempt employees are typically tracked using a time card system in which employees record the time they began and finished working each shift. Employees are often said to be "on the clock" between the time they clock in and the time they clock out, that is, the time for which they are being paid. The time before or after an employee's shift is referred to as "off the clock." When employees perform compensable work during a time for which they are not being paid, they are said to be performing "off-the-clock work," which may result in the employee initiating litigation to recover unpaid wages and overtime.

There are many ways that off-the-clock work may occur. Some of the more common allegations include employees starting work before clocking in, clocking out before finishing work, performing work from home but not reporting the time (including phone calls or emails), working through unpaid meal breaks, donning or doffing required uniforms or equipment before or after their shift, time shaving (i.e., paying employees for fewer hours than actually worked) or improper timeclock "rounding" practices. Employers can be liable for significant damages for not paying all time worked. Under the FLSA, violations are triggered if (a) the employee is not paid overtime when the unpaid time exceeds 40 hours in workweek, or (b) the employee is paid less than minimum wage when the unpaid hours result in the employee's hourly rate falling below the minimum amount.[8]

Evaluating off-the-clock work claims involves determining what activities constitute "work" (i.e., compensable activities) and then measuring how frequently these activities occur off the clock and their duration. Often this is accomplished using time-and-motion observation methods (live or video) or by analyzing electronic data such as computer logins, store alarm data, or email or phone timestamps.

Many organizations actively monitor employee timekeeping practices to ensure that employees are paid for all time worked and to avoid potential liability associated with employees working off the clock. For example, many managers regularly review employee time cards to ensure they are accurate. Implementation of electronic timekeeping systems also enhances the precision of time measurement because they are not susceptible to "rounding" that is common when employees self-report their time (e.g., report time to the nearest five minutes). However, employers sacrifice some of their ability to closely monitor employee timekeeping practices when employees work in more autonomous work settings. For example, monitoring the activities of remote employees is far more challenging than monitoring employees in the same

---

[8] For example, if an employee who is paid minimum wage works off the clock, their actual pay rate would fall below minimum wage when the unpaid time is added and divided by the amount paid.

physical workspace as their supervisor. In addition, the widespread use of company laptops or smartphones may also present a risk of noncompliance. These devices often give employees the ability to perform work at times outside of their work shift and can present an opportunity for off-the-clock work to occur if that time is not reported and paid.

Strategies to prevent this from occurring may include performing random audits of time records to ensure accuracy, training employees on proper timekeeping practices, or training managers not to contact non-exempt employees when they are off the clock (or ensure that the time is reported if they must). In some organizations, access to company resources such as email can be restricted when the employee is not clocked in or out of the office.

Though all organizations with non-exempt employee should be concerned with preventing off-the-clock work, changes in the nature of work in some organizations may present increased opportunities for noncompliance or create additional challenges in measuring compliance. The potential legal risks associated with off-the-clock work may warrant consideration of new strategies to minimize the risk, to the extent possible.

Pay Equity

In 1964 (the year after the Equal Pay Act was passed), the women's-to-men's earnings ratio was 59.10% in the United States, translating to a gender pay gap of approximately 41% (US Department of Labor, n.d.c). In contrast, in July 2018, the United States Department of Labor reported the women's-to-men's earnings ratio to be 81.30%, translating to a gender pay gap of approximately 19%[9] (US Bureau of Labor Statistics, 2018). Despite being reduced by 50% over the past 50 years, the national wage gap numbers are still striking. They do not, however, provide insight as to *why* the differences exist. For example, as indicated by the Women's Bureau at the Department of Labor, unequal distributions of men and women in lower-paying occupations and in capacities as caregivers account for significant proportions of the gap, although differences in negotiation willingness and strategies also may contribute (US Department of Labor, n.d.d). Of course, instances of illegal discrimination in compensation practices are potential explanations of unaccounted-for gaps, as well.

Conceptually, pay equity may be viewed through two lenses. Questions of external equity focus on pay relative to the relevant labor market; questions of internal equity, on the other hand, focus on pay relative to a comparative other within the same organization (Sady & Hanvey, 2018). Pay equity as it relates to equal employment opportunity (EEO) law concerns a specific type

---

[9] The gap further widens for Black/African American and Hispanic women, as their earnings are reported to be approximately 65% and 63% (respectively) of those reported for White men.

of internal equity question: Is an individual[10] paid fairly relative to (1) a comparative other(s) in the organization, (2) who does not share the same protected class status, (3) given the legitimate, nondiscriminatory reasons for observed pay differences?

When litigated, pay equity legal cases are often decided based on (1) whether aspects of the plaintiffs' and comparators' jobs are similar enough to allow comparison and (2) whether there are nondiscriminatory reasons for the pay differences. In order for other employees to be considered comparators, Title VII requires that they are "similarly situated,"[11] which the Equal Employment Opportunity Commission's (EEOC's) compliance manual defines as jobs that "generally involve similar tasks, require similar skill, effort, and responsibility, working conditions, and are similarly complex or difficult" (US Equal Employment Opportunity Commission, 2000). In addition, other objective factors, such as minimum qualifications, may also be important to consider in determining similarly situated.

If a group of similarly situated employees is established, regression analyses are typically used to evaluate whether the pay disparity between protected class subgroups (e.g., women versus men) is accounted for by legitimate, nondiscriminatory factors, such as prior job experience, tenure, education, or job performance (Paetzold & Willborn, 2013).[12] If the difference in average pay between protected class subgroups is not statistically significant after accounting (i.e. controlling) for the legitimate pay factors, illegal discrimination is not inferred.

The following examples of legitimate nondiscriminatory factors have proved important in noteworthy pay equity cases, but the list is in no way comprehensive:

- Educational backgrounds, experiences, and qualifications (*Warren v. Solo Cup Co.*, 2008);
- Prior work experience and actual job duties (*Coser v. Moore*, 1984);
- Actual job title or the job duties (*Anderson v. Westinghouse Savannah River Co.*, 2005);
- Type or level of the employees' applied skills (*Cooper v. S. Co.*, 2003);
- Skill, effort, or responsibility (*Sims-Fingers v. City of Indianapolis*, 2007).

Pay Equity over Time

In many ways, the pay equity legal landscape in the United States has changed very little in the past 50 years. Title VII of the Civil Rights Act of 1964 and the Equal Pay Act of 1963 are the prevailing standards by which

---

[10] Or a class of individuals who share protected class status (e.g., same sex).
[11] The standard for similarity under the EPA (1963) is *substantially equal*, which is typically interpreted as requiring a higher standard of similarity.
[12] The four factors listed are examples and are in no way comprehensive of the legitimate factors that may explain pay disparities.

claims of discrimination in pay are filed. Further, case law has not offered any particularly groundbreaking rulings to shift the way that pay equity is litigated. The past half-decade, however, has seen a proliferation of updated regulations that may influence the quantity and nature of pay equity issues looking forward.

It could be reasonably argued that the election of Barack Obama as president of the United States was the single biggest catalyst for the swell of attention on pay equity issues over the past decade. The first bill that President Obama signed into law was the Lilly Ledbetter Fair Pay Act (2009) (Stolberg, 2009) which amended the 180-day statute of limitations for filing an equal pay lawsuit under the Civil Rights Act (1964). The law specifies that the statute of limitations is not tied to the initial discriminatory pay action but rather resets with each paycheck that reflects the disparity created by the discriminatory pay action.

Under the Obama administration, pay equity became a major enforcement priority for the Office of Federal Compliance Programs (OFCCP), which enforces the affirmative action and anti-discrimination obligations of federal contractors and subcontractors (i.e. those that do business with the government and are therefore paid by taxpayers).[13] Unlike the complaint-driven investigations brought by the EEOC, investigations conducted by OFCCP are driven by annual audits of federal contractors' policies, programs, and human resource data. As part of the audit process, a contractor's compensation data may be analyzed to identify unexplained disparities in pay between protected class subgroups.

In 2013, OFCCP rescinded the President Bush–era pay equity enforcement standards and implemented Directive 2013-03 (referenced as *Directive 307*), which provided OFCCP greater latitude in their approach to grouping employees and analyzing statistical data as part of their investigations. On the heels of Directive 307, President Obama issued Executive Order 13665 (*Non-Retaliation for Disclosure of Compensation Information*) which protects applicants and employees from negative employment actions in response to their inquiry or discussion of the compensation of themselves and others. Such protections were already afforded in Section 7 of the National Labor Relations Act (NLRA),[14] but the executive order served to emphasize the commitment of the Obama administration to ensuring pay equity and to encourage transparency. As of the writing of this chapter in August 2018, Directive 307 was replaced by Directive 2018-05 (*Analysis of Contractor Compensation Practices during a Compliance Evaluation*). The new directive is intended to be more prescriptive than Directive 307 and "reinforces OFCCP's commitment to greater transparency, consistency and efficiency in compliance evaluations."

The most significant recent changes in the pay equity legal landscape in the United States have been at the state level. Amendments to state legislation have, in some ways, eclipsed the federal anti-discrimination standards. Although

---

[13] OFCCP is responsible for enforcing Executive Order 11246, which applies only to government contractors and subcontractors.
[14] Found in the "concerted activity" clause.

most of the 50 United States and territories have long had pay discrimination laws, up until this decade they have generally reflected the Equal Pay Act language.

In 2016, California passed the *California Fair Pay Act* (CFPA), which strengthened its compensation equity laws. Updated laws soon followed for many other states:

- New York Achieves Fair Pay (2016);
- Maryland Equal Pay for Equal Work Act (2016);
- Puerto Rico Equal Pay Act (2017);
- Oregon Equal Pay Act (2017);
- Washington – Equal Pay Opportunity Act (2018);
- New Jersey – Diane B. Allen Equal Pay Act (2018);
- Massachusetts Equal Pay Act (2018).

With California leading the way in updating legislation, cases filed under the CFPA are most likely to be filed and decided before cases in other states. Because no cases have yet been decided, opining on the courts' statutory interpretation of the CFPA is speculative; however, The California Commission on the Status of Women and Girls convened a statewide, multi-stakeholder Pay Equity Task Force that published a set of resources that interpret much of the CFPA in providing guidance.[15]

Although there are differences in the specific provisions of the state laws, there are also consistent themes that distinguish the state laws from the federal Equal Pay Act (1963):

- Use of "similar" or "comparable" in defining who can be compared to whom, as opposed to "equal work." Although ostensibly minor, the different language could allow broader groupings of comparators under the law.
- Allowing comparators to span multiple locations/establishments of an organization in one analysis, as opposed to limiting the comparators to one location/establishment.
- Requiring employers to explain "entire wage differential," which could be interpreted as requiring a differential that is exactly zero rather than one that does not meet accepted conventions of statistical significance.
- Limiting permissible explanations/defenses of a wage differential to "validated" or "bona fide" factors, rather than "any factor other than sex." This could require employers to show (1) that the pay factor was unbiased and actually relied upon in setting or changing pay and/or (2) that the pay factor qualifies as part of a clearly defined set of factors, such as a seniority system, a merit system, a system measuring production, geographic location, education, training, experience, or travel requirements.

---

[15] A variety of resources approved by the Pay Equity Task Force are available online at https://women.ca.gov/california-pay-equity-task-force/ca-pay-equity-resources/

- Limiting the influence of applicant salary history in setting starting pay, either by banning the request of such information from applicants or excluding prior salary history as a legitimate explanation for current pay.
- Expanding protection beyond just sex, and incorporating race/ethnicity (as with Title VII), or other categories such as gender identity.

For those interested in keeping abreast of new pay equity legislation, there are several continually updated online resources that provide summaries and heat maps of new pay legislation (e.g. http://salaryequity.com/).

The current attention to pay equity is not circumscribed by United States borders, as Sweden, Germany, Iceland, and the United Kingdom recently passed pay equity regulations. The UK pay gap reporting requirement has received the most recent focus, likely due to the public nature of the requirements. Starting this past April (April 4, 2018), organizations with 250 or more "relevant employees" in the United Kingdom (England, Scotland, and Wales) are required to annually report:

- The difference in mean and median "pay" between all male and female employees (part time, full time, all grades/levels);
- The proportion of men and women in each "pay quartile";
- The difference in mean and median "bonus" paid to male and female employees;
- The proportion of men and women receiving bonuses.

A director or equivalent is required to endorse the veracity of the information in the pay gap report in a written statement, and companies must publish the report on their own website for three years. Further, the UK government publishes the information from all annual reports in "league tables." These requirements may be a harbinger of continual efforts across the globe to increase pay transparency in an effort to ensure pay equality between men and women.

Increased pay equity regulations aside, the focus on pay equity is likely to expand due to the combination of human nature and the proliferation of available information about pay. With respect to human nature, aspects of pay equity are rooted in theories of organizational justice and psychological contracts. Perceptions of distributive justice (Adams, 1965) underlie claims of illegal pay discrimination, as the heart of such claims are perceptions that one person's (or protected class group's) input/output ratios are unequal to a comparative other(s). Procedural, interpersonal, and informational justice (Colquitt, 2001) perceptions may not only be correlated with fair and equitable compensation practices, but may also be antecedent to claims of discrimination in that employees with high perceptions of justice view their organizations' management and policies as fair, transparent, and in the employee's best interest. Similarly, one aspect of the psychological contract is that one will be paid fairly and in good faith for the contribution that one provides the organization (Rousseau, 1995). To the extent that technology companies like glassdoor.

com or LinkedIn.com allow applicants and employees greater visibility as to the pay of others in an organization, questions of justice and fairness are likely to increase.

Use of "Big Data" for Employment Decisions

One of the most exciting recent developments in human capital management, and perhaps the most ill-defined in terms of potential legal issues, pertains to the application of big data analytics to high-stakes employment decisions. It was not very long ago that the prospect of unproctored Internet testing for high-stakes employment decisions raised considerable alarm in terms of the reliability and validity of decisions based on test scores (Tippins et al., 2006). While it is now the norm to assess employment candidates using online assessments, the concerns raised during the nascent stages of the new technology did much to spur research that established the measurement invariance of electronic, remote assessment methods compared to traditional paper-and-pencil methods and to establish parameters of testing content and method parameters that help to ensure reliable and valid assessment scores (Meade, Michels, & Lautenschlager, 2007; Vandenberg & Lance, 2000). The application of big data analytic techniques to aid in human capital staffing is similarly fraught with unknown implications, and parameters around appropriate and legal use of such methods are likely to develop over time.

As noted by other organizational researchers, big data are defined by the amount of information available (volume), the degree of differences in the types of information available (variety), and the speed with which the information changes (velocity). Further, considerations of the trustworthiness (veracity) of the various data points are inherent in big data questions (Tonidandel, King, & Cortina, 2015). From a recruiting standpoint, access to such data is increasingly available to organizations given the proliferation of online footprints created by potential employees (through postings, social media accounts, and other professional and personal activities). Software programs such as Python make quick work of scraping and collating such information for huge numbers of people (Landers, Brusso, Cavanaugh, & Collmus, 2016). From a selection and promotion perspective, big data methods have been shown to be at least as good as traditional prediction methods (such as ordinary least squares regression) with large sample sizes, and better with the relatively small sample sizes that describe most historical criterion-related validation research (Putka, Beatty, & Reeder, 2017). As the complexity in both data and statistical methods increases, the ability of employers to explain their decision-making process and defend against challenges of illegal employment discrimination may increase in difficulty.

In October 2016, the EEOC held a public hearing on the use of big data in the employment context (US Equal Employment Opportunity Commission,

2016). One of the takeaways from the testimony of employment law and testing experts during the hearing was that, just as with traditional assessment, scoring, and prediction methods, the use of big data analytic tools in the employment space can be, but is not necessarily, fraught with legal issues. Ultimately, the appropriateness of the practice will be determined by the knowledge and sophistication of the practitioners designing and implementing the practice.

The Uniform Guidelines on Employee Selection Procedures ("Uniform Guidelines" or "UGESP") provide the standards by which federal enforcement agencies evaluate the evidence for the validity of a selection procedure, if that procedure is found to produce adverse impact. To the extent that big data methods are applied to source, identify, sort, and select human capital talent, aspects of the process may be challenged as discriminatory if protected class subgroup differences arise. Using typical challenges to the traditional testing paradigm to illustrate, several issues of defensibility might be anticipated:

1. **Data relevance and legality.** Sourcing applicant or employee data via web-scraping tools can lead to problems akin to the bycatch associated with commercial gillnetting – some of what is collected or used may be undesirable at best and illegal at worst. For example, job-unrelated information about criminal history, socioeconomic status, or disability could be problematic if used inappropriately. Moreover, whereas in traditional recruitment and selection processes, the provided candidate information is largely voluntary, big data tools may bypass consent and collate individuals' information without their expressed permission. While not necessarily illegal, increasing attention to privacy concerns and privacy rights may have future implications for the legality of such data collection.

2. **Dustbowl empiricism.** The sheer magnitude of available data points in a "big dataset" presents the opportunity for exploring sets of prediction models that modern computing power and analytic methods have made much more accessible. The ability to cycle through so much data to derive optimized prediction models is both powerful and potentially problematic if not closely monitored. Purely empirical approaches to prediction that are divorced from theory raise concerns long expressed about dustbowl empiricism (Mael & Ashforth, 1995; Mael & Hirsch, 1993); on the other hand, such explorations may open doors to new content knowledge (McAbee, Landis, & Burke, 2017). The challenge potentially facing organizations is explaining the "what" and "why" underpinning their prediction models, if protected class subgroup differences in employment outcomes result from the models. Being able to distinguish predictive factors that are *correlated with* protected class status from those that are *proxies for* protected class status is likely to distinguish practices that are successfully defended from those that are not. Further, temptations to incorporate tuning parameters into big data models that adjust based on protected class subgroup differences should be tempered by an understanding of within-group norming issues (Sackett & Wilk, 1994).

3. **The criterion problem.** The advent of big data methods does nothing to solve for the historical problem of appropriately defining performance (Austin & Villanova, 1992). The availability of robust data and sophisticated prediction methods may perpetuate problematic employment practices if the outcome predicted is one that has protected class subgroup differences and is difficult to defend as job-related. As much attention should be paid to the outcome side of the prediction equation as to the predictor side, lest "improvements" offered by big data analytic methods actually create or feed legal problems.

Conclusion

The legal risks associated with the changing nature of work warrant consideration in many organizations. In this chapter, we have highlighted four specific legal issues that have faced increased scrutiny in recent years – trends that we expect to continue. Looking ahead, we anticipate that work will continue to evolve, bringing a variety of new legal risks along with it. Political and social changes also play an important role in the forms of legal compliance that receive the most attention, which often translates into greater legal risk for organizations. It is therefore difficult to confidently predict what forms of legal compliance will be most heavily litigated in the future. However, we hope that the discussion offered here provides valuable examples for how changes to the nature of work can present new legal risks and encourages decision makers and practitioners to consider potential risks as work continues to change moving forward, regardless of the direction of that change.

Disclaimer

The views and opinions expressed in this chapter are those of the authors and do not necessarily reflect the opinions, position, or policy of Berkeley Research Group, LLC, DCI Consulting Group, Inc., or their other employees and affiliates.

References

Adams, J. S. (1965). Inequity in social exchange. In L. Berkowitz (Ed.), *Advances in experimental social psychology, Vol. 2* (pp. 267–299). New York, NY: Academic Press.

Austin, J. T., & Villanova, P. (1992). The criterion problem: 1917–1992. *Journal of Applied Psychology, 77*(6), 836–874.

Cohen, D. B., Aamodt, M. G., & Dunleavy, E. M. (2010). *Technical advisory committee report on best practices in adverse impact analyses*. Washington, DC: Center for Corporate Equality.

Colquitt, J. A. (2001). On the dimensionality of organizational justice: A construct validation of a measure. *Journal of Applied Psychology*, *86*(3), 386–400.

Gutman, A., Koppes, L., & Vodanovich, S. (2010). *EEO law and personal practices* (3rd ed.). New York, NY: Routledge, Taylor & Francis Group.

Hanvey, C. M. (2018). *Wage and hour law: Guide to methods and analysis*. New York, NY: Springer.

Hathaway, I., & Muro, M. (2016, October 13). Tracking the gig economy: New numbers. *The Brookings Institution*. Retrieved from www.brookings.edu/research/tracking-the-gig-economy-new-numbers/

Landers, R. N., Brusso, R. C., Cavanaugh, K. J., & Collmus, A. B. (2016). A primer on theory-driven webscraping: Automatic extraction of big data from the internet for use in psychological research. *Psychological Methods*, *21*, 475–492.

Leberstein, S. (2012). *Independent contractor misclassification imposes huge costs on workers and federal and state treasuries*. New York, NY: National Employment Law Project (NELP). Retrieved from http://nelp.org/content/uploads/2015/03/IndependentContractorCosts1.pdf

Mael, F. A., & Ashforth, B. E. (1995). Loyal from day one: Biodata, organizational identification, and turnover among newcomers. *Personnel Psychology*, *48*(2), 309–333.

Mael, F. A., & Hirsch, A. C. (1993). Rainforest empiricism and quasi-rationality: Two approaches to objective biodata. *Personnel Psychology*, 46(4), 719–738.

Manyika., J, Lund, S., Bughin, J., Robinson, K. Mischke, J., & Mahajan, D. (2016, October). Independent work: Choice, necessity, and the gig economy. *McKinsey Global Institute*. Retrieved from www.mckinsey.com/global-themes/employment-and-growth/independent-work-choice-necessity-and-the-gig-economy

McAbee, S. T., Landis, R. S., & Burke, M. I. (2017). Inductive reasoning: The promise of big data. *Human Resource Management Review*, *27*(2), 277–290.

Meade, A. W., Michels, L. C., & Lautenschlager, G. J. (2007). Are Internet and paper-and-pencil personality tests truly comparable? An experimental design measurement invariance study. *Organizational Research Methods*, *10*(2), 322–345.

Morris, S. B., & Dunleavy, E. M. (Eds.). (2016). *Adverse impact analysis: Understanding data, statistics, and risk*. New York, NY: Routledge.

Paetzold, R. L., & Willborn, S. L. (2013). *The statistics of discrimination: Using statistical evidence in discrimination cases*. Eagan, MN: WEST.

Putka, D. J., Beatty, A. S., & Reeder, M. (2017). Modern prediction methods: New perspectives on a common problem. *Organizational Research Methods*, *21*(3), 689–732.

Rousseau, D. (1995). *Psychological contracts in organizations: Understanding written and unwritten agreements*. Thousand Oaks, CA: Sage Publications.

Sackett, P. R., & Wilk, S. L. (1994). Within-group norming and other forms of score adjustment in preemployment testing. *American Psychologist*, *49*(11), 929–954.

Sady, K., Aamodt, M. G., & Cohen, D. (2015). Compensation equity: Who, what, when, where, why, and how. In C. Hanvey & K. Sady (Eds.), *Practitioner's guide to legal issues in organizations* (pp. 249–282). New York, NY: Springer.

Sady, K. & Hanvey, C. (2018). Pay equity. In C. Hanvey (Ed.), *Wage and hour law: Guide to methods and analysis* (pp. 171–184). New York, NY: Springer.

Seyfarth Shaw (2018). Annual workplace class action litigation report: An overview of 2017 in workplace class action litigation. *Labor Law Journal, 69*(1), 5–40.

Stolberg, S.G. (2009, January 29). Obama signs equal-pay legislation. *New York Times*. Retrieved from www.nytimes.com/2009/01/30/us/politics/30ledbetter-web.html

Tippins, N. T., Beaty, J., Drasgow, F., Gibson, W. M., Pearlman, K., Segall, D. O., & Shepherd, W. (2006). Unproctored internet testing in employment settings. *Personnel Psychology, 59*(1), 189–225.

Tonidandel, S., King, E. B., & Cortina, J. M. (Eds.). (2015). *Big data at work: The data science revolution and organizational psychology*. New York, NY: Routledge.

US Bureau of Labor Statistics. (2018). *Usual weekly earnings of wage and salary workers, second quarter 2018* (News Release USDL-18-1180). Retrieved from www.bls.gov/news.release/pdf/wkyeng.pdf

US Department of Labor. (n.d.a). *Minimum wage*. Retrieved from www.dol.gov/whd/minimumwage.htm

US Department of Labor. (n.d.b). *Misclassification of employees as independent contractors*. Retrieved from www.dol.gov/whd/workers/misclassification/

US Department of Labor. (n.d.c). *Breaking down the gender wage gap*. Retrieved from www.dol.gov/wb/media/gender_wage_gap.pdf

US Department of Labor. (n.d.d). *Women's earnings and the wage gap* [Issue Brief]. Retrieved from www.dol.gov/wb/resources/Womens_Earnings_and_the_Wage_Gap_17.pdf

US Department of Labor. (2013). *Child labor provisions for nonagricultural occupations under the Fair Labor Standards Act*. Retrieved from www.dol.gov/whd/regs/compliance/childlabor101_text.htm

US Department of Labor. (2014). *Fact sheet #13: Am I an employee? Employment relationship under the Fair Labor Standards Act* (FLSA). Retrieved from www.dol.gov/whd/regs/compliance/whdfs13.pdf

US Department of Labor. (2017a). *Minimum length of meal period required under state law for adult employees in private sector*. Retrieved from www.dol.gov/whd/state/meal.htm

US Department of Labor. (2017b). *Minimum paid rest period requirements under state law for adult employees in private sector*. Retrieved from www.dol.gov/whd/state/rest.htm

US Equal Employment Opportunity Commission. (2000). *EEOC compliance manual, section 10: Compensation discrimination*. Retrieved from www.eeoc.gov/policy/docs/compensation.html

US Equal Employment Opportunity Commission. (2016). *Use of big data has implications for equal employment opportunity, panel tells EEOC* [press release]. Retrieved fromwww.eeoc.gov/eeoc/newsroom/release/10-13-16.cfm

US Government Accountability Office. (2015). *Contingent workforce: Size, characteristics, earnings, and benefits* (GAO-15-168R). Retrieved from www.gao.gov/assets/670/669766.pdf

US Government Accountability Office. (2016). *Employment arrangements: Improved outreach could help ensure proper worker classification* (GAO-06-656). Retrieved from www.gao.gov/new.items/d06656.pdf

Vandenberg, R. J., & Lance, C. E. (2000). A review and synthesis of the measurement invariance literature: Suggestions, practices, and recommendations for organizational research. *Organizational Research Methods, 3*(1), 4–70.

Cases Cited

Anderson v. Westinghouse Savannah River Co., 406 F.3d 248, 263 (4th Cir. 2005)
Cooper v. S. Co., 260 F. Supp. 2d 1305, 1314, 1317 (N.D. Ga. 2003)
Coser v. Moore, 739 F.2d 746, 753 (2d Cir. 1984)
Dynamex operations West, Inc. v. Superior Court, 4 Cal.5th 903 (2018)
Sims-Fingers v. City of Indianapolis, 493 F.3d 768, 772 (7th Cir. 2007)
Warren v. Solo Cup Co., 516 F.3d 627, 630–31 (7th Cir. 2008)

Statutes and Regulations

Child Labor Regulations, Orders and Statements of Interpretation, 29 C.F.R. § 570.
Records to be Kept by Employers, 29 C.F.R. § 516.
Minimum Wage, 29 U.S.C. § 206.
Maximum Hours, 29 U.S.C. § 207.
Collection of Data, 29 U.S.C. § 211.
    Child Labor Provisions, 29 U.S.C. § 212.

8 The Rise and Decline of Organized Labor in the United States

American Unions from Truman to Trump

Raymond L. Hogler

At the end of World War II, membership density in American labor unions reached its historical peak of just over 34% of the eligible workforce (Freeman, 1999). The growth of union power began with Franklin D. Roosevelt's election in 1932 and the New Deal legislation of the 1930s. At the end of World War II, the 1946 congressional elections resulted in substantial gains for Republicans, who took control of both the House and the Senate, and whose immediate legislative objective was to curtail the influence of organized labor. Over President Truman's veto (Truman, 1947), Congress passed the Taft–Hartley Amendments to the National Labor Relations Act (NLRA) of 1935, and that legislation substantially modified the organizing and bargaining capabilities of labor unions.

Among its other features, Taft–Hartley enacted a series of union unfair labor practices, such as prohibiting secondary boycotts against employers, protecting employer speech opposing unionization, and authorizing states to ban compulsory payment of union dues by workers covered under a labor contract. The latter provision, referred to as "right to work," was codified in Section 14(b) of the Taft–Hartley Act (1947) and allows states to outlaw "the execution or application of agreements requiring membership in a labor organization as a condition of employment in any State or Territory in which such execution or application is prohibited by State or Territorial law." A total of 28 states have enacted right to work laws since Section 14(b), including Kentucky and Missouri in 2017 (National Conference of State Legislators, 2018).

In 1950, labor unions achieved a landmark collective bargaining success when the United Auto Workers and General Motors entered into a labor contract referred to as the "Treaty of Detroit" (Sugrue, 2012). The agreement established a compact between employers and employees under which basic compensation included wage rates, cost of living adjustments, pension protection, and healthcare (Levy & Temin, 2010). The labor relations accord between labor and management lasted until the mid-1970s, when economic conditions deteriorated and employers became unwilling to maintain high labor costs. The retrenchment of organized labor produced a drop in union membership from 22.2 percent to 15.3 percent between 1980 and 1990. During the same period, income inequality began to escalate, and by the 2016 election it had reached levels not seen since the late 1920s. Academic analysis suggested that union decline played a significant role in changing income distribution (Gordon, 2012). Inequality, declining economic opportunity, and the immiseration of white working-class men were determinative factors in the election of President Donald Trump in 2016 (Gould & Harrington, 2016). Under his administration, and absent the mitigating force of organized labor, American workers faced further economic disenchantment.

The institutional decay of America's organized labor movement, and the associated effects on work and workers, are best understood through a series of transformative historical events. Unions exist in an environment where changes in law, policy, and culture affect organizing and collective bargaining activities. This chapter surveys the evolving fortunes of American unions from the immediate postwar experience to the administration of President Trump. It begins with the set of institutional arrangements making up an era of labor–management cooperation from 1950 to 1978 (Edwards & Podgursky, 1986). The failure of the Labor Reform Bill of 1978, designed to facilitate union organizing, marked a shift in employer accommodation of unions and opened a new era of hostility to collective bargaining. According to Thomas Piketty and other economists, that same year marks the start of rising income inequality in the United States, and their research shows that union decline played an important role in that process (Cassidy, 2014).

The 2016 national elections signaled the demise of the American labor movement as a vital force in our political topography. Voters from such former union strongholds as Pennsylvania, Ohio, and Michigan switched allegiance from the Democratic to the Republican presidential candidate, disregarding the official labor position in the election. Voting patterns revealed the deep dissatisfaction of non-college educated, middle-aged white men who previously enjoyed comfortable incomes and secure work (Cohen, 2017). That demographic makes up the majority of union membership in the United States. More than any other factor, their abandonment of the Democratic Party and support for Donald Trump signifies the collapse of the American labor movement.

This chapter examines the themes sketched above. What becomes evident from the analysis is the key part unions played in our political economy during the postwar era and into the early years of the twenty-first century. As the nature of work evolves in developed countries, powerful forces will shape our responses to the attendant social and political change. Unions were instrumental in protecting the economic interests of workers. Whether they can do so in the future is an open question.

Union Power and the Politics of Class Forces, 1945–1976

The National Labor Relations (Wagner) Act of 1935 marked a revolutionary shift in American law when, for the first time, Congress enacted a federal statute governing private sector labor relations. Senator Robert

Wagner, who drafted the legislation, argued that protecting the right of workers to organize and bargain collectively would meliorate the economic disaster of the Great Depression. He added that his bill regulated national interstate commerce, which fell within the regulatory domain of federal power. Congress passed the bill, which one scholar described as the "most revolutionary law ever passed" in the United States (Klare, 1978), and President Roosevelt signed it on July 4, 1935. In October 1935, John L. Lewis and other labor leaders founded the Committee, later known as the Congress, of Industrial Organization and rapidly won union representation rights in the automobile and steel industries. The US Supreme Court declared in May 1937 that the NLRA was a constitutional exercise of federal power, which legitimated the institutional foundations of the labor movement (*Jones & Laughlin Steel Corp. v. NLRB*, 1937).

Following Roosevelt's death in April 1945, Harry Truman assumed the presidency of the United States. Truman faced difficult issues of reconversion at the end of the war, and, in response, he convened an industrial relations conference in November 1945 to deal with the transition to a peacetime economy. His approach, as he explained it, was to eliminate government controls on industry while minimizing disruption in the transition to a peacetime economy. Truman (1945a) cautioned the participants, "Our country is worried about our industrial relations. It has a right to be. That worry is reflected in the Halls of Congress in the form of all kinds of proposed legislation." The conference participants, despite Truman's urging, failed to resolve important differences between unions and management. A crucial point of disagreement dealt with the resolution of strikes, which had reached a historical peak in late 1945. As Truman (1945b) observed in his closing address, "on the all-important question of how to avoid work stoppages when these expedients have failed, the conference arrived at no accord. Failing in that, the conference was unable to attain the objective most necessary to successful reconversion." He warned that Congress would most likely act to resolve problematic labor relations issues, and a short time later, Congress passed the Taft–Hartley legislation (Labor Management Relations Act, 1947).

In its general approach and specific provisions, the Taft–Hartley amendments to the NLRA aimed to diminish the power of unions, protect the rights of individual union members, and strengthen employers' ability to resist organizing and collective negotiations. In their classic study, Harry Millis and Emily Brown (1950) analyzed the evolution of labor law during the period between 1937 and 1947. They particularly emphasized the public opposition against the wave of postwar strikes and the transformation in the political environment from the New Deal era to a Republican domination of Congress after the 1946 elections; as a consequence, when Truman vetoed the Taft–Hartley Bill, Congress promptly overrode his veto. Truman won reelection as president in 1948, but unions lacked the political power to restore the previous labor law environment.

The Taft–Hartley changes included prohibitions against certain union practices such as strikes against secondary employers, coercion or intimidation of employees, and other perceived abuses of union power. The statute set forth procedures for collective bargaining and the prevention of strikes. It also added Section 8(c) protecting management speech during organizing campaigns unless the speech contained "threats of reprisal or promise of benefits." Of particular importance, Section 14(b) of the Act gave states the authority to adopt "right to work" laws that outlawed the compulsory payment of union dues. Twenty-eight states have adopted such laws, and the right-to-work movement in the United States is a major reason for contemporary union decline (Hogler, 2015).

During the period from 1945 to 1964, middle-class incomes grew as workers bargained for higher wages, fringe benefits such as healthcare, paid vacations, and other elements of an employment relationship. In contrast to other industrial countries, the US employment system featured a preference for voluntary agreements between employers and employees about the terms of employment rather than government-mandated wages and benefits. The 1950 labor agreement between General Motors and the United Auto Workers (UAW) known as the "Treaty of Detroit" established a pattern of secure, stable, and well-paid jobs in an important economic sector. Walter Reuther, president of the UAW, agreed to a five-year contract that gave workers an initial wage increase followed by automatic cost-of-living adjustments and such fringe benefits as pensions, health insurance, vacations, and a robust grievance procedure with binding arbitration. Reuther's accomplishment stands as one of the milestones in American labor history (Barnard, 2004).

Even as American workers prospered, union density slipped steadily over the years from its peak of just over 34 percent of the nonagricultural work force in 1945 to just under 28 percent in 1964 (Freeman, 1999). Union leaders reacted to the situation with an effort to repeal what they regarded as the most odious provision of the Taft–Hartley Act, the Section 14(b) right to work provision. AFL-CIO president George Meany anticipated that democratic majorities in the House and Senate, and the support of President Lyndon Johnson, would ensure success of the bill. According to the *New York Times* (Pomfret, 1964), the American Federation of Labor and Congress of Industrial Organizations (AFL-CIO) believed that a repeal bill "would pass the Senate easily." When the legislation reached the Senate, however, Senator Everett Dirksen led a filibuster to prevent bringing the bill forward for a vote. Majority Leader Mike Mansfield attempted several times to end the filibuster but was unsuccessful. In October 1965 and January 1966, the Senate refused to vote on the bill and Mansfield lacked a two-thirds majority to halt debate. Senator Dirksen said, "We have the country behind us on this issue, and that is the reason that we are determined ... to fight to the finish." He added that the law was not the issue, but rather "the sovereign authority of the 50 states to legislate in this field if they so desire" (CQ Almanac, 1966). After the failure of repeal, George Meany warned that labor might not support Democratic political programs in the future.

Johnson declined to run for another term as president in 1968, and Richard Nixon, a Republican, won the election against the Democratic candidate, Hubert Humphrey. Nixon gained a second term in 1972, but he was forced to resign during the Watergate scandal in 1973. In 1976, Democrats regained control of Congress and the White House when Jimmy Carter succeeded Gerald Ford as president. With Carter's backing, labor mounted another campaign for legal reform and anticipated a quick victory given the Democratic majority in Congress. The Labor Reform Bill of 1977 proposed major revisions in the procedures for forming unions and negotiating labor agreements. It specifically allowed for union certification by means of signed authorization cards in place of secret ballot elections, and it gave union organizers access to the employer's workplace to respond to the employer's "captive audience" speeches to workers. It also modified the nature of employers' bargaining obligation under the law by strengthening penalties for a failure to bargain (Nash, 1978).

Labor's hopes for reform again confronted the political obstacle of a Senate filibuster, and the reform efforts ground to a halt after two contentious years. The failure of the pro-union bill had serious consequences. Gary Fink (1998), a labor historian, summarized the outcome with the following observation:

> The US Senate took its sixth and final cloture vote on June 22, seeking to stop a filibuster on S. 2467, the Labor Law Revision Bill of 1978. After securing fifty-eight of the sixty votes needed to end debate, leaders of the cloture effort saw their frail coalition begin to disintegrate. Majority Leader Robert Byrd then recommitted the bill to the Senate Human Resources Committee, thus ending the most ambitious effort since the New Deal to strengthen American workers' eroded collective bargaining rights under the National Labor
> Relations Act. (p. 239)

Following the defeat of the most comprehensive and far-reaching reform of the labor law since Taft–Hartley, labor leaders reacted angrily to their perceived betrayal by management. No longer did those leaders intend to participate in a "labor accord" through which the parties acted cooperatively for the benefit of workers as well as management. Unfortunately, political and economic conditions led to further union weakness over the next decade.

The election of Ronald Reagan in 1980 coincided with a series of events inimical to American unions. Economic growth in the latter 1970s faltered due to an increase in oil prices imposed by the Middle Eastern cartel that effectively controlled oil production. One analysis (Miller, 1983, p. 18) noted, "The period from the first quarter of 1979 through the end of 1982 opened with the dramatic shock in oil prices that sent inflation rocketing to an inordinately high rate." The high and persistent inflation during the Carter years led to an effort by employers to resist further wage and price increases. The Reagan administration responded to the inflationary pressures with a tight monetary policy that increased unemployment and dampened growth, and employers reacted by cutting wages and benefits and taking a militant stance toward union organizing. Reagan's decision to deal harshly with a rogue federal union sparked a decade of employer opposition to collective bargaining.

In the first year of Reagan's administration, employees of the Federal Aviation Administration represented by the Professional Air Traffic Controllers Organization (PATCO) began collective bargaining negotiations with the

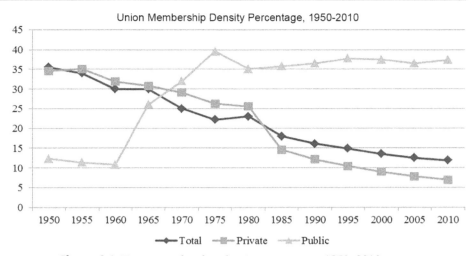

Figure 8.1 *Union membership density percentage*: 1950–2010.

government. As public employees, they bargained under the Federal Civil Service Reform Act of 1978, enacted during the Carter administration to regularize employment in the federal sector. The applicable law prohibits strikes by federal employees and punishes strikers through criminal sanctions. During his election campaign, Reagan assured air traffic controllers that he intended to correct many of the issues raised by the union, but some union demands proved to be unacceptable to the government and Reagan rejected them. The union called a strike on August 3, 1981, and two days later, President Reagan fired over 11,000 strikers. He also arrested a number of union leaders and seized the union's $3.5 million strike fund (Pardlo, 2017).

Analysts of the strike generally agree that Reagan's actions prompted employers throughout the country to resist unionism and wage increases. In his study of the event, labor historian Joseph McCartin (2011) argues that the government's opposition to the work action marked a turning point in American labor relations by fostering open hostility to the process of collective bargaining. Economic circumstances were favorable to management at the time because the unemployment rate exceeded 10 percent of the workforce and unions had less power to enforce bargaining demands. The combination of political and economic factors led to an accelerated rate of union decline during the period. Membership fell from 23 percent in 1980 to 16 percent in 1990, the most precipitous ten-year drop since the decade of 1920–1930. The decline continued into the 2010s, when it stabilized at 10.7 percent in 2017 (Hirsch & Macpherson, 2018). Figure 8.1 illustrates membership trends over six decades.

As union bargaining power eroded, trends in income distribution began to reverse previous patterns tending toward equality. According to research by Thomas Piketty and others, the share of income going to the upper tenth of the population during the 1980s rose while the share earned by the lower decile dropped rapidly. Piketty and his coauthors (2016) summarized their findings on an economics blog, where they wrote: "From 1980 to 2014, for example, none of the growth in per-adult national income went to the bottom 50 percent, while 32 percent went to the middle class (defined as adults between the median and the 90th percentile), 68 percent to the top 10 percent, and 36 percent to the top 1 percent" (Piketty, et al., 2016). They added a prescient comment on the consequences: "An economy that fails to deliver growth for half of its people for an entire generation is bound to generate discontent with the status quo and a rejection of establishment politics." Their cautionary observation foreshadows the election of Donald Trump.

Years of Desuetude, 1992–2016: Clinton, Bush, and Obama

Over three successive presidential administrations, labor failed to recover from the setbacks of the Reagan era, even though Democrats held majorities in Congress and the presidency at various times. The AFL-CIO lowered its ambitions for reform and endured several years of unfavorable political conditions. Following their defeat in the 1978 drive for labor law revision and the Republican presidencies of Ronald Reagan and George H. W. Bush, unions saw a new opportunity with the 1992 election of President Bill Clinton. Clinton successfully campaigned against Bush's reelection by attacking his economic policies, and Clinton's campaign strategy emphasized the relatively high levels of unemployment emerging during the Bush administration and Bush's failure to address the problems of American workers.

According to one report (Kelly, 1992), the Clinton campaign relied on three core campaign themes: "Change vs. more of the same. The economy, stupid. Don't forget health care." Clinton won the electoral college vote by a margin of 370 to George H. W. Bush's 160. Third-party candidate Ross Perot, an Independent, got over 19 million popular votes running on a platform that rejected ties to traditional party politics and emphasized voters' dissatisfaction with "politics as usual" (Holmes, 1992). Much of Perot's campaign foreshadowed the rise of Donald Trump in 2016 and his attacks on Hillary Clinton's neglect of white working-class voters. After her defeat, some Democratic leaders said of the campaign that the "emphasis on cultural issues has all but crippled them by diverting voters' attention from the core Democratic message of economic fairness" (Martin, 2016). In a broader context, Ms. Clinton's problematic relation with unions began during her husband's administration.

After the 1992 election in which organized labor supported Clinton's campaign, labor leaders brought forward a modest legislation revision that it believed would be an important step in restoring its bargaining power by changing the law regulating strikes. The Supreme Court's decision in *National Labor Relations Board v. Mackay Radio* (1938) gave employers the right to replace striking workers on a temporary or permanent basis by hiring new employees for their jobs. After Democrats swept the 1992 elections, they announced pro-union legislation to change the permanent replacement rule. Even though Democrats had control of both branches of Congress, a Republican filibuster in the Senate defeated the bill. In the Democrats' final effort to the push through the proposal, the bill came up for a Senate cloture vote in July 1994; it lost by seven votes (Dewar, 1994). Labor relations expert John Logan (2007, p. 610) offered several reasons for labor's defeat. Those reasons included President Clinton's lack of enthusiasm for the bill, a split among unions over the proper approach to legal change, and a lack of support for the bill on the part of politicians and the public. He added that the most important factor was "the determined opposition to labor law reform by employer groups and their congressional allies." The Clinton administration subsequently abandoned labor law reform as a political goal for the remainder of his presidency.

During George W. Bush's two terms in office from 2000 to 2008, Democrats attempted to revive labor law reform in the form of the Employee Free Choice Act. Representative George Miller (D-CA) introduced H.R.1696 in the House in 2005. The bill, known as the "Employee Free Choice Act," made union organizing much faster and simpler through a process of "card check certification" which allowed unions to gain certification by presenting signed authorization cards from a majority of employees requesting recognition and bargaining. The bill provided for third-party binding arbitration of collective bargaining disputes as a substitute for strikes. In addition, it increased the penalties for employer unfair labor practices. As the legislation moved through the House, Vice President Dick Cheney assured corporate leaders that President Bush intended to veto any pro-union measures that passed Congress (Patch, 2007). In the end, Senate Republicans successfully filibustered the bill, and it failed to move out of Congress.

The election of President Barack Obama and a Democratic Congress in 2008 offered yet another chance for unions. When Obama took office, Democrats held a majority of 57-41 in the Senate and 257-178 in the House. Sponsors of EFCA introduced another version of the bill, H.R. 1409, in March 2009. Some moderate Democratic senators objected to specific features of the legislation and indicated they would vote against it. Business leaders adamantly opposed any change at the federal level that would facilitate unionization and greater economic bargaining power for workers, despite the fact that many financial institutions had received generous government bailouts during the 2008 economic breakdown. As one commentator explained the complicity between the political arena and corporate interests (Stein, 2009):

> Three days after receiving $25 billion in federal bailout funds, Bank of America Corp. hosted a conference call with conservative activists and business officials to organize opposition to the US labor community's top legislative priority. Participants on the October 17 call – including at least one representative from another bailout recipient, AIG – were urged to persuade their clients to send "large contributions" to groups working against the Employee Free Choice Act (EFCA), as well as to vulnerable Senate Republicans, who could help block passage of the bill.

Opposition to reform proved successful in the early Obama administration and effectively stifled further efforts during his presidency.

Democrats failed to implement labor reforms in 2009, and in the 2010 congressional elections the political landscape changed significantly. Republicans gained 63 seats in the off-year election for a net majority of 242 seats to the Democratic Party's 193 seats (Election Results, 2010). Following the elections, the Obama administration abandoned legislative reforms to benefit organized labor. In his 2014 State of the Union address, President Obama did not mention any future initiatives to promote unions (Obama, 2014), and they continued to lose membership and influence.

The 2016 presidential election resulted in an unexpected victory for Donald Trump. Most political commentators believed that Hillary Clinton would carry working-class voters who traditionally voted for Democratic candidates, and she won the national popular vote by a margin of 65.8 million votes to Trump's 62.9 million (Presidential Election Results, 2016). Despite that, the key industrial states of Michigan, Wisconsin, and Pennsylvania, tilted the electoral college to Trump. As the *Washington Post* (Meko et al., 2016) summarized the outcome, "This election was effectively decided by 107,000 people in these three states. Trump won the popular vote there by that combined amount. That amounts to 0.09 percent of all votes cast in this election." The election also gave Republicans control of both houses of Congress and an opportunity to implement a new labor agenda based on Trump's campaign slogan to "make America great again." Although his campaign focused on improved economic conditions for American workers generally, Trump's actual legislative agenda delivered substantial tax cuts to wealthy citizens and increased the federal budget deficit (Thompson, 2018). As unemployment fell to historically low levels, workers' power to gain higher wages remained sluggish. Trump's formula for economic resurgence excluded labor unions and collective bargaining.

To reiterate, an important point about unions is that their ability to acquire resources for organizing and collective bargaining activities depends on a steady revenue stream of membership dues. The linchpin of dues collection is mandatory contribution from all covered members, just as all Americans are expected to pay taxes in support of government expenditures. Taft–Hartley's Section 14 (b), which is an exception to the principle of collective participation, gave states authority to prohibit "union security" clauses requiring dues payments from all members of the negotiating unit. Right-to-work laws weaken unions and their ability to fulfill basic functions. Within the early days of his administration, President Trump took actions that will enervate both private and public sector unions by reinforcing the idea that beneficiaries of a group effort can "opt out" of the collective body. That proposition is elaborated in the next section of this chapter.

The Trump Administration's Labor Policies

Donald Trump's presidential campaign rested on a promise to "make America great again." He did not present a specific economic program to achieve greatness, but his campaign generally focused on the renewal of American manufacturing and mining. In the first few months of his administration, President Trump made crucial appointments affecting organized labor both in the private and public sectors. First, he nominated Neil Gorsuch to replace Supreme Court Justice Antonin Scalia, who died unexpectedly in 2016. Gorsuch's appointment ensured a continuing majority of conservatives on the Court. According to *New York Times* legal expert Linda Greenhouse (2017), Gorsuch intends to base his doctrinal views on those of the staunchly conservative wing of the Court made up of Thomas, Alito, and Roberts. Gorsuch confirmed that expectation in June 2018 when he played a crucial role in undermining public sector unionism in the *Janus v. American Federation of State, County, & Municipal Employees* case by voting to overrule constitutional precedent that allowed unions to negotiate for compulsory dues payments (Liptak, 2018). The effort to limit union power began several years earlier, and Gorsuch made sure it would succeed.

In the case of *Knox v. Service Employees International Union* (2012), the Court laid the constitutional groundwork for banning compulsory dues payments in public union contracts by allowing covered workers to "opt in" to dues payments rather than forcing them to "opt out." Justice Alito, writing the majority opinion in *Knox*, proposed a constitutional principle that unions must assume that members prefer not to pay union dues if they have a choice, and the "default rule" should reflect that assumption. In his words: "Shouldn't the default rule comport with the probable preferences of most nonmembers? And isn't it likely that most employees who choose not to join the union that represents their bargaining unit prefer not to pay the full amount of union dues?" He reasoned that an opt-out system, which puts the burden on workers to declare their opposition to dues, creates a risk that the fees paid by nonmembers would be used for political and ideological ends with which they do not agree in violation of the First Amendment.

Alito presented no factual basis for his unusual position, and his stratagem of reasoning by rhetorical questions is hardly persuasive jurisprudence (Hogler, 2012). Presumably, if a majority of employees voted for union representation, they would want everyone to equitably share in the costs as well as the benefits of representation; and if most employees in the unit oppose union representation, they could simply vote out the union. As a basic precept of social order, if citizens cannot opt out of paying taxes for controversial expenditures such as wars in foreign countries, then why should such a rule apply to unions? Mancur Olson (1965) pointed out in an influential work that effective collective action necessarily requires that no one who benefits from a particular good should "free ride" on the efforts of others.

Whatever the intellectual shortcomings of the *Knox* decision, anti-union forces continued to press forward with a chain of litigation attempting to abolish public sector compulsory dues altogether. *Janus* represented the culmination of those efforts. The National Right to Work Legal Defense Foundation (2016), which represented the workers in *Janus* who objected to paying union dues, conceded at the outset that their claim conflicted with controlling legal precedent. Their argument was that the doctrine upholding public sector agency fees should be declared unconstitutional. In their words, "[Plaintiffs] Janus and Trygg submit that the [dues requirements] violate their First Amendment rights by forcing them to subsidize their unions' bargaining-related activities, notwithstanding their deeply help opposition to the positions their unions advance in collective bargaining" (NRWDLF, 2016, p. 5). Citing *Knox*, the plaintiffs attacked the cases upholding public sector fee payments, including the leading case of *Abood v. Detroit Bd. of Educ.*, 431 U.S. 209 (1977), and urged the Court to overrule those cases on First Amendment grounds.

The outcome of *Janus* after Gorsuch's appointment was predictable to any observer familiar with the legal environment. Justice Scalia's death in February 2016 temporarily halted the Court's attack on collective bargaining by creating a 4-4 deadlock on important labor issues, but when President Obama attempted to fill Scalia's seat, Senate Leader Mitch McConnell refused to bring Obama's appointment to a vote. Subsequently, President Trump's nominee proceeded quickly through the confirmation process because Republicans held a majority in the Senate.

The historical context of *Janus* extends back several decades. Scalia concurred in a 1991 case upholding compulsory fees, but he insisted that "a union cannot constitutionally charge nonmembers for any expenses except those incurred for the conduct of activities in which the union owes a duty of fair representation to the nonmembers being charged" (*Lehnert v. Ferris Faculty Association*, 1991). The *Janus* plaintiffs relied on the theory that public sector bargaining with a governmental employer is inherently political and "dictates that agency fees to support that speech cannot survive constitutional scrutiny" because they compel employees to engage in advocacy that is not consistent with their political beliefs (NRWLDF, 2016). That is, all public sector collective bargaining activities are necessarily political in nature because they seek to persuade elected officials of a particular course of action (Wellington & Winter, 1969). While the appointment of Justice Gorsuch guaranteed a setback for public unions, Trump's appointments to the National Labor Relations Board will prove equally devastating to private sector unions.

Following the 2008 election, President Obama's National Labor Relations Board (NLRB) appointees issued a number of rulings that a reconstituted Board challenged following Trump's appointment of two new members. Among the more controversial actions of the Obama Board were the reform of election procedures and decisions regarding joint employers, with the former most immediately affecting union organizing.

The Board's election rule, which was finalized in December 2014, featured major changes to update the process of union certification elections. According to the NLRB's (2014a) press release, a majority believed that "the rule will enable the agency to more effectively administer the National Labor Relations Act by modernizing its rules in light of modern technology, making its procedures more transparent and uniform across regions, and eliminating unnecessary litigation and delay." The modifications aimed to streamline Board functions by expediting elections, reducing unnecessary litigation, allowing for electronic filings, and requiring employers to provide unions seeking certification with employee telephone numbers and email addresses (NLRB, 2014b). Employer advocates characterized the Board's new rule as the "ambush election" rule, claiming that it gave unions an unfair advantage in the election process. After a federal district court upheld the rule, the Society for Human Resource Management (Shank, 2016) complained, "The court ruling upholding the NLRB union election rule is a loss for workers everywhere ... Employees need adequate time and information to make an informed decision about whether or not to join a union, and this decision prevents that." While the arguments failed to convince the district court, they prevailed with a Board dominated by new Trump appointees.

When the election rules were adopted, the Board had a full complement of five members. Three members supported the modifications, and Republican members Philip A. Miscimarra and Harry I. Johnson III dissented (NLRB, 2014b). The Board at Trump's inauguration in January 2017 consisted of two Democrats and one Republican. In September 2017, the Senate confirmed the second of Trump's Board appointments, a lawyer who specialized in labor cases representing management (Wheeler, 2017), and gave Republicans a 3-2 Board majority. With a pro-business majority, the Trump Board gained the power to reverse the election rules and return to the status quo ante (Stern, 2017). In addition, the Board has an opportunity to overturn some of the more controversial decisions of the Obama Board, including worker rights in disciplinary hearings, arbitration of employment disputes, and the statutory definition of an "employer" for purposes of representation and bargaining. The last issue has far-reaching implications for employers, as further explained below.

A case pending before the Board in 2017 affected various McDonald's franchises in the country and their relationship to the franchisor. After the filing of numerous unfair labor practice charges against the franchisees and the McDonald's corporation, the Board attempted to bring the cases together for resolution. The issue common to the complaints was whether McDonald's could be liable as a joint employer along with its various franchisees. Administrative Law Judge (ALJ) Lauren Esposito initially ruled that the cases should be consolidated for decision, noting that any outcome otherwise would mean the cases would not be decided for decades. In March 2018, McDonald's decided to avoid further litigation and a possible adverse result by offering to settle the case, and the NLRB accepted the offer (Wiessner, 2018).

The price of an unfavorable decision for employers was high. According to labor relations experts, "If McDonald's loses, it could face fundamental changes in its operating business model, the threat of unionization and collective bargaining across its more than 14,200 franchise outlets in the US, and increased vulnerability to all manner of litigation" (Knowledge @ Penn, 2016). Future joint employer cases will likely reverse the Obama Board's precedent; in fact, the Board made such a ruling in the *Hy-Brand Industrial Contractors* case, but its ruling was vacated when Member William Emanuel failed to recuse himself because of a conflict of interest (Seyfarth Shaw, LLC, 2018). The case remains pending.

Administrative degradation is not the only threat to labor; technology will also play a key role in determining work environments in the future. The erosion of collective bargaining systems threatens the effectiveness of worker involvement in decision making, which is one of the foundational elements of our labor law regime and also of unionism in the political economy generally (Freeman & Medoff 1984). Strong unions in the past successfully mediated the impacts of technological change by giving workers a voice in the employment relationship, but their future power to do so may be affected by labor-saving machines.

Work, Workers, and Technological Change

In October 2016, an eighteen-wheel tractor-trailer named "Otto" hauled 51,744 cans of beer from the Budweiser plant in Fort Collins, Colorado, to its destination in Colorado Springs, Colorado. The truck drove down Interstate 25 through the most congested traffic in the state and arrived safely at its destination. Unlike the other vehicles on the highway, Otto had no driver. *The Guinness Book of World Records* recognized the event and awarded Otto the title of "most miles driven by an unmanned vehicle." A news report (Chuang, 2017) commented, "While a man did sit in the driver's seat occasionally, he was recorded walking to the sleeper berth in the cab to read. But he was also monitoring the trip from the back seat. He never took the wheel, according to organizers of the experiment." Budweiser has a union contract at its Fort Collins plant, but the union has little control over the deployment of technological advancements.

The future impact of technology on workers, society, and the political economy engages some of the most influential thinkers in the country, such as Andrew McAfee and Erik Brynjolfsson (2017) at the Massachusetts Institute of Technology. In their highly publicized book, *Machine, Platform, Crowd: Harnessing Our Digital Future*, they examine the interaction between human labor and technology. Their treatment of future work frames the issue in three separate domains focusing on new technology that provides a platform accessible to anyone with a phone or computer. Uber, for example, revolutionized traditional modes of transportation by offering a means through which rides can be crowd sourced. The result is a decentralized system of transactions that lack the permanence and status of an "employment" relationship. The consequences, as one critic notes, may be problematic (Gilbey, 2017): "Some of these developments offer real, positive change – providing new ways to open up opportunities and advance the whole of society. Others merely offer a more cost-effective way of getting more for less from a population of workers already burdened with a gig economy and zero-hours contracts."

Technology likewise affects wealth distribution in advanced economies. In the three decades from the end of the Truman administration to the election of Ronald Reagan, measures of productivity and wage growth tracked closely together, but then they began to diverge significantly. As McAfee and Brynjolfsson explained in an interview (Bernstein & Raman, 2015), the divergence began in the 1980s as unions declined and technological development advanced rapidly. They said, "This phenomenon is what we call the Great Decoupling. The two halves of the cycle of prosperity are no longer married: Economic abundance, as exemplified by GDP and productivity, has remained on an upward trajectory, but the income and job prospects for typical workers have faltered." Workers with advanced skills gain increased income, while those in manual labor occupations see declining wages.

To illustrate, the *New York Times* (Irwin, 2017) published an article about two women janitors in the 1980s and 2017. The older woman started work for Eastman Kodak in Rochester, New York, cleaning offices during the Reagan era. Her employment package included health insurance, vacations, paid holidays, and other related benefits. She earned a college degree while working at the company and eventually became the chief technology officer. The second and younger woman cleans offices at the Apple campus in Cupertino, California. She is not an Apple employee but works for an independent cleaning service that has a contract to perform janitorial services. She has no prospects for advancement beyond her current job. Her situation reflects the bifurcation of permanent, well-compensated, and stable employment of the past into the contemporary trend toward an outsourced, low-wage, and uncertain environment for many workers. The pessimistic view is summed up in a recent commentary on the expansion of warehouse jobs announced by Amazon (Nolan, 2017): "There is zero doubt that the near and medium term will see millions of regular jobs–from taxi drivers to fast food workers to retail store employees of all types–disappear as they are replaced by computers and robots. The clock is ticking on many retail jobs. They simply will not exist for much longer."

Writing near the end of the nineteenth century, Edward Bellamy (1888) published a famous book titled *Looking Backward: 1889–2000*, which described the evolution of American society from a world of conflict and rapaciousness to one of tranquility and abundance. The protagonist of the book, Julian West, lives in Boston and is keenly aware of the economic inequality and suffering of Boston's working class. One evening West falls into a trance. When he awakes, it is the year 2000, and Bostonians live in a socialist paradise. West gradually comes to understand that new forms of society offer physical wellbeing and mental fulfillment where citizens voluntarily accept a form of militarized production that eliminates want and poverty.

West's utopia has failed to materialize, and even though living conditions now are far superior to those in 1889, economic deprivation has hardly disappeared. While job growth increased during 2017, wages remained relatively flat. One expert (Bernstein, 2017) assessed the situation in blunt terms: "But there is a big cloud in the job market sky: Wage growth is stalled out." Far from meliorating economic inequality, our institutions actively promote it. Whether the trend is sustainable is an important question moving into the future of work. President Trump's major economic initiative of tax reform offered little relief to lower-income American workers (Wasik, 2017), and his program of tariffs prompted retaliation from our trading partners which experts predict will result in slower future economic growth (Tankersley & Rappeport, 2018). Accordingly, the future direction of work is uncertain.

Conclusion

This chapter has traced the growth and decline of organized labor over the period from World War II up to President Trump's administration. Union membership density exceeded 30 percent of the workforce in 1945 and fell to just above 10 percent in 2017 (Ingraham, 2018). The deleterious consequences of a declining union movement are increasingly apparent. Real wages for middle-class American workers remained stagnant or declined following Ronald Reagan's election in 1980; and despite low unemployment rates following Donald Trump's inauguration, incomes for many Americans remained flat. A common explanation is that workers lack bargaining power to demand improvements in compensation and benefits. Employers, accordingly, respond to competitive pressures through lower labor costs.

The implications of a failing labor movement include a loss of middle-class incomes and increased wealth for those in the upper economic sectors. Levels of inequality in the United States now approach those immediately preceding the economic collapse of the late 1920s. The upheavals of the Great Depression and World War II eventually led to a period of unparalleled national prosperity from the 1950s to the late 1970s. Labor unions were the dominant feature of postwar employment relations, and as they declined, working-class incomes likewise fell. According to many commentators, the demographic tranche associated most strongly with unions – White, non-college educated, middle-aged men – brought Donald Trump to power by tilting the electoral college vote in three formerly industrial states. The conclusion is that strong unions carried us to economic prominence, and weak ones delivered us to economic anxiety and ensuing political turmoil.

References

Barnard, J. (2004). *American vanguard: The United Auto Workers during the Reuther years, 1935–1970*. Detroit, MI: Wayne State University Press.

Bellamy, E. (1888). *Looking backward, 2000–1887*. Boston, MA: Ticknor and Co.

Bernstein, J. (2017). Why wage growth is too slow and what to do about it. *Washington Post*, September 1. Retrieved from www.washingtonpost.com/news/postevery thing/wp/2017/09/01/.

Bernstein, A., & Raman, A. (2015). The great decoupling: An interview with Erik Brynjolfsson and Andrew McAfee. *Harvard Business Review*, June. Retrieved from https://hbr.org/2015/06/the-great-decoupling.

Cassidy, J. (2014). Piketty's inequality story in six charts. *New Yorker*, March 26. Retrieved from www.newyorker.com/news/john-cassidy/pikettys-inequality-story-in-six-charts.

Chuang, T. (2017). Self-driving truck's beer run on Colorado's Interstate 25 gets Guinness world record. *Denver Post*, June 29. Retrieved from www.denverpost.com/2017/06/29/self-driving-beer-truck-world-record/

Cohen, P. (2017). Immigrants keep an Iowa meatpacking plant alive and growing. *New York Times*, May 29. Retrieved from www.nytimes.com/2017/05/29/business/economy/.

CQ Almanac. (1966). 'Right to Work' repeal again loses in Senate. *Congressional Quarterly*, 22nd ed., 837–40 Retrieved from https://library.cqpress.com/cqalmanac/document.php?id=cqal66-1300523.

Dewar, H. (1994). Senate fails to break filibuster on striker replacement bill. *Washington Post*, July 13. Retrieved from www.washingtonpost.com/archive/politics/1994/07/13/ .

Edsall, T. (2017). The peculiar populism of Donald Trump. *New York Times*, February 2 Retrieved from www.nytimes.com/2017/02/02/opinion/the-peculiar-populism-of-donald-trump.html?emc=eta1.

Edwards, R., & Podgursky, M. (1986). The unraveling accord: American unions in crisis. In R. C. Edwards, P. Garonna and F. Todtling (Eds.), *Unions in crisis and beyond: Perspectives from six countries* (pp. 15–60). Dover, MA: Auburn House Publishing.

Election Results (2010). *New York Times*, November 8. Retrieved from www.nytimes.com/elections/2010/results/house.html.

Fink, G. (1998). Labor law revision and the end of the postwar labor accord. In K. Boyle (Ed.), *Organized labor and American politics, 1894–1994: The labor–liberal Alliance* (pp. 239–257). Albany, NY: State University of New York Press.

Freeman, R. (1999). Spurts in union growth: Defining moments and social processes. *National Bureau of Economic Research, Working Paper* No. 6012. Retrieved from www.nber.org/papers/w6012.pdf.

Freeman, R., & Medoff, B. (1984). *What do unions do?* New York, NY: Basic Books.

Gilbey, J. (2017). Book review: *Machine, platform, crowd: harnessing our digital future*, *Times Higher Education*, July 27 Retrieved from www.timeshighereducation.com/books/review-machine-platform-crowd-andrew-mcafee-and-erik-brynjolfsson-norton#survey-answer.

Gordon, C. (2012, June 5). Union decline and rising inequality in two charts. *Economic Policy Institute, Working Economics Blog*. Retrieved from www.epi.org/blog/union-decline-rising-inequality-charts/.

Gould, S., & Harrington, R. (2016, November 10). 7 charts show who propelled Trump to victory. *Business Insider*. Retrieved from www.businessinsider.com/exit-polls-who-voted-for-trump-clinton-2016-11.

Greenhouse, L. (2017). Trump's life-tenured judicial avatar. *New York Times*, July 6 Retrieved from www.nytimes.com/2017/07/06/opinion/gorsuch-trumpsupreme-court.html?mcubz=3&_r=0.

Hirsch, B., & Macpherson, D. (2018). Union membership and coverage database from the Current Population Survey. Retrieved from www.unionstats.com/.

Hogler, R. (2012). Constitutionalizing paycheck protection: What *Knox v. Service Employees International Union* means for American labor. *Labor Law Journal*, 64, 153–164.

Hogler, R. L. (2015). *The end of American labor unions: The right-to-work movement and the erosion of collective bargaining*. Santa Barbara, CA: ABC-CLIO.

Holmes, S. (1992). An eccentric but no joke: Perot's strong showing raises questions on what might have been, and might be. *New York Times*, November 5. Retrieved from www.nytimes.com/1992/11/05/us/1992-elections-disappointment-analysis-eccentric-but-no-joke-perot-s-strong.html.

Ingraham, C. (2018). Union membership remained steady in 2017. The trend may not hold. *Washington Post*, January 19. Retrieved from www.washingtonpost.com/news/wonk/wp/2018/01/19/ .

Irwin, N. (2017). To understand inequality, consider the janitors at two top companies, then and now. *New York Times*, September 3. Retrieved from: www.nytimes.com/2017/09/03/upshot/ .

Kelly, M. (1992). The 1992 campaign: The democrats – Clinton and Bush compete to be champion of change; Democrat fights perceptions of Bush gain. *New York Times*, October 31. Retrieved from www.nytimes.com/1992/10/31/us/.

Klare, K. E. (1978). Judicial deradicalization of the Wagner Act and the origins of modern legal consciousness, 1937–1941. *Minnesota Law Review*, *62*, 265–270.

Knowledge @ Penn (2016, Mar. 14). *How the McDonald's franchise labor case could upend an industry*. Retrieved from http://knowledge.wharton.upenn.edu/article/cappelli-mcdonalds/.

Knox v. Service Employees International Union (2012). 567 U.S. 310.

Labor Management Relations Act (LMRA) (1947). 29 U.S.C. § 141–197.

Lehnert v. Ferris Faculty Association. (1991). 500 U.S. 507.

Levy, F., & Temin, P. (2010). Institutions and wages in post–World War II America. In C. Brown, B. Eichengreen, & M. Reich (Eds.), *Labor in the era of globalization* (pp. 15–49). New York, NY: Cambridge University Press.

Liptak, A. (2018). Supreme Court ruling delivers a sharp blow to labor unions. *New York Times*, June 27. Retrieved from www.nytimes.com/2018/06/27/us/politics/supreme-court-unions-organized-labor.html.

Logan, J. (2007). The Clinton administration and labor law: Was comprehensive reform ever a realistic possibility? *Journal of Labor Research*, *28*, 609–628.

Martin, J. (2016). Pulling Democrats back to "It's the economy, stupid." *New York Times*, November 14. Retrieved from www.nytimes.com/2016/11/15/us/politics/democrats-economy.html.

McAfee, A., & Brynjolfsson, E. (2017). *Machine, platform, crowd: Harnessing our digital future*. New York, NY: W. W. Norton & Company.

McCartin, J. (2011). *Collision course: Ronald Reagan, the air traffic controllers, and the strike that changed America*. New York, NY: Oxford University Press.

Meko, T., Lu, D. & Gamio, G. (2016). How Trump won the presidency with razor-thin margins in in swing states. *Washington Post*, November 11. Retrieved from www.washingtonpost.com/graphics/politics/2016-election/swing-state-margins.

Miller, G. H. Jr. (1983, June). Inflation and recession, 1979–82: Supply shocks and economic policy. Federal Reserve Bank of Kansas City, *Economic Policy*, *3*, 8–21.

Millis, H., & Brown, E. (1950). *From the Wagner Act to Taft-Hartley: A study of national labor policy and labor relations*. Chicago, IL: University of Chicago Press.

Nash, P. (1978, Summer). The Labor Reform Act of 1977: A detailed analysis. *Employee Relations Law Journal*, 4(1), 59–80.

National Conference of State Legislatures. (2018). Right-to-work resources. Retrieved from www.ncsl.org/research/labor-and-employment/right-to-work-laws-and-bills.aspx.

National Labor Relations Board (NLRB). (2014a). NLRB issues final rule to modernize representation-case procedures. Retrieved from www.nlrb.gov/news-outreach/news-story/nlrb-issues-final-rule-modernize-representation-case-procedures.

National Labor Relations Board. (2014b). NLRB representation case-procedures fact sheet. Retrieved from www.nlrb.gov/news-outreach/fact-sheets/nlrb-representation-case-procedures-fact-sheet.

National Right to Work Legal Defense Foundation (NRWLDF). (2016). *Appellants' brief and short appendix*. Retrieved from www.nrtw.org/wp-content/uploads/2016/11/Janus-brief-Filed-with-short-appendix.pdf.

National Right to Work Legal Defense Foundation. (2017). *Right to work states*. Retrieved from www.nrtw.org/right-to-work-states/.

Nolan, H. (2017). Amazon warehouse employees are the most important workers in America. *Splinternews*. Retrieved from http://splinternews.com/amazon-warehouse-employees-are-the-most-important-workers.

Olson, M., Jr. (1965). *The logic of collective action*. Cambridge, MA: Harvard University Press.

Pardlo, G. (2017, February 12). The cost of defying the president. *New Yorker*. Retrieved from www.newyorker.com/culture/culture-desk/the-cost-of-defying-the-president.

Patch, J. (2007, February 14). Cheney says Bush will veto pro-union bill. *Politico*. Retrieved from www.politico.com/story/2007/02/cheney-says-bush-will-veto-pro-union-bill-002758.

Piketty, T., Saez, E., & Zucman, G. (2016). Economic growth in the United States: A tale of two countries. *Equitable Growth*. Retrieved from http://equitablegrowth.org/research-analysis/economic-growth-in-the-united-states-a-tale-of-two-countries/.

Pomfret, J. (1964). Labor maps fight on Taft-Hartley. *New York Times*, November 24. Retrieved from www.nytimes.com/1964/11/25/labor-maps-fight-on-tafthartley.html.

Presidential Election Results (2016). *New York Times*, November 8. Retrieved from www.nytimes.com/elections/results/president.

Seyfarth Shaw, LLC. (2018, February 27). NLRB vacates Hy-Brand decision and restores (for now) its broad Browning-Ferris Joint Employer Test. *Employer Labor Relations*. Retrieved from www.employerlaborrelations.com/2018/02/27/.

Shank, R. (2016, July 31). NLRB could implement significant changes to union election rules. *SHRM*. Retrieved from www.shrm.org/resourcesandtools/hr-topics/labor-relations/pages/quickie-election-rule-upheld.aspx.

Stein, S. (2009, March 12). Citigroup enters union fray with anti-EFCA call. *Huffington Post*. Retrieved from www.huffingtonpost.com/2009/03/12/citigroup-enters-union-fr_n_174106.html.

Stern, M. J. (2017, December 19). Donald Trump, union buster. *Slate*. Retrieved from www.slate.com/articles/news_and_politics/jurisprudence/2017/12/donald_trump_s_union_busting_appointees_just_incinerated_obama_s_labor_legacy.html.

Sugrue, T. (2012). Workers' paradise lost. *New York Times*, December 13. Retrieved from www.nytimes.com/2012/12/14/opinion/union-power-wanes-in-michigan.html.

Tankersley, J., & Rappeport, A. (2018). White House analysis finds tariffs will hurt growth, as officials insist otherwise. *New York Times*, June 7. Retrieved from www.nytimes.com/2018/06/07/us/politics/white-house-tariffs-growth.html.

Thompson, D. (2018). The GOP's tax-cut narrative is already unraveling. *The Atlantic*, February 28. Retrieved from www.theatlantic.com/business/archive/2018/02/trump-gop-tax-cut-narrative/554504/.

Truman, H. (1945a, Nov. 5). Address at the opening session of the Labor–Management Conference, Public Papers Harry S. Truman 1945–1953. *Harry S. Truman Library & Museum*. Retrieved from www.presidency.ucsb.edu/ws/index.php?pid=12300.

Truman, H. (1945b, Dec. 3). Special message to the Congress on Labor–Management Relations, Public Papers Harry S. Truman 1945–1953. *Harry S. Truman Library & Museum*. Retrieved from www.trumanlibrary.org/publicpapers/index.php?pid=494&st=labor+relations&st1

Truman, H. (1947, June 20). Veto of the Taft-Hartley Labor Bill. *The American Presidency Project*. Retrieved from www.presidency.ucsb.edu/ws/?pid=12675.

Wasik, J. (2017, November 29). How the GOP tax plan scrooges middle class, retired and poor. *Forbes*. Retrieved from www.forbes.com/sites/johnwasik/2017/11/29/.

Wellington, H., & Winter, R., Jr. (1969). The limits of collective bargaining in public employment. *Yale Law Journal*, 78, pp. 1107–1151.

Western, B. & Rosenfeld, J. (2011). Unions, norms, and the rise in US wage inequality. *American Sociological Review*, 76, 513–537.

Wheeler, L. (2017, September 25). *Senate confirms second Trump nominee to labor board. The Hill.* Retrieved from http://thehill.com/regulation/administration/352345-senate-confirms-second-trump-nominee-to-labor-board.

Wiessner, D. (2018, March 19). McDonald's agrees to settlement in franchisees' US labor case. *Reuters*. Retrieved from www.reuters.com/article/us-mcdonalds-nlrb/.

9 Changes in Organizational Income Inequality

The Causes and Consequences

Lixin Jiang

> Inequality, rather than want, is the cause of trouble.
>
> Confucius

It is undeniable that societal income inequality in the United States is at an all-time high (Thompson & Smeeding, 2014). However, the wage disparities between the heads of large American corporations and ordinary workers are the most extreme (Mishel, Gould, & Bivens, 2015). That is, as top managers pocket large monetary rewards, rank-and-file employees do not receive the fruits of economic growth (Mishel & Schieder, 2017) but suffer from wage stagnation (Davis & Cobb, 2010). Indeed, real wages of typical American workers have been stagnating for over three decades. According to Desilver (2014), the purchasing power of today's average hourly wage is about the same as it was in 1979 after adjusting for inflation. On the other hand, inflation-adjusted compensation of chief executive officers (CEOs) increased 997 percent from 1978 to 2014 (Mishel & Davis, 2015). Consequently, the average CEO compensation of the 350 largest companies in the United States was 271 times the annual average pay of typical workers in 2016 (Mishel & Schieder, 2017). In other words, an ordinary American worker would have to toil for almost a year to make what these CEOs made in one day. Although the ratio of CEO-to-worker pay has become smaller over the past few years (compared to 376-to-1 in 2000 and 303-to-1 in 2014), it is still astronomically larger than the ratio in the decades before the turn of the millennium (e.g., 20-to-1 in 1965; 30-to-1 in 1978; 59-to-1 in 1989; 123-to-1 in 1995; Mishel & Davis, 2015).

However, wage stagnation for rank-and-file employees was not created by abstract economic trends. Instead, those who have the most income, wealth, and power exert their influence on government policy to suppress employee wages (Mishel, 2015). In other words, the higher pay for CEOs does not reflect any increased contribution to corporate output. Rather, compensation for CEOs increases much faster than for any other groups. According to Mishel and Davis (2015), CEO pay grew twice as fast as corporate profits and more than five times faster than the pay of the top 0.1 percent of wage earners over the three decades from the 1980s to 2013.

Numerous studies in multiple fields (e.g., economics, political science, sociology, social epidemiology) have documented the ramifications of income inequality at the national level. Since wages are the primary source of income, a key culprit behind societal income inequality is pay dispersion within an organization (Bakija, Cole, & Heim, 2012; Cobb, 2016, Davis & Cobb, 2010; Lemieux, 2006; Sjöberg, 2009; Stainback, Tomaskovic-Devey, & Skaggs, 2010). For example, the growing compensation of executives was the largest factor in doubling the top 0.1 percent and top 1.0 percent share of overall household income growth from 1979 to 2007 (Bakija et al., 2012; Bivens & Mishel, 2013; Mishel & Davis, 2015). As a main source of societal income inequality, income disparities within an organization may have highly important consequences (Bapuji, 2015).

Researchers of organizational pay dispersion have distinguished horizontal and vertical pay dispersion. The former is defined as pay variation within levels and jobs and the latter is pay variation across levels (Shaw, 2014). The vast majority of studies have examined the former instead of the latter because one may expect to observe vertical pay dispersion within an organization where individuals have different skills, abilities, and responsibilities. As a result, the examinations of the causes and consequences of vertical pay dispersion, especially the aforementioned skyrocketing CEO-to-worker pay ratio, continue falling behind in the organizational literature, although vertical pay dispersion issues have garnered the most attention. However, the rising CEO-to-worker pay ratio may have negative consequences on employees because extreme power asymmetries in the workplace, signified by growing compensation differences between CEOs and their underlings, may make well-intentioned managers behave in a mean and selfish manner toward lower-level employees (Desai, Brief, & George, 2009; Kipnis, 1972; Zimbardo, 2007).

Below I first summarize the changes in reward distributions within organizations as a consequence of changes in employment relationships. Then I borrow the literature on power from social psychology to support the argument that the powerful are becoming more powerful at the expense of the powerless. Finally, I propose a new research agenda and some practical recommendations.

Changes in Employment Relationships and Reward Distribution

Bidwell, Briscoe, Fernandez-Mateo, and Sterling (2013) provide a comprehensive review on the influence of changes in employment relationships on the distribution of rewards within organizations. According to Bidwell et al. (2013), the middle of the twentieth century was dominated by the internal labor market where employment from external labor markets was insulated. However, the years since the 1970s witnessed a resurgence of external market forces. Due to the shift from the internal to the external labor market, lifetime employment, accompanied by nonwage benefits including health insurance and old age pensions, is replaced by a more flexible arrangement between employers and employees that enables organizations to adapt to emerging trends and markets.

What Are the Changes in Employment Relationships and Benefits?

Specifically, in response to the demands of external labor markets, organizations increasingly adopt pay-for-performance practices where workers are rewarded for their productivity (Heneman & Werner, 2005). As a means of reorganization and cost control (Hallock, 2009; Osterman, 1999), organizations are more likely to use layoffs as a normal business practice to restructure. Additionally, organizations growingly use contingent work (Houseman & Polivka, 2000; Kalleberg, 2000) through labor market intermediaries such as temporary help agencies (Cappelli & Keller, 2013) and outsource entire functions that were previously carried out internally (Abraham, 1990; Bidwell & Fernandez-Mateo, 2008). Consequently, tenure, especially among men (Farber, 2008), employees of large organizations (Bidwell, 2013), and employees in the private sector (Neumark, Polsky, & Hansen, 1999), has decreased substantially (Hollister, 2011).

Organizations also change their benefits practices (Fronstin, 2012; Maxwell, Briscoe, & Temin, 2000; Shuey & O'Rand, 2004). For example, in 1980, 70% of workers under age 65 received health insurance coverage from their employer. However, this number dropped to 54% in 2009 (Mishel, Bivens, Gould, & Shierholz, 2012). A decline in pensions was also observed in that 51% of employees were covered in 1980 compared with 43% in 2009 (Mishel et al., 2012). Moreover, only 26% of large employers provided retiree health benefits in 2011 versus 66% in 1988 (Kaiser Family Foundation/HRET, 2012). These numbers in health insurance coverage, pensions, and retiree health benefits indicate that many organizations are providing fewer benefits to their employees. For employees who do have access to benefits through their employer, however, the shift from the "defined benefit" format, that prescribes a specific benefit (e.g., a guaranteed retirement income) to workers with sufficient tenure, to the "defined contribution" format that provides a set amount of pretax money used toward the purchase of benefits (e.g., a 401k investment) in each year of employment has transferred market risk from employers to employees (Cobb, 2011; Munnell, Haverstick, & Sanzenbacher, 2006).

What Are Major Causes of Change?

The above-mentioned changes in employment relationships and benefits result from fundamental changes in the nature and requirements of work (Bidwell et al., 2013). As the United States has moved from national economics based on manufacturing to a global market based on technology and services, the nature of work changes and therefore the governance of employment practices must be updated. Some scholars have argued that technology, globalization, and demographic changes play an important role in changing employment practices. For example, firms and industries with high expenditures on information technology are more likely to lay off employees (Bidwell, 2013) and employ more contract agency and temporary help workers (Sahaym, Steensma, & Schilling, 2007). Globalization puts workers in one country in more direct competition with workers in other countries, often with large differences in wage levels (Shuman, 2017). For example, recent work found that China's manufacturing surge has a negative impact on American manufacturing employment and wages (Autor, Dorn, & Hanson, 2016). The nature of the workforce is also changing. Specifically, more women (Kalleberg, 2000; Pfeffer & Baron, 1988; Wiens-Tuers & Hill, 2002), older workers (Kalleberg, 2000), and younger generations (Smola & Sutton, 2002) who, to some extent, prefer nonstandard work arrangements are participating in the labor market.

Nevertheless, Bidwell et al. (2013) argue that there is no conclusive evidence suggesting that technological progress, global competition, and demographic shifts and preferences fully account for observed changes in employment patterns. Instead, they conclude that widespread changes in employment relationships are "the outcomes of struggles among stakeholders seizing opportunities to advance their own agendas and interests" (Bidwell et al., 2013, p. 76) by influencing government (Hacker & Pierson, 2010) in multiple areas including taxation, corporate governance, and financial deregulation (Baumgartner, Berry, Hojnacki, Kimball, & Leech, 2009) with the goal to increase employer flexibility and decrease employee protections.

Indeed, employees have lost power to employers, which is reflected by the decline in union membership. For example, union membership in the private sector fell from about 25% in 1970s to below 7% in 2012. A decrease in union membership helps to explain the changes in the employment relationship. Specifically, the union decline contributes to decreased employee tenure observed in recent years (Bidwell, 2013), increased wage inequality (Western & Rosenfeld, 2011), the growth in contingent work (Gramm & Schnell, 2001; Houseman, 2001), and reductions in health insurance and pensions (Buchmueller, DiNardo, & Valletta, 2002). For example, Banning and Chiles (2007) found that CEOs at nonunion firms earned nearly 20% more than their fellow executives in unionized companies. In contrast, workers in nonunion firms take home 80% of the earnings of their counterparts in union firms ($829 vs. $1,041; Bureau of Labor Statistics, 2018).

The shareholder value movement driving firms to solely focus on the return on corporate stock is another force behind shifting toward market-based employment practices. Indeed, shareholder pressures have caused firms to lay off employees (Budros, 1999), use equality incentives at the middle management level (Marler & Faugère, 2010), decrease defined benefit pensions (Cobb, 2012), and reduce retiree health benefits (Briscoe & Murphy, 2012).

What Are the Impacts of Change on Reward Distribution?

As a result, the aforementioned market-oriented employment relationship increases wage inequality. Performance (Lazear, 2000; Lemieux, Macleod, & Parent, 2009; Shearer, 2004), as opposed to employer characteristics (e.g., organizational size) and employee tenure, has played an important role in setting pay and other benefits. In past years, employment in large organizations was associated with higher pay. However, this advantage associated with employment in a large company decreased by nearly a third from 1988 to 2003 (Hollister, 2004). Rewards for tenure also decreased from 1983 to 1998 (DiPrete, Goux, & Maurin, 2002). Ironically, performance-based pay (e.g., bonus pay, commissions, or piece-rate contracts) translates into higher wage inequality. Using the Panel Study of Income Dynamics, Lemieux et al. (2009) found that 21% of the increased pay dispersion between 1976 and 1993 can be attributed to the growth of incentive pay. Moreover, performance-based pay (Castilla, 2008) and promotion (Castilla & Benard, 2010) may increase existing bias (e.g., race, gender). For example, an earlier study found that women's bonuses were 25% lower than men's even though their salaries were only about 1% lower (Elvira & Graham, 2002).

Not surprisingly, employee compensation differs depending on their employment status (e.g., regular employees, contingent workers, or outsourced workers). Contingent workers have lower pay and fewer benefits than regular workers, especially among blue-collar and pink-collar occupations (Kalleberg, Reskin, & Hudson, 2000). However, it is worth noting that high-skill temp workers (Barley & Kunda, 2004; Marler, Barringer, & Mikovich, 2002; Houseman, Kalleberg, & Erickcek, 2003) and independent contractors (Kunda, Barley, & Evans, 2002) make more than regular employees. Unfortunately, contingent work is more likely to be performed by low-skill workers (Kalleberg et al., 2000), women (Kalleberg et al., 2000; Segal & Sullivan, 1997), ethnic minority workers (Autor & Houseman, 2010), less experienced workers, and those who had recently been laid off (Bidwell & Briscoe, 2009). Without a formal relationship with an employer, contingent workers and outsourced workers do not receive benefits from an employer. Farber and Levy (2000) and Pierce (2001) have concluded that decreased employer-provided health and welfare benefits led to the rise of inequality during the 1980s and 1990s. Specifically, employer costs associated with health and pension benefits fell dramatically for low-income earners but rose for upper-income earners (Keene & Prokos, 2007; Little, 1995; Slottje, Woodbury, & Anderson, 2000).

As employment practices change, the relative share of wealth received by the organization's various stakeholders also changes. Cumulative evidence suggests that shareholders and their agents have received an increasing share of national wealth since the 1980s at the expense of employees. For example, the Bureau of Economic Analysis (2012) found that corporate profits in gross domestic product (GDP) increased from 6.1% in 1980 to 9.2% in 2011 while the share of workers' wages decreased from 60.1% to 55.2%. Although the benefits of layoffs brought to shareholders are debatable (Farber & Hallock, 2009), the use of outsourced and contingent workers (Lepak, Takeuchi, & Snell, 2003; Nayar & Willinger, 2001) and incentive pay (Banker, Lee, Gordon, & Srinivasan, 1996; Gerhart & Milkovich, 1990; Lazear, 2000) has increased employer profitability and stock returns. CEOs, whose compensation includes nonperformance-based pay (e.g., salary) and performance-based pay (e.g., stock-based compensation), clearly are benefiting from it (Mishel & Schieder, 2017), especially after the Clinton administration established Section 162(m) of the Internal Revenue Code in 1993. For example, from 1978 to 2000, the average inflation-adjusted CEO compensation of the 350 publicly owned US firms increased 1,270.8 percent while ordinary workers' compensation only increased 1.40 percent (Mishel & Davis, 2015).

While 162(m) states that publicly traded corporations can only deduct the first $1 million of salary, bonuses, stock grants, and other nonperformance-based pay to each of its top five executives, performance-based pay, such as non-equity incentive plans, stock options, stock appreciation rights, pensions, is fully deductible (Balsam, 2012). Not surprisingly, for executives who earn more than $1 million in cash compensation, Section 162(m) leads organizations to award executives more performance-based compensation (e.g., stock options; Balsam & Ryan, 2008). For example, over the 2007–2010 period, 55 percent of executive pay was based on performance and therefore deductible. In total, $121.5 billion in executive compensation of 32,492 examined corporations was deductible between 2007 and 2010 (Balsam, 2012). On the other hand, for executives making less than $1 million, Section 162(m) incites organizations to increase executives' cash compensation (Harris & Livingstone, 2002; Rose & Wolfram, 2002). Indeed, the number of executives pocketing more than $1 million nonperformance-based compensation increased from 3,379 in 2007 to 4,729 in 2010, despite fewer executives examined in 2010 ($N = 28,279$) compared to 2007 ($N = 38,511$; Balsam, 2012). Therefore, 162(m) does not decrease executive pay. Rather, the organizational practices encouraged by 162(m) result in an increase in executive pay and a decrease in corporate profits. Consequently, 162(m) hurts the shareholders and the US Treasury in that decreased company profits bring down both returns to the shareholders and the amount of profits subject to the corporate income tax (Balsam, 2012). These deductions cost the US Treasury an estimated $7.5 billion per year (Balsam, 2012).

Together, as the United States moved away from a closed, internal labor market to a system open to the influence of external market forces, employment practices have changed radically. For example, performance pay, the use of contingent work, layoffs, and outsourcing have become common practices. Employers also reduce their role in employee health and retirement benefits. These changes in employment patterns and benefits may be triggered by technological advancement, global competition, demographic change, union decline, and stakeholder value movement. As a result of changes in employment relationship and benefits, there is growing organizational reward inequality that is characterized by pay stagnation and decreased benefits among rank-and-file employees but increased pay and benefits among top managers (e.g., CEOs).

The Consequences of Skyrocketing CEO-to-Worker Pay Ratio: A Power Perspective

As previously mentioned, the past three decades have witnessed an unprecedented growing rate of compensation for CEOs and other top managers but wage stagnation for typical employees, resulting in unprecedented income inequality between executives and average employees. The skyrocketing CEO-to-worker pay ratio has wide-reaching implications for employees. Researchers in the pay dispersion area have used tournament theory (Lazear & Rosen, 1981), equity theory (Adams, 1963), and relative deprivation theory (Crosby, 1976) to explain the influence of pay variation in an organization. Each theory has received some empirical support (Shaw, 2014). Although these theories are helpful in explaining the consequences of horizontal pay dispersion, managerial power theory (Bebchuk & Fried, 2003, 2004) may be better to explain the negative implications of increasing CEO-to-worker pay ratio (i.e., vertical pay dispersion) on employees. Specifically, managerial power theory posits that perceived power asymmetries derived from the rising income inequality between CEOs and ordinary workers cause CEOs to behave in a mean and selfish manner towards their employees (Bebchuk & Fried, 2003, 2004; Desai et al., 2009).

Desai et al. (2009) propose that CEO compensation causes them to have power or the capacity to influence and control other people (French & Raven, 1959). By comparison, typical employees are powerless. Indeed, as early as 1967, Whistler, Meyer, Baum, and Sorensen argued that individual compensation in an organization provides information regarding their relative power and control. Therefore, CEO compensation is indicative of their formal power (Finkelstein, 1992; Hambrick & D'Aveni, 1992). Specifically, compensation committees, who are responsible for setting pay scales both across and within hierarchical levels, intentionally create pay differentials within an organization to indicate individuals' position and power. Thus, a CEO's compensation signals the CEO's power across organizations (Steers & Ungson, 1987; Ungson & Steers, 1984) and the CEO's importance in determining organizational outputs (Henderson & Frederickson, 1996). Substantial empirical evidence suggests that the higher the compensation, the higher is managerial power (Barkema & Pennings, 1998; Finkelstein & Hambrick, 1988, 1989, 1996; Lambert, Larcher, & Weigelt, 1993; Wade, O'Reilly, & Chandradat, 1990). CEO perceived power also increases as their compensation grows (Finkelstein, 1992). CEOs who perceive to be powerful are likely to act as if they were indeed more powerful; other organizational members are likely to accept CEO's power as a "fact of life" or a function of "doing business." Consequently, CEO's power goes unquestioned. Cumulative evidence suggests that the experienced and perceived power changes the way power holders think of themselves, their work, their subordinates, and the way they behave. Specifically, the power differences between CEOs and underlings cause CEOs to objectify workers (Van Kleef, De Dreu, Pietroni, & Manstead, 2006) and issue self-licenses to exploit them (Desai et al., 2009).

Kipnis (1972) suggests that those managers with high power tend to devalue the worth of their subordinates. They not only evaluate the quality of their employees' work as significantly poorer, but also prefer to maintain greater social distance from them (Kipnis, 1972). Because power holders typically control desired resources and outcomes, their ideas and views are readily accepted by subordinates (Kipnis, Schmidt, Price, & Stitt, 1981). Indeed, Mishel and Davis (2015) argue that "CEO pay does not reflect greater productivity of executives but rather the power of CEOs to extract concessions." Due to actor–observer differences in one's perception (Jones & Nisbett, 1972), power holders may be insensitive to the role that their power plays in producing such uncritical agreement and instead attribute it to the quality and value of their input. Consequently, they come to believe that their ideas and views are superior, implying that they are somehow special as compared to their subordinates, and thus deserving the resources, privileges, and other things that typically come with power. Furthermore, the experience of power results in a desire to influence subordinates. Once influence has been exerted, power holders begin to believe that subordinates cannot control their own actions (Kipnis et al., 1981). They attribute a subordinate's effort to the exertion of managerial power rather than to the subordinate's ability or motivation. As a result of devaluing the worth of their subordinates, power holders may come to perceive them as mere objects for manipulation in the service of power holders' own interests and goals (Kipnis et al., 1981). They may adjust their code of ethical behavior in order to rationalize such manipulation. Thus, over time, even the most well-intentioned individual has the potential to be corrupted by power (Zimbardo, 2007).

A wide range of studies suggest that power has negative implications in that power elicits behaviors that give priority to power holders' own interests, desires, and selfish ends (Kipnis, 1972, 1976). Power may increase displays of anger (Tiedens, 2000), the use of stereotypes (Fiske, 1993), and subordinate derogation (Georgesen & Harris, 1998, 2000). Additionally, power may decrease empathy and openness to others' perspectives, emotions, and attitudes (Anderson, Keltner, & John, 2003; Galinsky, Magee, Inesi, & Gruenfeld, 2006; Van Kleef et al., 2006). Power may also cause individuals to make self-serving performance evaluations (Georgesen & Harris, 1998), display selfish, self-destructive, and corrupt behaviors (Anderson & Galinsky, 2006; Chen, Lee-Chai, & Bargh, 2001; Galinsky, Gruenfeld, & Magee, 2003; Kipnis, 1972), pursue sexual motives (Bargh, Raymond, Pryor, & Strack, 1995; Pryor, 1987), and engage in sexual harassment (Pryor, LaVite, & Stoller, 1993) and sexual aggression (Groth, 1979). Lindskold and Aronoff (1980) found that in a prisoner's dilemma game, participants given power were significantly more deceitful and often competed after promising to cooperate. They were also substantially more exploitive, by continuing to compete with partners who consistently cooperated, than were those with equal or lower power. Thus, once again, power appears to have exerted a corrupting influence.

Taken together, the above theoretical rationale and empirical evidence suggest that an increase in vertical pay dispersion between CEOs and employees can lead CEOs to have a heightened sense of power, which, in turn, causes them to abuse employees. Greenhouse (2008) offered two examples that provide some support for this argument. Powerful FedEx executives misclassified FedEx drivers as independent contractors who have no right to unionize. As a result, FedEx was able to save on taxes, fringe benefits, healthcare costs, pensions, unemployment insurance, and other workers' costs but drivers were required to pay for their trucks, insurance, repairs, gas, and tires. However, FedEx still asked these independent contractors to wear the uniform and follow instructions about what to do, when to do it, how to do it, and when to take breaks (also see Berman, 2016; Wood, 2015). Another example involves managers at a Koch Foods poultry plant in Tennessee who ordered workers to only go to the restroom during their lunch and coffee breaks as a way to keep the assembly line operating non-stop and humiliated those who expressed a dire need to go to the toilet (Greenhouse, 2008). Empirically, Desai et al. (2009) revealed that companies in the top 100 list of best corporate citizens in 2006, which was compiled by Kinder, Lydenherg, Domini & Co. Company Profiles, awarded their CEOs less than the going rate for CEOs and that CEOs' compensation was negatively related to the human rights performance of the organization, a crude proxy for how employees may be treated in the organization. Moreover, top managers whose compensation skyrockets compared to average workers are more likely to adopt policies that damage workers' interests, such as deliberately violating safety norms, ignoring procedures, and laying off workers to sustain financial performance (Desai & Yao, 2015).

Indeed, vertical pay dispersion negatively impacts individual employees and employee relations (Akerlof & Yellen, 1990; Bapuji, 2015). Previous research has shown that pay dispersion within an organization decreases organizational justice, job satisfaction, employee cooperation, and innovation, but increases turnover rates (Pfeffer & Langton, 1993; Yanadori & Cui, 2013). Moreover, when executive compensation is high, employees are more cynical and display fewer organizational citizenship behaviors (Andersson & Bateman, 1997). Under economic inequality, the disadvantaged feel envy towards the advantaged and react in a way that hurts the advantaged even when such actions also hurt the disadvantaged themselves (Gino & Pierce, 2009). To get even with rewards inequality given by the organization, employees may resort to counterproductive behaviors, including decreased work effort and increased stealing (Greenberg, 1990). Relative wages are also found to be negatively associated with employee theft (Chen & Sandino, 2012). Using an experimental design, Guo, Libby, and Liu (2017) found that when vertical pay dispersion is high rather than low, subordinates are more likely to misreport costs. These translate into performance and financial consequences for organizations. Income inequality in an organization can harm interpersonal interactions because high levels of organizational inequality diminish employee generalized trust, identification with others, and cooperative behaviors (Bapuji, 2015). In his comprehensive review of pay dispersion research, Shaw (2014) concludes that unexplained or excessive pay dispersion negatively impacts individual, team, and organizational performance. For example, Connelly, Haynes, Tihanyi, Gamache, and Devers (2016) have found that organizations with high vertical pay dispersion between top management team members and non-top-level employees may inevitably fall into a "temporal trap" (Laverty, 1996) reaping short-term benefits at the expense of long-term gains.

Future Research

As mentioned before, outsized CEO compensation is accompanied by worker wage stagnation. However, research on the impact of worker wage stagnation on employees is scarce. Wage stagnation (i.e., depressed or flat wage growth below the rate of inflation) indicates that employees fail to receive resource gain in the form of income after their investment of energy, time, and effort at work (Benson, Probst, Jiang, Olson, & Graso, 2017). Consequently, employees may perceive a breach of psychological contract in that over time employees receive a relatively low level of compensation in exchange for job performance (Cropanzano & Prehar, 2001). Such a threat to employee resource investment (Hobfoll, 1989) leading to psychological contract breach (Turnley & Feldman, 1998) has negative consequences for employees. Indeed, Benson and colleagues found that wage stagnation resulted in decreased job satisfaction, which, in turn, led to reduced performance ratings. Future research should explore other negative consequences of wage stagnation on employees.

There has been a public outcry over widening organizational income inequality. Yet, little is known about the impact of organizational income inequality on employees (Bapuji, 2015; Connelly et al., 2016. On the one hand, tournament theory argues that employees at all levels may be inspired by high upper echelon level and therefore motivated to perform well. Indeed, Ding, Akhtar, and Ge (2009) have found that vertical pay dispersion was positively associated with product/service and quality sales growth. On the other hand, equity theory and relative deprivation theory propose that high pay dispersion causes ordinary employees to feel inequality, injustice, and jealousy, and therefore decreases their commitment and satisfaction (Finkelstein, Hambrick, & Cannella, 2009). Empirical studies have suggested that pay dispersion is related to lower performance-related outcomes (e.g., Bloom, 1999) and higher turnover rates (Riddell, 2011). Integrating both perspectives as well as the power perspective detailed in this chapter, future research may design innovative experiments to determine the optimal pay dispersion that motivates effort and enhances performance but also maintains organizational harmony and justice (Bapuji, 2015). Furthermore, an organization's relationships with customers and suppliers may also be influenced by pay dispersion (Connelly et al., 2016). For example, Poujol and Tanner (2009) found that high sales tournament reward dispersion causes salespeople to fail to maintain and develop lasting customer relationships. The influence of vertical pay inequality on employee cognitions, emotions, and behaviors as well as their relationships with coworkers, customers, and suppliers has not been adequately studied and is a ripe area for future investigations.

In addition to outcomes of organizational pay dispersion, even less is known about the antecedents of vertical pay dispersion (Gupta, Conroy, & Delery, 2012). Using a longitudinal (ten-year) sample of publicly traded corporates, Connelly et al. (2016) found that transient institutional investors with short time horizons and equity stakes in a large number of firms tend to pressure for higher top manager pay at the expense of employees and therefore increase CEO-to-worker pay dispersion, whereas dedicated investors with longer investment time horizons and equity stakes in a small number of firms are more likely to decrease CEO-to-worker pay dispersion. Continuing this line of research, future research may provide empirical evidence to clarify the sources of organizational pay dispersion.

Much current research on pay dispersion treats this variable in a vacuum without considering the influence of the wider social context surrounding organizations and their employees. However, because organizations are embedded within societies, various factors at the societal levels may positively or negatively influence organizations and their employees. Clearly, escalating CEO-to-worker pay ratio is not limited to the United States For example, Chinese smartphone maker Xiaomi Corp gave its CEO $1.5 million in stock, not contingent on companies meeting goals (Steinberg, 2018). Cultural variables (e.g., power distance) and societal factors (e.g., unemployment rate) may be particularly relevant to predict how employees may react to vertical pay dispersion.

For example, employee reactions to skyrocketing CEO-to-worker pay ratio may be influenced by the inequality present in the society (Bapuji, 2015; Bapuji & Neville, 2015). I propose two competing hypotheses regarding the impact of widening CEO-to-worker pay ratio on employees in the context of *low* (as opposed to high) societal income inequality. On the one hand, employees may react *negatively* because the low inequality in societal income contrasts intensely with high inequality within one's organization. Therefore, employees simply cannot accept the organizational practice that violates the existing social norm. On the other hand, employees may react *positively* because there are more social welfare resources within the social context with low income inequality (Zafirovski, 2005) to readily replace their threatened financial resources from the organization. Providing answers to this question will allow us to have a deeper understanding of the effects of pay dispersion and advance management theory and practice.

Practical Implications

Plato in *Laws* recommends that no one in a community should make more than five times the pay of the lowest-paid worker (Desai et al., 2009). In other words, he suggests setting limits for the poor as well as for the rich. His solution was echoed by J. P. Morgan, who stated that CEOs should make no more than 20 times the wages of a typical worker (Crystal, 1991). Indeed,

Canada's Lee Valley Tools, for example, has a maximum 10 to 1 ratio between its highest and lowest paid workers (Grant, 2014). Another example is Costco, whose CEO-to-worker pay ratio is 57:1. On the other end of the spectrum is Wal-Mart, whose CEO-to-worker pay ratio is 1034:1. Unfortunately, an average Wal-Mart worker only took home an annual wage of $19,177, thereby having to toil for more than a thousand years to earn the $22.2 million that Walmart's CEO pocketed in 2017 (Gelles, 2018).

Plato's recommendation is supported by experts. According to Mishel and Schieder (2017), since skyrocketing CEO pay is due to their power to set pay rather than their productivity, skills, or education, there would be no adverse consequence on corporate output or employment if CEOs earned less or were taxed more. Specifically, they recommend to "reinstate higher marginal income tax rates at the very top," "remove the tax break for executive performance pay," "set corporate tax rates higher for firms that have higher ratios for CEO-to-worker compensation," and "allow greater use of 'say on pay', which allows a firm's shareholders to vote on top executives' compensation."

As specified by Bebchuk and Fried (2003) and Crystal (1991), the board of directors, who determine CEO pay, should depend less on the executives they supervise and more on shareholders instead. In doing so, the board of directors might be mindful of possible repercussions from shareholders if they set the CEO compensation unwisely. Upon demonstrating that transient investors lead to high vertical pay dispersion while dedicated investors cause low vertical pay dispersion, Connelly et al. (2016) recommend managers to consider their existing governance structures, the kind of owners they would like to attract, and actions they might take to attract potential shareholders (Bushee, 2004). If organizations are to lower CEO pay packages, tax loopholes that allow corporate managers to avoid paying their fair share of taxes and enable corporates to deduct excessive pay packages as a "business expense" should be eliminated (Anderson, Cavanagh, Collins, Pizzigati, & Lapham, 2007).

CEO compensation is only part of the problem. The widening income inequality is also caused by employee wage stagnation. For decades, the typical American worker has seen their income growth barely keep up with inflation. Although the problem of wage stagnation is well recognized, less is known about how to tackle this problem. Accordingly, the Economic Policy Institute (2018) launched a multiyear research initiative to make wage growth a policy priority. For example, increasing the minimum wage would raise wages for millions of American workers. According to Denning (2018), unlike previous companies that considered the needs of all stakeholders including customers, employees, shareholders, and the community, contemporary corporates only focus on a single metric of performance – to maximize shareholder value at the expense of everything else. Without any consideration of the possible negative ramifications, employees are seen as expendable commodities. Denning argued that worker wage stagnation is a feature of the current economy because holding worker wages as low as possible allows corporates to secure short-term profits. Thus, Denning called for "a paradigm shift in management" and urged corporates to learn from the example of others (e.g., Apple, Google, Airbnb) offering new ways of running organizations.

The above suggestions to curb organizational income inequality, such as imposing new taxes, capping compensation levels, and increasing minimal wages, depend on government action and public policy measures. However, the effectiveness of these measures will be largely contingent upon the extent to which individuals and organizations comply with these regulations (Bapuji, 2015). As such, organizations need to play an active role to promote economic equality within and outside firms. Revealing the organizational consequences of pay dispersion may help managers and stakeholders to realize the harmful effect of economic inequality on organizations.

Conclusion

From 1978 to 2014, inflation-adjusted CEOs' compensation increased 997 percent whereas average employees' compensation only increased 11 percent (Mishel & Davis, 2015). In 2017 alone, Hock Tan of Broadcom earned $103.2 million and Frank Bisignano of First Data received $102.2 million as rewards (Gelles, 2018). These CEOs make more in one year than what average employees in their organization would earn in a lifetime. While social media criticize the widening pay dispersion within organizations, the academic community needs to work on understanding the consequences of employee wage stagnation, variables that may bring about vertical pay dispersion, as well as outcomes of such an outsized pay gap. I hope this review can provide some insights into the state of affairs and encourage future research to develop evidence-based social and organizational policy aimed at improving societal equality and human sustainability.

References

Abraham, K. G. (1990). Restructuring the employment relationship: The growth of market-mediated work arrangements. In K. G. Abraham & R. McKersie (Eds.), *New developments in the labor market: Toward a new institutional paradigm* (pp. 85–119). Cambridge, MA: MIT Press.

Adams, J. S. (1963). Toward an understanding of inequity. *Journal of Abnormal Psychology, 67*, 422–436.

Akerlof, G. A., & Yellen, J. L. (1990). The fair wage-effort hypothesis and unemployment. *Quarterly Journal of Economics, 105*(2), 255–283.

Anderson, C., & Galinsky, A. D. (2006). Power, optimism, and risktaking. *European Journal of Social Psychology, 36*, 511–536.

Anderson, C., Keltner, D. J., & John, O. P. (2003). Emotional convergence between people over time. *Journal of Personality and Social Psychology, 84*, 1054–1068.

Anderson, S., Cavanagh, J., Collins, C., Pizzigati, S., & Lapham, M. (2007). Executive excess 2008: How average taxpayers subsidize runaway pay. Retrieved from http://d3n8a8pro7vhmx.cloudfront.net/ufe/legacy_url/625/executive_excess_2008.pdf?1448063043

Andersson, L. M., & Bateman, T. S. (1997). Cynicism in the workplace: Some causes and effects. *Journal of Organizational Behavior, 18*(5), 449–469.

Autor, D. H., & Houseman, S. N. (2010). Do temporary help jobs improve labor market outcomes for low skilled workers? Evidence from "work first." *American Economic Journal: Applied Economics, 2*(3), 96–128.

Autor, D. H., Dorn, D., & Hanson, G. H. (2016). The China shock: Learning from labor-market adjustment to large changes in trade. *Annual Review of Economics, 8*, 205–240.

Bakija, J., Cole, A., & Heim, B. T. (2012). Jobs and income growth of top earners and the causes of changing income inequality: Evidence from US tax return data. Unpublished manuscript. Williams College, Williamstown, MA.

Balsam, S. (2012). Taxes and executive compensation. *Education Policy Institute*. Retrieved from www.epi.org/publication/taxes-executive-compensation/

Balsam, S., & Ryan, D. (2008). The effect of Internal Revenue Code Section 162 (m) on the issuance of stock options. In J. Hasseldine (Ed.), *Advances in Taxation* (pp. 3–28). Bingley, UK: Emerald Group Publishing Limited.

Banker, R. D., Lee, S. Y., Gordon, P., & Srinivasan, D. (1996). Contextual analysis of performance impacts of outcome-based incentive compensation. *Academy of Management Journal, 39*(4), 920–948.

Banning, K., & Chiles, T. (2007). Trade-offs in the labor union-CEO compensation relationship. *Journal of Labor Research, 28*(2), 347–357.

Bapuji, H. (2015). Individuals, interactions and institutions: How economic inequality affects organizations. *Human Relations, 68*(7), 1059–1083.

Bapuji, H., & Neville, L. (2015). Income inequality ignored? An agenda for business and strategic organization. *Strategic Organization, 13*(3), 233–246.

Bargh, J. A., Raymond, P., Pryor, J. B., & Strack, F. (1995). Attractiveness of the underling: An automatic power → sex association and its consequences for sexual harassment and aggression. *Journal of Personality and Social Psychology, 68*, 768–781.

Barkema, H. G. & Pennings, J. M. (1998). Top management pay: Impact of overt and covert power. *Organization Studies, 19*, 975–1003.

Barley, S. R., & Kunda, G. (2004). *Gurus, hired guns and warm bodies: Itinerant experts in a knowledge economy*. Princeton, NJ: Princeton University Press.

Baumgartner, F., Berry, J., Hojnacki, M., Kimball, D., & Leech, B. (2009). *Lobbying and policy change: Who wins, who loses, and why*. Chicago, IL: University of Chicago Press.

Bebchuk, L. A., & Fried, J. M. (2003). Executive compensation as an agency problem. *Journal of Economic Perspectives, 17*(3), 71–92.

Bebchuk, L., & Fried, J. (2004). *Pay without performance, Vol. 29*. Cambridge, MA: Harvard University Press.

Benson, W. L., Probst, T. M., Jiang, L., Olson, K. J., & Graso, M. (in press). Insecurity in the ivory tower: Direct and indirect effects of pay stagnation and job insecurity on faculty performance. *Economic and Industrial Democracy*.

Berman, J. (2016). FedEx to settle driver misclassification lawsuit for $240 million. *Logistics Management*. Retrieved from www.logisticsmgmt.com/article/fedex_to_settle_driver_misclassification_lawsuit_for_240_million

Bidwell, M. J. (2013). What happened to long-term employment? The role of worker power and environmental turbulence in explaining declines in worker tenure. *Organization Science, 24*(4), 1061–1082.

Bidwell, M. J., & Briscoe, F. S. (2009). Who contracts? Determinants of the decision to work as an independent contractor among information technology workers. *Academy of Management Journal, 52*(6), 1148–1168.

Bidwell, M.J., & Fernandez-Mateo, I. (2008). Three's a crowd? Understanding triadic employment relationships. In P. Cappelli (Ed.), *Employment relationships: New models of white collar work* (pp. 142–178). New York, NY: Cambridge University Press.

Bidwell, M., Briscoe, F., Fernandez-Mateo, I., & Sterling, A. (2013). The employment relationship and inequality: How and why changes in employment practices are reshaping rewards in organizations. *Academy of Management Annals, 7*(1), 61–121.

Bivens, J., & Mishel, L. (2013). The pay of corporate executives and financial professionals as evidence of rents in top 1 percent incomes. *Journal of Economic Perspectives, 27*, 57–78.

Bloom M. (1999). The performance effects of pay dispersion on individuals and organizations. *Academy of Management Journal, 42*, 25–40.

Briscoe, F., & Murphy, C. (2012). Sleight of hand? Practice opacity, third-party responses, and the interorganizational diffusion of controversial practices. *Administrative Science Quarterly, 57*(4), 553–584.

Buchmueller, T. C., DiNardo, J., & Valletta, R. G. (2002). Union effects on health insurance provision and coverage in the United States. *Industrial & Labor Relations Review, 55*(4), 610–627.

Budros, A. (1999). A conceptual framework for analyzing why organizations downsize. *Organization Science, 10*(1), 69–82.

Bureau of Labor Statistics (2018). Union members summary. Retrieved from www.bls.gov/news.release/union2.nr0.htm

Bushee, B. J. (2004). Identifying and attracting the "right" investors: Evidence on the behavior of institutional investors. *Journal of Applied Corporate Finance, 16*, 28–34.

Cappelli, P., & Keller, J. R. (2013). Classifying work in the new economy. *Academy of Management Review, 38*(4), 575–596.

Castilla, E.J. (2008). Gender, race, and meritocracy in organizational careers. *American Journal of Sociology, 113*(6), 1479–1526.

Castilla, E.J., & Benard, S. (2010). The paradox of meritocracy in organizations. *Administrative Science Quarterly, 55*(4), 543–676.

Chen, C. X., & Sandino, T. (2012). Can wages buy honesty? The relationship between relative wage and employee theft. *Journal of Accounting Research, 50*(4), 967–1000.

Chen, S., Lee-Chai, A.Y., & Bargh, J.A. (2001). Relationship orientation as moderator of the effects of social power. *Journal of Personality and Social Psychology, 80*, 183–187.

Cobb, J. A. (2011). *The employment contract broken? The (non) abandonment of defined benefit pensions (Working paper)*. Ann Arbor, MI: Wharton School of Business.

Cobb, J. A. (2012). *From the 'Treaty of Detroit' to the 401(k): The development and evolution of privatized retirement in the United States* (Doctoral dissertation, University of Michigan, Ann Arbor, MI, USA).

Cobb, J. A. (2016). How firms shape income inequality: Stakeholder power, executive decision making, and the structuring of employment relationships. *Academy of Management Review*, *41*(2), 324–348.

Connelly, B. L., Haynes, K. T., Tihanyi, L., Gamache, D. L., & Devers, C. E. (2016). Minding the gap: Antecedents and consequences of top management-to-worker pay dispersion. *Journal of Management*, *42*(4), 862–885.

Cropanzano, R., & Prehar, C.A. (2001). Emerging justice concerns in an era of changing psychological contracts. In R. Cropanzano (Ed.), *Justice in the workplace: From theory to practice*. Mahwah, NJ: Lawrence Erlbaum Associates, pp. 245–269.

Crosby, F. (1976). A model of egoistical relative deprivation. *Psychological Review*, *83* (2), 85–113.

Crystal, G. S. (1991). *In search of excess: The overcompensation of American executives*. New York, NY: W. W. Norton & Co.

Davis, G. F., & Cobb, J. A. (2010). Corporations and economic inequality around the world: The paradox of hierarchy. *Research in Organizational Behavior*, *30*, 35–53.

Denning, S. (2018). How to fix stagnant wages: Dump the world's dumbest idea. *Forbes*. Retrieved from www.forbes.com/sites/stevedenning/2018/07/26/how-to-fix-stagnant-wages-dump-the-worlds-dumbest-idea/#6b5bba771abc

Desai, S. D., Brief, A. P., & George, J. (2009). Meaner managers: A consequence of income inequality. In R. M. Kramer, A. E. Tenbrunsel, & M.H. Bazerman (Eds.), *Social decision making: Social dilemmas, social values, and ethical judgments*. New York, NY: Psychology Press, 315–334.

Desai, S.D., & Yao, T. (2015). Organizational income inequality: Rising wage disparities and worsening work conditions. Kenan-Flagler Business School Working paper.

Desilver, D. (2014). For most workers, real wages have barely budged for decades. *Pew Research Center*. Retrieved from www.pewresearch.org/fact-tank/2014/10/09/for-most-workers-real-wages-have-barely-budged-for-decades/

Ding, D. Z., Akhtar, S., & Ge, G. L. (2009). Effects of inter-and intra-hierarchy wage dispersions on firm performance in Chinese enterprises. *International Journal of Human Resource Management*, *20*(11), 2370–2381.

DiPrete, T. A., Goux, D., & Maurin, E. (2002). Internal labor markets and earnings trajectories in the post-Fordist economy: An analysis of recent trends. *Social Science Research*, *31*(2), 175–196.

Elvira, M. M., & Graham, M. E. (2002). Not just a formality: Pay system formalization and sex-related earnings effects. *Organization Science*, *13*(6), 601–617.

Farber, H. S. (2008). *Employment insecurity: The decline in worker–firm attachment in the United States (Working paper)*. Princeton University Industrial Relations Section.

Farber, H. S., & Hallock, K. F. (2009). The changing relationship between job loss announcements and stock prices: 1970–1999. *Labor Economics*, *16*(1), 1–11.

Farber, H. S., & Levy, H. (2000). Recent trends in employer-sponsored health insurance coverage: Are bad jobs getting worse? *Journal of Health Economics*, *19*, 93–119.

Finkelstein, S. (1992). Power in top management teams: Dimensions, measurement, and validation. *Academy of Management Journal*, *35*(3), 505–538.

Finkelstein, S., & Hambrick, D. C. (1988). Chief executive compensation: A synthesis and reconciliation. *Strategic Management Journal*, *9*, 543–558.

Finkelstein, S., & Hambrick, D. C. (1989). Chief executive compensation: A study of the intersection of markets and political processes. *Strategic Management Journal, 10*, 121–134.

Finkelstein, S., & Hambrick, D. C. (1996). *Strategic leadership: Top executives and their organizations.* Minneapolis, MN: West Publishing Company.

Finkelstein, S., Hambrick, D. C., & Cannella, A. A. (2009). *Strategic leadership: Theory and research on executives, top management teams, and boards.* New York, NY: Oxford University Press.

Fiske, S. T. (1993). Controlling other people: The impact of power on stereotyping. *American Psychologist, 48*, 621–628.

French, J. R. P., & Raven, B. (1959). The bases of social power. In D. Cartwright (Ed.), *Studies in social power* (pp. 150–167). Ann Arbor, MI: University of Michigan Press.

Fronstin, P. (2012). *Employment-based health benefits: Trends in access and coverage, 1997–2010 (Issue Brief No. 370).* Washington, DC: Employee Benefits Research Institute.

Galinsky, A. D., Gruenfeld, D. H., & Magee, J. C. (2003). From power to action. *Journal of Personality and Social Psychology, 85*, 453–466.

Galinsky, A. D., Magee, J. C., Inesi, M. E., & Gruenfeld, D. H. (2006). Power and perspectives not taken. *Psychological Science, 17*, 1068–1074.

Gelles, D. (2018). Want to make money like a C.E.O.? Work for 275 years. *New York Times*, May 25. Retrieved from www.nytimes.com/2018/05/25/business/highest-paid-ceos-2017.html

Georgesen, J. C., & Harris, M. J. (1998). Why's my boss always holding me down? A meta-analysis of power effects on performance evaluations. *Personality & Social Psychology Review, 2*, 184–195.

Georgesen, J. C., & Harris, M. J. (2000). The balance of power: Interpersonal consequences of differential power and expectancies. *Personality and Social Psychology Bulletin, 26*(10), 1239–1257.

Gerhart, B., & Milkovich, G. T. (1990). Organizational differences in managerial compensation and financial performance. *Academy of Management Journal, 33*(4), 663–691.

Gino, F., & Pierce, L. (2009). The abundance effect: Unethical behavior in the presence of wealth. *Organizational Behavior and Human Decision Processes, 109*(2), 142–155.

Gramm, C.L., & Schnell, J.F. (2001). The use of flexible staffing arrangements in core production jobs. *Industrial & Labor Relations Review, 54*(2), 245–258.

Grant, T. (2014). How One Company Levels the Pay Slope of Executives and Workers. *Globe and Mail*, January 13. Retrieved from www.theglobeandmail.com/news/national/time-to-lead/how-one-companylevels-the-pay-slope-of-executives-and-workers/article15472738/

Greenberg, J. (1990). Employee theft as a reaction to underpayment inequity: The hidden cost of pay cuts. *Journal of Applied Psychology, 75*(5), 561–568.

Greenhouse, S. (2008). *The big squeeze: Tough times for the American worker.* New York, NY: Knopf.

Groth, A. N. (1979). *Men who rape: The psychology of the offender.* New York, NY: Plenum Press.

Guo, L., Libby, T., & Liu, X. K. (2017). The effects of vertical pay dispersion: Experimental evidence in a budget setting. *Contemporary Accounting Research, 34*(1), 555–576.

Gupta, N., Conroy, S. A., & Delery, J. E. (2012). The many faces of pay variation. *Human Resource Management Review, 22*: 100–115.

Hacker, J. S., & Pierson, P. (2010). Winner-take-all politics: Public policy, political organization, and the precipitous rise of top incomes in the United States. *Politics & Society, 38*(2), 152–204.

Hallock, K. F. (2009). Job loss and the fraying of the implicit employment contract. *Journal of Economic Perspectives, 23*(4), 69–93.

Hambrick, D. C., & D'Aveni, R. A. (1992). Top team deterioration as part of the downward spiral of large corporate bankruptcies. *Management Science, 38*, 1445–1466.

Harris, D. G., & Livingstone, J. R. (2002). Federal tax legislation as an implicit contracting cost benchmark: The definition of excessive executive compensation. *Accounting Review, 77*(4), 997–1018.

Henderson, A. D., & Fredrickson, J. W. (1996). Information-processing demands as a determinant of CEO compensation. *Academy of Management Journal, 39*, 575–606.

Heneman, R. L., & Werner, J. M. (2005). *Merit pay: Linking pay to performance in a changing world*. Washington, DC: Information Age Publishing.

Hobfoll, S. E. (1989). Conservation of resources: A new attempt at conceptualizing stress. *American Psychologist, 44*(3), 513–524.

Hollister, M. N. (2004). Does firm size matter anymore? The new economy and firm size wage effects. *American Sociological Review, 69*(5), 659–676.

Hollister, M. N. (2011). Employment stability in the US labor market: Rhetoric vs. reality. *Annual Review of Sociology, 37*(1), 305–324.

Houseman, S. N. (2001). Why employers use flexible staffing arrangements: Evidence from an establishment survey. *Industrial & Labor Relations Review, 55*(1), 149–170.

Houseman, S. N., & Polivka, A. (2000). The implications of flexible staffing arrangements for job stability. In D. Newmark (Ed.), *On the job: Is long-term employment a thing of the past?* (pp. 427–462). New York, NY: Russell Sage Foundation.

Houseman, S. N., Kalleberg, A. L., & Erickcek, G. A. (2003). The role of temporary agency employment in tight labor markets. *Industrial & Labor Relations Review, 57*(1), 103–127.

Jones, E. E., & Nisbett, R.E. (1972). The actor and the observer: Divergent perceptions of causality. In E. E.Jones, D. E. Kanouse, H. H. Kelley, R. E. Nisbett, S. Valins, & B. Weiner (Eds.), *Attribution: Perceiving the cause of behavior* (pp. 79–94). Morristown, NJ: General Learning Press.

Kaiser Family Foundation/HRET. (2012). *Kaiser Family Foundation/Health Research & Educational Trust survey of employer-sponsored health benefits*. Retrieved from www.kff.org and as American Hospital Association/Health Research & Educational Trust catalog no. 097523.

Kalleberg, A. L. (2000). Nonstandard employment relations: Part-time, temporary and contract work. *Annual Review of Sociology, 26*, 341–365.

Kalleberg, A. L., Reskin, B. F., & Hudson, K. (2000). Bad jobs in America: Standard and nonstandard employment relations and job quality in the United States. *American Sociological Review, 65*(2), 256–278.

Keene, J., & Prokos, A. (2007). Comparing offers and take-ups of employee health insurance across race, gender, and decade. *Sociological Inquiry, 77*(3), 425–459.

Kipnis, D. (1972). Does power corrupt? *Journal of Personality and Social Psychology*, 24, 33–41.

Kipnis, D. (1976). *The powerholders.* Chicago, IL: University of Chicago Press.

Kipnis, D., Schmidt, S., Price, K., & Stitt, C. (1981). Why do I like thee: Is it your performance or my orders? *Journal of Applied Psychology*, 66, 324–328.

Kunda, G., Barley, S. R., & Evans, J. (2002). Why do contractors contract? The experience of highly skilled technical professionals in a contingent labor market. *Industrial & Labor Relations Review*, 55(2), 234–261.

Lambert, R. A., & Larcher, D. F., & Weigelt, K. (1993). The structure of organizational incentives. *Administrative Science Quarterly*, 38, 438–461.

Laverty, K. J. (1996). Economic "short-termism": The debate, the unresolved issues, and the implications for management practice and research. *Academy of Management Review*, 21, 825–860.

Lazear, E. P. (2000). Performance pay and productivity. *American Economic Review*, 90 (5), 1346–1361.

Lazear, E., & Rosen, S. (1981). Rank-order tournaments as optimum labor contracts. *Journal of Political Economy*, 89, 841–864.

Lemieux, T. (2006). Increasing residual wage inequality: Composition effects, noisy data, or rising demand for skill? *The American Economic Review* 96(3), 461–498.

Lemieux, T., Macleod, W. B., & Parent, D. (2009). Performance pay and wage inequality. *Quarterly Journal of Economics*, *124*(1), 1–49.

Lepak, D.P., Takeuchi, R., & Snell, S.A. (2003). Employment flexibility and firm performance: Examining the interaction effects of employment mode, environmental dynamism, and technological intensity. *Journal of Management*, 29, 681–703.

Lindskold, S., & Aronoff, J. R. (1980). Conciliatory strategies and relative power. *Journal of Experimental Social Psychology,16*, 187–198.

Little, J. (1995). The impact of employer payments for health insurance and social security on the premium for education and earnings inequality. *New England Economic Review*, , May/June, 25–40.

Marler, J. H., & Faugère, C. (2010). Shareholder activism and middle management equity incentives. *Corporate Governance: An International Review*, 18(4), 313–328.

Marler, J. H., Barringer, M. W., & Milkovich, G. T. (2002). Boundaryless and traditional contingent employees: Worlds apart. *Journal of Organizational Behavior*, *23*, 425–453.

Maxwell, J., Briscoe, F., & Temin, P. (2000). Corporate health care purchasing and the revised social contract with workers. *Business and Society*, 39, 281–303.

Mishel, L. (2015). Causes of wage stagnation. *Economic Policy Institute.* Retrieved from www.epi.org/publication/causes-of-wage-stagnation/

Mishel, L., & Davis, A. (2015). Top CEOs make 300 times more than typical workers: Pay growth surpasses stock gains and wage growth of top 0.1 percent. *Economic Policy Institute.* Retrieved from www.epi.org/publication/top-ceos-make-300-times-more-than-workers-pay-growth-surpasses-market-gains-and-the-rest-of-the-0-1-percent/

Mishel, L., & Schieder, J. (2017). CEO pay remains high relative to the pay of typical workers and high-wage earners. *Economic Policy Institute.* Retrieved from www.epi.org/publication/ceo-pay-remains-high-relative-to-the-pay-of-typical-workers-and-high-wage-earners/

Mishel, L., Bivens, J., Gould, E., & Shierholz, H. (2012). *The state of working America* (12th ed.). Ithaca, NY: Cornell University Press.

Mishel, L., Gould, E., & Bivens, J. (2015). Wage stagnation in nine charts. *Economic Policy Institute*. Retrieved from www.epi.org/publication/charting-wage-stagnation/

Munnell, A. H., Haverstick, K., & Sanzenbacher, G. (2006). *Job tenure and pension coverage* (Working Papers, pp. 1–35). Chestnut Hill, MA: Center for Retirement Research.

Nayar, N., & Willinger, G. L. (2001). Financial implications of the decision to increase reliance on contingent labor. *Decision Sciences, 32*(4), 661–681.

Neumark, D., Polsky, D., & Hansen, D. (1999). Has job stability declined yet? New evidence for the 1990s. *Journal of Labor Economics, 17*(4), S29–S64.

Osterman, P. (1999). *Securing prosperity*. Princeton, NJ: Princeton University Press.

Pfeffer, J., & Baron, J. N. (1988). Taking the workers back out: Recent trends in the structuring of employment. *Research in Organizational Behavior, 10,* 257–303.

Pfeffer, J., & Langton, N. (1993). The effect of wage dispersion on satisfaction, productivity, and working collaboratively: Evidence from college and university faculty. *Administrative Science Quarterly, 38*(3), 382–407.

Pierce, B. (2001). Compensation inequality. *Quarterly Journal of Economics, 116*(4), 1493–1525.

Poujol, F. J., & Tanner, J. F. (2009). The impact of contests on salespeople's customer orientation: An application of tournament theory. *Journal of Personal Selling and Sales Management, 30,* 33–46.

Pryor, J. B. (1987). Sexual harassment proclivities in men. *Sex Roles, 17,* 269–290.

Pryor, J. B., LaVite, C. M. & Stoller, L. M. (1993). A social psychological model for predicting sexual harassment. *Journal of Vocational Behavior,42,* 68–83.

Riddell, C. (2011). Compensation policy and quit rates: A multilevel approach using benchmarking data. *Industrial Relations: A Journal of Economy and Society, 50*(4), 656–677.

Rose, N. L., & Wolfram, C. (2002). Regulating executive pay: Using the tax code to influence chief executive officer compensation. *Journal of Labor Economics, 20*(S2), S138–S175.

Sahaym, A., Steensma, H. K., & Schilling, M. A. (2007). The influence of information technology on the use of loosely coupled organizational forms: An industry level analysis. *Organization Science,* 18(5), 865–880.

Segal, L. M., & Sullivan, D. G. (1997). The growth of temporary services work. *Journal of Economic Perspectives,* 11(2), 117–136.

Shaw, J. D. (2014). Pay dispersion. *Annual Review in Organizational Psychology and Organizational Behaviour, 1,* 521–544.

Shearer, B. (2004). Piece rates, fixed wages and incentives: Evidence from a field experiment. *Review of Economic Studies,* 71(2), 513–534.

Shuey, K., & O'Rand, A. (2004). New risks for workers: Pensions, labor markets, and gender. *Annual Review of Sociology, 30,* 435–477.

Shuman, M. (2017). Why wages aren't growing. *Bloomberg.* Retrieved from www.bloomberg.com/news/articles/2017-09-21/why-wages-aren-t-growing

Sjöberg, O. (2009). Corporate governance and earnings inequality in the OECD countries 1979–2000. *European Sociological Review, 25,* 519–533.

Slottje, D., Woodbury, S., & Anderson, R. (2000). Employee benefits and the distribution of income and wealth. In W. T. William, T. Alpert, & S. A. Woodbury (Eds.), *Employee benefits and labor markets in Canada and the United States* (pp. 349–378). Kalamazoo, MI: W. E. Upjohn Institute for Employment Research.

Smola, K. W., & Sutton, C. (2002). Generational differences: Revisiting generational work values for the new millennium. *Journal of Organizational Behavior, 23,* 363–382.

Stainback, K., Tomaskovic-Devey, D., & Skaggs, S. (2010). Organizational approaches to inequality: Inertia, relative power, and environments. *Annual Review of Sociology, 36,* 225–247.

Steers, R., & Ungson, G. R. (1987). Strategic issues in executive compensation decisions. In D. B. Balkin & L. R. Gomez-Mejia (Eds.), *New perspectives on compensation* (pp. 315–327). Englewood Cliffs, NJ: Prentice-Hall.

Steinberg, J. (2018). CEO's stock award from Chinese smartphone maker Xiaomi is one of the largest ever: Lei Jun gets about $1.5 billion ahead of company's listing in Hong Kong. *Wall Street Journal,* June 23. www.wsj.com/articles/ceos-stock-award-from-chinese-smartphone-maker-xiaomi-is-one-of-the-largest-ever-1529688807

Thompson, J., & Smeeding, T. (2014). Income inequality. *The Stanford Center on Poverty and Inequality.* Retrieved from https://inequality.stanford.edu/sites/default/files/media/_media/pdf/pathways/special_sotu_2014/Pathways_SOTU_2014_Income_Inequality.pdf

Tiedens, L. Z. (2000). Powerful emotions: The vicious cycle of social status positions and emotions. In N. M. Ashkanasy, C. E. Härtel, & W. J. Zerbe (Eds.), *Emotions in the workplace: Research, theory, and practice* (pp. 72–81). Westport, CT: Quorum Books/Greenwood Publishing Group.

Turnley, W. H., & Feldman, D. C. (1998). Psychological contract violations during corporate restructuring. *Human Resources Management 37*(1), 71–83.

Ungson, G. R, & Steers, R. M. (1984). Motivation and politics in executive compensation. *Academy of Management Review, 9,* 313–323.

Van Kleef, G. A., De Dreu, C. K. W., Pietroni, D., & Manstead, A. S. R. (2006). Power and emotion in negotiation: Power moderates the interpersonal effects of anger and happiness on concession making. *European Journal of Social Psychology, 36,* 557–581.

Wade J. B., O'Reilly, C. A., & Chandradat, I. (1990). Golden parachutes: CEOs and the exercise of social influence. *Administrative Science Quarterly, 35,* 587–603.

Western, B., & Rosenfeld, J. (2011). Unions, norms, and the rise in US wage inequality. *American Sociological Review, 76*(4), 513–537.

Whistler, T. L., Meyer, H., Baum, B. H., & Sorensen, P. F., Jr. (1967). Centralization of organizational control: An empirical study of its meaning and measurement. *Journal of Business, 40,* 10–26.

Wiens-Tuers, B., & Hill, E. (2002). How did we get here from there? Movement into temporary employment. *Journal of Economic Issues, 36*(2), 303–311.

Wood, R. W. (2015). FedEx settles independent contractor mislabeling case for $228 million. *Forbes.* Retrieved from www.forbes.com/sites/robertwood/2015/06/16/fedex-settles-driver-mislabeling-case-for-228-million/#793d62e7c22e

Yanadori, Y., & Cui, V. (2013). Creating incentives for innovation? The relationship between pay dispersion in RandD groups and firm innovation performance. *Strategic Management Journal, 34*(12), 1502–1511.

Zafirovski, M. (2005). Social exchange theory under scrutiny: A positive critique of its economic-behaviorist formulations. *Electronic Journal of Sociology, 2*(2), 1–40.

Zimbardo, P. (2007). *The Lucifer effect: Understanding how good people turn evil*. New York, NY: Random House.

10 Work and Employment in Fluid Organizational Forms

Jörg Sydow and Markus Helfen

Introduction

Despite all challenges and changes in recent years, work and employment continue to take place to a large extent within organizations. While it is true that some researchers emphasize the vanishing of large corporations and their decreasing importance for the organization of work and employment (Davis, 2016), formal organizations in capitalist as much as in other kinds of societies are unlikely to disappear. At the most, such organizations will continue to change in form. Nevertheless, the study of work and employment today needs to go beyond a "container view of organizations" (Winter, Berente, Howison, & Butler, 2014) that neglects how work and employment is organized outside the scope of classic formal hierarchies. Important examples of this sort of work are dependent self-employment and the acquisition of "jobs" with the help of online platforms in a spreading gig economy. According to estimates by McKinsey & Co., more than 160 million low- as well as high-skilled persons work in the United States and Western Europe in this new kind of economy, with more often than not severe consequences, not only for organizations, but also for individuals (Manyika et al., 2016). At the same time, nonstandard and precarious forms of work have proliferated across countries and industries (International Labour Office, 2016; Rubery, Grimshaw, Keizer, & Johnson, 2018).

Drivers of organizational innovation and transformation are to be found in fundamental social, technological and economic changes of societies. Within the current debates around buzzwords such as globalization, financialization, servitization, digitalization, virtualization, automation, aging, society, mass migration or de-unionization, very often technological and economic drivers are assumed implicitly or explicitly to be the key to their development. Nevertheless, it is important – once again – not to adopt a technologically or economically deterministic perspective (Winter et al., 2014). One should rather look for a theoretical perspective that reflects on the recursive constitution of structure and agency in and across organizations (e.g., Giddens, 1984). Thereby, it becomes possible to consider how different stakeholders – not only managers and workers, but also social movements, trade unions and non-governmental organizations (NGOs) – shape, the social organization of work and employment in practice: around technologies, inside and outside formal organizations, and on different national and transnational scales (e.g., Frenkel, 2001; Reinecke & Donaghey, 2015).

Obviously, labor, work, and employment are core categories of the social sciences with a considerable history of debating their proper understanding, also in relation to formal organization (e.g., Burawoy & Wright, 1990; Cohen, 2016; Delbridge & Sallaz, 2015; Edwards, 1990). In our context, in which we want to understand the connection of broader organizational and interorganizational changes and how they relate to work and employment (Kalleberg, 2001), we conceive both work and employment as being organized, either within or outside organizations. Since we use both these terms in order to come to an improved understanding of the implications of organizational innovation and transformation, we need to clarify these notions and their relationship.

In an organizational context, both concepts, work and employment, denote a structural arrangement for the exertion of human labor in time and space that can be thought of, at least in a first instance, as being independent of single individual actors. At second sight though, organized subjects – depending on their respective power – shape or at least co-shape work and employment. They do so in various constellations, i.e., as an individual job holder, a single employer, a line manager as well as a team of workers or within collectives in formal employee representation and participation as well as collective bargaining. Beyond this fundamental commonality, both terms look at similar and overlapping phenomena of the social organization of labor from different angles. The notion of work is much broader in that it denotes goal-directed human activity as a *conditio humana* to sustain life – also including its reproduction. Employment, by contrast, marks a special form of "economic" work (Cappelli & Keller, 2013), defined as activities undertaken for another party in exchange for some compensation, regulated either by a labor contract with an employer or by a contract with a customer in the case of self-employment (Davidov, 2014).

In addition, a concentration on the notion of work usually implies a more micro-level view on the performance of tasks within a broader labor process, whereas an analysis of employment comes along with a view on how the performance of work is embedded in wider employment relations. In other words, a focus on work gives rise to a concentration on "work relations," i.e., the action of workers with their object in the precise execution of work tasks – including technology and collaboration with coworkers. The term "employment relations," by contrast, provides a broader and at the same time narrower view: (1) broader in that the notion is reflective of the meso- or macro-embeddedness of performing work in societal context, i.e., links work to industrial relations embedded into the social institutions of an industry, a country or even a transnational space like the European Union or ASEAN; (2) narrower in that it confines itself to "dependent" work under the direction of an authority, however defined, but usually an employing organization.

In what follows, we start by discussing the so-called post-bureaucratic organization. From our view, post-bureaucracy is useful for introducing the rather general idea that organizational innovation and transformation affects work and employment in its broadest terms – though with some caveats concerning the size and nature of organizations. However, going beyond that term, we will highlight, define and analyze three dimensions we find helpful in substantiating the present trends towards more fluid forms of organizing: plurality, temporariness and partiality, and how these affect the current conditions of work and employment.

Plurality deals with the fact that the contracting of labor occurs in a multitude of arrangements involving often more than two actors. Thereby, employment inside and outside formal organizations is increasingly marked by triadic or triangulated relations which are, more generally, multiple rather than dyadic or bilateral (Havard, Rorive, & Sobczak, 2009; Marchington, Grimshaw, Rubery, & Willmott, 2005; Rubery, Cooke, Earnshaw, & Marchington, 2003). In these plural forms, the classical employer–employee relations are complemented, and sometimes replaced, by relations in which either buyer organizations or "labor intermediaries" (Bonet, Cappelli, & Hamori, 2013; Xhauflair, Huybrechts, & Pichault, 2018) join the setting. The archetypical example is temporary agency work, in which an agency arranges work of an employee for a third-party (Cappelli & Keller, 2013). Plural forms also include, however, a host of other arrangements in which sourcing agents (Sondararajan, Khan, & Tarba, 2018) are involved in co-shaping working conditions as well.

Temporariness deals with the fact that work and employment has become not only short-term but also marked by an institutionalized termination. The organizational forms contributing to this kind of temporality can be either of an ephemeral, very informal nature (e.g., a self-organized emergency response in the event of a major catastrophe) or formally set up and managed as in the case of most project-oriented arrangements. An example of the latter would be a project-based organization or project network (see below). Work and employment in the latter are said to be structured more by relational patterns than by hierarchical authority characteristic of the traditional employment relationship (Bechky, 2006).

Partiality is a related, but somewhat different concept that captures the idea that organizing in networks and some other structural arrangements does not necessarily combine all elements used to classify a "decided order" (Ahrne & Brunsson, 2011) as in the case of a "complete" organization, i.e. a clearly delineated membership, internal rules, monitoring, as well as incentives and sanctions. This incompleteness affects decisions on work and employment in several ways. In particular, the notion of partiality makes it easier to understand the organized character of plural and temporary arrangements outside formal organizations, but also the *unorganized* appearance of much of what is going on inside organizations. Prominent examples of organizational partiality are to be found not only in interorganizational networks, but also in markets, movements, and standard-setting.

Whilst discussing the development towards more post-bureaucratic organizational forms including their increased temporariness, plurality and partiality we will also highlight counter-movements that regulate work and employment conditions. While it is true that organizational innovation and transformation lead to an ever-growing diversity of work and employment arrangements, "legal frameworks create homeostatic pressures to sustain the distinctions across categories" (Cappelli & Keller, 2013, p. 576), most importantly and across most national institutions, between employment within an organization on the one hand and self-employment or contract work outside a formal organization on the other. At the same time, the struggle over the rules governing work – predominantly in terms of what is a type of work to be protected – creates regulatory paths along which the structuring of contract arrangements, social security systems, and other aspects of societal integration follows. In contrast to legal frameworks, the influence of individual and collective actors with their motives and mobilization power is, however, much more ambiguous and difficult to capture.

From Bureaucracies to Post-Bureaucratic Forms of Organizations?

Work and employment are shaped at least as much by organizations as by economics and technology (Trist, 1981; Winter et al., 2014), not to mention societal institutions, such as contract and labor law, trade unions, social movements, or professions. In consequence, formal organizational structures continue to matter when analyzing the development of work in and across organizations. Irrespective of whether they are publicly or privately owned, at least large organizations continue to be described as "bureaucratic," that is characterized by hierarchical order, formal rules, direct surveillance, and longer-term employment (Weber, 1968). Despite the fact that bureaucracy is obviously a matter of degree (Pugh, Hickson, Hinings, & Turner, 1968) and, perhaps even more importantly, not only has constraining but also enabling effects on organizations and their members (Adler & Borys, 1996; Styhre, 2007), scholars in the 1990s started speaking and writing about so-called "post-bureaucratic" forms of organizations.

Most prominently, Heckscher (1994) tried to define what was – at that time – the emerging post-bureaucratic form of organization, the (also admittedly ideal-type) properties of which are listed in Table 10.1. Joining this debate a decade later and focusing on work in projects as perhaps the most important form of temporary organizations, Hodgson (2004) sees this rhetoric as having ideas adopted from discussions about "flexible specialization," the "network organization," the "boundaryless organization" the "virtual organization," the "21st century organization" or the "new, knowledge- or internet-based economy." Nevertheless, this author, supported by many others (e.g., Alvesson & Thompson, 2005; Grey & Garsten, 2001; Johnson, Wood, Brewster, & Bookes, 2009; Oberg & Walgenbach, 2007; Sewell, 1998; Styhre, 2007), identifies the survival of bureaucratic elements in so-called post-bureaucratic organizations, not least power asymmetry and hierarchical authority. What is more, these bureaucratic elements are sometimes even strengthened by the introduction of new (more or

Table 10.1 *Characteristics of bureaucratic and post-bureaucratic organizations (based on Heckscher, 1994)*

Bureaucratic organization	Post-bureaucratic organization
Consensus through acquiescence to authority	Consensus through institutionalized dialogue
Influence based on formal position	Influence through persuasion/personal qualities
Internal trust	High need for internal trust
Emphasis on rules and regulations	Emphasis on organizational mission
Information monopolized at top of hierarchy	Strategic information shared in organization
Focus on rules for conduct	Focus on principles guiding action
Fixed (and clear) decision-making processes	Fluid/flexible decision-making processes
Communal spirit, friendship groupings	Network of specialized functional relationships
Hierarchical appraisal	Open and visible peer review processes
Definite and impermeable boundaries	Open and permeable boundaries
Objective rules to ensure equity of treatment	Broad public standards of performance
Expectation of constancy	Expectation of change

less bureaucratic) tools and techniques such as project management or cultural control through organizational missions (respectively). For this very reason, Hodgson (2004) prefers the term "re-bureaucratization" rather than "de-bureaucratization" for allegedly post-bureaucratic forms of organizations. According to this author, even if the organizational mission and strategic planning are emphasized, hierarchical coordination typically comes with rules and guidelines.

Nevertheless, some (for instance, agile) project management tool may well make a difference (Hodgson & Briand, 2013). Moreover, there is evidence for increasing autonomy being granted to employees within an organization, both in terms of scheduling and decision making (Wegman, Hoffman, Carter, Twenge, & Guenole, 2018). Others found that leaders reported that relationship-building and interpersonal skills are increasingly important in organizations to influence followers (Gentry, Harris, Baker, & Brittain Leslie, 2008). Beyond that, scholars lament the lack of empirical support for the post-bureaucratization thesis (e.g., Alvesson & Thompson, 2005; Styhre, 2007, pp. 95–101), not least with regard to implications for working conditions and employment relations.

An example of a post-bureaucratic organizational form within organizations is also the spread of so-called high-performance work systems. Core practices of high-performance work systems are: pay for performance, profit and gain sharing, team work, information sharing and participative decision making, selective hiring and extensive training, and providing job rotation and security (Posthuma, Campion, Masimova, & Campion, 2013). If not all, at least some of these practices have been increasingly employed, more often than not combined with developing a work climate and an organizational culture which allow for experimentation and exploration (Zhu, Gardner, & Chen, 2018). In general, post-bureaucratic forms of organization seem to rely on more than just high-performance work systems and practices and a more creativity-enhancing work environment. Commitment, identification, and even citizenship behavior (e.g., Blader, Patil, & Packer, 2017) seem additionally to ensure organizational control in such more fluid structures. The consequences for the organization of work and employment seem in any case to be much more ambivalent. For proponents, the participatory characteristics of employment practices following the ideal of a post-bureaucratic organization should be able to generate mainly self-motivated employees with shared objectives, taking on responsibility for the whole, thus allowing for a kind of creativity-enhancing mode of self-governance. A bit more defensively, some other authors argue that, at least if installed with a sufficient amount of job control and discretion, also regarding how to implement such systems, potential negative effects of this form on employees can be avoided and thus organizational performance improved (Jensen, Patel, & Messersmith, 2013). However, as Hodgson (2004) points out, post-bureaucratic forms are likely to rely on a third (ideal-) type of control which emphasizes organizational commitment and identification by means of trust and moral integrity (Willmott, 1993). With respect to forms of project-based organizing (see below), for instance, it is emphasized that "workers are controlled both structurally and normatively under project-management regimes" (Peticca-Harris, Weststar, & McKenna, 2015, p. 576).

Perhaps even more importantly, formal organizations and their employment relations have increasingly been interpenetrated by market- or market-like mechanisms (Godard, 2004; Kalleberg, 2001, 2009). According to Bidwell, Briscoe, and Fernandez-Mateo (2013), who review studies of work and employment in the United States, this interpenetration of hierarchical organization by such mechanisms is documented by (1) declining tenure, (2) increased restructuring through layoffs, (3) growing use of contingent workers, (4) increased outsourcing, (5) increased use of variable incentive pay, and (6) reduced employer role in benefits. At the same time, these authors mention two barriers towards an even more comprehensive and rapid interpenetration of organizations by market- or market-like mechanisms: the growing regulation of workplace practices and the increased influence of social movements on work and employment.

Two other caveats are needed: one concerning organizational size, another relating to ownership. For in contrast to large, diversified corporations, small and medium-sized firms as well as start-ups are believed to rely per se significantly less on bureaucratic forms of coordination and control (Mallett & Wapshott, 2017). As empirical studies have shown already, organizational size is indeed highly associated with the degree of bureaucratization (Child, 1984). It follows from this that the situation is quite different in organizations of a significantly smaller size, which more often than not serve as a model for the rejuvenation of large corporations (Baden-Fuller & Stopford, 1992). Such large corporations have in fact begun to collaborate with start-ups, for instance with the help of accelerator and incubator programs to benefit from the best of both bureaucratic and post-bureaucratic worlds. Regarding ownership, the difference between public organizations and private firms has, in view of the New Public Management movement and similar reform initiatives, diminished over the years and, via the systematic rather than random import of private-sector policies and practices (e.g., a performance management system), led to a kind of "hybrid model of employment" in which the public-sector ethos is more or less preserved (Conway, Fu, Monks, Alfes, & Bailey, 2015).

In conclusion, large bureaucratic organizations have experimented with some elements of the post-bureaucratic form. However, they have often combined the post-bureaucratic forms aimed at fostering commitment and creativity with market-like elements and organizational features which emphasize performance and goal alignment. In combination with practices of *re*bureaucratization, the resulting picture is fragmented and contradictory (Rubery, Earnshaw, Marchington, Cooke, & Vincent, 2002); not to mention that much work is organized by small and medium-sized firms and performed increasingly outside any formal type of organization.

Plurality of Working in Networked Organizations

The notion of the plurality of work, enabled essentially by network forms of organization (Powell, 1990), needs further clarification. One reason for much confusion is that network structures, i.e. complex constellations of vertical, horizontal and lateral relationships, can either come into being within organizations, or they can characterize (more or less temporary) relations among organizations. Another reason is that networks can be regarded either as a distinct organizational form of governance (Powell, 1990; Sydow, Schüßler, & Müller-Seitz, 2016), or adopted as a theoretical lens to study any kind of social system. In this latter case the notion of network theory has gained some popularity (Borgatti & Halgin, 2011). In all of these views, however, network structures are typically considered to allow for more fluid forms of exchange or organizing.

Nevertheless, even when looked at from a governance perspective, i.e., networks conceived as an organizational form that relies on trust and reciprocity rather than hierarchical fiat (Powell, 1990), the confusion persists. For many organizations have developed internal network structures by allowing more lateral communication or providing organizational units with greater autonomy (for instance, as profit centers). External network relations, often developed at the same time, result from closer collaboration among organizations that either did not have a relationship before, or previously only exchanged goods or services via fleeting market transactions. Such collaborative relationships may alternatively result from (quasi-)externalizing tasks and practices that were formerly carried out inside the boundaries of an organization (Sydow et al., 2016). While this latter strategy is commonly known as "outsourcing" (using outside resource), this very notion leaves the quality of business relationships open that emerge from respective outsourcing decisions.

This is unfortunate, at least in our context, because the resulting relationship can resemble either a rather ideal-type market transaction or one of different network modes of exchange; with diverging repercussions for work and employment performed within these relations. In what follows, we will concentrate on externalized or quasi-externalized work that typically comes along with sourcing goods and services or entire business processes (such as IT or HRM) from outside the boundaries of a focal organization, often, though not always, leading to interorganizational collaboration (or: external network relationships) that is then a substitute for intraorganizational collaboration (Davis-Blake & Broschak, 2009).

Pfeffer and Baron (1988) were among the first to point to the relevance of (quasi-)externalizing work with the help of more fluid organizational forms. Ashforth, George, and Blatt (2007) base their extensive review of the literature on the framework of these authors that usefully distinguishes employees (of a particular organization) – with regard to their "administrative attachment" – from independent contractors or freelancers. Using this framework, Ashforth and colleagues report not only important findings from empirical studies of nonstandard work but also discuss the blending, and hence pluralization, of standard and nonstandard work within a single organization – and the challenges that come along with it for management. For instance, in this latter regard these authors highlight the need to manage potential negative spillover effects from workers in nonstandard employment to those in standard employment and the tensions that may arise when workers of both kinds work side by side in the offices of factories.

However, as Ashforth and colleagues' (2007) review basically studies the experiences of nonstandard work arrangements, it is hard to isolate the importance of administrative attachment in relation to temporal and physical attachments (see also Davis-Blake & Broschak, 2009). Overall, the empirical studies reviewed lead to the conclusion that the experiences of individuals and the implications for organizations are not only very diverse, but can also be contradictory. For instance, and with particular reference to the administrative attachment, "nonstandard work is often associated with freedom, autonomy, and liberation from corporate control ... At the same time, many nonstandard workers also experience great constraints, whether self-imposed or imposed by others" (Ashforth et al., 2007, p. 80). An example for the former is a self-set milestone by either a self-employed worker or a project team; an example for the latter might be a delivery date asked for and sanctioned by a customer or issued onto the hand-held device of a driver through the algorithm of a delivery platform. The implications for the employing organization or the buying organization depend also on how these particular experiences are processed by the working individual. Another example is the experience of organizational boundaries by such workers because, as in the case of standard employment but also in much of temporary employment, these boundaries either continue to be clear-cut; or organizational boundaries are increasingly blurred – as is often assumed for forms of nonstandard employment that involve a third-party intermediary – with important implications for individual careers, identity formation and organizational commitment.

As already indicated, the situation is complicated because the (quasi-) externalization of work does not necessarily lead to nonstandard work arrangements in general. Rather, standard employment may be shifted from a focal organization wishing to adopt more lean structures to suppliers that are – because of significant wage differentials – more often than not located in developing countries and, for that very reason, can rely on more or less "standard" employment relations. This "interfirm transfer of jobs" (Davis-Blake & Broschak, 2009), as a consequence of decisions about make, buy or cooperate, often leaves a focal organization with not only less work, but also with changes in organizational structure and culture, new work designs, different skill requirements, career opportunities and perceived job security, changing work attitudes and supervisor–subordinate relationships, and most likely with more opportunities for experiencing – directly or indirectly (via coworkers) – working in triangular employment relations (see below).

Less with an eye on work and employment, but nevertheless highly relevant for this discussion, Gereffi, Humphrey, and Sturgeon (2005) distinguish three network types of transnational or even global value chain governance. These forms complement the traditional market mode of governance on the one hand (characterized by little explicit coordination beyond simple product and price specifications) and the hierarchical mode of governance (vertical integration) on the other (see also Sydow et al., 2016, pp. 12–15). The choice of one of these hybrid or network forms, which, according to Gereffi and colleagues, are importantly different with regard to the power relations between lead firms and suppliers, depends mainly upon three factors: the complexity of the information and knowledge to be transferred in the relationship; the ability to codify transactions and thus the need for transaction-specific investments; and the capabilities of suppliers with respect to the demands of the lead organization.

Modular governance is a first mode of network governance which makes use of the classic market mechanism more than the other two. Unlike market transactions, however, the information transmitted in modular value chains is more complex, although codified through standardized interfaces. Modular value chains are common in the electronics manufacturing industry, for instance. A second network mode of governance is termed by Gereffi and colleagues (2005) as being *relational*, as it continues with the original conception of a network as a long-term interorganizational arrangement based upon intensive communication and generalized reciprocity (rather than on short-term, price-coordinated exchanges). Examples of this type of global production and supply network are to be found in the automotive industry which, despite its increasing use of electronics and respective modularization strategies, continues to rely on relation-specific investments, face-to-face interaction and interorganizational trust. Buyers and suppliers in this industry tend to be mutually dependent, as suppliers have often developed strong capabilities that lead firms want to access as complementary competences. The third network mode of governance is appropriately termed *captive*, because here lead firms dominate a set of dependent suppliers that produce nonstandard items based on rather detailed product specifications. Captive suppliers have limited capabilities and are hardly able to innovate on their own and, in consequence, to develop into system suppliers. Lead firms develop incentives and control mechanisms to prevent captive suppliers from exiting the relationship. Examples of this type of governance are also to be found in the automotive industry, though less so between car manufacturers and system suppliers, and to a greater extent between the system and second- or third-tier suppliers.

The choice among relational vs. more market-based forms, as Lane and Probert (2009) show in their analysis of the global garment industry, depends not only on the transactional properties emphasized by Gereffi and colleagues, but also on the institutional context. Lane and Probert's study shows that in this highly competitive industry German clothing firms favored a relational approach based on longer-term cooperation, while Anglo-Saxon firms preferred more market-oriented, transactional forms of coordinating tasks across organizational boundaries. The authors explain this finding with the differences in the institutional environments of these two countries, not only with regard to labor and contract law but also to cultural practice.

The analysis of global production and supply networks was, for many years, quite ignorant regarding issues of work and employment, despite the abundance of "global work" (Hinds, Liu, & Lyon, 2011) and its many different manifestations. For that reason, Lakhani, Kuruvilla, and Avgar (2013) build on the framework developed by Gereffi et al. and inject agency – of labor and labor representatives – in order to shift the received theory of employment relations from the individual organization to the interorganizational network level. This also allows an equal emphasis on suppliers and, for a better understanding, "how connectedness between firms across national boundaries affects employment relations" (p. 443).

For the *modular* configuration Lakhani and colleagues (2013) postulate that it will "be associated with supplier employment relations systems that are characterized by low levels of lead firm influence, high levels of local institutional influence, moderate workforce skill levels, and moderate levels of employment stability" (p. 454). By contrast, the authors expect the *relational* approach to be associated with employment relations with suppliers "characterized by moderate levels of lead firm influence, dual lead and local institutional influence, high workforce skill levels, and high levels of employment stability" (p. 455). Finally, for *captive* configurations Lakhani et al. (2013) propose that, with the respective suppliers, employment relations systems will be associated "that are characterized by high levels of lead firm influence, dual lead and local institutional influence, low workforce skill levels and low levels of employment stability" (p. 456). These propositions are very plausible but still await empirical testing.

Based on the Lakhani et al. framework, Helfen, Schüßler and Sydow (2018) discuss further attempts to integrate employment relations into the literature on global production networks. Towards this end, they propose to acknowledge the centrality of multi-employer relations in current practice, i.e., of employment arrangements in which workers are faced with conditions set beyond the confines of their direct employer. Moreover, they introduce a network management perspective inspired by Giddens' (1984) structuration theory (Sydow et al., 2016; Sydow & Windeler, 1998), and explain how management practices of selecting, allocating, regulating and evaluating can affect multi-employer relations in such interorganizational networks.

Selecting network participants is a core task, because it heavily influences not only buyer–supplier relationships and horizontal interorganizational relations, but also the management of multi-employer relations. Selecting is typically a mutual process aimed at inclusion, typically dominated, however, by the lead organization and also including deselection aimed at the exclusion of members. Selection and deselection both influence how difficult or easy it will be to develop a common understanding among the network participants regarding, for instance, labor standards and/or trusting relationships with high relevance for multi-employer relations. Through the second practice of *allocating*, i.e., how tasks, resources and responsibilities are distributed among the network's participants, activities and practices are geared towards achieving the network's goals as well as those of its participants. Again, allocating work is likely to be dominated by the more powerful (i.e., lead) organization, including the provision of some organizations with more resources than others in order to manage employment relations and putting their vision of labor relations into reality along the global value chain. *Regulating*, the third practice, focuses on issuing, shaping, and enforcing the formal and informal network rules; it also includes goal-setting and involves issues of culture and ideology. Beyond the mere adoption of already institutionalized standards for regulating work across an interorganizational network (e.g., International Labour Office [ILO] conventions), regulating entails the question of who effectively controls what kinds of resources for rule-setting, and of who decides how earnings are to be distributed in the network. Both have obvious consequences for work and employment in the global production and supply network. Typically, selection, allocation and regulation build upon *evaluating* network participants, relationships, practices and outcomes. These evaluations, which are again characterized by power asymmetries in global production networks, go beyond "reflexive monitoring" (Giddens, 1984), and can include the contribution of organizations towards establishing and maintaining employment relations and practices considered to be "appropriate" for the network and its member organizations.

All these four practices of managing an interorganizational network in general and a global production and supply network in particular have direct and indirect implications for work and employment. These, however, are particularly difficult to isolate as, in reality, not only the three different modes of network governance can mix, amounting to what is sometimes called a "plural form" of governance (cf. Sydow & Helfen, 2017), but also management can enact these four distinct practices in different ways. In addition to this plurality, the different modes and practices – as well as their mix – may change over time, asking for a more dynamic theory of global production networks that takes the strategic agency of management as well as workers and their representatives more seriously (see also Helfen et al., 2018; Lakhani et al., 2013; Tampe, 2018).

In conclusion, the implications of the increasing plurality of work and employment arrangements, tightly connected to different forms and practices of networked organizations, are difficult to establish. Although most experts – in particular with an eye on global sourcing of services in developing countries – expect a downgrading of the conditions for work and employment, even if the firms themselves succeed in an economic upgrading (Barrientos, Gereffi, & Rossi, 2011), the potential for regulating the organization of work and employment in plural forms should be taken into account. However, given the spread of global production networks across very different institutional environments, this makes it even more difficult to come up with a clear-cut implications for work and employment. In consequence, we do not only need more differentiated theoretical frameworks originating from the work of Gereffi and others but much more empirical studies that connect the level of the work process with the organizational level of corporate or inter-corporate relations.

Working in Temporary Organizations

Temporary organizations can be either of an ephemeral, very informal nature, as in the case of self-organized emergency response in the event of a major catastrophe, or formally set up and managed as in the case of most project-oriented arrangements. In both cases, temporary organizations seem, at least at first sight, to qualify perfectly as post-bureaucratic forms. Bechky (2006), however, was among the first to point, on the basis of her ethnographic studies in the US film industry, to the rather organized character of such "temporary systems" (Goodman & Goodman, 1972). In particular, she discovered a structured role system that was deeply anchored in the industry or field, and enacted with the help of a number of practices in more or less idiosyncratic ways in the course of the film projects. Bechky contrasts such temporary organizations with traditional hierarchical or bureaucratic organizations and postulates that the former "are governed through networks of relationships rather than by lines of authority" (p. 3). While this may be correct for film projects that typically cut across organizational boundaries and hence rely "more heavily on social mechanisms such as reciprocity, socialization, and reputations" (ibid.), projects may well also be of an organizational kind in which hierarchy continues to be the central governance mechanism.

Because of the increasing diversity of temporary organizations, Bakker, DeFillippi, Schwab, and Sydow (2016) presented a typology distinguishing social systems in which either structures or actors (or both) may be of a temporary character. The most popular form of the latter, characterized by time-limited membership of organizational actors, is certainly *temporary employment*, no matter whether full time or part time. The most popular of the first kind are *projects* characterized by temporary structures but often carried out by permanent employees. Since another chapter of this volume (by Marcus Butts) deals with working time and temporary employment, we focus on working in organizational and interorganizational projects which, also with respect to the organization of work and employment, are of increasing importance (Burke & Morley, 2016; Lundin et al., 2015; Marsden, 2004).

Projects as temporary systems typically coexist within more permanent structures such as either formal organizations or interorganizational networks. This differentiation between organizations and interorganizational networks is crucially important because (intra)organizational projects, despite the coordinative relevance of informal relationships and norms also within organizations, can still be coordinated by hierarchical fiat. Interorganizational projects, by contrast and as mentioned before, have to rely on other network-like coordination mechanisms such as reciprocity and/or reputation. Going beyond this fundamental differentiation of intra- and interorganizational projects Lundin et al. (2015) point to an even greater diversity of organizational forms:

(1) *Intraorganizational projects* can be embedded in, and hence benefit from, the more permanent structures of either a project-supported organization (PSO) or a project-based organization (PBO). In PSOs projects only add flexibility to otherwise rather stable formal structures, while PBOs do most of their value-creating business with the help of these temporary systems. Popular examples of PBOs are not only professional consultancies, but also general contractors in the construction industry or engineering firms in the automotive industry.

(2) *Interorganizational projects* can either be unique without a history and a future or benefit from repeated collaboration within a project network (PNW). PNWs are also particularly common in the film, construction and consulting industries and, in the extreme case, may consist mainly of PBOs.

Most studies of temporary organizations, no matter whether PBOs, PSOs or PNWs, concentrate on managerial aspects. Lundin et al. (2015), nevertheless, compile a few findings from empirical research that address work and employment issues and point more often than not to their contradictory character. For instance, and with regard to PBOs:

> It is said that work in projects is task and action oriented, as well as perceived as stimulating by workers due to its problem solving character. Work in projects often includes direct dialogues with customers and members of other organizations, i.e. it is, to some extent at least, inter-organizational in its character. Work in projects, which promises therefore to be interesting, could simultaneously have stress caused by time limits and by responsibility laid on the individuals concerning both business results in the specific projects as well as the need to constantly perform to ensure their own future employability. Most importantly, project work is more likely to be associated with the "nonstandard employment relations" (Kalleberg, 2000; Lundin et al., 2015, p. 133)

With regard to PSOs, Lundin and colleagues (2015) refer to a study by Arvidsson (2009) and state:

> Like in PBOs, there are signs of stress resulting both from heavy workloads and from the uncertainties that are seen as a result of the two parallel structures and cultures of the organization. Employees we talked with expressed deep frustration over being uncertain as to which career path is best and what sort of experience would be most useful in the long run. In this case it seemed that a more permanent line-based organizational form produced relationships between managers and subordinates that tended to be more personal and long-term, with respect to both knowledge development and employment security. The line-based organization also gave the subordinates a fairly good idea of how their own careers are likely to progress, since the career ladder and associated requirements are clearly defined and relatively enduring. Some employees seemed to identify and feel loyalty with the line function in which they were employed while others seemed to be loyal to the projects in which they work. This in itself strengthened the tension between line functions and projects (Lundin et al., 2015, pp. 158–159)

However, studies of work and employment in project settings are not only quite rare, but they also, for instance, hardly differentiate between the degree of work routinization and standardization and/or the degree to which the individual's work situation is tied either to the temporary and/or the permanent parts of the larger organization. One difference may occur with regard to the visibility of performance differences among individuals, which – as Lundin and colleagues (2015, p. 142) speculate – may be much higher in PBOs than in other forms of temporary organizing. Because of the rather lean structure of the permanent organization in the case of a PBO (especially when compared with a PSO), the commitment of individuals may also easily become more tied to the particular project rather than to the overall organization. This aspect is captured by the concept of "project-citizenship behavior" (Braun, Ferreira, & Sydow, 2013) which in PBOs, as in other project-based forms of organizing, may either complement or be in conflict with citizenship behavior directed at the entire organization. Finally, across-project learning in this type of organizational form is particularly important and should not only be the responsibility of the permanent structure, but also be part of the task to be performed by individuals (Prencipe & Tell, 2001).

Dahlander and O'Mahony (2011) provide an example of a carefully designed study of project work, highlighting the role of lateral (or horizontal) authority for coordinating this type of work. In contrast to vertical authority, which is derived from the hierarchy of rank, this latter type of authority is based on expertise and typically exercised by peers – with respective effects on project workers. Their study of open source software projects shows that the coordination of such projects not only relies heavily on this particular type of authority, but also requires that project members spend a significant part of their working time coordinating project work. This, in turn, enables them to occupy more central, not necessarily more hierarchical ranks, probably captured by the concept of "boundaryless careers" (Arthur, 1994) which, in particular at least in PBOs and PSOs, may not be so boundaryless after all (Inkson, Gunz, Ganesh, & Roper, 2012).

Some equally rare studies focus on the downside of more often than not extreme work practices in terms of both long, uncompensated working hours and high work intensity "in a variety of employment relationships for various purposes at various times that are all dictated by the specification of the project" (Peticca-Harris et al., 2015, p. 573); or such studies of project work unearth job insecurity and inherent precarity even in the formal economy (Hewison, 2016; Hodgson, 2004). As a result, there is an urgent need for "project entrepreneurs" (Ferriani, Cattani, & Baden-Fuller, 2009) to maintain their employability by managing their project portfolio; a perspective that is well known to organizations (Beringer, Jonas, & Gemünden, 2012), but not necessarily to the individuals who would then be considered "portfolio workers" (Handy, 1989).

If temporariness mixes with plurality, as common in the film and television or logistics industries, the same concrete time-limited task may be carried out by someone in either a traditional, long-term employment relationship (full- or part-time) with either a direct employer or a temporary work agency, or by someone who is self-employed and acts as an independent (contract) worker or freelancer. Increasingly, all three kinds of work arrangements are likely to be found for carrying out the same task or project in time-space. These may be, as in the past, spatially bound (e.g., to an office or factory) or of an increasingly nomadic nature characterizing mobile work.

In sum, because of a lack of carefully crafted and conceptually differentiated research also in this field, the implications of working in temporary organizations are not much clearer than for working in or for networked organizations. Temporary forms of organization are well delineated and, as in the case of temporary employment, even have a long history of research to draw on. But in the case of project-based forms of organizing, a differentiated empirical approach is less common. As temporary forms rely more or less on permanent contexts, as in the case of organizations and interorganizational networks, knowledge of how to manage the interface between the temporary and the permanent – not least with respect to work and employment – would be particularly useful.

Working for Partial Organization?

Not least if enabled and reinforced by digital technologies and platforms, it is likely that more work has "to be performed outside organizational contexts" (Winter et al., 2014, p. 252). As should have already become clear by now, going beyond the hierarchical nesting of work into the employment practices within organizations by acknowledging more fluid organizational forms, however, does not imply that such practices are *less* organized, although the practices of organizing may take a different shape. This is nicely captured by the concept of partial organization. Ahrne and Brunsson (2011), who introduced this concept, aimed at using insights offered by organization theory to analyze more or less organized contexts such as markets, networks, communities, and standards.

Partial organization, according to these authors, exhibits a "decided order," that is, an order created by actors having made decisions about others, although not all of the five criteria of a "complete" organization may be met: (1) decisions on membership, (2) decisions on rules, (3) decisions on how to monitor members, (4) decisions about positive and negative sanctions, and (5) decisions about how to make decisions (e.g., about hierarchy). Even if only one of these five criteria is met, according to Ahrne and Brunsson (2011; 2019), it is a case of partial organization. Importantly, the concept of partial organization not only allows for different degrees of organization or "organizationality" (Dobusch & Schoeneborn, 2015), but also for the organizing of organizational environments, including even markets and social movements that are not only organized but also organize. Notably, partial organization refers to a lesser extent to a social system as an entity, but provides a process perspective on how systems are (partially) organized, thus capturing fluid organizational forms and practices also with regard to the stability that hitherto characterized them and, more often than not, now creates tensions that have to be managed in practice (Farjoun, 2010; Schreyögg & Sydow, 2010) by employers as much as by workers, contractors, and customers and/or their representatives.

While formal organizations may indeed become less relevant as direct employers, not only in face of nonstandard employment relationships that have increasingly entered organizations (Ashforth et al., 2007), these organizations are likely to continue to be influential in an indirect manner, not least contributing to the partial organization of markets, networks, communities, and standards. In any case, partial organization of such systems will survive and, consequently, the relevance of organization theory for a better understanding of work and employment in more or less organized systems.

The Future: No Limits?

Looking into the future, it is rather difficult to establish how work and employment will be affected by the lasting impact of the likely ongoing if not accelerating organizational innovation and transformation through plurality, temporality, and partiality as well as their respective combinations. However, it would be a mistake to understand these trends in organizing by examining their structural dimension alone. Flecker and Meil (2010), for example, report insights into changes of work and employment from several restructuring cases involving global software development and outsourced IT services such as call centers. While the external relations that resulted from the restructuring tended in the former case to be characterized as "captive," they were counterintuitively somewhat more likely to be of a "relational" quality in the latter. As a consequence of such restructuring, suppliers are likely to employ more staff in traditional employment – often at the expense of buyer organizations. Although a host of studies pinpoint the negative consequences of exploitative work and employment arrangements (among many others, Anner, Bair, & Blasi, 2013; Kalleberg, 2009; Weil, 2014), what this means exactly for work and employment conditions in the long run is nevertheless an open question. For example, Flecker and Meil (2010) note, at least for their captive cases of software development, some upgrading of working conditions over time, accompanied – also in their relational cases – by some direct or indirect re-bureaucratization.

However, this very outcome depends not only on the industry structure and governance of global production networks, but also on how suppliers, workers, and unions make use of their agency. Tampe (2018), for instance, demonstrates convincingly that sustainability standards do not per se lead to improved working conditions (in her case: in the Ecuadorian cocoa sector). Rather, improved outcomes for labor "are doubly contingent on first, favorable organizational outcomes that depend on diversified, learning-oriented buyer ties, and, second, on an organization's willingness to pass on these benefits to member farmers" (p. 44). This willingness is obviously also influenced by pressures from stakeholders. Frenkel, Rahman, and Rahman (2018) show a similar pattern in the garment industry of Bangladesh, where more long-term and cooperative relations seem to support the spread of improved working conditions with regard to health and safety (see also Kabeer & Mahmud, 2018, and, with regard to the global sports shoe industry, Frenkel, 2001). In order to give a final example: Sondararajan and colleagues (2018) point to the importance of local sourcing agents (here: in the Indian knitwear garment export industry) as a potential source of influence on working conditions in global production networks, as they can help transnational corporations (in particular those without subsidiaries) in respective countries to overcome the liability of being foreign. For these agents help to match buyers and suppliers who value humane working conditions by acquiring knowledge about field actors, gaining legitimacy in the relevant field, and translating the expectations of each party relating to the other. In some cases, these agents even take on a regulative intermediary role.

As argued above, both temporary and networked forms of organizing contribute to the spread of triangular work arrangements. That means that more and more people will have de facto more than one employer. However, such triangular or multi-employer relations may vary a lot, for instance with regard to who exactly exercises control over the labor process. This can continue to be the formal employer (including an intermediary such as a temp agency), the worker or contractor herself, or the client as the de facto employer. In some cases, the classic subordination of the worker under the control of the employer may be maintained. In others this subordination may be profoundly modified by the involvement of the client or, probably less likely, even diluted because the employee or self-employed alone (or together with the client) exerts a de facto control over the process (Havard et al., 2009).

Despite attempts of industrial relations scholars and practitioners to adapt their concepts and policies to these more fluid forms of work and employment (Bélanger & Edwards, 2013; Lakhani et al., 2013; Mironi, 2010), different analytical approaches may be needed that not only take the increasingly global aspect of work and employment into account, but also its virtualization and servitization. In practice, the representation of employees' interests and the influence of unions and other representational bodies to co-shape these forms are likely to decline further and ask for new policy approaches not only from unions and NGOs (Johnston & Land-Kazlaukas, 2018; Vandaele, 2018), governments and their agencies (Weil, 2014), but also from transnational bodies like the ILO and others (Anner, Bair, & Blasi, 2013; Donaghey, Reinecke, Nifourou, & Lawson, 2014). And managers, not least human resource managers, as well as workers/contractors and – in face of spreading co-creation (Sydow & Helfen, 2017; Vargo & Lusch, 2008) – increasingly customers, should fathom their strategic possibilities to (re)organize work in increasingly triangular employment relations in order to reconcile human needs and organizational goals more satisfactorily.

References

Adler, P. S., & Borys, B. (1996). Two types of bureaucracy: Enabling and coercive. *Administrative Science Quarterly*, *41*(1), 61–89.

Ahrne, G., & Brunsson, N. (2011). Organization outside organizations: The significance of partial organization. *Organization*, *18*(1), 83–104.

Alvesson, M., & Thompson, P. (2005). Post-bureaucracy. In Ackroyd, S., Batt, R., Thompson, P., & Tolbert, P. S. (Eds.), *The Oxford handbook of work and organization* (pp. 485–507). Oxford, UK: Oxford University Press.

Anner, M., Bair, J., & Blasi, J. (2013). Toward joint liability in global supply chains: Addressing the root causes of labor violations in international subcontracting networks. *Comparative Labor Law and Policy Journal*, *35*(1), 1–43.

Arthur, M. B. (1994). The boundaryless career: A new perspective for organizational inquiry. *Journal of Organizational Behavior*, *15*(4), 295–306.

Arvidsson, N. (2009). Exploring tension in projectified matrix organizations. *Scandinavian Journal of Management*, *25*(1), 97–107.

Ashforth, S. J., George, E., & Blatt, R. (2007). Old assumptions, new work: The opportunities and challenges of research on nonstandard employment. *Academy of Management Annals*, *1*(1), 65–117.

Baden-Fuller, C., & Stopford, J. M. (1992) *Rejuvenating the mature business: The competitive challenge*. London, UK: Routledge.

Bakker, R., DeFillippi, R. J., Schwab, A., & Sydow, J. (2016). Temporary organizing: Promises, processes, problems. *Organization Studies*, *37*(12), 1703–1719.

Barrientos, S., Gereffi, G., & Rossi, A. (2011). Economic and social upgrading in global production networks. *International Labour Review*, *150*(3–4), 319–340.

Bechky, B. A. (2006). Gaffers, gofers, and grips: Role-based coordination in temporary organizations. *Organization Science, 17*(1), 3–21.

Bélanger, J., & Edwards, P. (2013). The nature of front-line service work: Distinctive features and continuity in the employment relationship. *Work, Employment & Society, 27*(3), 433–450.

Beringer, C., Jonas, D., & Gemünden, H. G. (2012). Establishing project portfolio management: An exploratory analysis of the influence of internal stakeholders' interactions. *Project Management Journal, 43*(6), 16–32.

Bidwell, M., Briscoe, F., & Fernandez-Mateo, I. (2013). The employment relationship and inequality: How and why changes in employment practices are reshaping rewards in organizations. *Academy of Management Annals, 7*(1), 61–121.

Blader, S. L., Patil, S., & Packer, D. J. (2017). Organizational identification and workplace behavior: More than meets the eye. *Research in Organizational Behavior, 37*, 19–34.

Bonet, R., Cappelli, P., & Hamori, M. (2013). Labor market intermediaries and the new paradigm for human resources. *Academy of Management Annals, 7*(1), 341–392.

Borgatti, S. P., & Halgin, D. S. (2011). On network theory. *Organization Science, 22*(5), 1168–1181.

Braun, T., Ferreira, A., & Sydow, J. (2013). Citizenship behavior and effectiveness in temporary organizations. *International Journal of Project Management, 31*(6), 862–876.

Burawoy, M., & Wright, E. O. (1990). Coercion and consent in contested exchange. *Politics & Society, 18*(2), 251–266.

Burke, C. M., & Morley, M. J. (2016). On temporary organizations: A review, synthesis and research agenda. *Human Relations, 69*(6), 1235–1258.

Cappelli, P., & Keller, J. R. (2013). Classifying work in the New Economy. *Academy of Management Review, 38*(4), 575–596.

Child, J. (1984). *Organization* (2nd ed.). London, UK: Harper & Row.

Cohen, L. E. (2016). Jobs as Gordian knots: A new perspective linking individuals, task, organizations and institutions. *Research in the Sociology of Organizations, 47*, 25–59.

Conway, E., Fu, N., Monks, K., Alfes, K., & Bailey, C. (2015). Demands or resources? The relationship between HR practices, employee engagement, and emotional exhaustion within a hybrid model of employment relations. *Human Resource Management, 55*(5), 901–917.

Dahlander, L., & O'Mahony, S. (2011). Progressing to the center: Coordinating project work. *Organization Science, 22*(4), 961–979.

Davidov, G. (2014). Setting labour law's coverage: Between universalism and selectivity. *Oxford Journal of Legal Studies, 34*(3), 543–566.

Davis, G. F. (2016). *The vanishing American corporation.* San Francisco, CA: Berrett-Koehler.

Davis-Blake, A., & Broschak, J. P. (2009). Outsourcing and the changing nature of work. *Annual Review of Sociology, 35*, 321–340.

Delbridge, R., & Sallaz, J. J. (2015). Work: Four worlds and ways of seeing. *Organizations Studies, 36*, 1449–1462.

Dobusch, L., & Schoeneborn, D. (2015). Fluidity, identity, and organizationality: The communicative constitution of Anonymous. *Journal of Management Studies, 52*(8), 1005–1035.

Donaghey, J., Reinecke, J., Nifourou, C., & Lawson, B. (2014). From employment relations to consumption relations: Balancing labor governance in global supply chains. *Human Resource Management, 53*(2), 229–252.

Edwards, P. K. (1990). The politics of conflict and consent. How the labor contract really works. *Journal of Economic Behavior and Organization, 13*, 41–61.

Farjoun M. (2010). Beyond dualism: Stability and change as a duality. *Academy of Management Review, 35*, 202–225.

Ferriani, S., Cattani, G., & Baden-Fuller, C. (2009). The relational antecedents of project-entrepreneurship: Network centrality, team composition and project performance. *Research Policy, 38*, 1545–1558.

Flecker, J., & Meil, P. (2010). Organisational restructuring and emerging service value chains: Implications for work and employment. *Work, Employment and Society, 24*(4), 680–698.

Frenkel, S. (2001). Globalization, athletic footwear commodity chains and employment relations in China. *Organization Studies, 22*(4), 531–562.

Frenkel, S., Rahman, S., & Rahman, M. (2018). After Rana Plaza: Governance, processes and effects in Bangladesh's garment export factories. Paper presented at the workshop, 5 Years after Rana Plaza: Consequences for Labor Standards Improvements in Garment Supply Chains, Freie Universität Berlin, Berlin, Germany.

Gentry, W. A., Harris, L. S., Baker, B. A., & Brittain Leslie, J. (2008). Managerial skills: What has changed since the late 1980s. *Leadership & Organization Development Journal, 29*(2), 167–181.

Gereffi, G., Humphrey, J., & Sturgeon, T. (2005). The governance of global value chains. *Review of International Political Economy, 12*(1), 78–104.

Giddens, A. (1984). *The constitution of society*. Cambridge, UK: Polity.

Godard, J. (2004). A critical assessment of the high-performance paradigm. *British Journal of Industrial Relations, 42*(2), 349–378.

Goodman, L. P., & Goodman, R. A. (1972). Theater as a temporary system. *California Management Review, 15*, 103–108.

Grey, C., & Garsten, C. (2001). Trust, control and post-bureaucracy. *Organization Studies, 22*(2), 229–250.

Handy, C. (1989). *Age of unreason*. Boston, MA: Harvard Business School Press.

Havard, C., Rorive, B., & Sobczak, A. (2009). Client, employer and employee: Mapping a complex triangulation. *European Journal of Industrial Relations, 15*(3), 257–276.

Heckscher, C. (1994). Defining the post-bureaucratic type. In C. Heckscher & A. Donnellon (Eds.), *The post bureaucratic organization: New perspectives on organizational change* (pp. 14–62). London, UK: Sage.

Helfen, M., Schüßler, E., & Sydow, J. (2018). How can employment relations in global value networks be managed towards social responsibility? *Human Relations, 71*(12), 1640–1665.

Hewison, K. (2016). Precarious work. In S. Edgel, H. Gottfried, & E. Granter (Eds.), *The Sage handbook of the sociology of work and employment* (pp. 428–443). Los Angeles, CA: Sage.

Hinds, P., Liu, L., & Lyon, J. (2011). Putting the global in global work: An intercultural lens on the practice of cross-national collaboration. *Academy of Management Annals, 5*(1), 135–188.

Hodgson, D. E. (2004). Project work: The legacy of bureaucratic control in the post-bureaucratic organization. *Organization, 11*(1), 81–100.

Hodgson, D. E., and Briand, L. (2013). Controlling the uncontrollable: 'Agile' teams and illusions of autonomy in creative work. *Work, Employment and Society, 27*(2), 308–325.

International Labour Office (2016). *Non-standard employment around the world: Understanding challenges, shaping prospects.* Geneva, Switzerland: International Labour Office.

Inkson, K., Gunz, H., Ganesh, S., & Roper, J. (2012). Boundaryless careers: Bringing back boundaries. *Organization Studies, 33*(3), 323–340.

Jensen, J. M., Patel, P. C., & Messersmith, J. G. (2013). High-performance work systems and job control: Consequences for anxiety, role overload, and turnover intensions. *Journal of Management, 39*(6), 1699–1724.

Johnson, P., Wood, G., Brewster, C., & Bookes, M. (2009). The rise of post-bureaucracy: Theorists' fancy or organizational praxis? *International Sociology, 24*(1), 37–61.

Johnston, H., & Land-Kazlaukas, C. (2018). *Organizing on-demand: Representation, voice, and collective bargaining in the gig economy* (ILO Conditions of Work and Employment Series, No. 94). Geneva, Switzerland: International Labour Office.

Kabeer, N., & Mahmud, S. (2018). *Multi-stakeholder initiatives in Bangladesh in the aftermath of Rana Plaza: Global norms and workers' perspectives.* Paper presented at the workshop, 5 Years after Rana Plaza: Consequences for Labor Standards Improvements in Garment Supply Chains, Freie Universität Berlin, Berlin, Germany.

Kalleberg, A. L. (2000). Nonstandard employment relations: Part-time, temporary and contract work. *Annual Review of Sociology, 26*, 341–365.

Kalleberg, A. L. (2001). Organizing flexibility: The flexible firm in a new century. *British Journal of Industrial Relations, 39*(4), 479–504.

Kalleberg, A. L. (2009). Precarious work, insecure workers: Employment relations in transition. *American Sociological Review, 74*, 1–22.

Lakhani, T., Kuruvilla, S., & Avgar, A. (2013). From the firm to the network: Global value chains and employment relations theory. *British Journal of Industrial Relations, 51*(3), 440–472.

Lane, C., & Probert, J. (2009). *National capitalisms, global production networks.* Oxford, UK: Oxford University Press.

Lundin, R., Arvidsson, N., Brady, T., Ekstedt, E., Midler, C., & Sydow, J. (2015). *Managing and working in project society: Institutional challenges of temporary organizations.* Cambridge, UK: Cambridge University Press.

Mallett, O., & Wapshott, R. (2017). Small business revivalism: Employment relations in small and medium-sized enterprises. *Work, Employment and Society, 31*(4), 721–728.

Manyika, J., Lund, S., Bughin, J., Robinson, K., Mischke, J., & Mahajan, D. (2016). *Independent work: Choice, necessity, and the gig economy.* New York, NY: McKinsey Global Institute.

Marchington, M., Grimshaw, D., Rubery, J., & Willmott, H. (2005). *Fragmenting work: Blurring organizational boundaries and disordering hierarchies.* Oxford, UK: Oxford University Press.

Marsden, D. (2004). The 'network economy' and models of the employment contract. *British Journal of Industrial Relations, 42*(4), 659–684.

Mironi, M. (2010). Reframing the representation debate: Going beyond unions and non-union options. *Industrial and Labor Relations Review, 63*(3), 367–383.

Oberg, A., & Walgenbach, P. (2007). Post-bürokratische Organisation – Utopie und Alltag. Eine Fallstudie zur IT-gestützten Kommunikation. *Zeitschrift für Management, 2*(2), 168–197.

Peticca-Harris, A., Weststar, J., & McKenna, S. (2015). The perils of project-based work: Attempting resistance to extreme work practices in video game development. *Organization, 22*(4), 570–587.

Posthuma, R. A., Campion, M. C., Masimova, M., & Campion, M. A. (2013). A high performance work practices taxonomy: Integrating the literature and directing future research. *Journal of Management, 39*(5), 1184–1220.

Powell, W. W. (1990). Neither market nor hierarchy: Network forms of organization. *Research in Organizational Behavior, 12*, 295–336.

Prencipe, A., & Tell, F. (2001). Inter-project learning: processes and outcomes of knowledge codification in project-based firms. *Research Policy, 30*, 1371–1394.

Pugh, D. S., Hickson, D. J., Hinings, C. R., & Turner, C. (1968). Dimensions of organization structure. *Administrative Science Quarterly, 13*(1), 65–105.

Reinecke, J., & Donaghey, J. (2015). After Rana Plaza: Building coalitional power for labour rights between unions and social movement organisations. *Organization, 22*(5), 720–740.

Rubery, J., Cooke, F. L., Earnshaw, J., & Marchington, M. (2003). Inter-organizational relations and employment in a multi-employer environment. *British Journal of Industrial Relations, 41*(2), 265–289.

Rubery, J., Earnshaw, J., Marchington, M., Cooke, F. L., & Vincent, L. (2002). Changing organizational forms and the employment relationship. *Journal of Management Studies, 39*(5), 645–672.

Rubery, J., Grimshaw, D., Keizer, A., & Johnson, M. (2018). Challenges and contradictions in the 'normalising' of precarious work. *Work, Employment and Society, 32*(3), 509–527.

Schreyögg, G., & Sydow, J. (2010). Organizing for fluidity? On the dilemmas of new organizational forms. *Organization Science, 21*(6), 1251–1262.

Sewell, G. (1998). The discipline of teams: The control of team-based industrial work through electronic and peer surveillance. *Administrative Science Quarterly, 43*(2), 397–428.

Sondararajan, V., Khan, Z., & Tarba, S. Y. (2018). Beyond brokering: Sourcing agents, boundary work and working conditions in global supply chains. *Human Relations, 71*(4), 481–509.

Styhre, A. (2007). *The innovative bureaucracy*. London, UK: Routledge.

Sydow, J., & Helfen, M. (2017). *Production as a service: Plural network organization as a challenge for industrial relations*. Berlin, Germany: Friedich-Ebert-Foundation.

Sydow, J., Schüßler, E., & Müller-Seitz, G. (2016). *Managing inter-organizational relations*. London: Palgrave Macmillan.

Sydow, J., & Windeler, A. (1998). Organizing and evaluating interfirm networks: A structurationist perspective on network processes and effectiveness. *Organization Science, 9*(3), 265–284.

Tampe, M. (2018). Leveraging the vertical: The contested dynamics of sustainability standards and labour in global production networks. *British Journal of Industrial Relations, 56*(1), 43–74.

Trist, E. (1981). *The evolution of socio-technical systems* (Occasional Paper No. 2). Toronto, Canada: Ontario Quality of Working Life Center.

Vandaele, K. (2018). *Will trade unions survive in the platform economy? Emerging patterns of platform workers' collective voice in Europe* (Working Paper 2018.5). Brussels, Belgium: ETUI.

Vargo, S. L., & Lusch, R. F. (2008). Service-dominant logic: Continuing the evolution. *Journal of the Academy of Marketing Science, 36*(1), 1–10.

Weber, M. (1968). *Economy and society.* New York, NY: Bedminster Press.

Wegman, L. A., Hoffman, B. J., Carter, N. T., Twenge, J. M., & Guenole, N. (2018). Placing job characteristics in context: Cross-temporal meta-analysis of changes in job characteristics since 1975. *Journal of Management, 44*(1), 352–386.

Weil, D. (2014). *The fissured workplace: Why work became so bad for so many and what can be done to improve it.* Cambridge, MA: Harvard University Press.

Willmott, H. (1993). Strength is ignorance, slavery is freedom: Managing culture in modern organizations. *Journal of Management Studies, 30*, 515–552.

Winter, S., Berente, N., Howison, J., & Butler, B. (2014). Beyond the organizational 'container': Conceptualizing 21st century sociotechnical work. *Information and Organization, 24*, 250–269.

Xhauflair, V., Huybrechts, B., & Pichault, F. (2018). How can new players establish themselves in highly institutionalized labour markets? A Belgian case study in the area of project-based work. *British Journal of Industrial Relations, 56*(2), 370–394.

Zhu, Y. Q., Gardner, D. G., & Chen, H. G. (2018). Relationships between work team climate, individual motivation, and creativity. *Journal of Management, 44*(5), 2094–2115.

11 Changes in Worker Demographics

Shannon Cheng, Abby Corrington, Eden King, and Linnea Ng
[All authors contributed equally and authorship determined alphabetically]

To state simply that there have been changes in worker demographics is insufficient. There have been enormous, even seismic, shifts in the composition of the American workforce. Indeed, that the American workforce is increasingly diverse is axiomatic. But the specific manifestations, explanations, and consequences of such change – the details behind the axiom – are rarely probed by organizational psychologists. In this chapter, we will review evidence of changing demographics as it pertains to those identity groups that are traditionally cited as well as identity groups that are typically overlooked. In addition, we describe the rationale that helps to explain why these changes have emerged and thus why we might anticipate further shifts. Finally, we discuss potential implications of these changes for organizational theory and practice.

Demographic Changes, Projections, and Explanations

Our discussion of historical demographic changes and projections for future change considers evidence of trends in groups that are typically the focus of organizational scholarship (e.g., gender, race and ethnicity, age), as well as groups that are often overlooked by this scholarship (e.g., parents, multiracial individuals, immigrants, religious minorities, gender and sexual minorities, individuals with disabilities). The evidence we describe draws heavily from the national authority on the subject, the US Bureau of Labor Statistics (BLS). To assess past trends and determine future projections of the US workforce, defined as non-institutional (e.g., not in prison or mental health facilities) civilians (i.e., not in the Armed Forces) who are 16 years of age or older and employed or actively seeking employment, the BLS utilizes (1) population projections produced by the US Census Bureau, which considers trends in births, deaths, and immigration, and (2) historical trends in workforce participation for several demographic groups (BLS, 2015). Changes in the general population and workforce participation of different demographic groups can often be explained by a variety of psychosocial factors, which we will also explore as we examine how and why demographic patterns in the workplace continue to shift.

Gender

Historical and Projected Changes. From 1976 to 1996, the representation of women in the workforce increased from 40.5% to 46.2%; however, within the past two decades, this progress has plateaued around 46% (BLS, 2016; see Figure 11.1). Although men's participation in the workforce has steadily declined since the 1940s, women's participation has only declined since 1999 but is projected to continue declining in the next decade (Mosisa & Hipple, 2006; Toossi, 2015). This net decrease in both groups' workforce participation is buffered by the significant expected increase in population of both genders in the next decade (Toossi, 2015). The combined effects of these projections mean that while the growth rate of women in the workforce is slowing, it is still faster than that of men. As a result, focus has shifted from increasing workforce representation to decreasing the gender pay gap and increasing the representation of women in leadership positions. Indeed, the pay gap has narrowed; in 2015, women earned, on average, $0.83 for every $1 men earned, compared to $0.64 in 1980 (Cilluffo & Cohn, 2017). Women have made similar gains in attaining leadership positions, but inequality persists. For example, while women make up 51.5% of management, professional, and related positions (BLS, 2017a), they still only make up 19% of the US Congress and only 5% of *Fortune* 500 CEOs (Cilluffo & Cohn, 2017).

Explanations. Women's participation in the workforce increased dramatically following World War II due to a number of factors, primarily the demand for labor necessitated by the quickly expanding economy. Not only did the United

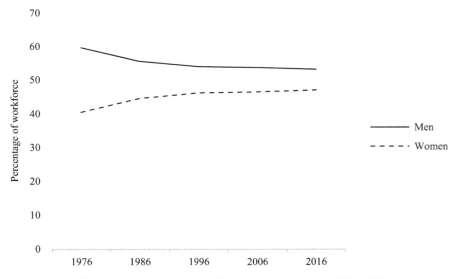

Figure 11.1 *Changing gender demographics in the workforce: 1976–2016. Data retrieved from BLS (see BLS, 2017b).*

States experience changes related to the general economy and education, such as market growth, improved standards of living, greater productivity, and increased college enrollment, it also witnessed progress on social fronts, including the civil rights movement, the push for women's rights, and equal opportunity employment legislation (Toossi, 2015). These social and economic changes created more supportive work environments and put women in a better position to work more.

In addition, the rise of the service sector and decline of the manufacturing sector provided women with more opportunities to join the workplace (Dunlop, 2009). In the past 75 years, the nature of work has shifted from jobs requiring more physical prowess – stereotypically expected of men, rather than women – to jobs requiring more mental prowess – held by both men and women. According to Eagly's (1987) social role theory, the principal cause of sex-based differences in social behavior is the divergent distribution of men and women into distinct social roles. Historically, women have assumed more communal roles and men have assumed more agentic roles, and for this reason, women are perceived to be more appropriate for service-oriented careers (e.g., social work), while men are perceived to have a better fit with leadership-oriented careers (e.g., management). Because the US economy has come to rely more heavily on service-oriented careers, women now compose a larger proportion of the workforce.

However, after the significant increase in workforce participation between World War II and 1999, participation rates of women have now started to decline. These changes are expected to continue, partly due to Baby Boomers reaching retirement age (Toossi & Morisi, 2017). Another potential reason for the plateauing of women's participation in the workforce could be the "glass ceiling" (US Federal Glass Ceiling Commission, 1995), which refers to the barriers preventing women from reaching many leadership positions – positions that men have historically held. As a result, although it is easier than before for women to enter the workforce, they still face many obstacles after they get in, which can significantly impact future projections of their participation in the workforce. For example, although the gender wage gap has narrowed since 1960, when women earned a mere 61 cents for every dollar men earned, they still earn only about 80 cents to the man's dollar (US Census Bureau, 2016). At the current rate, women will not reach pay equity until 2152 (AAUW, 2016). Moreover, women face stereotypes in the workplace that cause them to be perceived as less competent and capable than their male counterparts, and due to in-group favoritism, men tend to promote other men, rather than women (Reskin, 2000; Ridgeway & England, 2007). Beyond subtle bias and discrimination, women also tend to have smaller professional networks than men, reduced connections to high-status individuals, decreased access to workplace support and information (McGuire, 2002; Taylor, 2010). Each of these challenges reduces the likelihood that women will attain the same level of success as do men.

Race and Ethnicity

Historical and Projected Changes. The White population comprised over 80% of the US population until 1940, at which point the percentage held by this racial group began to decline (Sandefur, Martin, Eggerling-Boeck, Mannon, & Meier, 2001). Since then, the proportion of Hispanic and Asian individuals has increased considerably, while the percentage of the Black population has stayed relatively constant (Sandefur et al., 2001). Meanwhile, the percentage of the American Indian/Alaskan Native population has grown drastically, but still comprises only 1% of the population (Sandefur et al., 2001). Figure 11.2 demonstrates a recent subset of these historical trends, starting in 1976. The dramatic increase in racial diversity in the United States, particularly in recent years, is evidenced by the fact that from 2000 to 2010, 91.7% of the population growth was attributed to racial ethnic minorities, influenced by large past and continued immigration and higher fertility rates of ethnic minority groups compared to Whites (Passel, Cohn, & Lopez, 2011; Passel, Livingston, & Cohn, 2012).

In terms of future projections, by 2055, there will be no racial or ethnic majority (Cohn & Caumont, 2016). Specifically, by 2060, the White population is expected to comprise 69% (down from 78% in 2014) of the US population, the non-Hispanic White population is expected to comprise 44% (down from 62% in 2014), the Black/African American population is expected to comprise 14% (up from 13%), the Asian population is expected to comprise 9% (up from 5%),

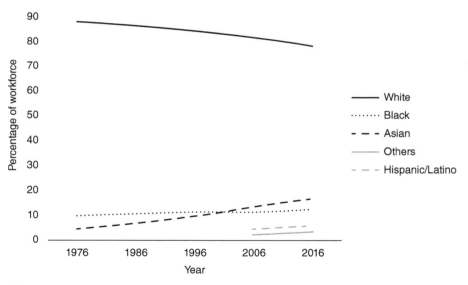

Figure 11.2 *Changing race and ethnicity demographics in the workforce: 1976–2016. Data for Asian and Other race categories were not collected before 2000. White, Black, Asian, and Other are races. Hispanic/Latino is an ethnicity that can be associated with any race. Percentages do not amount to 100. Data retrieved from BLS (see BLS, 2017b).*

and the American Indian/Alaska Native and Native Hawaiian/other Pacific Islander populations are expected to remain around 1% and 0.5%, respectively (US Census Bureau, 2015). Finally, the Two or More Races population is expected to comprise 6% of the total US population (up from 3% in 2014). Of note is that these numbers mean that within the next few decades, the United States is expected to become a "majority-minority" country, meaning that the non-Hispanic White population will total less than 50% of the total population (US Census Bureau, 2015). To put these percentages in perspective, relative to one another, the Two or More Races population is expected to grow the fastest, followed by the Asian population, then the Hispanic population (Hispanic origin is an ethnicity, so can be any race), then the Native Hawaiian/Other Pacific Islander population (particularly when considered both alone and in combination with other races), and finally the Black/African American and American Indian/Alaska Native populations (which are expected to increase only modestly; US Census Bureau, 2015).

These population changes certainly have implications for the workforce composition. Specifically, by 2050, the workforce participation rate for White individuals is projected to be 73.1%, 24.3% for those of Hispanic origin (can be of any race), 13.8% for Black, 8.3% for Asian, and 4.9% for all other groups (individuals classified as being of multiple race origin, American Indian/Alaska Native, and Native Hawaiian/Other Pacific Islander). These projected participation rates for each race and ethnicity category are all higher than the current rates, with the exception of the White race category (Toossi, 2006).

Explanations. The primary stimulus for population growth is the increase in the past several decades in the number of immigrants, who have high workforce participation rates (Toossi, 2015). Additionally, the White population has a lower fertility rate and fewer immigrants than other ethnic/racial groups (Toossi, 2015). This is in contrast to the sociological drivers of the increase in the Hispanic, Asian, and Black workforce. The Hispanic workforce is expected to increase due to high immigration and birth rates, as well as very high workforce participation rates (Toossi, 2015). With the exception of high birth rates, these are also the same reasons for the expected increase in the Asian workforce (Toossi, 2015). For the Black population, their increase in the workforce is due to high birth rates, a stable and continuous stream of Black immigrants, and Black women's elevated workforce participation rates (Toossi, 2015).

An additional explanation for the increase in racial and ethnic diversity of the workforce is the centrality of work for many immigrants. Research has shown that one of the main reasons individuals decide to emigrate to another country is enhanced work opportunities (Fassmann & Munz, 1994), and that individuals for whom work is more central to their lives are more likely to choose to emigrate to countries with better economic conditions (Boneva & Frieze, 2001). It follows, then, that increased immigration may lead to two changes in the US workforce: (1) an increase in racial/ethnic diversity, and (2) an increase in the value placed on work.

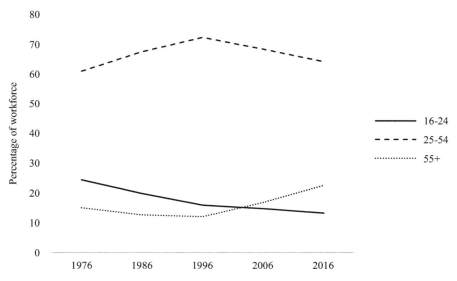

Figure 11.3 *Changing age demographics in the workforce: 1976–2016. Data retrieved from BLS (see BLS, 2017b).*

Age

Historical and Projected Changes. Over the past few decades, the US population has been increasingly characterized by higher life expectancy and lower birth rates, slowing overall population growth (Cohn & Caumont, 2016). Generally speaking, participation in the workforce is usually lower for the younger age group (16–24 years), increases for the prime working age group (25–54 years), and then declines quickly for the older age group (55 years and older; Toossi, 2015). While people are now working for longer before retiring, the Baby Boomer generation (born 1946–1964) is beginning to retire in large numbers, significantly impacting the composition of the workforce. Meanwhile, the participation rate in the workforce is still highest among 25- to 54-year-olds, but this rate has declined each year since 2000 (BLS, 2013). Among 16- to 24-year-olds, the workforce participation rate has also steadily decreased over the years from 24.3% in 1976 to 13.3% in 2016 (BLS, 2016; see Figure 11.3). As population growth slows but the population continues to get older, the BLS projects that the share of workers who are 55 years and older in the workforce will increase to 25.6% in 2022, due to a large share of 25- to 54-year-olds moving into this age group and continuing to work (BLS, 2013).

Explanations. A number of factors are at play with respect to the projected changes of these different age groups. For example, reasons for the declining workforce participation rate of the 16- to 24-year-old group include increased educational enrollment, economic dips, and job competition (Toossi & Morisi, 2017). Regarding education, enrollment in degree-granting postsecondary institutions increased by 21% between 1994 and 2004 and by another 17% between 2004 and 2014 (US Department of Education, 2016). This increase in the percentage of young people in school is attributable to several factors related to accessibility of college education, including (1) the economic benefits of education; (2) a decrease in the cost of college, with grants and education tax breaks; and (3) an expansion of community colleges (Aaronson, Fallick, Figura, Pingle, & Wascher, 2006). The fact that students are less likely to work than nonstudents renders increased educational enrollment a major factor in the decline in youth labor force participation (Aaronson et al., 2006b).

Regarding economic downturns, there is a cyclical tendency for people to withdraw from the workforce during times of diminished job opportunities (Aaronson et al., 2006). Those who withdrew during the recent economic downturn include young people between the ages of 16 and 24 years. By 2015, the US labor force participation rate was still three percentage points below the pre-recession 2007 rates, with no more than half of this decline attributable to demographic changes (Aaronson et al., 2014; Yagan, 2016). This suggests that most, but not all, people who withdrew from the workforce have reentered. In terms of job competition, younger individuals face competition for jobs from both older workers and foreign-born workers. The competition from the former stems from older workers living longer, healthier lives and having higher levels of education and skills than older workers did previously (Toossi & Morisi, 2017). Competition from the latter stems from an increase in the number of immigrants in the US workforce, which depresses wages for both low- and high-skilled native-born workers (Wolla, 2014). Other potential explanations for the decrease in the percentage of these younger workers include falling fertility rates, the evolving job market structure, globalization, and an increased demand for more educated workers (Aaronson, Park, & Sullivan, 2006; Katz & Krueger, 2017; Mosisa & Hipple, 2006; Toossi, 2015). In addition, the concept of "emerging adulthood," which is a prolonged exploration of oneself and one's interests during the late teens and twenties, is becoming more common and can also delay this group's entrance into the workforce (Arnett, 2000). According to the BLS (2013), the youth labor force (16 to 24 years old) is decreasing steadily from 16.9% in 1992 to a projected 11.3% in 2022. So although some students work part-time, many others simply delay entering the workforce until after they finish school.

The other group driving major changes in worker age demographics is the Baby Boomers, and several large-scale changes have taken place as this group has aged. First, Social Security reform legislation gradually increased the normal retirement age for receiving Social Security benefits. Second, the Senior Citizens Freedom to Work Act eliminated the earnings test for 65- to 70-year-old workers who received wages. Third, access to retiree health benefits diminished. Finally, healthcare costs increased (Mosisa & Hipple, 2006; Toossi, 2015). Given the incentives and opportunity to keep working, many older workers may choose this option, particularly if work is central to their identity (Diefendorff, Brown, Kamin, & Lord, 2002; Schmidt & Lee, 2008).

Understudied Groups

In contrast to the traditionally studied groups of gender, race and ethnicity, and age, much less data exists for understudied groups. As a result, less is known about their numbers and projections; however, we can reason about what might be expected based on recent trends and provide potential explanatory factors. In the following sections, we discuss parents, multiracial individuals, immigrants, religious minorities, gender and sexual minorities, and individuals with disabilities, with a brief note on intersecting identities as well.

Parents

Historical and Projected Changes. While the number of families in the United States with children (sons, daughters, stepchildren, or adopted children living in the household) below the age of 18 steadily increased from 32.7 million in 1993 to 35.9 million in 2007, since then this number has declined to 34.2 million in 2016 (BLS, 2017c). However, the percentage of married-couple families with at least one parent employed has remained relatively constant from 2007 (97.3%) to 2016 (96.8%); similarly, the percentage of married-couple families with both parents employed has also stayed relatively constant from 2007 (62.2%) to 2016 (61.1%). These numbers did experience dips from 2009 to 2011, possibly as an aftermath of the recession. When looking at single-parent families, in 2016, 72.5% of families with children maintained by women had the mother employed, and 82.6% of such families maintained by men had the father employed, compared to the 2007 values of 72.8% and 85.2%, respectively (BLS, 2017c). Consistent with trends over the past few decades, the participation rate for married mothers (67.9%) remained lower than the rate for mothers of other marital statuses (e.g., widowed, divorced, separated) (76.0%) in 2016. Also consistent with previous trends, the participation rates for fathers remained much higher than mothers, with 93.6% for married fathers and 87.7% for fathers of other marital statuses. These numbers indicate that even with an increase in the share of workers with family responsibilities in addition to their job responsibilities, women still typically carry more childrearing and household responsibilities, preventing them from engaging in the workforce as fully as men do.

Explanations. The proportion of children living in married-couple families has been declining over the past few decades, with divorce and cohabitation becoming more common, which may be partly due to improved societal attitudes towards premarital cohabitation and nonmarital childbearing (Daugherty & Copen, 2016). As previously discussed, the increase in the number of young adults in emerging adulthood may not only delay entrance into the workforce, but also delay marriage and family planning. This could help explain the record-high numbers of American adults who have never been married (Cohn & Caumont, 2016). Similarly, women are starting to wait longer to have children, choosing instead to focus more on their careers. The mean age of first-time mothers is 26.3 years in 2014, up from 24.9 years in 2000 and 21.4 in 1970 (Mathews & Hamilton, 2002, 2016). Despite these changes, it is still imperative to pay attention to parents in the workplace. The United States is the only industrialized nation that does not offer paid parental leave (Dell'Antonia, 2013), and although fathers have started to help out more at home, when a couple decides that one of them should leave the workforce to take care of the children, it is still usually women who drop out. Even when mothers stay in the workforce, the perception that work is taking priority over family can lead to feelings of guilt and counterproductive work behaviors (Morgan & King, 2012). This conflict between spending time with family while staying engaged in the workplace also impacts fathers, which further highlights the importance of understanding how parents, in both traditional and nontraditional families, participate in the workforce.

Multiracial Individuals

Historical and Projected Changes. In recent years, there has been growth in the number of multiracial people in the United States. According to the Census, these individuals make up about 2.1% of the population, but depending on the operationalization of multiracial identity this could be an underestimate of a group that constitutes up to 6.9% of the population (Pew Research Center, 2015d). This complicated tabulation is indicative of the varied ways in which multiracial individuals identify, i.e., as single race or multiracial, partially due to different racialized experiences. For example, Black/Other race multiracial individuals tend to have experiences more similar to Black individuals, whereas Native American/White multiracial individuals tend to have experiences more similar to White individuals (Pew Research Center, 2015d). As stated above, due to increasing rates of interracial marriage and multiracial births, it is anticipated that the multiracial population will continue to grow (Pew Research Center, 2015d). The multiracial population is young, as nearly half (46%) of multiracial Americans are younger than 18, compared to 23% of the overall American population. In addition, their birth rates are growing. In 1970, only 1% of babies living with two parents had parents with different racial backgrounds; in 2013, 10% of these babies had parents with different races. The profile of these younger multiracial individuals is also different than before; while Native American/White multiracial individuals are the majority among mixed-race adults, in 2013 the majority of mixed-race babies were either White/Black (36%) or White/Asian (24%). As this young group of multiracials moves to working age, they are expected to comprise a greater share of the workforce (Pew Research Center, 2015d).

Explanations. Because the Census Bureau only began allowing people to identify as more than one race in 2000, it is unclear how much of the increase in multiracial individuals is due to the fact that they are able to identify as such and how much it is due to an actual increase (Pew Research Center, 2015d). One potential explanation for the latter is a decline in social stigmatization of interracial marriages, many of which result in multiracial births (Associated Press, 2009; Pew Research Center, 2015d). This increased social acceptance may be ushered along by (and is reflected in) the popularity of influential multiracial figures in the United States, including a recent president (Barack Obama), athletes (e.g., Tiger Woods, Tony Parker), and actors (e.g., Vin Diesel, Olivia Munn).

However, another potential explanation for the unclear numbers may be that multiracial individuals make a decision to not identify as such. The Pew Research Center (2015d) found that only 39% of adults with a mixed racial background consider themselves as "mixed race or multiracial." These individuals cited multiple reasons for this identity gap, including because they only look like one race, they were raised as one race, they closely identify with one race, and they never knew the family member of a different race. In addition, some multiracial Americans have reported feeling pressured to identify as a single race, which can influence how they view and present themselves. Indeed, about 30% of multiracial adults say they have changed how they describe their race over time, going back and forth between identifying as multiracial or not (Pew Research Center, 2015d). Regardless of identification, it is clear that the number of multiracial individuals in America is increasing, and it is important to understand the unique challenges they may face in the workplace, such as identity management, and how to address them.

Immigrants

Historical and Projected Changes. Immigration has always defined the demographic identity of the United States, from early waves during the Industrial Revolution to the present. During the 1990s, there were over 10 million legal immigrants to the US, which was 40% higher than the 1980s and more than any other decade (Tindall & Shi, 2016). In 2016, immigrants comprised 16.9% of the US workforce (BLS, 2017b). In 2015, India and China overtook Mexico as the countries with the first and second greatest numbers of immigrants, respectively (Zong & Batalova, 2017). In 2016, Hispanic workers comprised 48.3% of nonnative labor, while Asian workers comprised 25.0% of nonnative labor (BLS, 2017d). From now through 2035, immigrants and their American-born children will significantly contribute to the population growth of working age individuals in the US (ages 25–64), as Baby Boomers begin to age out of the workforce (Zong & Batalova, 2017). By 2065, Asians are expected to comprise approximately 38% of immigrants in the US, and Hispanics are expected to comprise 31%, with White immigrants and Black immigrants comprising a smaller share, 20% and 9%, respectively (Passel & Cohn, 2017). The share of the US workforce comprised of immigrants has risen over the past couple decades, increasing from 13.3% in 2000 to 16.9% in 2016 (BLS, 2017d). If both legal and unauthorized immigration persist at their current rates, there will be

183.2 million working-age adults by 2035 (up from 173.2 million in 2015; Passel & Cohn, 2017). Of course, the actual immigration rate depends upon the policies created and enforced by the current and future legislatures (Ponnuru, 2017).

Explanations. In 1965, President Lyndon Johnson signed the Immigration and Nationality Services Act, eliminating discriminatory quotas based on national origin, which had been in effect since the 1920s (Tindall & Shi, 2016). This revolutionary change in immigration policy catalyzed the impressive growth of the US immigrant population that continues today. Immigrants from all over the world continue to come to the "land of opportunity," in hopes of freedom, job opportunities, and/or better lives for their families (Hudson & Schenck, 2001). As Baby Boomers reach retirement age, immigrants will take this group's place as the main driver of the expanding workforce. One reason for the important role of immigrants in the expanding workforce is that two-thirds of immigrants arriving in the United States between now and 2035 are expected to be between 25 and 64 years old, meaning they will be of prime working age (Passel & Cohn, 2017). In addition, more and more immigrants are entering with higher education. From 2011 to 2015, a higher percentage of immigrants had college degrees compared to native-born individuals, whereas before, a higher percentage of immigrants lacked GEDs in comparison to the native-born population (Zong & Batalova, 2017). This indicates that the types of immigrants joining the workforce may differ from those of the past, as recent immigrants arrive more educated and seek more highly skilled work. The change in educational profile among immigrants may also reflect the aforementioned shift in immigrants' countries of origin. Of course, these trends related to immigrants will all depend in part on dynamic immigration policies that vary across administrations.

Religious Minorities

Historical and Projected Changes. The proportion of Christian Americans is declining, from 78% in 2007 to 71% in 2014, while the number of American adults who do not identify with any organized religion continues to grow, up to 23% in 2015 (Cohn & Caumont, 2016). Additionally, the number of Americans who identify with non-Christian faiths also has risen between 2007 and 2014, increasing from 5% in 2007 to 6% in 2014, with particular growth among Muslims and Hindus (Pew Research Center, 2015b). By the year 2050, the proportion of Christians in the United States will have decreased from more than 75% in 2010 to 67%, and Islam will replace Judaism as the largest non-Christian religion (Pew Research Center, 2015c). While Christians will remain the largest religious group over the next few decades, both in the US and internationally, Islam is projected to grow faster than any other major religion. Hinduism and Buddhism are also becoming more prominent in the US, as well as other non-Christian faiths (Sherkat, 2014). Additionally, the religiously unaffiliated in the US are expected to increase from 16% in 2010 to 26% in 2050. As the religious makeup of the country shifts, the religious makeup of American organizations will also shift and become more diverse.

Religious minorities in the United States are also far more likely to have college degrees than their Christian counterparts. For individuals in the US who are 25 years old or older, 96% of Hindus, 75% of Jews, 54% of Muslims, 53% of Buddhists, and 44% of of those who are unaffiliated with a religion have a bachelor's degree or higher, while the same is true of only 36% of Christians (Pew Research Center, 2016). Although these data do not explain the increase in the number of Muslim, Hindu, and Buddhist individuals in the US, they do serve as indicators that religious minorities in the US may hold different types of careers than do Christians, particularly those jobs that require higher levels of education (e.g., medical professionals, academics, engineers).

Explanations. One potential explanation for the decrease in proportion of Christian Americans is the continued high rates of immigration and the resulting increase in cultural diversity in the United States For example, India and China, the two countries with the largest numbers of immigrants to the US, have large proportions of non-Christian individuals. As of 2011, India is 80% Hindu and 14% Muslim, while 50% of China's population is religiously unaffiliated (Central Intelligence Agency, 2011). Another explanation for the decrease in religiously affiliated people in the US is that they are older, while the unaffiliated group tends to be younger (Pew Research Center, 2015b). This lack of religiosity among young adults may be attributed to the fact that many people in this age group (Millennials) have parents who are Baby Boomers and have instilled in their children the importance of thinking for themselves and questioning authority – ideas that are in sharp contrast to the teachings of many religious organizations that emphasize obedience and deference to authority (Masci, 2016). This lack of trust in institutions does not stop at those that are religious; it extends to the labor market, government, and even marriage (Masci, 2016). Overall, a shift in the ideology of younger people has contributed to a decrease in the religiously affiliated in the US, which also impacts the proportion of religiously affiliated employees as these younger generations begin to enter the workforce.

Although religion is not usually encouraged as a topic of discussion in the workplace, issues related to religion often still come up, which can lead to interpersonal conflict within an organization. From 1997 to 2016, the number of claims filed for religious discrimination in the workplace has more than doubled, from 1,709 to 3,825 claims (US Equal Employment Opportunity Commission, 2016). As previously mentioned, organizations will continue to become more religiously diverse, with religious minorities often coming in with higher levels of education. To prevent further increases in religious conflict in the workplace, organizations need to better understand how to create supportive environments for religious minorities, such as educating employees about other religions to promote inclusive organizational cultures, as well as providing appropriate accommodations for non-Christian religious holidays or prayer spaces.

Gender and Sexual Minorities

Historical and Projected Changes. Over the past years, there has been an interest in research on gender and sexual minorities in the workplace, particularly due to the amount of discrimination they face and lack of federal protection (unlike many other minority groups). For example, Title VII of the Civil Rights Act of 1964 does not protect gender and sexual minorities (Unlawful Employment Practices, 2010). Since this is an invisible identity, meaning that there are no clear visible manifestations and the individual can choose whether or not to disclose, it is hard to obtain an accurate population count of gender and sexual minorities. Based on four recent national and two state population surveys, the Williams Institute estimates that there are approximately 9 million Americans that identify as lesbian, gay, bisexual, or transgender (LGBT; Gates, 2011). This number is likely to continue increasing, as younger generations become more comfortable with disclosing their identities. For example, nine in ten LGBT youth (ages 13–17) say they are out to their close friends, and 64% say they are out to their classmates (Human Rights Campaign [HRC], 2012).

Explanations. Similar to the case of multiracial people, it is unclear whether the recent and expected increase of LGBT people in the United States reflects an actual increase in the number of LGBT individuals, an increase in the number of those *who identify as such*, or simply better mechanisms for identifying LGBT people. Because the United States has no federal law prohibiting discrimination in the workplace on the basis of sexual orientation or gender identity (in fact, workers can be fired for being LGBT in 28 out of 50 states and for being transgender in 30), it is likely that many LGBT employees will remain "closeted" or decide not to disclose their sexual orientation or gender identity (HRC, 2016b; Steinmetz, 2017). Despite this lack of legal protection for LGBT employees, many organizations have voluntarily begun offering same-sex benefits to their employees. For example, 92% of *Fortune* 500 companies have nondiscrimination policies including sexual orientation, and 82% including transgender identity (HRC, 2016a). Moreover, 61% offer health benefits to their domestic partners, and 50% offer transgender-inclusive benefits (HRC, 2016a). Beyond workplace protections, the societal taboo against gender and sexual minorities is also declining, aided by the increased representation of LGBT individuals in the media, television, movies, and music (Ayoub & Garretson, 2017). The increase in LGBT employees in the workforce is likely attributable to this expanded acceptance, support, and normalization of the LGBT community in the United States.

Individuals with disabilities

Historical and Projected Changes. Individuals with disabilities (IWDs) have consistently comprised between 3.6% and 3.9% of the labor force from 2009, when the government began to collect data on disability status, through 2016 (BLS, 2017b). Since 2010, IWDs have shown consistent deficits in employment rates and median income levels, and greater unemployment rates in comparison to individuals without disabilities, with the employment gap increasing from 2010 to 2015 (Kraus, 2017). Additionally, a high percentage of IWDs are older in comparison to individuals without disabilities, creating an intersectional identity in the workplace (Kraus, 2017).

Scarce data exists on projections for IWDs. However, several groups have begun to prioritize this group of workers, developing strategies for closing the gap in employment between IWDs and the rest of the workforce. Recently, diversity and inclusion leaders at four *Fortune* 1,000 companies (Starbucks, Northrop Grumman, AT&T, and Ernst & Young) expressed their strong support for IWDs in the workplace and emphasized the benefits to hiring IWDs (Blahovec, 2016). The Coalition of State Governments also recently published a report on workforce development and IWDs. Moreover, a number of elected officials, including Delaware Governor John Carney, have offered their advice on best practices, including "making disability employment part of the state workforce development strategy, finding and supporting businesses hiring disabled workers, being a model employer by increasing the number of people with disabilities working in the state government, and providing youth with disabilities with career training" (Donnelly, 2017, p. 14). These efforts, in combination with educating organizations and the general public about disabilities, can help continue to increase the representation of IWDs in the workplace.

Explanations. Section 503 of the US Department of Labor's Rehabilitation Act (2014) requires "employers [to] take affirmative action to recruit, hire, promote, and retain these individuals (IWDs)" with a utilization goal of 7% for federal contractors and subcontractors. This legislation encourages employees to disclose their disabilities, and implores organizations to increase employment of IWDs; it has the potential to increase the disclosure of disability and the participation rates of IWDs in the workforce. However, the decision to disclose is not as easy as it seems. For example, even though disclosing allows IWDs to receive the proper accommodations from their employers, it can also enhance a person's experience of social stigma in the workplace. Many people assume that IWDs are unhappy, poorly adjusted, incapable, or overly dependent (Colella, 1994). They may be perceived as high in warmth but low in competence, which can create feelings of pity and engender paternalistic behaviors (Cuddy, Fiske, & Glick, 2007). As a result, others often view these individuals with sympathy, compassion, and social support, but also diminished expectations of job performance and ability (Stone & Colella, 1996). In addition, particularly for invisible disabilities, which have no clear visible manifestations, it may be hard for the individual to even detect, diagnose, and accept the presence of a disability (Santuzzi, Waltz, & Finkelstein, 2014). Therefore, while Section 503 is an important step in the right direction, there are many other factors that may currently prevent IWDs from disclosing their identities.

Education/SES

Historical and Projected Changes. We have grouped education and SES together because educational attainment and SES indicators are some of the most closely linked. For example, as educational attainment increases, unemployment rates decrease and earnings increase (Vilorio, 2016). There is a widening income gap between the impoverished and wealthy, with fewer Americans belonging to the middle class than in the past, including those in the workforce (Pew Research Center, 2015a). From 1971 to 2015, the middle class has shrunk from 61% to 50% of the population (Pew Research Center, 2015a). Income has become more polarized, with a greater proportion of the US population living with either little or excess income. Labor force participation rates are greater for higher economic classes (lower, middle, or upper class; Pew Research Center, 2015a). Differences in educational attainment are related to differences in social and economic mobility; amidst the widening of the economic gap, workers without a bachelor's degree have suffered the greatest loss in economic status (Pew Research Center, 2015a). Overall, educational attainment of the workforce has changed. From 1992 to 2016, there has been an increase in the percentage of the labor force with a bachelor's or advanced degree, and a decrease in the percentage of the labor force with a high school degree or less (Brundage, 2017). Currently, workers with some college or an associate's degree comprise the largest proportion of the workforce (Brundage, 2017). Both the educational and socioeconomic composition of the workforce have changed in related ways.

Explanations. These changes could indicate a changing workforce demand or changes in demographics of individuals entering the workforce. The recession, peaking in 2009, led to a loss of jobs in the United States. Since the recession, the recovery has led to growth in high-wage jobs and also recovery in low-wage jobs; however, we still have not fully recovered middle-wage jobs (Carnevale, Jayasundera, & Gulish, 2015). This may be attributable to differing levels of growth in fields with varying levels of wages. For high-wage jobs, managerial, STEM, and healthcare jobs experienced the most growth which may have outpaced industries and middle-wage roles (Carnevale et al., 2015). Jobs recovered since the recession have largely gone to college graduates (Carnevale et al., 2015). The loss of middle-wage jobs, defined as jobs falling in the middle third of wages, could contribute to the decline of the middle class (Carnevale et al., 2015). This change in the types of available jobs could lead to an increasing expectation that workers hold higher levels of education, since an increasing proportion of the workforce has a higher education. Higher education levels are correlated with higher wages, higher labor force participation rates, and lower unemployment rates (Brundage, 2017). Consequently, people could be obtaining higher levels of education to improve their employment and earning prospects. As mentioned earlier, the effects of education and SES may covary with other changing demographic features of the workforce. For instance, immigrants are becoming more educated and are projected to comprise an increasing proportion of the workforce. As the proportion of the workforce comprised of immigrants changes, so will the education and SES demographics of the workforce. This extends to other demographic shifts in the workforce for groups with varying levels of education.

A Note on Intersecting Identities

People cannot be represented by any single category. Instead, people have multiple identities that interact to determine their experience (Crenshaw, 1991). Examples of such intersections – which give rise to unique experiences – include a Black Muslim, a gay male, a Hispanic female, or even a White male. One intersectional trend that has appeared over the years is with respect to gender, ethnicity, and education. For example, since 1990, Black and Hispanic women (ages 25–34) have been consistently more likely to hold college degrees than their male counterparts (Ryan & Bauman, 2016). These educational patterns suggest that minority worker problems will become more concentrated among men (Lerman & Schmidt, 1999), which can impact not only the workplace, but also the dynamics at home, causing gender role shifts – as women in these communities are often better equipped than the men to obtain higher-paying jobs. Another trend that is highly likely with concealable identities, such as religious affiliation, sexual orientation, and some disabilities, is how individuals may be reluctant to disclose these identities when they are part of another, more salient stigmatized identity. For example, a Black individual or a woman may be even less likely to disclose that they have ADHD or identify with Buddhism, in order to prevent others from compounding the stigmas associated with their minority identities (Berdahl & Moore, 2006).

Implications of Changing Demographics

The historical trends and projected changes described here help to characterize the people who have and will engage in work in the United States. In addition, discussion of the sociological and psychological drivers of these changes helps to explain their occurrence. Taken together, this analysis points to new directions for organizational theory and practice.

Implications for Theory

In the course of their work lives, people will witness meaningful changes in the demographic composition of their organizations. The impact of such observations on individuals' attitudes, beliefs, and behaviors is an important direction for scholarly development. For example, although intersectionality theory

(Crenshaw, 1991) provides a strong theoretical foundation through which to understand the experiences of people who identify with multiple marginalized groups (e.g., Black women), organizational theories must go further to integrate the ways that both socially valued and devalued aspects of multiple categories influence our day-to-day (work) lives. Such theories are needed to understand the ways people view and understand themselves and the ways that people view and understand those who are different from themselves. A particular emphasis should be placed on efforts to study those categories which are typically overlooked but are nonetheless central to our identities; people's identities are derived not only from their gender, race and age but also their parental status, religion, sexual orientation, education and social class. In fact, people often cite these aspects of themselves as critical to their self-views (Crocker & Knight, 2005). Identity and interpersonal interactions are inherently complex phenomena that must be examined in more complex ways that better capture changing demographic realities.

Indeed, a range of theories could evolve to integrate diversity and/or social identities as potential exacerbating or attenuating factors. As one example, diversity has been considered in the context of leader–member exchange theory – a prominent theory of leader effectiveness. Evidence suggests that the quality of leaders' relationships with their followers can indeed vary as a function of relevant social identity characteristics (e.g., Dwertmann & Boehm, 2016). Might the same kind of effects apply to other kinds of leadership? Might diversity influence the magnitude or direction of effects that are presumed to be uniform? Identity moderates the effects of other, commonly studied, phenomena such as the consequences of procedural injustice (Armstrong-Stassen, 1998), the effectiveness of training (e.g., Shapiro, King, & Quinones, 2007), and reactions to recruitment messages (e.g., Avery, 2003). Future scholarship on a range of organizational phenomena should account for the potential influence of demographic differences.

Implications for Practice

If nothing else, the data summarized in this chapter should convince the reader of this: workplace diversity is unavoidable. Projections for continuing changes in the composition of the US workforce, coupled with growing recognition of the importance of multiple or intersecting identities, convey the certainty of diversity in organizations. Rather than focusing on numerical representation, then, human resource managers and diversity practitioners should shift their focus to the experience of inclusion. Indeed, McKay and colleagues (e.g., McKay, Avery, & Morris, 2008; McKay, Avery, Liao, & Morris, 2011) demonstrated that diversity increases firm profit only when people feel valued and respected. Creating a climate for diversity or inclusion (Dwertmann, Nishii, & van Knippenberg, 2016) is, of course, not as simple as having a Cinco de Mayo party or bringing in balloons for a new mom. Creating inclusiveness requires ongoing commitment (both top-down and bottom-up) to recognizing, respecting, and valuing differences. Inclusiveness requires that people listen open-mindedly to viewpoints that are different than their own, that they confront potential manifestations of prejudice, and that they actively seek out ways to connect with others. These are the characteristics of organizations and employees that will thrive with the changing workforce.

Conclusion

> Let us not act out of fear and misunderstanding, but out of the values of inclusion, diversity, and regard for all that make our country great.
>
> Loretta Lynch

The former US Attorney General succinctly summarized an objective that will serve organizations well. In light of dramatic changes in the composition of the US workforce described in this chapter, it is not hyperbole to suggest that failure to adapt will ensure failure to succeed. Organizations, and the scientists who study them, must overcome misunderstandings and work toward the ideals of inclusion that allow the benefits of diversity to be achieved.

References

Aaronson, S., Cajner, T., Fallick, B., Galbis-Reig, F., Smith, C., & Wascher, W. (2014). Labor force participation: Recent developments and future prospects. *Brookings Papers on Economic Activity*, *2014*(2), 197–275. https://doi.org/10.1353/eca.2014.0015

Aaronson, S., Fallick, B., Figura, A., Pingle, J. F., & Wascher, W. L. (2006). The recent decline in the labor force participation rate and its implications for potential labor supply. *Brookings Papers on Economic Activity*, *2006*(1), 69–154. https://doi.org/10.1353/eca.2006.0012

Aaronson, D., Park, K. H., & Sullivan, D. G. (2006). The decline in teen labor force participation. *Economic Perspectives*. https://papers.ssrn.com/sol3/papers.cfm?abstract_id=888529

American Association of University Women (AAUW). (2016). *The simple truth about the gender pay gap*. Retrieved from www.aauw.org/aauw_check/pdf_download/show_pdf.php?file=The-Simple-Truth

Armstrong-Stassen, M. (1998). The effect of gender and organizational level on how survivors appraise and cope with organizational downsizing. *Journal of Applied Behavioral Science*, *34*(2), 125–142. https://doi.org/10.1177/0021886398342001

Arnett, J. J. (2000). Emerging adulthood: A theory of development from the late teens through the twenties. *American Psychologist*, *55*(5), 469–480. https://doi.org/10.1037/0003-066X.55.5.469

Associated Press. (2009, May 28). *Multiracial America is fastest growing group*. NBC News. Retrieved from www.nbcnews.com/id/30986649/ns/us_news-life/t/multiracial-america-fastest-growing-group/#.Wb6sHmPADm0

Avery, D. R. (2003). Reactions to diversity in recruitment advertising – are differences black and white? *Journal of Applied Psychology, 88*(4), 672–679. https://doi.org/10.1037/0021-9010.88.4.672

Ayoub, P. M., & Garretson, J. (2017). Getting the message out: Media context and global changes in attitudes toward homosexuality. *Comparative Political Studies, 50*(8), 1055–1085. https://doi.org/10.1177/0010414016666836

Berdahl, J. L., & Moore, C. (2006). Workplace harassment: Double jeopardy for minority women. *Journal of Applied Psychology, 91*(2), 426–436.

Blahovec, S. (2016). Why hire disabled workers? 4 powerful (and inclusive) companies answer. *Huffington Post.* Retrieved from www.huffingtonpost.com/sarah-blahovec/why-hire-disabled-workers_b_9292912.html

Boneva, B. S., & Frieze, I. H. (2001). Toward a concept of a migrant personality. *Journal of Social Issues, 57*(3), 477–491. https://doi.org/10.1111/0022-4537.00224

Brundage, V. (2017). Profile of the labor force by educational attainment. *Bureau of Labor Statistics.* Retrieved from www.bls.gov/spotlight/2017/educational-attainment-of-the-labor-force/pdf/educational-attainment-of-the-labor-force.pdf

Bureau of Labor Statistics. (2013). Labor force projections to 2022: The labor force participation rate continues to fall. *Monthly Labor Review.* Retrieved from www.bls.gov/opub/mlr/2013/article/labor-force-projections-to-2022-the-labor-force-participation-rate-continues-to-fall-1.htm

Bureau of Labor Statistics. (2015). Understanding the 2014–24 projections. *Career Outlook.* Retrieved from www.bls.gov/careeroutlook/2015/article/projections-methodology.htm

Bureau of Labor Statistics. (2016). Labor force statistics from the current population survey. *US Department of Labor.* Retrieved from www.bls.gov/cps/tables.htm

Bureau of Labor Statistics. (2017a). Household data annual averages 2016. *US Department of Labor.* Retrieved from www.bls.gov/cps/cpsaat11.pdf

Bureau of Labor Statistics. (2017b). *Databases, table, & calculators by subject* [Database]. Retrieved from www.bls.gov/data/

Bureau of Labor Statistics. (2017c). *Employment characteristics of families summary* [Economic news release]. Retrieved from www.bls.gov/news.release/famee.nr0.htm

Bureau of Labor Statistics. (2017d, May 18). *Foreign-born workers: Labor force characteristics – 2016* [News Release]. Retrieved from www.bls.gov/news.release/pdf/forbrn.pdf

Carnevale, A. P., Jayasundera, T., & Gulish, A. (2015). Good jobs are back: College graduates are first in line. *Georgetown University Center on Education and the Workforce.* Retrieved from https://cew.georgetown.edu/wp-content/uploads/Good-Jobs_Full_Final.pdf

Central Intelligence Agency (2011). *The world factbook.* Retrieved from www.cia.gov/library/publications/the-world-factbook/fields/2122.html

Cilluffo, A., & Cohn, D. (2017, April 27). 10 demographic trends shaping the US and the world in 2017. *Pew Research Center.* Retrieved from www.pewresearch.org/fact-tank/2017/04/27/10-demographic-trends-shaping-the-u-s-and-the-world-in-2017/

Cohn, D., & Caumont, A. (2016, March 31). 10 demographic trends that are shaping the US and the world. *Pew Research Center.* Retrieved from www.pewresearch.org/

fact-tank/2016/03/31/10-demographic-trends-that-are-shaping-the-u-s-and-the-world/

Colella, A. (1994). Organizational socialization of employees with disabilities: Critical issues and implications for workplace interventions. *Journal of Occupational Rehabilitation*, *4*, 87–106. https://doi.org/10.1007/BF02110048

Crenshaw, K. (1991). Mapping the margins: intersectionality, identity politics, and violence against women of color. *Stanford Law Review*, *43*(6), 1241–1299. https://doi.org/10.2307/1229039

Crocker, J., & Knight, K. M. (2005). Contingencies of self-worth. *Current Directions in Psychological Science*, *14*(4), 200–203. https://doi.org/10.1111/j.0963-7214.2005.00364.x

Cuddy, A. J. C., Fiske, S. T., & Glick, P. (2007). The BIAS map: Behaviors from intergroup affect and stereotypes. *Journal of Personality and Social Psychology*, *92*(4), 631–648. https://doi.org/10.1037/0022-3514.92.4.631

Daugherty, J., & Copen, C. (2016). Trends in attitudes about marriage, childbearing, and sexual behavior: United States, 2002, 2006–2010, and 2011–2013. *National Center for Health Statistics*. Retrieved from www.cdc.gov/nchs/data/nhsr/nhsr092.pdf

Dell'Antonia, K. J. (2013, December 11). New act proposes national paid family leave policy. *New York Times*. Retrieved from https://parenting.blogs.nytimes.com/2013/12/11/new-act-proposes-national-paid-family-leave-policy/?_r=1

Diefendorff, J. M., Brown, D. J., Kamin, A. M., & Lord, R. G. (2002). Examining the roles of job involvement and work centrality in predicting organizational citizenship behaviors and job performance. *Journal of Organizational Behavior*, *23*, 93–108. https://doi.org/10.1002/job.123

Donnelly, G. (2017). See how your state ranks in employment among workers with disabilities. *Fortune*. Retrieved from http://fortune.com/2017/02/28/disability-employment-rank/

Dunlop, C. (2009). Female power; women in the workforce. *The Economist*. Retrieved from www.economist.com/node/15174418

Dwertmann, D. J., & Boehm, S. A. (2016). Status matters: The asymmetric effects of supervisor–subordinate disability incongruence and climate for inclusion. *Academy of Management Journal*, *59*(1), 44–64. https://doi.org/10.5465/amj.2014.0093

Dwertmann, D. J., Nishii, L. H., & van Knippenberg, D. (2016). Disentangling the fairness & discrimination and synergy perspectives on diversity climate: moving the field forward. *Journal of Management*, *42*(5), 1136–1168. https://doi.org/10.1177/0149206316630380

Eagly, A. H. (1987). *Sex differences in social behavior: A social-role interpretation*. Hillsdale, NJ: Erlbaum.

Fassmann, H., & Munz, R. (Eds.). (1994). *European migration in the late twentieth century: Historical patterns, actual trends, and social implications*. Laxenburg, Austria: International Institute for Applied Systems Analysis.

Gates, G. J. (2011, April). How many people are lesbian, gay, bisexual, and transgender? *The Williams Institute*. Retrieved from https://williamsinstitute.law.ucla.edu/research/census-lgbt-demographics-studies/how-many-people-are-lesbian-gay-bisexual-and-transgender/

Hudson, I. Z., & Schenck, S. (2001). America: Land of opportunity or exploitation? *Hofstra Labor and Employment Law Journal, 19*(2), 351–388.

Human Rights Campaign. (2012). Growing up LGBT in America. *Human Rights Campaign.* Retrieved from www.hrc.org/youth-report/view-and-share-statistics

Human Rights Campaign. (2016a). Corporate equality index 2017: Rating workplaces on lesbian, gay, bisexual and transgender equality. Retrieved from www.hrc.org/campaigns/corporate-equality-index

Human Rights Campaign. (2016b). *State maps of laws and policies.* Retrieved from www.hrc.org/state-maps

Katz, L. F., & Krueger, A. B. (2017). Documenting decline in US economic mobility. *Science, 356*(6336), 382–383. https://doi.org/10.1126/science.aan3264

Kraus, L. (2017). *2016 Disability Statistics Annual Report.* Durham, NH: University of New Hampshire. Retrieved from https://disabilitycompendium.org/sites/default/files/user-uploads/2016_AnnualReport.pdf

Lerman, R., & Schmidt, S. (1999). An overview of economic, social, and demographic trends affecting the US labor market. *US Department of Labor.* Retrieved from www.dol.gov/dol/aboutdol/history/herman/reports/futurework/conference/trends/Trendsintro.htm

Masci, D. (2016, January 8). Q&A: Why millennials are less religious than older Americans. *Pew Research Center.* Retrieved from www.pewresearch.org/fact-tank/2016/01/08/qa-why-millennials-are-less-religious-than-older-americans/

Mathews, T. J., & Hamilton, B. E. (2002). Mean age of mother, 1970–2000. *National Vital Statistics Reports, 51*(1), 1–14.

Mathews, T. J., & Hamilton, B. E. (2016). *Mean age of mothers is on the rise: United States, 2000–2014* (NCHS data brief no 232). Retrieved from www.cdc.gov/nchs/data/databriefs/db232.htm

McGuire, G. M. (2002). Gender, race, and the shadow structure. *Gender & Society, 16*(3), 303–322. https://doi.org/10.1177/0891243202016003003

McKay, P. F., Avery, D. R., Liao, H., & Morris, M. A. (2011). Does diversity climate lead to customer satisfaction? It depends on the service climate and business unit demography. *Organization Science, 22*(3), 788–803. https://doi.org/10.1287/orsc.1100.0550

McKay, P. F., Avery, D. R., & Morris, M. A. (2008). Mean racial-ethnic differences in employee sales performance: The moderating role of diversity climate. *Personnel Psychology, 61*(2), 349–374. https://doi.org/10.1111/j.1744-6570.2008.00116.x

Morgan, W. B., & King, E. B. (2012). The association between work–family guilt and pro-and anti-social work behavior. *Journal of Social Issues, 68*(4), 684–703. https://doi.org/10.1111/j.1540-4560.2012.01771.x

Mosisa, A., & Hipple, S. (2006). Trends in labor force participation in the United States. *Monthly Labor Review, 129*(35), 35–57.

Passel, J. S., & Cohn, D. (2017). Immigration projected to drive growth in US working-age population through at least 2035. *Pew Research Center.* Retrieved from www.pewresearch.org/fact-tank/2017/03/08/immigration-projected-to-drive-growth-in-u-s-working-age-population-through-at-least-2035/

Passel, J. S., Cohn, D., & Lopez, M. H. (2011). Hispanics account for more than half of nation's growth in past decade. Pew Research Center. Retrieved from www.pewhispanic.org/2011/03/24/hispanics-account-for-more-than-half-of-nations-growth-in-past-decade/

Passel, J. S., Livingston, G., & Cohn, D. (2012). Explaining why minority births now outnumber white births. *Pew Research Center*. Retrieved from www.pewsocialtrends.org/2012/05/17/explaining-why-minority-births-now-out number-white-births/

Pew Research Center. (2015a, December 9). The American middle class is losing ground. Retrieved from www.pewsocialtrends.org/2015/12/09/the-american-middle-class-is-losing-ground/

Pew Research Center. (2015b, May 12). America's changing religious landscape. Retrieved from www.pewforum.org/2015/05/12/americas-changing-religious-landscape/

Pew Research Center. (2015c, April 2). The future of world religions: Population growth projections, 2010–2050. Retrieved from www.pewforum.org/2015/04/02/religious-projections-2010-2050/

Pew Research Center. (2015d, June 11). Multiracial in America: Proud, diverse, and growing in numbers. Retrieved from www.pewsocialtrends.org/2015/06/11/multiracial-in-america/

Pew Research Center. (2016, December 13). Religion and education around the world. Retrieved from www.pewforum.org/2016/12/13/religion-and-education-around-the-world/

Ponnuru, R. (2017, September 27). Trump takes a (calculated) risk on immigration. *Bloomberg*. Retrieved from www.bloomberg.com/view/articles/2017-09-17/trump-takes-a-calculated-risk-on-immigration

Reskin, B. F. (2000). Getting it right: Sex and race inequality in work organizations. *Annual Review of Sociology*, 26(1), 707–709. https://doi.org/10.1146/annurev.soc.26.1.707

Ridgeway, C., & England, P. (2007). Sociological approaches to sex discrimination in employment. In F. J. Crosby, M. S. Stockdale, & S. A. Ropp (Eds.), *Sex segregation in the workplace: Trends, explanations, remedies* (pp. 189–211). Oxford: Blackwell.

Ryan, C. L., & Bauman, K. (2016, March). Educational attainment in the United States: 2015. *U.S Census Bureau*. Retrieved from www.census.gov/content/dam/Census/library/publications/2016/demo/p20–578.pdf

Sandefur, G. D., Martin, M., Eggerling-Boeck, J., Mannon, S. E., & Meier, A. M. (2001). An overview of racial and demographic trends. In N. J. Smeiser, W. J. Wilson, & F. Mitchell (Eds.), *America becoming: Racial trends and their consequences* (pp. 40–102). Washington, DC: National Academy Press.

Santuzzi, A. M., Waltz, P. R., Finkelstein, L. M., & Rupp, D. E. (2014). Invisible disabilities: Unique challenges for employees and organizations. *Industrial and Organizational Psychology*, 7(2), 204–219. https://doi.org/10.1111/iops.12134

Schmidt, J. A., & Lee, K. (2008). Voluntary retirement and organizational turnover intentions: The differential associations with work and non-work commitment constructs. *Journal of Business and Psychology*, 22(4), 297–309. https://doi.org/10.1007/s10869–008-9068-y

Shapiro, J. R., King, E. B., & Quinones, M. A. (2007). Expectations of obese trainees: How stigmatized trainee characteristics influence training effectiveness. *Journal *of Applied Psychology, 92*(1), 239–249. https://doi.org/10.1037/0021-9010.92.1.239

Sherkat, D. E. (2014). *Changing faith: The dynamics and consequences of Americans' shifting religious identities.* New York, NY: New York University Press. https://doi.org/10.18574/nyu/9780814741269.001.0001

Steinmetz, K. (2017, April 4). The NCAA lifted its North Carolina boycott. Here's what that could mean for LGBT rights. *Time.* Retrieved from http://time.com/4725014/ncaa-north-carolina-repeal-hb2-decision/

Stone, D. L., & Colella, A. (1996). A model of factors affecting the treatment of disabled individuals in organizations. *Academy of Management Review, 21*(2), 352–401. https://doi.org/10.5465/amr.1996.9605060216

Taylor, C. J. (2010). Occupational sex composition and the gendered availability of workplace support. *Gender & Society, 24*(2), 189–212. https://doi.org/10.1177/0891243209359912

Tindall, G. B., & Shi, D. E. (2016). *America: A narrative history* (10th ed.), Vol. 2. New York, NY: W. W. Norton & Company.

Toossi, M. (2006). A new look at long-term labor force projections to 2050. *Monthly Labor Review, 129*(11), 19–39.

Toossi, M. (2015). Labor force projections to 2024: The labor force is growing, but slowly. *Monthly Labor Review,* December. https://doi.org/10.21916/mlr.2015.48

Toossi, M., & Morisi, T. L. (2017). Women in the workforce before, during, and after the Great Recession. *Spotlight on Statistics.* Retrieved from www.bls.gov/spotlight/2017/women-in-the-workforce-before-during-and-after-the-great-recession/home.htm

Unlawful Employment Practices. (2010). 42 U.S.C. § 2000e-2.

US Census Bureau. (2015). *Projections of the size and composition of the US population: 2014 to 2060.* (Report No. P25–1143). Retrieved from www.census.gov/library/publications/2015/demo/p25-1143.html

US Census Bureau. (2016). *Income and poverty in the United States: 2015.* Retrieved from www.census.gov/data/tables/2016/demo/income-poverty/p60-256.html

US Department of Education, National Center for Education Statistics. (2016). *Digest of Education Statistics, 2015* (NCES 2016-014), Chapter 3. Retrieved from https://nces.ed.gov/fastfacts/display.asp?id=98

US Department of Labor. (2014). Regulations implementing Section 503 of the Rehabilitation Act. Retrieved from www.dol.gov/ofccp/regs/compliance/section503.htm

US Equal Employment Opportunity Commission. (2016). Charge statistics (charges filed with EEOC) FY 1997 through FY 2016. Retrieved from www.eeoc.gov/eeoc/statistics/enforcement/charges.cfm

US Federal Glass Ceiling Commission. (1995). A solid investment: Making full use of the nation's human capital. Retrieved from www.dol.gov/oasam/programs/history/reich/reports/ceiling2.pdf

Vilorio, D. (2016, March). Education Matters. *Career Outlook. US Census Bureau.* Retrieved from www.bls.gov/careeroutlook/2016/data-on-display/education-matters.htm

Wolla, S. A. (2014, May). *The economics of immigration: A story of substitutes and complements.* Retrieved from https://research.stlouisfed.org/publications/

page1-econ/2014/05/01/the-economics-of-immigration-a-story-of-substitutes-and-complements/

Yagan, D. (2016). Is the great recession really over? Longitudinal evidence of enduring employment impacts. Unpublished manuscript.

Zong, J., & Batalova, J. (2017). Frequently requested statistics on immigrants and immigration in the United States. *Migration Policy Institute.* Retrieved from www.migrationpolicy.org/article/frequently-requested-statistics-immigrants-and-immigration-united-states

12 Generational Changes in Personality, Values, and Abilities

Jorge Lumbreras and W. Keith Campbell

Defining Generations

A *generation* is a group of individuals who are born in a similar cohort (usually 17–20 years), experience a shared cultural context (usually national), and shape that cultural context (Gentile, Campbell, & Twenge, 2013). For example, the Baby Boomer generation was born in the United States from around 1946 to 1964. This generation experienced a similar culture and also changed the culture. The most common generations discussed in mass media and scholarly interests include the Silent Generation, Baby Boomers, Generation X (or GenX), and the Millennials (or GenMe).

It is important to note from the outset that *generations are fuzzy social constructs*. That is, the boundary of any generation is unlikely to be clear. You can see this in several obvious issues that arise in the discussion of generations. First, generational dates are somewhat arbitrarily set. Whether Generation X, for example, started in 1965 or 1962 or somewhere in between is not socially agreed upon. Second, the differences between generations are generally smooth, especially of general traits like personality or attitudes. The practical result is that someone born in 1966 as part of Generation X is likely to have more in common with the Baby Boomers born in 1964 than a Generation X member born in 1980. This is similar to a 13-year-old having more in common with a 12-year-old preteen than a 19-year-old teen. Third, generation descriptions are typically based on college graduates from more culturally generative states or locations. So, when we think of a generational exemplar we are likely to focus on only a certain face of the population, such as Baby Boomer college students protesting the Vietnam conflict or Millennial young people on the cutting edge of social media. Obviously, social and behavioral sciences are filled with fuzzy constructs – age, race, ethnicity, gender – but for some reason this has been a popular target for critique of generations research so it is important to address it upfront.

Generations can also be thought of as predictor variables in theoretically or practically significant research (e.g., Millennial status predicts ambition at work). These models can be easy to test (e.g., assess generation and other variable of interest then run comparison). But these easy tests often result in conclusions that are challenging to interpret.

Table 12.1 *Age, period and cohorts effects and generational differences*

Effect	Underlying Variable	Key Points	Example
Age	Biological age	Generational differences reflect age and will resolve with biological maturation	Millennials engage in risky behaviors; will resolve with age
Period	Cultural climate	Generational differences largely reflect broader culture changes; all ages should show similar changes	Millennials use smartphones; but so does everyone in culture
Cohort	Year of birth	Generational differences tied to specific birth cohort; likely to be carried with cohort	Millennials experienced massive educational cost increases; not shared with previous generations

In general, any association between generational status in an individual and an outcome variable (assuming proper sampling, measurement, etc.) can reflect an *age*, *period*, or *cohort* effect (see Table 12.1). Age effects are driven by the age of the individual and attributed to underlying developmental processes, so any cross-sectional study of generation status and an outcome variable will yield results that could be the result of participant age or could be a result of participant birth cohort. For example, a cross-sectional study that compares Generation X vs. Millennial work engagement will be testing people who differ on both age and birth cohort. This is important to resolve theoretically and practically because, for example, if the differences are developmental, the younger generation should look like the older generation after they mature. This has been the primary argument against the idea that Millennials are more narcissistic than previous generations (Roberts, Edmonds, & Grijalva, 2010) – young people are always narcissistic – although this argument does not explain why no data is showing elevated narcissism in the generations following the Millennials, called iGen, Generation Z, Homelanders, etc. (Aside: this uncertain naming process is more evidence for how generations are socially determined.)

The age vs. cohort challenge is relatively straightforward to address by examining cross-temporal data. For example, using historical data you can compare participants at the same age but born in different cohorts, such as 18-year-olds born in the 1960s vs. the 1990s. Any differences found in these comparisons are most likely the result of birth cohort or cultural effects: if people at the same age today are different than they were 40 years ago this is not typical development at work.

This, of course, brings up a greater challenge in generations work: untangling the influence of birth cohort from cultural period. For example, when you see Millennial workers on their smartphones all the time, is this something better predicted by their year of birth or the culture they are living in (and to make it even more complex, creating)? Period effects can be removed in cross-sectional studies – these are typically captured at one time point in one culture – but they are still theoretically very challenging. In the present example, should Millennials be described as smartphone-using? They use more smartphones than any previous generation, but smartphones are used across current generations as well – yet again, smartphones are used differently by different generational groups today, but these differences could also reflect age effects.

Fortunately, there are some emerging statistical models that can account for age, period, and cohort effects. One example is a Hierarchical Age–Period–Cohort (HAPC) model (Yang & Land, 2013) which is currently being used to disentangle the aforementioned effects by treating age as a fixed effect which is nested within crossed random effects of both birth cohort and time period. Unfortunately, the use of APC models is limited by available data. Furthermore, these models are so limited historically that they may not be useful to predict the longer-term trends in Millennials or iGen/GenerationZ. We have enough data to get some sense of the Baby Boom generation. They were born in a time when data collection was becoming more common; when they hit the 1960s data was commonly collected. And the Baby Boom is getting old enough that we have a lifespan's worth of data. We do not have this for any other group, at least not yet.

Overall, generational differences can come from or reflect multiple sources: age, period, or cohort. Most of the interest comes from cohort or period effects, but unfortunately these are very challenging to tease apart. Developmental effects are the least interesting from a generations perspective (although they are very important), but they can be controlled for using cross-temporal data.

Theoretical Approaches to Generations

There are several major theoretical challenges to understanding generations. We group these into six models. The first set of models focuses on how generations arise, the second set focuses additionally on the content of generations themselves.

How Generations Arise

There are two basic models of how generations arise, neither of which is well specified. The first is the classic sociological model (Manheim, 1952). Generations are largely products or consequences of historical or sociological forces. Imagine it this way: there are two groups of individuals born into very similar circumstances but at different sociohistorical periods. The difference between these groups will largely result from their shared experiences. This might mean experiencing a war together (like World War II), an economic collapse (like the Great Recession), or a technological breakthrough (like the Internet or radio). According to this model, generations are largely passively stamped by history, and major historical events will be especially important.

The second model takes a more cultural approach to generations (Gentile, Campbell, & Twenge, 2013). Culture can be thought of as a multilevel, interactive structure, with cultural ideas like "freedom," "equality," "individualism," or "God" on top, and individual self-concept, personality, and attitudes on the bottom. Mediating between these two are cultural structures such as economic systems, legal and educational systems, family systems, entertainment, etc. For example, in the United States a core belief in individualism will be reflected in the law (individual justice), education (individual merit), economics (individual opportunity), and self/personality (self-esteem, sense of uniqueness). Generational change thus happens when culture changes; the causal arrows are not clear. The sociological model hinges on the idea that culture is the main causal force; psychology tends to think of the individual (alone or with small groups) being the main causal force. We tend to be in the latter camp, given that we see culture as an emergent system of individual actions rather than the other way around, but note that even true emergent systems can have downward effects.

In sum, generations are linked to social and cultural structures according to the theories we know about. The scope and direction of this link is still unclear. Further, even if we could model how well generations track cultural change, we will then have another question to deal with: how does culture change? A large answer would touch on technology, contact with other cultures, disease, etc. We suspect that the answer to these questions will prove complex, highly probabilistic, and demand insights from some broader systems science (e.g., Berdahl et al., 2018).

The Content of Generations

In this section, we look at some models that focus more on generational content. That is, why is a particular generation the way it is? These models are both somewhat overlapping but have different scopes.

The *cyclical model* of generations (Strauss & Howe, 1992) is the most popular model out there. This model is heavily historical and stretches back centuries in the United States (and for this reason we will not be able to do it justice here). The main idea is that generations follow a cycle of four generations that repeat themselves such that the GI Generation (born 1901–1924) is characteristically the same as the Millennials (born 1982–2004). In the case of the Millennials and GI Generation, these are considered as "heroic" generations. They are tasked with rebuilding society. The previous generations, the Lost Generation (born 1883–1900) and Generation X (born 1961–1981), are similar, both being considered "nomadic." They are wandering after the spiritual highs of the previous generations. Missionary (born 1860–1882) and Baby Boomers (born 1943–1960) are considered "prophetic," or idealists who live during a revitalized time period. This model is fascinating in scope, but also challenging to test formally.

The *rising extrinsic individualism model* (Twenge, Campbell, & Freeman, 2012) suggests that generation changes are primarily seen in increasing individualism, especially with a more extrinsic focus. Specifically, the increasing individualism will move in the direction of individuals becoming more atomized but with a more extrinsic flavor. For example, the model does not predict greater self-sufficiency but instead more individuated consumer desires. This model held up well, but the Great Recession (2007–2009) has reset some priorities.

The *self-expressive liberation model* (e.g., Wetzel & Inglehart, 2010) is a similar model that sees and predicts rising individualism, but has a more hopeful and communal flavor to it. This research is based primarily on data from the World's Value Survey and is global rather than American in scope.

Economic models are a class of models that suggest generational differences are largely a reflection of economic factors. For example, personality may shift in the direction of extraversion and confidence needed for a modern consumer capitalist society (Jokela et al., 2017), and/or might vacillate with unemployment such that high unemployment in early adulthood tempers later narcissism and individualism (e.g., Bianchi, 2016).

The extended or *emerging adulthood model* is a hybrid developmental and generational model (Arnett, 2000). The idea is that developmental processes are changing such that there is a new phase of post-adolescence termed emerging adulthood. This time, from about ages 18 to 25, is a time when young people explore their environment before undertaking classic adulthood experiences like supporting oneself, starting a family, and purchasing a home. After the emerging adulthood phase, however, young people will go back to how they have always looked as adults. There is little empirical support for this second proposition – there just hasn't been enough history – but there are data linking later-onset adulthood with cultural individualism (Twenge & Campbell, 2018).

The *no change model* is very simple: generations are not different (Trzesniewski, & Donnellan, 2010). The secondary argument is often made that generations seem to get worse because we mistake developmental factors for generational factors. It is hard to imagine any support for this model because it is a null, but it is an important one. It is also likely that at long as generational changes and development factors align (e.g., the generations keep acting less mature at similar ages) it will be hard to tease these effects out.

How Do You Study Generations?

Generations can be studied with multiple variable types at different levels of analysis. This latter point is especially important to keep in mind as a generation can be analyzed at different levels. The most common approach for psychologists who are typically interested in individual psychological functioning is to look at aggregate individual qualities, such as personality traits, abilities, attitudes, and values. In its simplest form, you compare individuals' scores on these variables across different birth cohorts. Birth cohort means can be compared at the annual mean, five-year mean, or at the generation mean. Because most changes on these variables are continuous, the one- or five-year means are typically the most useful.

However, a generation can be studied by looking at other aspects of culture directly. These might be cultural products, like language use, naming practices, advertisements, or entertainment preferences. These might be demographic data like marriage and fertility rates, employment rates, and college attendance. And these might be material goods like home size and construction.

Variables in this second set are less familiar to psychologists, but are commonly used in samples where direct psychological assessments are not available. For example, a study of generational change in Ancient Rome might focus on labor, conflict, representations in arts and entertainment, and war. This type of historical work has been done (e.g., Winter, 2017) but with a focus on cultural rather than generational change. Soon it will be possible to build measures of cultural change directly from ongoing data flow (e.g., smartphones, television, or the web).

To use an example from a large study of narcissism in culture, data included self-report scales (personality, self-concept, attitudes, and values), and the cultural study of: song lyrics; pronoun use in books; house size and design; social media; cosmetic surgeries; classroom practices, etc. (Twenge & Campbell, 2009). The overall pattern of evidence was consistent with a rise in extrinsic individualism, including narcissism. However, there were inconsistent trends, such as the pattern of violence which made a long fall from the early 1990s.

Our suggestions for best practices include focus on using multiple assessments to the furthest extent possible. These might include psychological data, but other data that more directly assess culture are also important. Then it becomes a question of finding converging or diverging evidence. For example, imagine that you are interested in the work ethic of the next generation, iGen. First, you have to conceptualize and operationalize work ethic at multiple levels (e.g., individual; cultural), then you would need to measure it. You would start by looking for related constructs or items in the major longitudinal data sets, but then you would look to other sources. Are there surveys of business leaders on work ethic? Are there economic surveys on time use? Are there data on commuting habits? Are there data on academic major choice that might be relevant? Are people building and buying tools to make it easier to slack off at work? Are people taking medications to help or hurt the work ethic? To truly get at a question like this means thinking through a good deal of literature from many research areas.

A final word on best practices: Our cultural models of generations are built on the idea that there is a correlation or association between the culture and the traits of the people in it. For example, an individualistic culture is made of up individualistic individuals; collective cultures are made up of collective people. This quite often seems to be the case in most research, but there is no model that we are aware of that shows the regulation of this process. That is, what factors lead to a closer or more distant, even negative, association between the culture and the individual? It is almost certain that culture and individuals can cohere at times and not at others. In the United States, for example, the culture appears to be highly narcissistic as compared to the actual citizens (Miller et al., 2015).

Selected General Findings

We will provide an overview of some of the changes that we have seen across generations in regard to individualism. This is designed to provide a sample of what can be found with this approach to generations research, not to be an exhaustive review.

To begin, changes in personality are a mixed bag when it comes to generations. One widely discussed personality shift attributed to generations in the mass media is that Millennials are more narcissistic (i.e., have inflated self-views, strategies for maintaining said self-views, and exploitative relational styles) than previous generations (Twenge & Campbell, 2008). The original meta-analyses sparking this discussion provided evidence that narcissism was growing among recent college students, or young adults (Twenge et al., 2008). In contrast, two recent papers found no changes: one looking at male and female samples only (Roberts, Edmonds, & Grijalva, 2010) and one looking at two convenience samples collected after the original meta-analysis (Wetzel et al., 2017). This is a very tangled debate; I (W.K.C.) have a dog in the fight as well (for a list of further reading see the informative blog post by Twenge, 2013). At this point, the latest (but unpublished) data we have suggests that narcissism started reversing with the Great Recession. We are slowly uncovering the cultural changes this economic collapse brought about, and one seems to be lower narcissism (e.g., Park, Twenge, & Greenfield, 2017).

As will be discussed in the next section, other studies (e.g., Lyons & Kuron, 2014) find marked increases in individualism, at least when it comes to workplace settings. So context is important in considering whether there are changes in generations over time. Other personality changes that have been studied regarding generations over time include Big Five personality traits. Smits et al. (2011) present research from the Netherlands stretching from 1971 onwards, focusing on using a measure of the Big Five. One caveat which should be touched upon here is that generational research is not necessarily generalizable to other countries. No changes were found in openness to experience, conscientiousness, extraversion, agreeableness, or neuroticism, after considering some biases in the male and female subsamples (Smits et al., 2011). Interestingly, this contrasts with some other research such as Twenge (2009) who reported that neuroticism has increased across generations.

Now that we've discussed how personality has (or hasn't) changed across generations, we move on to the topic of attitudes, or how different cohorts feel or think about something. The research that has looked at general generational differences in attitudes includes reports by the Pew Research Center (2015, 2016), such as those regarding gay marriage and marijuana use. Keeping limitations of generational research in mind, attitudes have trended towards more leniency and open-mindedness on these modern-day issues. Overall, attitudes towards gay marriage have been increasingly positive across all age groups but much more prominently for so-called Millennials. In general, tolerance for other lifestyles and support for marijuana use is rising across the culture more broadly in APC models, rather than being limited to the Millennials (Twenge, Campbell, & Carter, 2017; Twenge, Carter, & Campbell, 2015a). At the same time, overall civic orientation in young people dropped from the mid-1960s to the late 2000s, which is consistent with an individualistic culture (Twenge, Campbell, & Freeman, 2012). A similar pattern is also found in the rapid rise in atheism, especially in young people (Twenge et al., 2015b). Importantly, the timing of these changes is not easily explained. That is, they are consistent with rising individualism, but there are clearly specific factors that played a role in these massive cultural changes.

With diversity in mind, demographic changes play a key part in how different generations shape their attitudes and values. An increasing minority (e.g., Latino/Hispanic, Black, Asian) population within the United States (Bureau of Labor Statistics, 2016) means American culture is and will continue to be different than in decades and cohorts past. With increases in multicultural initiatives throughout the United States, both in schools and the workplace, younger cohorts are becoming more aware of issues affecting not only themselves but people of different ages, race, ethnicity, sex, and various other identities.

Organization-Specific Findings

When it comes to organizations, research is considerably more succinct than that of the general population. This is possibly due to organizations wanting to gain any advantage possible when it comes to recruiting and selecting from a pool of fresh, young candidates. Regarding organizations, research is more focused on how generations have attributed to value and attitude changes (e.g., Lyons & Kuron, 2014; Twenge et al. 2010). Some studies find few to no significant generational differences in values or attitudes relevant to organizations (e.g., Wong, Gardiner, Lang, & Coulon, 2008), while others do (e.g., Campbell, Twenge, & Campbell, 2017; Twenge, Campbell, Hoffman, & Lance, 2010). Many of these studies should be taken with a grain of salt as they were conducted using cross-sectional methods, which were discussed earlier as confounding effects due to age and cohort.

In terms of personality, Lyons and Kuron's (2014) review of generational differences in the workplace summarizes generational differences as an increase in neuroticism, extraversion, and conscientiousness over time. The caveat to this evidence of generational differences is the suggestion that personality is not concrete up until 30 years of age (Terracciano et al., 2010) and Lyons and Kuron's (2014) claim is based on a study of young adult students. With that in mind, this could support the earlier claim, in tandem with increased positive self-view (Lyons & Kuron, 2014), that generations are becoming increasingly narcissistic over time.

Although conclusions on generational differences in personality are cautious, research on work values is clearer. Compared to the Baby Boomer generation, both Generation X and Millennials have more extrinsic values in the form of leisure time, status, and pay (Campbell, Twenge, & Campbell, 2017; Lyons & Kuron, 2014; Twenge, 2010; Twenge et al. 2010). In the same vein, Generation X and Millennials value work–life balance and their personal wellbeing more than Baby Boomers (Smola & Sutton, 2002). Millennials also seem to have fewer priorities on social values at work, and value working for a larger organization rather than their own business (Campbell, Twenge, & Campbell, 2017). This could be attributed, again, to the evidence that narcissism is increasing with generations or could be the result of the context in which younger generations live. This context refers to the increasing demand for young adults to continue their education beyond college and an increasingly stressful work environment (Wegman et al., 2018). Technology also allows work and nonwork life to creep into one another more easily, making work–life balance an absolute necessity for many entering the modern workforce at an early point in their careers. It could also be that when looking at "younger" generations, we are simply looking at young people who have a greater need for work–life balance than older adults who are closer to retirement and do not have children living with them.

Meanwhile, research points to positive trends in work attitudes when it comes to generational differences. Millennials seem to be more satisfied with their jobs than previous generations, although the results do not seem to differ much from Baby Boomers and GenX when it comes to turnover intentions, satisfaction with pay, benefits, or the work itself (Kowske, Rasch, & Wiley, 2010).

Overall, effect sizes may be too small to outweigh the costs of tailoring organizational and human resources policies to individual generations (Becton, Walker, & Jones-Farmer, 2014). The current outlook on how to incorporate generational research into organizations may be not to treat generations differently at all. This argument is embodied in Constanza & Finkelstein's (2015) piece on whether a focus on generational differences leads to stereotyping and a work-around to age discrimination. As we've discussed in this chapter, a major methodological issue with studying generations is an overabundance of cross-sectional studies which make it difficult to say whether differences are due to generation or age. By saying young people are part of one generation and old people are a different generation, organizations may simply be using "generation" as an alternative to age. This has obvious issues in that age is a protected class but generations are not yet – the courts have looked and we assume will continue looking at it – although generations are typically correlated with age at any time period.

Future Trends and Questions

Interest in generations is likely to continue as it is both fascinating and beneficial. In this section, we outline four key trends that are going to shape our understanding of generations going forward.

Diversity is a major trend in Europe and the Anglosphere, where immigration has been at high levels. On top of the diversity of citizens, there is a subsequent variation in reproduction. If immigrants have higher birth rates than other citizens, the demographic effects will be amplified. These transitions are challenging to predict. Imagine the trend in individualism in the United States, for example, if the more collectivistic groups – religious, ethnic, or otherwise cultural – continue reproducing at replacement rates while the more individualistic citizens lower their reproductive rates. And, at the same time, imagine that some members of the collectivistic groups are assimilating to the more individualistic US culture. These types of changes need to go into models, but that means a lot of guesswork.

Technological changes are similarly dramatic and hard to predict. In the case of generations, they have been shaped dramatically by war and finance. War, however, has changed dramatically in the United States because of technology. We simply do not fight large, troop-heavy ground wars like the First and Second World Wars. This means that the military experience will be shared by fewer and fewer people. Similarly with finance: the need to work has been central to generations, but it is materially possible for all citizens to now have a pretty remarkable life experience with little work. It will take awhile for nations to sort this out, and it might never get sorted, but the idea of the "job" outside a trade is relatively new and may not be here for long.

Social media allows people to form their own in- and outgroups fairly easily, meaning that they are more likely to engage only with people like themselves. This could harden values and attitudes towards several life aspects such as work, meaning generations could become their own "echo chambers." We are seeing this process occur in politics over time (e.g., Garimella & Weber, 2017) and on campuses through concept creep, polarization, and purification processes (e.g., Haidt, 2012). We are still trying to sort out the role of social media, and, to make matters more difficult for generations researchers, social media platform is confounded with age – and the younger people like photo-heavy content (e.g., SnapChat, Instagram) that is harder to analyze than word-heavy sites like Twitter.

The next generation, iGen, remains a challenge to describe. If the cyclical model is correct, the next generation will look like the Silent Generation who came of age in the 1950s. If the extrinsic individualism model is correct, we will get an iGen that is a road-weary and insecure continuation of the Millennials. And, of course, if the no-change model is correct, this next group is exactly like the previous ones. We will call them narcissistic and lazy, say they will be unable to contribute to the culture beyond adolescent pursuits, and then become surprised when they grow up and turn into us.

Future Research

Future research on generations needs to focus on time-lagged designs to better identify differences between not only cohorts, but also different age groups and time periods. The General Social Survey (GSS), a publicly available resource which surveys Americans at least every other year, is an example of a large data collection effort which is useful although not perfect for generations. By collaborating with the International Social Survey Program, the GSS has several "modules," or questions which are repeated every few years to different countries' equivalents of the GSS. This collaboration helps out generational research but is limited by time, or how far back we can study trends. To understand future, and current, generations, researchers need to stop relying on simple cross-sectional surveys. Collaborating with "big data" firms may be key to understanding generational differences for now, while efforts are built to study future cohorts.

Twenge (2010) stated that "one of the biggest challenges in research on generational differences is, to put it facetiously, the lack of a workable time machine" (p. 202). To put it simply, studying generational differences is difficult with the current data available to researchers, but continuing to collect it is vital to better understanding how generations work and how they impact the world of work.

References

Arnett, J. J. (2000). Emerging adulthood: A theory of development from the late teens through the twenties. *American Psychologist, 55*, 469–480.

Becton, J. B., Walker, H. J., & Jones-Farmer, A. (2014). Generational differences in workplace behavior. *Journal of Applied Social Psychology, 44*, 175–189.

Berdahl, A. M., Kao, A. B., Flack, A., Westley, P. A., Codling, E. A., Couzin, I. D., et al. (2018). Collective animal navigation and migratory culture: From theoretical models to empirical evidence. *Philosophical Transactions of the Royal Society B, 373*, 1–26.

Bianchi, E. C. (2016). American individualism rises and falls with the economy: Cross-temporal evidence that individualism declines when the economy falters. *Journal of Personality and Social Psychology, 111*, 567–584.

Bureau of Labor Statistics. (2016). *Labor force characteristics by race and ethnicity, 2016*. Retrieved from www.bls.gov/opub/reports/race-and-ethnicity/2016/pdf/home.pdf

Campbell, S. M., Twenge, J. M., & Campbell, W. K. (2017). Fuzzy but useful constructs: Making sense of the differences between generations. *Work, Aging and Retirement, 3*, 130–139.

Campbell, W., Twenge, J., & Carter, N. (2017). Support for marijuana (cannabis) legalization: Untangling age, period, and cohort effects. *Collabra: Psychology, 3*(1), 2. http://doi.org/10.1525/collabra.45

Costanza, D. P., & Finkelstein, L. M. (2015). Generationally based differences in the workplace: Is there a there there? *Industrial and Organizational Psychology, 8*, 308–323.

Garimella, V. R. K., & Weber, I. (2017). A long-term analysis of political polarization on Twitter. In *Proceedings of the 11th International Conference on Web and Social Media, May 15–18, 2017, Montreal, Quebec, Canada* (pp. 528–531). Association for the Advancement of Artificial Intelligence. Palo Alto, CA: AAAI Press.

Gentile, B., Campbell, W. K., & Twenge, J. M. (2013). *Generational cultures*. In A. B. Cohen (Ed.), *Culture reexamined: Broadening our understanding of social and evolutionary influences* (pp. 31–48). Washington, DC: American Psychological Association.

Haidt, J. (2012). *The righteous mind*. New York, NY: Random House.

Jokela, M., Pekkarinen, T., Sarvimäki, M., Terviö, M., & Uusitalo, R. (2017). Secular rise in economically valuable personality traits. *Proceedings of the National Academy of Sciences, 114*, 6527–6532.

Kowske, B. J., Rasch, R., & Wiley, J. (2010). Millennials' (lack of) attitude problem: An empirical examination of generational effects on work attitudes. *Journal of Business and Psychology, 25*, 265–279.

Lyons, S., & Kuron, L. (2014). Generational differences in the workplace: A review of the evidence and directions for future research. *Journal of Organizational Behavior, 35*, S139–S157.

Mannheim, K. (1952). *Essays on the sociology of knowledge*. London, UK: Routledge & Kegan Paul Ltd.

Miller, J. D., Maples, J. L., Buffardi, L., Cai, H., Gentile, B., Kisbu-Sakarya, Y., et al. (2015). Narcissism and United States' culture: The view from home and around the world. *Journal of Personality and Social Psychology, 109*(6), 1068–1089.

Park, H., Twenge, J. M., & Greenfield, P. M. (2017). American undergraduate students' value development during the Great Recession. *International Journal of Psychology, 52*, 28–39.

Pew Research Center. (2015). Section 1: Changing views of same-sex marriage. Retrieved from www.people-press.org/2015/06/08/section-1-changing-views-of-same-sex-marriage/

Pew Research Center. (2016). Support for marijuana legalization continues to rise. Retrieved from www.pewresearch.org/fact-tank/2016/10/12/support-for-marijuana-legalization-continues-to-rise/

Roberts, B. W., Edmonds, G., & Grijalva, E. (2010). It is developmental me, not generation me: Developmental changes are more important than generational changes in narcissism – Commentary on Trzesniewski & Donnellan (2010). *Perspectives on Psychological Science, 5*, 97–102.

Smits, I. A. M., Dolan, C. V., Vorst, H. C. M., Wicherts, J. M., & Timmerman, M. E. (2011). Cohort differences in big five personality factors over a period of 25 years. *Journal of Personality and Social Psychology, 100*, 1124–1138.

Smola, K.W., & Sutton, C. D. (2002). Generational differences: Revisiting generational work values for the new millennium. *Journal of Organizational Behavior, 23*, 363–382.

Strauss, W. & Howe, N. (1992). *Generations: The history of America's future, 1584 to 2069*. New York, NY: William Morrow.

Terracciano, A., McCrae, R. R., & Costa Jr, P. T. (2010). Intra-individual change in personality stability and age. *Journal of Research in Personality, 44*, 31–37.

Trzesniewski, K. H., & Donnellan, M. B. (2010). Rethinking "Generation Me": A study of cohort effects from 1976–2006. *Perspectives on Psychological Science, 5*, 58–75.

Twenge, J. M. (2009). Generational changes and their impact in the classroom: Teaching Generation Me. *Medical Education, 43*, 398–405.

Twenge, J. M. (2010). A review of the empirical evidence on generational differences in work attitudes. *Journal of Business and Psychology, 25*(2), 201–210.

Twenge, J. M. (2013, August 12). How dare you say narcissism is increasing? *Psychology Today*. Retrieved from https://psychologytoday.com/us/blog/the-narcissism-epidemic/201308/how-dare-you-say-narcissism-is-increasing.

Twenge, J. M., & Campbell, S. M. (2008). Generational differences in psychological traits and their impact on the workplace. *Journal of Managerial Psychology, 23*, 862–877.

Twenge, J. M., & Campbell, W. K. (2009). *The narcissism epidemic: Living in the age of entitlement*. New York, NY: Simon and Schuster.

Twenge, J. M., & Campbell, W. K. (2018). Cultural individualism is linked to later onset of adult-role responsibilities across time and regions. *Journal of Cross-Cultural Psychology, 49*(4), 673–682.

Twenge, J. M., Campbell, W. K., & Freeman, E. C. (2012). Generational differences in young adults' life goals, concern for others, and civic orientation, 1966–2009. *Journal of Personality and Social Psychology, 102*, 1045–1062.

Twenge, J. M., Campbell, S. M., Hoffman, B. J., & Lance, C. E. (2010). Generational differences in work values: Leisure and extrinsic values increasing, social and intrinsic values decreasing. *Journal of Management, 36*, 1117–1142.

Twenge, J. M., Carter, N. T., & Campbell, W. K. (2015a). Time period, generational, and age differences in tolerance for controversial beliefs and lifestyles in the United States, 1972–2012. *Social Forces, 94*, 379–399.

Twenge J. M., Carter, N. T., & Campbell, W. K. (2017). Age, time period, and birth cohort differences in self-esteem: Reexamining a cohort-sequential longitudinal study. *Journal of Personality and Social Psychology, 112*(5), e9–e17.

Twenge, J. M., Exline, J. J., Grubbs, J. B., Sastry, R., & Campbell, W. K. (2015b). Generational and time period differences in American adolescents' religious orientation, 1966–2014. *PLOS ONE, 10*(5), e0121454.

Twenge, J. M., Konrath, S., Foster, J. D., Keith Campbell, W., & Bushman, B. J. (2008). Egos inflating over time: A cross-temporal meta-analysis of the Narcissistic Personality Inventory. *Journal of Personality, 76*, 875–902.

Wegman, L. A., Hoffman, B. J., Carter, N. T., Twenge, J. M., & Guenole, N. (2018). Placing job characteristics in context: cross-temporal meta-analysis of changes in job characteristics since 1975. *Journal of Management, 44*, 352–386.

Welzel, C., & Inglehart, R. (2010). Agency, values, and well-being: A human development model. *Social Indicators Research, 97*, 43–63.

Wetzel, E., Brown, A., Hill, P. L., Chung, J. M., Robins, R. W., & Roberts, B. W. (2017). The narcissism epidemic is dead; long live the narcissism epidemic. *Psychological Science, 28*, 1833–1847.

Winter, D. G. (2017). *The power motive*. New York, NY: Free Press.

Wong, M., Gardiner, E., Lang, W., & Coulon, L. (2008). Generational differences in personality and motivation: Do they exist and what are the implications for the workplace? *Journal of Managerial Psychology, 23*, 878–890.

Yang, Y., & Land, K. C. (2013). *Age–Period–Cohort analysis: New models, methods and empirical applications*. Boca Raton, FL: CRC Press.

13 Changes in Work Behavior Patterns

Sara Jansen Perry, Emily M. David, and Lars U. Johnson

Work has become increasingly flexible over the last several decades, and flexibility is a top concern of many employees choosing between organizations (Burke & Ng, 2006; Global Workplace Analytics, 2017; Rau & Hyland, 2002). This increasing flexibility takes several forms, from the locations in which people work, to the type of work people call a career. Indeed, increasing flexibility has been an integral feature of the way the modern workforce approaches work. As we review the changing patterns in work behavior in this chapter, we describe three forms of flexibility – location, schedule, and work design – and then highlight one newer setting, or work arrangement, that accommodates all of these forms of flexible work – coworking. Coworking has yet to receive much attention in the industrial–organizational (I-O) psychology and organizational behavior literatures, but we posit that it may strike a much-needed balance, minimizing the challenges and maximizing the benefits of flexible work arrangements, while offering yet another option for how employees may choose to spend their working hours.

Background: Increasing Flexibility in Work Behavior Patterns

With each new generation that enters the workforce, more forms of flexibility are demanded (Sparrow, 2000). This is even more apparent as technology and automation usurps many traditional, routinized jobs, and more knowledge jobs emerge (Parker, Wall, & Cordery, 2001). As noted by Burke and Ng (2006), "knowledge workers don't like to be told what to do" (p. 90). So how should organizations best approach this new workforce and its demands for more flexibility? In contrast to other research that takes the perspective of how each entity can be more flexible (i.e., organizations, groups, and individuals being responsive to changes; Värlander, 2012), we explore the forms and implications of flexibility, as it is increasingly infused into work to meet these new worker demands. Autonomy (i.e., discretion to make work-related decisions; Parker et al., 2001) is one relevant construct in this discussion, but we focus more broadly as we explore flexibility in work patterns overall.

Drivers of Change

The prioritization of flexibility could well have emerged as downsizing became more prevalent over the past several decades. As Sparrow (2000) commented when describing downsizing trends over the last part of the twentieth century, "employees now worked in a permanent state of flux" (p. 205). As a result, employees were forced to change jobs more frequently than they would have liked. It is no surprise, then, that they began to see themselves as managers of their own work lives, and even their entire careers, rather than identifying strongly with their employing organization, or allowing that organization to hold such a powerful position determining the structure of their lives (Parker et al., 2001; Sparrow, 2000). In response, research on individualized work arrangements emerged (i.e., i-deals; Liao, Wayne, & Rousseau, 2016), as workers negotiated specialized deals to help them better manage demands in all domains of life. I-deals encompass many forms of flexibility (e.g., professional development opportunities, flexible schedules, and telecommuting) and appear to be beneficial for employees and organizations, when managed properly. This is just one example of how scholars have begun to study the ways in which workers expect more flexibility from organizations. Although we do not review research on i-deals here, we discuss three specific types of flexibility that are often part of i-deals – location, schedule, and work design – to provide a more in-depth review of the increasing prevalence of each type of flexibility, the challenges versus benefits of each, and future research directions. Efforts to understand how to implement these various forms of flexibility are likely to be beneficial, given research that suggests that flexible work arrangements have spillover effects on the employee, their workgroup, and their organization as a whole (e.g., Anderson, Coffey, & Byerly, 2002).

Location Flexibility

Location flexibility has been studied extensively in a body of literature centered on remote work. Remote work has been increasingly popular with the introduction of enabling technologies for doing all types of work from anywhere (Burke & Ng, 2006). Similar constructs that capture flexibility of work location (i.e., alternative work arrangements, or geographic alternatives to the central office) include telework, telecommuting, remote work, and flexspace (Allen, Golden, & Shockley, 2015; Bailey & Kurland, 2002; Gajendran & Harrison, 2007; Hill et al., 2008; Mokhtarian, Salomon, & Choo, 2005). Although scholars have spent a great deal of time attempting to define these concepts, the common thread is that, over time, more employees have been given the option, or sometimes the mandate, to work away from the traditional, central office of the organization (e.g., Bailey & Kurland, 2002; Hill et al., 2008; Mokhtarian et al., 2005; Sullivan, 2003; Wilks & Billsberry, 2007). This shifting of work settings from a centralized location to a remote, often isolated, location (i.e., home or another place away from coworkers and central office amenities) has been prolific. Statistics suggest that telecommuting rates have increased 140% over the past ten years, which is more than ten times faster than the workforce has grown overall (Global Workplace Analytics, 2017). Studies repeatedly show that employees are not at their desks 50–60% of the time, and therefore less dedicated office space is required, pushing some global organizations to revamp their offices to account for these trends (Global Workplace Analytics, 2017). A 2017 Gallup study surveying 15,000 American employees found that 31% worked remotely four to five days per week, up from 24% in the previous year, while lower-intensity remote work (those working remotely only one to two days per week) decreased at about the same rate (Chokshi, 2017).

Employees want location flexibility for a variety of reasons (Allen et al., 2015; Rau & Hyland, 2002), including to avoid long commutes, improve work–nonwork balance, and reduce the need to spend time and money physically preparing for the office environment (e.g., dressing up formally). Others have a desire for more variety in work environments, or wish to avoid contact with difficult people or situations (Allen et al., 2015; Bailey & Kurland, 2002; Beasley, Seubert, & Lomo-David, 2002; Hartig, Kylin, & Johansson, 2007). As people's lives get fuller with responsibilities and activities in all domains of life, work–nonwork boundaries have blurred somewhat, also explaining employees' increasing desire to work remotely. Richer technology has enabled this shift, since it allows for continuous improvements in the richness of communication among dispersed coworkers and seamless, 24/7 connection to work tasks (Burke & Ng, 2006).

Although the notion of "24/7 work" raises red flags for any occupational health expert (e.g., expectations for employees to be available via text or email at all times; Burke & Ng, 2006; Fenner & Renn, 2010), remote work is also associated with many benefits for organizations and individuals (e.g., Ludden, 2010). Meta-analytic research suggests that organizations benefit in terms of improved productivity, retention, and commitment (Martin & MacDonnell, 2012). For instance, JD Edwards' teleworkers are reportedly 20–25% more productive than their office-based counterparts, and American Express teleworkers reported even more productivity improvements at 43% (Global Workplace Analytics, 2017). Research also suggests significant cost savings in terms of energy and space for individuals, organizations, and their communities. For example, organizations could save as much as $11,000 per employee per year by allowing them to work from home just half the time (Global Workplace Analytics, 2017). Additionally, individual employees could save $2,000–$3,000 per year on commuting and other professional costs (e.g., dry cleaning and fuel; Breaugh & Farabee, 2012). Further, if employees with suitable jobs and a desire to work from home (an estimated 62 million employees) did so just half the time, greenhouse gas reductions would be the equivalent of taking New York State's entire workforce permanently off the road (Global Workplace Analytics, 2017). Interestingly, the United States Congressional Budget Office estimated their five-year cost of implementing telework throughout their agencies ($30 million) is less than a third of the cost of lost productivity from a single-day shutdown of federal offices in Washington, DC due to snow ($100 million; Global Workplace Analytics, 2017). Thus, programs allowing for location flexibility appear to also be good disaster readiness strategies (Donnelly & Proctor-Thomson, 2015). Scholarly research suggests organizations can also benefit when they can find remote workers closer to their customers (reducing the need for business travel), by improving the size and quality of the applicant pool, improving applicant attraction, and reducing physical barriers that might otherwise prevent certain types of employees from working (Alizadeh, 2009; Baker, Moon, & Ward, 2006). Other organizational benefits include higher morale, lower turnover, and reduced absenteeism (Breaugh & Farabee, 2012; Kurland & Bailey, 1999; Martin & MacDonnell, 2012).

At the individual level, employees also benefit (or assume they would benefit) from this form of flexibility. For example, 36% of employees say they would choose telework over a pay raise, 80% of employees consider telework a benefit they value (Global Workplace Analytics, 2017), and 94% of Americans say they would like to work remotely (Heby, 2017). Research suggests the most common individual benefits are higher productivity, motivation, commitment, wellbeing, satisfaction, and reduced work interference with family (but not necessarily family interference with work; Gajendran & Harrison, 2007; Golden, 2006a; Golden & Veiga, 2005; Golden, Veiga, & Simsek, 2006; Kurland & Bailey, 1999). These benefits also translate back to organizations, as individuals reciprocate through their attitudes and efforts on the job and toward the organization (Golden & Veiga, 2008).

One of the most-touted benefits of remote work that helps both organizations and individuals is the reduction of distractions. Estimates suggest businesses lose $600 billion per year on workplace distractions (Global Workplace Analytics, 2017). These may take the form of small talk, gossip, or the visual and audio distractions of simply working around other individuals (Sackett, 2002). These may also include the tendency to hold unnecessary meetings, versus communicating more efficiently or acting more independently when people are not as easily accessible (Fonner & Roloff, 2010). Research suggests that managers should encourage employees to keep clear boundaries between work and nonwork domains to help minimize work–family conflict and maximize performance, but this also creates a paradox, because employees who adopt this segmented approach are less likely to work in off-hours and may be harder to reach when needed (Lautsch, Kossek, & Eaton, 2009).

Of course, "working here, there, anywhere, and anytime" (Kurland & Bailey, 1999, p. 1) carries important challenges that must be addressed by individuals and their leaders who incorporate flexible location policies. Social isolation is a chief concern, which can lead to decreased performance and retention among those who do not get enough face-to-face interaction or at least have access to rich forms of communication technology (Golden, Veiga, & Dino, 2008). Further, it is simply harder to form strong bonds with a workgroup or the organization when working remotely (Bartel, Wrzesniewski, & Wiesenfeld, 2012). Questions also linger about the degree to which working remotely affects performance ratings and promotion potential. Some studies suggest performance ratings can improve, as long as flexible work policies are used properly (e.g., Kossek, Lautsch, & Eaton, 2006; Lautsch et al., 2009), whereas others suggest that the lack of 'face time' has damaging consequences for remote workers (e.g., Elsbach, Cable, & Sherman, 2010). Interestingly, however, meta-analytic evidence suggests that remote workers are not likely to think their own promotion potential is any lower; women are even likely to believe their promotion potential is higher when they work remotely more often (Gajendran & Harrison, 2007).

Other well-documented challenges include weaker organizational identification and loyalty, difficulty in accessing knowledge from people and resources in the office (and more risk in explicitly seeking help), and spillover of work-related stressors to the nonwork domain of life (or vice versa; Gajendran & Harrison, 2007; Golden & Schoenleber, 2014; Peters & van der Lippe, 2007). Exacerbating these challenges, office-based coworkers who do not have location flexibility may experience increased dissatisfaction as other employees work remotely more often (Golden, 2007). However, Lautsch et al. (2009) suggested that if managers of remote workers are proactive in sharing information, those employees may actually help their colleagues more. These findings underscore the fact that leadership behaviors and workgroup characteristics are critical factors to consider when considering an increase in employee location flexibility.

Of course, individual differences also affect the management of these benefits and challenges. Self-efficacy and self-regulation are important in helping employees implement structure in a remote work arrangement and to commit to both the flexible work arrangement and to their dispersed coworkers (Haines, St-Onge, & Archambault, 2002; Raghuram, Garud, Wiesenfeld, & Gupta, 2001; Workman, Kahnweiler, & Bommer, 2003). Emotional stability is also important to help employees manage challenges associated with remote work, including their ability to appropriately leverage autonomy when working away from the central office (Perry, Rubino, & Hunter, 2018). By extension, those with a strong need for autonomy may also fare better in remote work (O'Neill, Hambley, Greidanus, MacDonnell, & Kline, 2009), whereas those with high affiliation motivation or high need for achievement may be less well-suited, given their need for social interaction, attachment, and feedback (Haines et al., 2002; O'Neill et al., 2009).

In recent years, several large companies made headlines by cancelling or reducing their flexible location programs (e.g., Bhasin, 2013; Zenger, 2013), which may raise questions about the future efficacy of such programs. Some organizations cite reduced ability to collaborate and make decisions when more workers are remote, resulting in less innovation. Others were dissatisfied with productivity and engagement among remote workers in general. Still others have suggested that the findings in remote work research claiming increased productivity are misleading because many employees who claim to telework now are primarily doing so after normal work hours, thus simply adding more work hours to the day. However, a volumunious body of literature suggests that overall, remote work, and more broadly, location flexibility, is beneficial for all when properly managed. Successful implementation is more likely when a firm has reason to do business in dispersed areas (i.e., market demand; Neirotti, Paolucci, & Raguseo, 2013), and when the specific requirements of the job fit well with a flexible location. Success of such programs also depends on trust between managers and their teams (Bailey & Kurland, 2002), good communication among all parties (Lautsch et al., 2009), and a supportive organizational culture, starting with top leadership (Dikkers et al., 2007; Frye & Breaugh, 2004).

More than ever, it behooves organizations and scholars to find the appropriate implementation of this form of flexibility, as future generations will likely value it even more, and technology will continue to enhance the ability of more types of workers to work from anywhere, at any time. A good balance, enabling maximum productivity and protecting wellbeing across life domains, may exist somewhere around the 15-hour mark; individuals who work remotely more than 15 hours per week may see a plateau, and then decreasing job satisfaction (Golden, 2006b; Golden & Veiga, 2005). Industry studies suggest that optimal benefits (engagement, avoidance of distractions, and collaboration) may occur when workers are remote two to three (Global Workplace Analytics, 2017) or three to four days per week (Chokshi, 2017). Thus, recent statistics showing increases in very high-intensity remote work may be cause for concern; perhaps such arrangements have gone too far.

Future research should continue to explore the types of work location flexibility employees prefer and how managers can best provide those opportunities while still protecting organizational and employee interests, meaningful connections, wellbeing, and engagement. From a measurement standpoint, it is also important to consider differences in the meaning of constructs when they exist in a remote work setting versus a central office setting. For example, effective supervisor support or coworker support and interaction may involve very different behaviors for remote workers compared to on-site workers. Future research should also investigate which types of environments are best suited for different types of tasks (e.g., concentration or creativity) for a better understanding of the outcomes associated with remote work in various locations. As noted by Liegl (2014), although technology allows for "work 'anytime anywhere,' it becomes apparent that not all places seem to be equally suitable" (p. 163).

Schedule Flexibility

Scheduling flexibility (i.e., flextime) is another area in which employees' work behavior patterns have been changing, providing another form of flexibility to those jobs that do not allow for location flexibility. Traditionally, employees adhered mostly to organizationally set shifts, working only during their assigned shift. However, organizations have increasingly allowed employees to redefine their working hours in at least three ways. Some allow employees to choose their start and end times, but employees must still be present for a set number of hours. Compressed work weeks are another variation of this limited form of flexibility, which allows the organization to have predictability, with overlapping hours for all employees, but still allows individuals to better manage their non-work responsibilities. Other organizations offer more flexibility by requiring a certain number of hours to be worked, but allowing employees to choose when those hours occur. This may result in little overlap among employee work days, and thus may be better for less interdependent jobs and workgroups (Taskin & Edwards, 2007). On the bright side, this extreme form of scheduling flexibility may help employees by allowing them to work when they have maximum energy or concentration to devote to work (e.g., "morning" or "night" people). Finally, the most adaptable form of flextime focuses only on results produced by employees, without tracking or requiring any set number of hours (e.g., results-only work environment, ROWE; Ludden, 2010). This third category has received some negative press in conjunction with organizations cutting back their flexible work programs (e.g., Bhasin, 2013; Zenger, 2013), but scientific research suggests these programs can benefit employee wellbeing by improving employee control over their time (Moen, Kelly, & Lam, 2013). Another innovative flexible schedule offering is family-friendly vacation-by-the-hour, separate from normally allotted vacation time. Akin to family sick time, this allows employees to change schedules as needed without using their vacation or sick time, but they otherwise hold a normal, less flexible schedule (Johnson, 2007).

Compared to other research areas, work–family scholars have published the most on flextime, touting it as the more valuable form of flexibility for working parents (in contrast to location flexibility; Allen, 2001; Liao et al., 2016). Working from home or in other remote locations may be distracting or unfeasible for some employees with significant home responsibilities (Kossek et al., 2006; Lapierre & Allen, 2006; Shockley & Allen, 2007; Standen, Daniels, & Lamond, 1999). But scheduling flexibility still allows employees to manage their personal lives so that stressors from the nonwork domain do not derail them from committing to and engaging in their work, and employees may even perceive they have more time available for work (Moen et al., 2013; Rau & Hyland, 2002; Shockley & Allen, 2007). Consistent with this, the benefits of flextime include increased wellbeing, productivity, and satisfaction, and decreased absenteeism and work–family conflict. Just as with flexible work location, however, there may be a threshold after which the benefits of schedule flexibility diminish (more flexibility means less predictability and accountability), and those in certain jobs may not benefit as much (i.e., managers who need to be available during traditional hours, or among professionals who have significant autonomy in other forms; Allen, 2001; Baltes, Briggs, Huff, Wright, & Neuman, 1999; Breaugh & Frye, 2007; Liao et al., 2016).

One avenue for future research is examining the employee wellbeing implications of work that occurs in irregular or compressed timeframes. For example, some employees may feel pressure to get projects completed as quickly as possible, work during client daytime hours that differ from their own, or work nonstop during periods of high demand. Such pressure may ultimately heighten strain and work–family conflict, thus resulting in unwanted negative consequences of an otherwise beneficial offering.

Work Design Flexibility

Finally, work design is "the study, creation, and modification of the composition, content, structure, and environment within which jobs and roles are enacted" (Morgeson & Humphrey, 2008, p. 11). This is the broadest category of flexibility, encapsulating foundational work design theories (i.e., Hackman & Oldham, 1976; Humphrey, Nahrgang, & Morgeson, 2007), and new trends in redefining careers and work. As Morgeson and Humphrey (2008) noted, work design flexibility is increasingly an important consideration, as "workers are also proactive 'crafters' of their work roles, often dynamically redesigning their own work to suit their particular capabilities, interests, or situations" (pp. 3–4).

Flexibility in work design can benefit organizations who want to attract top talent by providing increasingly sought-after flexibility in the very definition of work. It can also mean defining work in such a way that it is accessible to more candidates. For example, redefining a job to include only aspects that can be accomplished by someone with disabilities or other limitations can help organizations benefit from a more diverse workforce. Similarly, job sharing has worked for individuals who strive to balance parenthood and career success (McManus, Korabik, Rosin, & Kelloway, 2002), especially in management or executive roles that are often so demanding that they preclude anyone who strives for work–life balance. Increased flexibility in the forms of contracting, part-time work, and job crafting has also empowered people who want to take an entrepreneurial approach to their career while still working with established organizations. Recent estimates suggest the American part-time remote workforce has increased 115% over the past decade, to 3.9 million workers (Guta, 2018). This source of talent is valuable for organizations that want to remain flexible to economic and project changes; they can hire highly qualified individuals for project work without the risk of unexpected and detrimental layoffs when demand decreases (Connelly & Gallagher, 2006; Guest, Oakley, Clinton, & Budjanovcanin, 2006).

Another way organizations offer more flexibility in work design, and simultaneously enhance innovation, is by offering traditional full-time employees the chance to work on autonomously defined projects for a certain percentage of their time. For example, P&G, Google, and 3M all have employee-driven innovation programs, rooted in the notion that increased flexibility enhances motivation, productivity, and creativity (Outthinker, 2017). Related to this, Haier (a Chinese company that manufactures home appliances) has self-managed innovation teams where an employee with a promising idea for a new product simply makes a proposal to create a cross-functional team tasked with developing a prototype (Kirkpatrick, 2017). These innovative, flexible forms of work design even go to the extreme in companies like Valve (a video game company), which invests heavily in hiring highly qualified employees, who are then, after onboarding, told simply to choose what they want to work on to make the company great (Burkus, 2016).

Perhaps as a result of these increasingly entrepreneurial and flexible mindsets, the "gig economy" has emerged, as well as an increase in the number of "digital nomads" and the rise of self-employed freelancers in the workforce (Burtch, Carnahan, & Greenwood, 2018; Spreitzer, Cameron, & Garrett, 2017). These trends were likely also amplified by the 2008 global financial crisis, forcing many workers into self-employment (Mariotti, Pacchi, & Di Vita, 2017); indeed, freelance knowledge workers have grown by more than a third since 2008 (IPSE, 2017). Freelance management systems have emerged in response, which are companies that act as a liaison between freelancers and clients. Many websites use competitive crowdsourcing to connect graphic design freelancers to individuals who need logos or websites. Other examples are Airbnb and Uber, which connect freelancers directly with consumers through reservation-booking software applications. These types of systems allow the freelancer to autonomously define their level of involvement in the gig and give them access to clients who need their services.

A significant benefit of these new forms of work is the removal of geographic boundaries, which potentially eliminates location conflicts between organizations and the top talent they wish to recruit (e.g., dual-career couples, or those otherwise unable to commute or relocate; Alizadeh, 2009; Baker et al., 2006). These trends also support the emergence of entrepreneurial mindsets among individuals valuing flexibility and personally meaningful work (Agrawal, Catalini, & Goldfarb, 2015; Spreitzer et al., 2017). Of course, drawbacks may also exist, including fewer opportunities for establishing strong personal connections or for identifying with a group of coworkers or a set organization, particularly when communication occurs through digital means (Claggett & Karahanna, 2018). If employees are too detached from their employer, they may be less likely to form long-term relationships or contribute to the organization in broader ways (e.g., citizenship; Meyer, Stanley, Herscovitch, & Topolnytsky, 2002).

Although many of these terms sound like buzzwords, and are, indeed, trendy, scientific research is critically needed to enhance our understanding on how they impact the workplace, employees, and the fundamental design of work. We need more evidence about how to best manage employees who crave more autonomy, collaboration, and a less formal environment. Business opportunities abound as well, with consulting companies sure to emerge that manage complex projects for clients while relying on freelancers to conduct the actual labor (Mulcahy, 2016). Rigorous studies are needed that explore intangible and tangible benefits of emergent work designs, including defining these new phenomena and exploring their effects on key work-related outcomes.

Emergence of Coworking Spaces as a New Workplace

Even as all of these forms of flexibility are infused throughout modern, global work patterns, people still crave and indeed, require, connection with other humans, as well as the ability to discuss ideas, share knowledge, access office technology, compare their own competence with others', and continuously hone their chosen craft (Deci & Ryan, 2000). The increasing flexibility we have discussed in terms of location, scheduling, and work design has somewhat limited employees in fulfilling these basic needs. For instance, some scholars lament that remote work is generally inefficient, stressful, boring, distracting, and/or isolating (e.g., Liegl, 2014). There is also something to be said for stability in fulfilling these needs and protecting one's wellbeing, even when the choice of location or other work-related decisions are up to the employee. One study found that home-based workers fared better in terms of work–life balance than virtual workers who work remotely in a multitude of (potentially unpredictable) locations (Hill, Ferris, & Martinson, 2003). Anyone who has tried to complete a work task at a café where the internet is not working or that is overcrowded can imagine the challenges faced by someone who routinely roams during their work day, versus someone who is rooted in one place, whether it be home or another stable remote location.

Coworking is a potential solution to addressing many divergent needs that are more challenging to meet in light of the increasing flexibility being offered. Almost two decades ago, Kurland and Bailey (1999) presented a typology describing unique ways employee needs might be met in the context of flexible work arrangements. What they proposed as "neighborhood work centers" (p. 55) have now evolved into coworking spaces or centers (Spinuzzi, 2012). In 2005, the first official coworking space opened in San Francisco, led by a software engineer named Brad Neuberg, as a potential solution for overly formal business centers and the challenges inherent in solo, work-at-home arrangements (Foertsch & Cagnol, 2013). In theory, coworking spaces are flexible, low-cost spaces that provide community, collaboration, and professional support in a vibrant atmosphere, outside of one's home.

Coworking spaces are defined as dedicated, membership-based spaces where independent workers (or multiple employees from the same business) can work autonomously, yet in the presence of others (Petriglieri, Ashford, & Wrzesniewski, 2018; Spinuzzi, 2012). At the most basic level, these communities provide office space and technology to individuals who otherwise would be working from home or in "third places" (e.g., libraries and cafés; Oldenburg, 1989). Beyond just providing space, however, these communities also bring diverse individuals together under one roof to share resources, ideas, and network contacts (Parrino, 2015). This new type of workplace provides opportunities for social connection, even if among people from very different professions and career paths. The structural features and policies of coworking spaces are typically designed to foster a sense of community, including digital applications and social networks, social events, newsletters, and published member directories. They also provide opportunities for continual learning and pooling of resources to gain benefits that larger organizations would normally offer, such as professional development workshops and buying power. Indeed, many have posited that this notion of community is precisely what differentiates coworking spaces from other open-space or shared office concepts; for instance, Capdevila (2015, p. 3) noted that key defining features are "the focus on the community and knowledge sharing dynamics." A final unique feature of these spaces is the often playful physical environment, designed to maximize social interaction and promote creativity through the use of varied workspaces and nontraditional, often fun, décor (van Meel, Martens, & van Ree, 2010).

Coworking spaces have grown exponentially from only a handful a decade ago to nearly 15,000 in 2017, with double that number expected by the year 2020 (GCUC, 2017; Statista, 2018). Some estimates suggest that the number of coworking members will rise to 5.1 million by 2022 (McBride, 2017). Members come from a variety of sectors, ranging from freelancers, consultants, small start-up businesses, large business touchdown spaces, and temporary project teams (Spinuzzi, 2012). Memberships are typically paid by the entity seeking out the space, whether it is the individual or their employing company.

The types and offerings of these spaces are as diverse as their members (Parrino, 2015). Typically, the floor plan is divided between dedicated desks, shared desks, private offices, shared conference rooms, and common/break areas, creating space for both the collaborative co-creation of goods and services and independent work (Bouncken & Reuschl, 2016). Although many are general and open to any interested party, some coworking spaces are more specialized, such as incubator spaces devoted to entrepreneurs and start-ups, or those who target a specific industry (e.g., communities of drafters and architects who need large printers). Still others are "maker spaces" that provide high-end technology and tools in a specially controlled environment to a variety of tinkerers, artists, and other professionals who need such resources. The innovativeness of the amenities in these spaces also varies based on the profiles of target members. In London, for instance, which boasts the highest number of coworking spaces of any city in the world (10 million square feet of real estate; Statista, 2018), potential members can find amenities like nap pods, hair salons, sand animation creation stations, selfie-corners, cake socials, showers, relaxation rooms, cafés, and entertainment. One Shanghai coworking space even featured a community pet tortoise that was used to predict the outcome of soccer matches for the 2018 World Cup.

Entrepreneurs establishing and overseeing coworking spaces also have a variety of motives. Some are simply opportunistic, capitalizing on these work trends (often by using their otherwise unoccupied commercial real estate). Others are more focused on building a profitable business, through large-scale, franchise or multi-location coworking models; these are sometimes impersonal as a result of this profit or growth focus. Still others intentionally seek to create a functional and inviting space that encourages a more personalized sense of community and productivity among their members. Thus, coworking spaces are diverse in their size and offerings, including in their level of intentionality.

The apparent benefits of coworking spaces include having a physical workspace with all the amenities of a traditional office, having a community of professionals with whom to interact when desired, and the influx of ideas of a diverse group of similar and dissimilar professionals sharing the space, while still maintaining one's own job and career autonomy. Customer contacts and collegial support may also emerge from the membership base, blending cooperation and competition dynamics that are separate from the politics occurring in a traditional workgroup within one organization. Despite their increased prevalence and intuitive benefits, however, scientific inquiry into coworking spaces has been scarce in the management and organizational psychology literature thus far. In two notable exceptions, Petriglieri et al. (2018) and Garrett, Spreitzer, and Bacevice (2017) agreed that one way coworking spaces may be highly beneficial is in the fostering of identity – toward the coworking community and one's profession – which may help in fostering positive emotions, a sense of purpose, and deep interpersonal connections.

Challenges also exist, such as the potential for conflict or stealing of ideas, or difficulty in forming relationships with highly dissimilar others (Guillaume, Brodbeck, & Riketta, 2012). There may also be some ambiguity about preferences and values of other members when members come from different work backgrounds and situations (from furniture selection to music preferences to type of work being conducted). The active role of the coworking center management may be important in addressing these challenges; they can help foster productive relationships among members, enforce community norms, and seek to proactively understand the diverse preferences of their members.

The coworking space model may appear similar to the organizational workplaces of the future, where space is used on an as-needed basis for work that is best performed there. Coworking spaces incorporate many of the principles from open-office layouts now being used in corporations, which include clear lines of sight across the office, but also offer flexible, non-dedicated work stations that allow employees to pick desks or alternative workspaces during the times they choose to work in the central office (i.e., hoteling, hot desking, free address; Kaufman, 2014; Lamagna, 2016). But we expect coworking spaces to overcome many of the drawbacks of the open office movement (e.g., lack of distraction-free areas or meaningful face-to-face communication, and concern about limiting the boundary of conversations; Bernstein & Turban, 2018; Hatch, 1987; Kaarlela-Tuomaala, Helenius, Keskinen, & Hongisto, 2009; Kaufman, 2014; Khazanchi, Sprinkle, Masterson, & Tong, 2018; Värlander, 2012). For example, Kaufman (2014, p. 1) noted that an open-plan office "ultimately damages workers' attention spans, productivity, creative thinking, and satisfaction." However, because coworking members are freed from the competitive, political, interrelated nature of work within a traditional, hierarchical organization, and are also armed with the knowledge that all those present *chose* to work within the same social space, these challenges may be minimized (Garrett et al., 2017). Further, many are motivated to join coworking spaces with the explicit aim of finding a community with work-related and socio-emotional support. In Spinuzzi's (2012) view, coworking spaces "combine social networking and working in a laid-back environment where the stress is gone" (p. 417).

Future research is needed to better understand the benefits and challenges associated with coworking spaces. As an example, we do not yet know whether certain types of individuals are more likely to thrive in coworking spaces. Given the challenges of open-plan workspaces with distractions, lack of privacy, and heightened noise (Kim & de Dear, 2013; Roper & Juneja, 2008), certain individuals (e.g., introverted workers or those low in social skill) may be poorly suited for coworking space membership. We also need to better understand how and when these spaces may contribute to organizational and individual productivity, employee wellbeing, and work engagement. Given that community and creativity are touted as benefits of these spaces, more field studies are needed comparing work conducted in these spaces with work conducted in other traditional and flexible locations. More quantitative work on identity formation in these spaces is also warranted, particularly among new freelancers and entrepreneurs who are still seeking to find their place in the market and their profession. It could be that people who foster productive connections with fellow members may also be empowered or emboldened to seek more productive connections with colleagues in their own organization or line of business. Moreover, future work should highlight the psychological effects of working more independently; as an example, freelancers may experience more strain given that their successes and failures are more personally impactful than when working as part of a group or organization.

Finally, there are also potential macro implications of coworking spaces. Namely, what is the potential impact on the broader community and on socio-economic inequality and/or inclusion in the workforce? Could coworking models offer flexibility to more employees that might not otherwise have it? For example, organizations that cannot feasibly allow work-at-home might consider such models for multiple groups of employees, perhaps based on home location or job type (Kurland & Bailey, 1999). Another question is, can exposure to diverse coworking members expose individuals to new areas of business and new ways of thinking? Further, how might certain groups of highly skilled service workers (e.g., physicians) respond to being excluded from the movement towards flexibility? Might these trends affect career choices among young people? Such research is critical so that scholars can provide informed recommendations on how to improve upon and maximally leverage flexible work patterns for the benefit of all.

Conclusions

Workers across the world have evolved in their patterns of work, and have increasingly demanded more flexibility. In this chapter, we have highlighted the increased flexibility infused into work locations, schedules, and most generally, into the design of jobs and careers. We have described one setting that incorporates and embraces all of these changes – coworking spaces – and we encourage continued research on these unique communities. We suggest that the emergence of these spaces has helped to ensure that loneliness and creative isolation are no longer limiting factors to increasing work flexibility.

As a worker-driven trend, the impacts of these changes in work pattern flexibility appear to be largely positive on employees and organizations, with a few important caveats. Although more research is needed, we optimistically expect that the future of work can be more rewarding and balanced, particularly for highly-skilled knowledge workers whose jobs are naturally positioned to capitalize on many forms of flexibility. Given changes in technology, these employees can be connected with potential clients around the globe and work from a variety of different locations. As they learn new skills, their job can change along with them in ways that they will likely find more meaningful than traditional organization-driven tasks.

Of course, we would be remiss if we did not also raise the question about those jobs that do not lend themselves to these forms of flexibility; might these trends in flexibility further bifurcate the "good" jobs from the "bad" jobs, or even separate "less flexible" high-status jobs from "better" high-status jobs? We suggest that perhaps it will not. Instead, we encourage researchers and organizations to consider the broader conceptualizations of flexibility we have only begun to define here, and seek ways to offer creative forms of flexibility to more types of employees even when some forms are not possible. As one example, how might employers offer factory or service employees, who have to be at a specific work location during a specific time, additional choices for how to navigate their work day and more broadly, their career within that organization? As another example, how might healthcare professionals, who are traditionally less flexible in terms of *where* they must practice medicine, capitalize on advances in technologies to embrace new forms of flexible practice? As a general rule, when one form of flexibility is not feasible for a particular job, we suggest that other forms of flexibility may be, and this broader view of flexibility can ensure that the changing nature of work may prove to be beneficial for all. Our hope is that more research into the forms and implications of flexibility will help guide employees and organizations towards a thriving future world of work.

Acknowledgements

We thank Meghan Savage and Ching-Yuan Meng for their help in conducting this research.

References

Agrawal, A., Catalini, C., & Goldfarb, A. (2015). *Slack time and innovation*. Cambridge, MA: National Bureau of Economic Research. http://dx.doi.org/10.3386/w21134

Alizadeh, T. (2009). Urban design in the digital age: a literature review of telework and wired communities. *Journal of Urbanism*, 2, 195–213.

Allen, T. D. (2001). Family-supportive work environments: The role of organizational perceptions. *Journal of Vocational Behavior, 58,* 414–435.

Allen, T. D., Golden, T. D., & Shockley, K. M. (2015). How effective is telecommuting? Assessing the status of our scientific findings. *Psychological Science in the Public Interest, 16,* 40–68.

Anderson, S. E., Coffey, B. S., & Byerly, R. T. (2002). Formal organizational initiatives and informal workplace practices: Links to work–family conflict and job-related outcomes. *Journal of Management, 28,* 787–810.

Bailey, D. B., & Kurland, N. B. (2002). A review of telework research: Findings, new directions, and lessons for the study of modern work. *Journal of Organizational Behavior, 23,* 383–400.

Baker, P. A., Moon, N. W., & Ward, A. C. (2006). Virtual exclusion and telework: Barriers and opportunities of technocentric workplace accommodation policy. *Work, 27,* 421–430.

Baltes, B. B., Briggs, T. E., Huff, J. W., Wright, J. A., & Neuman, G. A. (1999). Flexible and compressed workweek schedules: A meta-analysis of their effects on work-related criteria. *Journal of Applied Psychology, 84,* 496–513.

Bartel, C. A., Wrzesniewski, A., & Wiesenfeld, B. M. (2012). Knowing where you stand: Physical isolation, perceived respect, and organizational identification among virtual employees. *Organization Science, 23,* 743–757.

Beasley, R. E., Seubert, V. R., & Lomo-David, E. (2002). The effects of race on telecommuting motivators: Implications for the recruitment of minorities into open information technology positions. *Journal of Computer Information Systems, 42,* 21–25.

Bernstein, E. S., & S. Turban (2018). The impact of the 'open' workspace on human collaboration. *Philosophical Transactions of the Royal Society B.* Advance online publication.

Bhasin, K. (2013). Best Buy CEO: Here's why I killed the 'results only work environment'. *Business Insider.* Retrieved from www.businessinsider.com/best-buy-ceo-rowe-2013-3

Bouncken, R., & Reuschl, A. (2016). Coworking-spaces: How a phenomenon of the sharing economy builds a novel trend for the workplace and for entrepreneurship. *Review of Managerial Science, 12,* 317–334.

Breaugh, J. A., & Farabee, A. M. (2012). Telecommuting and flexible work hours: Alternative work arrangements that can improve the quality of work life. In *Work and Quality of Life* (pp. 251–274). Dordrecht: Springer.

Breaugh, J. A., & Frye, N. K. (2007). An examination of the antecedents and consequences of the use of family-friendly benefits. *Journal of Managerial Issues, 19,* 35–52.

Burke, R. J., & Ng, E. (2006). The changing nature of work and organizations: Implications for human resource management. *Human Resource Management Review, 16,* 86–94.

Burkus, D. (2016). Meet the 20-year-old company that operates without bosses. Retrieved from www.inc.com/david-burkus/how-this-company-runs-without-managers.html

Burtch, G., Carnahan, S., & Greenwood, B. N. (2018). Can you gig it? An empirical examination of the gig economy and entrepreneurial activity. *Management Science.* Advance online publication.

Capdevila, I. (2015). Co-working spaces and the localised dynamics of innovation in Barcelona. *International Journal of Innovation Management, 19*, 1–28.

Chokshi, N. (2017). Out of the office: More people are working remotely, survey finds. *New York Times*, February 15. Retrieved from www.nytimes.com/2017/02/15/us/remote-workers-work-from-home.html

Claggett, J. L., & Karahanna, E. (2018). Unpacking the structure of coordination mechanisms and the role of relational coordination in an era of digitally-mediated work processes. *Academy of Management Review 43*. https://doi.org/10.5465/amr.2016.0325

Connelly, C. E., & Gallagher, D. G. (2006). Independent and dependent contracting: Meaning and implications. *Human Resource Management Review, 16*, 95–106.

Deci, E. L., & Ryan, R. M. (2000). The "what" and "why" of goal pursuits: Human needs and the self-determination of behavior. *Psychological Inquiry, 11*, 227–268.

Dikkers, J. S. E., Geurts, S. A. E., den Dulk, L., Peper, B., Taris, T. W., & Kompier, M. A. J. (2007). Dimensions of work–home culture and their relations with the use of work–home arrangements and work–home interaction. *Work & Stress, 21*, 155–172.

Donnelly, N., & Proctor-Thomson, S. B. (2015). Disrupted work: Home-based teleworking (HbTW) in the aftermath of a natural disaster. *New Technology, Work & Employment, 30*, 47–61.

Elsbach, K. D., Cable, D. M., & Sherman, B. J. W. (2010). How passive 'face time' affects perceptions of employees: Evidence of spontaneous trait inference. *Human Relations, 63*, 735–760.

Fenner, G. H., & Renn, R. W. (2010). Technology-assisted supplemental work and work-to-family conflict: The role of instrumentality beliefs, organizational expectations and time management. *Human Relations, 63*, 63–82.

Foertsch, C., & Cagnol, R. (2013, September 2). The history of coworking in a timeline. Retrieved from www.deskmag.com/en/the-history-of-coworking-spaces-in-a-timeline.

Fonner, K. L., & Roloff, M. E. (2010). Why teleworkers are more satisfied with their jobs than are office-based workers: When less contact is beneficial. *Journal of Applied Communication Research, 38*, 336–361.

Frye, N. K., & Breaugh, J. A. (2004). Family-friendly policies, supervisor support, work–family conflict, family–work conflict, and satisfaction: A test of a conceptual model. *Journal of Business and Psychology, 19*, 197–220.

Gajendran, R. S., & Harrison, D. A. (2007). The good, the bad, and the unknown about telecommuting: Meta-analysis of psychological mediators and individual consequences. *Journal of Applied Psychology, 92*, 1524–1541.

Garrett, L. E., Spreitzer, G. M., & Bacevice, P. A. (2017). Co-constructing a sense of community at work: The emergence of community in coworking spaces. *Organization Studies, 38*, 821–842.

GCUC (Global Coworking Unconference Conference). (2017). 2018 global coworking forecast: 30,432 spaces and 5.1 million members by 2022. *GCUC*. Retrieved from https://gcuc.co/2018-global-coworking-forecast-30432-spaces-5-1-million-members-2022/

Global Workplace Analytics. (2017). 2017 state of telecommuting in the US. Retrieved from https://globalworkplaceanalytics.com/2017-state-of-telecommuting-in-the-us.

Golden, T. D. (2006a). Avoiding depletion in virtual work: Telework and the intervening impact of work exhaustion on commitment and turnover intentions.

Journal of Vocational Behavior, 69, 176–187. http://dx.doi.org/10.1016/j.jvb.2006.02.003

Golden, T. D. (2006b). The role of relationships in understanding telecommuter satisfaction. *Journal of Organizational Behavior, 27,* 319–340. http://dx.doi.org/10.1002/job.369

Golden, T. D. (2007). Co-workers who telework and the impact on those in the office: Understanding the implications of virtual work for co-worker satisfaction and turnover intentions. *Human Relations, 60,* 1641–1667.

Golden, T. D., & Schoenleber, A. H. (2014). Toward a deeper understanding of the willingness to seek help: The case of teleworkers. *Work, 48,* 83–90.

Golden, T. D., & Veiga, J. F. (2005). The impact of extent of telecommuting on job satisfaction: Resolving inconsistent findings. *Journal of Management, 31,* 301–318.

Golden, T. D., & Veiga, J. F. (2008). The impact of superior–subordinate relationships on the commitment, job satisfaction, and performance of virtual workers. *Leadership Quarterly, 19,* 77–88. http://dx.doi.org/10.1016/j.leaqua.2007.12.009

Golden, T. D., Veiga, J. F., & Dino, R. N. (2008). The impact of professional isolation on teleworker job performance and turnover intentions: Does time spent teleworking, interacting face-to-face, or having access to communication-enhancing technology matter? *Journal of Applied Psychology, 93,* 1412–1421.

Golden, T. D., Veiga, J. F., & Simsek, Z. (2006). Telecommuting's differential impact on work-family conflict: Is there no place like home? *Journal of Applied Psychology, 91,* 1340–1350. http://dx.doi.org/10.1037/0021-9010.91.6.1340

Guest, D. E., Oakley, P., Clinton, M., & Budjanovcanin, A. (2006). Free or precarious? A comparison of the attitudes of workers in flexible and traditional employment contracts. *Human Resource Management Review, 16,* 107–124.

Guillaume, Y. F., Brodbeck, F. C., & Riketta, M. (2012). Surface- and deep-level dissimilarity effects on social integration and individual effectiveness related outcomes in work groups: A meta-analytic integration. *Journal of Occupational & Organizational Psychology, 85,* 80–115.

Guta, M. (2018). 3.9 million Americans – including freelancers – now work from home at least half the week. *Small Business Trends.* Retrieved from https://smallbiztrends.com/2018/04/2018-remote-work-statistics.html

Hackman, J. R., & Oldham, G. R. (1976). Motivation through the design of work: Test of a theory. *Organizational Behavior & Human Performance, 16,* 250–279.

Haines III, V. Y., St-Onge, S., & Archambault, M. (2002). Environmental and person antecedents of telecommuting outcomes. *Journal of Organizational and End User Computing, 14,* 32–50.

Hartig, T., Kylin, C., & Johansson, G. (2007). The telework tradeoff: Stress mitigation vs. constrained restoration. *Applied Psychology: An International Review, 56,* 231–253.

Hatch, M. J. (1987). Physical barriers, task characteristics, and interaction activity in research and development firms. *Administrative Science Quarterly, 32,* 387–399.

Heby, R. (2017). 5 ways on-demand office space can improve employee satisfaction. Workforce Institute @ Kronos. Retrieved from https://workforceinstitute.org/5-ways-demand-office-space-can-improve-employee-satisfaction/

Hill, E. J., Ferris, M., & Martinson, V. (2003). Does it matter where you work? A comparison of how three work venues (traditional office, virtual office, and home office) influence aspects of work and personal/family life. *Journal of Vocational Behavior, 63*, 220–241.

Hill, J. E., Grzywacz, J., Allen, S., Blanchard, V., Matz-Costa, C., Shulkin, S., & Pitt-Catsouphes, M. (2008). Defining and conceptualizing workplace flexibility. *Community, Work & Family, 11*, 149–163.

Humphrey, S. E., Nahrgang, J. D., & Morgeson, F. P. (2007). Integrating motivational, social, and contextual work design features: A meta-analytic summary and theoretical extension of the work design literature. *Journal of Applied Psychology, 92*, 1332–1356.

IPSE (Association of Independent Professionals and the Self-Employed). (2017). Exploring the rise of self-employment in the modern economy. Retrieved from www.ipse.co.uk/uploads/assets/uploaded/59868faa-841d-496d-bba6891d417a7e94.pdf

Johnson, T. (2007). How to ask for flextime. *Good Morning America*. Retrieved from https://abcnews.go.com/GMA/CareerManagement/story?id=3098340&page=1

Kaarlela-Tuomaala, A., Helenius, R., Keskinen, E., & Hongisto, V. (2009). Effects of acoustic environment on work in private office rooms and open-plan offices – longitudinal study during relocation. *Ergonomics, 52*, 1423–1444.

Kaufman, L. (2014, December 30). Google got it wrong. The open-office trend is destroying the workplace. Workplaces need more walls, not fewer. *Washington Post*. Retrieved from www.washingtonpost.com/posteverything/wp/2014/12/30/google-got-it-wrong-theopen-office-trend-is-destroying-the-workplace/

Khazanchi, S., Sprinkle, T. A., Masterson, S. S., & Tong, N. (2018). A spatial model of work relationships: The relationship-building and relationship-straining effects of workspace design. *Academy of Management Review, 43*, 590–609.

Kim, J., & de Dear, R. (2013). Workspace satisfaction: The privacy–communication trade-off in open-plan offices. *Journal of Environmental Psychology, 36*, 18–26. http://dx.doi.org/10.1016/j.jenvp.2013.06.007

Kirkpatrick, D. (2017). Haier elevation. Retrieved from www.self-managementinstitute.org/haier-elevation

Kossek, E. E., Lautsch, B. A., & Eaton, S. C. (2006). Telecommuting, control, and boundary management: Correlates of policy use and practice, job control, and work–family effectiveness. *Journal of Vocational Behavior, 68*, 347–367.

Kurland, N. B., & Bailey, D. E. (1999). The advantages and challenges of working here, there, anywhere, and anytime. *Organizational Dynamics, 28*, 53–67.

Lamagna, M. (2016). The new office floor plans: Flexible or demoralizing? *MarketWatch*. Retrieved from www.marketwatch.com/story/in-todays-office-more-people-dont-have-a-desk-let-alone-an-office-2016-03-25

Lapierre, L. M., & Allen, T. D. (2006). Work-supportive family, family-supportive supervision, use of organizational benefits, and problem-focused coping: Implications for work–family conflict and employee well-being. *Journal of Occupational Health Psychology, 11*, 169–181.

Lautsch, B. A., Kossek, E. E., & Eaton, S. C. (2009). Supervisory approaches and paradoxes in managing telecommuting implementation. *Human Relations, 62*, 795–827.

Liao, C., Wayne, S. J., & Rousseau, D. M. (2016). Idiosyncratic deals in contemporary organizations: A qualitative and meta-analytical review. *Journal of Organizational Behavior, 37*, S9–S29.

Liegl, M. (2014). Nomadicity and the care of place – on the aesthetic and affective organization of space in freelance creative work. *Computer Supported Cooperative Work, 23*, 163–183.

Ludden, J. (2010). The end of 9-to-5: When work time is anytime. *NPR Morning Edition*. Retrieved from www.npr.org/templates/story/story.php?storyId=124705801&ps=rs?storyId=124705801&ps=rs

Mariotti, I., Pacchi, C., & Di Vita, S. (2017). Co-working spaces in Milan: Location patterns and urban effects. *Journal of Urban Technology, 24*, 47–66.

Martin, B. H., & MacDonnell, R. (2012). Is telework effective for organizations? A meta-analysis of empirical research on perceptions of telework and organizational outcomes. *Management Research Review, 35*, 602–616.

McBride, S. (2017) 2018 Global coworking forecast: 30,432 spaces and 5.1 million members by 2022. *GCUC*. Retrieved from http://usa.gcuc.co/2018-global-coworking-forecast-30432-spaces-5-1-million-members-2022/

McManus, K., Korabik, K., Rosin, H. M., & Kelloway, E. K. (2002). Employed mothers and the work–family interface: Does family structure matter? *Human Relations, 55*, 1295–1324.

Meyer, J. P., Stanley, D. J., Herscovitch, L., & Topolnytsky, L. (2002). Affective, continuance, and normative commitment to the organization: A meta-analysis of antecedents, correlates, and consequences. *Journal of Vocational Behavior, 61*, 20–52.

Moen, P., Kelly, E. L., & Lam, J. (2013). Healthy work revisited: Do changes in time strain predict well-being? *Journal of Occupational Health Psychology, 18*, 157–172.

Mokhtarian, P. L., Salomon, I., & Choo, S. (2005). Measuring the measurable: Why can't we agree on the number of telecommuters in the US? *Quality and Quantity, 39*, 423–452.

Morgeson, F. P., & Humphrey, S. E. (2008). Job and team design: Toward a more integrative conceptualization of work design, In J. Martocchio (Ed.), *Research in personnel and human resources management, Vol. 27* (pp. 39–91). Bingley, UK: Emerald Group Publishing Ltd.

Mulcahy, D. (2016, October 27). Who wins in the gig economy, and who loses? *Harvard Business Review, 94*. Retrieved from https://hbr.org/2016/10/who-wins-in-the-gig-economy-and-who-loses

Neirotti, P., Paolucci, E., & Raguseo, E. (2013). Mapping the antecedents of telework diffusion: Firm-level evidence from Italy. *New Technology, Work & Employment, 28*, 16–36.

Oldenburg, R. (1989). *The great good place: Café, coffee shops, community centers, beauty parlors, general stores, bars, hangouts, and how they get you through the day*. New York, NY: Paragon House Publishers.

O'Neill, T. A., Hambley, L. A., Greidanus, N., MacDonnell, R., & Kline, T. J. B. (2009). Predicting teleworker success: An exploration of personality, motivational, situational, and job characteristics. *New Technology, Work and Employment, 24*, 144–162.

Outthinker. (2017). 5 approaches to incentivizing innovation from P&G, 3M, Google, and more. Retrieved from https://outthinker.com/2017/06/14/5-approaches-incentivizing-innovation/

Parker, S. K., Wall, T. D., & Cordery, J. L. (2001). Future work design research and practice: Towards an elaborated model of work design. *Journal of Occupational and Organizational Psychology, 74,* 413–440.

Parrino, L. (2015). Coworking: Assessing the role of proximity in knowledge exchange. *Knowledge Management Research & Practice, 13,* 261–271.

Perry, S. J., Rubino, C., & Hunter, E. M. (2018). Stress in remote work: Two studies testing the Demand–Control–Person model. *European Journal of Work and Organizational Psychology, 27*(5), 577–593. doi: 10.1080/1359432X.2018.1487402

Peters, P., & van der Lippe, T. (2007). The time-pressure reducing potential of tele-homeworking: The Dutch case. *International Journal of Human Resource Management, 18,* 430–447.

Petriglieri, G., Ashford, S. J., & Wrzesniewski, A. (2018). Agony and ecstasy in the gig economy: Cultivating holding environments for precarious and personalized work identities. *Administrative Science Quarterly.* Advance online publication.

Raghuram, S., Garud, R., Wiesenfeld, B., & Gupta, V. (2001). Factors contributing to virtual work adjustment. *Journal of Management, 27,* 383–405.

Rau, B. L., & Hyland, M. M. (2002). Role conflict and flexible work arrangements: The effects on applicant attraction. *Personnel Psychology, 55,* 111–136.

Roper, K. O., & Juneja, P. (2008). Distractions in the workplace revisited. *Journal of Facilities Management, 6*(2), 91–109.

Sackett, P. R. (2002). The structure of counterproductive work behaviors: Dimensionality and relationships with facets of job performance. *International Journal of Selection and Assessment, 10,* 5–11.

Shockley, K. M., & Allen, T. D. (2007). When flexibility helps: Another look at the availability of flexible work arrangements on work–family conflict. *Journal of Vocational Behavior, 71,* 479–493.

Sparrow, P. R. (2000). New employee behaviours, work designs and forms of work organization: What is in store for the future of work? *Journal of Managerial Psychology, 15,* 202–217.

Spinuzzi, C. (2012). Working alone, together: Coworking as emergent collaborative activity. *Journal of Business and Technical Communication, 26,* 399–441.

Spreitzer, G. M., Cameron, L., & Garrett, L. (2017). Alternative work arrangements: Two images of the new world of work. *Annual Review of Organizational Psychology and Organizational Behavior, 4,* 473–499.

Standen, P., Daniels, K., & Lamond, D. (1999). The home as a workplace: Work–family interaction and psychological well-being in telework. *Journal of Occupational Health Psychology, 4,* 368–381.

Statista. (2018). Coworking spaces – Statistics & facts. Retrieved from www.statista.com/topics/2999/coworking-spaces/

Sullivan, C. (2003). What's in a name? Definitions and conceptualisations of teleworking and homeworking. *New Technology, Work and Employment, 18,* 158–164.

Taskin, L., & Edwards, P. (2007). The possibilities and limits of telework in a bureaucratic environment: Lessons from the public sector. *New Technology, Work and Employment, 22,* 195–207.

van Meel, J., Martens, Y., & van Ree, H. J. (2010). Planning office spaces. *A practical guide for managers and designers.* London: Laurence King.

Värlander, S. (2012). Individual flexibility in the workplace: A spatial perspective. *Journal of Applied Behavioral Science, 48,* 33–61.

Wilks, L., & Billsberry, J. (2007). Should we do away with teleworking? An examination of whether teleworking can be defined in the new world of work. *New Technology, Work and Employment, 22,* 169–177.

Workman, M., Kahnweiler, W., & Bommer, W. (2003). The effects of cognitive styles and media richness on commitment to telework and virtual teams. *Journal of Vocational Behavior, 63,* 199–219.

Zenger, J. (2013). Why are big companies calling their remote workers back into the office? *NBC News.* Retrieved from www.nbcnews.com/business/business-news/why-are-big-companies-calling-their-remote-workers-back-office-n787101.

PART III

Implications for Talent Management and Impact on Employees

14 Implications of the Changing Nature of Work for Selection

Brian D. Lyons, Alexander Alonso, Robert H. Moorman, and Ashley Miller

Implications for Selection

Efforts to understand how the changing nature of work will affect workforce plans are being shaped by forecasts of fundamental shifts in both the key competencies needed in future jobs and in our ability to predict what those specific competencies will be (Barley, Bechky, & Milliken, 2017). Mankins (2017) argues that "[d]igital transformation, the industrial internet, advanced analytics, artificial intelligence, robotics, machine learning and a plethora of other innovations are fundamentally changing the nature of work" (p. 1). These changes prompted the World Economic Forum (2016) to predict that "by 2020, more than a third of the desired core skill sets of most occupations will be comprised of skills that are not yet considered crucial to the job today" (para. 5). Further, the skill set disruptions brought on by technological and other changes will only accelerate the pace of change, inevitably impacting organizations' employee selection systems.

Reflecting this complexity of selection in today's workplace, popular press articles suggest that selection practices are increasingly diverging to reflect skill polarization in the workforce. For example, Glassdoor.com noted that organizations are taking more time to hire high-skill or knowledge-based jobs than ever before (Ell, 2017). Such time is ostensibly used to assess the critical knowledge, skills, abilities, and other characteristics (KSAOs) that are required in the job, thus maximizing hits and minimizing errors in selection. However, we are also in a technological era where online assessments are increasingly used and expedited feedback can be provided to applicants (McCarthy et al., 2017), which *should* reduce time-to-hire metrics (SHRM, 2016). In the presence of skill shortages, organizations may turn to employing gig workers, who comprise 20% to 30% of today's workforce in Europe and the United States (Manyika et al., 2016). Interestingly, these gig workers will likely never meet their employer (Barley et al., 2017), because organizations rely on technology to screen these workers for desirable competencies and onboard them quickly to realize faster returns in productivity.

Taken together, the inherent ambiguities of the changing nature of work, varying knowledge of desired competencies to address the changing nature of work, the simultaneous importance on both expediency and accuracy of hiring decisions, and changes in the employment relationship reflect a need for organizations to reexamine all stages of their selection system, beginning with how organizations define a job. That is, problems associated with the misidentification of critical competencies needed for present and future work as well as unnecessary delays in the selection process can be partly attributed to the way in which we typically define a job. We use traditional job analysis to define a job's specific tasks, duties, and responsibilities (TDRs) as well as its KSAOs to make inferences about the validity of tests used in a given selection system. However, as noted by Singh (2008), traditional job analysis is an outdated method to define a job in today's dynamic workplace.

In this chapter, we outline the need for organizations to adapt their selection systems to reflect the changing nature of work. First, we describe competency modeling and nine new competencies that are needed for today and tomorrow's workplace. Second, we identify predictor constructs and methods to measure these new competencies. Next, we examine administration trends and technology usage in selection. Finally, we recognize four challenges that organizations will face when advancing our solutions: (a) achieving buy-in for competency modeling; (b) the continued recognition of a criterion problem; (c) monitoring applicant reactions; and (d) acknowledging social and ethical issues that may arise with these proposed changes.

Competency Modeling and the New Competencies in Demand

Competency Modeling. Although not relatively new, one method to define jobs in a dynamic workplace is through use of competency modeling (Campion et al., 2011). Competency modeling defines the collection of KSAOs needed for effective performance, with competencies being derived at the organizational level and/or job level (Sanchez & Levine, 2009). In addition to addressing present demands, competency modeling can address future-oriented demands. Thus, instead of precisely defining TDRs of a given job, competency modeling primarily identifies general KSAOs that afford increased flexibility to adapt to new job demands. Competency modeling can also define what behaviors are necessary to effectively apply the competencies in varying contexts.

New Competencies in Demand. It is critical for industrial–organizational (I-O) psychologists, human resource (HR) practitioners, and affiliated professionals to acknowledge the new realities of work and focus efforts to build talent management systems with evolution in mind (Bersin, 2018; Boudreau, 2012; Boudreau & Ziskin, 2015). In particular, Boudreau (2012) and Bersin (2018) posit that new realities in society will yield significant shifts in the demands of work. Much of this has been borne out in the *Economist* Intelligence Unit (EIU) and the Society for Human Resource Management (SHRM) Foundation's (2014) joint research on the future of work, which leveraged more than

150 interviews with business leaders among the *Fortune* 100. Together, EIU and SHRM identified seven new realities in the workplace:

- An accelerating war for talent among knowledge workers;
- A need for transportability of skills and competencies;
- A drive for greater social responsibility among enterprises;
- An agile framework for adjusting to social and technological demand;
- A corps of aging workers to help reinstitute old skills in younger workers;
- An emphasis on knowledge management and transfer; and
- A drive for refined leadership development built on core competencies for complex problem solving.

A growing body of evidence supports these new realities. For example, Wegman et al. (2018) examined changes in job characteristics over time and found that jobs are now characterized by increased skill variety, autonomy, and interdependence. Reynolds, McCauley, and Tsacoumis (2018) also cite these new realities as the core of a recurring theme in talent management; namely how the continuing complexity of the criterion domain affects all aspects of talent management including selection, development, testing, credentialing, performance management, and beyond. While they cite these issues in the context of leaders, Silzer and Jeanneret (2011) also argue that this is a pervasive issue among all jobs in a more customized and complex social space. This suggests that there is even greater need for a focus on competencies needed to address the complex business problems of today and tomorrow.

Addressing this need, SHRM (2015, 2016) engaged in extensive qualitative and quantitative research to identify new competencies for the execution of work in the future. This research consisted of three primary tasks:

1. Boudreau and Ziskin (2015) conducted 63 interviews of chief human resource officers and thought leaders in the workforce space with the aim of identifying future-oriented talent needs;
2. SHRM researchers conducted an environmental scan of future competency models and perspectives shared by emerging leaders; and
3. SHRM researchers conducted representative surveys in 2014 and 2016 identifying human capital needs and challenges for the forthcoming ten-year period.

Together, these activities provided a good foundation for establishing competencies anticipated by the employer community in the era of the futurist. Derived from these activities, Table 14.1 presents the nine competencies needed for the execution of work in the present and future.

For the professions associated with talent management, it is now paramount that the focus shifts to addressing these new competencies in future-oriented job analyses, current-state job analyses, and all the offshoot products and services affiliated with them. Specifically, it is incumbent on I-O psychologists to focus efforts on building assessments of these competencies and ensuring validity of those assessments. Further, it is critical for HR practitioners to become more

Table 14.1 *Nine competencies that address the changing nature of work*

Competency	Definition	Sources
Social Entrepreneurship	The ability to assess the balance between operational efficiency and social demands with an eye toward eliminating marginalization, biases, and social harm.	Bersin (2018); Dees (2001); Martin and Osberg (2007)
Sensemaking Prediction	The ability to make sense of complex business problems without direction or background in the situation.	Ancona (2011); Soulier and Caussanel (2002)
Data Journalism	The skill of analyzing and presenting data in various technology-enabled modalities for the consumption of distinct audiences.	Royal and Blasingame (2015)
Reimagination	The ability to reinvent the methods by which an organization executes its operations while emphasizing the tenets of human-centered design and stakeholder value.	Vollmer, Egol, and Sayani (2014)
Experience Building	The skill of developing and designing unique or customizable employee and consumer experiences for retention.	Driggs and Rogers (2018)
Gig Project Management	The skill of managing complex projects based upon gig labor and acquiring temporary talent based upon task needs.	Daley (2017); Dixon (2017)
Knowledge Transfer	The ability to replicate the expertise, wisdom, and skills possessed by critical professionals in the heads and hands of their coworkers.	Trautman and McKee (2014); Wang (2016)
Workforce Engineering	The ability to drive a leading-edge digital agenda, including advanced analytics, leverage the latest advances in social engineering; and draw upon environmental influences to increase productivity and engagement.	Kane, Lajmi, and Hontalas (2018)
Analytical Application	The ability to integrate multifaceted sources of data into one cohesive thread and develop evidence-based strategy.	Ghasemaghaei, Ebrahimi, and Hassanein (2018)

familiar with the use of complex criteria and competencies as a means of managing talent. With this emphasis on core future competencies also comes a series of implications for practices related to employee selection, assessment, development, and performance management. We will explore the implications for selection in the following section.

How to Measure these Competencies in Selection

We recognize that not all the new competencies will be desired by an organization or all ranked as equally important by an organization, department, or job. But the measurement approach associated with a particular competency should be consistent across all competencies. Therefore, as with any new competency to measure for selection purposes, we first need to define the target construct (i.e., competency) and then weigh a variety of methods or tests to measure the construct against cost, adverse impact, and the validity properties of the new method or test. However, with the hope of accelerating the hiring process, we also have to evaluate the expediency with which the measure will generate useful feedback to both the hiring committee and the applicant.

Measurement Strategy. Given the relative novelty of the competencies needed in today's dynamic workplace, we acknowledge that science has indeed lagged behind practice – that is, very few academic studies have been undertaken to directly measure these new competencies and/or determine their criterion-related validity. We can, however, offer recommendations that balance validity, equity, and expediency concerns related to testing a particular competency. First, in the beginning of a selection system, we recommend that organizations embrace a sign-based approach to assess the new competencies. As mentioned by Wernimont and Campbell (1968), signs are commonly thought of as individual difference traits that relate to future performance (i.e., distal indicators) whereas samples are targeted behaviors that relate to future performance (i.e., proximal indicators). Although samples of future performance are theoretically preferred over signs of future performance in selection contexts (Wernimont & Campbell, 1968), the body of literature on the criterion-related validity of various predictor constructs and methods suggests otherwise. For example, meta-analytic results suggest that one of the most studied signs of future performance, general mental ability (GMA), is arguably the best predictor of future performance (Schmidt & Hunter, 1998). Conversely, Roth, Bobko, and McFarland's (2005) meta-analysis on the work sample test literature found a corrected criterion-related validity coefficient of .33, which was considerably lower than previously suggested by Schmidt and Hunter's (1998) meta-analysis. Taken together, considering the changing nature of work, organizations would be wise to study signs related to the new competencies instead of trying to sample behaviors associated with the competencies. The latter strategy may result in more error because desirable behaviors or TDRs may change more frequently than the desired traits that channel the specific behavior. Further, staging sample-based assessments later in the selection system will also save time and cost because fewer applicants will be assessed.

Similar to recommending signs, we also support an approach that emphasizes psychological fidelity over physical fidelity. Fidelity refers to the extent to which a measure or test is related to the performance domain (Ployhart, Schneider, & Schmitt, 2006) and a test's fidelity is composed of two dimensions, psychological fidelity and physical fidelity. If considering job performance as the ultimate criterion, then psychological fidelity is concerned with the degree to which a measure overlaps with the competencies required for successful job performance; physical fidelity, on the other hand, is concerned with the extent to which the measure is physically similar to the job performance domain. Given the emphasis of creative work over routine work (Hagel, 2018), the shift to more loosely defined work roles, and rapidly changing and volatile nature of the environment, we recommend placing a greater emphasis on how well a measure or test evaluates the competencies required in the performance domain rather than how well a measure or test captures the working environment (see Goldstein, Zedeck, & Schneider, 1993).

In support of these recommendations, we suggest that a sign-based, psychological fidelity approach addresses issues stemming from the changing nature of work, particularly the need to be agile in our assessment procedures and expedite the feedback generated by a selection process. Further, this approach inherently maximizes the use of online assessment rather than in-person evaluations of an applicant's qualifications, which should result in lower cost-per-hire values within a selection system. It is important to note that we are not advocating for the complete elimination of physical fidelity from test development or samples-based assessment; rather, we wish to infuse more technology toward the beginning of a selection system and allow behavioral assessment later in the process. For example, structured interviews can be administered virtually or via video-recorded prompts. Until virtual reality becomes ubiquitous in society, this method would lessen the importance of physical fidelity and using a pure samples-based approach; however, even moderately low-fidelity measures – hence, one lacking high physical fidelity – have the ability to generate favorable criterion-related validity (e.g., Lievens & Patterson, 2011; Motowidlo, Dunnette, & Carter, 1990).

Predictor Constructs and Selection Methods to Assess the New Competencies. What predictor constructs or specific selection methods would assess the new competencies? While traditional tests of job knowledge and work samples may be better suited to more static jobs, other methods such as GMA, situational judgment tests (SJTs), personality, biodata, structured interviews, and vocational interests may be more relevant in dynamic jobs. These predictor constructs and tests can be used to measure multiple competencies, which would be valuable when a particular competency is deemed highly important within a competency model.

In terms of which specific predictor constructs or selection methods may apply to the new competencies, there is some empirical work that offers guidance for future research. First, sensemaking prediction, analytical application, knowledge transfer, and gig project management competencies are becoming more and more necessary for job performance as job demands become less predictable. For example, sensemaking prediction skills help job incumbents understand ever more complex and novel business problems, while knowledge transfer then assists their efforts to communicate new understandings to others. Further, gig project management and knowledge transfer are important in the modern world of work because job holders are expected to fill in multiple organizational roles. A consultant, for example, may serve as a project manager for one client and then contribute as an analytics expert on another project. Similarly, sensemaking prediction, analytical application, and knowledge transfer would be more important as jobs change frequently and individuals must quickly learn and apply new technologies and techniques.

Together, the new competencies cited above are – to a degree – conceptually related to GMA. However, past studies have rarely sought to evaluate whether GMA can effectively predict these competencies. Thus, it is important that future research examines how conceptually related GMA is to each competency, and then assess relevant criteria associated with each competency. But prior research has found that GMA is already predictive of a variety of criteria, including job performance (Schmidt & Hunter, 1998), objective counterproductive work behaviors (Gonzalez-Mulé, Mount, & Oh, 2014), and off-duty deviance (Lyons et al., 2016). Kuncel, Hezlett, and Ones (2004), in particular, found that the Miller Analogies Test – a measure of verbal ability, a subcomponent of GMA – was a valid predictor of creativity, potential, and job performance. Likewise, in the project management literature, the ability to troubleshoot and solve problems was found to be a valid predictor of project success (Belout & Gauvreau, 2004). However, the use of a test that measures GMA (e.g., Wonderlic Cognitive Ability Test) will increase the probability of adverse impact via subgroup differences by race, regardless of how or where the measure of GMA is staged with other predictor constructs or tests within a selection system (e.g., Ryan, Ployhart, & Friedel, 1998). Consequently, organizations would be wise to measure the degree to which GMA directly relates to these competencies.

Structured interviews and SJTs could also be used to measure sensemaking prediction, analytical application, knowledge transfer, and gig project management. Analytical application, for example, could involve a scenario where the applicant recommends how they would structure a particular data set or analyze a particular problem. Similarly, SJTs involving resource allocation and time management could help measure the gig project management competency. Both structured interviews and SJTs have been used to measure constructs that are predictive of job performance (Christian, Edwards, & Bradley, 2010; Cortina et al., 2000); however, as noted previously, it is unclear whether these methods can be leveraged to measure these new competencies.

Second, competencies such as social entrepreneurship, experience building, and reimagination prepare job holders both to understand new environments and develop affirming employee and customer experiences. For example, social entrepreneurship skills help companies meet and exceed current and future societal expectations for socially responsible business practices. Similarly, reimagination skills would help companies address the demands of constantly changing markets to become sufficiently nimble. Finally, a competency in experience building may create unique and attractive employee and customer experiences allowing the company to become an employer of choice in a highly competitive labor market.

These competencies share conceptual roots with empathy, specifically being able to perceive social cues in the environment, understanding the business experience from the customer's or user's viewpoint, and engaging in perspective-taking behavior. Although assessing empathy will only measure a piece of these competencies, it appears to be a central trait in the channeling of these competencies into job-related behaviors. To measure empathy, studies have used items from Boyatzis, Goleman, and Rhee's (2000) Emotional Competence Inventory (ECI; e.g., Kellett, Humphrey, & Sleeth, 2002), Davis's (1980) Interpersonal Reactivity Index (e.g., Bakker & Demerouti, 2009), or created their own measure (e.g., Kellett, Humphrey, & Sleeth, 2006). While empathy has been shown to be related to leadership behavior (Kellett et al., 2002, 2006), less is known about its relationship with job performance. In addition, given the overlap between established predictor constructs (e.g., GMA, Big Five personality) and mixed/self-reported emotional intelligence (EI; Joseph, Jin, Newman, & O'Boyle, 2015), we would urge caution in using measures of mixed EI to measure empathy. We would also urge caution with screening for the opposite end of the continuum for empathy (e.g., sub-clinical psychopathy) as these measures could be framed as discriminatory under the Americans with Disabilities Act (Guenole, 2014). Clearly, more research is needed in the development of a construct-valid empathy scale and evaluating its criterion-related validity.

Third, social entrepreneurship and data-related competencies (e.g., analytical application and data journalism) could be measured via vocational interest inventories and biodata measures. In their review of the individual difference literature, Sackett, Lievens, Van Iddekinge, and Kuncel (2017) note that the study of vocational interests is reemerging in the literature. Measures of specific vocational interests show more promise in predicting job performance than general interest inventories, and they provide incremental variance in the prediction of job performance over GMA (Van Iddekinge, Roth, Putka, & Lanivich, 2011). A specific vocational interest could include items related to the desire to create social value in their work (social entrepreneurship; see Nga & Shamuganathan, 2010) or appeal in working with big data issues (data journalism). In addition, historical-based biodata items could also be created to determine an applicant's history of participating in social causes and experiences in handling and analyzing data. Behavioral consistency (see Schmidt & Hunter, 1998) could help explain why biodata items would be related to future job performance in jobs that value such competencies, but it is currently unknown if biodata items related to these competencies actually possess criterion-related validity. Both tests will also be costly to develop as they will be uniquely designed to fit the particular definition of each competency. Further, any discrimination issues (e.g., adverse impact) associated with interest inventories or biodata tests would be dependent on the content assessed. For example, if assessing applicants' vocational interests or biodata involving data analytics, then an organization may find subgroup differences between scores because of the underrepresentation of minorities in data-oriented careers (see Priceonomics, 2017; Zhang, 2017).

Fourth, the competency of knowledge transfer pertains to the ability and willingness to transfer tacit knowledge from training, mentoring, and/or experience to other colleagues in the organization. As mentioned before, knowledge transfer does have a conceptual underpinning in GMA; however, other predictor constructs and measures can potentially be used to assess this competency in selection. For example, those who are willing to share tacit knowledge are likely high in traits related to core self-evaluation (CSE): self-esteem, generalized self-efficacy, internal locus of control, and emotional stability. That is, an employee who is willing to share their knowledge with others has to be confident about their standing within the organization and not have any trepidation about making others more proficient in their work. CSE has been shown to be a valid predictor of job performance (Chang et al., 2012), and a 12-item scale of CSE has shown to possess construct validity (Judge, Erez, Bono, & Thoreson, 2003). It is unknown, however, whether CSE possesses incremental validity over other predictor constructs such as GMA and personality (Chang et al., 2012) and if subgroup differences exist. Since sharing information involves interpersonal communication, organizations may also use SJTs to measure applicants' interpersonal skills.

Finally, given its roots in analytics, planning, change, and redirection, workforce engineering is most likely important at the managerial level rather than lower-level jobs in the organization. While sign-based constructs such as GMA and conscientiousness may be measured, other behaviorally based assessments that evaluate specific experiences related to analytics, workforce planning, development, and readjustment are needed. Structured interviews, for example, could be created to maximize psychological fidelity (e.g., "Tell me about a time where you built a data-driven agenda within a particular product line") and an assessment center could require the applicant to present solutions to a workforce problem involving talent development or lack thereof. The criterion-related validity of GMA, conscientiousness, structured interviews, and assessment centers has been well documented (Cortina et al., 2000; Hurtz & Donovan, 2000; Meriac, Hoffman, Woehr, & Fleisher, 2008; Schmidt & Hunter, 1998). More importantly, structured interviews (Cortina et al., 2000) and assessment centers (Meriac et al., 2008) show incremental validity in predicting job performance beyond GMA and conscientiousness. However, similar to the other predictor constructs and tests, subgroup differences by race exist for both work sample tests and structured interviews (Ployhart & Holtz, 2008).

The studies mentioned above are used for illustrative purposes and do not represent an all-inclusive review of the extant literature. However, most of the studies mentioned are either indirect measures of the new competencies or meta-analytic reviews of the particular method or test. Thus, we need new individual studies that directly investigate predictive constructs or tests to measure these competencies and then determine their criterion-related validity. Until then, we acknowledge that any insight into the criterion-related validity of these new competencies is indirect and speculative.

Test Administration Trends

While it is clear each of these competencies has a foundation in existing bodies of research, many implications related to their inclusion rest in real-world application such as testing and test administration. Given their roots in complex criterion domains, it is important to note that testing for these competencies poses new challenges not easily addressed through technology alone. However, being able to assess complex competencies online rather than in person offers potential cost savings for organizations and an opportunity to provide expedited feedback to applicants. With this in mind, we note technological trends in the world of testing and test administration. In 2015, the Institute for Credentialing Excellence (ICE) identified three trends for changing the way we test competencies. These trends included:

1. *A renewed interest in assessment through observation by leveraging online proctoring technologies.* Specifically, ICE highlighted how using online proctoring provides a technologically assisted method for assessing a person's proficiency in handling novel situations or analyzing unique problems. Within a selection system, organizations could leverage online proctoring to observe applicant performance on various tests, such as work samples and role plays. While this technique remains experimental as users address privacy and security issues, experts such as Caveon Security Insights (2013) note their significant potential.
2. *A trend toward interaction-based simulations leveraging automated animation and natural language processing.* In thinking specifically about the need to assess more complex competencies, ICE identified the rise of automated animation (e.g., creating digital characters that animate themselves) and natural language processing as tools for enhancing the way we assess competencies. For example, Ang and Van Dyne (2008) identified the applicability of interaction-based simulations as a method to capture the proficiency of individuals in novel situations. The application of this technology lends credence when thinking of competencies such as workforce engineering and reimagination because it adds a rich assessment context typically only found in leadership assessments for individuals (Reynolds et al., 2018). In addition, automated animation simulations provide an opportunity to evaluate asymmetrical problem solving, which could be valuable when assessing the analytical application and experience-building competencies.
3. *A spike in the use of artificial intelligence to assess creativity.* In recent months, the testing community has been wrestling with a new reality around artificial intelligence: it can, in fact, reshape the way we look at computer adaptive testing and assessment. Specifically, testing houses such as Prometric are exploring the way new competency-based assessments including creativity tasks are being developed using artificial intelligence. This trend is one in its most nascent stages, but one with significant potential for changing the way competencies are assessed and tests are administered.

Challenges Arising from Assessing the New Competencies

There will be a variety of challenges to consider when attempting to assess the new competencies within a selection system. Below, we identify four challenges – achieving buy-in for competency modeling, continuing to recognize a criterion problem, monitoring applicant reactions, and acknowledging social and ethical issues – that may impede progress toward implementing our solutions and making transformative change to address the changing nature of work.

Achieving Buy-in for Competency Modeling. Gaining leadership buy-in means getting decision makers both to see the value competency modeling provides to the organization and actively advocate for its use across the various talent management functions (e.g., selection). To do this, leaders first must understand how competency modeling enables the organization to carry out business strategies and accomplish goals and objectives. Two strategies that may enhance leadership buy-in of competency models are communicating how competencies help companies (a) align success criteria and (b) adapt to new realities.

Aligning Success Criteria. A recent survey involving HR executives found that one of the top five challenges facing today's organizations is aligning people strategies to business objectives (King, 2018). Without this alignment, organizations may lack the talent to succeed; as a result, innovation suffers, loyalty and revenues may decline, and goals may be missed. One way to obtain better alignment is to use well-defined competencies that align with business priorities and are relevant to job performance (DDI, 2015). When used correctly, competencies help align the organization's HR systems by using a common framework for selecting, training, evaluating, compensating, and promoting (e.g., Green, 1999; Lawler, 1994; Schippmann et al., 2000). For example, competency models typically include descriptions of how the competencies change or progress with job level and even proficiency level (e.g., Martone, 2003; Rodriguez et al., 2002); consequently, they can easily be converted into rating scales for structured interviews, performance appraisals, job evaluations, measures of promotion readiness, and career development guides. This common framework allows for integration, prevents inconsistencies, and creates HR systems that reinforce one another by using the same KSAOs to maximize positive impact.

Adapting to New Realities. As job roles and tasks become more fluid due to strategic change and redirection, specific job analytic information related to job duties becomes quickly outdated. Competency modeling, by design, has a greater potential to adapt to these strategic changes than traditional job analysis (see Singh, 2008). An example of how competency models help organizations remain competitive and agile within these new realities is found in the outcomes of artificial intelligence advancements. As more traditional jobs become automated and new jobs require an understanding of nuance and emotion only possible by humans, organizations will need to identify clear soft skills for effective performance. However, in order to adapt to these new realities, organizations need to continuously monitor the validity of their competency model.

Continuing to Recognize a Criterion Problem. Not surprisingly, validly measuring the ultimate criterion of job performance has been an elusive problem within industrial psychology since the last century (see Austin & Villanova, 1992). However, with organizations either eliminating or truncating existing performance appraisals (Cappelli & Tavis, 2016) and work constantly changing to meet environmental demands, measuring the ultimate criterion like job performance will continue to be troublesome. If organizations eliminate performance appraisals, then any opportunity to conduct local criterion-related validity studies involving job performance dissipates. This drastic decision, of course, leaves the organization exposed legally (e.g., just cause termination) and will create equity issues (e.g., merit) within the workforce. In addition, organizations will have to rely on meta-analytic values of criterion-related validity of various predictor constructs or tests to substantiate their use in a selection system. However, this is worrisome because such meta-analytic values were likely computed from studies published prior to the Internet age (see Roth et al., 2005).

In lieu of completely eliminating performance appraisals, organizations seem to be trending in a direction where they are trading breadth and depth for generality and usability. For example, according to Buckingham and Goodall (2015), Deloitte's managers evaluate employee performance after every project with four general items, two of which are measured dichotomously, that focus on past and future performance (e.g., "This person is ready for promotion today"). Thus, organizations seem to be sacrificing a degree of validity of their performance appraisals for efficiency. This, in turn, may bias criterion-related validity values of various selection tests or predictor constructs.

Coupled with this tradeoff, if managers provide more autonomy to their workforce to meet the demands of the changing labor pool (Wegman et al., 2018), then there will be a reduced opportunity to observe subordinate performance and track critical incidents needed for valid evaluation. Organizations may then turn to peer assessment or results-oriented approaches (e.g., goal setting) to evaluate subordinate performance, but even those decisions can have precarious consequences. The nefarious activity at Wells Fargo in 2016, for example, demonstrates the caution associated with relying on results-oriented performance assessments.

Given the issues associated with validly measuring job performance, organizations may choose to measure additional criteria to evaluate the validity of various predictor constructs or tests. For instance, turnover costs, especially those within six months of employment, are troubling for any organization, and the tendency for younger generations to frequently change jobs exacerbates this costly problem (Backman, 2018). Organizations therefore may wish to use person–organization fit assessments (e.g., personality tests, structured interviews) to predict six-month retention rates or use tests that assess the knowledge transfer competency to mitigate any knowledge-related loss from frequent turnover events. Further, the dynamic nature of work increases the value of the future potential of an applicant relative to whether they meet the demands of the current job they are being selected for. In addition, organizations may wish to evaluate the propensity of deviance in applicants, either on-duty or even off-duty (see Lyons et al., 2016). Lastly, organizational citizenship behaviors could become more valuable as work becomes more interdependent than independent (Organ, 1983). Taken together, all of these situations suggest that organizations may encounter competing criteria to evaluate their applicant pool. Applicant scores on a test or battery of tests may suggest a future high-performer but also a greater propensity to leave the organization or commit deviant behaviors off-duty. Scores on another test may indicate high future potential but poor person–job fit. During the competency modeling process, organizations would be wise to also determine the workplace criteria they value the most, as such decisions will guide the strategy of future validation studies and avoid any confusion when competing results arise in test results.

Monitoring Applicant Reactions. From a stakeholder perspective, organizations should embrace the practice of monitoring applicant reactions to their selection system. Compared to the past, organizations are now able to access data related to applicant reactions to their selection systems on websites such as Glassdoor.com and Indeed.com. Ensuring applicants are at least satisfied with the selection process will likely lead to favorable future outcomes, such as the increased probability that they will apply again and eliciting positive perceptions about their brand as an employer (Hausknecht, Day, & Thomas, 2004). Regarding the latter, research has shown the powerful effects of having a positive brand or reputation as an employer. Collins and Han (2004) found that an organization's reputation had a direct effect on applicant quality and quantity. When a positive employer brand helps secure best places to work certifications, applicant pool quality increases, especially within smaller organizations (Dineen & Allen, 2016). Based on this evidence, organizations would be wise to monitor applicant reactions to their selection systems.

Considering our recommendations, however, we would expect some initial negative feedback from applicants. Specifically, although our recommendations focus on expediting the selection system by using predictor constructs and tests that are amenable to online assessment and high in psychological fidelity, they may produce initial negative reactions within the applicant pool. For example, leveraging online assessments (e.g., virtual realities) early in the selection process may likely feel impersonal to applicants, which may initially increase perceptions of unfairness by applicants. This feeling may be accentuated when the assessments do not place applicants in a realistic job environment during the process. Organizations that use video-based interviews at career fairs are likely experiencing this problem. Further, given the abstract nature of tests that measure GMA, applicants will likely have negative reactions toward these tests

(Hauseknecht et al., 2004), and we expect that such negative reactions will only increase over time as universities have begun eliminating GMA-related tests (e.g., ACT/SAT) in admissions processing (Sanchez, 2018).

However, three remedies can be implemented to assuage these negative reactions. First, organizations can provide clarity to each assessment by communicating why the particular measure is being used in a selection process, and this gesture could create more favorable applicant reactions than not providing such information (Ryan & Tippins, 2004). This information is likely conveyed on websites such as Glassdoor.com, so it is imperative that organizations monitor how publicly available their assessments are online. Next, the promise of providing immediate feedback after the completion of an assessment – a message as simple as saying they advanced to the next hurdle or they did not meet a desired cutoff – could help create favorable applicant reactions (McCarthy et al., 2017). Thus, organizations need their human resource information systems to be programmed to provide automated feedback after each assessment. Finally, surveying all applicants after a selection process has closed can only help the organization adapt its system to meet the demands of future applicant pools (see Bauer et al., 2001).

Acknowledging Social and Ethical Issues. The breadth, depth, and complexity of the competencies that will be required in a new paradigm of work may raise several social and ethical issues for organizations to address. One example is the potential reduction in the face validity of selection tests to measure the new competencies. Face validity – defined as the degree of perceived job relatedness of the selection method or test – often affects applicant perceptions of the fairness and appropriateness of selection measures (Smither et al., 1993). The increasing complexity of the competencies required in the new paradigm of work makes it more difficult to use measures that have a direct and obvious relationship with the job in question. For example, indirect measures of data journalism (e.g., GMA) will likely possess negative applicant reactions regardless of the job's content; however, even a direct measure of data journalism (e.g., transforming results from a table into a visual illustration) may result in poor face validity for jobs that do not directly involve data-oriented tasks *at the present time* but will in the future.

If perceptions of unfairness exist within a selection system, then it will likely increase the probability of litigation. Consistent with the Uniform Guidelines on Employee Selection Procedures (US Equal Employment Opportunity Commission et al., 1978), organizations may, among other strategies,– protect themselves against such litigation via a business necessity defense. For example, if organizations demonstrate that their measures of these competencies are related to a criterion of value to the business (e.g., job performance), then they may invoke a business necessity defense. Given the multifaceted nature of these competencies, this process may be more straightforward to demonstrate than content validity. In addition, since the competency model should reflect the foundation of successful organizational performance, measures of such competencies may be deemed a business necessity.

While the desired outcomes are equitable and accurate prediction from a measurement perspective *and* perceived fairness from an administration perspective, only the former is really a necessity. As inferred before, organizations are much more likely to achieve the latter in addition to the former if they appropriately communicate with and educate applicants and employees about their measurement methods and processes. Thus, it is incumbent upon organizations to educate its workforce within this new paradigm of work, so applicants and employees understand why measurement methods are changing and how they relate to effective job performance. Organizations should be transparent and share all information about the why the new competencies are needed and how they will be measured. Weaving in real success stories resulting from these new measurement methods can also help build support from applicants and employees, keeping diversity and job variety in mind when selecting people and jobs to highlight.

Finally, screening applicants' social media pages (e.g., Facebook) may become a popular method to indirectly evaluate competencies such as social entrepreneurship. That is, organizations could evaluate an applicant's civic engagement by examining their Facebook profile. According to a CareerBuilder survey, Salm (2017) reports that 70% of employers use social media to screen candidates before hiring, which is up significantly from 60% in 2016. However, unless social media content can be directly linked to job-related duties, we are against its future use because of invalid judgments inferred by profiles – lack of psychological fidelity – and discriminatory outcomes (i.e., adverse impact) that result (Van Iddekinge, Lanivich, Roth, & Junco, 2016). Put simply, due to inaccuracies in judgment and the high probability of implicit bias and/or adverse impact, organizations would be wise to discontinue this method to screen applicants.

Conclusion

We hope this chapter sheds new light on how organizations need to adapt their selection systems to meet the demands of the current and future workplaces. Organizations that embrace competency modeling, adapt how predictor constructs are measured and staged within a selection system, and emphasize the expediency of applicant feedback and selection decisions will likely have an advantage over others that are slow to adapt their selection practices. Clearly, additional research is needed with all aspects of our recommendations, and such applied work will only help our field become more noticeable within the C-suite.

References

Ancona, D. (2011). Sensemaking: Framing and acting in the unknown. In S. Snook, N. Nohria, & R. Khurana (Eds.), *The handbook for teaching leadership* (pp. 3–19). Thousand Oaks, CA: Sage Publications.

Ang, S., & Van Dyne, L. (2008). Conceptualization of cultural intelligence: Definition, distinctiveness, and nomological network. In S. Ang & L. Van Dyne (Eds.), *Handbook on cultural intelligence: Theory, measurement and applications* (pp. 3–15). Armonk, NY: M.E. Sharpe.

Austin, J. T., & Villanova, P. (1992). The criterion problem: 1917–1992. *Journal of Applied Psychology, 77*, 836–874.

Backman, M. (2018, June 11). Job hopping: Why Millennials resign nearly twice as often as older workers. Retrieved September 5, 2018, from www.usatoday.com/story/money/careers/employment-trends/2018/06/11/why-millennials-resign-more-than-older-workers/35921637/

Bakker, A. B., & Demerouti, E. (2009). The crossover of work engagement between working couples: A closer look at the role of empathy. *Journal of Managerial Psychology, 24*, 220–236.

Barley, S. R., Bechky, B. A., & Milliken, F. J. (2017). The changing nature of work: Careers, identities, and work lives in the 21st century. *Academy of Management Discoveries, 3*, 111–115.

Bauer, T. N., Truxillo, D. M., Sanchez, R. J., Craig, J. M., Ferrara, P., & Campion, M. A. (2001). Applicant reactions to selection: Development of the selection procedural justice scale (SPJS). *Personnel Psychology, 54*, 387–419.

Belout, A., & Gauvreau, C. (2004). Factors influencing project success: The impact of human resource management. *International Journal of Project Management, 22*, 1–11.

Bersin, J. N. (2018). 2018 Deloitte human capital trends report: The rise of the social enterprise. Retrieved August 6, 2018, from www2.deloitte.com/content/dam/insights/us/articles/HCTrends2018/2018-HCtrends_Rise-of-the-social-enterprise.pdf

Boudreau, J. W. (2012). Strategic I–O psychology lies beyond HR. *Industrial and Organizational Psychology: Perspectives on Science and Practice, 5*, 86–91.

Boudreau, J. W., & Ziskin, I. (2015). *Black holes & white spaces: Reimagining the future of work and HR with the CHREATE Project*. Alexandria, VA: HR People & Strategy.

Boyatzis, R. E., Goleman, D., & Rhee, K. S. (2000). Clustering competence in emotional intelligence: insights from the Emotional Competence Inventory. In R. Bar-On & J. D. A. Parker (Eds.), *The handbook of emotional intelligence: Theory development, assessment, and application at home, school and in the workplace* (pp. 343–361). San Francisco, CA: Jossey-Bass.

Buckingham, M., & Goodall, A. (2015). Reinventing performance management. *Harvard Business Review, 93*, 40–50.

Campion, M. A., Fink, A. A., Ruggeberg, B. J., Carr, L., Phillips, G. M., & Odman, R. B. (2011). Doing competencies well: Best practices in competency modeling. *Personnel Psychology, 64*, 225–262.

Cappelli, P., & Tavis, A. (2016). The performance management revolution. *Harvard Business Review, 94*, 58–67.

Caveon Security Insights. (2013). The good and bad of online proctoring. Retrieved August 6, 2018, from www.caveon.com/2013/03/15/the-good-and-bad-of-online-proctoring/

Chang, C. H., Ferris, D. L., Johnson, R. E., Rosen, C. C., & Tan, J. A. (2012). Core self-evaluations: A review and evaluation of the literature. *Journal of Management, 38*, 81–128.

Christian, M. S., Edwards, B. D., & Bradley, J. C. (2010). Situational judgment tests: Constructs assessed and a meta-analysis of their criterion-related validities. *Personnel Psychology, 63*, 83–117.

Collins, C. J., & Han, J. (2004). Exploring applicant pool quantity and quality: The effects of early recruitment practice strategies, corporate advertising, and firm reputation. *Personnel Psychology, 57*, 685–717.

Cortina, J. M., Goldstein, N. B., Payne, S. C., Davison, H. K., & Gilliland, S. W. (2000). The incremental validity of interview scores over and above cognitive ability and conscientiousness scores. *Personnel Psychology, 53*, 325–351.

Daley, C. (2017). Open-sourced AI: The next big step for the gig economy. Retrieved August 6, 2018, from https://aibusiness.com/ai-future-project-management-gig-economy/

Davis, M. H. (1980). A multidimensional approach to individual differences in empathy. *JSAS Catalog of Selected Documents in Psychology, 10*, 85.

Dees, J. G. (2001). The meaning of "social entrepreneurship." Retrieved August 6, 2018 from https://entrepreneurship.duke.edu/news-item/the-meaning-of-social-entrepreneurship/

Development Dimensions International (DDI). (2015). Competency management at its most competent. Retrieved August 6, 2018, from www2.deloitte.com/content/dam/Deloitte/za/Documents/human-capital/ZA_Competency_management_at_its_most_competent.pdf

Dineen, B. R., & Allen, D. G. (2016). Third party employment branding: Human capital inflows and outflows following "Best Places to Work" certifications. *Academy of Management Journal, 59*, 90–112.

Dixon, L. (2017). The future of the project management role. Retrieved August 6, 2018 from www.clomedia.com/2017/11/22/future-project-management/

Driggs, W., & Rogers, E. (2018). Building trusted relationships through analytics and experience. Retrieved August 6, 2018, from www.ey.com/Publication/vwLUAssets/EY-building-trusted-relationships-through-analytics-and-experience/$FILE/EY-building-trusted-relationships-through-analytics-and-experience.pdf

Economist Intelligence Unit & SHRM Foundation. (2014). Future trends in HR and work. Retrieved August 6, 2018, from http://futurehrtrends.eiu.com/report-2016/executive-summary/

Ell, K. (2017, August 9). It's taking longer than ever to get hired, Glassdoor survey shows. Retrieved August 6, 2018, from www.usatoday.com/story/money/2017/08/09/its-taking-longer-than-ever-get-hired-glassdoor-survey-shows/551001001/

Ghasemaghaei, M., Ebrahimi, S., & Hassanein, K. (2018). Data analytics competency for improving firm decision making performance. *Journal of Strategic Information Systems, 27*, 221–248.

Goldstein, I. L., Zedeck, S., & Schneider, B. (1993). An exploration of the job-analysis-content validity process. In N. Schmitt and W. C. Borman (Eds.), *Personnel selection in organizations* (pp. 3–34). San Francisco, CA: Jossey-Bass.

Gonzalez-Mulé, E., Mount, M. K., & Oh, I. S. (2014). A meta-analysis of the relationship between general mental ability and nontask performance. *Journal of Applied Psychology, 99*, 1222–1243.

Green, P. C. (1999). *Building robust competencies: Linking human resource systems to organizational strategies*. San Francisco, CA: Jossey-Bass Inc.

Guenole, N. (2014). Maladaptive personality at work: Exploring the darkness. *Industrial and Organizational Psychology: Perspectives on Science and Practice, 7*, 85–97.

Hagel III, J. (2018, August 21). 3 kinds of jobs that will thrive as automation advances. Retrieved September 10, 2018, from https://hbr.org/2018/08/3-kinds-of-jobs-that-will-thrive-as-automation-advances

Hausknecht, J. P., Day, D. V., & Thomas, S. C. (2004). Applicant reactions to selection procedures: An updated model and meta-analysis. *Personnel Psychology, 57*, 639–683.

Hurtz, G. M., & Donovan, J. J. (2000). Personality and job performance: The Big Five revisited. *Journal of Applied Psychology, 85*, 869.

Institute for Credentialing Excellence (ICE). (2015). Remote proctoring test delivery and trends: A report on options and considerations. Retrieved August 6, 2018, from www.credentialingexcellence.org/

Joseph, D. L., Jin, J., Newman, D. A., & O'Boyle, E. H. (2015). Why does self-reported emotional intelligence predict job performance? A meta-analytic investigation of mixed EI. *Journal of Applied Psychology, 100*, 298–342.

Judge, T. A., Erez, A., Bono, J. E., & Thoresen, C. J. (2003). The core self-evaluations scale: Development of a measure. *Personnel Psychology, 56*, 303–331.

Kane, J., Lajmi, M., & Hontalas, J. (2018). Next generation workforce: The new HR. *Accenture*. Retrieved August 6, 2018, from www.accenture.com/us-en/insight-next-generation-workforce

Kellett, J. B., Humphrey, R. H., & Sleeth, R. G. (2002). Empathy and complex task performance: Two routes to leadership. *Leadership Quarterly, 13*, 523–544.

Kellett, J. B., Humphrey, R. H., & Sleeth, R. G. (2006). Empathy and the emergence of task and relations leaders. *Leadership Quarterly, 17*, 146–162.

King, D. W. (2018, March). What's keeping HR up? *Human Resource Executive*. Retrieved August 6, 2018, from www.humanresourceexecutive-digital.com/humanresourceexecutive/march_2018?article_id=1361909&pg=25#pg25

Kuncel, N. R., Hezlett, S. A., & Ones, D. S. (2004). Academic performance, career potential, creativity, and job performance: Can one construct predict them all? *Journal of Personality and Social Psychology, 86*, 148–161.

Lawler III, E. E. (1994). From job-based to competency-based organizations. *Journal of Organizational Behavior, 15*, 3–15.

Lievens, F., & Patterson, F. (2011). The validity and incremental validity of knowledge tests, low-fidelity simulations, and high-fidelity simulations for predicting job performance in advanced-level high-stakes selection. *Journal of Applied Psychology, 96*, 927–940.

Lyons, B. D., Hoffman, B. J., Bommer, W. H., Kennedy, C. L., & Hetrick, A. L. (2016). Off-duty deviance: Organizational policies and evidence for two prevention strategies. *Journal of Applied Psychology, 101*, 463–483.

Mankins, M. (2017, September 7). How leading companies build the workforces they need to stay ahead. Retrieved May 25, 2018, from https://hbr.org/2017/09/how-leading-companies-build-the-workforces-they-need-to-stay-ahead

Manyika, J., Lund, S., Bughin, J., Robinson, K., Mischke, J., & Mahajan, D. (2016, October). Independent work: Choice, necessity, and the gig economy. Retrieved August 6, 2018, from www.mckinsey.com/featured-insights/employment-and-growth/independent-work-choice-necessity-and-the-gig-economy

Martin, R. L., & Osberg, S. (2007, Spring). Social entrepreneurship: The case for definition. *Stanford Social Innovation Review*. Retrieved August 6, 2018, from https://ssir.org/articles/entry/social_entrepreneurship_the_case_for_definition#

Martone, D. (2003). A guide to developing a competency-based performance-management system. *Employment Relations Today*, *30*, 23–32.

McCarthy, J. M., Bauer, T. N., Truxillo, D. M., Anderson, N. R., Costa, A. C., & Ahmed, S. M. (2017). Applicant perspectives during selection: A review addressing "so what?," "what's new?," and "where to next?" *Journal of Management*, *43*, 1693–1725.

Meriac, J. P., Hoffman, B. J., Woehr, D. J., & Fleisher, M. S. (2008). Further evidence for the validity of assessment center dimensions: A meta-analysis of the incremental criterion-related validity of dimension ratings. *Journal of Applied Psychology*, *93*, 1042–1052.

Motowidlo, S. J., Dunnette, M. D., & Carter, G. W. (1990). An alternative selection procedure: The low-fidelity simulation. *Journal of Applied Psychology*, *75*, 640–647.

Nga, J. K. H., & Shamuganathan, G. (2010). The influence of personality traits and demographic factors on social entrepreneurship start up intentions. *Journal of Business Ethics*, *95*, 259–282.

Organ, D. W. (1983). *Organizational citizenship behavior: The good soldier syndrome*. Lexington, MA: Lexington Books.

Ployhart, R. E., & Holtz, B. C. (2008). The diversity–validity dilemma: Strategies for reducing racioethnic and sex subgroup differences and adverse impact in selection. *Personnel Psychology*, *61*, 153–172.

Ployhart, R. E., Schneider, B., & Schmitt, N. (2006). *Staffing organizations: Contemporary practice and theory*. Mahwah, NJ: Lawrence Erlbaum Associates.

Priceonomics (2017). The data science diversity gap. *Forbes*. Retrieved September 4, 2018, from www.forbes.com/sites/priceonomics/2017/09/28/the-data-science-diversity-gap/#26b08345f58b

Reynolds, D. H., McCauley, C. D., & Tsacoumis, S. (2018). A critical evaluation of the state of assessment and development for senior leaders. *Industrial and Organizational Psychology: Perspectives on Science and Practice*.

Rodriguez, D., Patel, R., Bright, A., Gregory, D., & Gowing, M. K. (2002). Developing competency models to promote integrated human resource practices. *Human Resource Management*, *41*, 309–324.

Roth, P. L., Bobko, P., & McFarland, L. A. (2005). A meta-analysis of work sample test validity: Updating and integrating some classic literature. *Personnel Psychology*, *58*(4), 1009–1037.

Roth, P. L., Huffcutt, A. I., & Bobko, P. (2003). Ethnic group differences in measures of job performance: A new meta-analysis. *Journal of Applied Psychology*, *88*, 694–706.

Royal, C., & Blasingame, D. (2015). Data journalism: An explication. *ISOJ Journal*, *6*(1). Retrieved August 6, 2018, from https://isojjournal.wordpress.com/2015/04/15/data-journalism-an-explication/

Ryan, A. M., Ployhart, R. E., & Friedel, L. A. (1998). Using personality testing to reduce adverse impact: A cautionary note. *Journal of Applied Psychology, 83*, 298–307.

Ryan, A. M., & Tippins, N. T. (2004). Attracting and selecting: What psychological research tells us. *Human Resource Management*, *43*, 305–318.

Sackett, P. R., Lievens, F., Van Iddekinge, C. H., & Kuncel, N. R. (2017). Individual differences and their measurement: A review of 100 years of research. *Journal of Applied Psychology, 102*, 254–273.

Salm, L. (2017). 70% of employers are snooping candidates' social media profiles. Retrieved September 6, 2018, from www.careerbuilder.com/advice/social-media-survey-2017.

Sanchez, C. (2018, April 26). Study: Colleges that ditch the SAT and ACT can enhance diversity. Retrieved August 6, 2018, from www.npr.org/sections/ed/2018/04/26/604875394/study-colleges-that-ditch-the-sat-and-act-can-enhance-diversity

Sanchez, J. I., & Levine, E. L. (2009). What is (or should be) the difference between competency modeling and traditional job analysis? *Human Resource Management Review, 19*, 53–63.

Schippmann, J. S., Ash, R. A., Battista, M., Carr, L., Eyde, L. D., Hesketh, B. et al. (2000). The practice of competency modeling. *Personnel Psychology, 53*, 703–740.

Schmidt, F. L., & Hunter, J. E. (1998). The validity and utility of selection methods in personnel psychology: Practical and theoretical implications of 85 years of research findings. *Psychological Bulletin, 124*, 262–274.

Silzer, R. & Jeanneret, R. (2011). Individual psychological assessment: A practice and science in search of common ground. *Industrial and Organizational Psychology: Perspectives on Science and Practice, 4*, 270–296.

Singh, P. (2008). Job analysis for a changing workplace. *Human Resource Management Review, 18*, 87–99.

Smither, J. W., Reilly, R. R., Millsap, R. E., Pearlman, K., & Stoffey, R. W. (1993). Applicant reactions to selection procedures. *Personnel Psychology, 46*, 49–76.

Society for Human Resource Management (SHRM). (2015). SHRM research: Workforce readiness and skills shortages. Retrieved August 6, 2018, from www.shrm.org/hr-today/trends-and-forecasting/labor-market-and-economic-data/Documents/Workforce%20Readiness%20and%20Skills%20Shortages.pdf

Society for Human Resource Management (SHRM). (2016). The new talent landscape: Recruiting difficulty and skills shortages. Retrieved August 6, 2018, from www.shrm.org/hr-today/trends-and-forecasting/research-and-surveys/Documents/SHRM%20New%20Talent%20Landscape%20Recruiting%20Difficulty%20Skills.pdf

Soulier, E., & Caussanel, J. (2002). Narrative tools to improve collaborative sensemaking. *AAAI Technical Report* WS-02-09. Association for the Advancement of Artificial Intelligence. Retrieved August 6, 2018, from www.aaai.org/Papers/Workshops/2002/WS-02-09/WS02-09-002.pdf

Trautman, S., & McKee, M. (2014). The power of knowledge transfer: preserving your secret sauce while mitigating talent management risks. Retrieved August 6, 2018, from www.executivecoachglobal.com/the-power-of-knowledge-transfer-preserving-your-secret-sauce-while-mitigating-talent-management-risks/

US Equal Employment Opportunity Commission, Civil Service Commission, Department of Labor, & Department of Justice (1978). Adoption by four agencies of uniform guidelines on employee selection procedures. *Federal Register, 43*, 38290–38315.

Van Iddekinge, C. H., Lanivich, S. E., Roth, P. L., & Junco, E. (2016). Social media for selection? Validity and adverse impact potential of a Facebook-based assessment. *Journal of Management, 42*, 1811–1835.

Van Iddekinge, C. H., Roth, P. L., Putka, D. J., & Lanivich, S. E. (2011). Are you interested? A meta-analysis of relations between vocational interests and employee performance and turnover. *Journal of Applied Psychology*, *96*, 1167–1194.

Vollmer, C., Egol, M., & Sayani, N. (2014, Autumn). Reimagine your enterprise: Make human-centered design the heart of your digital agenda. *Strategy+Business.* Retrieved August 6, 2018, from www.strategy-business.com/article/00258?gko=6626b

Wang, K. (2016). Why collaborate? Three frameworks to understand business–NGO partnerships. Retrieved August 6, 2018, from http://blogs.worldbank.org/category/tags/knowledge-transfer

Wegman, L. A., Hoffman, B. J., Carter, N. T., Twenge, J. M., & Guenole, N. (2018). Placing job characteristics in context: Cross-temporal meta-analysis of changes in job characteristics since 1975. *Journal of Management*, *44*, 352–386.

Wernimont, P. F., & Campbell, J. P. (1968). Signs, samples, and criteria. *Journal of Applied Psychology*, *52*, 372–376.

World Economic Forum. (2016). The future of jobs. Retrieved August 6, 2018, from http://reports.weforum.org/future-of-jobs-2016/skills-stability/#view/fn-13

Zhang, V. (2017). Breaking down the gender gap in data science. Retrieved August 6, 2018, from www.forbes.com/sites/womensmedia/2017/08/03/breaking-down-the-gender-gap-in-data-science/#67b60ca4428

15 Implications of the Changing Nature of Work for Recruitment and Retention

Wayne F. Cascio

We live in a global world where technology, especially information and communication technology, is changing the manner in which businesses create and capture value, how and where we work, and how we interact and communicate. The term "technology" refers to the application of scientific knowledge for practical purposes, especially in industry – for example, "advances in computer technology" (Oxford Living Dictionaries, 2016). Consider five technologies that are transforming the very foundations of global business and the organizations that drive it: cloud and mobile computing, big data and machine learning, sensors and intelligent manufacturing, advanced robotics and drones, and clean-energy technologies (Wooldridge, 2015).

Digital technologies are not just helping people to do things better and faster, but they are enabling profound changes in the ways that work is done in organizations. Today, information and communication technology is heading toward a new stage that is based on ubiquitous computing. The concept of ubiquitous computing refers to an environment in which computational technology permeates almost everything, thereby enabling people to access and control their environment at any time and from anywhere – linking the physical world directly with the electronic space. The result is a ubiquitous space that allows a level of complexity, speed, and quality not possible before (Cascio & Montealegre, 2016). Here are just two examples:

- Computer networks allow employees to work from the office, their home, or anywhere. Employees are routinely collaborating with people they have never met, in places they have never visited, and staying connected with the office anywhere and anytime. This has enabled ubiquitous working environments that support different types of working styles and conditions (Maynard, Gilson, Jones-Young, & Vartiainen, 2017).
- Computer programs, intelligent robots, and other devices are used to perform an increasing variety of tasks with a high level of technical skills, and with benefits that include lower costs, higher quality, improved safety, and environmental protection. People, however, define, create, and maintain these automated programs, machines, and other devices (Broadbent, 2017).

All of this is prompting organizations to reexamine what a "job" actually is: how it is structured, how it should be reconfigured, or perhaps redefined, in an age of intelligent automation. How should companies rethink the value of a job, in terms of increased performance through machine intelligence? What sets of skills should companies invest in? Which jobs should remain within the company and which should be accessed via talent platforms or even shared with peers?

While it is true that advances in technology will continue to displace workers in a wide swath of our economy, when it comes to engaging and inspiring people to move in the same direction, empathizing with customers, and developing talent, humans will continue to enjoy a strong comparative advantage over machines (Cascio, 2017).

As the opening paragraphs make clear, many aspects of work are changing, but for purposes of assessing their impact on recruitment and retention, this chapter will focus on six key areas: (1) technology, (2) social media, (3) big data, (4) HR technology and information systems, (5) globalization, and (6) demographics. The chapter will begin with a brief review of changes in each of these areas and how they are affecting work. Next, we will consider how these same changes are affecting recruitment, recognizing that in the age of the Internet and social media, recruitment is, by definition, global. The chapter will conclude by offering research-based suggestions regarding what managers can do to maximize the retention of talent that they want to keep.

Technology and Changes in Work

Information and ideas are keys to success in economies everywhere because every country, every company, and every individual depends increasingly on knowledge. Computers have increasingly taken over such tasks as bookkeeping, clerical work, and repetitive production jobs in manufacturing. At the same time, countless white-collar jobs, such as many in customer service, have disappeared. Fortunately, history shows that technology-driven job destruction does not decrease overall employment – even while making some jobs obsolete. Ultimately, as workers adjust their skills and entrepreneurs create opportunities based on the new technologies, the number of jobs rebounds (Aeppel, 2015; Loten, 2017; Manyika et al., 2017). Decision makers cannot wait until evolving technologies disrupt the status quo. Rather, they need to understand how the competitive advantages on which they have based their strategies might erode or be enhanced a decade from now by emerging technologies. They need to understand how technologies might bring them new customers or force them to defend their existing bases, or inspire them to invent new strategies (Murray, 2015).

In the creative economy, the most important intellectual property is not software or music. Rather, it is the intellectual capital that resides in people. When assets were physical things like coal mines, shareholders truly owned them. But when the most vital assets are people, there can be no true ownership. The best that corporations can do is to create an environment that makes the best people want to stay (Friedman, 2016). Therein lies the challenge of attracting and retaining talent.

Like other new developments, there are negatives as well as positives associated with new technology, and they need to be acknowledged. Workers may be bombarded with mass junk email (spam), company computer networks may be attacked by hackers who can wreak havoc on the ability of an organization to function, and employees' privacy may be compromised. A comprehensive review of literature in this area revealed three lessons about the effects of ubiquitous computing. One, *the effect of ubiquitous computing on jobs is a process of creative destruction.* Ubiquitous computing is not the first technology to affect jobs. From steam engines to robotic welders to ATMs, technology has long displaced humans, often creating new and higher-skilled jobs in its wake. Two, *ubiquitous computing can be used to enable or to constrain people at work.* As an example, consider electronic monitoring systems. Evidence indicates that attitudes in general, and attitudes toward monitoring in particular, will be more positive when organizations monitor their employees within supportive organizational cultures (Alge & Hansen, 2014). Supportive cultures welcome employee input into the monitoring system's design, focus on groups of employees rather than singling out individuals, and focus on performance-relevant activities. Three, *ubiquitous computing is changing the nature of competition, work, and employment in ways that are profound and that need to be managed actively* (Cascio & Montealegre, 2017).

Beyond that, the ubiquitous presence of technology in our lives may limit opportunities to develop deep levels of self-awareness and to behave authentically, especially among those who spend lots of time in online worlds and working with avatars. Managers and organizations need to consider how to address the possibility of reduced self-awareness and authenticity among members of the digital workforce while also remaining aware of the ways that technology might be used to promote healthy identity development (Colbert et al., 2016).

So, what do changes in technology, especially artificial intelligence and machine learning, mean for jobs and work? IBM CEO Ginny Rometty was very clear on this point: "I do believe that when it comes to complete job replacement, it will be a very small percentage. When it comes to changing a job and what you do, it will be 100 percent" (Rometty, in Murphy, 2017, p. 64). A 2017 study by the McKinsey Global Institute supports her prediction: "Very few occupations – less than 5 percent – consist of activities that can be fully automated. However, in about 60 percent of occupations, at least one-third of the constituent activities could be automated, implying substantial workplace transformations and changes for all workers" (Manyika et al., 2017).

The potential impact of automation on employment, however, varies by occupation and sector. Activities most susceptible to automation include physical ones in predictable environments, such as operating machinery, preparing fast food, or collecting and processing data. This could displace large numbers of workers – for instance, in mortgage origination, paralegal work, accounting, and back-office transaction processing.

Just because tasks can be automated does not mean that they will be. Firms will need to consider the cost of developing and deploying automation solutions for specific uses in the workplace, the availability and cost of labor, and regulatory and social acceptance of automation.

Even when some tasks are automated, however, employment in those occupations may not decline but rather workers may perform new tasks. Automation will have a lesser effect on jobs that involve managing people, applying expertise, and social interactions, where machines are unable to match human performance – at least for now (Manyika et al., 2017).

Social Media and Changes in Work

Social media are important features of technological changes in work and they are here to stay. We are in near constant communication with one another, and our lives are chronicled for friends and followers in real time on social media. The use of Internet technologies makes those relationships easier to develop and maintain. How big is this phenomenon? Consider the top three social media and the number of users of each in 2017: Facebook (2.061 billion), YouTube (1.5 billion), and What'sApp (1.3 billion) (Statista, 2017). Social media include at least four major types: (1) social-networking sites, such as Facebook, LinkedIn, Instagram, and chat rooms; (2) blogs and microblogs, such as Twitter; (3) virtual worlds, such as Second Life; and (4) video-sharing websites, such as YouTube.

Today 72% of companies use social media to advertise their jobs, 59% find they get more referrals, and 50% get more applications by using social media. Fully 78% of recruiters have hired through social media, and 94% say they use or plan to use social media in recruiting talent. The top channels? LinkedIn, Facebook, and Twitter, pull in 96% of searching, 94% of contacting, and 92% of vetting candidates, respectively. Other networks, like YouTube, Yammer, and Jobster, are proving to be rich sources of talent as well (Society for Human Resource Management, 2016; Staff.com, 2016).

A recent Pew Research Center survey (Olmstead, Lampe, & Ellison, 2016) found that workers incorporate social media into a wide range of activities while on the job. Some of these activities are explicitly professional or job-related, while others are more personal in nature, as the following results show:

- 34% use social media while at work to take a mental break from their job
- 27% to connect with friends and family while at work
- 24% to make or support professional connections
- 20% to get information that helps them solve problems at work
- 17% to build or strengthen personal relationships with coworkers
- 17% to learn about someone they work with
- 12% to ask work-related questions of people *outside* their organization
- 12% to ask such questions of people *inside* their organization

Organizations are recognizing how popular social media is becoming in the workplace, and thus are developing policies surrounding its use. More than half of the employees surveyed said their employer has a policy about social media use at work.

A big appeal of social media is that they appear to be able to solve business challenges without any associated costs. Why hire a search firm when you can tap your personal/contact list to find candidates without charge? Why hire consultants when one of your "friends" can give you free advice? Why hire a coach when you can get a volunteer mentor from your current executives? The end result is that personal relationships with outsiders can become just as important as those with fellow employees. Will the promise of social media really play out as described? Maybe, but only if organizations can find ways to manage the risks that they entail.

Employees are integrating their use of Facebook, Twitter, Google, and other social media into their daily routines. Likewise, companies are integrating social media into their intranets, so that they can share internal information and knowledge with employees, and even with suppliers and customers if desired. Yet there are risks associated with doing this, and it is important to recognize them.

The top five social-media risks to business identified in a recent study are malware, brand hijacking, lack of content control, noncompliance with rules over record keeping, and unrealistic expectations of Internet performance (Wright, 2017a). Here are seven more: sexual harassment, defamation, libel, disclosure of confidential information or trade secrets, disclosure of customer lists, tort law violations (negative comments about employers), and theft of employer time. After all, the use of social media is not free. It only appears to be so because companies do not account for the time employees spend using social media. Studies show that at least some employees spend up to three hours per day on social networking websites (Weber, 2014)!

Big Data and Changes in Work

In business settings, it is hard to be convincing without data. If the data are developed systematically and comprehensively and are analyzed in terms of their strategic implications for a business or business unit, they are more convincing. Both internal and external data have always been available to researchers and organizations. Yet today's ubiquitous computing infrastructure, including, inter alia, industrial sensors and processors, speech-recognition and eye-tracking devices, mobile devices, radio-frequency identification and near-frequency-communication tags and labels, global positioning systems–enabled devices, smart televisions, car navigation systems, drones, wearable sensors, robots, and 3D virtual reality, allows individuals and organizations to collect enormous amounts of structured and unstructured data. In fact, we require the adjective "big" to distinguish this new paradigm of information and communication technology development.

At the same time, there are promises as well as perils associated with big data. Data are more widely available than ever before but to use the data wisely, decision makers must never lose sight of two paradoxes: (1) Many organizations are drowning in data but starved for information. (2) Data-driven decisions are evidence-based, yet there is still a great need for informed judgment and intuition (Cascio, 2019).

Users of big data seek to glean insights from analyzing the data and to use those insights to gain competitive advantage in the marketplace. "Big data" is the collection and analysis of the digital history created when people shop or surf the Internet, but it also includes the tests and measures of aptitudes, attitudes, behaviors, and competencies that employers compile about applicants and employees (King & Mrkonich, 2016). Three key features distinguish big data from more traditional approaches to analytics: volume, velocity, and variety (McAfee & Brynjolfsson, 2012). In terms of volume, the sheer amount of data that businesses can access has accelerated because most information is now in digital format and comes from many different sources. Consider the following examples. Zynga, a provider of social game services, processes 1 petabyte of data every day. A petabyte is a lot of data: the equivalent of 20 million four-drawer file cabinets filled with text. Google processes 20 petabytes of information per day! EMC Corp., a data-storage vendor, estimates that the amount of worldwide digital information doubles every two years (Roberts, 2013).

The variety of data includes sources of data both internal and external to HR and an enterprise. Examples include salary studies, industry benchmarks, and data published in print and digital media. Some of it is structured, like the information contained in relational databases in human resource information systems (HRIS), accounting, and enterprise resource planning systems. Other information is unstructured, like that found in answers to open-ended questions on employee-engagement surveys, social-media posts, blogs, wikis, emails, and videos. Velocity refers to the speed of data creation. Real-time, or nearly real-time, information makes it possible for an organization to be more agile than its competitors and to make the data actionable for business value.

Although the promise of big data is real, perils in the form of managerial challenges also abound. Here are four of them: Senior managers have to embrace big data, there is a pressing need to hire data scientists who can find meaningful patterns in the data, it is easy to mistake correlation for causation, and data alone never substitute for good judgment. Perhaps the biggest challenge is to be able to link the findings from big data to the competitive strategy of a business.

To the extent that managers can do that, there is great opportunity to gain competitive advantage. Here are three HR applications of big data:

- To improve recruiting processes, business subscribers to LinkedIn's Recruiter Service can access every LinkedIn profile, and then search for any number of criteria using standard LinkedIn filters.

- After finding that 30% of employees who got second opinions from top-rated medical centers ended up forgoing spinal surgery – which can cost $20,000 or more – Wal-Mart hired Castlight Healthcare to identify and communicate with workers suffering from back pain.
- Casino operator Caesar's wanted to know how much to pay prized employees to keep them from leaving. After analyzing pay and engagement scores for 5,000 workers who left, it found that attrition was 16% higher for those who earned below the midpoint of their salary range. Raising salary to the midpoint reduced attrition to 9%, but raising it higher than that had no effect and was just as effective as paying 10% above the midpoint (Silverman, 2016; Walker, 2012).

HR Technology: Human Resource Information Systems (HRIS)

A vast and ever-increasing array of HR technology is available to assist organizations with recruitment and staffing management: applicant-tracking software, Web-based applications, cloud computing, mobile apps, and video products. Organizations compete in talent markets, domestic and global, and HR technology often helps them attract and hire the best talent from those markets. As just one example, consider that individuals with disabilities play important roles in increasing diversity in organizations, and advances in assistive technology have dramatically increased job opportunities for them (Zielinski, 2016). Organizations benefit because they are able to recruit from a broader pool of applicants. Importantly, the costs of many assistive tools have dropped dramatically over the past decade, making them affordable for companies of all sizes.

At a general level, HR technology – most prominently in the form of HRIS – is used widely to source talent, to track applicants through the various steps of the recruitment-selection process, and to facilitate background investigations, job analyses, and applicant screening. Social media like LinkedIn and Web-based search engines enable firms to identify candidates ("How to use social media," 2016). Savvy recruiters are constantly looking for ways to poach high performers, and HR technology makes it easier than ever to find them.

A key feature of all modern HRIS systems is the use of relational databases that store data in separate files that can be linked by common elements, such as name, Social Security number, hiring status (full- or part-time), training courses completed, job location, mailing address, or birthdate, among others. A relational database lets a user sort the data by any of the fields.

Both large and small companies are eager to take advantage of the latest technology found in HRIS. Large employers want to upgrade their aging on-premise systems (platforms housed in privately controlled data centers) to cloud-based software-as-a-service (SAAS) systems: subscription-based software paid on a month-to-month basis. Small employers want to upgrade after years of using spreadsheets. Buyers in both groups need to be savvy consumers in order to choose wisely from the wide array of HRIS platforms that are available.

To do that, they must do seven things well (Cascio, 2019): (1) be very clear about exactly what they want their HRIS to do; (2) make the business case, for example, by aligning HR goals closely with an organization's business strategy and specifying the anticipated impact of the new system on the organization's bottom line; (3) systematically compare vendors; (4) match the technology to their organization's needs; (5) don't overlook finance or IT; (6) assess end users' experiences with the new system; and (7) address implementation issues, such as verifying the accuracy and integrity of the data in the new system.

HR technology has changed the ways that HR services are delivered and managed. Self-service portals promise faster execution of employee and manager transactions, with more informed users. At the same time, however, there is an urgent need to protect the integrity and privacy of employees' data and to ensure that all users are comfortable with the system. HR functions that can achieve those objectives will add genuine value to their organizations.

With respect to the adoption and implementation of HR technology, it can be used to enable or to oppress people at work. Self-determination theory is a particularly useful guide. That theory holds that self-motivation and wellbeing will be enhanced when innate needs for autonomy, competence, and relatedness are satisfied, and they will be diminished when these needs are thwarted (Ryan & Deci, 2017). Autonomy is the need to control one's actions, to be a causal agent in one's life. Competence is the need to experience mastery and to affect one's outcomes and surroundings. Relatedness is the need to feel interpersonally connected with others.

In practice, at least four considerations influence the adoption and implementation of workplace technologies. First, are they natural and easy to use? Usability concerns the interface between humans and technology, and it can be measured in terms of efficiency (time to complete a task), effectiveness (error rate), and user satisfaction. A second consideration is self-efficacy. People who feel competent to use, or to learn to use, new technology are likely to experience less anxiety when that new technology is introduced. A third consideration is economic. Does the new technology promise competitive advantage to an organization or to an individual in his or her personal life? If so, the organization or individual is more likely to implement it. Finally, it is also important to consider the role of social factors in the acceptance of technology. If friends, coworkers, or family members are using a particular technology – for example, a smartphone-payment system – peer pressure increases the likelihood of one's own adoption of it (Coovert & Thompson, 2014).

Globalization and Changes in Work

Other chapters in this volume (Murphy & Tierney, Chapter 3, this volume; Clott, Chapter 5, this volume) have discussed various aspects of globalization.

Hence, this section will be relatively brief. Globalization is the ability of any individual or company to compete, connect, exchange, or collaborate globally.

Indeed, the ability to digitize so many things, to send them anywhere and to pull them in from everywhere via our mobile phones and the Internet, has unleashed a torrent of global flows of information and knowledge. Global flows of commerce, finance, credit, social networks, and more are interlacing markets, media, central banks, companies, schools, communities, and individuals more tightly together than ever before. That same connectivity is also making individuals and institutions more interdependent. As author Tom Friedman notes, "Everyone everywhere is now more vulnerable to the actions of anyone anywhere" (2016, p. 27).

In no small part, the booming economies of recent years in developed countries have been fueled by globalization. Open borders have allowed new ideas and technology to flow freely around the globe, accelerating productivity growth and allowing companies to be more competitive than they have been in decades. Yet there is a growing fear on the part of many people that globalization benefits big companies instead of average citizens, as stagnating wages and growing job insecurity in developed countries create rising disenchantment. In theory, less-developed countries win from globalization because they get jobs making low-cost products for rich countries. Rich countries win because, in addition to being able to buy inexpensive imports, they also can sell more sophisticated products, like financial services, to emerging economies (Autor, Dorn, & Hanson, 2016). The problem, according to many experts, is that workers in the West are not equipped for today's pace of change, in which jobs come and go and skills can quickly become redundant (Brynjolfsson & McAfee, 2014; McKinsey Global Institute, 2016). In the public eye, multinational corporations are synonymous with globalization. In all of their far-flung operations, therefore, they bear a responsibility to be good corporate citizens, to preserve the environment, to uphold labor standards, to provide decent working conditions and competitive wages, to treat their employees fairly, and to contribute to the communities in which they operate.

Despite these concerns, economic interdependence among the world's countries will continue. Global corporations will continue to be created through mergers and acquisitions of unparalleled scope. These mega-corporations will achieve immense economies of scale and compete for goods, capital, and labor on a global basis. As a result, prices will drop, and consumers will have more options than ever (Ghemawat, 2017).

Another feature of globalization is that cheap labor and plentiful resources, combined with ease of travel and communication, have created global labor markets. This is fueling mobility as more companies expand abroad and people consider foreign postings as a natural part of their professional development. Beyond the positive effects that such circulation of talent brings to both developed and developing countries, it enables employment opportunities well beyond the borders of one's home country (Dulebohn & Hoch, 2017). This means that competition for talent will come not only from the company down the street but also from the employer on the other side of the world. It will be a seller's market, with talented individuals having many choices. Countries as well as companies will need to brand themselves as employers of choice in order to attract this talent (*Economist* Intelligence Unit, 2014; World Economic Forum & Boston Consulting Group, 2011).

Along with these trends, expect to see three more. The first is increasing workforce flux as more roles are automated or outsourced and more workers are contract-based, are mobile, or work flexible hours (McGovern, 2017). This may allow companies to leverage global resources more efficiently, but it also will increase the complexity of management's role. Second, expect more diversity as workers come from a greater range of backgrounds. Those with local knowledge of an emerging market, a global outlook, and an intuitive sense of the corporate culture will be particularly valued. Not surprisingly, talented young people will more frequently choose their employers based, at least in part, on opportunities to gain international experience. Finally, technical skills, although mandatory, will be less defining of the successful manager than the ability to work across cultures and to build relationships with many different constituents (Cascio, 2019).

Demographic Changes and Work

Other authors in this volume also discuss demographic changes (Cheng, Corrington, King, & Ng, Chapter 11, this volume) and we all agree that demographically, today's organizations are more diverse than ever before. They comprise more women at all levels; more multiethnic, multicultural workers; older workers; younger workers; more workers with disabilities; robots; and contingent workers. Consider some of the features of these changes.

Around the globe, the number as well as the mix of people available to work are changing rapidly. The U.S. labor force is aging, as the proportion of the labor force composed of people aged 55 and older rises from 19% in 2010 to 24% in 2050. By 2045 the non-Hispanic white population is projected to drop below 50%, with Hispanics making up more than a quarter of the population, and Asians, African Americans, and other ethnic groups constituting the rest (Overberg & Adamy, 2018). Immigration is projected to account for 88% of US population growth over the next 50 years, such that by 2055 there will be no majority racial or ethnic group.

Globally, the United Nations estimates that by 2060, for every 100 people of working age, there will be 30 people who are 65 and older. That is more than double the ratio of old to young people today. Because of low birth rates, the age wave is more acute in developed countries, increasing the cost of social programs and limiting economic growth. Younger migrants may ease that pain, however ("The first world is aging," 2015; Jordan, 2015).

In developed economies, many employers are unable to find people with the skill sets they need. By 2020, that talent gap could reach 1.5 million people in the United States and as many as 23 million in China (Lund, Ramaswamy, & Manyika, 2012; Qi, 2017). These trends have two key implications for managers: (1) The reduced supply of workers (at least in some fields) will make finding and keeping employees a top priority. (2) The task of managing a culturally diverse workforce, of harnessing the motivation and efforts of a wide variety of workers, will present a continuing challenge to management (Cascio, 2019).

Earlier we noted that more women than ever are found at all levels of organizations. Women constitute 47% of the US workforce, and they hold 52% of all managerial and professional positions. So much for the myth that women don't hold high-level business jobs because they supposedly don't aim high enough (Catalyst, 2016; U.S. Bureau of Labor Statistics, 2015). Age diversity is even more pronounced. At present, five generations comprise the US workforce: the *Silent Generation* (born 1930–1945); the *Baby Boom generation* (born 1946–1964); *Generation X* (born 1965–1980); *Generation Y*, also known as *Millennials* (born 1981–1995); and *Generation Z* (born 1996–2010).

Age-based stereotypes are common (Posthuma & Campion, 2009), particularly among older workers, but this is just as true for middle-aged and younger workers (Finkelstein, Ryan, & King, 2013). As those authors noted, supervisors can serve as powerful ambassadors of positive age-diverse interactions, both by embodying and facilitating positive views of outgroup members and by promoting open communication and treating people as individuals. To support an aging workforce, Truxillo, Cadiz, and Hammer (2015) outlined 11 possible interventions, from work redesign to optimizing total worker health.

In terms of generational similarities and differences, it is important to include sufficient experimental or statistical controls to avoid drawing inappropriate inferences from the data (see Kostanza Finkelstein, & Ravid, Chapter 2, this volume). That said, evidence from time-lag and cross-sectional studies suggests that, despite a number of similarities, the generations in today' s workplace differ in aspects of their personalities, work values and attitudes, leadership and teamwork preferences, leader behaviors, and career experiences (Lyons & Kuron, 2014; Twenge, 2010). Meta-analytic results, however, indicate that the relationships between generational membership and work-related outcomes (job satisfaction, organizational commitment, and intent to quit) are moderate to small, essentially zero in many cases. Differences that appear to exist are likely attributable to factors other than generational membership (Costanza, Badger, Fraser, Severt, & Gade, 2012). An overarching theme across studies, however, is that individualism characterizes all generations (Twenge, 2010). A question that remains, however, is the extent to which observed differences will remain stable or shift over time as the generations move through their respective life courses and career stages.

What are the implications for leaders? First, individual differences are always bigger than generational differences (Schumpeter, 2015). Generational differences are manifestations of broader trends in society and work that continue to evolve as the generations move through their respective life courses. Leaders cannot simply assume that past management practices will work in the modern context and that today's practices will work in the future (Lyons & Kuron, 2014). The bottom line is that workforce diversity is not just a competitive advantage. Today it's a competitive necessity.

Having examined some key trends in the world of work, the next sections of the chapter consider briefly how each one is affecting recruitment. Keep in mind that although we consider these trends separately, in reality they interact in tangible and intangible ways.

Implications of Technology for Recruitment

It is no exaggeration to say that the Internet has revolutionized recruitment practice. For the nearly 20% of the world's workforce who change jobs each year, there are more than 50,000 sites globally, as well as the ability to research employers and to network (Maurer, 2016a). Fully 92% of companies use social media for recruitment, and 45% of *Fortune* 500 firms include links to social media on their career-page sections. About a third of LinkedIn's revenue comes from corporate customers who buy rights for their recruiters to use LinkedIn's software as a service. This rapid evolution is expected to continue, with dynamic, customized job postings that use cookie-based targeting to communicate job advertisements to relevant individuals based on their online behaviors and the incorporation of mobile technology to access Internet-based job information (Dineen & Allen, 2014; Maurer, 2016b).

Implications of Social Media for Recruitment

Social media are inextricably linked to technology, and in this section we consider just two examples of how social media are revolutionizing the practice of recruitment. The first is LinkedIn. LinkedIn operates the world's largest professional network on the Internet, with more than 467 million members in more than 200 countries and territories. To put this fact into perspective, consider that professionals are signing up to join LinkedIn at a rate of more than two new members per second (About LinkedIn, 2017)! For a fee, organizations can sign up for a LinkedIn "Recruiter" account that allows access to the entire LinkedIn network. Designed specifically to match an organization's staffing workflow, Recruiter's user interface includes more than 20 advanced search filters. Alternatively, an organization can create a search based on its ideal candidate. It can contact potential candidates using "InMail" and incorporate collaboration and productivity features as well as administrative functions to manage accounts. On the supply side, potential applicants can receive email alerts for new jobs posted on LinkedIn that match advanced search criteria that they specify, or postings that are recommended to them from a feature called "Jobs You May Be Interested In" (LinkedIn talent solutions, 2017).

In 2017 Facebook made it possible for businesses to create job postings and for job seekers to apply for those openings directly on the social network in the United States and Canada. In 2018, it expanded this feature to more than 40 countries. Businesses and the more than 2 billion people on Facebook can use the feature for free, which is geared toward helping local businesses find candidates nearby. New features allow businesses to create job posts, manage applications, and schedule interviews, entirely on mobile devices. Job seekers can set up job alerts for the types of roles that interest them (Chaykowski, 2018). As these two examples show, social media are having a huge impact on the practice of recruitment.

Implications of Big Data for Recruitment

Over the past several years, applicant-tracking software (ATS) has helped many organizations eliminate operational problems in the recruitment process. Through cloud- or computer-based applications, firms have reengineered the entire recruitment process. ATS applications have evolved from résumé databases to well-rounded recruitment-optimization tools – cloud-based models that incorporate intuitive interfaces and tools that allow recruiters to cast a wider net for candidates (Maurer, 2017b; Zielinski, 2015, 2017).

Applicant-tracking systems such as IBM Kenexa BrassRing, Greenhouse, or SmartRecruiters have intuitive interfaces and tools as well as robust analytics with "dashboards" that illustrate key recruitment metrics (Maurer, 2017a; Zielinski, 2015). Fully 75% of hiring and talent acquisition managers use applicant tracking or recruiting software to improve the hiring process (Kandefer, 2017).

For example, organizations want to know how long it takes candidates to move through interview stages, how that influences dropout rates, and where recruiters spend the most time. IBM Watson helps recruiters measure the degree of effort required to fill certain job openings, helps prioritize job requisitions, accurately predicts the likelihood of candidates being successful, and performs social-media "listening" to create insights that help recruiters improve their messages to candidates. Greenhouse's ATS automatically sends a recruiter a pop-up email form when candidates are rejected, reminding him or her to communicate with that candidate. More broadly, the ability to communicate automatically with candidates as their applications move from one stage to another is a game changer for many companies, helping to improve the talent-acquisition process (Wright, 2017b; Zielinski, 2017).

Implications of HR Technology and Information Systems for Recruitment

Some applicant-tracking systems include features that record and analyze data to meet equal employment opportunity (EEO) and government-contractor requirements. They track where each applicant is in the recruitment process, and they generate reports that analyze the relative performance of alternative recruitment sources and strategies. To market their job openings more strategically, some employers are using real simple syndication (RSS) to reach job seekers via email or text message as soon as a new job is posted. Finally, some HRIS self-service portals allow applicants to manage multiple applications at once as their multimedia résumés display text, photos, videos, and sound. External websites like Glassdoor.com and TheJobCrowd.com allow job seekers to research an employer's brand and decide if they even want to apply for a job there. Those sites provide information about the culture and values of an organization and its senior managers, interview questions, and salaries. The sites are like "Trip Advisor" for jobs.

Implications of Globalization for Recruitment

Globalization is deepening and expanding, as most of the world continues to pursue free trade. At the same time, it is no exaggeration to say that the Internet has revolutionized recruitment practice. Why? Because that's where the action is. Despite the allure of commercial job search sites, evidence indicates that it took an average of about 15 applications to different employers to get a job through an online job site vs. 10 for those who applied directly to the company and 6 for those who were referred (Maurer, 2016a). The top ten job sites in 2017 were Indeed.com, CareerBuilder.com, Dice.com, Glassdoor.com, Idealist.com, LinkedIn.com, LinkUp.com, Monster.com, and SimplyHired.com (Doyle, 2017).

According to the McKinsey Global Institute, some 900 million people have international connections on social media, and 360 million take part in cross-border e-commerce (McKinsey Global Institute, 2016). Digital platforms for both traditional employment and freelance assignments are beginning to create more global labor markets as employers and job seekers find each other on the Internet. That allows companies to find the best person for a job anywhere in the world. In this increasingly digital era of globalization, companies can sell into fast-growing markets while keeping virtual teams connected in real time.

Implications of Demographics for Recruitment

Earlier we examined demographic trends in the United States and globally. Implications for organizations everywhere are clear. Their efforts to recruit new workers should focus on finding qualified employees who best fit the organization's values and HR practices rather than attempting to craft strategies to attract the average member of a generation. For example, an organization that emphasizes high commitment might emphasize work–life fit and flexible schedules, while looking for workers who are enthusiastic and hardworking, and who have the requisite skills and experience the organization needs (Cascio & Aguinis, 2019). In the future, organizations that thrive will be those that embrace the new demographic trends instead of fighting them. That will mean even more women and minorities in the workforce – and in the boardrooms.

Clearly, employers should use women and members of underrepresented groups (1) in their HR offices as interviewers; (2) on recruiting trips to high schools, colleges, and job fairs; and (3) in employment advertisements. These are necessary, but not sufficient, steps. Diverse candidates consider broader factors in their decisions to apply or to remain with organizations. One study found that although as many as 44% of African American candidates said they eliminated a company from consideration because of a lack of gender or ethnic diversity, three other diversity-related attributes affected their decisions to apply or remain: the ready availability of training and career-development programs, the presence of a diverse upper management, and the presence of a diverse workforce. It's not just hiring. People want to feel like they belong (Babcock, 2017; Volpone, Thomas, Sinisterra, & Johnson, 2014).

The key is to signal to prospective applicants from under-represented groups that an organization values diversity. Other ways to do that are to incorporate diversity into the corporate vision statement, for the CEO to meet regularly with employee resource groups, and to review diversity metrics and progress regularly. Above all, recognize two things: (1) It will take time to establish a credible, workable diversity-oriented recruitment program and (2) there is no payoff from simply waiting for members of under-represented groups to apply for jobs. Progressive organizations gather data on whom, when, and where they recruit and how they fare with different groups. The goal is to create a consistent corporate image that will support recruiting efforts across the board (Parsi, 2017).

Management Strategies to Maximize Retention

Who wouldn't want this job (Deal, 2007)?

- You are well paid
- You do interesting work
- You have the opportunity to advance
- You have the opportunity to learn and develop
- You have a supportive boss
- You work with peers and subordinates you trust
- You are treated with respect
- You have leaders who are credible and trustworthy
- And we might add, you have a pretty good fit between your work and your life

For many organizations, these are aspirational goals rather than features that employees actually experience every day at work. Yet they capture much of what we might call a "healthy" organization. Negative experiences on any one or more of them often lead employees to quit their jobs. In fact, research by the Society for Human Resource Management revealed that up to 20% of employee turnover happens within the first 45 days after hire (Provencher, 2018). This is why effective onboarding programs are so important. The best ones address issues such as the following (Cascio, 2019):

- *Entering a group* – concerns every new employee has about whether he or she will (a) be acceptable to the other group members, (b) be liked, and (c) be safe – that is, free from physical and psychological harm. These issues must be resolved before the new employee can feel comfortable and productive.
- *Naive expectations.* One reason employees often leave is that what they were told by recruiters does not match what they actually experienced on the job. Often, employees are on their own to figure out information about employee norms (rules or guides to acceptable behavior), company attitudes, or "what it really takes to get ahead around here." Simple fairness suggests that employees ought to be told about these intangibles. The bonus is that being up front and honest with them produces positive results. Indeed, an entire body of research on realistic job previews (RJPs) indicates that job acceptance rates will likely be lower for those who receive an RJP, but job survival rates will be higher (Hom, 2011; Landis, Earnest, & Allen, 2014; Phillips, 1998).
- *First-job environment.* The best programs use peers to socialize the new employee to desired job standards, they explain the how and the why of the new employee's first job assignment, and they are very clear about what she or he can expect to get out of it.

What does research tell us about why people quit their jobs? A study at Facebook uncovered three key reasons: the job wasn't enjoyable, people weren't able to use their strengths, and they were not growing in their careers. Among those who stayed, they found their work more enjoyable 31% more often, used their strengths 33% more often, and expressed 37% more confidence that they were gaining the skills and experiences they need to advance their careers (Goler, Gale, Harrington, & Grant, 2018). As these authors noted: "When you have a manager who cares about your happiness and your success, your career and your life, you end up with a better job, and it's hard to imagine working anywhere else."

Note the similarity of those findings to items in the bulleted list at the beginning of this section. Other research supports these findings (Rathi & Lee, 2017; Tian, Harvey, & Slocum, 2014). Employee engagement clearly plays an important role in retention (Harter, Schmidt, & Asplund, 2010; Harter, Schmidt, & Hayes, 2002; Kundu & Latta, 2017), but so also do factors such as short-term incentives, for example, "stay" bonuses and restricted stock units that vest over time (Miller, 2016) as well as employer branding (Tanwar & Prasad, 2016). The mission, vision, and purpose of a company are critical factors in retention (PwC International, 2016), and much can be learned from exit interviews, particularly about what works and what does not work inside an organization. Yet the most important measure of exit interviews is the positive change they generate (Spain & Groysberg, 2016).

Retention is a process that starts the first day an employee reports for work. Regular "check-ins" between managers and their direct reports should explore three themes: Are we helping you be effective in your current job? Are we helping you build a successful career? Are we helping you have a fulfilling life? (Spain & Groysberg, 2016). Some firms are using talent analytics to predict the likelihood that employees will stay or leave. While the content of their algorithms is typically proprietary, researchers recommend regular monitoring of factors such as job satisfaction, organizational commitment, job embeddedness, organizational shocks, and willingness to stay (Lee, Hom, Eberly, & Li, 2018).

Conclusion

Many factors are helping to shape the future world of work. We examined the impact of six of them briefly in this chapter: (1) technology, (2) social media, (3) big data, (4) HR technology and information systems, (5) globalization, and (6) demographics. Then we considered how each of these six areas is affecting recruitment. Finally, the chapter concluded with a short review of research-based strategies that managers can use to enhance the retention of the talent that they worked so hard to recruit.

References

About LinkedIn. Retrieved January 10, 2017, from https://press.linkedin.com/about-linkedin

Aeppel T. (2015, February 24). What clever robots mean for jobs: Experts rethink belief that tech always lifts employment as machines take on skills once thought uniquely human. *Wall Street Journal.* Retrieved February 25, 2015, from www.wsj.com/articles/what-clever-robots-mean-for-jobs-1424835002

Alge, B. J., & Hansen, S. D. (2014). Workplace monitoring and surveillance research since 1984: A review and agenda. In M. D. Coovert and L. F. Thompson (Eds.), *The psychology of workplace technology* (pp. 209–237). New York, NY: Routledge.

Autor, D. H., Dorn, D., and Hanson, G. H. (2016). The China shock: Learning from labor-market adjustment to large changes in trade. *Annual Review of Economics, 8,* 205–40.

Babcock, P. (2017, February 24). 5 steps to improve diversity recruiting. *SHRM online.* Retrieved February 26, 2017, from www.shrm.org/resourcesandtools/hr-topics/talent-acquisition/pages/five-steps-improve-diversity-recruiting.aspx

Broadbent, E. (2017). Interactions with robots: The truths we reveal about ourselves. *Annual Review of Psychology, 68,* 627–652.

Brynjolfsson, E. & McAfee, D. (2014). *The second machine age: Work, progress, and prosperity in a time of brilliant technologies.* New York, NY: W.W. Norton.

Cascio, W. F. (2017). How technology is changing work and organizations. In J. Markoff (Chair), *The future of work*. Symposium presented at the World Conference of Science Journalists, San Francisco, CA, October 2017.

Cascio, W. F. (2019). *Managing human resources: Productivity, quality of work life, profits* (11th ed.). New York, NY: McGraw-Hill.

Cascio, W. F., & Aguinis, H. (2019). *Applied psychology in talent management* (8th ed.). Thousand Oaks, CA: Sage.

Cascio, W. F., & Montealegre, R. (2016). How technology is changing work and organizations. *Annual Review of Organizational Psychology and Organizational Behavior*, *3*, 349–375.

Cascio, W. F., & Montealegre, R. (2017). Technology-driven changes in work and employment. *Communications of the ACM*, *60*(12), 60–67.

Catalyst. (2016, August 11). Women in the workforce: United States. Retrieved from www.catalyst.org/knowledge/women-workforce-united-states#footnoteref21_5e42rs9

Chaykowski, K. (2018, February 28). Facebook takes on LinkedIn and Glassdoor, expanding its job-posting tool to 40 countries. *Forbes*. Retrieved March 9, 2018, from www.forbes.com/sites/kathleenchaykowski/2018/02/28/facebook-expands-jobs-postings-to-40-countries-taking-on-linkedin-glassdoor/#4727c58a207f

Colbert, A., Yee, N., & George, G. (2016). The digital workforce and the workplace of the future. *Academy of Management Journal*, *59*, 731–739.

Coovert, M. D., and Thompson, L. F. (Eds.). (2014). *The psychology of workplace technology*. New York, NY: Routledge.

Costanza, D., Badger, J., Fraser, R., Severt, J., & Gade, P. (2012). Generational differences in work-related attitudes: A meta-analysis. *Journal of Business and Psychology*, *27*(4), 375–394.

Deal, J. J. (2007). *Retiring the generation gap*. New York, NY: Wiley.

Dineen, B. R., & Allen, D. G. (2014). Internet recruiting 2.0: Shifting paradigms. In K. Y. T. Yu & D. M. Cable (Eds.), *The Oxford handbook of recruitment*, Oxford, UK: Oxford University Press, pp. 382–401.

Doyle, A. (2017, January 31). Top 10 best job websites. Retrieved April 13, 2017, from www.thebalance.com/top-best-job-websites-2064080

Dulebohn, J. H., & Hoch, J. E. (2017). Virtual teams in organizations. *Human Resource Management Review*, *27*, 569–574.

Economist Intelligence Unit. (2014, February). *What's next: Future global trends affecting your organization*. Alexandria, VA: SHRM Foundation.

Finkelstein, L. M., Ryan, K., and King, E. B. (2013). What do the young (old) people think of me? Content and accuracy of age-based meta-stereotypes. *European Journal of Work and Organizational Psychology*, *22*(6), 633–657.

Friedman, T. L. (2016). *Thank you for being late: An optimist's guide to thriving in the age of accelerations*. New York, NY: Farrar, Straus & Giroux.

Ghemawat, P. (2017). Globalization in the age of Trump. *Harvard Business Review*, July–August, 10–23.

Goler, L., Gale, J., Harrington, B., & Grant, A. (2018). Why people really quit their jobs. *Harvard Business Review*, January. Retrieved from https://hbr.org/2018/01/why-people-really-quit-their-jobs?referral=03759&cm_vc=rr_item_page.bottom

Harter, J. K., Schmidt, F. L., & Hayes, T. L. (2002). Business-unit-level relationship between employee satisfaction, employee engagement, and business outcomes: A meta-analysis. *Journal of Applied Psychology*, *87*, 268–279.

Harter, J. K., Schmidt, F. L., & Asplund, J. W. (2010). Causal impact of employee work perceptions on the bottom line of organizations. *Perspectives on Psychological Science*, 5, 378–389.

Hom, P. W. (2011). Organizational exit. In S. Zedeck (Ed.), *Handbook of industrial and organizational psychology, Vol. 2* (pp. 325–75). Washington, DC: American Psychological Association.

How to use social media for applicant screening. (2016, August 10). Retrieved October 12, 2016, from www.shrm.org/resourcesandtools/tools-and-samples/how-to guides/pages/howtousesocialmediaforapplicantscreening.aspx

Jordan, M. (2015). Asians to surpass Hispanics as largest foreign-born group in US by 2055. *Wall Street Journal*, September 28. Retrieved from www.wsj.com/articles/asians-to-surpass-hispanics-as-largest-foreign-born-group-in-u-s-by-2055-1443412861

Kandefer, K. (2017, January 14). 50 recruitment stats HR pros must know in 2017. Retrieved October 21, 2017, from https://devskiller.com/50-recruitment-stats-hr-pros-must-know-2017/

King, A. G., and Mrkonich, M. (2016, October 7). The legal risks of "big data": What HR should know. Retrieved October 8, 2016, from www.shrm.org/resourcesandtools/legal-and-compliance/employment-law/pages/legal-risks-of-big-data.aspx

Landis, R. S., Earnest, D. R., & Allen, D. G. (2014). Realistic job previews: Past, present, and future. In K. Y. T. Yu and D. M. Cable (Eds.), *The Oxford handbook of recruitment*. Oxford, UK: Oxford University Press, pp. 423–436.

Lee, T. W., Hom, P., Eberly, M., & Li, J. (2018). Managing employee retention and turnover with 21st-century ideas. *Organizational Dynamics*, 47, 88–98.

LinkedIn talent solutions. Retrieved January 10, 2017, from https://business.linkedin.com/talent-solutions/recruiter

Loten, A. (2017). AI to drive job growth by 2020: Gartner. *Wall Street Journal*, December 15. Retrieved from https://blogs.wsj.com/cio/2017/12/15/ai-to-drive-job-growth-by-2020-gartner/

Lund, S., Ramaswamy, S, & Manyika, J. (2012). Preparing for a new era of work. *McKinsey Quarterly*, November. Retrieved from www.mckinsey.com/business-functions/organization/our-insights/preparing-for-a-new-era-of-work.

Lyons, S., & Kuron, L. (2014). Generational differences in the workplace: A review of the evidence and directions for future research. *Journal of Organizational Behavior*, 35, S139–S157.

Manyika, J., Lund, S., Chui, M., Bughin, J., Woetzel, J., Batra, P., Ko, R., & Sanghvi, S. (2017, November) What the future of work will mean for jobs, skills, and wages. *McKinsey Global Institute*. Retrieved November 15, 2017, from www.mckinsey.com/global-themes/future-of-organizations-and-work/what-the-future-of-work-will-mean-for-jobs-skills-and-wages

Maurer, R. (2016a, January 14). Internet is primary resource for job seekers worldwide. Retrieved January 26, 2016, from www.shrm.org/resourcesandtools/hr-topics/talent-acquisition/pages/internet-job-seekers-worldwide.aspx

Maurer, R. (2016b, February 2). The most sought-after talent prefer mobile recruitment. *SHRM online*. Retrieved February 14, 2016, from www.shrm.org/resourcesandtools/hr-topics/talent-acquisition/pages/talent-prefer-mobile-recruitment.aspx

Maurer, R. (2017a, February 23). 2017 recruiting trends point to technology driving change. *SHRM online*. Retrieved February 25, 2017, from www.shrm.org/resourcesandtools/hr-topics/talent-acquisition/pages/recruiting-trends-2017-technology-change.aspx

Maurer, R. (2017b, February 2). "Siri for recruiting" set to debut this year. *SHRM online*. Retrieved February 3, 2017, from www.shrm.org/resourcesandtools/hr-topics/talent-acquisition/pages/siri-for-recruiting-debut-2017-hiringsolved.aspx

Maynard, M. T., Gilson, L., Jones-Young, N. C., and Vartiainen, M. (2017). Virtual teams. In G. Hertel, D. Stone, R. Johnson, and J. Passmore. *The psychology of the internet at work*. Chichester, UK: Wiley-Blackwell.

McAfee, A., and Brynjolfsson, E. (2012). Big data: The management revolution. *Harvard Business Review*, October, pp. 60–67.

McGovern, M. (2017). *Thriving in the gig economy: How to capitalize and compete in the new world of work*. Wayne, NJ: Career Press/New Page Books.

McKinsey Global Institute. (2016, February). Digital globalization: The new era of global flows. Retrieved April 7, 2016, from www.mckinsey.com/business-functions/digital-mckinsey/our-insights/digital-globalization-the-new-era-of-global-flows

Miller, S. (2016, March 21). Private companies typically award an incentive pay mix. *SHRM online*. Retrieved March 22, 2016, from www.shrm.org/resourcesandtools/hr-topics/compensation/pages/incentive-pay-mix.aspx

Murphy, M. (2017). Debrief: Ginni Rometty. *Bloomberg Businessweek*, September 25, pp. 62–65.

Murray A. (2015, May 1). The new industrial revolution. *Fortune*, p. 6.

Olmstead, K., Lampe, C. & Ellison, N. B. (2016). Social media and the workplace. *Pew Research Center*. Retrieved January 10, 2018, from www.pewinternet.org/2016/06/22/social-media-and-the-workplace/

Overberg, P., & Adamy, J. (2018). Elderly in US are projected to outnumber children for first time. *Wall Street Journal*, March 13, p. A2.

Oxford Living Dictionaries. Retrieved December 29, 2016, from https://en.oxforddictionaries.com/definition/technology

Parsi, N. (2017, January 16). Workplace diversity and inclusion gets innovative. *SHRM online*. Retrieved January 19, 2017, from www.shrm.org/hr-today/news/hr-magazine/0217/pages/disrupting-diversity-in-the-workplace.aspx

Phillips, J. M. (1998). Effects of realistic job previews on multiple organizational outcomes: A meta-analysis. *Academy of Management Journal*, 41, pp. 673–690.

Posthuma, R. A., and Campion, M. A. (2009). Age stereotypes in the workplace: Common stereotypes, moderators, and future research directions. *Journal of Management*, 35, 158–188.

Provencher, T. (2018, February 13). Viewpoint: How to encourage new employees to stick around. *SHRM online*. Retrieved February 14, 2018, from www.shrm.org/resourcesandtools/hr-topics/employee-relations/pages/viewpoint-how-to-encourage-new-employees-to-stick-around.aspx

PwC International. (2016). Millennials at work. Retrieved May 12, 2017, from www.pwc.com/gx/en/financial-services/publications/assets/pwc-millenials-at-work.pdf

Qi, L. (2017). China lays out population forecast. *Wall Street Journal*, January 26, p. A7.

Rathi, N., & Lee, K. (2017). Understanding the role of supervisor support in retaining employees and enhancing their satisfaction with life. *Personnel Review, 46*, 1605–1619.

Roberts, B. (2013). The benefits of big data. *HRMagazine*, October, pp. 21–30.

Ryan, R. M., and Deci, E. L. (2017). *Self-determination theory: Basic psychological needs in motivation, development, and wellness.* New York, NY: Guilford.

Schumpeter. (2015). Myths about millennials. *The Economist*, August 1. Retrieved from www.economist.com/node/21660110#print

Silverman, R. E. (2016). Bosses tap outside firms to predict which workers might get sick. *Wall Street Journal*, February 16. Retrieved from www.wsj.com/articles/bosses-harness-big-data-to-predict-which-workers-might-get-sick-1455664940

Society for Human Resource Management. (2016, January 19). Managing and leveraging workplace use of social media. *SHRM online.* Retrieved August 18, 2017, from www.shrm.org/ResourcesAndTools/tools-and samples/toolkits/Pages/managingsocialmedia.aspx

Spain, E., & Groysberg, B. (2016). Making exit interviews count. *Harvard Business Review*, April, 88–95.

Staff.com. (2016). Social media for recruitment – infographic. Retrieved January 10, 2018, from https://blog.staff.com/social-media-for-recruitment-infographic/

Statista. (2017). The most famous social network sites worldwide as of September 2017, ranked by number of active users (in millions). Retrieved January 10, 2018, from www.statista.com/statistics/272014/global-social-networks-ranked-by-number-of-users/

Tanwar, K., & Prasad, A. (2016). Exploring the relationship between employer branding and employee retention. *Global Business Review, 17*(3S), 186S–206S.

The first world is aging. (2015). *Fortune*, October 1, p. 16.

Tian, X., Harvey, M., & Slocum, J. W. (2014). The retention of Chinese managers: The Chinese puzzle box. *Organizational Dynamics, 43*(1), 44–52.

Truxillo, D. M., Cadiz, D. M., & Hammer, L. B. (2015). Supporting the aging workforce: A review and recommendations for workplace intervention research. *Annual Review of Organizational Psychology and Organizational Behavior, 2*, 351–381.

Twenge, J. (2010). A review of the empirical evidence on generational differences in work attitudes. *Journal of Business and Psychology, 25*, 201–210.

U.S. Bureau of Labor Statistics. (2015, December). Women in the labor force: A databook. Retrieved from www.bls.gov/opub/reports/womens-databook/archive/women-in-the-labor-force-a-databook-2015.pdf

Volpone, S. D., Thomas, K. M., Sinisterra, P., and Johnson, L. (2014). Targeted recruiting: Identifying future employees. In K. Y. T. Yu and D. M. Cable (Eds.), *The Oxford handbook of recruitment.* Oxford, UK: Oxford University Press, pp. 110–125.

Walker, J. (2012). Meet the new boss: Big data. Companies trade in hunch-based hiring for computer modeling. *Wall Street Journal*, September 20, pp. B1, B2.

Weber, J. (2014). Should companies monitor their employees' social media? *Wall Street Journal*, October 22. Retrieved May 17, 2015, from www.wsj.com/articles/should-companies-monitor-their-employees-social-media-1399648685

World Economic Forum & Boston Consulting Group. (2011). *Global talent risk – Seven responses.* Cologny/Geneva, Switzerland: Author.

Wooldridge, A. (2015). The Icarus syndrome meets the wearable revolution. *Korn/Ferry Briefings on Talent and Leadership*, 6, pp. 27–33.

Wright, A. D. (2017a, March 6). Social postings still land employees in hot water. *SHRM online*. Retrieved March 8, 2017, from www.shrm.org/resourcesandtools/hr-topics/technology/pages/social-postings-still-land-employees-in-hot-water.aspx

Wright, A. D. (2017b, August 25). Job seekers are frustrated with automated recruiting. *SHRM online*. Retrieved August 26, 2017, from www.shrm.org/resourcesandtools/hr-topics/technology/pages/candidates-soured-too-much-technology.aspx

Zielinski, D. (2015, October 1). 7 reasons to love your ATS. *SHRM online*. Retrieved October 3, 2015, from www.shrm.org/hr-today/news/hr-magazine/pages/1015-applicant-tracking-systems.aspx

Zielinski, D. (2016). An HRM for everyone. *HR Magazine*, *61*(10), 47–50.

Zielinski, D. (2017, February 13). Recruiting gets smart thanks to artificial intelligence. *SHRM online*. Retrieved February 15, 2017, from www.shrm.org/resourcesandtools/hr-topics/technology/pages/recruiting-gets-smart-thanks-to-artificial-intelligence.aspx

16 Performance Management and the Changing Nature of Work

Deidra J. Schleicher and Heidi M. Baumann

Performance management (PM) has been defined as "a continuous process of identifying, measuring, and developing the performance of individuals and teams and aligning performance with the strategic goals of the organization" (Aguinis, 2013, p. 2). The vast majority of organizations (91%, according to Cascio, 2006) practice PM in one form or another, and PM has been the subject of an incredibly voluminous research literature in industrial–organizational psychology, human resources, and organizational behavior (as well as other fields). Like many other aspects of the world of work discussed in this handbook, PM has undergone substantial changes over the years (see, e.g., Hedge & Borman, 1995; Levy, Tseng, Rosen, & Lueke, 2017; Levy & Williams, 2004). This chapter will discuss both (a) the changing nature of PM practice and research as well as (b) the PM-related implications of other, more general, changes in the nature of work.

The Changing Nature of PM

PM Practice

In many ways, the PM landscape is very different than it was even just ten years ago. This is true for both research and practice, and because, historically, PM research tends to lag PM practice, we first discuss practice. There have been unprecedented changes to PM in practice, many with little substantiation or support from research (Levy et al., 2017). Some of these changes have been the subject of heated debates in the literature and amongst practitioners, such as doing away with performance ratings or other formal aspects of PM (e.g., Adler et al., 2016). As Levy et al. (2017) recently noted, one "can do a simple Google search [on PM] and tap into the uproar" (p. 156).

These more specific changes can be situated within the historical evolution of PM practices in general. First, as Alan Colquitt (2017) illustrates in his recent book, PM systems in organizations have evolved over time to address several different purposes and needs (ultimately, simultaneously), all reflecting varying historical influences (e.g., more objectively measuring performance to provide a better basis for promotion decisions; legal defensibility; management by objectives and total quality management, with the goal of restoring humaneness to

PM; and most recently, a focus on future performance and development; see also Cappelli & Tavis's 2016 discussion of the tug-of-war between accountability and development in PM over the decades). Unfortunately, as Colquitt (2017) eloquently notes, "All of these influences were additive, like barnacles attaching themselves to a log, one on top of the other" (p. 10), with the result being that PM systems in organizations today are simply asked to do too much.

Second, and related, PM has evolved over time to be much more than performance appraisal (PA). The term PM is generally agreed to have originated when practitioners (and eventually scholars) started talking about transforming PA from an event to a process (see Bretz, Milkovich, & Read, 1992; Kinicki, Jacobson, Peterson, & Prussia, 2013; Williams, 1997). PA has typically been conceptualized as "a discrete, formal, organizationally sanctioned event, usually not occurring more frequently than once or twice a year"; PM, on the other hand, is understood to be a broader set of ongoing activities aimed at managing employee performance (DeNisi & Pritchard, 2006, p. 254; Williams, 1997). PA also focuses more squarely on the measurement/assessment of performance; as such, it can be thought of as a subset of the broader phenomenon of PM (see Levy et al., 2017; Schleicher et al., 2018).

Third, partially in response to the "barnacle" situation noted above, there has been a growing trend recently to intentionally streamline PM processes in organizations. For example, in their book, *One Page Talent Management*, Effron and Ort (2010) advocate for streamlining PM processes (and other aspects of talent management) by removing their "low value" aspects; and Buckingham and Goodall (2015) report in *Harvard Business Review* how Deloitte recently greatly streamlined its PM processes. Falling into this category of PM change is the recent practice of eliminating performance ratings. Companies ranging from the technology sector to professional service firms to manufacturing are eliminating their formal rating process (Cappelli & Tavis, 2016), and this trend has resulted in a heated debate that spans both practice and research ("The pros and cons of retaining performance ratings were the subject of a lively, standing-room-only debate at the 2015 Society for Industrial and Organizational Psychology conference in Philadelphia," Adler et al., 2016). Many of the current efforts around streamlining PM processes are characterized by a concomitant increasing focus on development and learning. Cappelli and Tavis (2016), for example, describe the recent PM revolution as a shift "from accountability to learning" (p. 2); and Buckingham and Goodall (2015) describe one of the hallmarks of Deloitte's new system as "constant learning" (p. 42). Although this trend again in some ways feels cyclical, given admonitions from Deming and other Total Quality Management (TQM) devotees in the 1980s about performance appraisal being one of the "seven deadly diseases" of management and therefore something to be excised (Deming, 1986), the justification is somewhat different. The traditional TQM view of performance is that it is 90–95% about the system and processes, not individual employees; such a view would be at odds with even a more developmentally oriented, informal feedback view of PA and PM.

PM Research

Has PM research evolved in ways commensurate to changes in PM practice? A very recent review (Schleicher et al., 2018) comparing older and more recent work in this area suggests the answer is both yes and no. On the one hand, recent research has expanded to include examination of several explicitly development-focused PM approaches, such as "feedforward" interviews (Kluger & Nir, 2010) and strengths-based performance evaluation (Bouskila-Yam & Kluger, 2011). In addition, according to Schleicher et al. (2018), although the performance evaluation aspect of PM is still the most frequently studied component of PM (and in fact is more frequent in recent research compared to older research), feedback is the second most commonly studied component (and is also more frequently represented in recent, as opposed to older, research).

At the same time, performance ratings continue to receive a "disproportionate focus" (Adler et al. 2016) as outcomes of the PM process. Indeed, Schleicher et al. (2018) found that a full 76% of studies explicitly examining an outcome of PM focused on performance ratings; the next most common outcome was recommendations regarding administrative decisions (15% of these studies). Examination of feedback (6%), career planning (3%), and development plans (2%) as outcomes of PM is much less frequent in research. (These statistics refer to research that empirically examined the *quality of these types of outcomes* of PM; as noted in the prior paragraph, there is more research whose contextual focus is on the feedback component of PM.) In addition, there continues to be a lack of strong research on some aspects of PM that are a large focus in practice, such as coaching (see, e.g., Gregory & Levy, 2010, 2011, 2012; Gregory, Levy, & Jeffers, 2008). The elimination of performance ratings is another specific area where practice has far outpaced research, and there is unfortunately almost no empirical work examining what the impact of such a practice might be (see Payne & Mendoza, 2017). Finally, as Schleicher et al. (2018) point out, the research literature overall lacks sufficient evidence necessary for decisions related to streamlining various aspects of PM, as there has been no work directed at how essential each component of PM actually is (vis-à-vis the other components) and how the various components fit (e.g., interact with one another) within the broader PM system. In the absence of such evidence, they conclude that any recommendations such as doing away with performance ratings are premature. Thus, in these important ways, the research literature in PM still seems somewhat inadequate for addressing the key trends in the practice of PM.

A Systems-Based View of PM

Schleicher et al. (2018) have argued, based on the above observations, for a more explicit systems-based approach to the study of PM. A system, simply put, is a set of interrelated elements, such that a change in one element affects other elements in the system; and an open system is one that also interacts with its environment (Katz & Kahn, 1978). The interrelated components of a system are designed to work together and function as a whole to achieve a common purpose (Boulding, 1956). Although PM processes in organizations are often referred to as PM *systems*, historically PM has not been researched in this way. We adopt the Schleicher et al. systems-based PM model here, as it is instructive both with regard to the changing nature of PM as well as understanding the PM-related implications of other, more general, changes in the nature of work.

The pragmatic value of systems models such as this is in identifying which factors (out of a possibly infinite set) are most critical or important for understanding the functioning of the system (Nadler & Tushman, 1980). The need for this in the PM literature has been previously noted (Lawler, 2003), and it has become more pronounced over time, as the field has evolved from PA to the broader area of PM and as the relevant literature continues to grow at an exponential rate. At its broadest level, the Schleicher et al. (2018) model shows that understanding PM is a function of six critical components: Inputs, Tasks, Individuals, Formal Processes, Informal Processes, and Outputs. Here we briefly review each of these components, to set the stage for our discussion of how these components of PM have changed over time as well as how these PM components, theoretically, are likely to be impacted by the changing nature of work.

Schleicher et al. begin their model with a focus on the **Tasks** of PM. These refer to the "workflow" of the system (Nadler & Tushman, 1980), or the key activities involved in PM. These tasks represent the basic or inherent work to be done by the system, particularly in light of its strategy, and Schleicher et al. identify seven such tasks in PM: *setting performance expectations, observing employee performance, integrating performance information, the rendering of a formal summative performance evaluation, generating and delivering performance feedback, the formal performance review meeting, and performance coaching.*

Next, the **Inputs** represent the "givens" of the system – the materials the organization has to work with and the context in which it conducts its PM work. As such, they place demands and constraints on systems (Nadler & Tushman, 1980). Inputs include the environment (factors outside the PM system or the organization itself), resources, and strategy (organizational strategy, HR strategy, and, in this context, PM strategy; Collins-Camargo, Chuang, McBeath, & Bunger, 2014).

Third, **Individuals** refer to the characteristics and nature of the organizational members (their knowledge, skills, needs, personality, demographics, etc.) who perform the PM tasks; these are key factors thought to influence behavior on the tasks (Nadler & Tushman, 1980). The primary individuals implicated in PM tasks have traditionally been raters (especially managers) and ratees (employees).

Fourth, in this model, both formal and informal **Processes** are included. **Formal Processes** refer to structures, processes, and procedures that are explicitly developed to get individuals to perform PM tasks consistent with PM strategy and are often documented in writing. **Informal Processes**, in contrast, are unwritten, implicit, and emerge over time. They reflect both PM-related processes themselves (e.g., presence of informal feedback) as well as contextual factors that affect such processes (e.g., political climate surrounding PM).

Finally, **Outputs** refer to what is produced from the workflow of PM tasks. In the Schleicher et al. model these include the *performance rating(s)*; the *feedback generated and delivered*; the creation of a *development plan* or other *performance improvement plan*; *career planning*; *recommendations regarding administrative decisions*; and *documentation for legal purposes*.

Schleicher et al.'s (2018) review of the literature based on this model shows that both discussion and empirical examination of these various components of PM have changed over the years. For example, although PM research has historically underemphasized examination of Inputs, recent research has witnessed a significant increase in the study of Inputs. Indeed, it was this component of the Schleicher et al. model that has seen the greatest change in empirical research focus over time, in terms of number of studies. In addition, Schleicher et al. reported that recent research has broadened to examine multiple PM tasks beyond just evaluation, including feedback, coaching, and the setting of objectives (even though performance evaluation remains the most frequently studied task). Thus, it is not just that more recent PM research has shifted task focus, but that it tends to include a *broader* set of tasks, which is in-line with a systems-based evolution of PM. As discussed in the next section, some of these PM system components are more impacted by the changing nature of work than others, and we focus the remainder of the chapter on those.

The Changing Nature of Work and Its Implications for PM Systems

In this section we consider four aspects of the changing nature of work with particularly significant implications for PM systems: (a) changes in workers' skills and values, (b) shifts to flatter organizational structures and, consequently, expanded roles for employees, (c) advances in technology, and (d) globalization. First, Wegman et al. (2018) describe how both "popular and academic sources have proposed that employees increasingly value the opportunity for individual growth, skill development, flexibility, voice in important organizational decisions, and time spent completing significant and meaningful work" (p. 355). Further, Burke and Ng (2006) highlight the importance of continuous learning and updating of employees' knowledge and skills, given industry shifts to more knowledge-based work. Together these factors represent multiple changes in workers themselves which, as we discuss below, have significant implications for PM. Second, there are also significant changes in organizational structure, namely decentralization which leads to flatter organizations and, in turn, increases the need for collaboration between employees and results in various team-based structures (Burke & Ng, 2006). In addition, the increasing role scope and skill variety that accompany the flattening of organizational structures (Wegman et al., 2018) have some implications for how PM is done, as discussed further below. Third, organizations are increasingly impacted by changes in technology, and it has been suggested that technology is facilitating a new industrial revolution (editors' introduction to this handbook). Fourth, trends in globalization and related factors, such as outsourcing, global labor markets, the need for global collaboration, globally distributed works teams, and increased competition for talent, have far-reaching implications for both organizations and employees (Burke & Ng, 2006). In the remainder of the subsections here we consider recent research on three PM system components that have been particularly impacted by these changes in the nature of work: PM Inputs, Processes, and Individuals.

PM Inputs

Inputs are likely to be strongly implicated in the changing nature of work and its impact on PM. The PM literature has long acknowledged that such contextual variables are likely to be important for PM (e.g., Bretz et al., 1992; Ilgen et al., 1993; Klein, Snell, & Wexley, 1987; Murphy & Cleveland, 1991) while at the same time observing that very little empirical research exists on them. In their review, Levy and Williams (2004) labeled these factors "distal variables" ("broadly construed as contextual factors that affect many human resource systems, including [PA]," p. 885). They concluded in 2004 that such variables continue to receive very little research attention, other than a small number of studies on the impact of culture, climate, and technology in PA (e.g., Hebert & Vorauer, 2003; Miller, 2003). At the same time, they did identify the "context of PM" as an emerging theme in PM research, and it is one that has expanded over the years since their review.

The context surrounding PM has certainly undergone significant changes over the past few decades (den Hartog et al., 2004), including internationalization and the impact of culture and technology (Fletcher, 2001), as well as the emergence of new and different forms of organizations (see Burke & Ng, 2006; Knoke, 2000). Here we review the PM literature along several dimensions of context and other Inputs affected by the changing nature of work, including PM (a) in the global context; (b) under different ownership types and forms of organizational structure; and (c) in different industries/sectors of the economy. We then discuss the need for research to examine the PM-related implications of changes in other types of Inputs.

PM in a Global Context. Several recent studies have examined effects of the internationalization of an organization and of national culture on aspects of PM. First, regarding the former, stronger PM processes (e.g., more frequent and faster feedback, more comprehensive goal setting and performance evaluation), and better receptivity overall to PM, have been found in multinational (or more internationalized) firms as compared to domestic enterprises (Fee et al., 2011; Singh, Mohamed, and Darwish, 2013). It also appears that more globally integrated firms standardize their PM practices more than less integrated firms (except when the subsidiary is in a country with a more masculine culture than the firm's headquarters; see Claus & Briscoe, 2009, which provides a particularly good review of international PM research in general).

Second, national culture has been shown to be an important determinant of many aspects of PM, including choices about who should be evaluated and why (i.e., for what purpose). For example, Peretz and Fried (2012) examined approximately 6,000 organizations in 21 different countries and found that four cultural dimensions (i.e., power distance, individualism/collectivism, uncertainty avoidance, and future orientation) explained differences in PM practices across these organizations. They also found, importantly, that alignment between PM practices and the culture was important for outcomes. Research has also suggested that national culture can affect preferences for different types of PM (see Ellis, 2012), agreement between different rating sources (see Atwater, Smither, Wang, & Fleenor, 2009), and even the extent to which interpersonal affect biases performance ratings (see Varma, Pichler, & Srinivas, 2005). China is a specific cultural context that has been studied with some frequency in more recent PM research, and good discussions of PM in the Chinese context and the historical development of PM in China can be found in Taormina & Gao (2009) and in Tsai & Wang (2013, see pp. 2199–2200). Taken together, research in this area reveals that the alignment between national culture and aspects of PM appears to be particularly important for the effectiveness of PM.

PM across Ownership Type and Organizational Structure. Organizations have also changed with regard to form and structure (Burke & Ng, 2006; Knoke, 2000), and there has been greater growth in the private, as opposed to public, sector (Barua & Viechnicki, 2017). Some research has started examining the impact of these types of variables on PM, including public versus private organizations (e.g., Abu-Doleh & Weir, 2007; Shrivastava & Purang, 2011), whether organizations are management-controlled or owner-controlled (Silva & Tosi, 2004), and whether they are locally owned, foreign-owned, or jointly owned (Akuratiyagamage, 2005). This research suggests that private organizations tend to use PM more for key human capital decisions such as promotion and development, whereas public organizations tend to use PM more for legal compliance reasons (Abu-Doleh & Weir, 2007). In turn, private sector employees may perceive greater fairness and report higher satisfaction with PM than public sector employees (Shrivastava & Purang, 2011). Silva and Tosi (2004) found evidence of higher-quality performance evaluations in management-controlled than in owner-controlled firms, whereas Akuratiyagamage (2005) found no significant differences in type of PM across ownership type.

Organizational structure characteristics such as size, complexity, centralization, type of configuration, and union status, all of which have exhibited changes over the years (Burke & Ng, 2006), should theoretically impact PM.

Yet only a very few studies have examined such Input variables. Medcof and Song (2013) examined the PM-related implications of different HR configurations, finding that entrepreneurial (vs. cooperative) HR configurations resulted in less formal PM, less developmental feedback, and a weaker link between performance and compensation. Although unions have drastically declined in the US over the past 20 years (Dunn & Walker, 2016; see also Hogler, Chapter 9, this volume), union status is an example of an Input that could theoretically place constraints on PM, given that union employees' due process is mandated by the union contract and that PM elements such as goal setting must be implemented with safeguards (Brown & Warren, 2011). Yet Nurse (2005) found few differences between union and non-union employees' views of the procedural elements of PM, with the exception of interactional justice, which the non-union employees viewed significantly more positively than union employees.

Finally, research suggests that aspects of organizational culture and climate that are changing in recent times, including the extent to which the climate is participative and values employee engagement, also have implications for PM. For example, Tziner, Murphy, Cleveland, and Roberts-Thompson (2001) found that more participative climates can have a significant impact on raters' attitudes and behavior (in terms of rating elevation and discriminability); Haines and St-Onge (2012) found that a group-oriented culture where employee engagement is valued can strengthen the relationship between specific PM practices (e.g., rater training, multi-source feedback) and overall PM effectiveness; and Lievens, Conway, and De Corte (2008) found that, in more team-based cultures, more weight in the performance evaluation is given to citizenship behaviors and less to task performance, suggesting that raters may match their rating policy to the culture of the organization.

PM in Different Industries/Sectors. There have been shifts across the various sectors of the economy, with some sectors taking on greater (or lesser) significance over time (Knoke, 2000). This suggests the need to study PM across different sectors, particularly growing sectors such as technology and healthcare (Kacik, 2017). PM research has in fact recently begun to spread from primarily for-profit corporate settings to a number of different sectors and industries, including healthcare (e.g., Clarke, Harcourt, & Flynn, 2012) and not-for-profit contexts such as education (e.g., Irs & Türk, 2012) and especially public administration (e.g., Lee & Jimenez, 2011). As Lee and Jimenez have noted, PM is one of the key ingredients of a market-based public sector reform approach that has been gaining popularity in many countries, becoming "arguably one of the most important public management reform initiatives in the past two decades" (p. 168). Research in the nonprofit sector suggests that PM processes can generally be equally effective in this context (e.g., Becker et al., 2011). Rodwell and Teo (2008), for example, found that the effects of human capital-enhancing HR practices such as PM were generally similar in both for-profit and not-for-profit organizations (although some specific paths in the model differed by sector). At the same time, as systems theory would suggest, there are likely to be important differences in what specific PM process are most effective across different sectors. Thus, we believe it will become increasingly important for PM researchers to actively monitor growing sectors, especially those that are historically under-researched, to ensure that PM research is topical and providing much needed guidance in emerging industries.

Additional Research Needs on the Changing Nature of PM Inputs. Although recent research has demonstrated an increase in focus on Inputs (and other aspects of context) relative to older research, there remains an important need to study several additional aspects of the changing Inputs of PM. First, technology as a general input to PM systems should be examined. Although technical advancements in PM processes themselves have begun to be examined (see next section on changes in PM processes, and Krauss & Snyder, 2010), there has been little work on the PM-related implications of the more macro Input of general technological advances or development (Levy & Williams, 2004). For example, to the extent that an organization's investment in technology changes in accordance with organizational strategy, the PM system may be affected through vertical alignment considerations (Decramer, Smolders, & Vanderstraeten, 2013).

Second, research is needed on other "macro" Inputs, especially broader economic conditions. Such conditions obviously impact the resources available for PM, and earlier research (e.g., Balfour, 1992) has suggested that higher levels of investment in the PM system (with regard to, for example, training, materials, and other resources) are in fact positively associated with overall PM effectiveness. But as an Input, the broader economic conditions can also place both demands and constraints on PM systems. In fact, unlike some HR functions, economic crises seem to motivate an increasing interest in PM (Cabrera, Fernaud, Diaz, & Vilela, 2014). In higher education, for example, decreased resources resulting from fewer government funds have increased adoption of PM systems in attempts to increase efficiency and effectiveness (Decramer, Smolders, & Vanderstraeten, 2013). Yet there exists very little research empirically examining the implications of such changing economic conditions on the specifics of PM.

Third, the field also needs more research on *PM strategy* (i.e., what the organization is trying to accomplish with its PM system; Collins-Camargo et al., 2014). According to systems theory, the PM strategy should be critical, "because it determines the [PM] work to be performed by the organization and it defines desired [PM] outputs" (Nadler & Tushman, 1980), such as administrative decisions, development plans, career planning, and documentation. Yet there has been little empirical work in this area. The proposed central role of PM strategy necessitates greater attention to the various *purposes of PM*, which notably have evolved over time well beyond administrative decision making. As Levy and Williams (2004) noted, these systems also exist for purposes of employee development and for fostering feelings of ownership and perceptions of being valued and part of an organizational team. Additional categories of PM purpose that have been discussed in more recent research include employee socialization and organizational identification (Rahman, 2006; Wang, Tseng, Yen, & Huang, 2011); role definition and clarification (Youngcourt et al., 2007); cultural change (Wang et al., 2011); and organizational alignment (Ayers, 2013). Yet actual empirical examination of the effects of various purposes has generally been constrained to the more conventional purposes of PM, especially administration versus development (e.g., Boswell & Boudreau, 2000; Smither, London, & O'Reilly, 2005). And we know almost nothing about the implications of *changes* in PM purpose or other aspects of PM strategy over time within organizations.

Finally, given that Inputs appear to play a very important role in PM, we would encourage future researchers to be very explicit with regard to the context of the PM system under study, including national culture; industry; type of firm; organizational structure, strategy and culture; and especially purpose of the PM system. Our review of the literature suggests that very limited information on such Input variables is typically provided (for an exception, see Kleingeld, Van Tuijl, & Algera, 2004, who give a particularly detailed description of the PM context). And we found that more recent research is less, not more, likely to explicitly state the purpose of PM in the context under study. It is somewhat perplexing that, as the PM literature and our understanding of the importance of context in general (see Johns, 2018) have both evolved, recent researchers are less likely to describe this essential element. Such contextual descriptions will only become more important as the nature of work continues to evolve.

PM Processes

The changing nature of work also impacts many aspects of PM Processes, as discussed below. These changes have manifested most significantly with the Formal Processes of PM, but there are also impacts on Informal Process factors.

Technology and Online Systems. The advancement of technology in PM and the use of online systems is an area where PM practice has far outpaced research. In this area, the term "system" takes on an additional meaning; specifically, online PM systems fall under the broader umbrella of human resource information systems (HRIS; Payne, Horner, Boswell, Schroeder, & Stine-Cheyne, 2009). One empirical study found that online PM systems result in higher accountability and participation, but do not differ from traditional paper systems in terms of perceived security, user satisfaction, or utility (Payne et al., 2009). In another study, technology reduced feelings of social obligation such that peer evaluations conducted via email were more negative than peer evaluations completed on paper (Kurtzberg, Naquin, & Belkin, 2005).

Rating Format and Approach. As organizations decentralize and place greater emphasis on teamwork and collaboration, relative rating approaches may become less popular and more problematic. In particular, forced distribution rating systems (FDRS) have recently received considerable research attention, and studies demonstrate multiple hazards stemming from their use (e.g., Schleicher, Bull, & Green, 2009). Lawler (2003) describes FDRS as "an imposed bureaucratic solution to a real PM problem, rater leniency" (p. 403). In his study of 55 *Fortune* 500 companies, FDRS was found to accomplish its primary objective of differentiating employees, but this occurred at the expense of lowering the overall effectiveness of the PM system (as rated by senior HR executives in each company). In an organizational simulation, FDRS was linked to greater risk of an adverse impact violation, especially for larger organizations (Giumetti, Schroeder, & Switzer, 2015). Further, FDRS has been credited as a neutralizer of the relationship between psychological capital and performance (Rego, Marques, Leal, Sousa, & Pina e Cunha, 2010).

One issue related to specific PM approaches concerns the nature of the performance dimensions on which organizations focus. As the world of work changes, so too has this focus shifted, with organizations becoming increasingly concerned about such things as team-based behaviors, adaptability, innovation, and citizenship behaviors, in addition to task performance (Colquitt, 2017). In practice, performance ratings now include these varied dimensions, but research aimed at understanding how this might fundamentally change PM has been somewhat lagging. We know that such things as task performance, helping, voice, and organizational loyalty all exert an impact on overall evaluations (Whiting et al., 2008). We also know that the importance of these different dimensions varies based on the culture of the organization; in team-based cultures, more weight tends to be given to citizenship behaviors and less to task performance (Lievens, Conway, & DeCorte, 2008), suggesting that these dimensions are likely to continue to become more important over time, given changes in the nature of work.

Team-Based PM Approaches. Despite the increasing presence of teams in organizations and despite a direct reference to teams in textbook definitions of PM (e.g., "identifying, measuring, and developing the performance of individuals and teams." Aguinis, 2013, p. 2), there is a striking absence of empirical work on team-based PM specifically. Some conceptual work exists, including Duff's (2013) arguments that a servant leadership style might be particularly effective for coaching teams; and Rosen, Bedwell, Wildman, Fritzsche, Salas, and Burke's (2011) theoretical model of managing adaptive team performance (which includes behavioral markers for various steps in the process). Aguinis (2013) notes in his textbook that PM systems focused on managing team performance should target an individual's contribution to the team's performance, the team's performance as a whole, and individual performance, but such assertions have not been empirically tested. There is some indirect empirical evidence for changes in PM resulting from increased use of team-based structures, including studies that have expanded beyond in-role individual performance to find that employee behaviors important for team performance, such as organizational citizenship behavior and proactive behavior (Podsakoff, Ahearne, & MacKenzie, 1997), do relate positively to performance ratings (see Grant, Parker, & Collins, 2009; Whiting, Podsakoff, & Pierce, 2008).

Rating Sources. Decentralization and the associated focus on team structures can serve to make salient additional rating sources (e.g., peers) other than one's supervisor. Studies on rating source and the associated topic of multi-source rating systems are prevalent in the PM literature. Recent research finds evidence that rating source represents meaningful variance, as opposed to simply bias (Hoffman & Woehr, 2009), and that different rating sources demonstrate equivalence across measured performance constructs, making comparisons across raters meaningful (Woehr, Sheehan, & Bennet, 2005). Multiple studies found positive outcomes resulting from multi-source appraisal and feedback systems, including perceptions of a supportive culture and system effectiveness (Mamatoglu, 2008), increased fairness (Selvarajan & Cloninger, 2012), and a stronger effect on subordinate performance (Smither, London, & Reilly, 2005). Other studies have failed to support a relationship between use of multiple sources and overall PM effectiveness (Lawler & McDermott, 2003), and systems theory would suggest that lack of integration between multi-source feedback processes and other PM processes may account for the weak effects observed with employee behavior (Haines & St-Onge, 2012). Subordinates continue to emerge as the most lenient category of rater, and they are also more prone to cultural effects on their ratings compared to superiors or peers (Ng et al., 2011; van der Heijden & Nijhof, 2004). Quality of subordinate ratings increases under developmental purposes, but the same is not true of peer ratings (Greguras, Robie, Schleicher, & Goff, 2003). Finally, the inclusion of self-assessments can bias supervisor ratings (Chen & Kemp, 2012; Shore & Taschian, 2002, 2007), suggesting the importance of withholding managers' access to employee self-ratings until after their own ratings have been submitted (Randall & Sharples, 2012).

Employee Participation. Purported changes in workers' values over time suggest that employees increasingly desire voice in important organizational decisions, including participation in PM processes. Moreover, research shows that employee participation (both formal and informal) can have positive implications for PM. Specifically, involving employees during design and implementation of the PM system helps avoid potential issues (Becker et al., 2011), enhances perceptions of fairness and feedback utility (Tuytens & Devos, 2012), and results in greater satisfaction and performance (Kleingeld et al., 2004). Additionally, participation through self-ratings relates to increased opportunity to discuss performance issues in the appraisal interview (Inderrieden, Allen, &

Keaveny, 2004). More informally, voice during the performance review meeting relates positively to satisfaction with the appraisal and goal commitment (Kamer & Annen, 2010), and involvement in goal setting and more two-way communication relate positively to perceived appraisal fairness (Kavanagh, Benson, & Brown, 2007).

Feedback Environment. To the extent that modern work requires a greater variety of skills and employees appear increasingly interested in pursuing greater skill development and individual growth, the organization's feedback environment (an Informal PM Process factor) becomes critical. This consists of an employee's daily feedback-related interactions with his/her supervisor and coworkers (Steelman, Levy, & Snell, 2004), and Steelman et al. (2004) developed the Feedback Environment Scale as a diagnostic tool in this regard, useful for assessing and training managers on feedback and coaching tasks. The feedback environment relates positively to employee feedback orientation (Dahling et al., 2012; Linderbaum & Levy, 2010), perceived accuracy of feedback (Kinicki et al., 2004), the quality of coaching relationship formed (Gregory & Levy, 2011), and affective organizational commitment (Norris-Watts & Levy, 2004).

Additional Research Needs on the Changing Nature of PM Processes. Additional studies are needed that focus on process decisions regarding the use of technology in PM. Research in this area is particularly important given recent changes by companies who have eliminated performance ratings and increased frequency of formal feedback by implementing technology applications. As an example, IBM developed the ACE (Appreciation, Coaching, Evaluation) application to aid employees with requesting feedback from managers and teammates; the app has four main features including giving feedback, receiving feedback, participating in surveys, and reviewing feedback history (Lebowitz, 2016). Future research is needed to understand the impact of these and similar technological changes on employees' and managers' reactions, including fairness, satisfaction, and utility (Keeping & Levy, 2000). Related to the issue of doing away with formal ratings and moving to informal and more frequent feedback approaches, there is also a need to study the extent to which this is tied to greater autonomy and flexibility accompanying the "end of the job" era.

In addition, although PM research has already substantiated the criticality of employee participation and voice (Cawley, Keeping, & Levy, 1998), it would be interesting to investigate differences and interactions between formal and informal forms of voice. In the context of the changing nature of work, a first step might be explicitly asking employees whether formal (e.g., via self-ratings) or informal (e.g., through more frequent opportunities to speak during performance review meetings) participation better meets their desire to have a voice in important organizational decisions. Further, it is unclear whether formal and informal forms are compensatory for one another or whether employees instead view them as very distinct needs.

The Individuals of PM

The changing nature of work (and workers) also has particularly important implications for the Individuals of PM, including employees/ratees in PM and managers/raters in PM.

Employees/Ratees. Changes in employee demographics are part of the changing nature of work, and research has examined the impact of such demographic characteristics on PM, especially in terms of bias in the performance evaluation task. For example, research has found that women in line jobs receive lower performance ratings than women in staff jobs or men in either type of job (Lyness & Heilman, 2006). In addition, a recent study suggests that leaders with a greater percentage of Black employees are perceived as less competent and receive lower performance ratings, regardless of the leader's own race (Hernandez, Avery, Tonidandel, Hebl, Smith, & McKay, 2016).

As organizations become more global, the question of how cultural differences impact employees becomes especially relevant. Cultural variables represent a more recent focus for PM research, and links are being made between employees' cultural values and their preferences for particular PM practices. For instance, a study of expatriate New Zealanders in Belgium revealed distinct differences in preferences (e.g., for structured appraisals, involvement in goal setting) between these workers and native Belgians (Ellis, 2012).

As workers' desire for individual growth and skill development continue to increase, relevant PM-related individual differences of employees are likely to take on renewed importance. Most notable in this regard is the study of feedback orientation (FO), introduced by London and Smither (2002) and operationalized by Linderbaum and Levy (2010). This multidimensional construct represents an employee's overall receptivity to feedback, and research suggests FO relates to PM-related behaviors (e.g., intention to follow up on feedback), reactions (e.g., performance review meeting satisfaction; Dahling, Chau, & O'Malley, 2012; Linderbaum & Levy, 2010), the quality of coaching relationship with one's supervisor (Gregory & Levy, 2012), and indirectly to supervisor performance ratings and LMX through employees' feedback seeking (Dahling et al., 2012).

Managers/Raters. Similar to employees, cultural considerations regarding managers' role in PM are made more salient by recent trends towards globalization. Relevant research findings appear quite complex and contingency-based. For example, although ethnicity does not appear to affect attitudes toward PM (Rahman, 2006), raters' cultural value orientations can affect rating bias in multisource rating contexts (Ng, Koh, Ang, Kennedy, & Chan, 2011).

In addition, interdependence, an individual-level cultural variable reflecting the connectedness of a person to others, is associated with rater discomfort with evaluation and also more lenient ratings (Saffie-Robertson & Brutus, 2014). It also appears that raters high in bicultural identity integration may adjust evaluations to match the cultural setting (by, for example, giving less weight to situational factors in an American setting; Mok, Cheng, & Morris, 2010).

Increases in workers' desires for growth and development also have implications for managers/raters through constructs related to feedback and coaching, especially regarding raters' motives surrounding these PM activities. For example, recent research has found that raters who are motivated to assist ratees in identifying strengths and weaknesses provide ratings with less halo and leniency (Ng et al., 2011). In addition, female raters tend to provide more narrative comments than males (van der Leeuw et al., 2013), and in the context of the changing nature of workers, this becomes an increasingly important rater behavior.

Additional Research Needs on the Changing Nature of PM Individuals. An important area for future empirical work is the study of team-based PM, including testing the conceptual models and assertions discussed above. Further, studies should explicitly ask managers about how they weigh factors outside of individual performance (e.g., contributions to one's team) when evaluating employees involved in team-based work. Mixed methods approaches, including both qualitative and quantitative research, may be particularly useful in this area.

Continued research on feedback-related constructs within PM will also be important, given the changing nature of workers' values. Although to date FO has been primarily considered a characteristic of employees, managers' FO may be equally important. There is evidence that managers' own ratings can serve as an anchor for the appraisals they conduct on employees (Latham, Budworth, Yanar, & Whyte, 2008), and this phenomenon may also occur in terms of the feedback managers receive (i.e., in turn impacting the way in which they provide feedback to employees). We would expect many positive outcomes for managers who possess stronger FOs; however empirical evidence supporting this is needed.

We also recommend continued PM research on managers' and employees' cultural characteristics, especially given the increasingly global landscape of organizations. Multinational corporations (MNCs) must strike a difficult balance between standardized PM practices and more localized PM practices, and this has been found to be especially true for Western MNCs expanding into Asian countries (Claus & Briscoe, 2009). It may be the case that certain PM tasks, such as setting performance expectations, can be standardized because they are less impacted by cultural factors while other tasks, such as generating and delivering feedback, should be implemented in more localized forms. Further, outsourcing and growth in the number of contract workers employed by organizations (Burke & Ng, 2006) has interesting implications for

Individuals in terms of worker status being a relevant factor in PM. Contract workers' managers would have little opportunity to observe employees located physically at customer sites, and thus, may be required to rely on more objective measures or subjective information from other observers. How PM processes need to adapt for these and other "non-traditional workers" is an interesting and important avenue for future research.

Summary and Conclusions

As the material reviewed in this chapter suggests, PM has undergone significant changes over the years. To some extent this has always been the case (see Colquitt, 2017), but the rate and nature of change seems to be particularly pronounced in the past decade. It is clear also that PM practices will continue to be impacted by the changing nature of work. As such, our PM research needs to continue to evolve as well, to meet the realities of the changing nature of PM practice. Thus, we conclude this chapter with two general needs in the PM research literature that we view as particularly pressing in this regard.

First, there is much research evidence that a particular PM approach may be good (i.e., effective) for a particular organization, operating in a particular context and for a particular set of purposes; yet, as the congruence hypothesis of systems theory (Nadler & Tushman, 1980) would predict, what works or is a key requirement of PM in one context may not be so in another context. Indeed, the presence of extensive contingencies in PM calls into question the very notion of "best practices." Going forward, it is possible to build a list of evidence-based effective PM practices, but it will not be a simplistic list, and to do so we clearly need more research that examines the fit between (changing) Inputs and other systems components, as well as interactions amongst system components in general (given the internal interdependence principle of systems theory; Nadler & Tushman, 1980). Moreover, understanding the extensive contingencies within PM will necessitate research designs that measure variables from multiple PM system components at once and test their interactions. Our review suggests this is not at all the norm in the extant PM literature.

Second, there is very little longitudinal research in PM (i.e., research that explicitly looks at changes in PM components over time and their impact). The principle of adaptation within systems theory (Nadler & Tushman, 1980) argues that system inputs and outputs must be maintained at a favorable balance with the environment. Thus, PM systems must adapt to changing environmental conditions (i.e., Inputs) to maintain their effectiveness. We know, given the changing nature of work literature, that such Inputs are indeed changing. Yet there has been no substantive empirical research on how PM systems do and should *adapt* (i.e., how they change) in response to these shifting conditions. AsColquitt (2017) illustrates in his recent book on

PM, the historical form of adaptation of PM in organizations has been an additive one ("like barnacles attaching themselves to a log, one on top of the other," p. 10). There are likely to be much more functional approaches to the adaptation of PM systems, and examining these in future research will be critical for furthering our understanding of the interface between PM and the changing nature of work.

References

Abu-Doleh, J., & Weir, D. (2007). Dimensions of performance appraisal systems in Jordanian private and public organizations. *International Journal of Human Resource Management, 18*, 75–84.

Adler, S., Campion, M., Colquitt, A., Grubb, A., Murphy, K., Ollander-Krane, R., & Pulakos, E. D. (2016). Getting rid of performance ratings: Genius or folly? A debate. *Industrial and Organizational Psychology, 9*, 219–252.

Aguinis, H. (2013). *Performance management* (3rd ed.). Upper Saddle River, NJ: Pearson Prentice Hall.

Akuratiyagamage, V. M. (2005). Identification of management development needs: A comparison across companies of different ownership – foreign, joint venture and local in Sri Lanka. *International Journal of Human Resource Management, 16*, 1512–1528.

Atwater, L., Smither, J. W., Wang, M., & Fleenor, J. W. (2009). Are cultural characteristics associated with the relationship between self and others' ratings of leadership? *Journal of Applied Psychology, 94*, 876–886.

Ayers, R. S. (2013). Building goal alignment in federal agencies' performance appraisal programs. *Public Personnel Management, 42*, 495–520.

Balfour, D. L. (1992). Impact of agency investment in the implementation of performance appraisal. *Public Personnel Management, 92*, 1–15.

Barua, A., & Viechnicki, P. (2017). Looking for convergence: How is the government workforce similar to the private sector? *Deloitte Insights*, April 26.

Becker, K., Antuar, N., & Everett, C. (2011). Implementing an employee performance management system in a nonprofit organization. *Nonprofit Management and Leadership, 21*, 255–271.

Boswell, W. R., & Boudreau, J. W. (2000). Employee satisfaction with performance appraisals and appraisers: The role of perceived appraisal use. *Human Resource Development Quarterly, 11*, 283–299.

Boulding, K. E. (1956). General systems theory: The skeleton of science. *Management Science, 2*, 197–208.

Bouskila-Yam, O., & Kluger, A. N. (2011). Strength-based performance appraisal and goal setting. *Human Resource Management Review, 21*, 137–147.

Bretz, R. D., Milkovich, G. T., & Read, W. (1992). The current state of performance appraisal research and practice: Concerns, directions, and implications. *Journal of Management, 18*, 321–352.

Brown, T. C., & Warren, A. M. (2011). Performance management in unionized settings. *Human Resource Management Review, 21*, 96–106.

Buckingham, M., & Goodall, A. (2015). Reinventing performance management. *Harvard Business Review, 93*, 40–50.

Burke, R. J., & Ng, E. (2006). The changing nature of work and organizations: Implications for human resource management. *Human Resource Management Review, 16*, 86–94.

Cabrera, D. D., Fernaud, E. H., Díaz, R. I., Rodríguez, N. D., Vilela, L. D., & Sánchez, C. R. (2014). Factores relevantes para aumentar la precisión, la viabilidad y el éxito de los sistemas de evaluación del desempeño laboral. *Papeles del Psicólogo, 35*, 115–121.

Cappelli, P., & Tavis, A. (2016). The performance management revolution. *Harvard Business Review, 94*, 58–67.

Cascio, W. F. (2006). 10 global performance management systems. In G. K. Stahl & I. Björkman (Eds.), *Handbook of research in international human resource management* (pp. 176–196). Northampton, MA: Edward Elgar Publishing.

Cawley, B. D., Keeping, L. M., & Levy, P. E. (1998). Participation in the performance appraisal process and employee reactions: A meta-analytic review of field investigations. *Journal of Applied Psychology, 83*, 615–633.

Chen, Z., & Kemp, S. (2012). Lie hard: The effect of self-assessments on academic promotion decisions. *Journal of Economic Psychology, 33*, 578–589.

Clarke, C., Harcourt, M., & Flynn, M. (2012). Clinical governance, performance appraisal and interactional and procedural fairness at a New Zealand public hospital. *Journal of Business Ethics, 117*, 667–678.

Claus, L., & Briscoe, D. (2009). Employee performance management across borders: A review of relevant academic literature. *International Journal of Management Reviews, 11*, 175–196.

Collins-Camargo, C., Chuang, E., McBeath, B., & Bunger, A. C. (2014). Private child welfare agency managers' perceptions of the effectiveness of different performance management strategies. *Children and Youth Services Review, 38*, 133–141.

Colquitt, A. L. (2017). *Next generation performance management: The triumph of science over myth and superstition.* Charlotte, NC: Information Age Publishing.

Dahling, J. J., Chau, S. L., & O'Malley, A. (2012). Correlates and consequences of feedback orientation in organizations. *Journal of Management, 38*, 531–546.

Decramer, A., Smolders, C., & Vanderstraeten, A. (2013). Employee performance management culture and system features in higher education: Relationship with employee performance management satisfaction. *International Journal of Human Resource Management, 24*, 352–371.

Deming, W. E. (1986). *Out of the crisis.* Cambridge, MA: MIT Press.

den Hartog, D. N., Boselie, P., & Paauwe, J. (2004). Performance management: A model and research agenda. *Applied Psychology, 53*, 556–569.

DeNisi, A. S., & Pritchard, R. D. (2006). Performance appraisal, performance management and improving individual performance: A motivational framework. *Management and Organization Review, 2*, 253–277.

Duff, A. J. (2013). Performance management coaching: Servant leadership and gender implications. *Leadership & Organization Development Journal, 34*, 204–221.

Dunn, M., & Walker, J. ((2016). Union membership in the United States. Spotlight on Statistics, US Bureau of Labor Statistics (September).

Effron, M., & Ort, M. (2010). *One page talent management: Eliminating complexity, adding value.* Boston, MA: Harvard Business School Publishing.

Ellis, D. R. (2012). Exploring cultural dimensions as predictors of performance management preferences: The case of self-initiating expatriate New Zealanders in

Belgium. *International Journal of Human Resource Management, 23*, 2087–2107.

Fee, A., McGrath-Champ, S., & Yang, X. (2011). Expatriate performance management and firm internationalization: Australian multinationals in China. *Asia Pacific Journal of Human Resources, 49*, 365–384.

Fletcher, C. (2001). Performance appraisal and management: The developing research agenda. *Journal of Occupational and Organizational Psychology, 74*, 473–487.

Giumetti, G. W., Schroeder, A. N., & Switzer, I. S. (2015). Forced distribution rating systems: When does "rank and yank" lead to adverse impact?. *Journal of Applied Psychology, 100*, 180–193.

Grant, A. M., Parker, S., & Collins, C. (2009). Getting credit for proactive behavior: Supervisor reactions depend on what you value and how you feel. *Personnel Psychology, 62*, 31–55.

Gregory, J. B., & Levy, P. E. (2010). Employee coaching relationships: Enhancing construct clarity and measurement. *Coaching: An International Journal of Theory, Research and Practice, 3*, 109–123.

Gregory, J. B., & Levy, P. E. (2011). It's not me, it's you: A multilevel examination of variables that impact employee coaching relationships. *Consulting Psychology Journal: Practice and Research, 63*, 67–88.

Gregory, J. B., & Levy, P. E. (2012). Employee feedback orientation: Implications for effective coaching relationships. *Coaching: An International Journal of Theory, Research and Practice, 5*, 86–99.

Gregory, J. B., Levy, P. E., & Jeffers, M. (2008). Development of a model of the feedback process within executive coaching. *Consulting Psychology Journal: Practice and Research, 60*, 42–56.

Greguras, G. J., Robie. C., Schleicher, D. J., & Goff III, M. (2003). A field study of the effects of rating purpose on the quality of multisource ratings. *Personnel Psychology, 56*, 1–21.

Haines, V. Y., & St-Onge, S. (2012). Performance management effectiveness: Practices or context? *International Journal of Human Resource Management, 23*, 1158–1175.

Hebert, B. G., & Vorauer, J. D. (2003). Seeing through the screen: Is evaluative feedback communicated more effectively in face-to-face or computer-mediated exchanges? *Computers in Human Behavior, 19*, 25–38.

Hedge, J. W., & Borman, W. C. (1995). Changing conceptions and practices in performance appraisal. In A. Howard (Ed.), *The changing nature of work* (pp. 451–481). San Francisco,CA: Jossey-Bass.

Hernandez, M., Avery, D. R., Tonidandel, S., Hebl, M. R., Smith, A. N., & McKay, P. F. (2016). The role of proximal social contexts: Assessing stigma-by-association effects on leader appraisals. *Journal of Applied Psychology, 101*, 68–85.

Hoffman, B. J., & Woehr, D. J. (2009). Disentangling the meaning of multisource performance rating source and dimension factors. *Personnel Psychology, 62*, 735–765.

Ilgen, D. R., Barnes-Farrell, J. L., & McKellin, D. B. (1993). Performance appraisal process research in the 1980s: What has it contributed to appraisals in use? *Organizational Behavior and Human Decision Processes, 54*, 321–368.

Inderrieden, E. J., Allen, R. E., & Keaveny, T. J. (2004). Managerial discretion in the use of self-ratings in an appraisal system: The antecedents and consequences. *Journal of Managerial Issues, 16*, 460–482.

Irs, R., & Turk, K. (2012). Implementation of the performance-related pay in the general education schools of Estonia. *Employee Relations, 34*, 360–393.

Johns, G. (2018). Advances in the treatment of context in organizational research. *Annual Review of Organizational Psychology and Organizational Behavior.*

Kacik, A. (2017, October). Healthcare industry to create four million jobs by 2026. *Modern Healthcare.* www.modernhealthcare.com/article/20171027/NEWS/171029879

Kamer, B., & Annen, H. (2010). The role of core self-evaluations in predicting performance appraisal reactions. *Swiss Journal of Psychology, 69*, 95–104.

Katz, D., & Kahn, R. L. (1978). *The social psychology of organizations* (2nd ed.). New York, NY: Wiley.

Kavanagh, P., Benson, J., & Brown, M. (2007). Understanding performance appraisal fairness. *Asia Pacific Journal of Human Resources, 45*, 132–150.

Keeping, L. M. & Levy, P. E. (2000). Performance appraisal reactions: Measurement, modeling, and method bias. *Journal of Applied Psychology, 85*, 708–723.

Kinicki, A. J., Jacobson, K. J., Peterson, S. J., & Prussia, G. E. (2013). Development and validation of the performance management behavior questionnaire. *Personnel Psychology, 66*, 1–45.

Kinicki, A. J., Prussia, G. E., Wu, B. J., & McKee-Ryan, F. M. (2004). A covariance structure analysis of employees' response to performance feedback. *Journal of Applied Psychology, 89*, 1057–1069.

Klein, H. J., Snell, S. A., & Wexley, K. N. (1987). Systems model of the performance appraisal interview process. *Industrial Relations: A Journal of Economy and Society, 26*, 267–280.

Kleingeld, A., van Tuijl, H., & Algera, J. A. (2004). Participation in the design of performance management systems: A quasi-experimental field study. *Journal of Organizational Behavior, 25*, 831–851.

Kluger, A. N., & Nir, D. (2010). The feedforward interview. *Human Resource Management Review, 20*, 235–246.

Knoke, D. (2000). *Changing organizations: Business networks in the new political economy.* New York, NY: Routledge.

Krauss, A., & Snyder, L. A. (2009). Technology and performance management: What role does technology play in performance management? In J. W. Smither & M. London (Eds.), *Performance management: Putting research into action.* San Francisco, CA: Jossey-Bass.

Kurtzberg, T. R., Naquin, C. E., & Belkin, L. Y. (2005). Electronic performance appraisals: The effects of e-mail communication on peer ratings in actual and simulated environments. *Organizational Behavior and Human Decision Processes, 98*, 216–226.

Latham, G. P., Budworth, M., Yanar, B., & Whyte, G. (2008). The influence of a manager's own performance appraisal on the evaluation of others. *International Journal of Selection and Assessment, 16*, 220–228.

Lawler, E. E. (2003). Reward practices and performance management system effectiveness. *Organizational Dynamics, 32*, 396–404.

Lawler, E. E., & McDermott, M. (2003). Current performance management practices: Examining the varying impacts. *World at Work Journal, 12*, 49–60.

Lebowitz, S. (2016). After overhauling its performance review system, IBM now uses an app to give and receive real-time feedback. *Business Insider*, May 20. Retrieved from www.businessinsider.com/ibm-now-uses-the-ace-app-to-give-and-receive-real-time-feedback-2016-5

Lee, G., & Jimenez, B. S. (2011). Does performance management affect job turnover intention in the federal government? *American Review of Public Administration, 41*, 168–184.

Levy, P. E., Tseng, S. T., Rosen, C. C., & Lueke, S. B. (2017). Performance management: A marriage between practice and science – Just say "I do." In M. R. Buckley, A. R. Wheeler, & J. R. B. Halbesleben (Eds.), *Research in personnel and human resources management*, Vol. 35 (pp. 155–213). Bingley, West Yorkshire, England: Emerald Publishing Limited.

Levy, P. E., & Williams, J. R. (2004). The social context of performance appraisal: A review and framework for the future. *Journal of Management, 30*, 881–905.

Lievens, F., Conway, J. M., & De Corte, W. (2008). The relative importance of task, citizenship and counterproductive performance to job performance ratings: Do rater source and team-based culture matter? *Journal of Occupational and Organizational Psychology, 81*, 11–27.

Linderbaum, B. A., & Levy, P. E. (2010). The development and validation of the feedback orientation scale (FOS). *Journal of Management, 36*, 1372–1405.

London, M., & Smither, J. W. (2002). Feedback orientation, feedback culture, and the longitudinal performance management process. *Human Resource Management Review, 12*, 81–100.

Lyness, K. S., & Heilman, M. E. (2006). When fit is fundamental: Performance evaluations and promotions of upper-level female and male managers. *Journal of Applied Psychology, 91*, 777–785.

Mamatoglu, N. (2008). Effects on organizational context (culture and climate) from implementing a 360-degree feedback system: The case of Arcelik. *European Journal of Work and Organizational Psychology, 17*, 426–449.

Medcof, J. W., & Song, L. J. (2013). Exploration, exploitation and human resource management practices in cooperative and entrepreneurial HR configurations. *International Journal of Human Resource Management, 24*, 2911–2926.

Miller, J. S. (2003). High tech and high performance: Managing appraisal in the information age. *Journal of Labor Research, 24*, 409–424.

Mok, A., Cheng, C. Y., & Morris, M. W. (2010). Matching versus mismatching cultural norms in performance appraisal: Effects of the cultural setting and bicultural identity integration. *International Journal of Cross Cultural Management, 10*, 17–35.

Murphy, K. R., & Cleveland, J. N. (1991). *Performance appraisal: An organizational perspective*. Needham Heights, MA: Allyn & Bacon.

Nadler, D. A., & Tushman, M. L. (1980). A model for diagnosing organizational behavior. *Organizational Dynamics, 9*(2), 35–51.

Ng, K. Y., Koh, C., Ang, S., Kennedy, J. C., & Chan, K. Y. (2011). Rating leniency and halo in multisource feedback ratings: Testing cultural assumptions of power distance and individualism–collectivism. *Journal of Applied Psychology, 96*, 1033–1044.

Norris-Watts, C., & Levy, P. E. (2004). The mediating role of affective commitment in the relation of the feedback environment to work outcomes. *Journal of Vocational Behavior, 65*, 351–365.

Nurse, L. (2005). Performance appraisal, employee development and organizational justice: Exploring the linkages. *International Journal of Human Resource Management, 16*, 1176–1194.

Payne, S. C., Horner, M. T., Boswell, W. R., Schroeder, A. N., & Stine-Cheyne, K. J. (2009). Comparison of online and traditional performance appraisal systems. *Journal of Managerial Psychology, 24*, 526–544.

Payne, S. C., & Mendoza, A. (2017, April). Performance ratings: Does case law reveal more harm than good? Paper presented at the *Annual Conference of the Society for Industrial and Organizational Psychology*, Orlando, FL.

Peretz, H., & Fried, Y. (2012). National cultures, performance appraisal practices, and organizational absenteeism and turnover: A study across 21 countries. *Journal of Applied Psychology, 97*, 448–459.

Podsakoff, P. M., Ahearne, M., & MacKenzie, S. B. (1997). Organizational citizenship behavior and the quantity and quality of work group performance. *Journal of Applied Psychology, 82*, 262–270.

Rahman, S. A. (2006). Attitudes of Malaysian teachers toward a performance-appraisal system. *Journal of Applied Social Psychology, 36*, 3031–3042.

Randall, R., & Sharples, D. (2012). The impact of rater agreeableness and rating context on the evaluation of poor performance. *Journal of Occupational and Organizational Psychology, 85*, 42–59.

Rego, A., Marques, C., Leal, S., Sousa, F., & Pina e Cunha, M. (2010). Psychological capital and performance of Portuguese civil servants: Exploring neutralizers in the context of an appraisal system. *International Journal of Human Resource Management, 21*, 1531–1552.

Rodwell, J. J., & Teo, S. T. T. (2008). The influence of strategic HRM and sector on perceived performance in health services organizations. *International Journal of Human Resource Management, 19*, 1825–1841.

Rosen, M. A., Bedwell, W. L., Wildman, J. L., Fritzsche, B. A., Salas, E., & Burke, C. S. (2011). Managing adaptive performance in teams: Guiding principles and behavioral markers for measurement. *Human Resource Management Review, 21*, 107–122.

Saffie-Robertson, M. C., & Brutus, S. (2014). The impact of interdependence on performance evaluations: The mediating role of discomfort with performance appraisal. *International Journal of Human Resource Management, 25*, 459–473.

Schleicher, D. J., Baumann, H. M., Sullivan, D. W., Levy, P. E., Hargrove, D. C., & Barros-Rivera, B. A. (2018). Putting the system into performance management systems: A review and agenda for performance management research. *Journal of Management, 44*, 2209–2245.

Schleicher, D. J., Bull, R. A., & Green, S. G. (2009). Rater reactions to forced distribution rating systems. *Journal of Management, 35*, 899–927.

Selvarajan, T. T., & Cloninger, P. A. (2012). Can performance appraisals motivate employees to improve performance? A Mexican study. *International Journal of Human Resource Management, 23*, 3063–3084.

Shore, T. H., & Tashchian, A. (2002). Accountability forces in performance appraisal: Effects of self-appraisal information, normative information, and task performance. *Journal of Business and Psychology, 17*, 261–274.

Shore, T. H., & Tashchian, A. (2007). Effects of feedback accountability and self-rating information on employee appraisals: A replication and extension. *Psychological Reports, 100*, 1091–1100.

Shrivastava, A., & Purang, P. (2011). Employee perceptions of performance appraisals: A comparative study on Indian banks. *International Journal of Human Resource Management, 22*, 632–647.

Silva, P., & Tosi, H. L. (2004). Determinants of the anonymity of the CEO evaluation process. *Journal of Managerial Issues, 16*, 87–102.

Singh, S., Mohamed, A. F., & Darwish, T. (2013). A comparative study of performance appraisals, incentives and rewards practices in domestic and multinational enterprises in the country of Brunei Darussalam. *International Journal of Human Resource Management, 24*, 3577–3598.

Smither, J. W., London, M., & Reilly, R. R. (2005). Does performance improve following multisource feedback? A theoretical model, meta-analysis, and review of empirical findings. *Personnel Psychology, 58*, 33–66.

Steelman, L. A., Levy, P. E., & Snell, A. F. (2004). The feedback environment scale: Construct definition, measurement, and validation. *Educational and Psychological Measurement, 64*, 165–184.

Taormina, R. J., & Gao, J. H. (2009). Identifying acceptable performance appraisal criteria: An international perspective. *Asia Pacific Journal of Human Resources, 47*, 102–125.

Tsai, C., & Wang, W. (2013). Exploring the factors associated with employees' perceived appraisal accuracy: A study of Chinese state-owned enterprises. *International Journal of Human Resource Management, 24*, 2197–2220.

Tuytens, M., & Devos, G. (2012). Importance of system and leadership in performance appraisal. *Personnel Review, 41*, 756–776.

Tziner, A., Murphy, K. R., Cleveland, J. N., & Roberts-Thompson, G. P. (2001). Relationships between attitudes toward organizations and performance appraisal systems and rating behavior. *International Journal of Selection and Assessment, 9*, 226–239.

van der Heijden, B. I. J. M., & Nijhof, A. H. J. (2004). The value of subjectivity: Problems and prospects for 360-degree appraisal systems. *The International Journal of Human Resource Management, 15*, 493–511.

van der Leeuw, R. M., Overeem, K., Arah, O. A., Heineman, M. J., & Lombarts, K. M. J. M. H. (2013). Frequency and determinants of residents' narrative feedback on the teaching performance of faculty: Narratives in numbers. *Academic Medicine, 88*, 1324–1331.

Varma, A., Pichler, S., & Srinivas, E. S. (2005). The role of interpersonal affect in performance appraisal: Evidence from two samples – the US and India. *International Journal of Human Resource Management, 16*, 2029–2044.

Wang, H., Tseng, J., Yen, Y., Huang, I. (2011). University staff performance evaluation systems, organizational learning, and organizational identification in Taiwan. *Social Behavior and Personality, 39*, 43–54.

Wegman, L. A., Hoffman, B. J., Carter, N. T., Twenge, J. M., & Guenole, N. (2018). Placing job characteristics in context: Cross-temporal meta-analysis of changes in job characteristics since 1975. *Journal of Management, 44*, 352–386.

Whiting, S. W., Podsakoff, P. M., & Pierce, J. R. (2008). Effects of task performance, helping, voice, and organizational loyalty on performance appraisal ratings. *Journal of Applied Psychology, 93*, 125–139.

Williams, M. J. (1997). Performance appraisal is dead. Long live performance management. *Harvard Management Update, 2*, 1–6.

Woehr, D. J., Sheehan, M. K., & Bennett, W. (2005). Assessing measurement equivalence across rating sources: A multitrait–multirater approach. *Journal of Applied Psychology, 90*, 592–600.

Youngcourt, S. S., Leiva, P. I., & Jones, R. G. (2007). Perceived purposes of performance appraisal: Correlates of individual- and position-focused purposes on attitudinal outcomes. *Human Resource Development Quarterly, 18*, 315–343.

17 Implications of the Changing Nature of Work for Training

Tiffany M. Bisbey, Allison Traylor, and Eduardo Salas

The nature of work is transient. As new technologies and capabilities take root in the workplace, new patterns are established that define our industrial era. This is evidenced by the American Industrial Revolution, when manufacturing replaced agriculture as the economic pillar of the country and immigration soared (Hirschman & Mogford, 2009). Over the last century and through scientific intervention, researchers have improved the efficiency of work by recognizing the potential of the workforce in affecting organizational success. We saw the birth of organizational psychology and uncovered methods of leveraging employee knowledge, skills, and attitudes (KSAs) to improve performance. We built training and development programs, and revealed best practices for employee learning – all designed around the traditional world of work.

Today, we are experiencing a new revolution – one characterized by globalization, unique organizational structures, and a technological boom that is advancing capabilities faster than they can be learned and adopted. In this new world, the traditional paradigm for training and development is shifting alongside the demands of modern society. Organizational scientists and practitioners are at the forefront of shaping the contemporary workplace, and we have a responsibility to be responsive to the needs sparked by global changes. The goal of this chapter is to outline implications for the science and practice of training as the workplace continues to evolve. Along the way, we provide guidance for training a labor force that thrives in this technologically and socially complex world. Our hope is to spark research for building training and development systems that are compatible with the 'new normal'.

The issues described here and throughout this volume create conditions that implicate the methods used to train employees, the types of training programs offered, and the skills necessary for an effective workforce. In this chapter, we provide an overview of the substantive issues within the area of training as the nature of work changes, highlighting key findings and opportunities for future research. We begin with a brief summary of the science of training and of what we know about effective training. Next, we draw on our expertise and research in training to describe our vision for how the practice will change in response to the evolving nature of work. We conclude with a list of steadfast best practices to guide us through these changes and make recommendations for future research.

The Science of Training

Skilled employees provide organizations with competitive advantage, so workers must continuously learn and develop their KSAs to remain relevant. The interest in human capital has kept psychologists interested in training and development for over 100 years (see Bell, Tannenbaum, Ford, Noe, & Kraiger, 2017). Organizations in the United States spend an estimated $177 billion annually on formal training programs (Carnevale, Strohl, & Gulish, 2015) – and for good reasons. Training enhances the capacity for organizations to perform effectively by adapting, innovating, improving safety, and achieving goals (Salas, Tannenbaum, Kraiger, & Smith-Jentsch, 2012). It has been used to reduce errors in aviation and the military, and has even been shown to improve patient mortality rates in healthcare settings (Hughes et al., 2016). Training is effective, and the extent of its effectiveness is largely dependent on its design, delivery, and implementation (Salas et al., 2012). Insights from the science of training give guidance for leveraging these factors before, during, and after training to maximize training effectiveness. We preface our discussion of training implications with a brief overview of lessons from a century of training research.

Before Training

Before designing a training program, it is essential to determine what and who should be trained and to identify factors that might impact training effectiveness (Goldstein & Ford, 1993). This is known as a training needs analysis. A complete needs analysis involves examining core job functions and the KSAs required to complete tasks (i.e., job-task analysis), organizational alignment with priorities and readiness to support training (i.e., organizational analysis), and those who lack the necessary KSAs and what they require in order to reap learning benefits (i.e., person analysis; for more in-depth information on training needs analyses, see Salas et al., 2012). The science is clear on this recommendation: the needs analysis is one of the most important steps of designing a training initiative. It is also important to prepare the organization for the upcoming intervention by discussing expectations with employees and leaders, fostering honest perceptions of training utility, and showing commitment to employee development (Salas et al., 2012). This means that organizational leadership must prioritize the learning initiative so that employees do the same and approach the event fully engaged and ready to learn.

In preparing for training and throughout implementation, it is important to encourage positive attitudes and perceptions towards the initiative. This might include building trainee self-efficacy and motivation to learn, which often go hand-in-hand. Research shows that those with high self-efficacy are also more motivated to learn and achieve greater learning outcomes (Chen, Gully, Whiteman, & Kilcullen, 2000). Having a supportive supervisor can also improve trainee motivation (Salas & Cannon-Bowers, 2001). Supervisors can support their employees by listening to their concerns, respecting and responding to their needs, and showing an interest their professional development by offering a useful training opportunity. Employees should also perceive that the training will teach them useful, job-relevant KSAs; otherwise, they may disengage and show little motivation to perform well throughout the training (Knowles, Holton, & Swanson, 2005).

During Training

The design of the training program is also important for effective learning. A good design starts with a strategy focused on the transfer of trained KSAs to on-the-job performance. Maximizing training transfer involves four key steps: (1) convey the information that needs to be learned, (2) demonstrate how the appropriate behaviors might look in context, (3) provide opportunities for practice, and (4) provide evaluative feedback (Salas & Cannon-Bowers, 2001). Meta-analytic evidence suggests that well-designed training programs have many opportunities for trainees to make errors and learn to cope with them in practice (Keith & Frese, 2008). Cultivating a space where suboptimal performance is safe (or even encouraged) is a key component of effective training in jobs where errors can have extreme consequences, such as in medicine or aviation. Accordingly, we see many resources devoted to developing high-fidelity simulations in which trainees can commit errors safely and get experience managing performance before, during, and after errors without the real-life consequences. The progression of technology has substantially advanced simulation capabilities and will continue to provide great opportunities for training in high-risk contexts.

After Training

After the training program is complete, there are several factors of the design, delivery, and implementation that can still influence the transfer of trained KSAs to on-the-job performance. One of the most crucial insights from the science of training is the importance of evaluations. Training evaluations result in evidence regarding the utility of the program to inform feedback given to stakeholders, marketing campaigns for the program, and future decisions about training use or redesigns to optimize the program (Kraiger, 2002). The most commonly used framework for evaluating training efforts is Kirkpatrick's (1994) four-level model that assesses trainee reactions, learning, transfer of learned behaviors, and organizational results. Additional evaluation measures can also be built into the design of the program, such as with internal referencing strategy. Using this method, trainees are assessed before and after training on relevant and irrelevant content, and the extent of training effectiveness is demonstrated by more growth on the relevant content than on the irrelevant content (Haccoun & Hamtiaux, 1994). Although less common in the organizational literature, internal referencing strategy can provide robust evaluation results in research situations where the use of a control group might be unfeasible or impracticable. All training interventions should be critically and consistently evaluated to produce the richest information possible related to its effectiveness.

Organizational leaders should do all that they can do to foster a supportive climate and provide the resources that employees need to carry out work using their new skills, as well as opportunities to practice them and outlets for future questions (Martin, 2010; Quiñones, Ford, Sego, & Smith, 1995). Relatedly, trainees should be encouraged to use debriefing strategies in order to share in their experiences using trained KSAs on the job, uncover obstacles to transfer, and collectively recognize ineffective practices moving forward (Smith-Jentsch, Cannon-Bowers, Tannenbaum, & Salas, 2008). All of these methods support effective and sustained training transfer. It is about considering the training initiative as a single piece of an organizational change initiative. Training is not a panacea, but a single tool that can mobilize change through employee learning and dedication to a new way of working.

Summary

The science of training has yielded many guidelines for researchers and practitioners interested in maximizing training effectiveness. As the world of work evolves, research will naturally follow suit. What impact is this evolution having on the science of training? We describe our vision for how the changing nature of work impacts the way we train employees and think about training, while recognizing that much more will stay the same than will change. We note that none of the changes discussed in this chapter limit the usefulness or validity of the information culminated throughout a century of scientific study. Rather, we stand by these foundations and provide a list of steadfast best practices to guide us through workplace changes (see Table 17.1).

Implications of the Changing Nature of Work for Training

It is important to remember that the workplace is a dynamic system with many interconnected parts; macro- and micro-level changes influence one another, and the combination of multiple changes can create conditions that impact the way employees are trained. To provide an organized structure for discussing these effects, we classify workplace changes into four broad categories while acknowledging that their interdependence necessitates some crossover in the topics we cover. We discuss implications related to: (a) the changing composition of the workforce, (b) macrolevel industrial changes, (c) technological advancement, and (d) changes in typical employee behavior patterns. Within each section, we examine how changes in the workplace can influence training design, delivery, and implementation. We forgo a comprehensive review of these changes to avoid redundancy with other chapters in this volume

Table 17.1 *Nine best-practices for training effectiveness*

Practical Recommendations	Suggested Resources
Before training 1) Conduct a needs analysis before designing a training program to determine priorities and organizational readiness 2) Prepare the training environment by encouraging transparent discussions about training utility and the benefits of participation	Burke & Hutchins, 2008; Kraiger, 2008; Salas, Tannenbaum, Kraiger, & Smith-Jentsch, 2012; Tracey, Hinkin, Tannenbaum, & Mathieu, 2001
During training 3) Leverage information presentation, demonstration, practice, and feedback with considerations for context in the design of a training program 4) Sustain a supportive learning climate throughout the training program by using leaders to encourage positive attitudes and perceptions	Cannon-Bowers, Rhodenizer, Salas, & Bowers, 1998; Noe & Colquitt, 2002; Salas & Cannon-Bowers, 2001; Sitzmann, Bell, Kraiger, & Kanar, 2009
After training 5) Evaluate the training program to determine its effectiveness 6) Motivate and facilitate long-term sustainability by maintaining a supportive climate and encouraging ongoing learning	Kirkpatrick, 1994; Kraiger, 2002; Phillips, 2012; Senge, Kleiner, Roberts, Ross, & Smith, 2014; Wenger, McDermott, & Snyder, 2002
Recommendations for moving forward 7) Monitor market trends with an eye on the 'big picture' to recognize factors with potentially salient impacts for training content, design, and delivery 8) Be responsive to trainee needs both inside and outside of the organization to consider designs that are compatible with idiosyncratic lifestyles and career paths 9) Seek insight from research to build evidence-based training programs	

and devote our discussion to their implications for training and development (we refer the reader to Part II of this volume for more background information and in-depth discussions of each change in the workplace).

Workforce Composition Is Changing

Globalization and expanding demographic ranges are creating a diverse workforce with a wide variety of values, experiences, and KSAs. As a result, practitioners must adapt the content of training programs to meet the needs of today's market and equip employees with the skills necessary to perform in this new environment. Toossi (2012) predicts a more culturally- and age-diverse American workforce than ever before by 2050, projecting that non-Hispanic white Americans will make up less than 50% of the country's employees. The content trained will continue to be driven by the need for KSAs relevant to managing and working with a diverse range of employees. Furthermore, novel design and delivery methods will help ensure that these skills translate to the fastest-growing sector of the labor force – older employees.

In 2018, over 76,000 cases of employment discrimination were filed to the United States Equal Employment Opportunity Commission (EEOC, 2019). Projections indicate that the American workforce will only continue to diversity in the future (Sommers & Franklin, 2012). Organizational leaders often look to diversity training to prepare their employees for these demographic shifts (Dobbin & Kalev, 2016). Diversity training is intended to reduce prejudice, increase awareness, and encourage positive attitudes toward working with others from different backgrounds (Roberson, Kulik, & Tan, 2012, p. 341). Although research has provided mixed results regarding the efficacy of these programs, meta-analytic findings indicate that the positive effects of diversity training are greatest when accompanied by additional long-term initiatives targeting both diversity awareness and skills (Bezrukova, Spell, Perry, & Jehn, 2016). Similarly, globalization is increasing the need for cross-cultural training (Chebium, 2015). Cross-cultural training programs focus on improving the competencies that enable employees to effectively interact and collaborate with individuals from other cultures (Bird, Mendenhall, Stevens, & Oddou, 2010). Research supports the use of cross-cultural training, suggesting its effectiveness at improving the interpersonal skills and job performance of global workers (Black & Mendenhall, 1990).

Shifting demographic composition also demands retraining of older adults. As younger employees likely benefit from recent schooling, older employees must rely on their organizations to provide skills training; this is especially important in technology-based industries (Beier, 2008). Advances in modern technology (discussed in a later section) often require highly skilled workers, decreasing the demand for less-skilled workers who are not as efficient at interacting with technology (Berman et al., 1994; Yan, 2006). As high-skilled employees are in demand, low-skilled workers (some who may have been with the company for many years) will need to be educated and trained to remain competitive members of the workforce. The specific content trained will vary across organizations and objectives, but will likely include more technical-skill training or retraining for interacting with technology.

The shifting age-demographic will almost certainly result in one of the most drastic socially driven implications for training delivery and implementation. Aging often coincides with a decline in cognitive performance, which can impact how older employees learn and interpret training information. Research suggests that, under some conditions, the correlation between age and learning performance is negative due to cognitive and motivational differences in younger and older learners (Callahan, Kiker, & Cross, 2003; Charness, 2009; Kubeck, Delp, Haslett, & McDaniel, 1996); however, providing older trainees with fewer time restrictions, more structure, and appropriate framing of training events may encourage learning and minimize any group differences (Beier, 2008, 2012; Moseley & Dessigner, 2007; Wolfson, Cavanagh, & Kraiger, 2014; Young, 2017). Research also indicates that providing an outline of training content helps trainees focus on key themes, and might be particularly useful for older learners (Mayer, 1979; Wolfson & Kraiger, 2014). Although training older employees may necessitate more work in providing additional accommodations, organizations must be cautious not to marginalize this sector of workers by neglecting their training needs.

To summarize, researchers should work to provide instructional solutions that satisfy all demographic ranges of trainees, and practitioners should conduct needs assessments to reveal the specific training considerations that may be necessary for their particular workforce composition. The streamlined travel industry and widespread use of social media make it simple to cross geographical and social boundaries both physically and digitally, making individuals from all walks of life more connected than ever before. We anticipate and encourage more interventions geared at fostering values for all types of diversity and effective cross-cultural collaboration.

The Organizational Landscape Is Changing

More technology in the workplace can mean that certain jobs might become obsolete due to automation. An obvious example can be seen in factories or manufacturing companies where machines can work faster, yield a higher quantity, and produce higher-quality output than human employees. The transition from a manufacturing- and services-based market to a knowledge- and idea-based economy is contributing to a workplace characterized by rapid changes, ill-defined job requirements, and complex problems that require creativity and collaboration to solve. Creative ideas and innovation are driving global business (Adler, 2001), as evidenced by popular and international organizations like Google, Apple, and Amazon.com. The KSAs required for success are harder to define in this dynamic environment, creating a need for better strategies in defining jobs and roles to inform training (Singh, 2008).

The relatively fluid nature of work is making the boundaries of specific roles less clear. Job descriptions are becoming broader, focusing more on competencies (e.g., *critical thinking* and *problem solving*) instead of specific skills (e.g., proficiency in Microsoft Office applications). The taskwork required for a particular position can change at any time, and employees are expected to adapt to new procedures (Singh, 2008). Transportable-skills training (e.g., team training) will continue to be important, as workers can utilize these skills across performance contexts. The possibility for rapid change is due, in part, to the current knowledge-based market (Cascio, 2019). Modern organizations are placing more value on innovation and looking for ways to leverage knowledge for competitive advantage, resulting in a surge of technological advancements with shorter life-cycles (Cooke, 2001; Powell & Snellman, 2004).

New technology certainly impacts the technical skills we train for; but non-technical skills (i.e., "soft skills") are also being spotlighted, such as those related to competencies like creativity, problem solving, and adaptability (e.g., see Carnevale et al., 2015, PayScale, 2016).

Unfortunately, these ambiguous constructs are the focus of much debate in the literature regarding their definition, appropriate breadth, and potential overlap with related constructs. This has resulted in areas of research lacking theoretical development. Essentially, the requirements for effective performance are more broad and ill-defined than the more-observable KSAs required in the traditional workplace. This could mean that employees may benefit from being trained 'broader' rather than 'deeper' in a particular domain. Related theory might be informed through qualitative interviews with managers to provide rich insight to how these competencies might look in the context of work. Researchers should continue to make progress in defining these constructs and their lower-level components so that they can be targeted in training initiatives. Without a concrete understanding of the specific KSAs captured by these constructs, the effects of our efforts to develop the workforce in this regard will be limited.

The structure of work is also evolving as corporations downsize and practice flatter hierarchies (Malone, 2004), coinciding with an increase in the use of teams across industries (Cross, Rebele, & Grant, 2016). Flat hierarchies are characterized by decentralized management and distributed decision making (Malone, 2004). Not only does this highlight the importance of training general teamwork skills, but also the importance of integrating teamwork considerations with concepts traditionally studied at the individual level. For instance, a good 'problem solver' may or may not be effective in collaborating with a team to solve problems. Researchers should work to develop training programs that fully integrate teamwork concepts to develop valuable skills that twenty-first-century workers need.

Another structural change is an increase in the use of contract-based employees (Bonet, Cappelli, & Hamori, 2013; McGovern, 2017), meaning that those who work for a particular company might not be fully employed by that company at all. These nonstandard work arrangements challenge traditional perspectives of organizational boundaries, as well as the roles and responsibilities of each party in an employment relationship. As a result, more employees are taking charge of their own professional development. Workers are relying less on employers for training and opting for independent programs that offer certificates, skills badges, or micro-credentials. For example, massive open online courses (or MOOCs) are self-paced e-learning programs. MOOCs can cover both technical and nontechnical skills, with topics ranging from sophisticated data-analysis to business negotiations. These courses are typically provided by universities through an online platform (e.g., Coursera, edX), attracting trainees with a desirable brand image (e.g., Harvard, MIT, Wharton) and the convenience of an at-home or on-the-go education.

In summary, macrolevel changes in the economy trickle down to necessitate an emphasis on innovation, nontechnical skills training, and team-based work.

Researchers should work to define and develop twenty-first-century skills, while practitioners should find ways to include nontraditional employees in workplace interventions or capitalize on the flourishing market for self-managed learning. We expect to see an increase in self-selected and e-learning programs, as they provide flexible solutions for nontraditional employees who may not receive developmental opportunities from the organizations to which they are contracted. This increase will likely coincide with advancements in technology.

Technology Is Changing

The exponential growth of technological capabilities is a trending topic in both academic writing and the popular press (Brynjolfsson, Rock, & Syverson, 2017). Beyond offering new methods of approaching training, technology will also impact the standard organizational structure and roles played by employees (see Cascio & Montealegre, 2016). Incorporating new technology into existing organizations requires effective change implementation practices. Organizations often invest in new technology with the intent of enhancing performance, but productivity can suffer if employees are not prepared to handle such changes in work structure. Adopting and integrating new technology into an existing work system requires a new set of skills (Bartel, Ichniowski, & Shaw, 2007). These changes demand not only new technical competencies, but also nontechnical competencies to equip employees with the KSAs necessary for managing the new system and shifts in traditional roles. Organizations that take a holistic approach to change implementation by supplementing a new technology with training outperform those that neglect the need for training (Boothby, Dufour, & Tang, 2010). Preparedness training is one example of an intervention that can help in implementing a new technology. This type of training encourages positive attitudes toward upcoming changes; allowing employees to accept, adopt, and adapt to the new system with ease (Ouadahi, 2008). As organizations incorporate more technology that changes the way work is carried out, we will see more information from scholars interested in facilitating effective change implementation.

We are also seeing more training and development approaches that incorporate micro-learning and learning games. Gamification of training involves integrating features of video games with training content to supplement instruction and engage trainees at a relatively low cost. Recent research indicates that gamification could add to the perceived value of training for employees and enhance their learning experience (Landers & Armstrong, 2017). Micro-learning is another technologically driven training enhancement that provides flexibility in where employees complete training sessions, as well as the functionality to train using mere fragments of time; although research shows only a limited understanding of the effectiveness of micro-learning, it is certainly shaping the education industry's approach to technological innovations in the classroom (Job & Ogalo, 2012). Many speculate that the use of online-based learning will provide opportunities to meet these needs (e.g., Gatta, 2008); but researchers caution practitioners to give special attention to program usability, user proficiency with computers and motivation, and support for older employees to ensure training effectiveness (Lim, Lee, & Nam, 2007). Meta-analytic evidence indicates that web-based instructional methods can be as effective as classroom-based approaches, particularly when web-based methods provide opportunities for practice and feedback (Sitzmann, Kraiger, Stewart, & Wisher, 2006). In addition, programs combining web- and classroom-based instruction tend to be more effective than those including only one instructional method (Sitzmann et al., 2006).

With innovations in virtual reality and AI on the rise, advanced technology is becoming more affordable and accessible by the general population. Greater access to advanced technology enables us to do more than ever before as organizational researchers and practitioners. Inevitably, we will continue to see increased human interaction with technology and interdisciplinary collaboration to design efficient systems. As we look to automation for efficiency and opportunities to reduce liability from human error, the skill sets necessary for effectiveness are evolving. We will continue to see new methods of delivering training content that incorporate newfound capabilities (e.g., e-learning programs), which will further allow researchers to investigate the effectiveness of new learning methods.

Worker Behavioral Patterns Are Changing

A growing labor force with many different types of people and lifestyles is revealing values of flexibility and autonomy, and this extends into perspectives of career development. Millennial workers place greater importance on rapid career advancement and the development of new skills than older generations, ultimately leaving their jobs more quickly in pursuit of new opportunities (Ng, Schweitzer, & Lyons, 2010). Accordingly, organizations are advertising flexible benefits as a method to attract young talent (Rau & Hyland, 2002); an issue of growing importance, as rapid changes in the market position workforce talent as a key source of competitive advantage (see Boudreau & Ramstad, 2005). Fortunately, technological advancements provide novel solutions (e.g., MOOCs) that complement new behavioral patterns of the workforce with self-directed or self-paced learning.

Research has long indicated the efficacy of training strategies focused on the learner in combination with more traditional instructional methods like classroom-style lectures (e.g., behavior modeling; Simon & Werner, 1996). Technology has enhanced these approaches by providing organizations with the resources to adapt training programs to a self-paced format that matches idiosyncratic lifestyles, giving employees more autonomy over when and where they develop their skills. This might be in the form of short lessons on a smartphone app or on the Internet, or even on-the-job with feedback from sociometric badges that collect real-time data throughout performance episodes. These methods of learning and assessing learning should be investigated further by researchers to determine their efficacy as training tools. We need a better understanding of the mechanisms behind informal training to determine and improve upon its utility as a method of organizational training.

Workers are also spending less time developing tenure with a single organization, in favor of job-hopping as a way to rapidly advance their careers in a competitive market. Organizations will need to respond to the needs of this generation of workers by providing individualized opportunities for career development (Burke & Ng, 2006). Additionally, job descriptions are becoming harder to define as job duties are becoming less structured in nature and requiring more tacit skills. These factors increase the demand for training focused on KSAs that are more transferable across job contexts, such as soft skills related to interpersonal communication or teamwork (Robles, 2012). For example, leadership training is effective in eliciting not only positive reactions from training participants, but also attitudinal and behavioral change (Lacerenza, Reyes, Marlow, Joseph, & Salas, 2017).

The behavioral norms of the labor force are shifting, both within and outside of the workplace. These shifts can be considered micro-level changes that are driven by all of the issues discussed in this chapter (e.g., cultural changes, globalization, technological advancements). Fortunately, technology and new approaches to training content have facilitated organizations' responses to these changes. As a result, today's employees are receiving more adaptive and tailored training than ever before.

Implications for Dominant Training Paradigms

All of the changes and implications discussed provide a new lens for examining the impact of training initiatives, and in some ways might affect the way we think about training research in general. As workforce composition expands beyond the traditional demographic majorities, we are able to learn more about training effectiveness across subgroups. As the selection of training delivery and implementation methods broadens, we will be confronted with new challenges to traditional paradigms of thought. Methods that proved effective in the past may need additional considerations to serve the same benefits to all learners. The theories built around the conventional world of work may or may not apply to our 'new normal'. This means that researchers need to reevaluate our models of training effectiveness. We should test our theories against new training methods and designs, with our diverse workforce, to reveal opportunities to discover more about what works and why.

Training researchers will benefit from collaborations with social, education, and cognitive psychologists to build new theories and design programs that maximize learning for trainees of all ages and backgrounds. Technology-driven trends also encourage interdisciplinary collaboration. Human-factors and information-technology professionals will complement research teams as we learn more about how the usability of different devices and digital platforms impacts training effectiveness. Technological advancements might also allow us to reexamine old questions with new perspectives. For instance, e-learning and smartphone-based apps afford new means for studying massed versus different levels of distributed practice across demographic groups (Kraiger, 2014). Digital forms of spaced practice (e.g., through a smartphone app with learning games) simplify and allow for more data collection across multiple time points, potentially revealing deeper insight to within-person effects like those related to affect or motivation. We also see opportunities to study the effects of feedback delivery throughout learning initiatives, a key factor in trainee motivation to learn (Noe, 1986).

The traditional purpose of training is to provide workers with the KSAs necessary to be effective employees. With the changes discussed in this volume, auxiliary purposes served by training are beginning to receive recognition. We are interested in seeing how organizations start to capitalize on these effects. For instance, Cascio (2019) suggests that satisfied employees serve as brand ambassadors; and providing training signals to employees that the organization cares about their professional development – positioning training as an avenue to enhance brand imaging. Training might also be used as a way to enhance employee commitment to the organization (see Tannenbaum, Mathieu, Salas, & Cannon-Bowers, 1991) in a time when professional development and continuous learning is held in high esteem by the workforce and job-hopping is common. Employers should do all they can to foster a climate where employees want to stay; providing training and development opportunities that allow them to continuously learn could be one way to achieve this.

We also recognize a greater question of accountability in preparing the workforce. With wide recognition of a skills gap, stakeholders wonder whether it is the responsibility of the K-12 education system, postsecondary institutions, or corporate training programs to ensure workers have the KSAs needed in today's organizations. We see this as a great opportunity for qualitative research that provides a richer understanding of the various needs and expectations across all levels of the labor market. Baldwin, Ford, and Blume (2017) note that it is vital to know what it is like to be in each person's shoes (e.g., employee, trainer, leader) in the context of an organization in order to maximize the transfer of learned behaviors. Qualitative findings can inform the way we define and measure twenty-first-century skills, clarify and align the goals of all participants from workers to policy makers, and lead to effective training designs that leverage the benefits of the contemporary workplace.

Conclusion

The way people learn has not changed; what is changing is the organizational expectations on how to deliver and implement training (see Table 17.2). Global changes are impacting the way we think about and carry

Table 17.2 *Summary of training implications*

Changes in the Modern Workplace	Implications for Training Content and Objectives	Implications for Training Design and Delivery	Suggestions for Training Research and Practice
Workforce Composition *more diversity in culture and age*	• Retraining of older adults for in-demand skills • More cross-cultural competence and diversity training	• Fewer time restrictions for older employees • Offer training outlines to summarize learning content	• Research: uncover instructional solutions that satisfy all demographic ranges of trainees • Practice: conduct needs assessments to reveal the specific training considerations necessary for a particular organization
Organizational Landscape *little clarity in roles and necessary skills, flat organizations*	• More of a focus on 'soft skills' • Greater use of self-selected training	• Integration of technical and nontechnical skills training in a single intervention • More micro-credentials and skills badges	• Research: define and develop twenty-first-century skills; fuse frameworks for technical and nontechnical skill development • Practice: incorporate nontraditional employees in training interventions
Technology *new solutions alter system structures, novel training methods*	• More preparedness training to manage shifting roles • Training technical skills that adapt to swift-changing technology	• Gamification of training • More online platforms and e-learning programs (MOOCs)	• Research: uncover methods of facilitating change implementation; collaborate across disciplines to design effective systems • Practice: give special attention to program usability, user proficiency, and trainee motivation
Behavioral Patterns *employee desire for autonomy, rapid career advancement*	• More leadership-based training • More adaptive and tailored training	• More programs offering a self-paced format • Greater use of micro-learning (e.g., with smartphone apps)	• Research: examine the effectiveness of informal learning, as well as new assessment techniques • Practice: provide individualized opportunities for development

out work, mobilizing an evolution in organizational science and practice. No longer is it the norm to work in homogeneous groups with typical employment arrangements and nine-to-five shifts. Significant changes, such as the current influx of technology and diversity, can reveal gaps in what we know about training; but they also reveal opportunities for us to improve training with newfound capabilities. The focus of this chapter is on the impact we anticipate seeing in training research and practice as the workplace continues to evolve, but we close by reiterating the strong foundation of evidence that precedes us. We rely on that foundation to aid us in pioneering new territories in training, to continue the legacy of evidence-based training, and to drive the development of a workforce that thrives in our dynamic world of work.

Acknowledgements

This work was supported in part by grants NNX16AP96G and NNX16AB08G from The National Aeronautics and Space Administration (NASA) to Rice University.

References

Adler, P. S. (2001). Market, hierarchy, and trust: The knowledge economy and the future of capitalism. *Organization Science, 12*, 215–234. doi: 10.1287/orsc.12.2.215.10117

Baldwin, T. T., Ford, J. K., & Blume, B. D. (2017). The state of transfer of training research: Moving toward more consumer-centric inquiry. *Human Resource Development Quarterly, 28*, 17–28. doi: 10.1002/hrdq.21278

Bartel, A., Ichniowski, C., & Shaw, K. (2007). How does information technology affect productivity? Plant-level comparisons of product innovation, process improvement and worker skills. *Quarterly Journal of Economics, 122*, 1721–1758. doi: 10.1162/qjec.2007.122.4.1721

Beier, M. E. (2008). International review of industrial and organizational psychology. In G. P. Hodgkinson & J. K. Ford (Eds.), *International Review of Industrial and Organizational Psychology, 2008*. Chichester, UK: John Wiley & Sons.

Beier, M. E., Teachout, M. S., & Cox, C. B. (2012). The training and development of an aging workforce. In W. C. Borman & J. W. Hedge (Eds.), *The Oxford handbook of work and aging* (pp. 436–453). New York, NY: Oxford University Press

Bell, B. S., Tannenbaum, S. I., Ford, J. K., Noe, R. A., & Kraiger, K. (2017). 100 years of training and development research: What we know and where we should go. *Journal of Applied Psychology, 102*, 305–323. doi: 10.1037/apl0000142

Berman, E., Bound, J., & Griliches, Z. (1994). Changes in the demand for skilled labor within US manufacturing: evidence from the annual survey of manufactures. *Quarterly Journal of Economics, 109*(2), 367–397.

Bezrukova, K., Spell, C. S., Perry, J. L., & Jehn, K. A. (2016). A meta-analytical integration of over 40 years of research on diversity training evaluation. *Psychological Bulletin, 142*, 1227–1274. doi: 10.1037/bul0000067

Bird, A., Mendenhall, M., Stevens, M. J., & Oddou, G. (2010). Defining the content domain of intercultural competence for global leaders. *Journal of Managerial Psychology*, *25*, 810–828. doi: 10.1108/02683941011089107

Black, J. S., & Mendenhall, M. (1990). Cross-cultural training effectiveness: A review and a theoretical framework for future research. *Academy of Management Review*, *15*, 113–136. doi: 10.2307/258109

Bonet, R., Cappelli, P., & Hamori, M. (2013). Labor market intermediaries and the new paradigm for human resources. *Academy of Management Annals*, *7*, 339–390. doi: 10.1080/19416520.2013.774213

Boothby, D., Dufour, A., & Tang, J. (2010). Technology adoption, training and productivity performance. *Research Policy*, *39*, 650–661. doi: 10.1016/j.respol.2010.02.011

Boudreau, J. W., & Ramstad, P. M. (2005). Talentship, talent segmentation, and sustainability: A new HR decision science paradigm for a new strategy definition. *Human Resource Management*, *44*, 129–136. doi: 10.1002/hrm.20054

Brynjolfsson, E., Rock, D., & Syverson, C. (2017). *Artificial intelligence and the modern productivity paradox: A clash of expectations and statistics (No. w24001)*. Cambridge, MA: National Bureau of Economic Research. doi: 10.3386/w24001

Burke, L. A., & Hutchins, H. M. (2008). A study of best practices in training transfer and proposed model of transfer. *Human Resource Development Quarterly*, *19*, 107–128. doi: 10.1002/hrdq.1230

Burke, R. J., & Ng, E. (2006). The changing nature of work and organizations: Implications for human resource management. *Human Resource Management Review*, *16*, 86–94. doi: 10.1016/j.hrmr.2006.03.006

Callahan, J. S., Kiker, D. S., & Cross, T. (2003). Does method matter? A meta-analysis of the effects of training method on older learner training performance. *Journal of Management*, *29*, 663–680. doi: 10.1016/S0149-2063_03_00029-1

Cannon-Bowers, J. A., Rhodenizer, L., Salas, E., & Bowers, C. A. (1998). A framework for understanding pre-practice conditions and their impact on learning. *Personnel Psychology*, *51*, 291–320. doi: 10.1111/j.1744-6570.1998.tb00727.x

Carnevale, A. P., Strohl, J., & Gulish, A. (2015). *College is just the beginning: Employers' role in the $1.1 trillion postsecondary education and training system* (Report No. ED558166). Washington, DC: Georgetown University Center on Education and the Workforce. Retrieved from https://files.eric.ed.gov/fulltext/ED558166.pdf

Cascio, W. F. (2019). Training trends: Macro, micro, and policy issues. *Human Resource Management Review*, *29*, 284–297.

Cascio, W. F., & Montealegre, R. (2016). How technology is changing work and organizations. *Annual Review of Organizational Psychology and Organizational Behavior*, *3*, 349–375. doi: 10.1146/annurev-orgpsych-041015-062352

Charness, N. (2009). Skill acquisition in older adults: Psychological mechanisms. In S. J. Czaja & J. Sharit (Eds.), *Aging and work* (pp. 232–258). Baltimore, MD: Johns Hopkins University Press.

Chebium, R. (2015, January 7). How to create an effective cross-cultural training program. Retrieved from www.shrm.org/hr-today/news/hr-magazine/pages/010215-cross-cultural-training.aspx

Chen, G., Gully, S. M., Whiteman, J. A., & Kilcullen, R. N. (2000). Examination of relationships among trait-like individual differences, state-like individual differences, and learning performance. *Journal of Applied Psychology*, *85*, 835–847. doi: 10.1037/0021-9010.85.6.835

Cooke, P. (2001). Regional innovation systems, clusters, and the knowledge economy. *Industrial and Corporate Change*, *10*, 945–974. doi: 10.1093/icc/10.4.945

Cross, R., Rebele, R., & Grant, A. (2016). Collaborative overload. *Harvard Business Review*, *94*, 74–79.

Dobbin, F., & Kalev, A. (2016). Why diversity programs fail. *Harvard Business Review*, *94*(7), 14.

Equal Employment Opportunity Commission. (2018). Charge statistics. Retrieved from www1.eeoc.gov/eeoc/statistics/enforcement/charges.cfm

Gatta, M. (2008). Low-skill workers, technology, and education: A new vision for workforce development policy. *Economic & Labour Relations Review*, *19*, 109–127. doi: 10.1177/103530460801900108

Goldstein, I. L., & Ford, K. J. (1993). Training in organizations: Needs assessment, development, and evaluation. Pacific Grove, CA: Brooks.

Haccoun, R. R., & Hamtiaux, T. (1994). Optimizing knowledge tests for inferring learning acquisition levels in single group training evaluation designs: The internal referencing strategy. *Personnel Psychology*, *47*, 593–604. doi: 10.1111/j.1744-6570.1994.tb01739.x

Hirschman, C., & Mogford, E. (2009). Immigration and the American industrial revolution from 1880 to 1920. *Social Science Research*, *38*, 897–920. doi: 10.1016/j.ssresearch.2009.04.001

Hughes, A. M., Gregory, M. E., Joseph, D. L., Sonesh, S. C., Marlow, S. L., Lacerenza, C. N., ... & Salas, E. (2016). Saving lives: A meta-analysis of team training in healthcare. *Journal of Applied Psychology*, *101*, 1266–1304. doi: 10.1037/apl0000120

Job, M. A., & Ogalo, H. S. (2012). Micro-learning as innovative process of knowledge strategy. *International Journal of Scientific and Technology Research*, *1*(11). Retrieved from www.ijstr.org/final-print/dec2012/Micro-Learning-As-Innovative-Process-Of-Knowledge-Strategy.pdf

Keith, N., & Frese, M. (2008). Effectiveness of error management training: A meta-analysis. *Journal of Applied Psychology*, *93*, 59–69. doi: 10.1037/0021-9010.93.1.59

Kirkpatrick, D. L. (1994). *Evaluating training programs: The four levels.* San Francisco, CA: Berrett-Koehler. (Original work published 1959.)

Knowles, M. S., Holton, E. F., & Swanson, R. A. (2005). *The adult learner: The definitive classic in adult education and human resource development* (6th ed.). Boston, MA: Elsevier.

Kraiger, K. (2002). Decision-based evaluation. In K. Kraiger (Ed.), *Creating, implementing, and maintaining effective training and development: State-of-the-art lessons for practice* (pp. 331–375). San Francisco, CA: Jossey-Bass.

Kraiger, K. (2008). Transforming our models of learning and development: Web-based instruction as enabler of third-generation instruction. *Industrial and Organizational Psychology*, *1*, 454–467. doi: 10.1111/j.1754-9434.2008.00086.x

Kraiger, K. (2014). Looking back and looking forward: Trends in training and development research. *Human Resource Development Quarterly*, *25*, 401–408. doi: 10.1002/hrdq.21203

Kubeck, J. E., Delp, N. D., Haslett, T. K., & McDaniel, M. A. (1996). Does job-related training performance decline with age? *Psychology and Aging, 11*, 92–107. doi: 10.1037/0882-7974.11.1.92

Lacerenza, C. N., Reyes, D. L., Marlow, S. L., Joseph, D. L., & Salas, E. (2017). Leadership training design, delivery, and implementation: A meta-analysis. *Journal of Applied Psychology.* doi: 10.1037/apl0000241

Landers, R. N., & Armstrong, M. B. (2017). Enhancing instructional outcomes with gamification: An empirical test of the Technology-Enhanced Training Effectiveness Model. *Computers in Human Behavior, 71*, 499–507. doi: 10.1016/j.chb.2015.07.031

Lim, H., Lee, S.-G., & Nam, K. (2007). Validating E-learning factors affecting training effectiveness. *International Journal of Information Management, 27*, 22–35. doi: 10.1016/j.ijinfomgt.2006.08.002

Malone, T. (2004). *The future of work: How the new order of business will shape your organization, your management style, and your life.* Boston, MA: Harvard Business School Press.

Martin, H. J. (2010). Workplace climate and peer support as determinants of training transfer. *Human Resource Development Quarterly, 21*, 87–104. doi: 10.1002/hrdq.20038

Mayer, R. E. (1979). Can advance organizers influence meaningful learning? *Review of Educational Research, 49*, 371–383. doi: 10.3102/00346543049002371

McGovern, M. (2017). *Thriving in the gig economy: How to capitalize and compete in the new world of work.* Wayne, NJ: Career Press.

Moseley, J. L., & Dessigner, J. C. (2007). *Training older workers and learners: Maximizing the performance of an aging workforce.* San Francisco, CA: Wiley & Sons.

Ng, E. S. W., Schweitzer, L., & Lyons, S. T. (2010). New generation, great expectations: A field study of the millennial generation. *Journal of Business and Psychology, 25*, 281–292. doi: 10.1007/s10869-010-9159-4

Noe, R. A. (1986). Trainees' attributes and attitudes: Neglected influences on training effectiveness. *Academy of Management Review, 11*, 736–749. doi: 10.5465/AMR.1986.4283922

Noe, R. A., & Colquitt, J. A. (2002). Planning for training impact: Principles of training effectiveness. In K. Kraiger (Ed.), *Creating, implementing, and managing effective training and development* (pp. 53–79). San Francisco, CA: Jossey-Bass.

Ouadahi, J. (2008). A qualitative analysis of factors associated with user acceptance and rejection of a new workplace information system in the public sector: A conceptual model. *Canadian Journal of Administrative Sciences, 25*, 201–213. doi: 10.1002/cjas.65

PayScale (2016). *2016 workforce-skills preparedness report.* Seattle, WA: PayScale, Inc. Retrieved from www.payscale.com/data-packages/job-skills

Phillips, J. J. (2012). *Handbook of training evaluation and measurement methods.* London, UK: Routledge.

Powell, W. W., & Snellman, K. (2004). The knowledge economy. *Annual Review of Sociology, 30*, 199–220. doi: 10.1146/annurev.soc.29.010202.100037

Quiñones, M. A., Ford, J. K., Sego, D. J., & Smith, E. M. (1995). The effects of individual and transfer environment characteristics on the opportunity to perform trained tasks. *Training Research Journal, 1*, 29–48.

Rau, B. L., & Hyland, M. A. M. (2002). Role conflict and flexible work arrangements: The effects on applicant attraction. *Personnel Psychology, 55*, 111–136. doi: 10.1111/j.1744-6570.2002.tb00105.x

Roberson, L., Kulik, C. T., & Tan, R. Y. (2012). Effective diversity training. In Q. M. Roberson (Ed.), *The Oxford handbook of diversity and work* (pp. 341–365). New York, NY: Oxford University Press.

Robles, M. M. (2012). Executive perceptions of the top soft skills needed in today's workplace. *Business Communication Quarterly, 75*, 453–465. doi: 10.1177/1080569912460400

Salas, E., & Cannon-Bowers, J. A. (2001). The science of training: A decade of progress. *Annual Review of Psychology, 52*, 471–499. doi: 10.1146/annurev.psych.52.1.471

Salas, E., Tannenbaum, S. I., Kraiger, K., & Smith-Jentsch, K. A. (2012). The science of training and development in organizations: What matters in practice. *Psychological Science in the Public Interest, 13*(2), 74–101. doi: 10.1177/1529100612436661

Senge, P. M., Kleiner, A., Roberts, C., Ross, R. B., & Smith, B. J. (2014). *The fifth discipline fieldbook: Strategies and tools for building a learning organization.* New York, NY: Crown Publishing Group.

Simon, S. J., & Werner, J. M. (1996). Computer training through behavior modeling, self-paced, and instructional approaches: A field experiment. *Journal of Applied Psychology, 81*, 648–659. doi: 10.1037/0021-9010.81.6.648

Singh, P. (2008). Job analysis for a changing workplace. *Human Resource Management Review, 18*, 87–99. doi: 10.1016/j.hrmr.2008.03.004

Sitzmann, T., Bell, B. S., Kraiger, K., & Kanar, A. M. (2009). A multilevel analysis of the effect of prompting self-regulation in technology-delivered instruction. *Personnel Psychology, 62*, 697–734. doi: 10.1111/j.1744-6570.2009.01155.x

Sitzmann, T., Kraiger, K., Stewart, D., & Wisher, R. (2006). The comparative effectiveness of web-based and classroom instruction: A meta-analysis. *Personnel Psychology, 59*, 623–664. doi: 10.1111/j.1744-6570.2006.00049.x

Smith-Jentsch, K. A., Cannon-Bowers, J. A., Tannenbaum, S. I., & Salas, E. (2008). Guided team self-correction: Impacts on team mental models, processes, and effectiveness. *Small Group Research, 39*, 303–327. doi: 10.1177/1046496408317794

Sommers, D., & Franklin, J. C. (2012). Overview of projections to 2020. *Monthly Labor Review, 135*(1), 3–20.

Tannenbaum, S. I., Mathieu, J. E., Salas, E., & Cannon-Bowers, J. A. (1991). Meeting trainees' expectations: The influence of training fulfillment on the development of commitment, self-efficacy, and motivation. *Journal of Applied Psychology, 76*, 759–769. doi: 10.1037/0021-9010.76.6.759

Toossi, M. (2012). Projections of the labor force to 2050: A visual essay. *Monthly Labor Review, 135*(10), 3–16.

Tracey, J. B., Hinkin, T. R., Tannenbaum, S., & Mathieu, J. E. (2001). The influence of individual characteristics and the work environment on varying levels of training outcomes. *Human Resource Development Quarterly, 12*, 5–23.

Wenger, E., McDermott, R. A., & Snyder, W. (2002). *Cultivating communities of practice: A guide to managing knowledge.* Boston, MA: Harvard Business School Press.

Wolfson, N. E., Cavanagh, T. M., & Kraiger, K. (2014). Older adults and technology-based instruction: Optimizing learning outcomes and transfer. *Academy of Management Learning & Education, 13*, 26–44. doi: 10.5465/amle.2012.0056

Wolfson, N. E., & Kraiger, K. (2014). Cognitive aging and training: The role of instructional coherence and advance organizers. *Experimental Aging Research, 40*, 164–186. doi: 10.1080/0361073X.2014.882206

Yan, B. (2006). Demand for skills in Canada: the role of foreign outsourcing and information-communication technology. *Canadian Journal of Economics/ Revue canadienne d'économique, 39*(1), 53–67.

Young, C. K. (2017). *Age and training: A meta-analysis examining training features* (Doctoral dissertation). Retrieved from ProQuest Dissertations & Theses. (Accession No. 2018-13260-247).

18 Leader Behaviors and the Changing Nature of Work

John W. Michel and Gary Yukl

Introduction

For decades, scholars have sought to understand the behaviors that leaders in organizations use to accomplish their objectives. The research has examined how leader behaviors are related to the performance and satisfaction of followers or subordinates, and how the leadership situation influences a leader's choice of behaviors and the effectiveness of the behaviors. Much of the early leadership research only examined one or two broad behavior constructs (e.g., consideration and initiating structure, transformational and transactional leadership). Although the broad behaviors can be useful, it is more important to examine results for the specific, component behaviors in each broad construct. The effects of the component behaviors will vary depending on the leadership situation, and major changes in the situation can change the relative importance of the component behaviors. The purpose of this chapter is to discuss why focusing on a leader's flexibility in using specific component leader behaviors is important as the nature of work changes. We accomplish this objective by exploring some specific ways in which work is changing, and by suggesting how leaders could respond to such changes. We begin with a description of a leader behavior taxonomy that was especially helpful for understanding how leaders will need to adapt their behavior to changes in the nature of work and the workplace. We will also explore how some traits, values, and skills of leaders help to explain how they can effectively lead others as the nature of work changes.

Types of Leadership Behavior

The most useful way to describe leadership behavior is with a hierarchical taxonomy that includes four broad behavior constructs: task-oriented behavior, relations-oriented behavior, change-oriented behavior, and external behavior (Yukl, 2012, 2013). Each broad construct has a different primary objective and includes specific component behaviors that are useful for achieving that objective.

Broad task-oriented and relations-oriented behaviors were identified in some of the early research on leader behavior used to influence subordinates or followers (Fleishman, 1953; Halpin & Winer, 1957). The behavior category labeled "Initiating structure" involves a concern for task objectives, and the behavior labeled "Consideration" involves a concern for relationships. Drawing on this early work, other leader researchers proposed similar broad behavior categories such as goal emphasis and supportive leadership (Bowers & Seashore, 1966), instrumental leadership and supportive leadership (House, 1971), and performance and maintenance behavior (Misumi & Peterson, 1985). The task-oriented behaviors are used to improve the efficiency and reliability of current operations and to ensure that work unit members understand task procedures, objectives and priorities. Specific task-oriented behaviors include setting goals and assigning tasks, monitoring performance and providing feedback, coordinating work among employees, providing contingent rewards and punishments, and resolving operational problems. Relations-oriented behaviors are used to maintain high task motivation, confidence, cooperation, and mutual trust for members of the work unit. Specific relations-oriented behaviors include providing support and encouragement, developing employee skills and confidence through coaching and mentoring, consulting with employees on important decisions, involving subordinates in making decisions that affect them, and encouraging cooperation and teamwork. Recent meta-analyses of the hundreds of studies conducted on task-oriented and relations-oriented behaviors found that these behavior categories are related to indicators of leadership effectiveness (Burke et al., 2006; DeRue, Nahrgang, Wellman, & Humphrey, 2011; Judge, Piccolo, & Ilies, 2004).

Starting in the early 1980s, the leadership literature was dominated by research on charismatic and transformational theories of leadership (Bass, 1985). An important contribution of these theories was an emphasis on change-oriented behaviors. However, it was not until the 1990s that change-oriented behaviors were recognized as a distinct category of leadership behaviors (Ekvall & Arvonen, 1991; Yukl, 1999; Yukl, Gordon, & Taber, 2002). Change-oriented behaviors are used to adapt to the demands, threats, and opportunities affecting the leader's work unit or organization. Specific change-oriented behaviors include communicating an inspiring vision for the work unit or organization, proposing major changes in objectives or strategies for attaining them, influencing the implementation of major changes, encouraging innovative thinking, and facilitating collective learning. These behaviors are especially relevant for executive leaders and are more effective in dynamic, uncertain work environments. Research has found a positive relationship between change-oriented leader behaviors and outcomes such as job attitudes, managerial effectiveness, and independent ratings of leader performance (Gil, Rico, Alcover, & Barrasa, 2005; Michel, Lyons, & Cho, 2010).

The task-oriented, relations-oriented, and change-oriented behaviors were usually defined in terms of behaviors leaders use with subordinates or followers, but it has long been recognized that external-focused behaviors are also relevant for managerial effectiveness (e.g., Mintzberg, 1973). External leadership behaviors are used to promote and defend the interests of the work unit or organization, to identify and understand threats and opportunities in the external environment, and to obtain necessary resources, support, and information for the survival and success of the leader's group or organization. Specific external leadership behaviors include networking, external monitoring, and representing (Yukl, 2012). Networking includes developing and maintaining good relationships with constituents both inside and outside the organization who can provide important information, resources, and political support. External monitoring involves gathering information about important events and changes in the external environment, identifying strengths, weaknesses, opportunities, and threats for the organization, and identifying best practices to help the organization maintain a competitive advantage. Representing involves promoting and defending the reputation of the group or organization, lobbying for resources and support from peers and superiors, negotiating agreements with outsiders such as clients and suppliers, and engaging in political tactics to influence superiors and governmental agencies. Research on external behaviors is limited, but this research has found a positive relationship with managerial effectiveness (Hassan, Prussia, Mahsud, & Yukl, 2018; Kim & Yukl, 1995), group performance (Ancona & Caldwell, 1992; Druskat & Wheeler, 2003), and organizational performance (Grinyer, Mayes, & McKiernan, 1990).

Adapting Behavior to the Leadership Situation

Several situational leadership theories describe the relationship of broad or specific leader behaviors to outcomes in different situations. For example, Vroom and Yetton (1973) found that managers made more successful decisions when they used the specific decision procedures proposed in their normative decision model. Involving other people such as subordinates in making a leader decision was more effective when subordinates or followers shared the leader's objectives, had relevant knowledge not possessed by the leader, and their cooperation was needed to implement the decision. Research on the multiple-linkage model (Yukl, 1989, 2012) suggested that the types of tasks performed by subordinates determine which specific leadership behaviors are most relevant. For example, it is more important to clarify task goals and work procedures when the tasks are novel and complex. It is more important to provide support and encouragement when the work is difficult and stressful. Other research suggests that leaders use different behaviors depending on the skills and motives of subordinates (Hersey & Blanchard, 1984) or the nature of the exchange relationship with each subordinate (Graen & Uhl-Bien, 1995).

Flexible leadership theory can be useful for understanding leadership and the changing nature of work, because it draws on several relevant literatures (such as leadership, human resource management, strategic management and organizational change) to explore how leaders effectively influence employees, teams and organizations (Yukl & Lepsinger, 2005; Yukl & Mahsud, 2010). According to the theory, it is especially important for leaders to be flexible in their use of leadership behaviors when the situation is changing. Which broad and specific behaviors are most relevant also depends on the performance determinant a leader wants to influence. Task-oriented behaviors are very relevant for improving efficiency, relations-oriented behaviors are very relevant for improving employee commitment to task objectives and mutual trust and cooperation, and the change-oriented and external behaviors are very relevant for facilitating adaptation to a changing situation and new threats and opportunities for the work unit or organization. Top executives have the most responsibility for making major changes in an organization, but the support of managers at all levels is needed to effectively implement these changes. Effective adaptation often requires not only actions by individual leaders in an organization, but also some changes in management programs and organizational structures. Here again, top management usually has the primary responsibility for such changes.

As the nature of the work changes, leaders need to be flexible and adaptive in how they respond to the changes. Yet, little recent empirical research on how leaders adapt their behavior to changing situations has been conducted thus far, especially with respect to the changing nature of work. The implications of workplace changes have been discussed by Burke and Ng (2006) and by the SHRM Foundation (*Economist* Intelligence Unit, 2014). We will focus on three broad types of changes facing organizations in the future: demographic changes, technological changes, and strategic changes. Moreover, we will consider how the skills, values, and integrity of leaders affect how well they can lead others as the nature of work changes.

Implications of Changes in the Leadership Situation

Changes in workplace demographics, technology and innovation, and globalization will influence how work is done and the types of leadership behavior likely to be effective. Some of the specific changes include the following: (1) demographic changes with regard to worker gender, race, and age; (2) increase in the use of artificial intelligence in the workplace; (3) changes in the forms of work, specifically an increase in contingent work, telework, and distributed work; (4) a more highly educated workforce; (5) a drive for innovation and working in the gig economy; (6) changes in occupations and work tasks; and (7) an increase in global strategic alliances and a more global workforce. In the following sections, we discuss each of these changes and the implications for effectively leading subordinates, teams and organizations in the future.

Demographic Changes

As described by Burke and Ng (2006), a number of demographic changes will have a powerful effect on the nature of work in organizations. These changes include an aging workforce, generational differences, and increased workforce diversity. Each of these demographic changes is discussed in detail in the following sections.

The Aging Workforce. As the Baby Boom generation reaches retirement age, coupled with lower birth rates, organizations need to prepare to accomplish more work with fewer human resources. In fact, by 2030 approximately one in five people will be 65 or older (Ortman, Velkoff, & Hogan, 2014). In addition to a potentially smaller workforce, the retirement of older workers also means a potential loss of tacit knowledge from the organization. In preparation for the looming retirement of the Baby Boom generation, leaders need to retain and employ older workers in ways that will be most useful for an organization. The Society for Human Resource Management's 2014 Survey on Aging (SHRM Foundation, 2014a) found that retaining older workers is important because respondents believe they possess more knowledge and skills than younger workers, are more responsible than younger workers, act more professionally and have a stronger work ethic than younger workers, and can help the organization retain tacit knowledge through mentorship. In light of these changes, leaders should find ways to get older workers to stay longer with the organization, consider how to modify policies and practices to appeal to older workers, and determine how to facilitate knowledge transfer from older workers nearing retirement (Kelly, 2015).

Leaders can draw on various behaviors, skills and programs in response to these issues. To create greater appeal to older workers, leaders can emphasize relations-oriented behaviors and programs. For example, one way to retain older workers beyond retirement age is to implement programs geared toward these workers, such as part-time, telework, or flexible work arrangements. Additionally, leaders can increase retention of older workers by providing support and encouragement and letting older workers know that the organization cares about their wellbeing and values their contributions (Eisenberger, Stinglhamber, Vandenberghe, Sucharski, & Rhoades, 2002). Finally, to facilitate knowledge transfer, leaders can implement training and mentoring programs that use older workers to teach younger workers.

Generational Differences/Life Stage. With a large proportion of the workforce getting older, organizations are paying closer attention to how employees of different ages work together. Three different generations currently comprise the workforce: the Baby Boom Generation (1943–1963), Generation X (1964–1980), and the Millennial Generation (1981–2000). Differences among employees from these generational cohorts are expected because the life experiences, and the historical and social life events (e.g., wars, disasters, economic fluctuations, technological advances), for a particular generational cohort differ from those for other generational cohorts (Kupperschmidt, 2000).

While some research has shown that differences between generations can affect the attitudes, behaviors, values, and expectations of people (Macky, Gardner, & Forsyth, 2008), other researchers have found similarities among generations with respect to engagement, commitment, preferences for learning, and job performance (Gentry, Griggs, Deal, Mondore, & Cox, 2011). In fact, despite the often popular focus on generational differences, research has found that differences between employees may be more a function of a person's position in the life stage and career stage rather than a generational difference per se (SHRM Foundation, 2014b). A person's life and career stages determine what they expect and need to be happy and productive. Some issues are common among employees regardless of life and career stage. For example, employees with young children, regardless of age, have more in common because of their need to balance work and life issues, and single employees regardless of age have more discretionary time and are less tied down. However, other issues are different depending on a person's life and career stage. Employees in their late 60s are focusing on transitioning from work to retirement; whereas, employees in their late 20s and early 30s are more focused on getting promoted and taking on more managerial experiences.

As such, managers should be keenly aware of where employees are in their life and career stage and lead them accordingly. Employees in the early career stage are in their early 20s and just trying to navigate the working world beyond college. For employees in the early career stage, leaders may want to strongly emphasize task-oriented behaviors such as clarifying expectations and monitoring performance, but in a supportive way that encourages younger employees to get engaged and work hard (Gentry et al., 2011). Employees in the second career stage (in their late 20s and early 30s) are primarily focused on getting promoted and moving into supervisory or managerial roles. When leading employees in this second career stage, leaders may want to focus more attention on providing coaching and mentoring to them. Employees in the third (mid-30s to early 50s) and fourth (late 50s through 60s) career stages have many years of experience and have achieved many promotions and professional accomplishments. For employees in the third and fourth career stage, leaders should consider delegating more important decisions, as long as the employee has demonstrated high levels of ability. Leaders should also consider asking these employees to serve as coaches and mentors to younger employees in an effort to build identity and commitment to the organization. Finally, employees who are in their late 60s can be used for assignments with a time horizon appropriate for their retirement plans, and they may also want to serve as a coach and mentor to young employees to ensure that important tacit knowledge is retained in the organization.

Workforce Diversity. Organizations continue to experience an increase of workforce diversity with respect to gender and racial differences in the workplace. As of 2016, women were estimated to make up nearly 47% of the labor force in the United States, and nearly 52% of these women held management and professional positions (Center for American Progress, 2017). However, in 2016 only around 5% of CEOs at S&P 500 companies were women, and women had only about 20% of board seats of the *Fortune* 500 companies (Kinicki &

Fugate, 2018). Furthermore, the gender wage pay gap continues as women only earn approximately 80% of what their male counterparts earn on average (Anonymous, 2018), despite the fact that women have earned the majority of bachelor's and master's degrees in recent years (US Census Bureau, 2017).

Similarly, racial groups are expected to continue to experience discrimination and their own glass ceiling, despite the fact that the US workforce is becoming increasingly diverse. In fact, the US Census Bureau predicts that between 2012 and 2060 there will be continued growth in the Asian American, Hispanic American, and African American populations, and by 2060 these minority groups are expected to constitute approximately 60% of the workforce (Toossi, 2016). Despite this growth. Hispanics and African Americans currently hold fewer professional and managerial jobs, they earn less, and the number of race-based discrimination charges examined by the Equal Employment Opportunity Commission increased from 294 in 1995 to 678 in 2015 (Kinicki & Fugate, 2018).

In response to these challenges, leaders need to be keenly aware of their values, biases, and actions when supervising people from such a diverse workforce. Organizations should be careful to ensure that those promoted into leadership roles embody the values essential for ethical leaders. One especially important value is integrity, which refers to dealing with others in an open and honest way, keeping promises and commitments, and not attempting to manipulate or deceive others. Another important value is humility, which refers to treating others with dignity and respect, admitting limitations and mistakes, and emphasizing contributions of others. Fairness and justice is another important value, and it refers to encouraging and supporting the fair treatment of others, speaking out against unfair or unjust practices, and refraining from commonly held stereotypes and prejudices when managing people different from oneself.

Drawing on their own value systems, leaders should foster an organizational climate that supports and encourages diversity. First, leaders should look for ways to foster appreciation and tolerance for diversity. For instance, they can do so by setting a good example, encouraging respect and understanding of differences, celebrating different beliefs and traditions, and encouraging and supporting others who demonstrate tolerance for diversity. Furthermore, leaders should facilitate equal opportunity and reduce discrimination in personnel decisions (Cox & Blake, 1991). People involved in selecting and promoting employees should be trained to become aware of and to reduce biases based on racial, ethnic, or gender stereotypes. Leaders should also make a conscious effort to ensure that employees from different racial and ethnic backgrounds and genders are given equal opportunities in mentoring and coaching programs, and in training, and equal promotional opportunities. Leaders can also implement a diversity training program that creates a better understanding of diversity problems and helps employees become more self-aware about stereotyping and intolerance (Cox & Blake, 1991).

Technological Changes

Technology is rapidly changing the way work gets done. As new technologies are invented, work is becoming cheaper, faster and more efficient to accomplish in many cases. It has become easier to analyze massive amounts of data to make decisions (big data), and to share data and information easily and quickly around the world. Two types of technological change that are likely to be of particular relevance to leaders are artificial intelligence and distributed work.

Artificial Intelligence. The continued development of computers and "artificial intelligence" (AI) will eliminate some types of jobs and change the nature of work for managers. For example, a well-developed AI program can handle many of the monitoring and reporting tasks for managers. AI can also be used to sift through big data and help managers make better decisions with the data. In fact, a study by Frey and Osborne (2013) found that 47% of jobs in America are at high risk of becoming automated, and other research has found that AI-enabled automation of knowledge work could lead to a possible $9 trillion reduction in labor costs (*Economist*, 2017). Although increased automation may improve efficiency and process reliability, too much AI may lead to decreases in employee commitment, satisfaction and wellbeing, especially if the AI technologies are used only to reduce costs by replacing employees with machines. Kolbjørnsrud, Amico, and Thomas (2016) provided some suggestions for how AI can help to redefine the work of employees and their managers. Since managers spend upwards of 54% of their time on administrative coordination and control activities, AI technology can be used to sift through huge amounts of data quickly, allowing managers and employees to dedicate more time to understanding what the data mean in the context of the organization's strategy and culture. Also, when leaders redesign work so that less-desirable tasks are accomplished through AI, employees have more time to focus on tasks that have greater purpose and impact for them.

Accordingly, to effectively lead in the AI era, leaders need to be humble, adaptable, have a strong vision, and promote employee engagement (Chamorro-Premuzic, Wade, & Jordan, 2018). When adopting AI technology, it is important for leaders to demonstrate humility by being aware about what they do not know, and to trust those around them to provide their expertise. Leaders also need to be adaptable when implementing AI technologies. For example, leaders should be open to new and innovative ways of getting work accomplished in their groups and be able to reassure employees that AI is being adopted to make work more efficient and reliable, and not simply to automate work and reduce the workforce. Finally, leaders should encourage innovative thinking and collaborate with employees in adopting AI initiatives, so that employees feel part of the decision-making and implementation processes.

Distributed Work. Due to increases in mobile technologies (e.g., laptops, cellphones), communication systems, long commutes, and the desire for more flexible work arrangements, there is an increased desire for distributed or remote work (telecommuting, interacting online). Workers today prefer to work outside the office in hotel spaces, coffee shops, or even in airports between client visits, rather than commuting long distances to office spaces that have a lot of interruptions (Fried & Hansson, 2013; Hansson, 2013). One study found that on average, managers only spend about 40% of their time in a traditional office, 30% of their time in a home office, and the remainder of their time in other locations (Ware, 2011). Working remotely is also becoming more popular with the advent of online meeting platforms such as Google Hangouts, Go to Meeting, and Skype. These technologies allow members to effectively engage with their teams despite being physically separated. For example, it is possible that holographic projection technology could be used to make it appear that team members are sitting around the same conference table, even though they are actually in different parts of the country.

Managing employees remotely carries additional challenges not often encountered when managing employees in person. Some of the unique challenges about managing employees remotely include relinquishing control and allowing for more autonomy, knowing when and how much to communicate with employees, setting expectation, but not micro-managing employees, and whether to focus on time on task versus completion of work (Hearn, 2016). Furthermore, some managers believe that working remotely can hurt communication, collaboration, efficiency and effectiveness within a workgroup. In a now famous move, Marissa Mayer, CEO of Yahoo, wrote a memo explaining that to become a truly great place to work, it was important for employees to work side-by-side and that telework would be discouraged moving forward (Tkaczyk, 2013). Despite potential issues, working remotely makes sense for many employees and managing remote employees does not require a different skill set for managers (Knight, 2015). However, it is important that managers set clear expectations and help remote employees to identify with and feel connected to the others in the workgroup. To ensure that employees understand expectations and boundaries while working remotely, it is important for managers to set specific goals, rules, and policies that help to establish a clear understanding for employees regarding how they should spend their time, report progress on goals, and deal with any unexpected interruptions or delays in getting work accomplished (Knight, 2015). Managers can also use different relations-oriented behaviors including developing collective identification through the use of ceremonies, symbols, and rituals; encouraging social interactions among members through teambuilding or other fun work events; conducting process analysis sessions; and increasing incentives for mutual cooperation. Managers can also provide support to employees working remotely by serving as a coach, facilitator, and consultant. This support includes obtaining any information, resources, and political support the team needs to be successful. It is also important to provide the technological support needed to ensure that online systems work effectively and the team is able to communicate effectively.

Despite the benefits of distributed work, being constantly connected can lead to issues such as increased stress and burnout for employees who are constantly checking email, taking phone calls after work hours, reviewing reports and responding to customers, long after the traditional work day has ended (Golden, 2006). As such, the lines between work and family have become increasingly blurred as technologies have made it easier to work from anywhere at any time (Golden, Veiga, & Simsek, 2006). In an effort to reduce work–family conflict that employees may experience due to distributed work, leaders can provide social support to employees. In addition to providing instrumental and emotional support to help employees conserve resources and deal with potential stress and burnout related to their work (Halbesleben, 2006), recent research has demonstrated that leaders can provide support to help employees attain a balance between their responsibilities at home and work (Kossek, Pichler, Hammer, Bodner, & Hammer, 2014). Such family support includes providing flexible work schedules, allowing employees to bring children to work when needed, and simply demonstrating an interest in the issues employees may be facing outside of work (Bagger & Li, 2014). Given that work–life conflict is common and supervisor family support has been shown to reduce work–family conflict (Kossek et al., 2014) and increase performance (Bagger & Li, 2014) beyond traditional forms of social support, the future leader behavior literature should consider including family support as an important component behavior and train leaders how and when to use such behaviors to improve the attitudes and behaviors of their employees.

Potential Problems Involving Technology. The increased use of technology helps to make work more efficient, but organizations have experienced a number of related problems in recent years, including threats to customer data privacy due to cybersecurity hacks, the weaponization of AI systems, and ransomware in the cloud (Giles, 2018). In addition to loss of important data, technology threats can also cause disruptions in the work flow. To deal with these problems, leaders need to anticipate potential cyber threats facing the organization and put in place policies and practices to protect the company secrets and customer data. In particular, leaders can employ individual specialists (or a team of them) to keep the organization up-to-date about evolving vulnerabilities from hackers and to identify and protect points of weakness in the organization's IT systems. Leaders should also develop clear security policies and practices that become part of the organizational culture. It is important to clearly communicate the policy to all employees and to provide adequate rewards to employees for identifying and preventing any cybersecurity threats.

Changes in Occupations and Work Tasks

The nature of occupations and how work is accomplished is also changing. Many jobs are becoming increasingly complex due to interactions between human skills and rapidly changing technologies (Grant & Parker, 2009;

Wegman, Hoffman, Carter, Twenge, & Guenole, 2018). Along with the increase of technology is an increased emphasis on continuous innovation to develop and maintain a sustainable competitive advantage. Moreover, there is a growing interest in the "gig economy," which includes a greater emphasis on independent contractors and shorter-term employment agreements. Managers need to create conditions that support these changes.

Knowledge Workers (More Highly Educated Workforce). There is a greater number of knowledge workers in the economy than ever before (Bureau of Labor Statistics, n.d.). Knowledge workers are necessary as work is quickly becoming more cognitively complex, collaborative, and more dependent on technological competence. Most knowledge workers like more autonomy, conduct work that is more conceptual than tangible in nature, desire continued training and developmental opportunities, and expect higher salaries and benefits packages. Also, the retention of good knowledge workers will become more important because of their special skills. Leaders should empower such workers and provide adequate recognition and developmental opportunities to ensure valued knowledge workers remain with the company. Leaders should also include knowledge workers in the process of making decisions about major changes for which they have relevant knowledge.

Drive for Innovation. In a recent article from the Forbes Coaches Council (2017), increases in innovation are evident as 63% of companies are hiring chief innovation officers and more than 90% are using technology to develop new products or services. According to Mumford, Scott, Gaddis, and Strange (2002), leading innovation is an unusually complex process that requires expertise from the leader. The changes require more encouragement by leaders of innovation within the firm, more encouragement and facilitation of collective learning, more encouragement of innovative thinking by employees, and more empowerment of employees to participate in innovative efforts. At the same time, leaders need to provide support and encouragement so that employees feel psychologically safe to try new initiatives and to learn from their failures. Leaders will also have to develop capabilities to manage the increased rate of change in products and services due to an increase in innovation.

Gig Economy. The gig economy refers to an increased propensity for organizations to hire independent contractors on a short-term basis (Alton, 2018). Features that attract people to engage in the gig economy include working as a "free agent" for any company depending on need, being paid for limited contracts, and having multiple sources of income. According to a report by CareerCast.com (Strauss, 2017), some jobs that have become popular in the gig economy include multimedia artists, accountants, management analysts, and software and web developers. Organizations that participate in the gig economy will likely experience a major shift in organizational culture (Schneider, 1987). Because employees who engage in the gig economy are looking for alternative work arrangements marked by greater flexibility, organizations may experience greater fluctuation of employees in and out of the workplace. This volatility in employment could lead to the development of an organizational culture that is weak or differentiated (Schneider, Salvaggio, & Subirats, 2002), which means that members may have a difficult time understanding how to respond to the environment. Leaders need to create a strong purpose based on important values and lead by example to model the importance of these values. To ensure that employees focus on the tasks and responsibilities needed to get work accomplished effectively, leaders should clarify employee expectations about what is required to accomplish goals and outcomes. It is also important to carefully monitor the operations of independent contractors operating in the gig economy until they establish a level of rapport and trust with the employee.

Global and Strategic Changes

There are a number of changes related to globalization. Improvements in technology, transportation, and supply chain management have increased competition both nationally and globally. Regardless of whether an organization operates globally, most organizations will be affected in one way or another by the global environment or workforce. As a result of these changes, leaders need to become attuned to globalization issues and adopt strategies to get the most out of a global workforce and global competition.

Global Strategic Alliances. Few industries are immune to increased global competition, and strategic alliances and international cooperative agreements are becoming increasingly popular. Data from the Securities Data Corporation, suggests that the number of strategic alliances have increased approximately 25% each year over the past decade (UK Essays, 2015). A strategic alliance is a long-term cooperative agreement between two or more independent companies to manage a specific project with the goal of improving the competitive advantage of those involved in the alliance (Dussauge & Garrette, 1999). The key parameters of strategic alliances according to Dussauge and Garrette include opportunism, necessity, and speed. Some strategic alliances to improve global competitive advantage were used by Google and Lycos Europe, Bayer Healthcare and Intendis, Fiat and Chrysler, and City Bank and American Express. In order to identify opportunities for strategic alliances, leaders need to engage in external monitoring to understand their competition, network with others in the industry to gather information and gain political support, encourage innovation in order to maintain a competitive advantage, and envision and encourage change when necessary. Leaders also need to manage fluid external dependencies and shifting alliances by effectively using their social and professional networks to help their organizations compete in the global economy.

Global Workforce and Careers. A positive benefit of competing in the global economy is access to a global workforce. In his book *The World Is Flat* (2005),

Thomas Friedman estimates that the global labor market has grown by 5 billion people. As such, savvy organizations are expanding their reach for talent to candidates from all over the world. However, employing a global workforce creates additional challenges for leaders. Employing a global workforce can increase diversity in the workforce, but managers have to engage in more virtual work with employees working in different time zones, differences in language, and cultural barriers (Burke & Ng, 2006). Other challenges with managing a global workforce include deploying the skills where needed regardless of geographic location, spreading knowledge throughout the organization regardless of where it originates, and identifying who has the ability to function effectively in the organization's different regions (Roberts, Kossek, & Ozeki, 1998). As organizations move beyond their home borders, leaders must seek to understand the new markets and environments. Organizations in Europe and Asia-Pacific have made a more significant jump from individual to collective leadership approaches in the past decade than have US organizations. As organizations become more global, leaders will have to think about which behaviors are appropriate for the particular performance determinant they face, but also which behaviors are most relevant for the cultural context.

Leader Values and Integrity

In recent years, the leadership literature has placed greater emphasis on understanding the importance of a leader's values and integrity (Brown & Treviño, 2006). Theories such as servant leadership theory (Greenleaf, 1977), spiritual leadership theory (Fry, 2003), and authentic leadership theory (Avolio, Gardner, Walumbwa, Luthans, & May, 2004) have emphasized values such as honesty, altruism, compassion, fairness, courage, stewardship, and humility. Proponents of ethical-based theories contend that leaders whose behavior reflects these values will be more effective because ethical leaders seek to build mutual trust and respect in their work groups. Ethical leaders also work hard to foster a fair and collaborative work environment and resolve conflicts using integrative solutions (Yukl, 2013). More work is needed to further examine the extent to which leader values and integrity influence the relationships between specific component behaviors and leader effectiveness. For example, it is plausible to expect that followers will be more open to influence from leaders who exhibit high levels of integrity, empathy, and fairness toward them. Alternatively, followers who perceive a leader as unethical and dishonest may be more skeptical of the leader's influence attempts. However, research examining leader values and integrity as a boundary condition of effective leader behavior is still very limited, and more studies are needed to understand how leader values influence the use of the specific behaviors and the effects of the behaviors.

Leader Traits and Skills

Leadership scholars have long sought to identify traits and skills that distinguish leaders from non-leaders and predict leader advancement and success. The leader traits most consistently related to these outcomes included achievement motivation, energy level, dominance (or socialized need for power), extraversion, agreeableness, conscientiousness, and honesty/integrity (DeRue et al., 2011; Hoffman, Woehr, Maldagen-Youngjohn, & Lyons, 2011).

Although there is a general understanding of the leader traits and behaviors that predict leader effectiveness, little research has been conducted to integrate the leader trait and leader behavior literature. One exception is a meta-analysis conducted by DeRue and colleagues (DeRue et al., 2011). In this study, the authors examined the relationships between leader traits, leader behaviors and leadership effectiveness outcomes. An important contribution of this paper is the integration of traits and behaviors in predicting leader effectiveness. In terms of comparing the relative importance of traits and behaviors, the results demonstrated that behaviors were more important predictors of leader effectiveness. However, the results also indicate that leader behaviors mediate some relationships between traits and leader effectiveness. For example, task competence–related attributes (e.g., intelligence, conscientiousness) were most predictive of leader effectiveness through task-oriented leadership; whereas, interpersonal attributes (e.g., extraversion, agreeableness) were most predictive of leader effectiveness through relations-oriented leadership. Moreover, both types of traits were similarly related to leader effectiveness through change-oriented behaviors.

A potential implication of these findings is that leaders need to be aware of their dominant traits and think about what behaviors they may draw on most often when leading others. For example, extraverted leaders may draw on consultative or collaborative decisions because of their decision to create a more social environment; whereas, introverts may be more likely to delegate decision-making authority in order to give followers an opportunity to engage in introspection and reflection. Likewise, leaders high in openness to experience may be more likely to encourage innovation and creativity in their work groups; whereas, leaders lower in openness to experience may draw more heavily on setting specific goals and structuring work. Based on these assertions, future research should further investigate the extent to which specific traits influence leader effectiveness through some leader behaviors and not others.

Leader skills are state-like individual differences that involve the ability to perform some type of activity or task more or less effectively. The early literature identified three broad categories of leader skills: technical skills, interpersonal skills, and conceptual skills (Katz, 1955). Technical skills are primarily concerned with knowledge about methods, processes, and equipment for conducting work and factual knowledge about the organization and its products and services. Specific technical skills include technical knowledge and organizing and planning. Interpersonal skills include social skills and an ability to empathize and communicate effectively with others. Specific interpersonal skills include empathy, charm, diplomacy, and oral communication. Conceptual skills include foresight, intuition, and good judgment when making sense of ambiguous situations. Specific conceptual skills include analytical ability, deductive and inductive reasoning, logic, and concept formation. Other more specific types of skills that have been explored in the leadership literature include political skills (Ferris, Treadway, Perrewé, Brouer, Douglas, & Lux, 2007), emotional (Goleman, Boyatzis, & McKee, 2002) and social (Zaccaro, Gilbert, Thor, & Mumford, 1991) intelligence, and competencies involving the ability to use specific types of behavior such as planning and coaching (e.g., Mumford, Campion, & Morgeson, 2007).

In their meta-analysis of research on leader skills, Hoffman and colleagues found that leader effectiveness was most strongly related to interpersonal skills, oral communication, management skills, problem-solving skills, and decision-making skills (Hoffman et al., 2011). Though not equivalent to actual behavior, skills can help some leaders select and use specific component behaviors more effectively. It is plausible that similar to traits, the effects of leader skills on leader effectiveness is also mediated by leader behaviors. For example, task-oriented behaviors likely serve to primarily mediate technical skills, relations-oriented behaviors likely mediate interpersonal skills, and change-oriented behaviors likely mediate conceptual skills. The research on how skills can enhance the effects of leader behavior is still very limited, and more studies are needed to discover how a leader's skills influence the choice of behaviors and leader flexibility in adapting behavior to different situations.

Summary and Recommendations

As the nature of work and the workplace changes, leaders need to be flexible and adaptive to be effective. Past theory and research has identified a wide range of leader behaviors and management programs that appear relevant for some situations. However, there has been little research to directly study how effectiveness of specific behaviors is related to changes in the leadership situation. It seems likely that all the change-oriented leadership behaviors and some of the external behaviors are becoming more important for understanding and adapting to the increasingly uncertain external environment for most organizations. Some of the relations-oriented behaviors also seem likely to become more important as the workforce becomes more diverse and unstable. Problem solving will probably be the most important task-oriented behavior in an uncertain and turbulent future world, and some of the other specific task behaviors may also become more important. Table 18.1 briefly summarizes the earlier description of specific behaviors likely to become more important in the future. Conceptual and interpersonal skills are likely to become more important for most leaders, and some types of technical skills will also become more important. As yet there is little direct evidence to support most of these predictions.

To improve leadership theory and practice, scholars need to pay more attention to the way leaders change their behavior to cope with different situations and to adapt effectively to changes in the nature of work and the

Table 18.1 *Examples of leadership behaviors that are becoming more important*

Task-oriented behaviors:
Manage the increased rate of change in products and services
Manage complex new technologies and work processes
Use new computer-based methods of monitoring the work
Anticipate and resolve an increased number of crises and disruptions
Plan ways to prevent cyber-attacks and attempts to steal company secrets

Relations-oriented behaviors:
Encourage cooperation and teamwork for a less stable, more diverse workforce
Empower skilled employees to help make decisions about necessary changes
Provide more support to employees with work–life conflicts and family problems
Encourage and support more appreciation of diversity and equal opportunity
Encourage older employees to stay longer and serve as mentors to young employees

Change-oriented behaviors:
Encourage and facilitate more innovation and flexibility by employees
Encourage and facilitate collective learning and new knowledge diffusion
Lead multi-functional project teams and task forces to implement changes
Implement more frequent changes in work processes and products or services
Develop support for major changes easily misperceived as threats to job security

External behaviors:
Manage fluid external dependencies and shifting strategic alliances
Monitor and understand the external threats and opportunities
Manage global projects involving different cultures
Make effective use of social and professional networks
Manage more virtual project teams and remote employees

workplace. The focus should be on specific behavior rather than the broad, often poorly defined meta-categories that have dominated so much of the past leadership research. Flexible, adaptive leadership cannot be understood by only examining a few broad behaviors. Examining specific behaviors also makes it easier to identify behaviors that mediate the relationship of traits and values to measures of leader effectiveness. It is also important in future research to examine not only the results for individual behaviors, but also the joint and interactive effects among the different behaviors. For example, more supportive behaviors may be appropriate when advocating innovative change to develop a sense of psychological safety within the work group. Similarly, not all respondents will be equally responsive to all leader behaviors. For example, Michel and Tews (2016) noted that followers may be more or less responsive to certain leader behaviors depending on the nature of the relationship between the leader and follower. In general, these authors found that whereas task-oriented behaviors were equally effective in influencing all followers, relations-oriented and change-oriented behaviors were only effective in influencing followers when there was a high-quality LMX relationship. The authors reasoned that followers in high-quality LMX relationships were more responsive to relations and change behaviors because of the feelings of trust, admiration, and respect they had for the leader; whereas, low-quality LMX followers were more skeptical of why the leader was being so supportive or asking them to change. Alternatively, task-oriented behaviors were presumed to influence low-quality LMX followers because these behaviors provide clarification and structure for the expectations needed to fulfill the economic exchange with the leader. Accordingly, future research should explore different combinations of component behaviors and the extent to which different component behaviors are equally effectively for all employees.

In summary, there is a need for more research on how leaders adapt their behavior to changing situations, and also on how the use of different behaviors has increased or decreased as the nature of work, organizations, and societies has been changing. Progress in learning more about these subjects will require much better research designs than the typical survey study with a convenience sample that is found in much of the recent leadership research. Well-designed studies on leader behavior in different or changing situations will make it easier to identify the individual behaviors and patterns of behavior most relevant for flexible, adaptive leadership of organizations in the twenty-first century. Three promising types of studies are field experiments, diary incidents, and simulations.

Field experiments are rare because they are difficult to conduct in real organizations, but a few have been conducted with good results (e.g., Dvir & Shamir, 2003; Hand & Slocum, 1972; Latham & Saari, 1979; Martin, Liao, & Campbell, 2013; Seifert & Yukl, 2010). A longitudinal field experiment would involve training one sample of similar managers to use behaviors expected to be relevant for a new or changing situation. After an appropriate period of time in which managerial effectiveness can be determined, the results for the trained managers can be compared to results for an untrained control group that is less likely to use the behaviors. The findings could be used to identify what training to provide to the managers in the control group and perhaps follow-up training to the experimental group of managers.

Another good research method that should be used more often in research on leader adaptation to change is a longitudinal diary study. Leaders and subordinates in several similar subunits of an organization could keep a weekly diary in which they record incidents describing leader behavior over a period of time in which the changes occur, with follow-up measures on the effectiveness of each leader in implementing the changes (e.g., boss ratings, subordinate attitudes and performance). Diary incidents can also be used to examine the behaviors leaders use in different situations. The behaviors that are most relevant for effectiveness in each situation can be identified, and behavior questionnaires can also be used at the end of the period of study to provide an additional way to measure leader behavior.

A third methodology that should be used more often in future leader behavior research is simulations and leadership games, which have been used to some extent in the leadership literature (Avolio, Waldman, & Einstein, 1988;

Drescher, Korsgaard, Welpe, Picot, & Wigand, 2014). Future research could adopt a simulation game (e.g., the Global Alliance Game, 2012), with several competing teams. Some participants would be asked to serve as the leader of each team during the simulation, and the leader behaviors could be recorded during each session of the simulation and coded into the different leadership behaviors. The simulation could involve changes in the situation such as new threats and opportunities for the teams. For an experimental design in a simulation study, the leaders could be trained in advance to use two or three different patterns of behavior to determine which one is most effective.

References

Alton, L. (2018, January 24). Why the gig economy is the best and worst development for workers under 30. *Forbes.* Retrieved from www.forbes.com/sites/larryalton/2018/01/24/

Ancona, D. G., & Caldwell, D. F. (1992). Bridging the boundary: External activity and performance in organizational teams. *Administrative Science Quarterly, 37,* 634–665.

Anonymous. (2018). Pay Equity & Discrimination. Retrieved June 21, 2018, from https://iwpr.org/issue/employment-education-economic-change/pay-equity-discrimination/

Avolio, B. J., Gardner, W. L., Walumbwa, F. O., Luthans, F., & May, D. R. (2004). Unlocking the mask: a look at the process by which authentic leaders impact follower attitudes and behaviors. *Leadership Quarterly, 15*(6), 801–823.

Avolio, B. J., Waldman, D. A., & Einstein, W. O. (1988). Transformational leadership in a management game simulation. *Group & Organization Management, 13*(1), 59–80.

Bagger, J., & Li, A. (2014). How does supervisory family support influence employees' attitudes and behaviors? A social exchange perspective. *Journal of Management, 40*(4), 1123–1150.

Bass, B. M. (1985). *Leadership and performance beyond expectations.* New York, NY: Harper.

Bowers, D. G., & Seashore, S. E. (1966). Predicting organizational effectiveness with a four-factor theory of leadership. *Administrative Science Quarterly, 11,* 238–263.

Brown, M. E., & Treviño, L. K. (2006). Ethical leadership: A review and future directions. *Leadership Quarterly, 17*(6), 595–616.

Bureau of Labor Statistics, U. (n.d.). STEM 101: Intro to tomorrow's jobs. Retrieved from www.bls.gov/ooq

Burke, C. S., Stagl, K. C., Klein, C., Goodwin, G. F., Salas, E., & Halpin, S. M. (2006). What type of leadership behaviors are functional in teams? A meta-analysis. *Leadership Quarterly, 17*(3), 288–307.

Burke, R. J., & Ng, E. (2006). The changing nature of work and organizations: Implications for human resource management. *Human Resource Management Review, 16*(2), 86–94.

Center for American Progress. (2017). The women's leadership gap. Retrieved July 19, 2018, from www.americanprogress.org/issues/women/reports/2017/05/21/432758/womens-leadership-gap/

Chamorro-Premuzic, T., Wade, M., & Jordan, J. (2018). As AI makes more decisions, the nature of leadership will change. *Harvard Business Review*, 2–7. Retrieved from https://hbr.org/2018/01/as-ai-makes-more-decisions-the-nature-of-leader ship-will-change

Cox, T. H., & Blake, S. (1991). Managing cultural diversity: Implications for organizational competitiveness. *Academy of Management Executive*, 5(3), 45–56.

DeRue, D. S., Nahrgang, J. D., Wellman, N., & Humphrey, S. E. (2011). Trait and behavioral theories of leadership: An integration and meta-analytic test of their relative validity. *Personnel Psychology*, 64(1), 7–52.

Drescher, M. A., Korsgaard, M. A., Welpe, I. M., Picot, A., & Wigand, R. T. (2014). The dynamics of shared leadership: Building trust and enhancing performance. *Journal of Applied Psychology*, 99(5), 771–783.

Druskat, V. U., & Wheeler, J. V. (2003). Managing from the boundary: The effective leadership of self-managed work teams. *Academy of Management Journal*, 46(4), 435–457.

Dussauge, P., & Garrette, B. (1999). *Cooperative strategy: Competing successfully through strategic alliances*. Chichester, UK: Wiley.

Dvir, T., & Shamir, B. (2003). Follower developmental characteristics as predicting transformational leadership: A longitudinal field study. *Leadership Quarterly*, 14(3), 327–344.

Economist, (2017). The future of work. Artificial intelligence: Anything you can do, AI can do better. So how will it change the workplace? Retrieved June 22, 2018, from http://webcache.googleusercontent.com/search?q=cache:BFG_OxtrgHcJ: learnmore.economist.com/story/

Economist Intelligence Unit. (2014). *What's next: Future global trends affecting your organization. Evolution of work and the worker*. New York, NY: SHRM Foundation and Economist Intelligence Unit. Retrieved from www.shrm.org/hr-today/news/hr-magazine/Documents/

Eisenberger, R., Stinglhamber, F., Vandenberghe, C., Sucharski, I. L., & Rhoades, L. (2002). Perceived supervisor support: Contributions to perceived organizational support and employee retention. *Journal of Applied Psychology*, 87(3), 565–573.

Ekvall, G., & Arvonen, J. (1991). Change-centered leadership: An extension of the two-dimensional model. *Scandinavian Journal of Management*, 7, 17–26.

Ferris, G. R., Treadway, D. C., Perrewé, P. L., Brouer, R., Douglas, C., & Lux, S. (2007). Political skill in organizations. *Journal of Management*, 33, 290–320.

Fleishman, E. A. (1953). The description of supervisory behavior. *Personnel Psychology*, 37, 1–6.

Forbes Coaches Council (2017). What can your organization do to become more innovative? Retrieved June 12, 2018, from www.forbes.com/sites/forbescoaches council/2017/07/13/what-can-your-organization-do-to-become-more-innova tive/#55d311cf4bfa

Frey, C. B., & Osborne, M. A. (2013). The future of employment: How susceptible are jobs to computerisation? Retrieved from www.oxfordmartin.ox.ac.uk/down loads/academic/The_Future_of_Employment.pdf

Fried, J., & Hansson, D. H. (2013). *Remote: Office not required*. London, UK: The Crown Publishing Group.

Fry, L. W. (2003). Toward a theory of spiritual leadership. *Leadership Quarterly*, *14*(6), 693–727.

Gentry, W. A., Griggs, T. L., Deal, J. J., Mondore, S. P., & Cox, B. D. (2011). A comparison of generational differences in endorsement of leadership practices with actual leadership skill level. *Consulting Psychology Journal*, *63*(1), 39–49.

Gil, F., Rico, R., Alcover, C. M., & Barrasa, Á. (2005). Change-oriented leadership, satisfaction and performance in work groups. *Journal of Managerial Psychology*, *20*(3/4), 312–328.

Giles, M. (2018). Six cyber threats to really worry about in 2018. Retrieved June 12, 2018, from www.technologyreview.com/s/609641/six-cyber-threats-to-really-worry-about-in-2018/

Global Alliance Game | Carpenter Strategy Toolbox. (2012). Retrieved July 24, 2018, from https://carpenterstrategytoolbox.com/2012/07/25/global-alliance-game/

Golden, T. D. (2006). Avoiding depletion in virtual work: Telework and the intervening impact of work exhaustion on commitment and turnover intentions. *Journal of Vocational Behavior*, *69*(1), 176–187.

Golden, T. D., Veiga, J. F., & Simsek, Z. (2006). Telecommuting's differential impact on work–family conflict: Is there no place like home? *Journal of Applied Psychology*, *91*(6), 1340–1350.

Goleman, D., Boyatzis, R. E., & McKee, A. (2002). *Primal leadership: Realizing the power of emotional intelligence.* Boston, MA: Harvard Business School Press.

Graen, G. B., & Uhl-Bien, M. (1995). Relationship-based approach to leadership: Development of leader-member exchange (LMX) theory of leadership over 25 years: Applying a multi-level multi-domain perspective. *Leadership Quarterly*, *6*(2), 219–247.

Grant, A. M., & Parker, S. K. (2009). Redesigning work design theories: the rise of relational and proactive perspectives. *Academy of Management Annals*, *3*(1), 317–375.

Greenleaf, R. K. (1977). *Servant leadership: A journey into the nature of legitimate power and greatness.* Mahwah, NJ: Paulist Press.

Grinyer, P. H., Mayes, D., & McKiernan, P. (1990). The sharpbenders: Achieving a sustained improvement in performance. *Long Range Planning*, *23*, 116–125.

Halbesleben, J. R. B. (2006). Sources of social support and burnout: a meta-analytic test of the conservation of resources model. *Journal of Applied Psychology*, *91*(5), 1134–45.

Halpin, A. W., & Winer, B. J. (1957). A factorial study of the leader behavior descriptions. In R. M. Stogdill & A. E. Coons (Eds.), *Leader behavior: Its description and measurement.* Columbus, OH: Bureau of Business Research, Ohio State University.

Hand, H. H., & Slocum, J. W. (1972). A longitudinal study of the effect of a human relations training program on managerial effectiveness. *Journal of Applied Psychology*, *56*, 412–418.

Hansson, D. H. (2013). A new workplace manifesto: In praise of freedom, time, space, and work. Retrieved July 19, 2018, from www.fastcompany.com/3020833/a-new-luxury-manifesto-in-praise-of-freedom-time-space-and-working-remotely

Hassan, R., Prussia, G., Mahsud, R., & Yukl, G. (2018). How leader networking, external monitoring, and representing are relevant for effective leadership. *Leadership and Organization Development Journal, 39*(4), 454–467.

Hearn, S. (2016). The modern challenges of managing remote performance. Retrieved July 19, 2018, from www.entrepreneur.com/article/284150

Hersey, P., & Blanchard, K. H. (1984). *The management of organizational behavior* (4th ed.). Englewood Cliffs, NJ: Prentice Hall.

Hoffman, B. J., Woehr, D. J., Maldagen-Youngjohn, R., & Lyons, B. D. (2011). Great man or great myth? A quantitative review of the relationship between individual differences and leader effectiveness. *Journal of Occupational and Organizational Psychology, 84*(2), 347–381.

House, R. J. (1971). A path–goal theory of leader effectiveness. *Administrative Science Quarterly, 16,* 321–339.

Judge, T. A., Piccolo, R. F., & Ilies, R. (2004). The forgotten ones? The validity of consideration and initiating structure in leadership research. *Journal of Applied Psychology, 89*(1), 36–51.

Katz, R. L. (1955). Skills of an effective administrator. *Harvard Business Review*, January–February, 33–42.

Kelly, B. K. (2015). *The aging workforce: Four steps to maximize older workers in your organization.* Chapel Hill, NC: UNC Kenan-Flager Business School, University of North Carolina.

Kim, H., & Yukl, G. (1995). Relationships of self-reported and subordinate-reported leadership behaviors to managerial effectiveness and advancement. *Leadership Quarterly, 6,* 361–377.

Kinicki, A., & Fugate, M. (2018). *Organizational behavior: A practical, problem-solving approach* (2nd ed.). Columbus, OH: McGraw-Hill.

Knight, R. (2015). How to manage remote direct reports. *Harvard Business Review Digital Articles*, 2–6. Retrieved from http://search.ebscohost.com/login.aspx?direct=true&db=buh&AN=118666569&site=ehost-live

Kolbjørnsrud, V., Amico, R., & Thomas, R. J. (2016). How artificial intelligence will redefine management. *Harvard Business Review*, July, 1–7. Retrieved from https://hbr.org/2016/11/how-artificial-intelligence-will-redefine-management

Kossek, E. E., Pichler, S., Hammer, L. B., Bodner, T., & Hammer, L. B. (2014). Workplace social support and work–family conflict: A meta-analysis clarifying the influence of general and work–family-specific supervisor and organizational support, workplace social support and work–family conflict construct definitions and linkages. *Personnel Psychology, 64*(2), 1–15.

Kupperschmidt, B. R. (2000). Multigeneration employees: Strategies for effective management. *Health Care Manager, 19,* 65–76.

Latham, G. P., & Saari, L. (1979). The application of social learning theory to training supervisors through behavioral modeling. *Journal of Applied Psychology, 64,* 239–246.

Macky, K., Gardner, D., & Forsyth, S. (2008). Generational differences at work: Introduction and overview. *Journal of Managerial Psychology, 23,* 857–861.

Martin, S. L., Liao, H., & Campbell, E. M. (2013). Directive versus empowering leadership: A field experiment comparing impacts on task proficiency and proactivity. *Academy of Management Journal, 56*(5), 1372–1395.

Michel, J. W., Lyons, B. D., & Cho, J. (2010). Is the full-range model of leadership really a full-range model of effective leader behavior? *Journal of Leadership & Organizational Studies, 18*(4), 493–507.

Michel, J. W., & Tews, M. J. (2016). Does leader–member exchange accentuate the relationship between leader behaviors and organizational citizenship behaviors? *Journal of Leadership & Organizational Studies, 23*(1), 13–26.

Michel, J. W., Tews, M. J. & Allen, D. G. (2019). Fun in the workplace: A review and expanded theoretical perspective. *Human Resource Management Review, 29,* 98–110.

Mintzberg, H. (1973). *The nature of managerial work.* New York, NY: Harper & Row.

Misumi, J., & Peterson, M. (1985). The performance-maintenance (PM) theory of leadership: Review of a Japanese research program. *Administrative Science Quarterly, 30,* 198–223.

Mumford, M. D., Scott, G. M., Gaddis, B., & Strange, J. M. (2002). Leading creative people: Orchestrating expertise and relationships. *Leadership Quarterly, 13*(6), 705–750.

Mumford, T. V., Campion, M. A., & Morgeson, F. P. (2007). The leadership skills strataplex: Leadership skill requirements across organizational levels. *Leadership Quarterly, 18*(2), 154–166.

Ortman, J. M., Velkoff, V. A., & Hogan, H. (2014). An aging nation: The older population in the United States population estimates and projections current population reports. Retrieved from www.census.gov/population

Roberts, K., Kossek, E. E., & Ozeki, C. (1998). Managing the global workforce: Challenges and strategies. *Academy of Management Executive, 12*(4), 93–106.

Schneider, B. (1987). The people make the place. *Personal Psychology, 40,* 437–453.

Schneider, B., Salvaggio, A. N., & Subirats, M. (2002). Climate strength: A new direction for climate research. *Journal of Applied Psychology, 87*(2), 220–229.

Seifert, C. F., & Yukl, G. (2010). Effects of repeated multi-source feedback on the influence behavior and effectiveness of managers: A field experiment. *Leadership Quarterly, 21*(5), 856–866.

SHRM Foundation (2014a). *The aging workforce – state of older workers in US organizations.* Alexandria, VA: Society for Human Resource Management.

SHRM Foundation (2014b). *What's next: Future global trends affecting your organization. Evolution of work and the worker.* New York, NY: Society for Human Resource Management.

Strauss, K. (2017, March 8). 10 great "gig economy" jobs for 2017. *Forbes.* Retrieved from www.forbes.com/sites/karstenstrauss/2017/03/08/10-great-gig-economy-jobs-for-2017/#1403e24c25c9

Tkaczyk, C. (2013). Marissa Mayer breaks her silence on Yahoo's telecommuting policy. *Fortune.* Retrieved July 19, 2018, from http://fortune.com/2013/04/19/marissa-mayer-breaks-her-silence-on-yahoos-telecommuting-policy/

Toossi, M. (2016). A look at the future of the US labor force to 2060. *Spotlight on Statistics: US Bureau of Labor Statistics.* Retrieved June 22, 2018, from www.bls.gov/spotlight/2016/a-look-at-the-future-of-the-us-labor-force-to-2060/home.htm

UK Essays (2015). Why have strategic alliances grown in popularity? Retrieved June 13, 2018, from www.ukessays.com/essays/business-strategy/strategic-alliances-is-the-cause-of-popularity.php

US Census Bureau. (2017). Educational attainment in the United States. Retrieved June 21, 2018, from www.census.gov/data/tables/2017/demo/education-attainment/cps-detailed-tables.html

Vroom, V. H., & Yetton, P. W. (1973). *Leadership and decision making.* Pittsburgh, PA: University of Pittsburgh Press.

Ware, J. (2011). The changing nature of work: What's in it for me? Retrieved June 22, 2018, from www.Slideshare.Net/Jpware/The-Changing-Nature-Of-Work-Whats-In-It-For-Me

Wegman, L. A., Hoffman, B. J., Carter, N. T., Twenge, J. M., & Guenole, N. (2018). Placing job characteristics in context: Cross-temporal meta-analysis of changes in job characteristics since 1975. *Journal of Management, 44*(1), 352–386.

Yukl, G. (1989). Managerial leadership: A review of theory and research. *Journal of Management, 15*(2), 251–289.

Yukl, G. (1999). An evaluative essay on current conceptions of effective leadership. *European Journal of Work and Organizational Psychology, 8*(1), 33–49.

Yukl, G. (2012). Effective leadership behavior: What we know and what questions need more attention. *Academy of Management Perspectives, 26*, 66–85.

Yukl, G. (2013). *Leadership in organizations* (8th ed.). Upper Saddle River, NJ: Pearson.

Yukl, G., Gordon, A., & Taber, T. (2002). A hierarchical taxonomy of leadership behavior: Integrating a half century of behavior research. *Journal of Leadership and Organizational Studies, 9*(1), 15–32.

Yukl, G., & Lepsinger, R. (2005). Why integrating the leading and managing roles is essential for organizational effectiveness. *Organizational Dynamics, 34*(4), 361–375.

Yukl, G., & Mahsud, R. (2010). Why flexible, adaptive leadership is important. *Consulting Psychology Journal, 62*(2), 81–93.

Zaccaro, S. J., Gilbert, J. A., Thor, K. K., & Mumford, M. D. (1991). Leadership and social intelligence: Linking social perspectiveness and behavioral flexibility to leader effectiveness. *Leadership Quarterly, 2*, 317–342.

19 The Changing Nature of Teams
Recommendations for Managing Twenty-First-Century Teamwork

Justin M. Jones, Gouri Mohan,
Hayley M. Trainer, and Dorothy R. Carter

The twentieth century was characterized by dramatic changes in the way organizations structured work. The rising economic tide driven by the industrial revolution created an economy fueled by innovation and competition. Complex socioeconomic forces incentivized organizations to globalize and gave rise to work that required adaptability, advanced technologies, speed, and specialization. These changes signaled the end of solitary functional work and the birth of collaborative, dynamic, and highly specialized work structured around *teams* (Kozlowski & Bell, 2003; Kozlowski & Ilgen, 2006; Mathieu, Heffner, Goodwin, Salas, & Cannon-Bowers, 2000).

In turn, the importance of teamwork to the twentieth-century economy sparked an extensive body of scientific research focused on the drivers of team effectiveness. This stream of research convincingly demonstrates that team members' *thoughts* (e.g., team cognitive states such as shared mental models; Mathieu et al., 2000), *feelings* (e.g., team affective states such as trust or cohesion; Beal, Cohen, Burke & McLendon, 2003; De Jong & Elfring, 2010; Langfred, 2004), *motivational states* (e.g., collective efficacy; Marks, 1999), and *teamwork behavioral processes* (e.g., communication, coordination; Marks, Mathieu, & Zaccaro, 2001), significantly impact team performance. Thus, a key responsibility of any team leader or manager is to help facilitate the thoughts, feelings, motivations, and behaviors needed to meet team task demands (Hackman, 1998; Zaccaro, Rittman, & Marks, 2001).

In the twenty-first century, the need for teamwork is continuing to intensify, posing new challenges for managing teams. For instance, many important and complex human endeavors – such as addressing demands related to climate change (Weaver et al., 2014), cybersecurity (Steinke et al., 2015), counterterrorism (Spitzmuller & Park, 2018), global health (Gittell, Godfrey, & Thistlethwaite, 2013), or long-duration space exploration (Mesmer-Magnus, Carter, Asencio, & DeChurch, 2016) – are demanding equally complex patterns of teamwork across collectives that are substantially larger, more diverse, and geographically distributed than many teams of the previous century. Further challenging team management, many organizations have decentralized managerial duties and instilled teams with substantial authority to manage themselves. Moreover, advanced technologies are continuing to reshape the nature of teamwork by allowing for technologically mediated communication and virtual collaboration across unprecedented degrees of space and time. In fact, recent advancements in robotics and artificial intelligence suggest that certain

Table 19.1 *The changing nature of teamwork: recommendations for management*

Reality	Defining Characteristics	Recommendations for Managing Teamwork
#1: Complex Problems Require Adaptive Patterns of Teamwork across Small and Large Groups	• Fluidity in team memberships, roles and structures • Increasing use of ad hoc and short-term teams • Teams working closely with other teams • Working on multiple teams simultaneously and over time	• Emphasize coordination and collaboration • Allow teams to make and recover from mistakes during training • Socialize new team members through coaching and formal socialization procedures • Create processes to retain specialized knowledge within teams • Train employees on general teamwork skills, emphasize learning and sharing, and implement cross-training to reduce the impact of dynamism
#2: Teams are Assembled and Led by Team Members as well as Managers	• Shared, dynamic, and informal leadership among team members • Team self-assembly • Teams comprised of short-term freelance workers • Teaming with crowds	• Create a psychologically safe environment and help secure resources for the team • Facilitate effective team assembly through assembly technology, or informing others about employee profiles • Train employees on how to provide leadership behaviors regardless of role, through training or coaching
#3: Technology is Interwoven with Teamwork	• Technology is an integral part of teamwork processes • Virtual collaboration is the norm • Rise of artificial intelligence, decision-making tools, and co-bots • Teaming with robots is becoming a reality	• Make sure that the forms of technology used match the task being performed • Consider the strengths and weaknesses of the different forms of teammates when creating teams • Allow employees sufficient time to train with new technologies or robotic team members to facilitate shared knowledge and trust

technologies will not be merely "tools" used by humans, but instead, will be akin to actual "team members."

The changing nature of teamwork is shifting what it means to "manage" a team. In this chapter, we aim to illustrate how teams are changing and the implications of these changes for managing teamwork. We identify *three key realities* of twenty-first-century teamwork, summarized in Table 19.1: (1) organizational challenges are demanding complex and fluid patterns of teamwork across small and large teams; (2) teams are being assembled and led by members as well as managers; and (3) technology is increasingly interwoven with teamwork. Complex and fluid teamwork configurations, self-assembled and self-managed teams, and advanced technologies present both benefits as well as challenges for management. Therefore, within each subsection, we provide suggestions for those who aim to facilitate teamwork in modern organizations.

Reality #1: Complex Problems Require Adaptive Patterns of Teamwork across Small and Large Groups

On October 1, 2017, a gunman opened fire on a crowd of concert-goers at a music festival on the Las Vegas Strip in Nevada. This event activated a complex "rescue task force" comprised of paramedics, police officers, hospital workers, and many others who worked together to save as many lives as possible. Since 2010, the police and fire departments of Clark County, Nevada, had been collaborating to prepare for large-scale disaster response, but the 2017 shooting was the first time the two agencies launched their joint task force in response to a real event. The proactive preparation, which included providing cross-training to paramedics regarding police skills such as kicking down doors and treating the wounded in live-fire environments, allowed the two agencies to rapidly coordinate a rescue task force that assessed the safety of the environment while also treating and transporting the wounded to trauma centers as swiftly as possible (Bui, Zapotosky, Barrett, & Berman, 2017). Ultimately, the rescue task forces played a vital role in reducing the devastating impact of the Las Vegas tragedy (Ackers, 2017) and are now used as a model for fire and police departments across the country (Torres-Cortez, 2017).

Importantly, the response to the Las Vegas tragedy epitomizes a reality that many organizations are facing: complex problems are requiring adaptive patterns of teamwork across small and large groups. Specifically, this example demonstrates that many organizational challenges are far beyond the scope of any single small team, and instead, require *multiple* distinct groups or teams from different backgrounds and areas of expertise to coordinate their actions. Moreover, today's teams and systems are required to respond *adaptively* to dynamic situations characterized by unexpected events and changes both external as well as internal to the team – often, while constituent members are dividing their attention and efforts across multiple *other* teams. We review these three characteristics of the first "reality" in the following sections.

Multiteam Systems

The need for coordinated teamwork across complex "teams of teams" has started to permeate the scientific literature on organizations over the past two decades. Research on these *multiteam systems* recognizes that modern workplaces often require teams to work in collaboration with other teams in order to solve broad problems (e.g., Mathieu et al., 2001; Shuffler & Carter, 2018;

Zaccaro, Marks, & DeChurch, 2012). Defined formally, multiteam systems constitute human systems comprised of "two or more teams that interface directly and independently in response to environmental contingencies toward the accomplishment of collective goals" (Mathieu et al., 2001, p. 290).

When working properly, a multiteam system will combine the unique knowledge and abilities possessed by members of multiple component teams synergistically to achieve outcomes that no single team could handle working in isolation. The reality, of course, is that collaboration across multiple teams does not always go as planned. Indeed, vast differences between component teams, with regard to their goals, areas of expertise, norms, work processes, or social contexts can create serious divisions between teams that inhibit inter-team coordination and detract from multiteam system performance (Connaughton, Williams, & Shuffler, 2012; Luciano, DeChurch, & Mathieu, 2018; Sullivan, Lungeanu, DeChurch, & Contractor, 2015). On the other hand, if component teams are *not* differentiated sufficiently, constituent members may believe their unique contributions are unnoticed, and thus, they may lack motivation to work on behalf of the system (Hogg, van Knippenberg, & Rast, 2012).

Adaptive Team Performance in Response to External and Internal Changes

The second reality reflected by the Las Vegas shooting example is that twenty-first-century teams need to be capable of rapidly *adapting* to changes stemming from the external embedding environment as well as changes internal to the team. According to Gorman, Cooke, and Amazeen (2010), team adaptivity is "the altering of structure in accordance with changes in the environment" (p. 295). Adaptivity in teams and multiteam systems is particularly critical in highly dynamic operating environments, where teams encounter unexpected and/or novel events. For instance, in the Las Vegas shooting example, although the agencies had been working together for several years to prepare for eventual disasters, the specific event was still unexpected and required the component teams in the rescue task forces to adapt. Hospital staff needed to adjust to the unexpectedly high volume of patients by altering their usual communication patterns and seeking help from off-duty staff, and triage nurses needed to understand exactly which capabilities and skill sets were possessed by other hospital staff and organize patients accordingly.

In addition to encountering changes in the external operating environments, many teams in modern organizations experience substantial *internal* changes, such as shifts in team composition (i.e., the configuration of member attributes; Levine & Moreland, 1990) as certain team members leave and others join. Indeed, as modern workers are more likely to change jobs, organizations, and careers, teams have become increasingly unstable. To this end, today's teams are rarely static entities with stable group membership, but rather are often flexible groupings with fluid memberships (Mathieu, Tannenbaum, Donsbach, & Alliger, 2014). Scholars have argued that changes to team composition affect team members' thoughts, feelings, and behavioral processes (Bell, Brown, Colaneri, & Outland, 2018). However, findings related to the effects of dynamic team composition on team performance are equivocal. On one hand, as team members leave and new members join, these turnover processes may help the team produce more unique ideas (Gruenfeld, Martorana, & Fan, 2000). On the other hand, research suggests that there are significant challenges associated with team composition shifts. For example, changes in team composition can disrupt team processes and norms, diminish team human and social capital, and reduce team performance (Hausknecht & Holwerda, 2013). Moreover, teams with high turnover may be particularly prone to relying on previously constructed knowledge (Lewis, Belliveau, Herndon, & Keller, 2007), and thus, may be less able to respond adaptively to new challenges in the external environment.

Multiteam Memberships

The third reality reflected by the Las Vegas shooting example is that, in many workplaces, employees must distribute their time and efforts across multiple teams, simultaneously, or over time. Due in part to technological innovation, organizations now face immense competition on a global scale, requiring them to become more efficient in their efforts. As a result, employees are now expected to take on diverse roles working across disciplines, functions, and groups to optimize their work as part of organizations that have abandoned functional structures. For instance, in the Las Vegas example, meeting the needs of each *patient* represented a unique team or system task involving specific sets of actors (e.g., police, firefighters, hospital staff with specific areas of expertise), and members of the rescue task forces were required to split their attention across multiple patients (i.e., different "teams").

Organizational researchers are increasingly emphasizing the importance of considering the impact of employees' *"multiteam memberships"* on outcomes in the workplace (O'Leary, Mortensen, & Woolley, 2011). Membership on multiple teams has certain advantages such as offering learning opportunities through exposure to diverse knowledge (O'Leary et al., 2011). However, multiteam memberships can also increase people's teamwork demands and reduce the likelihood that they will receive social support from teammates (Pluut, Flestea, & Curşeu, 2014). There are also inherent "switching costs" when people transition from working on one team to another (Bertolotti, Mattarelli, Mortensen, O'Leary, & Incerti, 2013). Issues related to division of attention can be compounded by issues of temporal misalignment across teams, which are likely to arise when team members' schedules do not overlap (Mortensen, Woolley, & O'Leary, 2007).

Managing Complex Forms of Teamwork

Recent research has suggested several ways in which leaders and/or managers can help facilitate adaptive team and multiteam system performance. For example, Firth and colleagues showed that *frame-of-reference training*, which provides component teams with a common language and standardized criteria for judging their own and others' performance, facilitates multiteam coordination and performance, likely due to a reduction in idiosyncrasies, errors, and inefficiencies in between-team processes (Firth, Hollenbeck, Miles, Ilgen, & Barnes, 2015). Likewise, Asencio and colleagues argue that using tools such as *multiteam charters* that establish clear norms and guidelines related to interteam coordination and communication facilitates multiteam system performance (Asencio, Carter, DeChurch, Zaccaro, & Fiore, 2012).

Notably, empirical studies demonstrate that multiteam systems function most effectively when a formally defined "leadership" or "integration" team assumes primary responsibility for system planning and decision-making and is focused on facilitating both *intra*-team as well as *inter*-team interactions in support of superordinate goals (Davison, Hollenbeck, Barnes, Sleesman, & Ilgen, 2012; DeChurch & Marks, 2006; De Vries, Hollenbeck, Davison, Walter, & Van der Vegt, 2016; Lanaj, Foulk, & Hollenbeck, 2018; Lanaj, Hollenbeck, Ilgen, Barnes, & Harmon, 2013; Murase, Carter, DeChurch, & Marks, 2014). However, case studies also suggest that many systems, particularly those that are ad hoc and form quickly in response to an unexpected environmental change, do not have the benefit of a formalized leadership team, particularly during initial phases of task performance (Beck & Plowman, 2014; Edmondson & Harvey, 2018).

To enhance adaptability, Burke, Stagl, Salas, Pierce, and Kendall (2006) emphasize the importance of allowing team members to make and recover from mistakes during training, as mistakes represent unexpected and novel experiences. In contexts where there are frequent changes in team composition, managers may need to emphasize team *socialization* processes. Socialization enables new team members to develop shared understanding with incumbents, gain team knowledge, and learn team goals and norms. Therefore, socialization plays a critical role in ensuring that new team members develop their identity with the team and "get up to speed" as quickly as possible. Similarly, managers and team incumbents need to help "coach" new team members on relevant aspects of the team. A study of extreme action teams found that in highperforming medical teams, leaders delegated leadership responsibilities to incumbent subordinates while they trained new team members (Klein, Ziegert, Knight, & Xiao, 2006). Through this act of dynamic delegation, leaders were able to create action teams which trained new team members quickly, coordinated their actions, and were better able to endure changing team composition (Klein et al., 2006). Further, managers can reduce the potentially negative effects of losing specialized team members by taking steps to retain the tacit knowledge of team members. For example, managers can utilize management information systems that allow members to "store" their specialized knowledge for future use, preventing loss of critical information.

An often unexpected challenge for managers of teams comprised of individuals who are members of multiple *other* teams is that the managers do not have full control over team members' schedules and activities. Further, managers often need to coordinate their team's activities with managers of other teams, creating the potential for leadership ambiguity and confusion. Managers must be cognizant of the increasing demands and stressors placed upon employees who work on multiple teams and take these demands into account when planning and assigning tasks. Organizations can help ensure that potential teammates are prepared for shifts in team composition and multiteam membership demands by training employees on general teamwork skills (Edmondson, 2012). Indeed, skills such as communication, coordination, and planning are transferable, and thus, help ensure that teams can be high-functioning quickly.

In summary, teamwork has grown in complexity and fluidity in order to cope with the dynamic and multifaceted challenges that twenty-first-century organizations currently face. Whereas interdependent systems, adaptive performance, and multiteam memberships are often *necessary* in order to meet the demands of today's problems, they also present critical challenges for managers of teams. Further complicating team management, as we describe next, many of the key responsibilities of team managers (e.g., assembling teams, leading teams) are being handled by the team members themselves.

Reality #2: Teams Are Assembled and Led by Team Members as Well as Managers

Zooniverse is an online citizen-science project repository launched in 2009 that has positioned more than one million citizens – most of whom are *not* formally trained scientists – at the leading edge of scientific discovery. The purpose of Zooniverse is to connect volunteers to complex scientific projects requiring the active participation of numerous human contributors (Cox et al., 2015). In doing so, Zooniverse accomplishes three objectives. First, Zooniverse helps to reduce large and complex datasets into formats that can be easily analyzed by scientists while increasing the probability of serendipitous discoveries (Fortson et al., 2012). Second, by creating research teams comprised of a few scientist project leaders and a crowd of civilian volunteers, scientists are spending less resources, producing research faster, and analyzing data more accurately than they could on their own. In fact, one of the advantages of "crowdsourced science" is its speed and accuracy (Sauermann & Franzoni, 2015). A final objective of Zooniverse is to engage the public in order to educate and change attitudes towards science (Lintott et al., 2008). As a means to this end, the Zooniverse enables anyone with a computer to help scientists with an array of fascinating projects including identifying planets, mapping the structure of cells, or even characterizing patterns of penguin behavior (Cox et al., 2015). The impact of Zooniverse has been nothing short of astounding. As of October 2018, Zooniverse has almost 1.3 million research volunteers working on over 30 projects. These efforts have resulted in a number of scientific discoveries and over 250 scholarly publications (Simpson, Page, & De Roure, 2014).

Interestingly, the collaboration sparked by platforms such as Zooniverse also calls into question certain simplifying assumptions about what it means to "manage" teamwork. Organizations like Zooniverse are loosely bound and self-organized, resulting in a structure with unrivaled flexibility as people join and leave project teams at will. Similarly, organizations such as *Uber* have achieved scale at unprecedented rates by using short-term freelance employees who work as part of the "gig economy" (Kuhn, 2016). Whereas prior research has often assumed that key duties of team management–such as selecting team members, assigning individual and team goals, and coordinating, directing, and motivating the team – were centralized into the hands of one or a few key formal leaders or managers, in reality these duties are often distributed and handled both formally as well as informally. Indeed, in modern organizations, multiple people often share in responsibility for assembling and leading teams.

Shared Responsibility for Team Assembly

Even organizations with more traditional organizational structures, such as Google, are relatively more flexible than many organizations of the previous century. For instance, Google allows many employees to spend approximately 20% of their time working on solo and/or collaborative projects of their own choosing. In other words, employees at many organizations are "self-assembling" into teams.

Allowing teams to self-assemble may have certain advantages, such as increased team member satisfaction and autonomy (Wax, 2015). Google's flexible structure has supported the development of innovations such as Google News (Hayes, 2008) and wheelchair-accessible routes in Google Maps (D'Onfro, 2018). However, providing employees with the authority to self-assemble into teams also presents new issues. For instance, issues of bias and discrimination may be more likely to occur in self-assembled team contexts than manager-assembled teams because people may tend to team up with individuals who are similar to themselves on surface and deep level attributes (Hinds, Carley, Krackhardt, & Wholey, 2000). More "homogeneous" teams may struggle to generate creative or innovative outputs (Guimera, Uzzi, Spiro, & Amaral, 2005; Uzzi, Mukherjee, Stringer, & Jones, 2013). Self-assembled teams also tend to have fuzzy boundaries, which can create ambiguity about who is on the team and who is not (Wang & Hicks, 2015) and may lead to a lack of identification within the team. Finally, it may be difficult for people to assemble the most effective teams given that they may lack a complete picture of the organizational environment and/or the knowledge, skills, and abilities possessed by other potential teammates.

Shared Responsibility for Team Leadership

The flexibility afforded by many modern organizational structures also calls into question traditional scholarly depictions of leadership. Whereas research on leadership has often assumed that leadership originates only from one or a few "formal" leaders (e.g., team managers), in many organizational contexts, leadership responsibilities are distributed or shared by multiple individuals who influence one another both formally as well as informally over time (Carson, Tesluk, & Marrone, 2007; Carter, DeChurch, Braun, & Contractor, 2015; DeRue & Ashford, 2010; Pearce & Conger, 2003).

Shared or distributed forms of leadership have a number of benefits. For example, shared forms of leadership can enhance team performance by allowing teams to capitalize on the unique skills and expertise held by different team members (Aime, Humphrey & DeRue, 2014; Friedrich, Vessey, Schuelke, Ruark, & Mumford, 2009). In fact, distributed forms of leadership are often necessary as organizations increasingly employ self-managed or ad hoc teams to cope with dynamic, complex, and competitive environments. However, the complexity of shared leadership can also create challenges.

For example, the presence of multiple leaders may create confusion for team members trying to figure out who to go to for direction and advice. If informal leaders emerge based on surface level characteristics (e.g., personality or gender), rather than task-based competence, team performance is likely to suffer (Joshi & Knight, 2015; Lanaj & Hollenbeck, 2015). Additionally, shared leadership structures may require that team or system members trust one another and share a common collective identity – developing these relationships may be challenging in contexts where members divide their attention across multiple teams. Furthermore, teams may need substantial time and interaction experience before being willing to "share" in leadership. Yet, lengthy interaction and preparation is not always possible in ad hoc and short-term teams. A final challenge associated with informal and shared forms of leadership is that they may not be appropriate for certain tasks or teams. Indeed, shared leadership is most appropriate for complex and highly interdependent tasks (Carson et al., 2007).

Managing Teams Assembled and Led by Team Members

When teams are assembled and led by constituent team members, members of "management" may feel as though they do not have a role in ensuring that the team performs effectively and achieves its goals. On the contrary, there are significant contributions to be made by management, and they are likely to have a significant influence on the ultimate success or failure of their teams. For example, one important function for managers in organizations that allow team self-assembly is to create a work environment which supports effective team self-assembly processes. To do so, managers should work to develop a collaborative culture and encourage employees to explore working relationships with people from diverse backgrounds. Managers should also provide employees with sufficient information so that they can make informed assembly decisions. To do so, they may leverage technologies designed to help teams assemble more effectively (Contractor, 2013) or utilize organizational social networks to educate people on areas of expertise distributed throughout the organization.

Likewise, the informal and distributed nature of leadership in teams does not make formal leaders obsolete. Formal leaders can support teams in effectively distributing and sharing leadership (Friedrich, Griffith, & Mumford 2016; Friedrich et al., 2009; Klein et al., 2006). For example, prior research shows that formal leaders' communication styles, network development and leader–team exchange relationships are associated with the development of shared leadership (Friedrich et al., 2016). Leader characteristics such as intelligence, agreeableness, and low prior experience are associated with their employment of such behaviors, suggesting that formal leader selection, training, and ongoing leadership development continue to be important in twenty-first-century teams. However, leadership development initiatives should also incorporate approaches that expand entire *teams'* leadership capacity (Day, Gronn, & Salas, 2004). For example, leadership development approaches targeting teams may be more effective to the extent that these approaches enhance the team members' abilities to understand and leverage the patterns of social relationships within and external to the team (Cullen-Lester, Maupin, & Carter, 2017).

In summary, modern organizations, such as Zooniverse, Uber, or Google are becoming less reliant on formal management to facilitate teamwork and are instead distributing traditional duties – such as assembling and leading teams – to the team members themselves. Although teams that assemble and lead themselves afford new possibilities (e.g., serendipitous discoveries, greater efficiency, higher team satisfaction), these features of twenty-first-century teams also present new challenges for management.

Reality #3: Technology Is Interwoven with Teamwork

The third reality is that technology is now tightly interwoven with teamwork processes. In fact, certain technologies (e.g., robotics) may be more appropriately conceptualized as "team members" rather than "tools used by team members." The United States Army, for example, is already using human–robot teams or "manned–unmanned teams" (MUM-Ts) to improve combat effectiveness. In Iraq and Afghanistan, Apache helicopter pilots are teaming up with Army Shadow and Eagle drones in order to enhance their view of the battlefield and ability to identify and eliminate targets (Osborn, 2016). The pilots are given the ability to control both the flight path and the sensors (e.g., infrared cameras) onboard the drones, although the majority of their functions are autonomous. Footage from the drones is then streamed live to a monitor inside the helicopter cockpit. According to the Army, these human–robot teams allow for dynamic and fast-moving targets to be tracked and pursued, even from long distances (Osborn, 2016). With the help of these autonomous systems, pilots are able to see where their target is before even taking off, giving them the ability to adjust their plans in real time. Furthermore, the continuous view of the target ensures that pilots are always situationally aware and are not entering into surprising or potentially dangerous situations.

Teaming with Technology

The use of MUM-Ts in the U.S. Army is providing a glimpse into what teaming with technology may look like in the future. Yet, almost all of today's teams are virtual to some degree. For instance, most teams leverage technologies such as telecommunication and/or collaboration tools to complement their current capabilities. Moreover, the use of AI and robotics in the workplace is growing exponentially. Some of these technologies are widespread, such as co-bots and decision-making tools. Co-bots are robots which perform simple repetitive tasks in order to free human workers to perform higher level functions. Amazon for example, currently uses co-bots in order to retrieve items for shipping within its various distribution centers (Marr, 2018). Some of these technologies are more novel. For example, some organizations have begun to utilize advanced robotics with sensory, physical, and processing abilities that may surpass those of humans.

Certainly, advanced technologies are facilitating teamwork and the capacity of humans to tackle important problems. However, like the other two realities of twenty-first-century teamwork, teaming with technology presents a number of challenges. For example, in highly virtual and geographically distributed teams, some team members may never meet one another face-to-face. In such contexts, the development of team affective, behavioral, and cognitive psychological states and processes can be difficult. Indeed, prior research suggests that cross-cultural teams often suffer from a weakened shared team identity and greater emotional conflict due to an over-reliance on virtual communication, which may ultimately lead to a reduction in the team-oriented efforts of members (Gelfand, Erez, & Aycan, 2007). An increased reliance on technology can also hinder the development of shared perceptions of knowledge important to the team, which are critical for teams to leverage resources. Finally, exclusive electronic dependence and geographic dispersion has been shown to negatively affect the innovation capability of virtual teams (Gibson & Gibbs, 2006).

Human–robot teams are presenting additional challenges for managing twenty-first-century teamwork. One such challenge is that sometimes human weakness can be inadvertently transmitted to their robot teammates. For example, Amazon recently developed an AI and trained it to read resumes using biased decision-making rules, resulting in sexist selection decisions against women (Grossman, 2018). A possible lesson to learn from Amazon's foray into AI is that robots are strongly influenced by their environment, as they learn and adapt according to the information that surrounds them. As such, it will be important to determine how the work environment surrounding robots can be structured so as to facilitate desired decisions and behaviors.

Another key hurdle to integrating robots and humans in team contexts is determining whether robots can participate in important teamwork processes. In fact, relatively little is known currently about the nature of key team-level phenomena (e.g., team affect, team behavior, team cognition) – which have been studied extensively for decades in human teams – within human–*robot* teams. Previously, managers were only responsible for facilitating thoughts, feelings, motivations, and behaviors among humans. However, managers will now have to balance human-to-robot and robot-to-robot relationships as well. Critically, it is likely that these different relationships will manifest themselves in different ways within the team setting; however, further research in this area is necessary in order to fully understand the differential effect of these different relationships on various aspects of teamwork.

Part of learning how robots will operate as part of the team involves understanding how they might contribute to team-level phenomena such as affective, behavioral, and cognitive processes. In terms of team affect, there is still much to be learned about trust between humans and robots, especially within team environments (Hancock et al., 2011). Moreover, there are likely to be key differences in the nature of human versus robot "motivation." Although robots can demonstrate goal-directed behavior, these behaviors can be problematic as robots relentlessly pursue their objectives and do not have a sense of self-preservation (Groom & Nass, 2007). Another critical part of teamwork that is taken for granted in human teams is ensuring that team members are thinking on the same page, or what team scientists refer to as "team cognition." From what we currently know, robotic team cognition seems to be a distinct possibility. For example, robots are capable of sharing information with others, whether they be other robots or humans, and can be designed to share unique information more than their human counterparts; processes which are essential for aligning team cognitions. Arguably some of the most important processes of an effective team, however, are behavioral. Many behaviors typical of human teams, such as back-up behaviors (i.e., providing support) and implicit coordination, may either look entirely different, or cease to exist when robots are part of the team. Whereas it appears that there are some hurdles to integrating robots into teams, there is also promise that, as technology continues to improve, robots will increasingly become better teammates with humans.

Managing Teamwork Intertwined with Technology

The growing streams of research on virtual teams and human–robot teaming suggests a number of best practices for managing teamwork that is intertwined with technology. For example, in order to ensure team effectiveness, it is important for teams to use technologies that are well suited to team tasks. Insufficient task–technology fit–that is, when technology does not provide adequate richness for the task being performed – may hinder team trust, motivation and confidence and encourage unnecessary conflicts. In particular, it is important to ensure that communication and collaboration technologies match the information-processing and coordination demands of the team (Maruping & Agarwal, 2004).

When leading human–robot teams in particular, it is critical to understand the strengths and weaknesses of different types of team members. Robots are optimized for tasks associated with decision making, danger, or the use of advanced sensory or physical capabilities. Contrarily, humans have unique abilities such as feeling and detecting emotion in others and pattern recognition.

Effectively using these two "forms" of team members to complement each other is essential in order to take full advantage of human–robot teams (Groom & Nass, 2007). For example, there is preliminary research that shows allocating repetitive and time-consuming tasks, such as planning, to robot team members increases human team member effectiveness (Gombolay, Wilcox, & Shah, 2018). Indeed, teams may be best served by using technology for functions where humans have been found to be fallible, such as entering into dangerous environments or making decisions (Groom & Nass, 2007).

Further, effective human–robot interaction and development of trust requires practice. Training as a team with robot team members allows for everyone to establish a shared mental model – or understanding – of the teamwork, taskwork, and the robot team members' capabilities. For example, geographically distributed robotic surgery teams have benefited from integrating communication and coordination training into their practices, enabling them to reduce surgery preparation time and time spent communicating (Cunningham, Chellali, Jaffre, & Classe, 2013). Thus, having the team train together with robot teammates prior to task performance may allow for the team members to experience the robot's perceptions, as well as its strengths and limitations, while also facilitating shared language and understanding.

For managers of human–robot teams, fostering positive human-to-robot relationships may be important given that humans may begin to feel devalued in relation to the robots. On the other hand, managing human–robot teams may also require managers to *reduce* the strength of certain human–robot bonds. For example, soldiers in the U.S. Army have shown strong attachments to their robot teammates. In fact, it is quite common for soldiers to give robots awards, name them after spouses, and even hold funerals for their destroyed counterparts. One robot is even reported to have received a purple heart and a full burial detail with a 21-gun salute (Carpenter, 2013). Developing attachments to robot teammates could be problematic if such attachments prevent individuals from using robots for their intended purposes, thereby putting humans at risk. Moreover, there is also the possibility that humans will tend to blindly trust robots, believing them to be infallible. For example, students developing a robot to guide people out of burning buildings unexpectedly found that users would follow the robot through buildings they were familiar with even when it led them away from the exit or made wrong turns (Robinette, Li, Allen, Howard, & Wagner, 2016). Future research will need to identify ways to counteract these potentially harmful beliefs if humans and robots are to work together effectively.

Conclusion

This chapter identifies three key realities of teamwork in modern organizations and advances multiple suggestions for managing twenty-first-century teamwork. We argue that teams are increasingly fluid and dynamic, assembled and led by team members as well as managers, and that teamwork is inextricably linked with technology. These new frontiers in teamwork undoubtedly present critical challenges for managers. However, they also provide organizations with new avenues for addressing the most important problems facing our species.

References

Ackers, M. (2017). One unit standing together: Police and firefighters learned from past tragedies, using different tactic to save lives. *Las Vegas Sun*, October 22. Retrieved from https://lasvegassun.com/news/2017/oct/22/one-unit-standing-together-police-and-firefighters/

Aime, F., Humphrey, S., DeRue, D. S., & Paul, J. B. (2014). The riddle of heterarchy: Power transitions in cross-functional teams. *Academy of Management Journal*, *57*(2), 327–352.

Asencio, R., Carter, D. R., DeChurch, L. A., Zaccaro, S. J., & Fiore, S. M. (2012). Charting a course for collaboration: A multiteam perspective. *Translational Behavioral Medicine*, *2*(4), 487–494.

Beal, D. J., Cohen, R. R., Burke, M. J., & McLendon, C. L. (2003). Cohesion and performance in groups: A meta-analytic clarification of construct relations. *Journal of Applied Psychology*, *88*(6), 989–1004.

Beck, T. E., & Plowman, D. A. 2014. Temporary, emergent interorganizational collaboration in unexpected circumstances: A study of the *Columbia* space shuttle response effort. *Organization Science*, *25*, 1234–1252.

Bell, S. T., Brown, S. G., Colaneri, A., & Outland, N. (2018). Team composition and the ABCs of teamwork. *American Psychologist*, *73*(4), 349–362.

Bertolotti, F., Mattarelli, E., Mortensen, M., O'Leary, M., & Incerti, V. (2013). How many teams should we manage at once? The effect of multiple team membership, collaborative technologies, and polychronicity on team performance. *34th International Conference on Information Systems, December 15–18, 2013*. Association for Information Systems, Milan, Italy. Retrieved from https://dblp.org/db/conf/icis/icis2013

Bui, L., Zapotosky, M., Barrett, D., & Berman, M. (2017). At least 59 killed in Las Vegas shooting rampage, more than 500 others injured. *Washington Post*, October 2. Retrieved from www.washingtonpost.com/news/morning-mix/wp/2017/10/02/

Burke, C. S., Stagl, K. C., Salas, E., Pierce, L., & Kendall, D. (2006). Understanding team adaptation: A conceptual analysis and model. *Journal of Applied Psychology*, *91*(6), 1189–1207.

Carpenter, J. (2013). The quiet professional: An investigation of US military explosive ordnance disposal personnel interactions with everyday field robots (Unpublished doctoral dissertation). University of Washington, USA.

Carson, J. B., Tesluk, P. E., & Marrone, J. A. (2007). Shared leadership in teams: An investigation of antecedent conditions and performance. *Academy of Management Journal*, *50*(5), 1217–1234.

Carter, D. R., DeChurch, L. A., Braun, M. T., & Contractor, N. S. (2015). Social network approaches to leadership: An integrative conceptual review. *Journal of Applied Psychology*, *100*, 597–622. http://dx.doi.org/10.1037/a0038922

Connaughton, S. L., Williams, E. A., & Shuffler, M. L. (2012). Social identity issues in multiteam systems: Considerations for future research. In Zaccaro, S. J., Marks, M. A., & DeChurch, L. (Eds.), *Multiteam systems: An organization form for dynamic and complex environments* (pp. 109–140). New York, NY: Routledge Taylor & Francis Group.

Contractor, N. (2013). Some assembly required: Leveraging Web science to understand and enable team assembly. *Philosophical Transactions of the Royal Society A: Mathematical, Physical and Engineering Sciences, 371*(1987), 20120385. doi:10.1098/rsta.2012.0385

Cox, J., Oh, E. Y., Simmons, B., Lintott, C., Masters, K., Greenhill, A., ... & Holmes, K. (2015). Defining and measuring success in online citizen science: A case study of Zooniverse projects. *Computing in Science & Engineering, 17*(4), 28–41.

Cullen-Lester, K. L., Maupin, C. K., & Carter, D. R. (2017). Incorporating social networks into leadership development: A conceptual model and evaluation of research and practice. *Leadership Quarterly, 28*(1), 130–152.

Cunningham, S., Chellali, A., Jaffre, I., Classe, J., & Cao, C. G. (2013). Effects of experience and workplace culture in human–robot team interaction in robotic surgery: A case study. *International Journal of Social Robotics, 5*(1), 75–88.

Davison, R. B., Hollenbeck, J. R., Barnes, C. M., Sleesman, D. J., & Ilgen, D. R. (2012). Coordinated action in multiteam systems. *Journal of Applied Psychology, 97*(4), 808–824.

Day, D. V., Gronn, P., & Salas, E. (2004). Leadership capacity in teams. *Leadership Quarterly, 15*(6), 857–880.

DeChurch, L. A., & Marks, M. A. (2006). Leadership in multiteam systems. *Journal of Applied Psychology, 91*(2), 311–329.

De Jong, B. A., & Elfring, T. (2010). How does trust affect the performance of ongoing teams? The mediating role of reflexivity, monitoring, and effort. *Academy of Management Journal, 53*(3), 535–549.

DeRue, D. S., & Ashford, S. J. (2010). Who will lead and who will follow? A social process of leadership identity construction in organizations. *Academy of Management Review, 35*(4), 627–647.

De Vries, T. A., Hollenbeck, J. R., Davison, R. B., Walter, F., & Van der Vegt, G. S. (2016). Managing coordination in multiteam systems: Integrating micro and macro perspectives. *Academy of Management Journal, 59*(5), 1823–1844.

D'Onfro, J. (2018, March 18). These Google employees used their "20 percent" time to improve Maps for people in wheelchairs. *Business Insider*. Retrieved from www.businessinsider.com/google-20-percent-time-policy-2015-4

Edmondson, A. C. (2012). *Teaming: How organizations learn, innovate, and compete in the knowledge economy*. San Francisco, CA: Jossey-Bass.

Edmondson, A. C., & Harvey, J. F. (2018). Cross-boundary teaming for innovation: Integrating research on teams and knowledge in organizations. *Human Resource Management Review, 28*(4), 347–360.

Firth, B. M., Hollenbeck, J. R., Miles, J. E., Ilgen, D. R., & Barnes, C. M. (2015). Same page, different books: Extending representational gaps theory to enhance performance in multiteam systems. *Academy of Management Journal, 58*(3), 813–835.

Fortson, L., Masters, K., Nichol, R., Borne, K., Edmondson, E., Lintott, C., ... & Wallin, J. (2012). Galaxy zoo: Morphological classification and citizen science.

In M. J., Way, J. D., Scargle, K. M., Ali, & A. N., Srivastava (Eds.), *Advances in machine learning and data mining for astronomy* (pp. 213–236). Boca Raton, FL: CRC Press.

Friedrich, T. L., Griffith, J. A., & Mumford, M. D. (2016). Collective leadership behaviors: Evaluating the leader, team network, and problem situation characteristics that influence their use. *Leadership Quarterly, 27*, 312–333.

Friedrich, T. L., Vessey, W. B., Schuelke, M. J., Ruark, G. A., & Mumford, M. D. (2009). A framework for understanding collective leadership: The selective utilization of leader and team expertise within networks. *Leadership Quarterly, 20*(6), 933–958.

Gelfand, M. J., Erez, M., & Aycan, Z. (2007). Cross-cultural organizational behavior. *Annual Review of Psychology, 58*(20), 1–35.

Gibson, C. B., & Gibbs, J. L. (2006). Unpacking the concept of virtuality: The effects of geographic dispersion, electronic dependence, dynamic structure, and national diversity on team innovation. *Administrative Science Quarterly, 51*(3), 451–495.

Gittell, J. H., Godfrey, M., & Thistlethwaite, J. (2013). Interprofessional collaborative practice and relational coordination: Improving healthcare through relationships. *Journal of Interprofessional Care, 27*(3), 210–213.

Gombolay, M. C., Wilcox, R. J., & Shah, J. A. (2018). Fast scheduling of robot teams performing tasks with temporospatial constraints. *IEEE Transactions on Robotics, 34*(1), 220–239.

Gorman, J. C., Cooke, N. J., & Amazeen, P. G. (2010). Training adaptive teams. *Human Factors, 52*(2), 295–307.

Groom, V., & Nass, C. (2007). Can robots be teammates?: Benchmarks in human–robot teams. *Interaction Studies, 8*(3), 483–500.

Grossman, D. (2018). Amazon fired its resume-reading AI for sexism. Retrieved from www.popularmechanics.com/technology/robots/a23708450/amazon-resume-ai-sexism/

Gruenfeld, D. H., Martorana, P. V., & Fan, E. T. (2000). What do groups learn from their worldliest members? Direct and indirect influence in dynamic teams. *Organizational Behavior and Human Decision Processes, 82*(1), 45–59.

Guimera, R., Uzzi, B., Spiro, J., & Amaral, L. A. N. (2005). Team assembly mechanisms determine collaboration network structure and team performance. *Science, 308*(5722), 697–702.

Hackman, J. R. (1998). Why teams don't work. In R. S. Tindale, L. Heath, & J. Edwards (Eds.), *Theory and research on small groups* (pp. 245–267). New York, NY: Plenum.

Hancock, P. A., Billings, D. R., Schaefer, K. E., Chen, J. Y., De Visser, E. J., & Parasuraman, R. (2011). A meta-analysis of factors affecting trust in human–robot interaction. *Human Factors, 53*(5), 517–527.

Hausknecht, J. P., & Holwerda, J. A. (2013). When does employee turnover matter? Dynamic member configurations, productive capacity, and collective performance. *Organization Science, 24*(1), 210–225.

Hayes, E. (2008, May 12). Google's 20 percent factor. *ABC News*. Retrieved from https://abcnews.go.com/Technology/story?id=4839327&page=1

Hinds, P. J., Carley, K. M., Krackhardt, D., & Wholey, D. (2000). Choosing work group members: Balancing similarity, competence, and familiarity. *Organizational Behavior and Human Decision Processes, 81*(2), 226–251.

Hogg, M. A., Van Knippenberg, D., & Rast III, D. E. (2012). Intergroup leadership in organizations: Leading across group and organizational boundaries. *Academy of Management Review, 37*(2), 232–255.

Joshi, A., & Knight, A. P. (2015). Who defers to whom and why? Dual pathways linking demographic differences and dyadic deference to team effectiveness. *Academy of Management Journal, 58*(1), 59–84.

Klein, K. J., Ziegert, J. C., Knight, A. P., & Xiao, Y. (2006). Dynamic delegation: Shared, hierarchical, and deindividualized leadership in extreme action teams. *Administrative Science Quarterly, 51*(4), 590–621.

Kozlowski, S. W. J., & Bell, B. S. (2003). Work groups and teams in organizations. In W. C. Borman, D. R. Ilgen, & R. J. Klimoski (Eds.), *Handbook of psychology, Vol. 12: Industrial and organizational psychology* (pp. 333–375). London, UK: Wiley.

Kozlowski, S. W. J., & Ilgen, D. R. (2006). Enhancing the effectiveness of work groups and teams. *Psychological Science in the Public Interest, 7*(3), 77–124.

Kuhn, K. M. (2016). The rise of the "Gig Economy" and implications for understanding work and workers. *Industrial and Organizational Psychology, 9*(1), 157–162.

Lanaj, K., Foulk, T. A., & Hollenbeck, J. R. (2018). The benefits of not seeing eye to eye with leadership: Divergence in risk preferences impacts multiteam system behavior and performance. *Academy of Management Journal, 61*(4), 1554–1582.

Lanaj, K., & Hollenbeck, J. R. (2015). Leadership over-emergence in self-managing teams: The role of gender and countervailing biases. *Academy of Management Journal, 58*(5), 1476–1494.

Lanaj, K., Hollenbeck, J. R., Ilgen, D. R., Barnes, C. M., & Harmon, S. J. (2013). The double-edged sword of decentralized planning in multiteam systems. *Academy of Management Journal, 56*(3), 735–757.

Langfred, C. W. (2004). Too much of a good thing? Negative effects of high trust and individual autonomy in self-managing teams. *Academy of Management Journal, 47*(3), 385–399.

Levine, J. M., & Moreland, R. L. (1990). Progress in small group research. *Annual Review of Psychology, 41*(1), 585–634.

Lewis, K., Belliveau, M., Herndon, B., & Keller, J. (2007). Group cognition, membership change, and performance: Investigating the benefits and detriments of collective knowledge. *Organizational Behavior and Human Decision Processes, 103*(2), 159–178.

Lintott, C. J., Schawinski, K., Slosar, A., Land, K., Bamford, S., Thomas, D., ... & Murray, P. (2008). Galaxy Zoo: morphologies derived from visual inspection of galaxies from the Sloan Digital Sky Survey. *Monthly Notices of the Royal Astronomical Society, 389*(3), 1179–1189.

Luciano, M. M., DeChurch, L. A., & Mathieu, J. E. (2018). Multiteam systems: A structural framework and meso-theory of system functioning. *Journal of Management, 44*(3), 1065–1096.

Marks, M. A., Mathieu, J. E., & Zaccaro, S. J. (2001). A temporally based framework and taxonomy of team processes. *Academy of Management Review, 26*(3), 356–376.

Marr, B. (2018, August 29). The future of work: Are you ready for smart cobots? *Forbes*. Retrieved from www.forbes.com/sites/bernardmarr/2018/08/29/the-future-of-work-are-you-ready-for-smart-cobots/#174e49e522b3

Maruping, L. M., & Agarwal, R. (2004). Managing team interpersonal processes through technology: A task–technology fit perspective. *Journal of Applied Psychology*, *89*(6), 975–990.

Mathieu, J. E., Heffner, T. S., Goodwin, G. F., Salas, E., & Cannon-Bowers, J. A. (2000). The influence of shared mental models on team process and performance. *Journal of Applied Psychology*, *85*(2), 273–283.

Mathieu, J. E., Marks, M. A., & Zaccaro, S. J. (2001). Multi-team systems. In N. Anderson, D. S. Ones, H. K. Sinangil, & C. Viswesvaran (Eds.), *Organizational psychology, Vol. 2: Handbook of industrial, work and organizational psychology* (pp. 289–313). London, UK: Sage.

Mathieu, J. E., Tannenbaum, S. I., Donsbach, J. S., & Alliger, G. M. (2014). A review and integration of team composition models: Moving toward a dynamic and temporal framework. *Journal of Management*, *40*(1), 130–160.

Mesmer-Magnus, J. R., Carter, D. R., Asencio, R., & DeChurch, L. A. (2016). Space exploration illuminates the next frontier for teams research. *Group & Organization Management*, *41*(5), 595–628.

Mortensen, M., Woolley, A. W., & O'Leary, M. B. (2007). Conditions enabling effective multiple team membership. In K. Crowston, S. Sieber, & E. Wynn (Eds.), *Virtuality and virtualization* (pp. 215–228). New York, NY: Springer Science +Business.

Murase, T., Carter, D. R., DeChurch, L. A., & Marks, M. A. (2014). Mind the gap: The role of leadership in multiteam system collective cognition. *Leadership Quarterly*, *25*(5), 972–986.

O'Leary, M. B., Mortensen, M., & Woolley, A. W. (2011). Multiple team membership: A theoretical model of its effects on productivity and learning for individuals and teams. *Academy of Management Review*, *36*(3), 461–478.

Osborn, K. (2016, June 6). Real-time drone footage just gave the Apache a deadly advantage. *Business Insider*. Retrieved from www.businessinsider.com/real-time-drone-footage-for-apache-2016-6

Pearce, C. L., & Conger, J. A. (2003). *Shared leadership: Reframing the hows and whys of leadership*. Thousand Oaks, CA: Sage.

Pluut, H., Flestea, A. M., & Curşeu, P. L. (2014). Multiple team membership: A demand or resource for employees? *Group Dynamics: Theory, Research, and Practice*, *18*(4), 333–348.

Robinette, P., Li, W., Allen, R., Howard, A. M., & Wagner, A. R. (2016). Overtrust of robots in emergency evacuation scenarios. *11th ACM/IEEE International Conference on Human–Robot Interaction, March 7–10, 2016, Christchurch, New Zealand*. Association for Computing Machinery/Institute of Electrical and Electronic Engineers. Retrieved from http://humanrobotinteraction.org/2016/

Sauermann, H., & Franzoni, C. (2015). Crowd science user contribution patterns and their implications. *Proceedings of the National Academy of Sciences*, *112*(3), 679–684.

Shuffler, M. L., & Carter, D. R. (2018). Teamwork situated in multiteam systems: Key lessons learned and future opportunities. *American Psychologist*, *73*(4), 390–406.

Simpson, R., Page, K. R., & De Roure, D. (2014). Zooniverse: Observing the world's largest citizen science platform. In *Proceedings of the 23rd International Conference on World Wide Web (WWW '14 Companion)* (pp. 1049–1054). New York, NY: ACM Press.

Spitzmuller, M., & Park, G. (2018). Terrorist teams as loosely coupled systems. *American Psychologist*, *73*(4), 491–503.

Steinke, J., Bolunmez, B., Fletcher, L., Wang, V., Tomassetti, A. J., Repchick, K. M., ... & Tetrick, L. E. (2015). Improving cybersecurity incident response team effectiveness using teams-based research. *IEEE Security & Privacy*, *13*(4), 20–29.

Sullivan, S. D., Lungeanu, A., DeChurch, L. A., & Contractor, N. S. (2015). Space, time, and the development of shared leadership networks in multiteam systems. *Network Science*, *3*(1), 124–155.

Torres-Cortez, R. (2017, October 7). Firefighters' training kicked in, helping curb shooting death toll. *Las Vegas Sun*. Retrieved from https://lasvegassun.com/news/2017/oct/07/firefighters-training-kicked-in-helping-curb-shoot/

Uzzi, B., Mukherjee, S., Stringer, M., & Jones, B. (2013). Atypical combinations and scientific impact. *Science*, *342*(6157), 468–472.

Wang, J., & Hicks, D. (2015). Scientific teams: Self-assembly, fluidness, and interdependence. *Journal of Informetrics*, *9*(1), 197–207.

Wax, A. (2015). *Self-assembled teams: Attraction, composition, and performance* (Unpublished doctoral dissertation). Georgia Institute of Technology, USA.

Weaver, C. P., Mooney, S., Allen, D., Beller-Simms, N., Fish, T., Grambsch, A. E., ... & Langner, L. (2014). From global change science to action with social sciences. *Nature Climate Change*, *4*(8), 656–659.

Zaccaro, S. J., Marks, M. A., & DeChurch, L. A. (2012). Multiteam systems: An introduction In *Multiteam systems* (pp. 18–47). New York, NY: Routledge.

Zaccaro, S. J., Rittman, A. L., & Marks, M. A. (2001). Team leadership. *Leadership Quarterly*, *12*(4), 451–483.

20 Managing Employees across the Working Lifespan

Cort W. Rudolph and Hannes Zacher

The global workforce is aging and becoming increasingly age-diverse (Rudolph, Marcus, & Zacher, 2019). For instance, the dependency ratio (reflecting the number of people of traditional "working age" – between 16 and 64 years – divided by the number of "older people" – those 65 years and over) is declining globally. Such declines are noted in both developed and developing countries, including the United States (i.e., shifting from 4.6 working age adults to each older person in 2014 to a projected 1.9 by 2100) and India (i.e., shifting from 10.9 working age adults to each older person in 2014 to a projected 2.3 by 2100; Gerland et al., 2014; see also Cheng, Corrington, King, & Ng, Chapter 11 in this volume). Organizational researchers and practitioners have therefore paid increasing attention to the issue of managing employees of different ages. Whereas some approach this issue from a generational perspective (Twenge & Campbell, 2008), others have favored a lifespan developmental approach to attracting, motivating, leading, and retaining younger, middle-aged, and older workers (Rudolph, 2016).

With respect to the former, generational explanations (i.e., attributing observations of various work-related phenomena to generations and differences that are assumed to exist between them) have typically been adopted uncritically by organizational researchers, and until recently this has gone unchecked (see also Costanza, Finkelstein, Imose, & Ravid, Chapter 2 in this volume). Research concerning the influence of generations at work has at best been equivocal; however, mounting evidence suggests that the generations concept does not hold up to conceptual and empirical scrutiny. For example, there is scant evidence that generational differences exist in work outcomes (e.g., Costanza, Badger, Fraser, Severt, & Gade, 2012), common methodologies used to study generational effects do not triangulate upon the same conclusions (Costanza, Badger-Darrow, Yost, & Severt, 2017; Rudolph, 2015), and there has been recent doubt cast on the structure of generational groupings as they are commonly understood – even by researchers who would otherwise support their existence (e.g., Campbell, Twenge, & Campbell, 2017).

We have recently adopted a more critical perspective on the study of generations, which is grounded in the traditions of sociological constructionism (Rudolph & Zacher, 2015) and lifespan developmental psychology (e.g., Rudolph & Zacher, 2017a, 2017b; Zacher, 2015a). The social constructivist perspective suggests that generations are one means of understanding and communicating the complexities of age. However, our constructivist perspective also warns of the potential pitfalls associated with "generationalized" thinking and encourages individuals to transcend the limitations of this necessarily reductionist mode of sensemaking. Similarly, by recognizing the role of historical events and life histories, the lifespan perspective provides a means of integrating the idea that the generations concept attempts to convey with an understanding of the way in which continuous processes affect individual developmental trajectories. These ideas have recently culminated in a formal call for a moratorium on generations research in the organizational sciences (see Rudolph & Zacher, 2017a).

In this chapter, we focus on answering the question, "What bearing does the changing nature of work present to workers of different ages and life and career stages?" To answer this question, we adopt the lifespan perspective (Baltes, Reese, & Lipsitt, 1980; see Rudolph, 2016, for a systematic review of the lifespan perspective applied to the study of working) as an organizing framework. In brief, the lifespan perspective suggests that individual development is continuous, multicausal, multidimensional, and multidirectional (Baltes, 1987). In other words, the lifespan perspective accounts for the idea that different factors such as abilities, skills, and motives can change in positive (i.e., gains – for example, accruing job knowledge over time) or negative (i.e., losses – for example, reduced psychomotor abilities with increasing age) ways, or remain stable across the lifespan. Moreover, the lifespan perspective offers that individuals' developmental pathways are jointly influenced by internal factors (e.g., those that are genetically determined; specific behaviors that one engages in), and by external factors in individuals' sociocultural and historical context (Baltes, 1987). While the lifespan perspective has thus far served as a useful guide for challenging prevailing thought about aging at work, we currently lack a codified framework of practical recommendations regarding how to best apply lifespan thinking to the management of an aging and age-diverse workforce. To address this gap, and to move us beyond overgeneralized and misguided assumptions regarding the influence of generations at work, we have organized this chapter around the seven axioms of lifespan development outlined by Baltes (1987). These seven axioms serve as core tenets of the lifespan perspective and serve to guide clearer thinking about the process of aging at work. Below, we introduce the lifespan perspective in more detail. Then, we outline these seven axioms of lifespan development, and discuss how each has important implications for understanding the aging workforce and how to manage workers across the lifespan. To fit with the overall theme of this volume, we integrate observations about relevant intersections between the lifespan perspective and the changing nature of work throughout this discussion.

An Introduction to the Lifespan Perspective

The lifespan developmental perspective emerged in the late 1970s as a meta-theoretical framework to integrate a variety of specific theories of human development and aging (i.e., ontogeny). Accordingly, there is no single lifespan theory per se; rather, various theories of human development are subsumed underneath the larger umbrella of the lifespan perspective (e.g., Baltes, Lindenberger, & Staudinger, 2006; Brandtstädter, 1999; Carstensen, Isaacowitz, & Charles, 1999; Featherman & Lerner, 1985; Heckhausen & Schulz, 1995). The lifespan perspective is inherently multidisciplinary, and it informs the way that various fields of inquiry understand the experiences and behaviors of individuals over time, embedded within multiple social, cultural, and historical contexts (Baltes, 1987; Baltes et al., 1980). Unlike traditional perspectives that posit discrete and normative stages of development (e.g., Erikson, 1950; Levinson, 1986; Piaget, 1976), lifespan researchers are concerned with continuous normative developmental trajectories (e.g., average age-graded declines in fluid cognitive abilities). Moreover, lifespan researchers investigate how distinct personal (e.g., individual differences) or idiosyncratic factors (e.g., job loss) and contexts (e.g., organizational climate) serve to differentially modify these continuous developmental trajectories.

The lifespan perspective additionally acknowledges that individual development is not only a product of the context in which it takes place, but that individuals also actively shape their own development and their environmental contexts (i.e., humans are both products *and* producers of their developmental course; Lerner & Busch-Rossnagel, 1981; Zacher, Hacker, & Frese, 2016). Such notions of developmental contextualism are hallmarks of developmental systems theory, a lifespan theory proposed by Lerner and colleagues (Featherman & Lerner, 1985; Ford & Lerner, 1992; Lerner, 1996; Lerner & Kauffman, 1985). According to developmental systems theory, individual agents and the environments in which they are embedded are mutually interactive, such that agent–environment interactions impact both contextual characteristics and person-level physiological and psychological characteristics. Thus, to the extent that context interacts with and shapes individuals, their individual characteristics and behavior may in turn also shape the macrosystemic context (i.e., via various emergent processes; see Kozlowski & Klein, 2000). For example, motivational changes at the individual level (i.e., manifesting as large-scale shifts in patterns of individual-level behaviors; for example, noted patterns in the desire to work longer and past traditional/normative retirement ages; see Beehr & Bennett, 2015) may lead to aggregate level sociocultural (e.g., changing attitudes toward older workers) and economic changes (e.g., organizations designing systems to better accommodate older workers and to sustainably prolong working lives).

Baltes' (1987) Seven Axioms of Lifespan Development

In a seminal work, Baltes (1987) outlines seven tenets of the lifespan perspective, which have served as axioms that have guided thinking about aging from a lifespan perspective. Importantly, these axioms can likewise be applied to understanding the aging workforce and how to manage workers across the lifespan. As suggested by Baltes (1987), "For many researchers, the life-span orientation entails several prototypical beliefs that, in their weighting and coordination, form *a family of perspectives* that together specify a coherent metatheoretical view on the nature of development. The significance of these beliefs lies not in the individual items but in the pattern" (p. 612). In brief, these axioms of the lifespan perspective suggest that development: (i) is a lifelong process, (ii) is multidirectional, (iii) implies gains and losses, (iv) is modifiable, (v) is historically embedded, (vi) is contextualized, and (vii) is multidisciplinary. We explore these seven axioms in more detail below, and in a select review of the literature, exemplify their application to understanding the aging workforce. In doing so, we specifically tie these principles to examples of existing theory and research that can inform our goal of understanding how to manage workers across the lifespan.

Axiom I: Development Is a Lifelong Process. The first axiom of the lifespan perspective defines ontogenetic development as a lifelong process. Early theoretical models of human development favored discontinuous or staged views of the developmental course (e.g., Erikson, 1950; Kohlberg, 1987; Piaget, 1976). The lifespan perspective represents a distinct departure from such models; by recognizing development as a continuous and lifelong process, no particular age period or stage is more or less important for determining the course of development. Additionally, both continuous (i.e., cumulative) and discontinuous (i.e., innovative) activities constitute the continuum of the developmental process (Baltes, 1987).

Research on career development (e.g., Phillips, 2015; Vondracek, Lerner, & Schulenberg, 1986) and leadership development (e.g., Day, 2011) both well embody these principles. Research on career development has long adopted a lifespan perspective to address both early, mid-career, and later-career development processes (Feldman, 2002). For example, recent work has adopted longitudinal research designs and applied sophisticated statistical procedures to model variability in career development growth trajectories. For example, Zwaan, ter Bogt, and Raaijmakers (2010) studied a sample of aspiring Dutch pop musicians over the course of three years. Using a growth mixture model, four distinct patterns of career development were uncovered: upward, downward, stable-successful, and stable-unsuccessful. Moreover, successful pop musicians were found to have higher social support, stronger professional attitudes, and larger professional networks than other musicians. Similarly, Upadyaya and Salmela-Aro (2015) used growth mixture modeling to assess a five-wave longitudinal study of career development in Finnish youth transitioning from education to work. Results suggest that career engagement and satisfaction develop in parallel over time, but that there are different latent categories of positive school-to-career transitions (i.e., high and low) that define the unfolding of these career development indicators. Also adopting a longitudinal design and applying a lifespan theoretical lens to early career development, Hirschi, Niles, and Akos (2011) investigated predictors and outcomes of active engagement in career preparation in a sample of Swiss adolescents who were surveyed three times throughout their eighth-grade year. The results of this study suggest that initial self-exploration, environmental exploration, and active career planning related positively to later interindividual increases in career decidedness and career choice congruence. Finally, considering later-life adult career development and adopting a lifespan perspective, Beier, Torres, and Gilberto (2017) have more recently discussed and conceptually integrated various principles of autonomous learning with principles derived from both lifespan and modern career theories. Specifically, Beier and colleagues propose a model whereby autonomous learning serves as an intermediary mechanism linking developmental goals and associated self-regulation mechanisms (i.e., selection, optimization, and compensation strategies; perceptions of time) to career development outcomes.

To some extent, studying leadership development necessitates the adoption of a lifespan perspective. For example, as suggested by Day and colleagues (2014), "if leadership is a process and not a position, and leadership development is a longitudinal process involving possibly the entire lifespan, then we need to put forward comprehensive process models and test them appropriately" (Day, Fleenor, Atwater, Sturm, & McKee, 2014, p. 79). Indeed, in their integrative perspective on leadership development, Day, Harrison, and Halpin (2012) emphasize that effective leadership is the product of developing experientially derived competencies that accrue over the lifespan. To this end, both career and leadership development research address aspects of the changing nature of work. Specifically, the promotion of lifelong learning has been offered as a facet of changes to the psychological contract (e.g., Rousseau, 1995, 1996), and similar ideas are reflected in modern career theories (e.g., Hall & Mirvis', 1995, protean career model).

With respect to managing an aging workforce, it must be recognized that the principle of lifelong development suggests that employees are not static entities. It is important to acknowledge that development does not "stop" once one reaches adulthood. For instance, research has shown average age-related changes in cognitive abilities (Baltes, Staudinger, & Lindenberger, 1999), personality (Roberts, Walton, & Viechtbauer, 2006), and work motives (Kooij, de Lange, Jansen, Kanfer, & Dikkers, 2011) in adult populations. These age-related factors, in turn, may have implications for job attitudes and performance across the lifespan. It is also important to understand how both continuous and discontinuous processes contribute to dynamics in development, and to recognize that humans are dynamic entities. More specifically, the lifespan perspective recognizes continuous processes as those that are cumulative in nature, whereas discontinuous processes are understood as innovative in nature. For example, predictable declines in physical functioning that limit the scope of job responsibilities over the course of normal development are considered continuous, cumulative processes. On the contrary, the sudden experience of job loss would constitute a discontinuity to one's normative developmental course. Of note, discontinuities are not necessarily unexpected occurrences; the lifespan perspective recognizes that individuals can exercise varying degrees of agency upon the progression of their own developmental course. Moreover, the duration of such events can have either a short-term (e.g., a three-month expatriate job assignment) or long-term (e.g., the onset of a permanent disability that substantially limits one's work options) influence as such. Perhaps more important than duration, however, is the consequent influence that such discontinuities have upon one's normative developmental course. Overall, the axiom of lifelong development suggests that managers should adopt a long-term developmental perspective on employees, careers, and their own leadership that takes normative (or average) age-related changes and the possibility of ad hoc idiosyncratic changes across the working lifespan into account.

Axiom II: Development Is Multidirectional. The axiom of multidirectionality suggests the possibility of pluralism (i.e., variability or heterogeneity) in trajectories of developmental change across functional domains (Baltes, 1987). For example, one such system may demonstrate gains over time (e.g., job knowledge), whereas another shows losses over time (e.g., physical strength), and such dynamics are even plausible within the same sphere of functioning. For example, research concerning aging and emotions at work has found an age-related advantage in perceiving one's own emotions and emotion regulation processes (e.g., Scheibe & Zacher, 2013; Toomey & Rudolph, 2018). In contrast, the ability to perceive other people's emotions correctly appears to decline with age (Doerwald, Scheibe, Zacher, & Van Yperen, 2016). To this end, Carstensen's (1991, 1996) lifespan theory of socioemotional selectivity (SST) posits that age-related enhancements in emotion self-perception and regulation capacity occur, in part, due to shifting goal horizons that are associated with reduced time perspectives and increasing age (e.g., Carstensen et al., 1999). More nuanced theories of age and emotion regulation similarly assert such an age-related advantage in emotion regulation, but also challenge certain basic assumptions about this process. For example, the selection, optimization, and compensation – emotion regulation model (SOC-ER; Urry & Gross, 2010) posits that older adults maintain high levels of psychological wellbeing by selecting and optimizing specific emotion regulation processes, which serve to compensate for age-related changes in both internal and external resources. This model suggests that whereas younger adults have a higher capacity to engage internal cognitive control in service of emotional regulation via reappraisal, losses of control require older adults to rely more on external encouragement from others to facilitate situational selection as a mode of emotion regulation. Similarly, the strength and vulnerability integration model (SAVI; Charles, 2010) predicts age-related benefits in the management of emotions related to transient (e.g., day-to-day) stressors, but age-related declines in emotion regulation capacities in the face of chronic stressors.

Outside of conceptual models of emotion regulation, empirical cognitive aging research speaks to multidirectional developmental trajectories (see

Salthouse, 2012, for a review and implications for the work context). For example, classic works demonstrate the stability of crystallized mental abilities (i.e., cognitive pragmatics) and the decline of fluid mental abilities (i.e., cognitive mechanics) over time (Baltes, Dittmann-Kohli, & Dixon, 1984; Dixon & Baltes, 1986). These functions are echoed in conceptual works: for example, Kanfer and Ackerman (2004) discuss how these multidirectional cognitive ability dynamics serve to account for shifting work motivations and work performance across the adult lifespan.

Considering how this axiom can be applied to managing an aging workforce, it must be understood that knowledge, skills, abilities, and other factors change in multiple directions across time. The assumption that "aging implies decline" is misguided from this lens, and may lead to overgeneralizations and mischaracterizations of older workers, particularly in relation to declining abilities (e.g., Posthuma & Campion, 2009). This axiom also suggests that work systems could be optimally designed to incorporate those characteristics of workers that are likely to change across the lifespan (e.g., increased job knowledge; higher capacities for emotional regulation). For example, job knowledge can be transferred from older to younger workers via purposefully implemented knowledge-sharing programs (e.g., DeLong, 2004). Additionally, jobs requiring direct customer interactions may be best suited for older individuals, who are better at adaptively integrating emotional experiences at work (e.g., Toomey & Rudolph, 2017). It is also important to afford workers those resources that serve to facilitate age-conditional functioning in various domains. In their lifespan model of job design, Truxillo, Cadiz, Rineer, Zaniboni, and Fraccaroli (2012) argued that job autonomy, skill variety, social support, and task significance are more important for motivating older workers. In contrast, these researchers posit that skill variety, job complexity, and job feedback are particularly important to younger workers. Several of the model's propositions have received support in empirical studies (e.g., Zacher, Dirkers, Korek, & Hughes, 2017; Zaniboni, Truxillo, & Fraccaroli, 2013). Regarding the changing nature of work more generally, some cross-temporal evidence has suggested that certain perceived job characteristics – including skill variety – have increased over time (Wegman et al., 2018).

Axiom III: Development Implies Gains and Losses. This axiom defines successful development as a positive ratio of age-related gains to losses across the lifespan. That is to say, success in development occurs to the extent that one's available pool of developmental resources (e.g., accrued knowledge and skills; physical and cognitive abilities; social connections; culture, see Baltes, 1987) outweighs those lost in the process of aging. Conceptual models of successful aging at work (Zacher, 2015b) reflect this idea and further elaborate on the need to view success in terms of positive age-related trajectories in work outcomes. Other successful aging models (Kooij, 2015) offer instead that success is realized through continuous efforts at maintaining person–environment fit – a process that, in itself, is also resource intensive. These perspectives are complementary to the extent that one can maintain an array of resources (e.g., personal, contextual) to support positive long-term trajectories of person–environment fit across time.

Research regarding the influence of cognitive decrements for the health and wellbeing of older workers speaks to such gain/loss dynamics over time. For example, Infurna and Andel (2017) investigated how levels of episodic memory at retirement and rates of change in episodic memory before and after retirement are associated with functional health and wellbeing (i.e., disability, cardiovascular disease, and mortality risk) following retirement. Results suggest that those individuals with higher levels of episodic memory at the time of retirement, and relative stability in episodic memory prior to and following retirement, had a lower risk likelihood for impaired functional health and wellbeing following retirement. In another area of study, Wang, Burlacu, Truxillo, James, and Yao (2015) showed that, relative to younger workers, older workers have higher levels of feedback orientation related to social awareness, but lower levels of feedback orientation related to utility. These age-related differences in feedback orientation were found to moderate relationships between feedback characteristics (i.e., delivery, favorability, quality) and reactions to feedback.

In terms of managing an aging workforce, this axiom suggests that organizations must be cognizant of the role that age-related decrements in resources (i.e., relative to those gained over time – for example, job knowledge, work experience, and emotional competencies) play in defining the long-term success of their employees. One means of addressing this is to design and implement active interventions that support the long-term health and wellbeing of workers of all ages. In doing so, it is important to focus on changing those features of the work environment that benefit individuals regardless of their age. For example, research shows that workers of all ages benefit from the implementation of flexible work policies that allow them to dictate when, where, and how their work is performed (Rudolph & Baltes, 2017). Of note, shifts from standard work patterns to increasing flexible work have been noted as a facet of the changing nature of work (e.g., Rousseau, 1995, 1996). Organizations may also be well served to develop systems to translate the gained resources and accrued experiences of older employees (i.e., those that constitute "success" at work) into long-term strategies (e.g., via knowledge management systems; see DeLong, 2004; Slagter, 2007). For instance, Kooij, van Woerkom, Wilkenloh, Dorenbosch, and Denissen (2017) showed that older employees who participated in a job-crafting intervention were subsequently better able to adjust their jobs to their personal strengths. Finally, organizations could consider placing older workers in work roles that better suit their needs and capabilities, for instance, serving in mentoring and organizational ambassador roles (Calo, 2005).

Axiom IV: Development Is Modifiable. Modifiability is defined by intraindividual plasticity (i.e., the potential for within-person and over-time dynamics). As such, multiple developmental courses are possible; however, the core function of development is the search for and realization of such plasticity and an acknowledgement of its constraints (Baltes, 1987). To some extent the concept of plasticity reflects notions of adaptability (e.g., Rudolph, Lavigne, & Zacher, 2016) and proactivity (e.g., Parker & Bindl, 2016), both of which have been noted as important person-level variables for successfully navigating dynamic and changing work environments. Research concerning so-called recurrent novelty at work speaks to the capacity for and consequences of intra-individual plasticity for cognitive functioning and performance. To this end, Oltmanns and colleagues (2017) explored the extent to which the cumulative effects of repeated exposure to work-task changes among manufacturing employees with low levels of job complexity influence grey matter volume and cognitive functioning over 17 years. Previous research has associated low-complexity jobs with decreased cognitive functioning (e.g., Fisher et al., 2014; Schooler, Mulatu, & Oates, 1999). This study found that work-task changes were associated with better processing speed and working memory capacity, as well as higher grey matter volume in those brain regions that have been associated with learning. Thus, recurrent novelty in the form of changing job tasks may serve to counteract those declines in cognitive functioning that have been associated with low-complexity jobs.

Mirroring these findings more generally, researchers have recognized the importance of adopting an age-conscious approach to job design (e.g., Truxillo et al., 2012). For example, Zaniboni and colleagues (2013) report two time-lagged studies in which higher task variety was associated with lower work-related burnout and turnover intentions for younger workers compared to older workers, and higher skill variety was associated with lower turnover intentions for older workers compared to younger workers. Core principles of action regulation theory would likewise support the conclusion that the design of jobs and job processes needs to be optimized to facilitate healthy workforce aging as well as promote positive cognitive and personality development over time (Zacher et al., 2016).

The principle of plasticity has a number of important implications for managing an aging workforce beyond its direct relevance to active job (re)design efforts. As such, it is important for organizations to recognize that certain elements within the immediate work and organizational context, including perceived job characteristics, can serve to support or diminish long-term success outcomes for workers of all ages. While objective job characteristics themselves may not be immediately modifiable in light of certain organizational constraints (e.g., the more-or-less rigid structure of certain routinized jobs; provisions for safety), it has been posited that certain proactive work behaviors aimed at changing one's perceived job resources and demands, including specific efforts directed toward job crafting (Rudolph, Katz, Lavigne, & Zacher, 2017), may be particularly efficacious for maintaining long-term person–environment fit (see Kooij, Tims, & Kanfer, 2015). Managers also need to be aware of the fact that workers' ability to learn and develop does not diminish with advancing age; however, research suggests that, due to age stereotypes and negative feedback, older workers may have reduced self-efficacy for learning (Maurer, 2001). Thus, it is vital that organizations design and implement training and development programs that take into account the experience and motives of workers of different ages (Beier, Teachout, & Cox, 2012).

Axiom V: Development Is Historically, Socially, and Culturally Embedded. Beyond those previously mentioned influences, the course of people's development can vary substantially with historical, social, and cultural conditions (Baltes, 1987). Such so-called period effects suggest that a range of sociocultural conditions that emerge over time can influence the experiences of any given individual. Such experiences could shape the way in which people's development unfolds. Of note, this axiom directly speaks against the possible role that generational differences may play in affecting work outcomes, as the concept of historical embeddedness suggests the role that contemporaneous influences can play in shaping developmental trajectories, whereas generational differences theories implicate birth cohorts as the mechanisms of such change.

Notable examples of the role of such historical influences are represented in research by Bianchi (2013, 2014), which addresses how contemporaneous economic conditions influence work outcomes. For example, across a series of studies, Bianchi (2013) demonstrated that economic conditions at the time of college graduation predicted later-life job satisfaction, and these effects held when controlling for different industry and occupational choices. More recently, Bianchi (2014) offered three studies which demonstrate that entering adulthood during economic recessions (compared to coming of age in more prosperous times) is associated with lower levels of narcissistic personality later in life. In our critique of the generational differences literature, we offer a review of various studies of similar historical/contemporaneous period effects (e.g., daylight savings time, earthquakes, unionization), which have been shown to exert demonstrable influences on important work outcomes (see Rudolph & Zacher, 2017a, table 1).

Applied to the management of an aging workforce, this axiom suggests that it is critical for organizations to recognize the potentially important role that current work and life contexts and events can have for shaping the behavior of their employees. It is important to note that while such effects may manifest as short-term changes, from the research reviewed here, such differences can also have long-lasting influences on important attitudes and personality characteristics that organizations value (e.g., job satisfaction). It is likewise critical to recognize that historical influences are not the results of so-called "generational" (i.e., birth cohort) effects, although these two possible explanations are often unduly and inappropriately conflated in the literature (e.g., via the so-called "cross-temporal meta-analysis" methodology; see Twenge et al., 2008 for an example of such a study that intractably conflates cohort and historical period effects with one another; see also Rudolph & Zacher, 2017a, 2018 for related critiques of this method).

Axiom VI: Development Is Contextualized. Contextualization, in this regard, suggests that individual development is the result of the dialectics and interactions of three distinct systems of influences: normative age-graded, history-graded, and non-normative (Baltes, 1987). Normative age-graded influences refer to those systems of developmental influence that are typically encountered by most people but that manifest as interindividual differences. Such influences may include the normal course of biological maturation associated with aging (e.g., declines in physical functioning and fluid cognitive abilities) and prototypical socialization events (e.g., education, family, retirement). Mirroring to some extent the axiom of historical embeddedness, history-graded influences refer to those systems of developmental influence that are linked to the specific time period in which individuals develop (Baltes, 1987). For instance, many people born in the United States during the first half of the twentieth century were influenced by the Great Depression (Elder, 1999). As noted by Zacher (2015a) and Rudolph and Zacher (2017a), history-graded developmental influences differ from the concept of "generations," in that they do not imply that individuals must be categorized on the basis of broad birth year ranges, or via assumptions about shared life experiences. Rather, the lifespan perspective offers that history-graded influences serve as features of one's biography that can potentially impact each individual's developmental outcomes, again manifesting as interindividual differences. Finally, non-normative influences manifest as unique, idiosyncratic effects for each particular individual. Such unique influences could include the sudden onset of an illness, a severe work accident, the loss of a long-term partner or relative, financial gains, or unplanned early retirement.

One example of research on non-normative influences can be found in Roberts and Robins' (2004) study on the influence of stability and change in person–environment fit in relation to personality development over time. Using a four-year longitudinal study of college students, this study found that higher levels of initial person–environment fit were associated with overall higher personality consistency and changes in personality, including higher self-esteem, and lower agreeableness and neuroticism, over time. Similar research by Roberts, O'Donnell, and Robins (2004) links changes in life goals across various domains with changes in personality traits across a four-year timeframe. Indeed, modern neosocioanalytic (Roberts & Wood, 2006) and sociogenomic (Roberts, 2018) models of personality development both posit that mechanisms approximating non-normative systems of developmental influence can have profound effects on personality change and development across the lifespan.

In a different regard, Heckhausen's research on school-to-work transitions directly considers the interplay of various developmental influences, and notably the role of normative developmental influences. For example, in a longitudinal study of such transitions, Heckhausen and Tomasik (2002) investigated vocational aspirations of German high school students who were applying for vocational training programs. Such school-to-work transitions are one type of critical transitional period that represents a normative developmental experience. The findings of this study suggest that applicants shift their perception of vocational ideals (i.e., "dream jobs") to vocational preferences (i.e., jobs they were *interested* in) as the apprenticeship deadline approaches. Additionally, observed relationships between such perceptions and reports of primary and secondary control striving behaviors provide some evidence for the role that shifting control strategies serve as a means for coping with the perception of restricted career choices.

The axiom of contextualization has several implications for managing an aging workforce. Most notably, it suggests a need for organizations to recognize that not only normative patterns of aging, but also idiosyncratic influences, can have an important impact on employees' development at work. In other words, while knowledge of average age-related trends may provide managers with a general idea of the typical strengths and potential weaknesses of younger and older employees, they also need to consider the important role of interindividual differences and unexpected life and work events (Zacher, Kooij, & Beier, 2018). If managers are unaware of the substantial heterogeneity among both younger and older workers in terms of abilities, skills, and motives – and that such variability tends to further increase with advancing age – they may fall victim to an ecological fallacy, whereby inferences are made about individuals based on their age group membership (see also Costanza, Finkelstein, Imose, & Ravid, Chapter 2 in this volume).

Axiom VII: Development Is Multidisciplinary. The final axiom of the lifespan perspective suggests that development must be understood through the lenses of multiple scientific disciplines. Accordingly, any understanding of development is incomplete without recognizing myriad factors (e.g., biological, sociolocultural). This means that a purely psychological (or sociological, biological, gerontological, etc.) perspective is but a partial and incomplete representation of the totality of human ontogeny (Baltes, 1987). Consequently, when applying this final axiom, aging at work must be understood from multiple perspectives, and the integration of multidisciplinary perspectives is indeed necessary to gain a complete picture of our aging workforce.

To this end, the socio-gerontological life course theory is a corollary metatheoretical perspective with roots in the sociological tradition (e.g., Elder, 1998). The life course perspective describes the dynamic role of human agency bounded by the constraints of various contextual and structural factors (i.e., institutions such as family, organizations, countries). Like the lifespan perspective, life course theory emphasizes the notion that there are individualized developmental trajectories. However, where lifespan theories describe development as a continuous process, the life course perspective offers that development can be described as a series of age-graded roles that people assume over time (Shanahan, 2000). These roles can be defined in terms of their timing (e.g., historical period, chronological age) or their sequencing (i.e., the normative sequencing of life events). With an emphasis on the bounded role of individual agency, various choices and actions occur within contexts (i.e., defined as those limits that are imposed by one's embeddedness in various historical, cultural, or social circumstances) and combine to shape the construction of an individual's life course trajectory.

Considering phenomena relevant to the aging workforce, retirement research has for some time adopted such an eclectic, multidisciplinary lifespan/life course perspective (see Wang & Shi, 2014, for a review). For example, Damman, Henkens, and Kalmijn (2013) adopted a multidisciplinary perspective to explore how life histories (i.e., an inherently life course concept) are related to retirement adjustment outcomes (i.e., an inherently psychological concept) in a three-wave panel study. Results suggest that, in general, the longer people have been retired, the less likely they are to miss work-related social contacts. However, interesting demographic patterns were also noted in this study: for example, divorced retirees without a partner were more likely to miss the social dimensions that were provided to them via working. Additionally, steeper upward career paths were found to be associated with lower financial retirement adjustment difficulties, but they were also associated with higher difficulties adjusting to the loss of perceived status (i.e., identity) following retirement. Similarly adopting a multidisciplinary approach to the study of retirement, research by Donaldson, Earl, and Muratore (2010) explores the intersection of individual (e.g., demographics, health), psychosocial (e.g., mastery, planning), and organizational factors (e.g., conditions of workforce exit) that influence the process of retirement adjustment. Among other things, the results of this study suggest that a higher personal sense of mastery (i.e., an individual-level psychological variable) and more favorable organizational factors (i.e., various contextual conditions surrounding one's exit from their employer prior to retirement) significantly predicted adjustment to retirement.

With respect to managing an aging workforce, this final axiom suggests that it is of vital importance to recognize that important age-related work outcomes are multiply determined. The multidisciplinary perspective requires one to think beyond common explanations of behavior, and to seek more comprehensive models to describe such behaviors. Multidisciplinary models of development necessarily have to examine predictors and outcomes on multiple conceptual and analytical levels. For instance, administrative science and business scholars focus not only on individual-level psychological variables, but also on organizational level factors such as age diversity, organizational age discrimination climate, and firm performance (Kunze, Boehm, & Bruch, 2011). Moreover, based on research in social and cross-cultural psychology, aging researchers have argued that individual age and central cultural values (e.g., individualism–collectivism) present in different countries interact in predicting outcomes such as age discrimination (Marcus & Fritzsche, 2016). In summary, managers should be aware that age-related processes and outcomes are simultaneously shaped by a multitude of factors that reside at different conceptual levels and that may be studied in different scientific disciplines, including psychology, business, sociology, medicine, anthropology, and others (cf. Baltes, 1987).

Summary and Conclusions

This chapter presents the lifespan developmental perspective as an integrative meta-theoretical framework for understanding the myriad complexities associated with the proposition of managing an increasingly aging workforce. In particular, we have focused on exploring how adopting a lifespan perspective on aging at work can aid in circumventing the notable shortcomings associated with the popular notion of generational differences. We introduced the lifespan perspective broadly, and then outlined its development as a mode of thinking about human development. Seven axioms of the lifespan perspective were outlined, and select primary empirical research and theory in the work and organizational psychology domain that exemplify these axioms were reviewed. Additionally, we presented a number of specific practical recommendations for how to apply these seven axioms to the management of an aging workforce.

Our hope is that this review of the lifespan perspective and associated examples from the literature, and the practical advice derived thence will serve to guide future thinking about the management of the aging workforce. One important implication of the adoption of a lifespan perspective for the management of an aging workforce is the refocusing and reemphasis on the entirety of the adult lifespan, not just upon "older workers" (see Rudolph, Toomey, & Baltes, 2017). Early perspectives on so-called "age management," or the specific strategic focus on managing age at work, typically focused solely on the implications of an aging workforce for the management of older workers (e.g., Naegele & Walker, 2010; Walker, 2005). As it emphasizes that no particular age or stage holds dominance over any other, a broader adoption of the lifespan perspective necessitates the consideration of workers of all ages (and the aging process per se), not just a focus on older workers specifically. Thus, from a lifespan perspective, we would argue that the general notion of age management must be recast in terms of any number of age-conscious processes that serve to accomplish core human resources management (HRM) practices.

Indeed, more recent works have begun to adopt such a broader perspective on age management. For example, Böhm, Schröder, and Kunze (2013) conceptualize age management in terms of "HRM dimensions employed to manage human resources with an explicit focus on the demands of an ageing workforce" (p. 216). Adopting this conceptualization, Böhm and colleagues (2013) provide a framework for organizing age management principles around sets of guidelines that specify best practices for actively managing age across a number of organizational processes, including recruiting, training and lifelong learning, career management and redeployment, flexible work time and work arrangements, health management and workplace accommodations, performance measurement and remuneration, and transitions to retirement (see Böhm et al., 2013, p. 226; Table 12.1, in this volume.). We suspect that an even more complete typology of successful age management strategies will emerge with the continued adoption of the lifespan perspective on managing the aging workforce advocated for here.

Although we would argue that the adoption of broader, lifespan-informed practices for age management is important for the long-term management of an aging workforce, it is also important to recognize that the general notion of generational differences is incompatible with the core tenets of lifespan perspective. It should be clear from the theory and research reviewed here that the notion of generational differences as they are commonly (and incorrectly) understood to affect work processes and outcomes cannot be accommodated within the boundaries of the lifespan perspective. Accordingly, adopting a lifespan perspective to the management of the aging workforce requires us, as a field, to move beyond the notable pitfalls in generationalized thinking that have been offered elsewhere (e.g., Rudolph & Zacher, 2015, 2017a, 2017b), and strongly cautioned against again here. Perhaps the best "practical" advice that can be gleaned from the preceding review is that aging is a far more complicated, nuanced, and individualized process than generational perspectives would have one believe. With great hope, we therefore advance the preceding lifespan perspective as a path toward an enhanced understanding of the interesting, important implications of the universal process of aging at work. We think that these ideas inform a better way forward, as we strive to understand the changing nature of work.

Acknowledgement

The authors would like to acknowledge and thank Rachel S. Rauvola for her assistance in the preparation of this work.

References

Baltes, P. B. (1987). Theoretical propositions of life-span developmental psychology: On the dynamics between growth and decline. *Developmental Psychology, 23*, 611–626.

Baltes, P. B., Dittmann-Kohli, F., & Dixon, R. A. (1984). New perspectives on the development of intelligence in adulthood: Toward a dual-process conception and a model of selective optimization with compensation. In P. B. Baltes & O. G. Brim, Jr. (Eds.), *Life-span development and behavior, Vol. 6* (pp. 33–76). New York, NY: Academic Press.

Baltes, P. B., Lindenberger, U., & Staudinger, U. M. (2006). Lifespan theory in developmental psychology. In W. Damon & R. M. Lerner (Eds.), *Handbook of child psychology, Vol. 1: Theoretical models of human development* (6th ed., pp. 569–664). New York, NY: Wiley.

Baltes, P. B., Reese, H. W., & Lipsitt, L. P. (1980). Life-span developmental psychology. *Annual Review of Psychology, 31*, 65–110.

Baltes, P. B., Staudinger, U. M., & Lindenberger, U. (1999). Lifespan psychology: Theory and application to intellectual functioning. *Annual Review of Psychology, 50*, 471–507.

Beehr, T. A., & Bennett, M. M. (2015). Working after retirement: Features of bridge employment and research directions. *Work, Aging and Retirement, 1*, 112–128.

Beier, M. E., Teachout, M. S., & Cox, C. B. (2012). The training and development of an aging workforce. In J. W. Hedge & W. C. Borman (Eds.), *The Oxford handbook of work and aging* (pp. 436–453). New York, NY: Oxford University Press.

Beier, M. E., Torres, W. J., & Gilberto, J. M. (2017). Continuous development throughout a career: A lifespan perspective on autonomous learning. In J. E. Ellingson & R. A. Noe (Eds.), *Autonomous learning in the workplace* (pp. 179–200). New York, NY: Taylor & Francis.

Bianchi, E. C. (2013). The bright side of bad times: The affective advantages of entering the workforce in a recession. *Administrative Science Quarterly, 58*, 587–623.

Bianchi, E. C. (2014). Entering adulthood in a recession tempers later narcissism. *Psychological Science, 25*, 1429–1437.

Böhm, S. A., Schröder, H. S., & Kunze, F. (2013). Comparative age management: Theoretical perspectives and practical implications. In J. Field, R. Burke, & C. L. Cooper (Eds.), *The SAGE handbook of work, aging, and society* (pp. 211–237). Thousand Oaks, CA: Sage.

Brandtstädter, J. (1999). The self in action and development: Cultural, biosocial, and ontogenetic bases of intentional self-development. In J. Brandtstädter & R. M. Lerner (Eds.), *Action and self development: Theory and research through the life span* (pp. 37–65). Thousand Oaks, CA: Sage.

Calo, J. (2005). The generativity track: A transitional approach to retirement. *Public Personnel Management, 34*, 301–312.

Campbell, S. M., Twenge, J. M., & Campbell, W. K. (2017). Fuzzy but useful constructs: Making sense of the differences between generations. *Work, Aging and Retirement, 3*, 130–139.

Carstensen, L. L. (1991). Selectivity theory: Social activity in life-span context. *Annual Review of Gerontology and Geriatrics, 11*, 195–217.

Carstensen, L. L. (2006). The influence of a sense of time on human development. *Science, 312*, 1913–1915.

Carstensen, L. L., Isaacowitz, D. M., & Charles, S. T. (1999). Taking time seriously: A theory of socioemotional selectivity. *American Psychologist, 54*, 165–181.

Charles, S. T. (2010). Strength and vulnerability integration: A model of emotional well-being across adulthood. *Psychological Bulletin, 136*, 1068–1091.

Costanza, D. P., Badger, J. M., Fraser, R. L., Severt, J. B., & Gade, P. A. (2012). Generational differences in work-related attitudes: A meta-analysis. *Journal of Business and Psychology, 27*, 375–394.

Costanza, D. P., Badger-Darrow, J. B., Yost, A. B., & Severt, J. B. (2017). A review of analytical methods used to study generational differences: Strengths and limitations. *Work, Aging and Retirement, 3*, 149–165.

Damman, M., Henkens, K., & Kalmijn, M. (2013). Missing work after retirement: The role of life histories in the retirement adjustment process. *The Gerontologist, 55*, 802–813.

Day, D. V. (2011). Integrative perspectives on longitudinal investigations of leader development: From childhood through adulthood. *Leadership Quarterly, 22*, 561–571.

Day, D. V., Fleenor, J. W., Atwater, L. E., Sturm, R. E., & McKee, R. A. (2014). Advances in leader and leadership development: A review of 25 years of research and theory. *Leadership Quarterly, 25*, 63–82.

Day, D. V., Harrison, M. M., & Halpin, S. M. (2012). *An integrative approach to leader development: Connecting adult development, identity, and expertise.* New York, NY: Routledge.

DeLong, D. W. (2004). *Lost knowledge: Confronting the threat of an aging workforce.* New York, NY: Oxford University Press.

Dixon, R. A., & Baltes, P. B. (1986). Toward life-span research on the functions and pragmatics of intelligence. In R. J. Sternberg & R. K. Wagner (Eds.), *Practical intelligence: Origins of competence in the everyday world* (pp. 203–235). New York, NY: Cambridge University Press.

Doerwald, F., Scheibe, S., Zacher, H., & Van Yperen, N. W. (2016). Emotional competencies across adulthood: State of knowledge and implications for the work context. *Work, Aging and Retirement, 2*, 159–216.

Donaldson, T., Earl, J. K., & Muratore, A. M. (2010). Extending the integrated model of retirement adjustment: Incorporating mastery and retirement planning. *Journal of Vocational Behavior, 77*, 279–289.

Elder, G. H. (1998). The life course as developmental theory. *Child Development, 69*, 1–12.

Elder, G. H. (1999). *Children of the Great Depression: Social change in life experience.* Boulder, CO: Westview Press.

Erikson, E. H. (1950). *Childhood and society*. New York, NY: Norton.

Featherman, D. L., & Lerner, R. M. (1985). Ontogenesis and sociogenesis: Problematics for theory and research about development and socialization across the lifespan. *American Sociological Review, 50*, 659–676.

Feldman, D. C. (2002). Stability in the midst of change: A developmental perspective on the study of careers. In D. C. Feldman (Ed.), *Work careers: A developmental perspective* (pp. 3–26). San Francisco, CA: Jossey-Bass.

Fisher, G. G., Stachowski, A., Infurna, F. J., Faul, J. D., Grosch, J., and Tetrick, L. E. (2014). Mental work demands, retirement, and longitudinal trajectories of cognitive functioning. *Journal of Occupational Health Psychology, 19*, 231–242.

Ford, D. H., & Lerner, R. M. (1992). *Developmental systems theory: An integrative approach.* Thousand Oaks, CA: Sage.

Gerland, P., Raftery, A. E., Ševčíková, H., Li, N., Gu, D., Spoorenberg, T., ... & Wilmoth, J. (2014). World population stabilization unlikely this century. *Science, 346*, 234–237.

Hall, D. T., & Mirvis, P. H. (1995). The new career contract: Developing the whole person at midlife and beyond. *Journal of Vocational Behavior, 47*(3), 269–289.

Heckhausen, J., & Schulz, R. (1995). A life-span theory of control. *Psychological Review, 102*, 284–304.

Heckhausen, J., & Tomasik, M. J. (2002). Get an apprenticeship before school is out: How German adolescents adjust vocational aspirations when getting close to a developmental deadline. *Journal of Vocational Behavior, 60*, 199–219.

Hirschi, A., Niles, S. G., & Akos, P. (2011). Engagement in adolescent career preparation: Social support, personality and the development of choice decidedness and congruence. *Journal of Adolescence, 34*, 173–182.

Infurna, F. J., & Andel, R. (2017). The impact of changes in episodic memory surrounding retirement on subsequent risk of disability, cardiovascular disease, and mortality. *Work, Aging and Retirement*.

Kanfer, R., & Ackerman, P. L. (2004). Aging, adult development, and work motivation. *The Academy of Management Review*, 29, 440–458.

Kohlberg, L. (1987). *The Measurement of moral judgement*. Cambridge, UK: Cambridge University Press.

Kooij, D. T. (2015). Successful aging at work: The active role of employees. *Work, Aging and Retirement*, 1, 309–319.

Kooij, D. T. A. M., de Lange, A. H., Jansen, P. G. W., Kanfer, R., & Dikkers, J. S. E. (2011). Age and work-related motives: Results of a meta-analysis. *Journal of Organizational Behavior*, 32, 197–225.

Kooij, D. T., Tims, M., & Kanfer, R. (2015). Successful aging at work: The role of job crafting. In P. M. Bal, D. T. A. M. Kooij, & D. M. Rousseau (Eds.), *Aging workers and the employee–employer relationship* (pp. 145–161). Zurich, Switzerland: Springer International Publishing.

Kooij, D. T., van Woerkom, M., Wilkenloh, J., Dorenbosch, L., & Denissen, J. J. (2017). Job crafting towards strengths and interests: The effects of a job crafting intervention on person–job fit and the role of age. *Journal of Applied Psychology*, 102, 971–981.

Kozlowski, S. W. J., & Klein, K. J. (2000). A multilevel approach to theory and research in organizations: Contextual, temporal, and emergent processes. In K. J. Klein & S. W. J. Kozlowski (Eds.), *Multilevel theory, research and methods in organizations: Foundations, extensions, and new directions* (pp. 3–90). San Francisco, CA: Jossey-Bass.

Kunze, F., Boehm, S. A., & Bruch, H. (2011). Age diversity, age discrimination climate and performance consequences: A cross organizational study. *Journal of Organizational Behavior*, 32, 264–290.

Lerner, R. M. (1996). Relative plasticity, integration, temporality, and diversity in human development: A developmental contextual perspective about theory, process, and method. *Developmental Psychology*, 32, 781–786.

Lerner, R. M., & Busch-Rossnagel, N. A. (1981). *Individuals as producers of their development: A life-span perspective*. New York, NY: Academic Press.

Lerner, R. M., & Kauffman, M. B. (1985). The concept of development in contextualism. *Developmental Review*, 5, 309–333.

Levinson, D. J. (1986). A conception of adult development. *American Psychologist*, 41, 3–13.

Marcus, J., & Fritzsche, B. A. (2016). The cultural anchors of age discrimination in the workplace: A multilevel framework. *Work, Aging and Retirement*, 2, 217–229.

Maurer, T. J. (2001). Career-relevant learning and development, worker age, and beliefs about self-efficacy for development. *Journal of Management*, 27, 123–140.

Naegele, G., & Walker, A. (2010). Age management in organisations in the European Union. In M. Malloch (Ed.), *The Sage handbook of workplace learning* (pp. 251–267). London, UK: Sage.

Oltmanns, J., Godde, B., Winneke, A. H., Richter, G., Niemann, C., Voelcker-Rehage, C., ... & Staudinger, U. M. (2017). Don't lose your brain at work: The role of recurrent novelty at work in cognitive and brain aging. *Frontiers in Psychology, 8*, e2598. doi: 10.3389/fpsyg.2017.00117.

Parker, S. K., & Bindl, U. K. (Eds.). (2016). *Proactivity at work: Making things happen in organizations*. New York, NY: Taylor & Francis.

Phillips, S. D. (2015). Lifespan career development. In P. J. Hartung, M. L. Savickas, & W. B. Walsh (Eds.), *APA handbook of career intervention, Vol. 1: Foundations* (pp. 99–113). Washington, DC: APA.

Piaget, J. (1976). Piaget's theory. In *Piaget and his school* (pp. 11–23). Heidelberg, Germany: Springer Berlin.

Posthuma, R. A., & Campion, M. A. (2009). Age stereotypes in the workplace: Common stereotypes, moderators, and future research directions. *Journal of Management, 35*, 158–188.

Roberts, B. W. (2018). A revised sociogenomic model of personality traits. *Journal of Personality*.

Roberts, B. W., O'Donnell, M., & Robins, R. W. (2004). Goal and personality trait development in emerging adulthood. *Journal of Personality and Social Psychology, 87*, 541–550.

Roberts, B. W., & Robins, R. W. (2004). Person–environment fit and its implications for personality development: A longitudinal study. *Journal of Personality, 72*, 89–110.

Roberts, B. W., Walton, K. E., & Viechtbauer, W. (2006). Patterns of mean-level change in personality traits across the life course: A meta-analysis of longitudinal studies. *Psychological Bulletin, 132*, 1–25.

Roberts, B. W., & Wood, D. (2006). Personality development in the context of the neo-socioanalytic model of personality. In D. K. Mroczek & T. D. Little (Eds.), *Handbook of personality development* (pp. 11–39). Mahwah, NJ: Lawrence Erlbaum Associates.

Rousseau, D. M. (1995). *Psychological contracts in organizations: Written and unwritten agreements*. Newbury Park, CA: Sage.

Rousseau, D. M. (1996). Changing the deal while keeping the people. *Academy of Management Executive, 10*, 50–59.

Rudolph, C. W. (2015). A note on the folly of cross-sectional operationalizations of generations. *Industrial and Organizational Psychology, 8*, 362–366.

Rudolph, C. W. (2016). Lifespan developmental perspectives on working: A literature review of motivational theories. *Work, Aging and Retirement, 2*, 130–158.

Rudolph, C. W., & Baltes, B. B. (2017). Age and health jointly moderate the influence of flexible work arrangements on work engagement: Evidence from two empirical studies. *Journal of Occupational Health Psychology, 22*, 40–58.

Rudolph, C. W., Katz, I. M., Lavigne, K. N., & Zacher, H. (2017). Job crafting: A meta-analysis of relationships with individual differences, job characteristics, and work outcomes. *Journal of Vocational Behavior, 102*, 112–138.

Rudolph, C. W., Lavigne, K. N., & Zacher, H. (2016). Career adaptability: A meta-analysis of relationships with measures of adaptivity, adapting responses, and adaptation results. *Journal of Vocational Behavior, 98*, 17–34.

Rudolph, C. W., Marcus, J., & Zacher, H. (2019). Global Issues in Work, Aging, and Retirement. In K. Shultz & G. Adams (Eds.), *Aging & work in the 21st century* (2nd ed.). New York, NY: Routledge/Psychology Press.

Rudolph, C. W., Toomey, E., & Baltes, B. B. (2017). Considering age diversity in recruitment and selection: An expanded work lifespan view of age management. In J. McCarthy & E. Parry (Eds.), *Handbook of age diversity and work* (pp. 607–638). London, UK: Palgrave-Macmillan.

Rudolph, C. W. & Zacher, H. (2015). Intergenerational perceptions and conflicts in multi-age and multigenerational work environments. In L. Finkelstein, D. Truxillo, F. Fraccaroli, F., & R. Kanfer (Eds.), *Facing the challenges of a multi-age workforce: A use-inspired approach* (pp. 253–282). New York, NY: Psychology Press.

Rudolph, C. W. & Zacher, H. (2017a). Considering generations from a lifespan developmental perspective. *Work, Aging and Retirement, 3*, 113–129.

Rudolph, C. W. & Zacher, H. (2017b). Myths and misconceptions about leading generations: Setting the record straight. In T. A. Scandura & E. Mouriño (Eds.), *Leading diversity in the 21st century* (pp. 243–278). Charlotte, NC: Information Age Publishing.

Rudolph, C. W. & Zacher, H. (2018). The kids are alright: Taking stock of generational differences. *The Industrial and Organizational Psychologist, 55.* http://my.siop.org/tip/jan18/editor/ArtMID/13745/ArticleID/248/The-Kids-Are-Alright-Taking-Stock-of-Generational-Differences-at-Work

Salthouse, T. A. (2012). Consequences of age-related cognitive declines. *Annual Review of Psychology, 63*, 201–226.

Scheibe, S., & Zacher, H. (2013). A lifespan perspective on emotion regulation, stress, and well-being in the workplace. In P. L. Perrewé, C. C. Rosen, & J. R. B. Halbesleben (Eds.), *The role of emotion and emotion regulation in job stress and well-being* (pp. 163–193). Bingley, UK: Emerald Group Publishing Limited.

Schooler, C., Mulatu, M. S., & Oates, G. (1999). The continuing effects of substantively complex work on the intellectual functioning of older workers. *Psychology and Aging, 14*, 483–506.

Shanahan, M. J. (2000). Pathways to adulthood in changing societies: Variability and mechanisms in life course perspective. *Annual Review of Sociology, 26*, 667–692.

Slagter, F. (2007). Knowledge management among the older workforce. *Journal of Knowledge Management, 11*, 82–96.

Toomey, E. C., & Rudolph, C. W. (2018). Age-conditional effects in the affective arousal, empathy, and emotional labor linkage: Within-person evidence from an experience sampling study. *Work, Aging and Retirement, 4*, 145–160.

Truxillo, D. M., Cadiz, D. M., Rineer, J. R., Zaniboni, S., & Fraccaroli, F. (2012). A lifespan perspective on job design: Fitting the job and the worker to promote job satisfaction, engagement, and performance. *Organizational Psychology Review, 2*, 340–360.

Twenge, J. M., & Campbell, S. M. (2008). Generational differences in psychological traits and their impact on the workplace. *Journal of Managerial Psychology, 23*, 862–877.

Twenge, J. M., Konrath, S., Foster, J. D., Campbell, W. K., & Bushman, B. J. (2008). Egos inflating over time: A cross-temporal meta-analysis of the Narcissistic Personality Inventory. *Journal of Personality, 76*(4), 875–902.

Upadyaya, K., & Salmela-Aro, K. (2015). Development of early vocational behavior: Parallel associations between career engagement and satisfaction. *Journal of Vocational Behavior, 90*, 66–74. doi: 10.1016/j.jvb.2015.07.008

Urry, H. L., & Gross, J. J. (2010). Emotion regulation in older age. *Current Directions in Psychological Science, 19*, 352–357.

Vondracek, F. W., Lerner, R. M., & Schulenberg, J. E. (1986). *Career development: A life-span developmental approach*. Hillsdale, NJ: Lawrence Erlbaum.

Walker, A. (2005). The emergence of age management in Europe. *International Journal of Organisational Behaviour, 10*, 685–697.

Wang, M., Burlacu, G., Truxillo, D., James, K., & Yao, X. (2015). Age differences in feedback reactions: The roles of employee feedback orientation on social awareness and utility. *Journal of Applied Psychology, 100*, 1296–1308.

Wang, M., & Shi, J. (2014). Psychological research on retirement. *Annual Review of Psychology, 65*, 209–233.

Wegman, L. A., Hoffman, B. J., Carter, N. T., Twenge, J. M., & Guenole, N. (2018). Placing job characteristics in context: Cross-temporal meta- analysis of changes in job characteristics since 1975. *Journal of Management*. doi: 10.1177/0149206316654545

Zacher, H. (2015a). Using lifespan developmental theory and methods as a viable alternative to the study of generational differences at work. *Industrial and Organizational Psychology, 8*, 342–346.

Zacher, H. (2015b). Successful aging at work. *Work, Aging and Retirement, 1*, 4–25.

Zacher, H., Dirkers, B. T., Korek, S., & Hughes, B. (2017). Age-differential effects of job characteristics on job attraction: A policy-capturing study. *Frontiers in Psychology, 8*, 1124. doi: 10.3389/psyg.2017.01124

Zacher, H., Hacker, W., & Frese, M. (2016). Action regulation across the adult lifespan (ARAL): A meta-theory of work and aging. *Work, Aging and Retirement, 2*, 286–306.

Zacher, H., Kooij, D. T. A. M., & Beier, M. E. (2018). Active aging at work: Contributing factors and implications for organizations. *Organizational Dynamics*.

Zaniboni, S., Truxillo, D. M., & Fraccaroli, F. (2013). Differential effects of task variety and skill variety on burnout and turnover intentions for older and younger workers. *European Journal of Work and Organizational Psychology, 22*, 306–317.

Zwaan, K., ter Bogt, T. F., & Raaijmakers, Q. (2010). Career trajectories of Dutch pop musicians: A longitudinal study. *Journal of Vocational Behavior, 77*(1), 10–20. doi: 10.1016/j.jvb.2010.03.004

21 Implications of the Changing Nature of Work for Employee Attitudes and Work Perceptions

Lauren A. Wegman and Brian J. Hoffman

Documented in academic work (i.e., Howard, 1995; National Academy of Sciences, 1999; Wegman, Hoffman, Carter, Guenole, & Twenge 2018), and outlined in the earlier chapters in this volume, the modern workplace, worker, and even the work itself appear to be substantially different from those of years past. With these changes, what is required for successful work performance has subsequently shifted (see Chapter 16, this volume, on implications for performance management), and thus, modern employees face different challenges and demands as they perform their work roles compared to their counterparts 50, 30, even as recently as five years ago. For example, well documented is the shift from manufacturing to service (Howard, 1995), only to be somewhat supplanted recently with the knowledge economy (Felin, Zenger, & Tomsik, 2009), comparatively requiring a greater emphasis on interpersonal relationships (National Academy of Sciences, 1999) and demanding a highly competent, capable, and an involved workforce (Kessels, 2001). Similarly, due to globalization and resulting competition pressures, organizations need a more flexible, agile structure and many have flattened levels of management, at the same time pushing decision-making autonomy to lower levels of employees (Howard, 1995; National Academy of Sciences, 1999), and resulting in a greater need for a flexible, responsible, and resourceful workforce. Perhaps most obviously, technological innovations have allowed for better coordination across functional and geographic boundaries but also have produced more information, data, and available knowledge creating a demand for an intelligent workforce to manage the influx of information (Potosky & Lomax, 2013).

To the extent that these changes and others have contributed to positive (or negative) outcomes for employees, we would expect to see shifts in employees' perceptions of work engagement. The objective of this chapter is to offer a perspective on the possible implications of the changes on six common employee engagement indicators: perceived organizational support, organizational commitment, organizational justice perceptions, job satisfaction, psychological stressors, and employee burnout. In the following sections, we first summarize significant, large-scale trends that have been linked to a change in employee engagement over time. We then conclude with a review of available literatures that describe ways in which each of our six employee engagement indicators may have changed.

Context around Changes: National Trends and Social Indicators

Past analyses of changes in work and workers largely relied on social indicators and macroeconomic trends to describe changes in work. Below we summarize the changes that have been anecdotally linked to changes in employee engagement, concentrating on four large-scale changes (adapted from the National Academy of Sciences' 1999 categorization and the work of Johns 2006 on contextual changes): changes in technology, workforce composition, occupational/industry shifts, and organizational restructuring. For a more in-depth review of documented changes, please see the chapters in Part II of this volume.

Technology Innovation

Rapid advancements in technology and consumer adoption of these new, and ever-increasingly, sophisticated technologies have fundamentally altered work practices (Coovert & Thompson, 2013), making technology one of the most cited reasons for changes in work.

Using Technologies at Work

Changes in technology may have broad effects on the workplace and the individuals within it. For instance, according to the upgrading hypothesis (Blauner, 1964; Gallie, 1978), when technology innovations are introduced into work settings they can result in greater skills demands (e.g., learning, integrating, monitoring). "Technologies ... can force the complete reengineering of an office job, and a shift in the knowledge, skills, and abilities of office workers" (Coovert, 1995, p. 176). Due to the pressure to master new technology, some suggest more stress is placed on employees (Van der Spiegel, 1995). Given the increased speed with which new technologies are introduced to the workplace, negative reactions such as these may be on the rise. On the other hand, technology has also been heralded as a way to increase work resources, possibly leading to an increase in positive work perceptions in more recent years. For instance, technology enables workers to complete more work in less time compared to previous decades. Specifically, automation technologies have begun to replace menial and routine job tasks, freeing up employees' time for more complex assignments (Cappelli, Bassi, Katz, Knoke, Osterman, & Useem, 1997) but technology may eventually replace workers in some jobs (Nixon & Spector, 2013), possibly resulting in greater levels of job insecurity.

Technology Enabling New Ways to Work

Perhaps the most radical contribution afforded from recent advances in technology is in the freedom organizations (and individuals) have in deciding when and where work should take place. For example, organizations have the ability to utilize e-learning technology for training and onboarding of new workers, and conference/video calls can unite stakeholders located in various parts of the world. Employees are increasingly working from home, with some even varying the time of the day (and night) they work. Taken together, this paints a very different picture of the modern workplace compared to the workplace of past decades, and without recent technological gains these freedoms would not have been possible. However, enabling technology has been called a double-edged sword (Coovert & Thompson, 2013; Lewis & Roper, 2008). While some researchers promote a positive view of the effect of technology on employee attitudes, others suggest negative outcomes for employees. For example, evidence has been found for increased work–life balance as a result of flexible policies and procedures (Bryant, 2000; Felstead, Jewson, Phizacklea, & Walters, 2002) and flextime has been linked to increased work motivation (Barney & Elias, 2010). Conversely, others propose flexible technologies have aided in the feeling of "never being off the clock" (Deal, Altman, & Rogelberg, 2010, p.195) often citing evidence of increased hours worked while flexing (Noonan & Glass, 2012), inability to detach during vacation (Galinsky, Bond, Kim, Backon, Brownfield, & Sakai, 2005), and the greater value placed on leisure time (Twenge, Campbell, Hoffman, & Lance, 2010). Some evidence suggests that technology's impact on employee engagement depends on the degree of control afforded from the technology. In their review of the literature, Nixon and Spector (2013) concluded that when technology enabled employee flexibility in scheduling (e.g., telecommuting), employees experienced greater perceptions of control and were better able to handle demanding work. On the other hand, technology-enabled "supplemental work," or work outside normal working hours facilitated by communication devices, contributes to decreased control perceptions and possibly negative effects on engagement levels.

Workforce Composition

Another commonly cited trend is the changing composition of the workforce. Stemming in part from changing labor laws and immigration patterns (Borjas, 2008; Mishel, Bernstein, & Allegretto, 2007), the last few decades have witnessed shifts in the demographic composition of the workforce (Howard, 1995; National Academy of Sciences, 1999). Although many of these shifts are being seen across industrialized countries, in order to make the amount of information manageable, this review focuses on changes in the US workforce.

Working with Diverse Groups

Workplace diversity has been found to have an effect on worker attitudes across varying organizational relationships (e.g., supervisor and subordinate dyads, Wesolowski & Mossholder, 1997; work group relations, Riordan & Shore, 1997). Demographic diversity in the workplace influences day-to-day social exchanges

(Thomas & Chrobot-Mason, 2005), and increased work team diversity is thought to increase the salience of social categories (e.g., gender, race, ethnicity), possibly leading to the development of in-group/out-group distinctions (Brief, 2008).

Women's Roles and Dual-Earning Families

Another implication resulting from changes in workforce demographic composition has been shifts in perceptions of women's roles. According to social identity theory (Ashforth & Mael, 1989; Capozza & Brown, 2000; Tajfel & Turner, 1985), as individuals take on multiple roles, they are able to express different aspects of their identity and therefore feel greater fulfillment. A Gallup poll from 1936 asked a nationally representative sample (of both men and women) whether a married woman, with a husband capable of supporting her, should have a job herself. Eighty-two percent of the sample in 1936 responded that she should not work. This question was asked again in 1996, however, this time with 83% responding that she should indeed work (Caplow, Hicks, & Wattenberg, 2001). Given this trend, it would not be at all surprising if women held fundamentally different attitudes toward perceptions of work. With greater numbers of women in the workplace, there has been an associated increase in dual-income families (i.e., only 40.5% of females participated in the labor force in 1970; this increased to 61% in 2010; US Census Bureau, 2012). Although having dual incomes may increase perceptions of security as well as family income, it also could contribute to difficulties balancing work and family demands (Hammer, Allen, & Grigsby, 1997). Research has indicated that employed married men are increasingly stepping in to help out with household chores and childcare activities (Hill, Hawkins, Ferris, & Weitzman, 2001). However, household tasks remain largely gender-segregated, with men more likely to perform more timing-flexible tasks (e.g., repairing household objects, yard care) and women engaging in more time-sensitive tasks (e.g., food preparation, childcare; Milkie & Peltola, 1999). Perceptions of greater demands, fewer resources, and burnout may result from the struggle to balance work and family roles. Furthermore, as an employee moves up the organizational hierarchy, work responsibility and work demands tend to increase. As women increasingly gain access to management positions (i.e., close to 35% of managers were female in 1970 compared to over 50% in 2010; US Census Bureau, 1975–2011 [1985, 1992], 2012), their work responsibilities will likely become more challenging and time-intensive.

Occupational/Industry Shifts

The occupational composition of the United States has drastically shifted over the course of the last century (US Bureau of Labor Statistics, 2006). Specifically, there has been a large growth in service occupations, a smaller decrease in manufacturing occupations, and a large growth in professional/technical fields along with managerial (US Bureau of Labor Statistics, 2006).

Shift from Manufacturing to Service

The growth in service occupations coupled with the decrease in manufacturing, suggests the knowledge, skills, and abilities (KSAs) critical to performance in service jobs (e.g., interpersonal skills, emotion regulation, agreeableness) will be increasingly important relative to KSAs important in manufacturing (e.g., psychomotor skills, physical skills). In support of this, interdependence, or the degree to which employees must work with others in order to accomplish job tasks, has been found to be increasingly important in more recent years (Wegman et al., 2018). Some believe the interpersonal aspects associated with service roles may serve to bolster positive employee perceptions (e.g., social support from coworkers and supervisors) and decreased stress (Lloyd, King & Chenoweth, 2002). Supporting this, interdependence is positively associated with satisfaction (Humphrey, Nahrgang, & Morgeson, 2007). On the other hand, the demands of service work may be seen as overly taxing, resulting in negative work attitudes and burnout. For instance, due to the demands to coordinate with others (Kiggundu, 1983), task interdependence has been linked to work role stress (Wong, DeSanctis, & Staudenmayer, 2007). In addition, increased exposure to customers and dependence on coworkers is potentially demanding on emotional labor resources and, accordingly, has been linked to burnout and job dissatisfaction (Grandey, 2000; Hochschild, 1983; Morris & Feldman, 1996, 1997; Wharton, 1993).

The Rise of Knowledge Work

The group of occupations that have seen the most growth since the early 1900s are professional/technical jobs (i.e., under 5% of the workforce in 1910 and rising to close to 25% in 2000; US Bureau of Labor Statistics, 2006). Knowledge-based work consists of cognitively demanding jobs involving the creation, packaging, sharing, and manipulation of knowledge (Arthur, Defillippi, & Lindsay, 2008). According to the National Academy of Sciences (1999), employee success in the knowledge economy is contingent on employee cognitive and interactive skills. Similar to how the manufacturing–service shift has presumably resulted in an increased demand for soft skills over physical and psychomotor skills, the skills associated with knowledge work are possibly in higher demand in more recent years. However, with the organizational need for speed and continued technological innovation, knowledge KSAs may not be enough. For example, commentators have predicted that even highly intelligent employees may face becoming obsolete if they do not keep up with the cutting edge practices and new technologies (Nixon & Spector, 2013).

Reorganizing Work Structures

As external demands such as globalization, deregulation, and competition (Andreu & Sieber, 2001) have increased, the marketplace may have become increasingly unstable. Two ways that organizations have responded to threatening external demands and increasing flexibility is by introducing more flattened hierarchies (Howard, 1995) and organizing work teams (Appelbaum & Batt, 1994).

Skill Demands and Span of Control

With increased market instability and competition, employees are thought to play a greater role in organizational success (National Academy of Sciences, 1999). Furthermore, with the trend in flatter hierarchies and broadening job scope, fewer workers are responsible for larger segments of work (Howard, 1995). Supporting this, a recent meta-analysis found that modern employees report greater on-the-job skill variety and a broader scope of responsibility compared to years past (Wegman et al., 2018). Similarly, when asked to retrospectively compare modern work conditions to work 20–30 years ago, the "greater need to regularly improve work skills" was the most commonly listed difference (Taylor, Funk, & Craighill, 2006). Based on this, is seems possible that organizational demands pressure employees to constantly update their skills. This explanation is consistent with the increasing percentage of the US workforce holding college degrees since the 1970s (US Census Bureau, 1975–2011 [1992], 2012). To the extent that work increasingly requires the use of novel skills, and given the close association between skill variety and engagement (Crawford, LePine, & Rich, 2010), it seems possible that employee engagement might also have increased (e.g., Ryan & Deci, 2000). However, if pressures to gain skills become too strong, instead of being viewed as a challenge associated with growth and development, they could be perceived as a hindrance, and result in increased burnout.

Teams

According to the National Academy of Sciences (1999), the increased organizational use of teams is "[a]mong the most visible changes in the structure of work" (p. 270). Organizing work into teams reflects the corporate need for increased communication, coordination, and troubleshooting among all functional organizational levels (National Academy of Sciences, 1999). In this way, team assignments may aid in organizational adaptability. Because team-based structures are drastically different from independent positions, different skill sets are needed for successful team performance. In their review of the team literature, Stevens and Campion (1994) identified interpersonal skills (i.e., conflict resolution, collaboration, and communication) and self-management skills (i.e., goal setting, planning, and coordination) as the most import KSAs for team success. Due to the organizational need for teams, there is possibly an increased demand for employees who have these team KSAs. However, employees fitting this bill seem to be in short supply. A report by the Society for Human Resource Management listed interpersonal skills among the top rated deficiencies of employees entering the workforce (2008 a, b). Given the organizational demand for teams coupled with the fact that many employees may lack the KSAs necessary for successful team performance, it is possible that employees may be struggling to perform in team-based settings.

Layoffs

Mass layoffs occurred so frequently during the 1980s and 1990s that researchers have called this time period "the era of organizational restructuring" (Allen, Freeman, Russell, Reizenstein, & Rentz, 2001). During this time, many of the downsized positions were thought previously "untouchable" (e.g., white-collar, managerial, professional, salaried, college graduate; American Management Association, 1996; Cappelli, 1999). Although the era of restructuring is past, downsizing is still a threat to the modern workplace. Past studies consistently support a negative relationship between job security and various employee attitudes (Staufenbiel & König, 2010; Sverke, Hellgren, & Näswall, 2002). For example, "survivors" of organizational downsizings often exhibit a phenomenon coined "layoff survivor sickness" (Noer, 1990, 1993, 1997) consisting of negative work attitudes, psychological health, and physical health–related effects (Kozlowski, Chao, Smith & Hedlund, 1993). Furthermore, with job stability in question, some have proposed that the once strong psychological contract binding individual employees to the organization is now broken (Rousseau & Wade-Benzoni, 1995).

Summary. All in all, the large-scale changes outlined above describe a modern workplace relatively different to workplaces of the past – one which is more diverse, technologically savvy, and needing to compete on a global scale. These demands have resulted in flatter hierarchies and work groups. Service and knowledge–based work has been on the rise and has led to a decrease in once sought-after psychomotor skills in exchange for "soft skills" and cognitive ability. The following section contains a qualitative review investigating the impact of possible changes on the five employee engagement indicators.

Changes in Employee Reactions to and Attitudes toward Work

Using the documented trends described above, we linked these national trends and social indicators to possible changes in specific indicators of employee engagement: perceived organizational support, organizational commitment, organizational justice perceptions, job satisfaction, psychological stressors, and burnout. We selected these six variables because: (a) they are commonly examined in the management literature, (b) there is reason to expect that the levels of these have changed in recent years, (c) they have been consistently linked with outcomes of interest to organizations, and (d) they are representative of the types of attitudinal and perceptual variables commonly assessed in practice within organizations.

Perceived Organizational Support. Perceived organizational support (POS) describes the organization's commitment to an employee, as perceived by the employee (Rhoades & Eisenberger, 2002). According to social exchange theory (Meyer & Allen, 1997; Mottaz, 1988; Rhoades & Eisenberger, 2002), when an employee believes their company invests resources in them, the employee is more likely to repay the organization by investing resources and loyalty back into the company (Eisenberger, Huntington, Hutchison, & Sowa, 1986; Meyer & Allen, 1997). As described above, with increases in restructuring and downsizing, it is possible that greater strain has been placed on the once strong employee–employer relationship (Rousseau & Wade-Benzoni, 1995). Previously downsized individuals are thought to develop negative attitudes about work in general (Feldman, Leana, & Bolino, 2002), and survivors of downsized departments were found to report lower levels of POS compared to employees from non-downsized teams (Knudsen, Johnson, Martin, & Roman, 2003). Furthermore, 25% of downsized surviving employees reported feeling they could easily be impacted in a future downsizing event while only 7% of employees who have not directly experienced a downsizing event also felt this way (Taylor et al., 2006).

Regardless of downsizing experience, there is some evidence that, as a whole, employees today experience more negative feelings about their work and workplace. In a series of national surveys on the public opinion of business corporations, sentiment was the lowest on record in recent years, with more than half of employees sampled (i.e., 62%) holding an unfavorable view of organizations, generally speaking (Dimock, Doherty, & Tyson; 2013). Consistent with this it has recently been estimated that only 25% of US employees think their organization is worthy of their loyalty (Keiningham & Aksoy, 2009) and over half (i.e., 56%) of employees retrospectively reported that their current employer is less loyal compared to their employer 20–30 years ago (Taylor et al., 2006).

Finally, the resources that organizations invest in their employees have also changed (Cappelli, 2015). Historically, organizations provided employees with developmental opportunities needed for effective job performance and advancement. However, in recent years employees are increasingly responsible for acquiring needed skills either through securing informal development opportunities or seeking out skill-building external to their organization (Cappelli, 2015). In this way, organizations are investing less in systematic and programmatic development for their employees relative to past years. Taken together, with increased organizational restructuring initiatives and the increasingly negative view of business, it is possible that POS has decreased in recent years.

Organizational Commitment. Mowday, Steers, and Porter (1979) define organizational commitment (OC) as "the relative strength of an individual's identification with and involvement in a particular organization" (p. 226). According to social exchange theory (Rhoades & Eisenberger, 2002; Meyer & Allen, 1997; Mottaz, 1988), low levels of POS on the part of the organization often result in low employee commitment to the organization. As discussed above, given the mass layoffs since the 1990s, many organizations seem to be embracing flatter, more flexible hierarchies. Ongoing structural changes to organizational hierarchies are purported to have altered the employee–employer psychological contract, presumably impacting OC (Bal, Lange, Jansen, & Van der Velde, 2008; Zhao, Wayne, Glibkowski, & Bravo, 2007). Psychological contract breach occurs when the employee believes that the organization has failed to keep its obligations (Morrison & Robinson, 1997), and downsizings are a commonly listed culprit of breach (Allen et al., 2001; Gakovic & Tetrick, 2003; Robinson, 1996). Two recent meta-analyses found employee perceptions of psychological contract breach to be moderately related to decreased commitment ($\rho = -.39$ to $-.38$; Bal et al., 2008; Zhao et al., 2007). Coupled with this, a retrospective survey found that 62% of employed respondents agreed that "job security" has decreased relative to 20–30 years ago (Taylor et al., 2006), possibly meaning that employees have little trust in their organizations.

Perhaps the strongest support for a decrease in OC is evidenced with the trend in job hopping in which employees seem to jump from job to job relatively quickly. A longitudinal study conducted by the US Department of Labor (2004) indicated that in a 20-year period, men held an average of 10.4 jobs and women 9.9 jobs on average (between the ages of 18 and 38). This equates to a getting a new job almost every two years and is a contrast to the traditional "job for life" mentality which was thought to exist predominantly only a few decades back (Cappelli, 1999; Howard, 1995). Possibly, a lack of commitment to the organization is behind these relatively frequent job changes. Supporting this, in their retrospective survey, Taylor et al. (2006) found 51% of respondents agreed that employees are less committed to their current employers relative to 20–30 years back.

Generational change studies have examined possible shifts in OC across time (e.g., Costanza, Badger, Fraser, Severt, & Gade, 2012; Lub, Bijvank, Bal, Blomme, & Schalk, 2012). The literature, however, is contradictory when drawing conclusions regarding generational differences in OC, with some authors reporting generational differences and others finding no differences in OC (e.g., Benson & Brown, 2011; Cennamo & Gardner, 2008; Lub et al., 2012). Pulling from Costanza et al.'s (2012) meta-analysis, the evidence for decreases in OC across generations is mixed, with no strong trends in more or less commitment across generations. However, the generational literature examining OC is limited regarding what can be detected and what inferences can be drawn (Gentile, Wood, Twenge, Hoffman, & Campbell, 2014). Costanza et al.'s (2012) meta-analysis is somewhat limited by the relatively small number of studies available to look at each relationship and confidence intervals that generally contain zero. Due to the limitations of the generational change literature, coupled with increased breaches to the psychological contract and the job hopping trend, it is possible that OC has decreased across time.

Fairness Perceptions. Organizational justice perceptions stem from employee judgments regarding fairness of organizational systems (Colquitt, Conlon,

Wesson, Porter, & Ng, 2001). Like POS and OC, significant changes to organizational structures possibly have led to changes in employee perceptions of fairness. However, in the case of organizational justice, it is not so much that changes have occurred, but how the changes were handled. It has been well documented that decisions made by business leaders during organizational redesigns make or break the initiative (Cappelli et al., 1997). Successful organizational adaptation is increasingly reliant on the leader's ability to generate employee support and enthusiasm for proposed changes, rather than merely trying to overcoming employee resistance (Kotter, 2002). Research has identified that perceptions of justice in the change process yield a strong influence on remaining employees. For example, in downsizings, the perceived fairness in treatment of those who were let go seems to greatly color surviving employees' work perspectives and behaviors (Brockner, 1988). Given the negative perception many Americans seem to hold toward organizations in general (Dimock et al., 2013), and to their employer specifically (Keiningham & Aksoy, 2009; Taylor et al., 2006), it is possible that past organizational redesigns may not have been handled justly. Adding to this, after a downsizing, many companies try to forge a new psychological contract with the remaining employees, one that greatly reduces the organization's obligations but adds greater responsibility and requirements to employees (e.g., greater workload, more direct reports; Cappelli et al., 1997). To the extent that employees do not feel adequately compensated for their increased work efforts, organizational justice perceptions will potentially suffer.

Shifts in workplace composition may also have had an impact on perceptions of organizational justice. As our brief discussion above shows, the modern workforce is quite different than in years past. Due to conflict and discrimination that can arise when differences become salient (Pfeffer, 1983), employee perceptions of fairness may have decreased over time. Minority group members may experience workforce discrimination in functions including: unfair processes and decisions in selection, termination, rewards, and compensation. Aside from decreased fairness perceptions of minority group members, majority members also may hold greater injustice perceptions in more recent years. For example, government-initiated diversity empowerment programs (e.g., Affirmative Action) have in some cases been fought with various forms of backlash (Kidder, Lankau, Chrobo-Mason, Mollica, & Friedman, 2004; Stockdale & Crosby, 2004). Based on the surge of large-scale organizational change initiatives, the negative psychological effects of downsizing, and the changing composition of the American workforce, we propose employee perceptions of organizational justice to have decreased across time.

Job Satisfaction. Job satisfaction has been defined as "employee's affective reactions to a job based on comparing actual outcomes with desired outcomes" (Fields, 2002, p. 1). With restructuring initiatives designed to flatten organizational hierarchies and as a result expand any given employee's contribution to their company's success, jobs may be requiring more of employees' time, energy, and resources and subsequently may be contributing to decreased levels of job satisfaction. Specifically, a large national study of US employees estimated that one out of every three employees is "chronically overworked" (e.g., feelings of being overwhelmed by how much must be done, feelings of not having enough time to complete work; Galinsky et al., 2005). Feeling overworked was found to be correlated with negative work attitudes including anger toward the employer and resentment toward coworkers (Galinsky et al., 2005). The downstream potential effects of high numbers of overworked employees are becoming evident, with some studies reporting employees seemingly less motivated to seek and accept advancement opportunities (Families and Work Institute & American Business Collaboration, 2004) and reporting employees to be placing a higher premium on leisure (Kennedy, Smith, Wells, & Wellman; 2008; Taylor et al., 2006; Twenge et al., 2010).

To add to this, there is some retrospective evidence suggesting employees believe their jobs and work lives are less satisfying today compared to years gone by. Specifically, 59% of respondents sampled agreed that today, versus 20 or 30 years ago, employees must continuously work harder to earn their living, and 39% agree overall perceptions of work-related experiences are getting more negative as time goes on (Taylor et al., 2006). From the perspective of the employee, the organization offers no reparation for perceived damages (e.g., psychological breach, increased workload); however, the employee cannot simply lessen work performance without the possibility of termination. In other words, "[t]hey are tied to the company because they feel they have to be, and their performance does not decrease because they are afraid of being fired" (Cappelli, 1999, p. 131), and some commentators believe business leaders are aware of employee morale being at an all-time low (Cappelli, 1999). Because organizational performance has not been greatly impacted, low work morale levels have received little attention from leadership (Cappelli, 1999).

As with OC, some research has sought to examine the possibility of changes in job satisfaction across generations (e.g., Benson & Brown, 2011; Costanza et al., 2012; Kowske, Rasch, & Wiley, 2010; Wilson et al., 2008), but the evidence is mixed, with some studies finding decreases in job satisfaction (Benson & Brown, 2011; Wilson, Squires, Widger, Cranley, & Tourangeauet, 2008) and others increases (Kowske et al., 2010). In an attempt to clarify generational trends, Costanza et al. (2012) conducted a meta-analysis of primary cross-sectional studies examining shifts in common job attitudes across generations. Their meta-analysis provides some support, albeit weak, for a decrease in job satisfaction with more recent generations. Altogether, given the increased likelihood for chronically overworked employees, the fear of termination, and some support from the generational change literature, it seems job satisfaction may be decreasing as time goes on.

Stress Perceptions. Karasek (1979) describes psychological stressors as "an independent variable that measures stress sources, such as work load demands, present in the work environment" (p. 287). In other words, psychological stressors reflect the degree to which an employee perceives the work environment as having stressful situations. Although ease and flexibility are often cited as organizational benefits of a constantly connected workforce (Baltes, Briggs, Huff, Wright, & Neuman, 1999; Hill et al., 2001; Valcour & Hunter, 2005), they seem to come at a tradeoff to employee stress levels (Madden & Jones, 2008). As stated above, Van der Spiegel (1995) proposed that increased technological demands result in "technostress," and recent survey-based research lends support to this proposition. For instance, of employees who have access to communication and information technologies at home, 46% reported an increase in work demands and hours worked, 49% reported elevated stress, and 49% reported the communication technologies made it difficult to "disconnect" from work (Madden & Jones, 2008). Furthermore, when asked to what degree communication and information technologies have led to increased work demands, 46% reported that demands have "intensified" and an additional 15% reported that demands have increased "a lot." Madden and Jones (2008) concluded: "those who are most tethered to work are more likely to say that their gadgets and connectivity have increased demands that they work more hours" (p. iv).

With both knowledge and service occupations placing significant pressures on their workers, occupational shifts may also have contributed to greater psychological stressors. Knowledge work consists of complex and often ambiguous tasks in which employees often utilize higher-order skills such as analyzing, evaluating, and creating. Cognitive complexities have been proposed to increase stress perceptions (Karasek, 1979) and these skills can lead to a depletion of resources and feelings of cognitive fatigue (Cohen & Spacapan, 1978; Cohen, 1980). Service-based jobs holders may experience their own set of unique stressors. Increased exposure to customers, the need to manage client relationships, and pressure from management to provide excellent customer service may prove taxing on employees' emotional labor resources (Fried, Levi, & Laurence, 2008; National Academy of Sciences, 1999). The trend in teamwork, and the associated increase in interdependent work (Wegman et al., 2017), may be leading to an increase in stress perceptions in more recent years. For example, a recent study found team member relationship conflict to be positively related to stress perceptions which were found to be associated with decreased job satisfaction and performance (Hon & Chan, 2013). In support, Stevens and Campion (1994) list "conflict resolution" as one of the most important KSAs for work team performance. Due to stress resulting from availability of communication technology, the cognitive complexities of knowledge-based work, and the increased need to work together with others (e.g., customers, team members), we propose psychological stressors to have increased with time.

Burnout. Burnout is "a syndrome of emotional exhaustion, depersonalization, and reduced personal accomplishment that can occur among individuals who work with people in some capacity" (Maslach, Jackson, & Leiter, 1996, p. 4).

As is evident from the national trends reported above, organizations increasingly need to evolve in the marketplace in order to beat competitors and remain profitable. Demands resulting from downsizing initiatives (i.e., heavy workload, greater role responsibility, stress; Maslach & Leiter, 2008), highly complex work (National Academy of Sciences, 1999), pressures to learn new technology (Van der Spiegel, 1995), and increased performance-monitoring techniques (Varca, 2006), have each been proposed to increase perceptions of work overload (i.e., too much work, too little time) and result in greater levels of burnout (Brantely, 1993; Shirom, Westman, Shamai, & Carel, 1997). To meet pressing organizational demands, employees are working longer hours (Ng & Feldman, 2008). Although in the short term, this may lead to increased employee output, in the long run, increased hours worked have negative effects on both employee wellbeing (e.g., physical and mental health, burnout) and organizational productivity (Ng & Feldman, 2008; Robinson, Flowers, & Carroll, 2001; Spence & Robbins, 1992). For example, the results of a study conducted by the Centers for Disease Control and Prevention linked overworked symptoms (e.g., feeling too tired, high work commitments, long work hours) to poor nutrition and inactivity at work (Blackford, Jancey, Howat, Ledger, & Lee, 2012). Furthermore, overworked employees report greater stress, depression, and poor overall health (Galinsky et al., 2005). With burnout a key mediator between job demands and health outcomes (Schaufeli & Bakker, 2004), it seems that overworked employees may also be experiencing greater burnout. Taken together, it is possible that burnout has increased in more recent years.

Summary

Based on the evidence cited above, it seems possible for the modern workforce to hold more negative attitudes toward work compared to employees of previous decades. From this, workers could be described as stressed and possibly inclined to experience conflict in terms of their role within the organization as well as balancing work and family demands. Additionally, we speculate that the modern workforce possibly feels uncommitted and unjustly treated, and as a result could be experiencing lowered levels of job satisfaction and increased burnout. Implications of this possibility of a negative workforce and future research are discussed below.

Conclusion and Future Directions

In this chapter, we discussed trends in macro contextual factors of work and explored their possible impact on employees' work attitudes and work perceptions. From this review, there is evidence to suggest that workers have a more negative view of their organizations in terms of POS, organizational commitment, perceptions of fairness, job satisfaction and levels of stress and burnout compared to employees working in previous decades. Although this chapter is only speculative, the possibility of a more negative workforce is troubling, especially given the link between some work perceptions and employee physical and mental health (i.e., burnout, stress, role overload; Galinsky et al., 2005; Karasek & Theorell, 1990).

If indeed the modern workforce is holding greater negative work perceptions and these impact worker wellbeing, an increase in health-related issues may occur. A greater focus on the identification of specific approaches to assuage burnout perceptions, possibly through working to decrease role overload (i.e., role conflict, role ambiguity, work–family conflict), might be helpful. Similarly, to the extent that job satisfaction has decreased across time, a subsequent drop in performance and worker productivity is possible. Future research dedicated to understanding methods to maintain high levels of job satisfaction while employees are experiencing work overload could be fruitful. Recognizing the cost, organizations have attempted to initiate policies and procedures geared toward reducing work–family conflict perceptions of their employees (Grover & Crooker, 1995; Frye & Breaugh, 2004). However, given the mixed meta-analytic findings evaluating the effectiveness of organizational programs designed to reduce work–family conflict (e.g., Allen, Johnson, Kiburz, & Shockley, 2013; Byron, 2005; Gajendran & Harrison, 2007; Mesmer-Magnus & Viswesvaran, 2006; Michel, Kotrba, Mitchelson, Clark, & Baltes, 2011), it seems more research is need to understand what additional methods (or combination of methods) will be most beneficial.

While this chapter is only qualitative, through our review of the available literature, we found a dearth of empirical research examining the changing nature of work and its effect on employees. While one of the main challenges of examining changes over time is methodological, we encourage more work in this space, possibly in the form of cross-temporal meta-analyses (discussed in Chapter 1, this volume). Finally, to the extent that attitudinal variables are indeed changing over time, there may be a need to reevaluate current measures. For example, Dekas, Bauer, Welle, Kurkoski, and Sullivan (2013), showed that some traditional organizational citizenship behavior items are "less appropriate in a modern work context" (p. 232), as they are less functionally relevant to modern work roles. While only an example, there might be value in following suit of Dekas et al. and reevaluating current scales for relevance to modern organizations.

In closing, we have attempted to summarize the literature as it relates to implications of the changing nature of work on employee attitudes and work perceptions. While this qualitative summary is not an empirical examination of changes across time, it is our hope that this work encourages greater research into the changing nature of work and its implications. Given the central role of work in employees' lives, it is critical for researchers and organizations to work together to ensure a positive, healthy workforce for the future.

References

Allen, T. D., Freeman, D. M., Russell, J. E., Reizenstein, R. C., & Rentz, J. O. (2001). Survivor reactions to organizational downsizing: Does time ease the pain? *Journal of Occupational and Organizational Psychology, 74*, 145–164.

Allen, T. D., Johnson, R. C., Kiburz, K., & Shockley, K. M. (2013). Work–family conflict and flexible work arrangements: Deconstructing flexibility. *Personnel Psychology*, 66, 345–376.

American Management Association. (1996). *1996 AMA survey on downsizing, job elimination and job creation.* New York, NY: American Management Association. Retrieved from www.copyrightreviews.com/5046137/1996-ama-survey-on-downsizing-job-elimination-and-job-creation

Andreu, R., & Sieber, S. (2001). Rally racing: knowledge and learning requirements for a winning team. *Knowledge and Process Management, 8*, 91–98.

Appelbaum, E., & Batt, R. (1994). *The new American workforce transforming work systems in the United States.* Ithaca, NY: ILR Press.

Arthur, M. B., Defillippi, R. J., & Lindsay, V. J. (2008). On being a knowledge worker. *Organizational Dynamics, 37*, 365–377.

Ashforth, B. E., & Mael, F. (1989). Social identity theory and the organization. *Academy of Management Review, 14*, 20–39.

Bal, P. M., De Lange, A. H., Jansen, P. G., & Van Der Velde, M. E. (2008). Psychological contract breach and job attitudes: A meta-analysis of age as a moderator. *Journal of Vocational Behavior, 72*, 143–158.

Baltes, B. B., Briggs, T. E., Huff, J. W., Wright, J. A., & Neuman, G. A. (1999). Flexible and compressed workweek schedules: A meta-analysis of their effects on work-related criteria. *Journal of Applied Psychology, 84*(4) 496–513.

Barney, C. E., & Elias, S. M. (2010). Flex-time as a moderator of the job stress–work motivation relationship: A three nation investigation. *Personnel Review, 39*, 487–502.

Benson, J., & Brown, M. (2011). Generations at work: Are there differences and do they matter? *International Journal of Human Resource Management, 22*, 1843–1865.

Blackford, K., Jancey, J., Howat, P., Ledger, M., & Lee, A. H. (2012). Office-based physical activity and nutrition intervention: Barriers, enablers, and preferred strategies for workplace obesity prevention, Perth, Western Australia, 2012. *Preventing Chronic Disease, 10.*

Blauner, R. (1964). *Alienation and freedom: The factory worker and his industry.* Chicago, IL: University of Chicago Press.

Borjas, G. (2008). Labor outflows and labor inflows in Puerto Rico. *Journal of Human Capital, 2*, 32–68.

Brantely, P. J. (1993). Daily stress and stress related disorders. *Annals of Behavioral Medicine, 15*, 17–25.

Brief, A. P. (2008). *Diversity at work.* New York, NY: Cambridge University Press.

Brockner, J. (1988). The effects of work layoffs on survivors: Research, theory, and practice. *Research in Organizational Behavior, 10*, 213–256.

Bryant, S. (2000). At home on the electronic frontier: Work, gender and the information highway. *New Technology, Work and Employment, 15*, 19–33.

Byron, K. (2005). A meta-analytic review of work–family conflict and its antecedents. *Journal of Vocational Behavior, 67*, 169–198.

Caplow, T., Hicks, L., & Wattenberg, B. J. (2001). *The first measured century: An illustrated guide to trends in America, 1900–2000.* Washington, DC: AEI Press.

Capozza, D., & Brown, R. (Eds.). (2000). *Social identity processes: Trends in theory and research.* Thousand Oaks, CA: Sage.

Cappelli, P. (1999). *The new deal at work: Managing the market-driven workforce.* Boston, MA: Harvard Business School Press.

Cappelli, P. H. (2015). Skill gaps, skill shortages, and skill mismatches: Evidence and arguments for the United States. *ILR Review, 68*(2), 251–290.

Cappelli, P., Bassi, L., Katz, H., Knoke, D., Osterman, P., & Useem, M. (1997). *Change at work.* New York, NY: Oxford University Press.

Cennamo, L., & Gardner, D. (2008). Generational differences in work values, outcomes and person–organization values fit. *Journal of Managerial Psychology, 23*, 891–906.

Cohen, C. (1980). After effects of stress on human performance and social behavior: A review of research and theory. *Psychological Bulletin, 88*, 82–108.

Cohen, S., & Spacapan, S. (1978). The after effects of stress: An attentional interpretation. *Environmental Psychology and Nonverbal Behavior, 3*, 43–57.

Colquitt, J. A., Conlon, D. E., Wesson, M. J., Porter, C. O., & Ng, K. Y. (2001). Justice at the millennium: A meta-analytic review of 25 years of organizational justice research. *Journal of Applied Psychology, 86*(3), 425–445.

Coovert, M. D. (1995). Technological changes in office jobs (pp. 175–208). In A. Howard (Ed.), *The changing nature of work.* San Francisco, CA: Jossey-Bass.

Coovert, M. D., & Thompson, L. F. (Eds.). (2013). *The psychology of workplace technology.* New York, NY: Routledge.

Costanza, D. P., Badger, J. M., Fraser, R. L. Severt, J. B., & Gade, P. A. (2012). Generational differences in work-related attitudes: A meta-analysis. *Journal of Business and Psychology, 27*, 375–394.

Crawford, E. R., LePine, J. A., & Rich, B. L. (2010). Linking job demands and resources to employee engagement and burnout: a theoretical extension and meta-analytic test. *Journal of Applied Psychology, 95*, 834–848.

Deal, J. J., Altman, D. G., & Rogelberg, S. G. (2010). Millennials at work: What we know and what we need to do (if anything). *Journal of Business and Psychology, 25*, 191–199.

Dekas, K. H., Bauer, T. N., Welle, B., Kurkoski, J., & Sullivan, S. (2013). Organizational citizenship behavior, version 2.0: A review and qualitative investigation of OCBs for knowledge workers at Google and beyond. *Academy of Management Perspectives, 27*, 219–237.

Dimock, M., Doherty, C., & Tyson, A. (2013). Favorable views of business, labor rebound. *Pew Research Center.* Retrieved from www.people-press.org/files/legacy-pdf/6-27-13%20Business%20and%20Labor%20Release.pdf

Eisenberger, R., Huntington, R., Hutchison, S., & Sowa, D. (1986). Perceived organizational support. *Journal of Applied Psychology, 71*, 500–507.

Families and Work Institute & American Business Collaboration. (2004) Gender & generation within the workplace. *The American Business Collaboration.*

Retrieved from www.abcdependentcare.com/docs/ABC-generation-gender-workplace.pdf.

Feldman, D. C., Leana, C. R., & Bolino, M. C. (2002). Underemployment and relative deprivation among re-employed executives. *Journal of Occupational and Organizational Psychology*, 75, 453–471.

Felin, T., Zenger, T. R., & Tomsik, J. (2009). The knowledge economy: Emerging organizational forms, missing microfoundations, and key considerations for managing human capital. *Human Resource Management*, 48, 555–570.

Felstead, A., Jewson, N., Phizacklea, A., & Walters, S. (2002). The option to work at home: Another privilege for the favoured few? *New Technology, Work and Employment*, 17, 204–223.

Fields, D. (2002). *Taking the measure of work: A guide to scales for organizational research and diagnosis*. Thousand Oaks, CA: Sage Publications.

Fried, Y., Levi, A. S., & Laurence, G. (2008). Job design in the new world of work. In S. Cartwright & C. L. Cooper (Eds.), *Oxford handbook of personnel psychology* (pp. 587–597). New York, NY: Oxford University Press.

Frye, N. K., & Breaugh, J. A. (2004). Family-friendly policies, supervisor support, work–family conflict, family–work conflict, and satisfaction: A test of a conceptual model. *Journal of Business and Psychology*, 19, 197–220.

Gajendran, R. S., & Harrison, D. A. (2007). The good, the bad, and the unknown about telecommuting: meta-analysis of psychological mediators and individual consequences. *Journal of Applied Psychology*, 92, 1524–1541.

Gakovic, A., & Tetrick, L. E. (2003). Psychological contract breach as a source of strain for employees. *Journal of Business and Psychology*, 18, 235–246.

Galinsky, E., Bond, J., Kim, S., Brownfield, E., & Sakai, K. (2005). When the way we work becomes too much. Retrieved from www.familiesandwork.org

Gallie, D. (1978). *In search of the new working class: Automation and social integration within the capitalist enterprise*. Cambridge, MA: Cambridge University Press.

Gentile, B., Wood, L. A., Twenge, J. M., Hoffman, B. J., Campbell, W. K. (2014). The problem of generational change: Why cross-sectional designs are inadequate for investigating generational differences. In C. E. Lance & R. J. Vandenberg (Eds.), *Statistical and methodological myths and urban legends* (2nd ed.) (pp.100–111). New York, NY: Taylor & Francis.

Grandey, A. (2000). Emotion regulation in the workplace: A new way to conceptualize emotional labor. *Journal of Occupational Health Psychology*, 5, 95–110

Grover, S. L., & Crooker, K. J. (1995). Who appreciates family-responsive human-resource policies: The impact of family-friendly policies on the organizational attachment of parents and non-parents. *Personnel Psychology*, 48, 271–288.

Hammer, L. B., Allen, E., & Grigsby, T. D. (1997). Work–family conflict in dual-earner couples: Within-individual and crossover effects of work and family. *Journal of Vocational Behavior*, 50, 185–203.

Hill, E. J., Hawkins, A. J., Ferris, M., & Weitzman, M. (2001). Finding an extra day a week: The positive influence of perceived job flexibility on work and family life balance. *Family Relations*, 50, 49–58.

Hochschild, A. R. (1983). *The managed heart: Commercialization of human feeling*. Berkeley, CA: University of California Press.

Hon, A. H., & Chan, W. W. (2013). The effects of group conflict and work stress on employee performance. *Cornell Hospitality Quarterly, 54*, 174–184.

Howard, A. (Ed.) (1995). *The changing nature of work.* San Francisco, CA: Jossey-Bass.

Humphrey, S. E., Nahrgang, J. D., & Morgeson, F. P. (2007). Integrating motivational, social, and contextual work design features: A meta-analytic of the summary and theoretical extension work design literature. *Journal of Applied Psychology, 92*, 1332–1356.

Johns, G. (2006). The essential impact of context on organizational behavior. *Academy of Management Review, 31*, 386–408.

Karasek, R. A. (1979). Job demands, job decision latitude, and mental strain: Implications for job design, *Administrative Science Quarterly, 24*, 285–308.

Karasek, R., & Theorell, T. (1990). *Healthy work: Stress, productivity, and the reconstruction of working life.* New York, NY: Basic Books.

Keiningham, T. L., & Aksoy, L. (2009). *Why loyalty matters: The groundbreaking approach to rediscovering happiness, meaning, and lasting fulfillment in your life and work.* Dallas, TX: BenBella Books.

Kennedy, T. L., Smith, A., Wells, A. T., & Wellman, B. (2008). Networked families. *Pew Internet & American Life Project*, 1–44. Retrieved from www.pewinternet.org/Reports/2008/Networked-Families.aspx

Kessels, J. W. (2001). Learning in organisations: A corporate curriculum for the knowledge economy. *Futures, 33*, 497–506.

Kidder, D. L., Lankau, M. J., Chrobot-Mason, D., Mollica, K. A., & Friedman, R. A. (2004). Backlash toward diversity initiatives: Examining the impact of diversity program justification, personal and group outcomes. *International Journal of Conflict Management, 15*, 77–102.

Kiggundu, M. N. (1983). Task interdependence and job design – test of a theory. *Organizational Behavior and Human Performance, 31*, 145–172.

Knudsen, H. K., Johnson, A. J., Martin, J. K., & Roman, P. M. (2003). Downsizing survival: The experience of work and organizational commitment. *Sociological Inquiry, 73*, 265–283.

Kotter, J. (2002). Managing change: The power of leadership. *Balanced Scorecard Report, 4*, 6–9.

Kowske, B. J., Rasch, R., & Wiley, J. (2010). Millennials'(lack of) attitude problem: An empirical examination of generational effects on work attitudes. *Journal of Business and Psychology, 25*, 265–279.

Kozlowski, S. W. J., Chao, G. T., Smith, E. M., & Hedlund, J. (1993). Organizational downsizing: Strategies, interventions, and research implications. In C. L. Cooper & I. Robertson (Eds.), *International Review of Industrial and Organizational Psychology* (pp. 262–332). Chichester, UK: John Wiley.

Lewis, S., & Roper, I. (2008). Flexible working arrangement: From work–life to gender equity policies. In C. L. Susan and G. Cooper, *The Oxford handbook of personnel psychology* (pp. 411–437). Oxford: Cartwright.

Lloyd, C., King, R., & Chenoweth, L. (2002). Social work, stress and burnout: A review. *Journal of Mental Health, 11*, 255–265.

Lub, X., Nije Bijvank, M., Matthijs Bal, P., Blomme, R., & Schalk, R. (2012). Different or alike? Exploring the psychological contract and commitment of different generations of hospitality workers. *International Journal of Contemporary Hospitality Management, 24*, 553–573.

Madden, M., & Jones, S. (2008). Networked workers. *Pew Internet & American Life Project.* Retrieved from www.pewinternet.org/Reports/2008/Networked-Workers.aspx

Maslach, C., Jackson, S. E., & Leiter, M. P. (1996). *Maslach burnout inventory manual* (3rd ed.). Palo Alto, CA: Consulting Psychologists Press.

Maslach, C., & Leiter, M. P. (2008). Early predictors of job burnout and engagement. *Journal of Applied Psychology, 93*(3), 498–512.

Mesmer-Magnus, J. R., & Viswesvaran, C. (2006). How family-friendly work environments affect work/family conflict: A meta-analytic examination. *Journal of Labor Research, 27*, 555–574.

Meyer, J. P., & Allen, N. J. (1997). *Commitment in the workplace: Theory, research, and application.* Thousand Oaks, CA: Sage.

Michel, J. S., Kotrba, L. M., Mitchelson, J. K., Clark, M. A., & Baltes, B. B. (2011). Antecedents of work–family conflict: A meta-analytic review. *Journal of Organizational Behavior, 32*, 689–725.

Milkie, M. A., & Peltola, P. (1999). Playing all the roles: Gender and the work–family balancing act. *Journal of Marriage and the Family, 61*, 476–490.

Mishel, L., Bernstein, J., & Allegretto, S. (2007). *The state of working America 2006/2007.* Ithaca, NY: ILR Press.

Morris, J. A., & Feldman, D. C. (1996). The dimensions, antecedents, and consequences of emotional labor. *Academy of Management Review, 21*, 986–1010.

Morris, J. A., & Feldman, D. C. (1997). Managing emotions in the workplace. *Journal of Managerial Issues, 9*, 257–274.

Morrison, E. W., & Robinson, S. L. (1997). When employees feel betrayed: A model of how psychological contract violation develops. *Academy of Management Review, 22*, 226–256.

Mottaz, C. J. (1988). Determinants of organizational commitment. *Human Relations, 41*, 467–482.

Mowday, R. T., Steers, R. M., & Porter, L. W. (1979). The measurement of organizational commitment. *Journal of Vocational Behavior, 14*, 224–247.

National Academy of Sciences (1999). *The changing nature of work: Implications for occupational analysis.* Washington, DC: National Academy Press.

Ng, T. W., & Feldman, D. C. (2008). Long work hours: A social identity perspective on meta-analysis data. *Journal of Organizational Behavior, 29*, 853–880.

Nixon, A. E., & Spector, P. E. (2013). The impact of technology on employee stress, health, and well-being. In M. D. Coovert & L. Foster Thompson (Eds.), *The psychology of workplace technology* (pp. 238–260). New York, NY: Routledge.

Noer, D. M. (1990). Layoff survivor sickness: A new challenge for supervisors. *Supervisory Management, 35*, 1–2.

Noer, D. M. (1993). *Healing the wounds.* San Francisco, CA: Jossey-Bass.

Noer, D. M. (1997). *Breaking free: A prescription for personal and organizational change.* San Francisco, CA: Jossey-Bass.

Noonan, M. C., & Glass, J. L. (2012). The hard truth about telecommuting. *Monthly Labor Review, 135*, 38–45.

Pfeffer, J. (1983). Organizational demography. In L. L. Cummings & B. M. Staw (Eds.), *Research in organizational behavior* (pp. 299–357). Greenwich, CT: JAI Press.

Potosky, D., & Lomax, M. W. (2013). Leadership and technology: A love–hate relationship. In M. D. Coovert & L. F. Thompson (Eds.), *The psychology of workplace technology*, (pp. 118–146). New York, NY: Routledge.

Rhoades, L., & -714berger, R. (2002). Perceived organizational support: A review of the literature. *Journal of Applied Psychology, 87*(4), 698–714.

Riordan, C. M., & Shore, L. M. (1997). Demographic diversity and employee attitudes: An empirical examination of relational demography within work units. *Journal of Applied Psychology, 82*(3), 342–358.

Robinson, B. E., Flowers, C., & Carroll, J. (2001). Work stress and marriage: A theoretical model examining the relationship between workaholism and marital cohesion. *International Journal of Stress Management, 8*, 165–175.

Robinson, S. L. (1996). Trust and breach of the psychological contract. *Administrative Science Quarterly, 41*(4), 574–599.

Rousseau, D. M. & Wade-Benzoni, K. A. (1995). Changing individual–organization attachments: A two-way street. In A. Howard (Ed.), *The changing nature of work*, (pp. 290–321). San Francisco, CA: Jossey-Bass.

Ryan, R. M., & Deci, E. L. (2000). Self-determination theory and the facilitation of intrinsic motivation, social development, and well-being. *American Psychologist, 55*(1), 68–78.

Schaufeli, W. B., & Bakker, A. B. (2004). Job demands, job resources, and their relationship with burnout and engagement: A multi-sample study. *Journal of Organizational Behavior, 25*, 293–315.

Shirom, A., Westman, M., Shamai, O., & Carel, R. S. (1997). Effects of work overload and burnout on cholesterol and triglycerides levels: The moderating effects of emotional reactivity among male and female employees. *Journal of Occupational Health Psychology, 2*(4), 275–288.

Society for Human Resource Management. (2008a). *SHRM 2007 Symposium on the Workforce Readiness of the Future US Labor Pool: Executive summary*. Alexandria, VA: Author.

Society for Human Resource Management. (2008b). Workforce readiness weekly survey. *Society for Human Resource Management*. Retrieved from www.shrm.org/surveys.

Spence, J. T., & Robbins, A. S. (1992). Workaholism: Definition, measurement, and preliminary results. *Journal of Personality Assessment, 58*, 160–178.

Staufenbiel, T., & König, C. J. (2010). A model for the effects of job insecurity on performance, turnover intention, and absenteeism. *Journal of Occupational and Organizational Psychology, 83*, 101–117.

Stevens, M. J., & Campion, M. A. (1994). The knowledge, skill, and ability requirements for teamwork: Implications for human resource management. *Journal of Management, 20*, 503–530.

Stockdale, M. S., & Crosby, F. J. (2004). *The psychology and management of workplace diversity*. Malden, UK: Blackwell Publishing.

Sverke, M., Hellgren, J., & Näswall, K. (2002). No security: A meta-analysis and review of job insecurity and its consequences. *Journal of Occupational Health Psychology, 7*(3), 242–264.

Tajfel, H. & Turner, J. C. (1985). The social identity of theory of intergroup behavior. In S. Worchel & W. G. Austin (Eds.), *Psychology of intergroup relations* (pp. 7–24). Chicago, IL: Nelson-Hall.

Taylor, P., Funk, C., & Craighill, P. (2006). Public says American work life is worsening, but most workers remain satisfied with their jobs. *Pew Social Trends*. Retrieved from http://pewsocialtrends.org/files/2010/10/Jobs.pdf

Thomas, K. M., & Chrobot-Mason, D. (2005). Group-level explanations of workplace discrimination. In R. L. Dipboye, & A. Colella (Eds.), *Discrimination at work: The psychological and organizational bases* (pp. 63–88). Mahwah, NJ: Lawrence Erlbaum Associates.

Twenge, J. M., Campbell, S. M., Hoffman, B. J., & Lance, C. E. (2010). Generational differences in work values: Leisure and extrinsic values increasing, social and intrinsic values decreasing. *Journal of Management, 36*, 1117–1142.

US Census Bureau. (1975–2011). *Statistical abstracts of the United States: 1975–2011.* Washington, DC: Author. Retrieved from www.census.gov/compendia/statab/

US Census Bureau. (2012). *Statistical abstracts of the United States: 2012.* Washington, DC: Author. Retrieved from www.census.gov/compendia/statab/

US Department of Labor, Bureau of Statistics (2004). Number of jobs held, labor market activity, and earnings growth among younger baby boomers: Recent results from a longitudinal survey. Retrieved from www.bls.gov/nls/nlsy79r20.pdf

US Department of Labor, Bureau of Statistics (2006). Occupational changes: Then and now. Retrieved from www.bls.gov/opub/ted/2006/apr/wk1/art04.htm

Valcour, P. M., & Hunter, L. W. (2005). Technology, organizations, and work–life integration. In EE Kossik & SJ Lambert (Eds.), *Work and life integration: Organizational, cultural, and individual perspectives* (pp. 61–84). London, UK: Lawrence Erlbaum.

Van der Spiegel, J. (1995). New information technologies and changes in work. In A. Howard (Ed.), *The changing nature of work* (pp. 97–111). San Francisco, CA: Jossey-Bass.

Varca, P. E. (2006). Telephone surveillance in call centers: Prescriptions for reducing strain. *Managing Service Quality, 16*, 290–305.

Wegman, L. A., Hoffman, B. J., Carter, N. T., Twenge, J. M., & Guenole, N. (2018). Placing job characteristics in context: Cross-temporal meta-analysis of changes in job characteristics since 1975. *Journal of Management, 44*, 352–386.

Wesolowski, M. A., & Mossholder, K. W. (1997). Relational demography in supervisor–subordinate dyads: Impact on subordinate job satisfaction, burnout, and perceived procedural justice. *Journal of Organizational Behavior, 18*, 351–362.

Wharton, A. S. (1993). The affective consequences of service work: Managing emotions on the job. *Work and Occupations, 20*, 205–232.

Wilson, B., Squires, M., Widger, K., Cranley, L., & Tourangeau, A. (2008). Job satisfaction among a multigenerational nursing workforce. *Journal of Nursing Management, 16*, 716–723.

Wong, S. S., DeSanctis, G., & Staudenmayer, N. (2007). The relationship between task interdependency and role stress: A revisit of the job demands–control model. *Journal of Management Studies, 44*, 284–303.

Zhao, H. A. O., Wayne, S. J., Glibkowski, B. C., & Bravo, J. (2007). The impact of psychological contract breach on work-related outcomes: A meta-analysis. *Personnel Psychology, 60*, 647–680.

22 Implications of the Changing Nature of Work for the Interface between Work and Nonwork Roles

Jeffrey H. Greenhaus and Gerard A. Callalan

A significant challenge facing contemporary employees is how to fashion a life that enables them to be engaged, effective, and satisfied not only at work but in other important domains as well. Many workers enact multiple roles – employee, family member, friend, neighbor, community volunteer, leisure enthusiast – and their successful navigation of these roles affects their wellbeing (Carmeli & Russo, 2016). The intersection, or interface, between a person's work and nonwork pursuits is influenced by many factors that arise from changes in the nature of work (Greenhaus & Kossek, 2014; Ramarajan & Reid, 2013). Over the past several decades, changes in the economy, organization strategies, government policies, and societal and cultural norms have created substantial demands – and have provided significant resources – for individuals as they manage different spheres of their lives (Greenhaus & Powell, 2017). The aim of this chapter is to examine how these factors, which are broadly changing the nature of work and employment, affect the interface between the work and nonwork domains.

The chapter begins with a brief discussion of the interface between work and nonwork domains. We then highlight five important elements of the changing nature of work: (1) the nonpermanence of employment relationships, (2) globalization and international careers, (3) advances in technology, (4) task and social contexts of work, and (5) generational forces in the workplace. Next, we discuss the impact of these changes on the work–nonwork interface of employees juggling multiple roles, and identify individual, organizational, and societal actions that can help employees manage the work–nonwork interface in this rapidly changing work environment.

The Work–Nonwork Interface

Ever since Kanter (1977) laid to rest the myth that work and family represent "separate" and unconnected worlds, there has been an explosion of research designed to understand how different spheres of activity intersect in a person's life. This research was largely driven by the recognition that the extensive participation of women, single parents, and dual-earner partners in the workplace meant that an increasingly high proportion of the workforce had to contend with the demands arising from multiple life roles.

The early research on the work–family interface often adopted a conflict perspective (Greenhaus & Beutell, 1985) in which participation in multiple roles was potentially incompatible. Each role presents a set of demands or stressors that can drain resources (e.g., time, energy) that are available for other roles (Ten Brummelhuis & Bakker, 2012). Moreover, reflecting the bidirectional nature of the work–family interface, extensive demands at work (e.g., role overload, role conflict) can interfere with family life (work-to-family conflict), whereas extensive demands at home (e.g., responsibility for dependant care, conflict with partner) can interfere with work life (family-to-work conflict) (Michel, Kotrba, Mitchelson, Clark, & Baltes, 2011).

The early research has evolved in several directions, two of which are particularly relevant to this chapter. First, the initial emphasis on conflict has been accompanied by an increasing recognition that participation in a role can enrich (Greenhaus & Powell, 2006) or facilitate (Wayne, Grzywacz, Carlson, & Kacmar, 2007) effective participation in another role. In other words, whereas demands that arise in a role can produce conflict or interference with another role, resources that are acquired in a role, such as financial assets, social capital, development of skills, emotional and psychological reserves, and task flexibility, can enhance or enrich performance and positive affect in another role (Greenhaus & Powell, 2006). As with work–family conflict, work–family enrichment is bidirectional. Work-related resources (e.g., social support at work, job autonomy) can enrich family life, and family-related resources (e.g., social support from family members, being married) can enrich work life (Lapierre, Li, Kwan, Greenhaus, DiRenzo, & Shao, 2018).

Second, the initial focus has expanded, in aspiration if not in practice, to consider the interface between work and a range of other roles, rather than solely the family role. This broader focus, variably referred to as work–home, work–life, and work–nonwork, recognizes that many employees not only participate in work and family roles, but also in community, political, religious, leisure, and self-development activities. We prefer the term work–nonwork interface to represent this broader perspective rather than the narrower term work–home and the popular but imprecise term work–life, which seems to assume that work is not part of life (Casper, Vaziri, Wayne, De Hauw, & Greenhaus, 2018).

Conflict and enrichment are not the only constructs that capture the work–nonwork interface. However, they are important to consider because extensive conflict can restrict employees' opportunity to be engaged, effective, and satisfied in work and nonwork roles, and extensive enrichment can increase employees' engagement, effectiveness, and satisfaction across different parts of life (Casper et al., 2018). Of particular significance to this chapter, the work-related demands that produce conflict and the work-related resources that enable enrichment stem from the nature of work and the relationships between employees and their employers (Sinclair, Morgan, & Johnson, Chapter 23, this volume).

The Changing Nature of Work

In this section, we discuss five components of the changing nature of work. We then identify the implications of the contemporary work scene for the intersection of work and nonwork lives.

Nonpermanent Employment Relationships

The early part of the twenty-first century has witnessed a seismic shift in employment relationships from an assumption of some level of permanence to an expectation of little or no permanence (Kalleberg, 2009; Valletta & van der List, 2015). This shift has spawned new terms to describe evolving employment relationships, including gig employment, precarious work, independent contract work, temporary service personnel, freelancers, app-enabled workers, and on-demand workers (Horowitz, 2015; Irwin, 2016; Kalleberg, 2009; Weber & Silverman, 2015). All of these terms tend to fall under the umbrella of "alternative work arrangements" (Cappelli & Keller, 2013a; Spreitzer, Cameron, & Garrett, 2017), and the common element in these arrangements is the lack of permanence in the relationship between the employee and the employer (Callanan, Perri, & Tomkowicz, 2017). The substantial growth of nonpermanent work affiliations is evident in the United States (Katz & Krueger, 2017, 2019) and Europe (Vacas-Soriano, 2015).

A confluence of economic, technological, global, and social forces (Spreitzer et al., 2017) has put extensive pressure on organizations to maximize shareholder wealth (Callanan, 2015), often accomplished through cost cutting and more on-demand work scheduling that has led to the well-documented change in the psychological contract between employers and employees from a longer-term relational focus, based on mutual loyalty and job security, to a shorter-term transactional bond whereby employment is contractual by nature and is based on the mutual provision of economic benefit to the employer and the worker (Cappelli & Keller, 2013b; Coyle-Shapiro & Shore, 2007; Ng, Feldman, & Lam, 2010; Rousseau, 1995; Smithson & Lewis, 2000).

An important consequence of the shift to nonpermanent employment is the decline in job security experienced by workers in the United States and throughout other economically developed parts of the world (Brochu & Morin, 2012; Fullerton & Wallace, 2005; Kalleberg, 2009). Moreover, the temporary nature of jobs (or "gigs") requires individuals to make frequent choices whether to accept each new potential work arrangement with a real or implied recognition of the attendant opportunity costs of continuing to pursue a short-term and less permanent arrangement instead of pursuing longer-term and possibly full-time employment (Callanan et al., 2017).

Globalization and International Careers

The globalization of business that has accelerated in the twenty-first century has radically altered worldwide commercial practices and permanently changed business relationships. Nearly all companies throughout the industrialized world, regardless of size, now have commercial interests and dealings that span the globe. This growth in cross-border business activity has commensurately reshaped career patterns, with many managers and professionals either in international careers or facing the potential to undertake one. An *international career*, in which work unfolds over an extended period of time and across the boundaries of countries and geographic regions (Shaffer, Kraimer, Chen, & Bolino, 2012; Tams & Arthur, 2007), can take different forms (Greenhaus, Callanan, & Godshalk, 2019).

An *expatriate career assignment* – whether corporate-initiated or self-initiated – involves the physical relocation of the individual from his or her home (or base) country to an operation in a foreign country, normally for some set period of time (Baruch, Dickmann, Altman, & Bournois, 2013; Selmer, 2006; Shaffer et al., 2012). A *virtual expatriate* is an employee of a parent company who, through the use of various forms of communication technology, is able to coordinate the work of employees who are working at foreign units of the parent company in other parts of the world without physically relocating out of the home country (Baugh, Sullivan, & Carraher, 2013). With *flexpatriation*, the employee regularly travels to and lives in multiple host countries for project-based or troubleshooting work assignments that usually last one or two months (Mayerhofer, Hartmann, Michelitsch-Riedl, & Kollinger, 2004). An international career could also involve periodic *international work assignments* where the employee is required to travel to, and work in, one or more foreign countries on an ad hoc basis that typically ranges from a few days up to a month or more in duration. Finally, an *immigrant worker* is an expatriate who establishes a more permanent legal residence in the host country, normally remaining in the host country on a longer-term basis (Baruch et al., 2013).

The globalization of the economy has produced a number of opportunities for employees as well as demands with which employees need to cope. Depending on the particular type of international career, employees can gain a better understanding and appreciation of global business practices, an enhanced degree of professional development and advancement potential, and personal growth and development for themselves (and potentially their family) through exposure to peoples and cultures throughout the world (Baruch et al., 2013; Ramaswami, Carter, & Dreher, 2016; Westman, Etzion, & Chen, 2008). At the same time, as we discuss shortly, international careers can increase employees' work pressures and place demands on their family lives.

Advances in Technology

The rapid advancements in communication, production, and artificial intelligence (AI) technologies have dramatically altered the employment picture (Autor, 2015; Colbert, Yee, & George, 2016; Holland & Bardoel, 2016). Many jobs and careers have changed profoundly, while others have disappeared completely (Ewing, 2017). Broadly speaking, technological advancements have created new business applications and industries that did not previously exist, and have also eliminated industries and jobs through the process of creative destruction, which has revised ways of working in terms of employee options and employer demands and expectations (Bughin, Chui, & Manyika, 2010; Ewing, 2017; Ten Brummelhuis, Bakker, Hetland, & Keulemans, 2012).

For example, the "uberization" of the worldwide economy reflects the influence of instantaneous and mobile communications technology combined with new methods of work deployment and working arrangements (Manjoo, 2015) that allow jobs and workers to become on-demand, thereby permitting rapid movement from one nonpermanent job or assignment to another. In terms of creative destruction, occupations that require less intensive skill sets and positions with traditionally low barriers to entry have already disappeared due to advancements in technology, with many more occupations to follow suit. Moreover, knowledge workers, who were generally considered winners in the contemporary employment landscape, are seeing jobs and careers threatened as new software is automating knowledge-based work. Indeed, professions generally protected from an external threat of job loss due to high barriers to occupational entry, including ones requiring a high level of education, licensure or certification, and membership in professional sanctioning bodies, are facing job losses due to advances in technology. In the current and future work environment, it is likely that fewer workers will be necessary as technology and AI eliminate tasks and services that historically had a high human component in their delivery (Frey, 2015).

The Task and Social Context of Work

Recent research has documented the extent to which job characteristics have changed over the past several decades. Wegman, Hoffman, Carter, Twenge, and Guenole (2018) found linear increases in two task characteristics – skill variety and job autonomy – and one social characteristic – interdependence with others – and attribute these changes to broad environmental trends such as advanced technology, movement toward a knowledge economy, leaner organizations, and team-based projects. There was also some indication that perceptions of task identity and task significance have waned in recent decades, possibly due to increased automation that fractionates work functions (identity) and downsizing that results in overqualified employees working in lower-level jobs (significance).

A companion study (Wegman & Hoffman, 2017) explored changes in the psychological experience of working over recent decades. Increases in role conflict, emotional exhaustion, and work–family conflict led Wegman and Hoffman to suggest that modern work is taking a psychological toll on employees whose overload and subsequent exhaustion may restrict their ability to manage their work *and* nonwork demands. Moreover, declines in job satisfaction, and especially in satisfaction with supervisors and coworkers, suggest that the increasing interdependence of the workplace (Wegman et al., 2018) may make work more "socially demanding" and conflictual, resulting in declining relationship satisfaction at work (Wegman & Hoffman, 2017).

Generational Influences in the Contemporary Workplace

The importance of generational differences is grounded in the idea that each generation of individuals displays discernible values, traits, experiences, and shared life events that make one generation unique compared with others (Lumbreras & Campbell, Chapter 12, this volume; Costanza, Finkelstein, Imose, & Ravid Chapter 2, this volume; Hansen & Leuty, 2012; Joshi, Dencker, & Franz, 2011; Joshi, Dencker, Franz, & Martocchio, 2010; Lyons, Schweitzer, & Ng, 2015). To the extent that different generations of employees have distinctive values and attitudes (Becton, Walker & Jones-Farmer, 2014; Cogin, 2012; Hansen & Leuty, 2012; Lyons & Kuron, 2013; Lyons et al., 2015; Sullivan, Forret, Carraher, & Mainiero, 2009; Twenge, Campbell, Hoffman, & Lance, 2010), they may have varying reactions to the changing nature of work. While there is some disagreement over the terminology used to describe each generation of employees, the most commonly used terms are the "Baby Boom," or those born during the two decades after the end of World War II, "Generation X," or those born during the period from the mid-1960s until the end of the 1970s, and "Generation Y" or "Millennials," consisting of those born in the final 20 years of the twentieth century.

Within the United States, the Baby Boom generation consists of roughly 78 million people, all of whom will be of the "traditional" retirement age of 65 by the year 2030 (Colby & Ortman, 2014). Baby Boom employees face a number of challenges, including maintaining their competency in an era of rapid technological change and minimal mobility opportunities for older workers, deciding whether and when to retire, acquiring sufficient financial resources to retire at a time of their choosing (Boveda & Metz, 2016; DeSilver, 2016), and dealing with health issues that could restrict the number of hours they devote to work.

In broad terms, intergenerational studies indicate that Generations X and Y employees, at least in comparison with the older Baby Boom generation, tend to rate work as less central to their total lives, place a high value on leisure time, seek out self-enhancement and asceticism, show a greater degree of openness to change, express a lower work ethic, and consistently score highly on individualistic traits (Cogin, 2012; Lyons, Higgins, & Duxbury 2007; Lyons & Kuron, 2013; Lyons et al., 2015; Ng, Schweitzer, & Lyons, 2010; Twenge et al., 2010). Although some commentators have referred to the Millennial generation as "Gen Me" or the "narcissistic generation" (Arnett, 2013), Millennials also value traditional work qualities such as prospects for advancement, training and developmental opportunities, and working for an ethical organization (Ng et al., 2010). Particularly relevant to this chapter, younger workers, especially those in the Millennial generation, place substantial emphasis on employment flexibility to achieve a greater balance between work demands and nonwork interests (Cogin, 2012; Lyons & Kuron, 2013).

The Changing Nature of Work and the Work–Nonwork Interface

The structure and context of work affect the intersection or interface between work and other parts of life for a growing segment of the workforce. Moreover, because changes in the nature of work present employees with both stressful demands *and* the potential to acquire resources, recent changes in work can have negative (conflict) *and* positive (enrichment) effects on employees' life outside of work. As we discuss these consequences, it is important to recognize that conflict and enrichment are not generally mutually exclusive (Powell & Greenhaus, 2006). Not only do employees experience multiple aspects of work, some of which are demands (e.g., time pressures) and others of which are resources (e.g., support), but even one particular aspect of work such as job autonomy can be both a stressor and a resource (Wegman & Hoffman, 2017).

Work-Related Demands

A widespread employee reaction to the current landscape of work is a diminished level of job security created by transactional psychological contracts, extensive job loss, and the growth of temporary, alternative work arrangements. Quite apart from the actual loss of employment, feelings of insecurity regarding employment and employability produce physical and mental distress that can spill over to other parts of life (Shoss, 2017) producing conflict between the roles (Richter, Näswall, & Sverke, 2010). Moreover, the insecurity associated with "at-will" employment practices and the widespread use of alternative work arrangements can produce a sense of career instability (Callanan et al., 2017) that might discourage employees from spending time or investing emotionally in other parts of their lives.

The lack of permanence in jobs creates other forms of unpredictability, such as a loss of certainty of a paycheck and the tenuous nature or unavailability of benefits, such as child- and elder care. Because weekly and monthly income in alternative work arrangements can face substantial swings, financial planning for everyday expenses becomes difficult or impossible, especially for low- and moderate-income households (Hannagan & Morduch, 2015). People in alternative work arrangements also often give up the "social insurance" that usually results from permanent and longer-term employment relationships (Fleming, 2017; Irwin, 2016). Employee benefits, such as pensions, health insurance, workers compensation, medical leave, and unemployment insurance, which would normally be available to permanent full-time workers and their households, typically are not available to temporary part-time workers and those in on-demand work arrangements. As a result, the ability to make long-term life choices concerning marriage, family, child- and elder care, home ownership, and retirement are compromised (Callanan et al., 2017; Fleming, 2017).

In addition, alternative work arrangements can create havoc scheduling life events such as childcare and medical appointments because day-to-day and week-to-week work schedules can vary widely (Henly & Lambert, 2014; Lambert, Haley-Lock, & Henly, 2012; Martin, Sinclair, Lelchook, Wittmer, & Charles, 2012). The newly created term "clopening" has been used to describe the situation in which employees have to "close" a store or a business at night and then "open" the store the next morning, usually after getting only a few hours of sleep (Kantor, 2014). Employees who are involved in clopening often are given little or no advance notice that they will have to work these shifts with short turnaround times (Greenhouse, 2015).

Increasing demands at work are not limited to employees working in non-permanent, alternative arrangements. To the extent that contemporary work is taking a psychological toll on employees through role conflict, emotional exhaustion, and interpersonal demands (Wegman & Hoffman, 2017; Wegman et al., 2018), negative emotions can spill over into the home, debilitating life outside of work (Ilies, Schwind, Wagner, Johnson, DeRue, & Ilgen, 2007). A recent diary study revealed that incivility at work increases employees' daily hostility, which subsequently increases their anger and withdrawal at home (Lim, Ilies, Koopman, Christoforou, & Arvey, 2018). Therefore, when the changing nature of work produces conflictual relationships (Wegman & Hoffman, 2017), the resultant strain can deteriorate relationships in other life domains.

The changing nature of work also presents employees with difficulties in managing the boundaries between work and other life domains. Despite the benefits of technology-enabled telework (to be discussed below), telecommuters must learn how to manage the boundary between work and home so that their physical presence at home enables them to attend to family-related matters when necessary without impairing their performance on the job, or requiring them to work additional hours (Noonan & Glass, 2012). One risk of telework is the blurring of the boundary between work and home (Olson-Buchanan & Boswell, 2006) that can "increase interrole interruptions and distractions and, thus, role conflict" (Allen, Golden, & Shockley, 2015, p. 47).

Moreover, whether or not they telecommute, advances in communication and information technology (e.g., computers, tablets, and smart phones) can "electronically tether" employees to an employer that expects them to be available and responsive to work demands 24/7, including while on vacation (Greenhaus & Kossek, 2014). Organizational expectations that employees prioritize work over other parts of life put pressure on employees to increase the permeability of their home boundary so that they can attend to work matters at home outside of normal work hours (Capitano, 2016). This technology-enabled constant connection to work can lead to "job creep" (Kossek, Thompson, & Lautsch, 2015), which in turn increases conflict between work and nonwork domains (Butts, Becker, & Boswell, 2015; Diaz, Chiaburu, Zimmerman, & Boswell, 2012; Matusik & Mickel, 2011; Piszczek, 2017). In addition, work that crosses the home boundary on a regular basis does not permit employees time to recover from the strain experienced at work (Sonnentag & Fritz, 2007), with subsequent declines in work engagement and performance (Sonnentag, 2012). Additionally, the impact of technology-enabled intrusion of work into the home domain is exacerbated for employees in global careers who need to communicate with colleagues or customers from countries in different time zones.

Globally infused work experiences place other demands on employees as well. Not only can the anticipated effect of an international assignment on family relationships dictate whether an expatriation or other foreign assignment is actually undertaken (Richardson, 2006), but the assignment's effect on family members can determine whether a successful adjustment to the assignment is achieved (Lazarova, Westman, & Shaffer, 2010). If the family does not accompany the employee, the employee may be concerned with whether the family can properly manage day-to-day activities in the absence of the employee. Whether due to this concern or simply loneliness, the absence of the employee's family in the host country might restrict the employee's effective functioning in the work role. On the other hand, if the family does accompany the employee on the international assignment, the inability of the family to adjust to the assignment can be a factor in causing a suboptimal experience or the ultimate failure of the assignment (Lazarova et al., 2010).

Resources

As noted earlier, the changing nature of work not only produces work-related demands but also provides opportunities and resources in several respects. For example, nonpermanent and nonroutine jobs not only allow flexibility for the employing (or contracting) organization, but they also may offer flexibility to employees in terms of the basis of the employment relationship, the scheduling of work, and where the work is to be accomplished (Spreitzer et al., 2017). For some individuals, contractual work, part-time employment, and agency work provide a way to achieve autonomy in the terms of the employment relationship and overall career management (Greenhaus & Kossek, 2014; Spreitzer et al., 2017). In this sense, the individual can set the terms for when to enter the workforce and when to exit as required by various life events (e.g., birth of a child, divorce). In addition, even when employed or "contracted with" on a regular basis, the individual can decide the timing of when to work. For example, individuals engaged as drivers by Uber and other similar firms can opt to be on-the-clock or off-the-clock depending on life circumstances and choices. This scheduling flexibility allows individuals to adapt and meld their work hours to daily nonwork demands related to household chores, childcare requirements, and leisure interests.

Advances in communications technology have allowed virtual work and both part-time and full-time telecommuting to proliferate, whether on contractual or permanent work arrangements. Between 20 and 25% of all workers in the United

States are performing some or all of their work at home (Bureau of Labor Statistics, 2016, 2017; Irby, 2014). Depending on whether the off-site work is synchronous (work is performed at a specified time) or asynchronous (work is performed primarily at the discretion of the worker), the individual has options and flexibility in addressing family and other nonwork demands. In addition, the individual saves time and energy by not having to deal with a daily commute to and from the place of employment, thus increasing scheduling flexibility and decreasing stress. Although the extent to which telework reduces work–family conflict and increases work attitudes and performance is complex and depends on a variety of situational factors (Allen et al., 2015), it seems to have the potential to promote positive outcomes for employees and employers (Gajendran & Harrison, 2007). Similar to the impact of telework, the benefits to employees of flexibility in their timing or scheduling of work depend on a variety of factors, including the attitude of supervisors toward flexibility, the frequency of changes in daily work schedules, and the manner in which employees manage the boundary between work and other parts of life (Kossek, Lautsch, & Eaton, 2005).

Increasing levels of job autonomy in recent decades, attributed to a knowledge economy with lean organizations in which employees are required to have more discretion in how to perform their job (Wegman et al., 2018), also has the potential to enrich life outside of work. Autonomy at work is a resource that can enhance employees' growth opportunities and positive affect at work (Bakker, ten Brummelhuis, Prins, & van der Heijden, 2011; Janssen, Peeters, de Jonge, Houkes, & Tummers, 2004), which can spill over to promote high performance and positive affect in other parts of life (Greenhaus & Powell, 2006). Not surprisingly, autonomy at work has been shown to be a strong predictor of work-to-family enrichment (Lapierre et al., 2018).

International careers involving foreign travel or relocation can also have positive consequences for the connections between work and nonwork domains (Mäkelä, Kinnunen, & Suutari, 2015). For example, intermittent international business travel can, at times, serve as a needed respite for the employee from the demands of his or her family life. In this sense, the international travel and the break from personal interactions on the home front can allow for a "recharging of the batteries" and an overall reduction in the stresses felt by the employee and his or her partner (Westman et al., 2008; Westman, Etzion, & Gattenio, 2008). Moreover, on more permanent international assignments, the supporting presence of a partner and family can facilitate a more positive adjustment to the international assignment for the employee (Greenhaus & Kossek, 2014). Expatriation assignments can also provide opportunities for employees, spouses, and children to experience other cultures and travel widely from the host country base, thereby enriching the quality of family life (Greenhaus & Powell, 2017).

Generational Influences on Employees' Work and Nonwork Lives

The changing nature of work provides resources in some circumstances and produces considerable demands and stressors in others. The mixed consequences of changes in work are perhaps best illustrated by considering the generational composition of the workforce (Cheng, Corrington, King, & Ng,Chapter 11, this volume). The ability of some Baby Boomers to remain active in the workforce beyond the standard retirement age, by choice or economic necessity, is a case in point. The availability of temporary and/or part-time positions, often with flexible work schedules and at remote locations, can enable employees to gradually reduce their involvement in work at a trajectory they prefer, earn income to support themselves and their families, maintain a work identity that provides a purpose in life, and experience positive emotions at work that can spill over into other parts of their lives, in effect providing a "bridge" between a career-oriented job and full retirement (Callanan & Greenhaus, 2008). However, for some Baby Boomers, this strategy could leave little time for nonwork activities and relationships that would normally blossom during late career and into retirement.

The changing nature of work could also prove a boon to the many Millennials who place a strong emphasis on flexibility and balance in life, adopting a "whole-life" perspective to their careers (Briscoe, Hall, & DeMuth, 2006; DiRenzo, Greenhaus, & Weer, 2015) in which they are concerned not only about meaningful experiences at work but also with the impact of their career on their overall life (Cogin, 2012; Lyons & Kuron, 2013; Winter & Jackson, 2014). However, if working in temporary, transactional, and often remote employment arrangements prevents employees from spending sufficient time in an organizational setting to learn the "realities" of organizational life, foster lasting supportive relationships, and develop a portfolio of technical and leadership skills to help them develop over time, their work experiences may not provide sufficient financial, social, or psychological resources to enrich other parts of their life.

Individual, Organizational, and Societal Actions

In this section, we identify actions that individuals, organizations, and societies can take to enhance employees' and families' wellbeing. The relevance of these actions does not stem directly from the changing nature of work but rather their importance is intensified in light of the changes. In addition, our discussion is based on the belief that although employees and their families can (and should) take responsibility for managing their careers and their lives, their actions are likely to be more effective and contribute more to their wellbeing when organizations and societies provide appropriate support for their efforts.[1]

---

[1] Many of the ideas expressed in this section of the chapter are based on or consistent with recommendations provided by Greenhaus and Powell (2017).

Individual Actions

We advocate that employees and their families make "work–nonwork decisions" as they navigate their involvement in different parts of life. A work–nonwork decision is a choice that is made in one part of life (e.g., work) that is informed by consideration of another part of life (e.g., nonwork). Work-related decisions (such as taking or quitting a job, pursuing a particular career path, going from full-time to part-time or the reverse) that are informed by nonwork considerations (e.g., family responsibilities, volunteer commitments, friendships) can help employees experience greater balance in life because a broader range of values or needs is taken into account than if the decision had been based exclusively on work-related factors.

Consider an employee who accepts a new job in a different organization (or one gig rather than another), at least in part, because flexibility in the hours or location of work enables the employee to meet his or her dependant care responsibilities. The employee has made a work decision informed by consideration of his or her nonwork commitments, and presumably will be better able to meet family responsibilities while also working on a job that meets work-related needs. It is not that work-related factors (challenge, prospects for advancement) are ignored in such decisions, but rather that they are supplemented by consideration of nonwork factors.[2]

There are several factors that can determine the effectiveness of a work–nonwork decision. First, employees need to understand their identities, values, needs, and aspirations (at work and outside of work) to make decisions that are compatible with these qualities. Such self-awareness enables individuals to seek out employment opportunities that can potentially meet a wide range of needs. Moreover, employees in committed relationships need to understand their partner's identities, values, needs, and aspirations so that the family (not only the employee) can benefit from the decision. Second, employees need to supplement their self-awareness with an awareness of the demands and resources associated with different options in the environment. In other words, an employee cannot leverage self-insight into an effective decision in the absence of accurate assessments of job characteristics, organizational culture, family demands, the needs of a friend, and so on. Third, employees should be proactive in anticipating changes, gathering information, weighing alternatives, and making decisions rather than waiting for others to take the initiative.

We therefore see the virtue of employees adopting a protean career orientation (PCO) whereby they engage in proactive, self-directed actions intended to help them meet personally-meaningful values and goals at work and in life (Briscoe et al., 2006). A strong PCO enables employees to acquire sufficient

---

[2] Although we focus on work decisions in this chapter, an individual can also make a decision in a nonwork domain (e.g., to move to another region of the country) that is informed, at least in part, by work-related considerations (e.g., a fertile area to open a new business).

human, social, and psychological capital to enhance their employability and their feelings of work–nonwork balance (DiRenzo et al., 2015). Moreover, in the context of work–nonwork decision making, a strong PCO must be accompanied by strong commitments to the needs of other stakeholders (e.g., family, friends, community) with whom the employee shares similar goals.

Proactive work–nonwork decision making is particularly relevant to our discussion because many of the changes in work highlighted in this chapter have implications for employees' nonwork commitments. We have seen that nonpermanent employment arrangements, advanced technology, globalization, and the task and social context of work can confront employees with stressful demands that interfere with their nonwork life, but also present opportunities and resources that can potentially enrich life outside work. As a result, individuals need to understand the positive and negative features of different work environments and make informed decisions that are as compatible as possible with their work and nonwork aspirations.

We identify additional individual actions that support work–nonwork decision making in the midst of the changing nature of work. First, it is important for employees to manage the permeability of their role boundaries. The permeability of the boundary around a role (e.g., family) refers to the extent to which the boundary permits aspects of other roles (e.g., work, communities, hobbies) to enter the role. Impermeable boundaries keep matters from other roles out, and permeable boundaries allow matters from other roles to enter the domain. Individuals differ in how much permeability they prefer as well as how much permeability their circumstances permit. We noted earlier that advances in technology increasingly permit work to be performed in locations outside the office, and that employees can become "tethered" electronically to their organization by work-related requests (emails, texts, conference calls) at home outside of "normal" work hours. Employees who generally prefer an impermeable boundary at home (keeping work out) may be faced with strong pressures from their employer to construct a more permeable home boundary so they can be accessible to the organization at virtually all times. Therefore, employees need to understand their preferences, their family's preferences, and their organization's preferences to juggle potentially conflicting expectations. It also requires sufficient insight (and courage) to know when to comply with personal, family, and organizational expectations.

Moreover, even teleworkers, whose very job hinges on advanced information and communication technology, may have significant boundary management challenges because working from home can blur work and home boundaries that share the same physical space. Therefore, teleworkers need to address the permeability of the work role boundary (When should I stop work to attend to a family member's need? Should I have a "do not disturb" policy when I am at my workspace at home?) to assure that they are meeting work responsibilities while meeting family members' urgent needs.

Second, making effective work–nonwork decisions often requires employees to communicate and problem-solve with important stakeholders in their organization, family, or community. Communication is essential to (a) clarify performance expectations that others hold about us, (b) obtain information about available resources (e.g., an organization's relocation practices, a community's job training center), (c) seek support (e.g., flexibility from a supervisor, job leads from a neighbor or friend), and (d) determine actions that can meet the needs of multiple stakeholders, including ourselves (Friedman, 2008). Ongoing communication with partners in a committed relationship is especially important to assure collaboration in making decisions that affect the entire family. As one specific example, employees considering an international assignment should consult their family to decide whether to accept the assignment and, if it is accepted, how to assure that the assignment will be successful, not only from the vantage point of the employee's career but from the family's perspective as well.

Given the heightened feelings of job insecurity due to a turbulent economy, transactional psychological contracts, uncertainties associated with nonpermanent work arrangements, and the looming possibility of job loss, it is important for employees to understand and manage their emotions. Because negative emotions can restrict the exploration of a broad range of potential actions (Lerner, Li, Valdesolo, & Kassam, 2015; Mellers, Schwartz, & Ritov, 1999; Sweeny, 2008), employees should work toward reducing the impact of negative emotions on decision making, by labeling and understanding the source of the negative emotion (Bazerman & Moore, 2013; Lieberman, Eisenberger, Crockett, Tom, Pfeifer, & Way, 2007), and/or by reappraising and reframing the situation that produced the negative information from a hindrance or threat to an opportunity to improve life (Podsakoff, LePine, & LePine, 2007).

Organizational and Societal Actions

Although we have recommended that individuals make proactive decisions that take their work *and* nonwork lives into account, most people don't have full control over their circumstances. Many organizations constrain individuals' decisions because of the absence of supportive policies and practices, and many countries constrain decisions by the absence of supportive laws and public policies. For example, full-time employees who want to move into a part-time job to better meet their family responsibilities may not be able to do so easily if their company does not provide part-time options and the country in which they live does not mandate all employers of a certain size to provide part-time opportunities. Or, individuals who would like to accept a temporary gig assignment to maximize schedule flexibility may feel unable to do so because their health insurance is provided by their current employer.

Formal organizational practices include parental supports (e.g., paid leaves), dependant care assistance (e.g., elder care referrals), flexible work arrangements (e.g., flextime, telework), and informational supports (e.g., employee assistance programs, hot lines). Of course, there is no guarantee that the mere availability of such practices will enable employees to make effective work–nonwork decisions, improve their quality of life, and be productive on the job. The effectiveness of these practices depends on a variety of factors, including whether they are properly implemented, whether employees are encouraged to use (rather than be punished for using) them, and whether the formal practices are accompanied by informal support from managers and coworkers and a supportive organizational culture (Greenhaus & Powell, 2017). Still, these practices should generally make it more feasible for employees and their families to make decisions that can potentially enable them to be engaged, effective, and satisfied in different parts of their life.

Similarly, nations vary widely in the extent to which their laws and public policies help their citizens make decisions and take actions that work for them, their families, and their employers. Societal supports include mandating employers to provide parental leave, part-time jobs for those who want them, vacations and holidays; placing limits on the number of hours that employees can work; and funding dependant care (e.g., daycare or after-school care) services through subsidies or tax credits. As with organizational practices, societal laws and policies do not guarantee that employees can make decisions that enable them to be engaged, effective, and satisfied in different parts of their life. Moreover, some policies can have mixed consequences. For example, mandating opportunities for part-time employment can permit many workers to remain in the workforce while meeting responsibilities to their family or community, but the employees may receive lower pay, fewer benefits, and restricted opportunities for advancement. Nevertheless, it is important for countries to understand their citizens' work *and* nonwork goals, identify whether there are gaps between aspirations and experience, and develop policies that address these gaps and are consistent with the values of the citizenry.

Conclusions

The changing nature of work discussed in this chapter has produced a variety of work demands or stressors that can interfere with life outside of work, including job insecurity, financial instability, unpredictability of work schedules, pressures to be accessible regularly to the organization electronically, emotional exhaustion, and the unique challenges associated with the pursuit of international assignments. However, changing employment practices have also provided significant resources, at least for some employees: flexibility in the scheduling and location of work, enhanced levels of autonomy or discretion on the job, and exposure to different cultures for those whose careers cross national boundaries.

To cope with the demands and take advantage of the resources, we encourage employees to make proactive employment decisions that take all important facets of their life into account: work, family, community, and self-development.

The efficacy of work–nonwork decisions – that often involve boundary management, communication and problem solving with stakeholders, and the management of emotions – can hinge on the support that individuals and their families receive from the organizations for which they work and the societies in which they live.

References

Allen, T., Golden, T. D., & Shockley, K. M. (2015). How effective is telecommuting? Assessing the status of our scientific findings. *Psychological Science in the Public Interest*, *16*, 40–68.

Arnett, J. J. (2013). The evidence for generation we and against generation me. *Emerging Adulthood*, *1*, 5–10.

Autor, D. H. (2015). Why are there still so many jobs? The history and future of workplace automation. *Journal of Economic Perspectives*, *29*, 3–30.

Bakker, A. B., ten Brummelhuis, L. L., Prins, J. T., & van der Heijden, F. M. M. A. (2011). Applying the job demands–resources model to the work–home interface: A study among medical residents and their partners. *Journal of Vocational Behavior*, *79*, 170–180.

Baruch, Y., Dickmann, M., Altman, Y., & Bournois, F. (2013). Exploring international work: Types and dimensions of global careers. *International Journal of Human Resource Management*, *24*, 2369–2393.

Baugh, S. G., Sullivan, S. E., & Carraher, S. M. (2013). Global careers in the United States. In C. Reis & Y. Baruch (Eds.). *Careers without borders* (pp. 297–322). New York, NY: Routledge.

Bazerman, M. H., & Moore, D. (2013). *Judgments in managerial decision making* (8th ed.). Hoboken, NJ: Wiley.

Becton, J. B., Walker, H. J., & Jones-Farmer, A. (2014). Generational differences in workplace behavior. *Journal of Applied Social Psychology*, *44*, 175–189.

Boveda, I., & Metz, A. J. (2016). Predicting end-of-career transitions for baby boomers nearing retirement age. *Career Development Quarterly*, *64*, 153–168.

Briscoe, J. P., Hall, D T., & DeMuth, R. L. (2006). Protean and boundaryless careers: An empirical exploration. *Journal of Vocational Behavior*, *69*, 30–47.

Brochu, P. & Morin, L. (2012). Union membership and perceived job insecurity: Thirty years of evidence from the American General Social Survey. *Industrial & Labor Relations Review*, *65*, 263–285.

Bughin, J., Chui, M., & Manyika, J. (2010). Clouds, big data, and smart assets: Ten tech-enabled business trends to watch. *McKinsey Quarterly*, August, 1–14.

Bureau of Labor Statistics, (2016, July 8). 24 percent of employed people did some or all of their work at home in 2015. *The Economics Daily*. Retrieved from www.bls.gov/opub/ted/2016/24-percent-of-employed-people-did-some-or-all-of-their-work-at-home-in-2015.htm

Bureau of Labor Statistics, (2017, June 27). American time use survey – 2016 results. *BLS News Release*. Retrieved from www.bls.gov/news.release/pdf/atus.pdf.

Butts, M. M., Becker, W. J., & Boswell, W. R. (2015). Hot buttons and time sinks: The effects of electronic communication during nonwork time on emotions and work–nonwork conflict. *Academy of Management Journal*, *58*, 763–788.

Callanan, G. A. (2015). They reap, but do not sow: How multi-national corporations are putting an end to virtuous capitalism. *Business and Society Review*, 120, 363–384.

Callanan, G. A., & Greenhaus, J. H. (2008). The baby boom generation and career management: A call to action. *Advances in Developing Human Resources*, 10, 70–85.

Callanan, G. A., Perri, D. F., & Tomkowicz, S. (2017). Career management in uncertain times: Challenges and opportunities. *Career Development Quarterly*, 65, 353–365.

Capitano, J. (2016). *When work enters the home: Antecedents of role boundary permeability behavior.* (Unpublished doctoral dissertation, Drexel University, Philadelphia, PA.)

Cappelli, P., & Keller, J. (2013a). Classifying work in the new economy. *Academy of Management Review*, 38, 575–596.

Cappelli, P., & Keller, J. (2013b). A study of the extent and potential causes of alternative employment arrangements. *ILR Review*, 66, 874–901.

Carmeli, A., & Russo, M. (2016). The power of micro-moves in cultivating regardful relationships: Implications for work–home enrichment and thriving. *Human Resource Management Review*, 26, 112–124.

Casper, W. J., Vaziri, H., Wayne, J. H., DeHauw, S., & Greenhaus, J. H. (2018). The jingle-jangle of work–nonwork balance: A comprehensive and meta-analytic review of its meaning and measurement. *Journal of Applied Psychology*, 103: 182–214.

Cogin, J. (2012). Are generational differences in work values fact or fiction? Multi-country evidence and implications. *International Journal of Human Resource Management*, 23, 2268–2294.

Colbert, A., Yee, N., & George, G. (2016). The digital workforce and the workplace of the future. *Academy of Management Journal*, 59, 731–739.

Colby, S. L., & Ortman, J. M. (2014). The baby boom cohort in the United States: 2012 to 2060. *US Census Bureau Current Population Reports, May*. Retrieved from www.census.gov/prod/2014pubs/p25-1141.pdf

Coyle-Shapiro, J., & Shore, L. (2007). The employee–organization relationship: Where do we go from here? *Human Resource Management*, 17, 166–179.

DeSilver, D. (2016). More older Americans are working, and working more, than they used to. *Pew Research Center*, Retrieved from www.pewresearch.org/fact-tank/2016/06/20/more-older-americans-are-working-and-working-more-than-they-used-to

Diaz, I., Chiaburu, D., Zimmerman, R. D., & Boswell, W. R. (2012). Communication technology: Pros and cons of constant connection to work. *Journal of Vocational Behavior*, 80, 500–508.

DiRenzo, M. S., Greenhaus, J. H., & Weer, C. H. (2015). Relationship between protean career orientation and work–life balance: A resource perspective. *Journal of Organizational Behavior*, 36, 538–560.

Ewing, J. (2017). Robocalypse now? Central bankers argue whether automation will kill jobs. *New York Times*, June 28. Retrieved from www.nytimes.com

Fleming, P. (2017). The human capital hoax: Work, debt and insecurity in the era of uberization. *Organization Studies*, 38, 691–709.

Frey, T. (2015). 101 endangered jobs by 2030. *Journal of Environmental Health*, 77, 40–42.

Friedman, S. D. (2008). Be a better leader, have a richer life. *Harvard Business Review*, 86(4), 112–118.

Fullerton, A. S., & Wallace, M. (2005). Traversing the flexible turn: US workers' perceptions of job security, 1977–2002. *Social Science Research*, *36*, 201–221.

Gajendran, R. S., & Harrison, D. A. (2007). The good, the bad, and the unknown about telecommuting: Meta-analysis of psychological mediators and individual consequences. *Journal of Applied Psychology*, *92*, 1524–1541.

Greenhaus, J. H., & Beutell, N. J. (1985). Sources of conflict between work and family roles. *Academy of Management Review*, *10*(1), 76–88.

Greenhaus, J. H., Callanan, G. A., & Godshalk, V. M. (2019). *Career management for life* (5th ed.). New York, NY: Routledge.

Greenhaus, J. H., & Kossek, E. E. (2014) The contemporary career: A work–home perspective. *Annual Review of Organizational Psychology and Organizational Behavior*, *1*, 361–388.

Greenhaus, J. H., & Powell, G. N. (2006). When work and family are allies: A theory of work–family enrichment. *Academy of Management Review*, *31*(1), 72–92.

Greenhaus, J. H., & Powell, G. N. (2017). *Making work and family work: From hard choices to smart choices*. New York, NY: Routledge.

Greenhouse, S. (2015). In service sector, no rest for the working. *New York Times*, February 21. Retrieved from www.nytimes.com

Hannagan, A., & Morduch, J. (2015). Income gains and month-to-month income volatility: Household evidence from the US Financial Diaries. *US Financial Diaries Project*, October, 1–28. Retrieved from https://wagner.nyu.edu/files/faculty/publications/

Hansen, J. C. & Leuty, M. E. (2012). Work values across generations. *Journal of Career Assessment*, *20*, 34–52.

Henly, J. R., & Lambert, S. (2014). Unpredictable work timing in retail jobs: Implications for employee work–life outcomes. *Industrial and Labor Relations Review*, *67*, 986–1016.

Holland, P., & Bardoel, A. (2016). The impact of technology on work in the twenty-first century: exploring the smart and dark side. *International Journal of Human Resource Management*, *27*, 2579–2581.

Horowitz, S. (2015). Help for the way we work now. *New York Times*, September 7. Retrieved from www.nytimes.com

Ilies, R., Schwind, K. M., Wagner, D. T., Johnson, M. D., DeRue, D. S., & Ilgen, D. R. (2007). When can employees have a family life? The effects of daily workload and affect on work–family conflict and social behaviors at home. *Journal of Applied Psychology*, *92*, 1368–1379.

Irby, C. M. (2014). All in a day's work: overcoming telework challenges. *Monthly Labor Review*, December.

Irwin, N. (2016). With "gigs" instead of jobs, workers bear new burdens. *New York Times*, March 31. Retrieved from www.nytimes.com

Janssen, P. P. M., Peeters, M. C. W., de Jonge, J., Houkes, I., & Tummers, G. E. R. (2004). Specific relationships between job demands, job resources and psychological outcomes and the mediating role of negative work–home interference. *Journal of Vocational Behavior*, *65*, 411–429.

Joshi, A., Dencker, J. C., & Franz, G. (2011). Generations in organizations. *Research in Organizational Behavior*, *31*, 177–205.

Joshi, A., Dencker, J. C., Franz, G., & Martocchio, J. J. (2010). Unpacking generational identities in organizations. *Academy of Management Review, 35*, 392–414.

Kalleberg, A. L. (2009). Precarious work, insecure workers: Employment relations in transition. *American Sociological Review, 74*, 1–22.

Kanter, R. M. (1977). *Work and family in the United States: A critical review and agenda for research and policy.* New York, NY: Russell Sage Foundation.

Kantor, J. (2014). As shifts vary, family's only constant is chaos. *New York Times*, August 14. Retrieved from www.nytimes.com

Katz, L. F., & Krueger, A. B. (2017). The role of unemployment in the rise of alternative work arrangements. *American Economic Review, 107*, 388–392.

Katz, L. F., & Krueger, A. B. (2019). The rise and nature of alternative work arrangements in the United States, 1995–2015. *ILR Review, 72*(2), 382–416.

Kossek, E. E., Lautsch, B. A., & Eaton, S. C. (2005). Flexibility enactment theory: Implications of flexibility type, control, and boundary management for work–family effectiveness. In E. E. Kossek & S. J. Lambert (Eds.), *LEA's organization and management series. Work and life integration: Organizational, cultural, and individual perspectives* (pp. 243–261). Mahwah, NJ: Lawrence Erlbaum Associates.

Kossek, E. E., Thompson, R. J, & Lautsch, B. A. (2015). Balanced workplace flexibility: Avoiding the traps. *California Management Review, 57*, 5–25.

Lambert, S. J., Haley-Lock, A., & Henly, J. R. (2012). Schedule flexibility in hourly jobs: Unanticipated consequences and promising directions. *Community, Work & Family, 15*, 293–315.

Lapierre, L. M., Li, Y., Kwan, H. K., Greenhaus, J. H., DiRenzo, M. S., & Shao, P. (2018). A meta-analysis of the antecedents of work–family enrichment. *Journal of Organizational Behavior, 39*, 385–401.

Lazarova, M. B., Westman, M., & Shaffer, M. A. (2010). Elucidating the positive side of the work–family interface on international assignments: A model of expatriate work and family performance. *Academy of Management Review, 35*, 93–117.

Lerner, J. S., Li, Y., Valdesolo, P., & Kassam, K. S. (2015). Emotion and decision making. *Annual Review of Psychology, 66*, 799–823.

Lieberman, M. D., Eisenberger, N. I., Crockett, M. J., Tom, S. M., Pfeifer, J. H., & Way, B. M. (2007). Putting feelings into words: Affect labeling disrupts amygdala activity in response to affective stimuli. *Psychological Science, 18*, 421–428.

Lim, S., Ilies, R., Koopman, J., Christoforou, P., & Arvey, R. D. (2018). Emotional mechanisms linking incivility at work to aggression and withdrawal at home: an experience-sampling study. *Journal of Management, 44*, 2888–2908.

Lyons, S. T., Higgins, C., & Duxbury, L. (2007). An empirical assessment of generational differences in basic human values. *Psychological Reports, 101*, 339–352.

Lyons, S. T., & Kuron, L. (2013). Generational differences in the workplace: A review of the evidence and directions for future research. *Journal of Organizational Behavior, 35*, 139–157.

Lyons, S. T., Schweitzer, L., & Ng, E. S. W. (2015). How have careers changed? An investigation of changing career patterns across four generations. *Journal of Managerial Psychology, 30*, 8–21.

Mäkelä, L., Kinnunen, U., & Suutari, V. (2015). Work-to-life conflict and enrichment among international business travelers: The role of international career orientation. *Human Resource Management, 54*, 517–531.

Manjoo, F. (2015). Uber's business model could change your work. *New York Times*, January 28. Retrieved from www.nytimes.com

Martin, J. E., Sinclair, R. R., Lelchook, A. M., Wittmer, J. L., & Charles, K. E. (2012). Non-standard work schedules and retention in the entry-level workforce. *Journal of Occupational and Organizational Psychology, 85*, 1–22.

Matusik, S. F., & Mickel, A. E. (2011). Embracing or embattled by converged mobile devices? Users' experiences with a contemporary connectivity technology. *Human Relations, 64*, 1001–1030.

Mayerhofer, H., Hartmann, L. C., Michelitsch-Riedl, G., & Kollinger, I. (2004). Flexpatriate assignments: A neglected issue in global staffing. *International Journal of Human Resource Management, 15*, 1371–1389.

Mellers, B., Schwartz, A., & Ritov, I. (1999). Emotion-based choice. *Journal of Experimental Psychology: General, 128*, 332–345.

Michel, J. S., Kotrba, L. M., Mitchelson, J. K., Clark, M. A., & Baltes, B. B. (2011). Antecedents of work–family conflict: A meta-analytic review. *Journal of Organizational Behavior, 32*, 689–725.

Ng, E. S. W., Schweitzer, L., & Lyons, S. T. (2010). New generation, great expectations: A field study of the millennial generation. *Journal of Business Psychology, 25*, 281–292.

Ng, T. W. H., Feldman, D. C., & Lam, S. S. K. (2010). Psychological contract breaches, organizational commitment, and innovation-related behaviors: A latent growth modeling approach. *Journal of Applied Psychology, 95*, 744–751.

Noonan, M. C., & Glass, J. L. (2012). The hard truth about telecommuting. *Monthly Labor Review, 135*, 38–45.

Olson-Buchanan, J. B., & Boswell, W. R. (2006). Blurring boundaries: Correlates of integration and segmentation between work and nonwork. *Journal of Vocational Behavior, 68*, 432–445.

Piszczek, M. M. (2017). Boundary control and controlled boundaries: Organizational expectations for technology use at the work–family interface. *Journal of Organizational Behavior, 38*, 592–611.

Podsakoff, N. P., LePine, J. A., & LePine, M. A. (2007). Differential challenge stressor–hindrance stressor relationships with job attitudes, turnover intentions, turnover, and withdrawal behavior: A meta-analysis. *Journal of Applied Psychology, 92*, 438–454.

Powell, G. N., & Greenhaus, J. H. (2006). Is the opposite of positive negative? Untangling the complex relationship between work–family enrichment and conflict. *Career Development International, 11*, 650–659.

Ramarajan, L., & Reid, E. (2013). Shattering the myth of separate worlds: Negotiating nonwork identities at work. *Academy of Management Review, 38*, 621–641.

Ramaswami, A., Carter, N. M., & Dreher, G. F. (2016). Expatriation and career success: A human capital perspective. *Human Relations, 69*, 1959–1987.

Richardson, J. (2006). Self-directed expatriation: Family matters. *Personnel Review, 35*, 469–486.

Richter, A., Näswall, K., & Sverke, M. (2010). Job insecurity and its relation to work–family conflict: Mediation with a longitudinal data set. *Economic and Industrial Democracy, 31*, 265–280.

Rousseau, D. M. (1995). *Psychological contracts in organizations: Understanding written and unwritten agreements*. Newbury Park, CA: Sage.

Selmer, J. (2006). Expatriate experience. In J. H. Greenhaus & G. A. Callanan (Eds.), *Encyclopedia of career development* (pp. 306–307). Thousand Oaks, CA: Sage.

Shaffer, M. A., Kraimer, M. L., Chen, Y., & Bolino, M. C. (2012). Choices, challenges, and career consequences of global work experiences: A review and future agenda. *Journal of Management, 38*, 1282–1327.

Shoss, M. K. (2017). Job insecurity: An integrative review and agenda for future research. *Journal of Management, 43*(6), 1911–1939.

Smithson, J., & Lewis, S. (2000). Is job insecurity changing the psychological contract? *Personnel Review, 29*, 680–702.

Sonnentag, S. (2012). Psychological detachment from work during leisure time: The benefits of mentally disengaging from work. *Current Directions in Psychological Science, 21*, 114–118.

Sonnentag, S., & Fritz, C. (2007). The recovery experience questionnaire: Development and validation of a measure for assessing recuperation and unwinding from work. *Journal of Occupational Health Psychology, 12*, 204–221.

Spreitzer, G. M., Cameron, L., & Garrett, L. (2017). Alternative work arrangements: Two images of the new world of work. *Annual Review of Organizational Psychology and Organizational Behavior, 4*: 473–499.

Sullivan, S. E., Forret, M. L., Carraher, S. M., & Mainiero, L. A. (2009). Using the kaleidoscope career model to examine generational differences in work attitudes. *Career Development International, 14*, 284–302.

Sweeny, K. (2008). Crisis decision theory: Decisions in the face of negative events. *Psychological Bulletin, 134*, 61–76.

Tams, S., & Arthur, M. (2007). Studying careers across cultures: Distinguishing international, cross-cultural, and globalization perspectives. *Career Development International, 12*, 86–98.

Ten Brummelhuis, L. L., & Bakker, A. B. (2012). A resource perspective on the work–home interface: The work–home resources model. *American Psychologist, 67*(6), 545–556.

Ten Brummelhuis, L. L., Bakker, A. B., Hetland, J., & Keulemans, L. (2012). Do new ways of working foster work engagement? *Psicothema, 24*, 113–120.

Twenge, J. M., Campbell, S. M., Hoffman, B. J., & Lance, C. E. (2010). Generational differences in work values: Leisure and extrinsic values increasing, social and intrinsic values decreasing. *Journal of Management, 36*, 1117–1142.

Vacas-Soriano, C. (2015). *Recent developments in temporary employment: Employment growth, wages and transitions*. Dublin, Ireland: Eurofound.

Valletta, R., & van der List, C. (2015). Involuntary part-time work: Here to stay? *FRBSF Economic Letter*, June 8, 1–5.

Wayne, J. H., Grzywacz, J. H., Carlson, D. S., & Kacmar, K. M. (2007). Work–family facilitation: A theoretical explanation and model of primary antecedents and consequences. *Human Resource Management Review, 17*, 63–76.

Weber, L., & Silverman, R. E. (2015). On demand workers: "We are not robots." *Wall Street Journal*, January 27. Retrieved from www.wsj.com.

Wegman, L. A., & Hoffman, B. J. (2017). The United States at work: A review and cross-temporal meta-analysis of changes in the psychological experience of working. Paper presented in B. Hoffman & L. Wegman (Chairs), The

Changing Nature of Work: Empirical Trends and Organizational Responses. Symposium presented at the annual meeting of the Society for Industrial and Organizational Psychology, Orlando, FL.

Wegman, L. A., Hoffman, B. J., Carter, N. T., Twenge, J. M., & Guenole, N. (2018). Placing job characteristics in context: Cross-temporal meta-analysis of changes in job characteristics since 1975. *Journal of Management, 44*, 352–386.

Westman, M., Etzion, D., & Chen, S. (2008). Crossover of positive experiences from business travelers to their spouses. *Journal of Managerial Psychology, 24*, 269–284.

Westman, M., Etzion, D., & Gattenio, E. (2008). International business travels and the work–family interface: A longitudinal study. *Journal of Occupational and Organizational Psychology, 81*, 459–480.

Winter, R. P., & Jackson, B. A. (2014). Expanding the younger worker employment relationship: Insights from values-based organizations. *Human Resource Management, 53*, 311–328.

23 Implications of the Changing Nature of Work for Employee Health and Safety

Robert R. Sinclair, John Morgan, and Elyssa Johnson

The effects of changes in the structure and organization of work on workers' safety, health, and wellbeing are a fundamental concern for both researchers and practitioners focused on improving the quality of work life. Aside from sleep, workers spend substantially more of their adult lives working than in any other activity, leading to work being a major influence on health. According to estimates from the International Labor Organization (2014), occupational injuries and illnesses kill over 2.3 million workers each year – approximately 6,300 workers each day, with millions more experiencing nonfatal injuries and illnesses. Moreover, at least in the United States, work has been among the top sources of stress in annual surveys for over a decade, with financial, personal, and family health concerns following closely behind (American Psychological Association [APA], 2017).

Unsafe and unhealthy working conditions also create significant costs for employers: US companies spent over $50 billion in direct workers' compensation costs (e.g., lost productivity, work stoppages, administrative costs) in 2010 alone (Liberty Mutual Research Institute for Safety, 2012), and employers spend an estimated $2 in indirect costs for every $1 in direct costs of injuries (Huang, Leamon, Courtney, Chen, & DeArmond, 2011). Poor employee health also threatens organizational productivity and profitability (Loeppke et al., 2009; Mitchell & Bates, 2011). Costs associated with obesity, depression, back pain, and other chronic conditions are estimated to exceed 10% of total labor costs (Collins et al., 2005), and unhealthy employees cost the US economy an estimated $1.3 trillion annually; including $1.1 trillion in lost productivity costs and $277 billion associated with medical treatments (DeVol & Bedroussian, 2007).

In addition to costs directly associated with healthcare, organizations have increasingly offered compensation and benefits programs designed to attract today's workers and to be responsive to their diverse set of needs. A survey conducted by Fractl (2017) showed that a wide variety of benefits ranging from health insurance to flexible work schedules to free coffee and meals play a significant role in individuals' job choices. Traditional benefit packages, including health insurance, are increasingly being supplemented by perquisites (Jensen, McMullen, & Stark, 2007). Some examples of perquisites include meals, onsite health facilities and concierge services. Aside from attracting new employees, perquisites have the goal of reducing stress and improving physical and mental wellbeing (Clark, 2007). However, research is inconclusive on whether perquisites contribute above and beyond traditional benefits in predicting outcomes such as organizational commitment and turnover (Dale-Olsen, 2006; Renaud, Morin, & Bechard, 2017). While many organizations have sought creative ways to engage and reward employees, it is important to note that real wages have remained flat or fallen for most workers (Mishel, Gould, & Bivens, 2015) and, as shown in the annual APA surveys cited above, economic stressors continue to be a major concern for many employees.

The main theme of this volume is to understand the changing nature of work. The nature and pace of changes to jobs present significant challenges to researchers seeking to understand the health implications of these changes, as well as to government and organizational leaders seeking to craft appropriate policy solutions. Indeed, a 2002 report issued by the National Institute of Occupational Safety and Health noted that "revolutionary changes in the organization of work have far outpaced our knowledge about the implications of these changes for the quality of working life and for safety and health on the job" (NIOSH, 2002, p. 1). Although some of the issues have changed since 2002, the general concern remains the same: changes to work organization represent an important threat to workers' occupational health. On the other hand, not all the news is bad. Some changes in work organization have the potential to improve certain aspects of workers' lives and/or their work-related wellbeing.

Given the importance of the changing nature of work to occupational health, the goals of our chapter are to (1) provide a brief overview of occupational health psychology and describe the NIOSH concept of work organization to link the changing nature of work to occupational health, (2) present the Job Demands–Resources model as a theoretical framework to account for the effects of work organization on employee health, and (3) describe several key trends in the nature of work organization with regard to their implications for occupational health. We will discuss research in five key areas including (1) employment relationships, (2) work schedules, (3) technology, (4) lean production, and (5) safety and wellness interventions.

Occupational Health Psychology and Work Organization

Occupational Health Psychology (OHP) concerns "the application of psychological principles to improving the quality of work-life, and to protecting and promoting the safety, health, and wellbeing of workers" (NIOSH 2010). Space constraints prevent a detailed review, but the historical trends contributing to the emergence of OHP have been discussed in a variety of excellent sources (e.g., Barling & Griffiths, 2011; Schonfeld & Chang, 2017). Sinclair and Cheung (2015) characterized OHP as focusing on four broad types of health promotion efforts, all of which might be affected by the changing nature of work. *Physical injury prevention* focuses on reducing physical harm, such as physical injuries/illnesses. *Physical health promotion* involves efforts to promote healthy behavior such as through organizational wellness programs. *Psychological disorder prevention* focuses on ameliorating work-related causes of mental health problems. Finally, *psychological health promotion* involves understanding the role of work in positive mental health states such as a sense of meaning and purpose at work.

OHP can be contrasted with other fields in terms of its focus on primary prevention (cf. Tetrick & Quick, 2003) – efforts to prevent health problems before they occur through changes in the work environment when possible. Sinclair and Cheung (2015) noted that OHP also addresses organizationally-valued outcomes such as retention, job performance, and organizational functioning but retains a primary focus on worker safety, health, and wellbeing. Our chapter adapts an OHP perspective as we primarily focus on how the changing nature of work influences worker safety, health, and wellbeing.

The social, political, technological, economic, etc. trends reflecting the changing nature of work have been discussed extensively in several excellent chapters in this volume. The most important trends related to worker safety, health, and wellbeing are referred to by NIOSH as changes in work organization. NIOSH (2009) describes work organization as the way in which work processes are designed, performed, and managed, and how organizational practices and characteristics (e.g., managerial strategies and policies) influence job designs. Various scholars have extended the idea of work organization to also discuss "healthy work organization" to highlight distinctions between healthy and unhealthy work processes and practices (e.g., DeJoy, Wilson, Vandenberg, McGrath-Higgins, & Griffin-Blake, 2010; Landsbergis, 2003).

Any particular aspect of work organization may create multiple demands and resources for workers. For example, workers who work on schedules consisting of longer work hours on fewer days (e.g., four 10-hour shifts or three 12-hour shifts) may experience benefits such as shift-related premiums, increased numbers of consecutive days off, or greater flexibility to attend to family role demands, even as they face health threats such as extended consecutive exposure to physical hazards (e.g., chemicals, poor air quality), greater demands for recovery time, limited opportunities for healthy behavior on working days, and increased fatigue. To provide a framework for general understanding of these effects, we integrated the NIOSH discussion of work organization with the Job Demands–Resources model (JD-R; Bakker & Demerouti, 2007).

The JDR model describes the role of demands and resources as influences on employee health and performance outcomes. Demands are physical, social, psychological, or organizational characteristics of a job that require sustained effort; examples of demands associated with the changing organization of work include team conflict, long work hours, and adapting to new technologies. Resources are aspects of a job that help employees accomplish work tasks, reduce demands, or enable personal growth. Examples of resources associated with the changing nature of work include team social support, flexibility afforded by new types of work schedules, and the beneficial effects of new technologies at work. The central proposition of the JD-R model is that dual

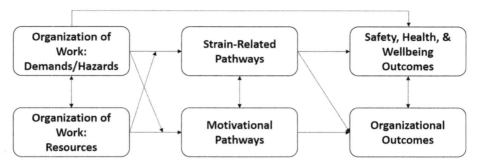

Figure 23.1 *Linking the organization of work to occupational health outcomes.*

processes link these work organization factors to employee health and performance outcomes such that demands are thought to be associated with mental and physical resource depletion whereas resources have an energizing motivational function. The job strain associated with demands is typically viewed as influencing health outcomes such as burnout, whereas the motivational effects of job resources influence employee performance and retention outcomes through their effects on outcomes such as work engagement

As shown in Figure 23.1, this model can be extended to account for changes in the nature of work. Thus, changing work organization may create both new demands and new resources that subsequently influence work outcomes through their impacts on worker strain and motivation (see Greenhaus & Callanan, Chapter 22, this volume). Figure 23.1 also shows, consistent with the JD-R model, that demands and resources may interact to influence worker strain and motivation, such that high resources and low demands would be viewed as the optimal combination for having highly motivated workers with limited job strain. Finally, although they are not typically presented in JD-R research, our model includes direct pathways from demands to the outcomes to reflect the idea that some work organization-related hazards may affect outcomes through pathways other than strain/engagement. For example, workplace violence and safety hazards influence employee health not just through their effects on strain but also through their direct impacts on employee health. A great deal of research supports the basic propositions of the JD-R model (cf. Bakker & Demerouti, 2017), and the model provides a straightforward framework for understanding how the changing nature of work might influence employee safety, health, and wellbeing. In the remainder of this chapter, we review several trends associated with the changing nature of work and discuss their implications for occupational health.

The Changing Employment Relationship

One fundamental change in the organization of work is the relationship between employees and their employer. While this relationship used to be secure and well-defined for most workers, it has become increasingly amorphous. The term "Alternative work arrangements" has been used to define this increased flexibility (Spreitzer, Cameron, & Garrett, 2017), with the extreme end of freelance workers being called "the gig economy" (Kuhn, 2016). This change has left employers wondering how best to retain their employees in a constantly shifting market while employees may suffer negative health outcomes from their newfound job insecurity.

At least for the foreseeable future, a substantial portion of jobs will be fulltime weekday positions where work is performed in a traditional office. However, alternative work arrangements are growing steadily as jobs become more flexible in the employment relationship, work schedule and where the work is completed (Spreitzer et al., 2017). Though there are multiple dimensions to alternative work arrangements, we will focus on flexibility in the employment relationship for the purposes of this chapter. Overall, the percentage of individuals employed via an alternative work arrangement grew from 10.1% to 15.8% from 2010 to 2015 (Katz & Krueger, 2019). However, alternative work arrangements vary greatly in what type of jobs are included and the sorts of problems these workers face that pose risks for employee health and wellbeing.

Individuals choose alternative work arrangements for a variety of reasons. Previously researchers assumed that individuals choose alternative working arrangements only when typical work arrangements are not available (Spreitzer et al., 2017). Current research shows that individuals often seek out independent work for the freedom and flexibility it allows, along with the opportunity to do work that is more meaningful to them. Alternative work arrangements may also extend to freelancers. Freelancers are usually defined as employees who complete short-term work on a per-contract basis and tend to be more vulnerable than other independent contractors, since their contracts are usually nonrecurring and less stable (Kuhn, 2016). Freelancers have historically been an under-studied population, possibly due to difficulty in recruiting adequate samples of them (Bergman & Jean, 2016). The rise of online platforms to connect freelancers with potential clients, such as Uber and Taskrabbit, has enabled freelancers to find greater success in supporting themselves. However, due to the legal precariousness of some of these companies (Lowe, 2017), freelancers may find themselves with even less job security in the very near future. Researchers should make an effort to further study these more vulnerable populations to understand what it means to be a truly independent worker as the "gig economy" continues to grow (Kuhn, 2016).

The rise of alternative work arrangements may also reflect a growing trend in general transience of employees, most notably younger employees who stay at their jobs three years or less (Bureau of Labor Statistics [BLS], 2013). As a result, employers are seeking new ways to retain these younger employees. Indeed, several chapters in this volume provide useful guidance on understanding and responding to issues related to managing younger workers (cf. Cheng, Corrington, King, & Ng, Chapter 11, this volume; Costanza, Finkelstein, Imose, & Ravid, Chapter 2, this volume; Rudolph & Zacher, Chapter 20, this volume). Campione (2015) examined how effective various corporate offerings were at keeping younger workers satisfied at their jobs and concluded that negative factors that drive employees to leave (e.g., long, irregular work hours) had stronger effects than positive factors that entice employees to stay (e.g., pay, flextime, coworker support). These results suggest that it is especially important to attend to the negative aspects of work organization.

With the changing employment relationship, one of the major areas of concern is job insecurity. Job insecurity is a perceived threat to the continuity and stability of employment (Shoss, 2017) and is clearly related to the unstable nature of alternative work arrangements. Job insecurity is a subjective, future-focused phenomenon, meaning that it relies on one's perceptions of their job events that may cause one harm in the future (De Witte, 1999; Boswell, Olson-Buchanan, & Harris, 2014). Shoss (2017) proposes self-employment as a predictor of job insecurity, due to self-employment's unstable nature. Further, in a qualitative study, 54 self-employed individuals in a variety of industries described either job or income insecurity as a source of work stress (Schonfeld & Mazzola, 2015). Most of these threats related to a lack of work or losing business and how these threats affect their income. The stressful effects of job insecurity have been shown to lead to lower physical and psychological health, regardless of occupational status (Sverke, Hellgren, & Naswall, 2002). Cheng and Chan (2008) subsequently showed that the relationship between job insecurity and health depends on organizational tenure and age, with older and longer tenured employees suffering worse effects. This may be because these employees may be more invested in their job, or feel they would not be able to find new employment if they lost their job. Regardless, future research should examine how older employees fare in alternative work arrangements, as they may be more vulnerable as a result of the increased insecurity.

Schedule Flexibility

Nonstandard work schedules have become increasingly common, with as many as 90% of adults having worked a nonstandard schedule at some point in their life (Presser & Ward, 2011). Nonstandard schedules can be defined as any schedule outside of the usual daytime shift, whether night, split, or flexible hours. These nonstandard schedules provide opportunities for employers to match the preferences of their employees, which in turn can affect those employees' work–family balance. Shiftwork that interferes with sleep can have serious health consequences, which in turn affects employees' work quality (Mullins, Cortina, Drake, & Dalal, 2014). Being sleep-deprived does not simply affect one aspect of job performance, but appears to cause multiple health problems. This provides more incentive for employers to be open to implementing flexible schedules.

Some employees naturally have a biological clock in which their prime working hours are after the sun goes down. These night owls may experience great difficulty when constrained to a traditional work schedule, suffering from chronic insomnia and the various health outcomes that stem from it (Hatoum et al., 1998). Sõõru, Hein, and Hazak (2017) argue that trying to force these employees to stick to a nine-to-five schedule will be ineffective in the long run, as natural sleeping habits are an individual difference which cannot be changed (Veatch, Keenan, Gehrman, Malow, & Pack, 2017). Instead, employers should implement flexible schedules which match an employee's preference and help the employee maintain a better quality of life.

In addition to night owls, there are other types of employees who may desire flexible working arrangements (FWAs). Those who prefer to integrate their work and nonwork roles instead of maintaining strict boundaries tend to desire flextime more strongly (Thompson, Payne, & Taylor, 2015). However, flexible schedules are also more desirable in a job overall, being viewed as a nice bonus in addition to other offerings (Islam & Wentworth, 2014). This is especially true among employees who must balance additional roles, such as employed students and working parents. FWAs are a particularly desirable job characteristic for those prioritizing work–family balance. This can take the form of flextime, voluntary part-time work, or telecommuting, all of which can help maintain work–life balance (Dizaho, Salleh, & Abdullah, 2017). Timms et al. (2015) demonstrated that FWAs were associated with outcomes such as reduced turnover intentions and psychological strain (but interestingly also lower work engagement over time, possibly due to a lack of unofficial organizational support, which made FWAs appear undesirable and potentially career-harming).

If FWAs are not available, or if employees are unable to work 40 hours per week due to caregiving responsibilities, multiple jobs, etc., they may turn to part-time work (cf. Lyonette 2015). Part-time work may lead to better work–life balance and life satisfaction, but often comes with career costs. Part-time workers tend to experience lower pay, lower status, and fewer improvement/promotion opportunities (Lyonette, Baldauf, & Behle, 2010). Like other alternative work arrangements, employees may have to choose whether to prioritize their work or home life, and staying part-time can be a way to focus on the latter.

We have already explored the effects sleepiness can have on productivity (Mullins et al., 2014), but what about the more permanent effects it can have on employee health? Night shift workers in particular are more susceptible to health problems, though perhaps not directly. Ramin et al. (2015) found that night shift employees were more likely to be obese, to smoke, and to become sleep-deprived. Given the many health problems associated with these outcomes (Hatoum et al., 1998; Sturm, 2002), night shift workers are clearly less likely to be healthy. Eating habits may help explain the increased obesity rates, as rotating shift workers (who work both the night and day shifts) have been found to have worse diets and less consistency in eating times (Yoshizaki et al., 2016). Training managers to recognize and help their employees get enough sleep is an important step in helping employees with nonstandard schedules so those employees can stay healthy and productive, and guidelines for this are already being developed (Caruso, 2015).

Intuitively, one would think long work hours would show a similar relationship with negative health outcomes, and there is evidence to suggest this may be the case (Barnett, 2006). However, Ganster, Rosen, and Fisher (2016) conducted a meta-analysis and found that this may not necessarily be true. They found that, overall, longer work hours were not strongly associated with negative health and wellbeing outcomes, such as coronary heart disease, obesity, stress, and depression. However, the effects of long work hours varied considerably across demographic groups, with younger and male workers potentially finding themselves more vulnerable to negative effects. Future research should consider further examination of these individual differences and other possible moderators of the relationship between long work hours and health/wellbeing.

Overall, work schedules are much more diverse than in the past. Now, more than ever, employers recognize the potential benefits of matching employees' schedules to their preferences, family obligations and other needs. However, many employees still work on schedules that represent potential threats to their health and wellbeing. Many questions remain about how to best design and manage work schedules to increase worker health and improve organizational productivity. Thus, work schedule research should continue to be a fruitful area of occupational health research in the years to come.

Technology and Health

The next key topic relating to the changing nature of work is the impact of technology, most notably with regard to employees' increased ability to work remotely. As more employees are remotely connecting to their workplace, new benefits and problems are emerging. The positives include the ability to telework and be a part of a virtual team that does not have to meet in person. However, with more remote connections, it is more important (and often more challenging) to maintain a distinct work–life balance as workers may have a decreased ability to fully disengage from work and experience accompanying health problems.

According to a study by the Pew Research Center, 64% of Americans own a smartphone, almost doubling the percentage who owned a smartphone in 2011 (Smith, 2015). Out of these individuals, 46% viewed the devices as an item they cannot live without, often relying on them for work-related tasks and to connect with others. Concurrently, more individuals participate in virtual teams and telework than ever before. For example, from 1995 to 2015 the percentage of individuals who reported they have telecommuted rose from 9% to 37% (Jones, 2015).

As we consider the implications of technology for occupational health, it is first necessary to understand how differing levels of connectivity play a role in influencing employees' behaviors and wellbeing. MacCormick, Dery, and Kolb (2012) describe three main levels of connectivity: hyper connectivity, hypo connectivity. and dynamic connectivity. First, hyper connectivity reflects extreme levels of connectivity. High connectivity may be appealing because it allows individuals to always be connected and up to date on organizational decisions; however, hyper connectivity is associated with disengagement, decreased alignment with self and organizational goals, and increased burnout. This is explained by the distracting influence technology has along with a lack of recovery time (MacCormick et al., 2012). The opposite of hyper connectivity is hypo connectivity, or low usage of technology. Individuals at this level of connectivity fear being connected 24/7 and actively avoid technology advances. Lastly, dynamic connectivity refers to individuals who can freely move between connection levels as needed and who may, as a result, experience benefits such as increased autonomy, flexibility, responsiveness and feedback. The ability to shift between connectivity levels enables these individuals to maximize the benefits of technology while avoiding some of its negative consequences.

When employees do not manage their connectivity levels carefully there are negative outcomes for an individual's wellbeing, specifically regarding stress. In the workplace there are already a number of stressors, but with the continually increased amount of technology has come the idea of "technostress." Technostress, originally coined by Craig Brod, is a modern disease caused by one's inability to cope or deal with information communication technology in a healthy manner (Ayyagari, Grover & Purvis, 2011). Individuals suffering from technostress have been shown to have lower productivity and job satisfaction, along with decreased commitment to their organization (Ragu-Nathan, Tarafdar, Ragu-Nathan, & Tu, 2008; Tarafdar, Tu, Ragu-Nathan, & Ragu-Nathan, 2007). Research has shown there are a number of aspects of using technology that contribute to technostress including work overload, technology invading personal life and privacy, complexity of technology, technology threatening job security and role ambiguity (Ayyagari et al., 2011; Tarafdar et al., 2007). Further, specific factors about technology relating to its usability, intrusive features and pace of change all predict the stressors that lead to technostress (Ayyagari et al., 2011).

Similar to technostress is workplace telepressure, a construct that looks specifically at the preoccupation and urge to immediately respond to work-related messages that come via technology. With the intense urge to respond to messages experienced with workplace telepressure, the intended benefits of being able to be flexible with digital messages are lost (Barber & Santuzzi, 2015). As a result of workplace telepressure, employees reported less psychological detachment and poorer sleep quality along with higher levels of burnout and health-related absenteeism. Barber and Santuzzi (2015) found that workplace norms and technology overload were a stronger predictor of workplace telepressure as compared to personality characteristics or other individual differences.

New communication technologies may have both positive and negative outcomes for occupational health. On the one hand, the use of technology for work can hinder recovery processes, which are a vital component of recovery

(Etzion, Eden, & Lapidot, 1998), leading to higher levels of work-related exhaustion (Derks, van Mierlo, & Schmitz, 2014). On the other hand, Ragsdale and Hoover (2016) found that employees' attachment to cell phone use moderated the relationship between cell phone use and occupational health. Specifically, the relationship of cell phone use with emotional exhaustion and work–family conflict was weaker for employees who were more attached to their cell phones, while the relationship of technology use with engagement was stronger for those who were more attached. The authors suggested that employees who are more attached to cell phones may use them more effectively to manage work tasks. Communication technologies also can serve as a resource that enhances access to social support, internal resources, and feelings of higher control over one's work, therefore helping employees rather than causing harm (Day, Scott, & Kelloway, 2010; Ragsdale & Hoover, 2016). Additionally, using technology for personal use during the workday can act as a recovery experience, buffering against emotional exhaustion (Ragsdale & Hoover, 2016).

What can organizations do to promote the benefits of technology and to avoid its negatives? Employers should promote more segmentation norms and emphasize boundary management, thus creating a culture with strict work–home boundaries to limit the work-to-home spillover provided by technology (Derks et al., 2014). Some organizations have gone a step further, implementing specific policies limiting the use of work email and such technologies to when individuals are actually at work (Barber & Santuzzi, 2015). For example, Volkswagen has limited work-related email use to 30 minutes before and after a shift to facilitate detachment from work ("Volkswagen turns off," 2012). Other organizations have created policies that reward employees for taking "wireless vacations" – avoiding work-related technology use while on vacation (Richardson, 2017).

Lean Production

Lean production, also commonly referred to as the Toyota Production System, Total Quality Management, Continuous Quality Improvement, etc., refers to a set of manufacturing techniques developed in Japan, particularly in the automotive industry and transported to US manufacturing through popular books such as *The machine that changed the world* (Womack, Jones, & Roos, 1990). Lean production is not one technique but rather a bundle of processes aimed at maximizing the efficient use of resources in manufacturing systems through techniques such as just-in-time inventory management, continuous improvement in productivity and quality, and elimination of various types of waste in production processes (cf. Landsbergis, Cahill, & Schnall, 1999; Mehri, 2006).

Lean production techniques have been touted as constituting a revolutionary set of changes in manufacturing associated with general improvements in production quality and quantity. However, they are not without their critics.

Relatively early in the adoption of lean processes in the United States, labor advocates criticized lean production techniques in terms of their physical health implications for workers, based on the argument that one of the proximal consequences of lean manufacturing is that workers are asked to work faster and harder so as to maintain desired standards of efficiency and therefore are at greater risk of injury (cf. Babson, 1995). Other early reviews expressed concerns about job strain and risks of musculoskeletal disorders in organizations that adopt lean techniques (Landsbergis et al., 1999). And, in a classic example of participant observer research, Mehri (2006) wrote about lean production based on his work as an "insider" at a Toyota Production facility, concluding:

> What will change over the next 30 years? I fear that little will happen. There are some who continue to accept the *tatemae* without understanding the *honne* it belies. Toyota was recently lauded for the reduced design time in production of the Prius. But never is the impact on the health and safety of engineers mentioned. Like I was, I suspect engineers and production employees were simply pressed, intimidated, and overloaded to get the job done. (p. 41)

Despite these concerns, adoption of lean production techniques seems to be increasing and several recent studies have examined its implications for productivity and health in varied settings, including healthcare (Benders, Bleijerveld, & Schouteten, 2017; Hasle, Nielson, & Edwards, 2016; von Thiele Schwarz, Augustsson, Hasson, & Stenfors-Hayes, 2015), the public sector (Baines, 2010; Carter et al., 2011; Radnor & Osborne, 2013), and manufacturing (Carter et al., 2011; Oudhuis & Tengblad, 2013). These studies, when taken as a whole, appear to reach decidedly mixed (at best) conclusions about the benefits of lean production, particularly for employees' health. For example, a review by Toivanen and Landsbergis (2013) concluded that lean production was associated with high stress levels as well as mixed effects for musculoskeletal problems and sickness, and noted a need for future research focusing on cardiovascular health issues. Similarly, Halse, Bojesen, Jensen, and Bramming (2012) found that implementing lean production practices had mostly negative effects for employees including mental health effects such as tension, exhaustion, and depression. Overall, this literature suggests that implementing lean production techniques may lead to both mental and physical health concerns for employees, although these effects may depend on how lean production systems are implemented as well as on certain factors in the work environment, with stronger negative effects noted for less complex jobs (Halse et al., 2012) and better effects observed in the presence of job control and social support (Koukoulaki, 2014).

The Changing Nature of Occupational Health Interventions

As the nature of work organization has changed, so too have the interventions implemented by organizations to address those changes. Interventions have expanded to include new intervention targets and have shifted to emphasize integrated efforts to simultaneously achieve multiple health outcomes. Organizations increasingly recognize that healthy work includes both physical and psychological health and includes health concerns directly experienced at work and those influenced by the work–family interface. For example, the APA Center for Organizational Excellence's Psychologically Healthy Workplace Award (PHWA) program recognizes organizations that effectively address a comprehensive set of occupational health outcomes (Grawitch & Ballard, 2016). The PHWA program identifies five aspects of a psychologically healthy workplace: (1) employee involvement, (2) work–life balance, (3) employee growth and development, (4) employee recognition, and (5) health and safety. PHWA award winners outperform national averages on several desirable outcomes, including employee retention, employee satisfaction, and participation in wellness programs. This section will explore the current state of research for three intervention types that might help create such a workplace: wellness programs, Total Worker Health™ interventions, and work–family interventions.

Following the implementation of the Affordable Care Act, many organizations began implementing wellness programs (Koh & Sebelius, 2010). Wellness programs are services sponsored by an organization to improve the health of their employees, whether through directing employees to make gains outside of work or by creating facilities and programs onsite (Wolfe, Parker, & Napier, 1994). Evidence shows that such programs are effective; Parks and Steelman (2008) found that employees who participate in wellness programs tend to show lower absenteeism and higher job satisfaction. Wellness programs also may generate a concrete return on investment (ROI): as much as $4.33 for every $1 spent on the wellness program (Light, Kline, Drosky, & Chapman, 2015). It is worth noting, however, that there is very little standardization with regard to what goes into ROI calculations (Goetzel et al., 2014), so the ROI of wellness programs remains an open question. Thus, although the benefits of wellness programs are still being debated (Goetzel et al., 2014), they appear to have great potential to improve employee health and reduce costs.

Wellness programs have come under increased legal scrutiny related to their voluntary nature and the use of biometric data in such programs. Some have even suggested that biometric data may be the future of employee wellness programs (Ho, 2017). The EEOC recently released their "final rules" for employee wellness programs, suggesting that they be fully voluntary, be "reasonably designed" (not overly burdensome or unnecessarily intrusive), and be accessible to employees with disabilities (Miller, 2017). Biometric data, such as blood glucose or cholesterol, is not specifically defined as intrusive and may provide employees specific insight into their health (Fu et al., 2016). However, some have pointed out that the wellness program practice of tying employees' financial incentives to their status on biometric measures may raise concerns about adverse impact, given the gender and ethnic differences on such measures (cf. Switzer et al., 2017). Thus, wellness programs are likely to be increasingly utilized to support employee health, although the nature of the data used to guide such programs will likely continue to evolve.

Work–family interventions are a far newer brand of intervention than employee wellness programs, but have encountered some of the same setbacks, the foremost being the question of whether they actually work. Interestingly, multiple intervention attempts targeting work–family conflict have succeeded with regard to other outcomes, but have had much lower success with alleviating work–family conflict itself (Allen & Martin, 2017). This may be because many interventions focus on schedule flexibility or telecommuting options rather than directly addressing conflict (Hammer, Demsky, Kossek, & Bray, 2016). Interventions have also suffered from low quality control, as some studies have been lacking in methodological rigor, which has hurt the reputation of work–family interventions (Kossek, Hammer, Kelly, & Moen, 2014). All is not lost, however, as success stories do exist for interventions successfully reducing work–family conflict, even if indirectly (Karlson, Eek, Orbaek, & Osterberg, 2009). And, as stated previously, interventions have improved other desirable outcomes for employees and organizations, such as better health and reduced absenteeism.

As noted above, one of the trends in workplace health interventions is increased integration of intervention efforts across various occupational health goals and targets. Historically, the various programs intended to assist employees (such as wellness programs, safety policies, and employee assistance programs) tend to be isolated from each other, limiting their effectiveness (Schill & Chosewood, 2013). Yet, occupational health concerns often reflect both safety and wellness issues operating in concert. For example, obese workers may take more time to recover from physical injuries and smokers may have more adverse reactions to poor air quality concerns. Although the need for integrated responses to managing worker safety and health has been recognized for several decades, empirical research on the effectiveness of such programs has been somewhat lacking until relatively recently.

NIOSH's Total Worker Health™ (TWH™) program is one such effort to address occupational health concerns with an integrated approach (NIOSH, 2012; Schill & Chosewood, 2013). Schill and Chosewood (2013) define Total Worker Health™ as a "strategy integrating occupational safety and health protection with health promotion to prevent worker injury and illness and to advance worker health and well-being" (p. S8). TWH™ programs adopt a systematic approach to integrate multiple organizational systems addressing the protection and promotion of employees' *total* health, safety, and wellbeing.

Anger et al. (2015) examined 17 studies that tackled both safety and health in their intervention. All but one showed improvements for employees related to injuries or health conditions, suggesting these integrated approaches are often achieving their goals. However, only one study, Hunt et al.'s (2005) Wellworks-2 program, specifically addressed the effectiveness of integrated approaches. Additionally, only one study provided materials to replicate their intervention, so identifying best practices currently requires examination of the academic literature. A report by NIOSH (2012) summarized the relevant research at the time and proposed a four-phase implementation model consisting of diagnosis, strategic and tactical planning, intervention, and measurement. The future of TWH™ interventions will include identifying best practices and standardization, as the success rate appears to be quite good.

Generally, the current state of intervention research is promising. Wellness programs and TWH™ interventions show fairly strong ROI and positive health outcomes. Work–family interventions, on the other hand, are still in the early stages of being developed but should not be discounted as an improvement strategy. In addition to the types discussed above, mindfulness interventions to manage stress are growing in popularity and research interest, though questions have been raised about the validity of mindfulness intervention research (Jamieson & Tuckey, 2017). As organizations try to improve conditions for their employees through interventions, they should strive to follow current best practices, and researchers need to help identify those practices to facilitate more effective interventions in the future.

Conclusions

This chapter has presented a brief review of several trends related to the changing nature of work and discussed their implications for occupational health. Predicting the future is challenging as the only certainty with regard to the changing nature of work is that it will likely continue to change; new threats and opportunities will likely continuously come into focus. Additionally, governmental and organizational responses to major societal challenges such as global warming and the associated rise of the green economy and the impact of automation on the nature and availability of jobs will stimulate even more changes in the future; whether these changes will be for the better or worse with regard to workers' occupational health remains to be seen and needs to continue to be studied.

References

Allen, T. D., & Martin, A. (2017). The work–family interface: A retrospective look at 20 years of research in JOHP. *Journal of Occupational Health Psychology*, *22*, 259–272. https://doi.org/10.1037/ocp0000065

American Psychological Association (2017). Stress in America: The state of our nation. *Stress in America™ Survey*. Retrieved November 14, 2017, from www.apa.org/news/press/releases/stress/2017/state-nation.pdf

Anger, W. K., Elliot, D. L., Bodner, T., Olson, R., Rohlman, D. S., Truxillo, D. M., ... & Montgomery, D. (2015). Effectiveness of Total Worker Health interventions. *Journal of Occupational Health Psychology*, *20*, 226–247. https://doi.org/10.1037/a0038340

Ayyagari, R., Grover, V., & Purvis, R. (2011). Technostress: Technological antecedents and implications. *Management Information Systems Quarterly*, *35*, 831–858.

Babson, S. (Ed.) (1995) *Lean work: Empowerment and exploitation in the global auto industry*. Detroit, MI: Wayne State University Press.

Baines, D. (2010). "If we don't get back to where we were before": Working in the restructured non-profit social services. *British Journal of Social Work, 40*, 928–945. https://doi.org/10.1093/bjsw/bcn176

Bakker, A. B., & Demerouti, E. (2007). The Job Demands–Resources model: State of the art. *Journal of Managerial Psychology, 22*, 309–328.

Bakker, A. B., & Demerouti, E. (2017). Job Demands-Resources theory: Taking stock and looking forward. *Journal of Occupational Health Psychology, 22*, 273–285.

Barber, L. K., & Santuzzi, A. M. (2015). Please respond ASAP: Workplace telepressure and employee recovery. *Journal of Occupational Health Psychology, 20*, 172–189.

Barling, J., & Griffiths, A. (2011). A history of occupational health psychology. In J. C. Quick & L. E. Tetrick (Eds.), *Handbook of occupational health psychology* (2nd ed., pp. 21–34). Washington, DC: American Psychological Association.

Barnett, R. C. (2006). Relationship of the number and distribution of work hours to health and quality-of-life (QOL) outcomes. In P. L. Perrewe' & D. C. Ganster (Eds.), *Research in occupational stress and well-being, Vol. 5: Employee health, coping, and methodologies* (pp. 99–138). Amsterdam: Elsevier.

Benders, J., Bleijerveld, H., & Schouteten, R. (2017). Continuous improvement, burnout and job engagement: A study in a Dutch nursing department: Continuous improvement, burnout and job engagement. *International Journal of Health Planning and Management, 32*, 481–491. https://doi.org/10.1002/hpm.2355

Bergman, M. E., & Jean, V. A. (2016). Where have all the "workers" gone? A critical analysis of the unrepresentativeness of our samples relative to the labor market in the industrial–organizational psychology literature. *Industrial and Organizational Psychology: Perspectives on Science and Practice, 9*, 84–113.

Boswell, W. R., Olson-Buchanan, J. B., & Harris, T. B. (2014). I cannot afford to have a life: Employee adaptation to feelings of job insecurity. *Personnel Psychology, 67*, 887–915. doi:10.1111/peps.12061

Bureau of Labor Statistics, (2013). Economic news release: Employee tenure summary. Retrieved November 14, 2017, from: http://data.bls.gov/cgi-bin/print.pl/news.release/tenure.nr0.htm.

Campione, W. A. (2015). Corporate offerings: Why aren't Millennials staying? *Journal of Applied Business & Economics, 17*, 60–75.

Carter, B., Danford, A., Howcroft, D., Richardson, H., Smith, A., & Taylor, P. (2011). 'All they lack is a chain': Lean and the new performance management in the British civil service. *New Technology, Work and Employment, 26*, 83–97.

Caruso, C. C. (2015). Reducing risks to women linked to shift work, long work hours, and related workplace sleep and fatigue issues. *Journal of Women's Health, 24*, 789–794. https://doi.org/10.1089/jwh.2015.5481

Cheng, G. H.-L., & Chan, D. K.-S. (2008). Who suffers more from job insecurity? A meta-analytic review. *Applied Psychology: An International Review, 57*, 272–303. https://doi.org/10.1111/j.1464-0597.2007.00312.x

Clark, A. D. (2007). The new reality: Using benefits to attract and retain talent. *Employment Relations Today (Wiley), 34*, 47–53. doi:10.1002/ert.20164

Collins, J. J., Baase, C. M., Sharda, C. E., Ozminkowski, R, J., Nicholson, S., Billotti, G. M., ... & Berger, M. L. (2005). The assessment of chronic health conditions on work performance, absence, and total economic impact for employers. *Journal of Occupational and Environmental Medicine, 47*, 547–557.

Dale-Olsen, H. (2006). Wages, fringe benefits and worker turnover.: https://doi.org/10.1016/j.labeco.2004.03.005

Day, A., Kelloway, K. E., & Scott, N. (2010). Information and communication technology: Implications for job stress and employee well-being. In *New developments in theoretical and conceptual approaches to job stress* (pp. 317–350). Bingley, UK: Emerald Group Publishing Limited. doi:10.1108/S1479-3555(2010)0000008011

DeJoy, D. M., Wilson, M. G., Vandenberg, R. J., McGrath-Higgins, A. L., & Griffin-Blake, C. S. (2010). Assessing the impact of healthy work organization intervention. *Journal of Occupational and Organizational Psychology, 83*, 139–165.

Derks, D., van Mierlo, H., & Schmitz, E. B. (2014). A diary study on work-related smartphone use, psychological detachment and exhaustion: Examining the role of the perceived segmentation norm. *Journal of Occupational Health Psychology, 19*, 74–84. doi:10.1037/a0035076

DeVol, R., & Bedroussian, A. (2007). *An unhealthy America. The economic burden of chronic disease*. Santa Monica, CA: Milken Institute.

De Witte, H. (1999). Job insecurity and psychological well-being: Review of the literature and exploration of some unresolved issues. *European Journal of Work and Organizational Psychology, 8*, 155–177. doi:10.1080/135943299398302

Dizaho, E. K., Salleh, R., & Abdullah, A. (2017). Achieving work life balance through flexible work schedules and arrangements. *Global Business & Management Research, 9*, 455–465.

Etzion, D., Eden, D., & Lapidot, Y. (1998). Relief from job stressors and burnout: Reserve service as a respite. *Journal of Applied Psychology, 83*, 577–585. doi:10.1037/0021-9010.83.4.577

Fractl (2017). *2017 employee benefits study*. Retrieved November 1, 2017, from www.frac.tl/employee-benefits-study/

Fu, P. L., Bradley, K. L., Viswanathan, S., Chan, J. M., & Stampfer, M. (2016). Trends in biometric health indices within an employer-sponsored wellness program with outcome-based incentives. *American Journal of Health Promotion, 30*, 453–457.

Ganster, D. C., Rosen, C. C., & Fisher, G. G. (2016). Long working hours and well-being: What we know, what we do not know, and what we need to know. *Journal of Business and Psychology*. https://doi.org/10.1007/s10869-016-9478-1

Goetzel, R. Z., Henke, R. M., Tabrizi, M., Pelletier, K. R., Loeppke, R., Ballard, D. W., ... & Metz, R. D. (2014). Do workplace health promotion (wellness) programs work? *Journal of Occupational and Environmental Medicine, 56*(9), 927–934. https://doi.org/10.1097/JOM.0000000000000276

Grawitch, M. J., & Ballard, D. W. (2016). *The psychologically healthy workplace: Building a win–win environment for organizations and employees*. Washington, DC: American Psychological Association.

Hammer, L. B., Demsky, C. A., Kossek, E. E., & Bray, J. W. (2016). Work–family intervention research. In T. D. Allen & L. Eby (Eds). *The Oxford handbook of work and family* (pp. 349–361). Oxford, UK: Oxford University Press. https://doi.org/10.1093/oxfordhb/9780199337538.013.27

Hasle, P., Bojesen, A., Jensen, P. L., & Bramming, P. (2012). Lean and the working environment: A review of the literature. *International Journal of Operations & Production Management, 32*, 829–849.

Hasle, P., Nielsen, A. P., & Edwards, K. (2016). Application of lean manufacturing in hospitals–the need to consider maturity, complexity, and the value concept: Application of lean manufacturing in hospitals. *Human Factors and Ergonomics in Manufacturing & Service Industries, 26,* 430–442. https://doi.org/10.1002/hfm.20668

Hatoum, H. T., Kong, S. X., Kania, C. M., Wong, J. M., & Mendelson, W. B. (1998). Insomnia, health-related quality of life and healthcare resource consumption. A study of managed-care organisation enrollees. *Pharmacoeconomics, 14,* 629–637.

Ho, S. (2017). The future of workplace wellness programs. *Strategic HR Review, 16,* 2–6. https://doi.org/10.1108/SHR-11-2016-0101

Huang, Y., Leamon, T. B., Courtney, T. K., Chen, P. Y., & DeArmond, S. (2011). A comparison of workplace safety perceptions among financial decision-makers of medium- vs. large-size companies. *Accident Analysis and Prevention, 43,* 1–10

Hunt, M. K., Lederman, R., Stoddard, A. M., LaMontagne, A. D., McLellan, D., Combe, C., ... & Sorensen, G. (2005). Process evaluation of an integrated health promotion/occupational health model in WellWorks-2. *Health Education & Behavior: The Official Publication of the Society for Public Health Education, 32,* 10–26.

International Labor Organization (2014). *Global employment trends 2014: Risk of a jobless recovery? International Labour Office.* Geneva: ILO. Retrieved November 14, 2017, from: www.ilo.org/wcmsp5/groups/public/—dgreports/—dcomm/—publ/documents/publication/wcms_233953.pdf.

Islam, S., & Wentworth, D. K. (2014). Work experience and gender effects on the work schedule preferences of undergraduate accounting students. *Accounting and Finance Research, 3,* 127–142. https://doi.org/10.5430/afr.v3n3

Jamieson, S. D., & Tuckey, M. R. (2017). Mindfulness interventions in the workplace: A critique of the current state of the literature. *Journal of Occupational Health Psychology, 22,* 180–193. https://doi.org/10.1037/ocp0000048

Jensen, D., McMullen, T., & Stark, M. (2007). *The manager's guide to rewards: What you need to know to get the best for – and from – your employees.* New York, NY: AMACOM/American Management Association.

Jones, J. M. (2015). *In US, telecommuting for work climbs to 37%.* Retrieved November 1, 2017, from http://news.gallup.com.libproxy.clemson.edu/poll/184649/telecommuting-work-climbs.aspx

Karlson, B., Eek, F., Ørbæk, P., & Österberg, K. (2009). Effects on sleep-related problems and self-reported health after a change of shift schedule. *Journal of Occupational Health Psychology, 14,* 97–109. https://doi.org/10.1037/a0014116

Katz, L. F., & Krueger, A. B. (2019). The rise and nature of alternative work arrangements in the United States, 1995–2015. *Industrial and Labor Relations Review, 72,* 382–416.

Koh, H. K., & Sebelius, K. G. (2010). Promoting prevention through the Affordable Care Act. *New England Journal of Medicine, 363,* 1296–1299. https://doi.org/10.1056/NEJMp1008560

Kossek, E. E., Hammer, L. B., Kelly, E. L., & Moen, P. (2014). Designing work, family & health organizational change initiatives. *Organizational Dynamics, 43,* 53–63. https://doi.org/10.1016/j.orgdyn.2013.10.007

Koukoulaki, T. (2014). The impact of lean production on musculoskeletal and psychosocial risks: An examination of sociotechnical trends over 20 years. *Applied Ergonomics*, *45*(2), 198–212. https://doi.org/10.1016/j.apergo.2013.07.018

Kuhn, K. M. (2016). The rise of the "Gig Economy" and implications for understanding work and workers. *Business Horizons*, *56*, 39–50. https://doi.org/10.1016/j.bushor.2012.09.002

Landsbergis, P. A. (2003). The changing organization of work and the safety and health of working people: A commentary. *Journal of Occupational and Environmental Medicine*, *45*, 61–72.

Landsbergis, P. A., Cahill, J., & Schnall, P. (1999). The impact of lean production and related new systems of work organization on worker health. *Journal of Occupational Health Psychology*, *4*, 108–130.

Liberty Mutual Research Institute for Safety (2012, Winter). *2010 Workplace Safety Index, from research to reality* [online]. Hopkinton, MA: Liberty Mutual. Retrieved November 14, 2017, from: www.libertymutual.com/researchinstitute

Light, E. M. W., Kline, A. S., Drosky, M. A., & Chapman, L. S. (2015). Economic analysis of the Return-on-Investment of a worksite wellness program for a large multistate retail grocery organization: *Journal of Occupational and Environmental Medicine*, *57*, 882–892. https://doi.org/10.1097/JOM.0000000000000486

Loeppke, R., Taitel, M., Haufle, V., Parry, T., Kessler, R., & Jinnett, K. (2009). Health and productivity as a business strategy: a multiemployer study. *Journal of Occupational & Environmental Medicine*, *51*, 411–428.

Lowe, M. (2017). Uber's gambit: Reassessing the regulatory realities of the "Gig Economy." *Cornell HR Review*, 1–5.

Lyonette, C. (2015). Part-time work, work–life balance and gender equality. *Journal of Social Welfare and Family Law*, *37*, 321–333. https://doi.org/10.1080/09649069.2015.1081225

Lyonette, C., Baldauf, B., & Behle, H. (2010). "Quality" part-time work: A review of the evidence. Government Equalities Office (March). Retrieved November 1, 2017, from: http://citeseerx.ist.psu.edu/viewdoc/download?doi=10.1.1.459.4508&rep=rep1&type=pdf

MacCormick, J. S., Dery, K., & Kolb, D. G. (2012). Engaged or just connected? Smartphones and employee engagement. *Organizational Dynamics*, *41*, 194–201.

Mehri, D. (2006). The darker side of lean: An insider's perspective on the realities of the Toyota Production System. *Academy of Management Perspectives*, *20*, 21–42.

Miller, O. Z. (2017). EEOC final rules on employer wellness programs. *Employee Relations Law Journal*, *42*, 51–56.

Mishel, L., Gould, E., & Bivens, J. (2015). Wage stagnation in nine charts. *Economic Policy Institute*, 6.

Mitchell, R. J., & Bates, P. (2011). Measuring health-related productivity losses. *Population Health Management*, *14*, 93–98.

Mullins, H., Cortina, J., Drake, C., & Dalal, R. (2014). Sleepiness at work: A review and framework of how the physiology of sleepiness impacts the workplace. *Journal of Applied Psychology*, *99*(6), 1096–1112. https://doi.org/10.1037/a0037885

National Institute for Occupational Safety and Health (NIOSH) (2009). *Work organization and stress-related disorders.* Retrieved from www.cdc.gov/niosh/programs/workorg/

National Institute for Occupational Safety and Health (NIOSH) (2002). *The changing organization of work and the safety and health of working people.* Retrieved from www.cdc.gov/niosh/docs/2002-116/pdfs/2002-116.pdf

National Institute for Occupational Safety and Health (NIOSH) (2012). *Research compendium: The NIOSH Total Worker Health™ Program: Seminal research papers 2012.* Washington, DC: US Department of Health and Human Services, Public Health Service, Centers for Disease Control and Prevention, National Institute for Occupational Safety and Health, DHHS (NIOSH) Publication No. 2012-146, 2012 May: 1–214.

Oudhuis, M., & Tengblad, S. (2013). Experiences from implementation of lean production: Standardization versus self-management: A Swedish case study. *Nordic Journal of Working Life Studies, 3*, 31.

Parks, K. M., & Steelman, L. A. (2008). Organizational wellness programs: A meta-analysis. *Journal of Occupational Health Psychology, 13*, 58–68. https://doi.org/10.1037/1076-8998.13.1.58

Radnor, Z., & Osborne, S. P. (2013). Lean: A failed theory for public services? *Public Management Review, 15*, 265–287. https://doi.org/10.1080/14719037.2012.748820

Ragsdale, J. M., & Hoover, C. S. (2016). Cell phones during nonwork time: A source of job demands and resources. *Computers in Human Behavior, 57*, 54–60.

Ragu-Nathan, T. S., Tarafdar, M., Ragu-Nathan, B. S., & Tu, Q. (2008). The consequences of technostress for end users in organizations: Conceptual development and empirical validation. *Information Systems Research, 19*, 417–433.

Ramin, C., Devore, E. E., Wang, W., Pierre-Paul, J., Wegrzyn, L. R., & Schernhammer, E. S. (2015). Night shift work at specific age ranges and chronic disease risk factors. *Occupational and Environmental Medicine, 72*, 100–107. https://doi.org/10.1136/oemed-2014-102292

Renaud, S., Morin, L., & Béchard, A. (2017). Traditional benefits versus perquisites: A longitudinal test of their differential impact on employee turnover. *Journal of Personnel Psychology, 16*, 91–103. doi:10.1027/1866-5888/a000180

Richardson, K.M. (2017). Managing employee stress and wellness in the new millennium. *Journal of Occupational Health Psychology, 22*, 423–428.

Schill, A. L., & Chosewood, L. C. (2013). *The NIOSH Total Worker Health^{TM} program: an overview.* LWW.

Schonfeld, I. S., & Chang, C-H. (2017). *Occupational health psychology.* New York, NY: Springer.

Schonfeld, I. S., & Mazzola, J. J. (2015). A qualitative study of stress in individuals self-employed in solo businesses. *Journal of Occupational Health Psychology, 20*, 501–513. doi:10.1037/a0038804

Shoss, M. K. (2017). Job insecurity: An integrative review and agenda for future research. *Journal of Management, 43*, 1911–1939. doi: 0149206317691574.

Sinclair, R. R. & Cheung, J. H. (2015). Occupational health. In S. K. Whitbourne (Ed.), *The encyclopedia of adulthood and aging* (pp. 993–997). Hoboken, NJ: Wiley-Blackwell. doi: 10.1002/9781118528921.wbeaa166

Smith, A. (2015). *US smartphone use in 2015.* Retrieved November 1, 2017, from www.pewinternet.org/2015/04/01/us-smartphone-use-in-2015/

Sõõru, E., Hein, H., & Hazak, A. (2017). Why force owls to start work early? The work schedules of R&D employees and sleep. *TUT Economic Research Series, 25*. Retrieved from http://www.tutecon.eu/index.php/TUTECON/article/view/25

Spreitzer, G. M., Cameron, L., & Garrett, L. (2017). Alternative work arrangements: Two images of the new world of work. *Annual Review of Organizational Psychology and Organizational Behavior, 4*, 473–499.

Sturm, R. (2002). The effects of obesity, smoking and drinking on medical problems and costs. *Health Affairs, 21*, 245–253. https://doi.org/10.1377/hlthaff.21.2.245

Sverke, M., Hellgren, J., & Naswall, K. (2002). No security: A meta-analysis and review of job insecurity and its consequences. *Journal of Occupational Health Psychology, 7*, 242–264.

Switzer, F. S., Cheung, J. H., Burns, D. K., Sinclair, R. R., Roth, P., McCubbin, J., & Tyler, P. (2017). Carrots, not sticks: Adverse impact and wellness programs. *Journal of Occupational and Environmental Medicine, 59*, 250–255.

Tarafdar, M., Tu, Q., Ragu-Nathan, B. S., & Ragu-Nathan, T. S. (2007). The impact of technostress on role stress and productivity. *Journal of Management Information Systems, 24*, 301–328.

Tetrick, L. E., & Quick, J. C. (2003). Prevention at work: Public health in occupational settings. In L. E. Tetrick & J. C. Quick (Eds). *Handbook of occupational health psychology* (pp. 3–17). Washington, DC: American Psychological Association.

Thompson, R. J., Payne, S. C., & Taylor, A. B. (2015). Applicant attraction to flexible work arrangements: Separating the influence of flextime and flexplace. *Journal of Occupational and Organizational Psychology, 88*, 726–749. https://doi.org/10.1111/joop.12095

Timms, C., Brough, P., O'Driscoll, M., Kalliath, T., Siu, O. L., Sit, C., & Lo, D. (2015). Flexible work arrangements, work engagement, turnover intentions and psychological health: Flexible work arrangements, work engagement, turnover intentions and psychological health. *Asia Pacific Journal of Human Resources, 53*, 83–103. https://doi.org/10.1111/1744-7941.12030

Toivanen, S., & Landsbergis, P. (2013). Lean och arbetstagarnas hälsa [Lean and worker health]. In P. Sederblad & L. Abrahamsson (Eds.), *Lean i arbetslivet* [Lean in working life]. Stockholm: Liber.

Veatch, O. J., Keenan, B. T., Gehrman, P. R., Malow, B. A., & Pack, A. I. (2017). Pleiotropic genetic effects influencing sleep and neurological disorders. *The Lancet Neurology, 16*, 158–170.

"Volkswagen turns of Blackberry e-mail after work hours." (2012). Retrieved from: www.bbc.com/news/technology-16314901

Von Thiele Schwarz, U., Augustsson, H., Hasson, H., & Stenfors-Hayes, T. (2015). Promoting employee health by integrating health protection, health promotion, and continuous improvement: A longitudinal quasi-experimental intervention study. *Journal of Occupational and Environmental Medicine, 57*, 217–225.

Wolfe, R., Parker, D., Napier, N. (1994). Employee health management and organizational performance. *Journal of Applied Behavioral Science, 30*, 22–42.

Womack, J. P., Jones, D.T., & Roos, D. 1990. *The machine that changed the world.* New York, NY: Harper Perennial.

Yoshizaki, T., Kawano, Y., Noguchi, O., Onishi, J., Teramoto, R., Sunami, A., ... & Togo, F. (2016). Association of eating behaviours with diurnal preference and rotating shift work in Japanese female nurses: A cross-sectional study. *BMJ Open, 6*, e011987. https://doi.org/10.1136/bmjopen-2016-011987

24 The Dark Side of Workplace Technology

Cyber-Related Counterproductive Work Behavior, Workplace Mistreatment, and Violation of Workplace Ethics

David J. Howard and Paul E. Spector

There is perhaps no workplace factor that has a bigger negative impact on employee behavior than technology. Technology has had a monumental impact on both the physical aspects of the workplace and how workers perform their jobs, transitioning from a largely paper-and-pencil office to the computerized world we live in today that can allow for more efficient performance of job tasks and the ability to work remotely. Furthermore, information and communication technologies (ICT) have changed the way that people behave and communicate in the workplace. ICT advances have created new devices and media for interactions among employees and between employees and the public (e.g., customers). At the same time, electronic access to organizational and personal information has created the means for employees to intentionally or unintentionally misuse ICT devices and an organization's sensitive data. Thus, these technologies have provided new opportunities for organizational insiders and outsiders to engage in counterproductive work behavior (CWB; behavior that harms organizations or people in organizations), and unethical behaviors, including workplace mistreatment.

The workplace mistreatment literature falls within the domain of occupational health psychology, linking workplace experience to employee health and wellbeing. The proliferation of the Internet and ICT usage in today's changing workplace has led to new cyber-occupational health psychology (C-OHP) constructs being studied, including cyber incivility and cyberbullying. CWB research focuses on the actor's behavior, with much of it concerned with the impact of these behaviors on organizational functioning. Again, we find that technology has created new opportunities for employees to engage in cyber-CWB (C-CWB) with behaviors like cyberloafing, cyber-sabotage, and cyber-theft. This chapter has three goals: (1) to present a brief overview of counterproductive work behaviors and workplace mistreatment, (2) review the current literature that focuses on newer technology-driven C-CWB and C-OHP constructs, and (3) to discuss the ethical implications involved with organizations attempting to minimize C-CWB using workplace monitoring methods.

Counterproductive Work Behaviors and Workplace Mistreatment

Counterproductive work behaviors (CWBs) are intentional acts that harm or are intended to harm the organization or people in organizations (Spector & Fox, 2005). The definition of CWB reveals the boundary condition that the behavior must be a volitional act, one that the employee purposefully commits. For example, if an employee's assigned workload was too high for him or her to be able to complete all tasks, that employee would not be committing a CWB if failing to complete a task because his or her intention was to complete their assigned work, but the workload level made it impossible. However, if the same employee was sabotaging a team's production tasks so they were unable to complete their work, then the employee would be committing a CWB. Additionally, there is no boundary condition with regard to intent to harm; only that the purposeful behavior, either directly or indirectly, harms the organization or coworkers (Jex & Britt, 2014, p. 178). Unless the behavior is accidental (a common occurrence in cybersecurity behaviors discussed later in the chapter), if subsequent harm occurs to a coworker or the organization, it is considered a CWB.

Workplace mistreatment occurs when an employee experiences a harmful physical (e.g., being hit) or psychological (e.g., being yelled at) incident at work (Cortina & Magley, 2003, p. 247). Similar to CWB, workplace mistreatment is an overarching term used to describe a variety of behaviors that have negative effects on workers and organizations. Workplace mistreatment constructs generally examined from the target's perspective include abusive supervision, bullying, incivility, interpersonal conflict, and social undermining (Hershcovis, 2011), and the constructs are typically differentiated by the frequency, intensity or severity, and intentionality of the behaviors. Workplace bullying (sometimes referred to as mobbing) is the persistent exposure to interpersonal aggression and mistreatment from supervisors, subordinates, or colleagues (Einarsen, Hoel, & Notelaers, 2009) from which they have difficulty defending themselves (Yang, Caughlin, Gazica, Truxillo, & Spector, 2014), including abuse, ridicule, teasing, and social exclusion (Einarsen, 2000). The frequency and at times escalating nature of the hostile coworker relationship is one of the defining characteristics of bullying (Einarsen et al., 2009), and may also occur in conjunction with a power imbalance among organization members (Hershcovis, 2011; Niedl, 1996). Because the targets of bullying often feel defenseless and are subject to harassment for extended periods of time, the outcomes of bullying can be severe and long-lasting, impacting the victim's mental health and well-being (Van den Brande, Baillien, De Witte, Vander Elst, & Godderis, 2016) as well as organizational outcomes such as turnover, worker's compensation and litigation (Hoel, Sheehan, Cooper, & Einarsen, 2011).

Workplace incivility refers to "rude, condescending, and ostracizing acts that violate workplace norms of respect, but otherwise appear mundane" (Cortina, Kabat-Farr, Magley, & Nelson, 2017, p. 299). Workplace incivility is a low intensity behavior and may be limited to a single event. Unlike other CWB/mistreatment constructs, employees who commits uncivil acts might not realize their actions were interpreted by coworkers in this manner, nor did they necessarily intend to cause harm to others. Perhaps because of this, the prevalence of workplace incivility is extremely high, with as many as 98% of employees reporting having been the recipient of workplace incivility at some point, and nearly half reporting incivility on a weekly basis (Porath & Pearson, 2013). The negative outcomes associated with being the target of workplace incivility are far-reaching, including affective (e.g., anger and other emotions), cognitive (e.g., lower motivation and perceptions of fairness), and behavioral (e.g., retaliation) effects (Schilpzand, de Pater, & Erez, 2016). Furthermore, Andersson and Pearson's (1999) work reports an escalating "tit-for-tat" among coworkers occurring with workplace incivility.

C-CWB and Workplace Mistreatment

Tepper's (2000) seminal article "Consequences of abusive supervision" begins with the following quote from the 1994 film *Swimming with Sharks*, starring Kevin Spacey as an abusive supervisor and Frank Whaley as his assistant:

> "What did I tell you the first day? Your thoughts are nothing; you are nothing ... if you were in my toilet bowl I wouldn't bother flushing it. My bath mat means more to me than you ... you don't like it here, leave!"

The quote is shocking in its display of behavior from one organization member toward another and the movie is filled with abusive supervision, bullying, incivility, and retaliation. However, a viewing of the film today proves just how much the workplace has changed in the past two decades. No longer is wearing a wired headset for one's work phone considered an extravagant luxury, and no longer are employees using pay phones to return phone calls to a number sent on a pager. The employee of today is often contacted through email and text message, both during work hours and away from the office, and it is commonplace for employees to use laptops and smartphones for work. Personal computers and other ICT devices have thoroughly changed the workplace of today, allowing for more efficiency and productivity, but at the same time these technologies present the opportunity for employees to engage in new forms of C-CWB and worker mistreatment. This chapter reviews the literature for four of these behaviors: cyberloafing, cyber incivility, cyberbullying, and insider threats to cybersecurity.

Cyberloafing

Each spring, the National Collegiate Athletic Association (NCAA) hosts the Division 1 basketball tournament known as March Madness, where 68 teams from colleges and universities around the United States vie to be crowned that season's champion. The tournament is a widely viewed affair that has increasingly been streamed by workers online, as many of the games occur during regular workday hours on Thursday and Friday for two consecutive weeks. Challenger, Gray & Christmas (2016) estimate the total loss to organizations from their employees' lost productivity regarding the 2016 March Madness tournament approaches $4 billion. It is easy to understand the concern that employers have regarding their employees' personal Internet usage during work, as the current total estimated costs to US businesses approaches $85 billion annually (Zakrzewski, 2016). The ubiquity of Internet access through smartphones, combined with the popularity of social networking websites (e.g., Facebook, Instagram, Twitter) and websites such as YouTube, Reddit, E-bay, and Amazon, has forced organizations to consider how to manage their employees' cyberloafing habits.

Cyberloafing is an employee's voluntary usage of the Internet to engage in non-work-related web browsing and personal email communication during office hours (Lim, 2002). In recent years, cyberloafing has become pervasive in the workplace, with up to 90% of employees admitting to browsing the Internet for personal use while at work (Lim & Teo, 2005) and 96% receiving personal email during work (Blanchard & Henle, 2008). Cyberloafing behaviors have been classified into two broad categories: minor cyberloafing (e.g., checking personal email at work, browsing news websites) and serious cyberloafing (e.g., online gaming and gambling, visiting adult-oriented websites), with the percentage of workers committing serious cyberloafing infractions fewer than those who commit minor behaviors (Blanchard & Henle, 2008).

While there is agreement in the extant literature that cyberloafing is a CWB, there is disagreement regarding to which CWB category cyberloafing belongs. Lim (2002) originally categorized cyberloafing as a form of production deviance ("purposeful failure to perform job tasks effectively the way they are supposed to be performed," Spector et al., 2006, p. 449) because of the relatively minor nature of cyberloafing compared to more severe CWBs such as sabotage, and this classification remains popular among researchers (e.g., Blanchard & Henle, 2008; Restubog et al., 2011). Alternately, cyberloafing has been described as a withdrawal construct (Askew et al., 2014). Withdrawal behaviors are those that reduce the amount of time worked that is required by the organization (Spector et al., 2006) and include arriving late to work, taking longer lunch breaks than allowed, and leaving early (Krischer, Penney, & Hunter, 2010). Research shows that the average amount of time workers spend on cyberloafing varies from around one hour to half the day, and it is clear that when employees are using the Internet for their personal use they are not performing the job as the organization requires. Further evidence for cyberloafing as a withdrawal behavior exists with its significant correlation with lateness, absenteeism, extended breaks, and leaving early (Askew et al., 2014). We agree with Askew et al. (2014) that cyberloafing more closely aligns with withdrawal behaviors.

Much like other CWBs, it is important for organizations to be able to understand the mechanisms behind why people cyberloaf when they should be performing their duties. The theory of planned behavior (TPB) has emerged as a theoretical framework to study cyberloafing. While emotion-based theories and models have dominated research to examine reactive CWBs (i.e. CWBs resulting from negative emotions caused by one's work environment), TPB can be particularly useful in examining the nature of instrumental CWBs. Instrumental CWBs are "based primarily on "cold" cognitions, plans, and personal or professional strategies, as opposed to "hot" emotions and associated cognitive processes" (Fox & Spector, 2010, p. 94). TPB states that social norms, attitudes, and perceived behavioral control lead to behavior through intentions (Ajzen, 1985). The norms in an organizational context are behaviors considered acceptable among coworkers, even though the behavior may not be officially condoned by the company, and social norms have proven to be one of the best predictors of cyberloafing (e.g., Askew et al., 2014; Blanchard & Henle, 2008; Restubog et al., 2011). Lim and Chen (2012) found employees thought cyberloafing for 75 minutes a day was an acceptable amount and often employees feel that their web browsing habits do not affect the organization, nor are their browsing habits dissimilar from their coworkers'. Cyberloafing attitudes in the TPB model can be measured by asking workers how they feel about cyberloafing, for example, with items from Askew et al. (2014) asking "participants to rate the extent to which they think cyberloafing is valuable, enjoyable, beneficial, and good" (p. 514).

In addition to directly asking respondents their attitudes about cyberloafing, other attitudinal variables, such as job involvement (Liberman, Seidman, McKenna, & Buffardi, 2011) and organizational justice (Lim, 2002), have also been found to predict cyberloafing. When considering why workers cyberloaf and their perceived control with regard to browsing the Internet at work, one cannot help but think that sometimes the answer is the most obvious one: they cyberloaf because they can. Even in the early twenty-first century, Internet access at work was largely able to be monitored and controlled by information technology (IT) departments. However, the rise of smartphone technology and unlimited data plans gives workers easy access to the Internet without having to use their employer's Internet connection. The ability to loaf is even greater if the employee is not being closely monitored (a topic we will cover more at length at the end of this chapter) and many workers can make it look like they are working while they browse the Internet on their work PC (Lim & Teo, 2005). The physical transformation of the workplace to now include teleworkers (working from home or away from the office) has allowed cyberloafing to flourish, and O'Neill, Hambley, and Bercovich (2014) find cyberloafing behaviors to negatively relate to job satisfaction for these workers.

Not all researchers believe that cyberloafing is entirely bad for organizations though, and the popular press certainly seems to agree with the notion that some cyberloafing is good for the employee. Specifically, there appears to be a relationship between organizational stressors and cyberloafing, and browsing the Internet can be a palliative way for workers to cope with stress in the workplace (Anandarajan & Simmers, 2005). Occupational stressors that relate to loafing behavior include both role conflict and role ambiguity having a positive relationship with cyberloafing (Blanchard & Henle, 2008). Role conflict exists when demands a worker receives are inconsistent or at odds with each other, and role ambiguity exists when there are unclear job requirements (Rizzo, House, & Lirtzman, 1970). Blanchard and Henle (2008) also found that a negative relationship exists between role overload (i.e. too much to do in too little time) and cyberloafing, such that those who were high in role overload did not cyberloaf as much. Blanchard and Henle's results were supported by Krajcevska, Pindek, and Spector (2017), who found that those experiencing low workload were more apt to cyberloaf, and that the relationship between workload and cyberloafing was possibly mediated by job boredom.

Cyber Incivility

The proliferation of Internet access in the workplace has also allowed for workers to freely communicate with others in an immediate manner through email, and smartphone access has made texting coworkers possible. No longer do you have to wait for the postman or fax machine to send and receive information. Now you can transmit messages rapidly by just typing and hitting "send." Communicating through ICTs has proven invaluable for organizations and their workers. In a study of individuals who have Internet access at work, the Pew Research Center found a large percentage of employees believe email (61%), Internet (54%), and smartphones (24%) are now "very important" to perform their job (Purcell & Rainie, 2014). Though email and texting allow for near instantaneous transmission of communication and for many they are much faster and more efficient to use, tradeoffs exist when using ICTs instead of face-to-face interactions in the workplace. One of the biggest downsides to ICT usage is the loss of important facial expressions, body language and voice inflections that are apparent to others in face-to-face communication. The potential for emails and text messages to be construed as uncivil regardless of intent is likely higher than with in-person communication because of the missing contextual cues and the likelihood that we perceive ourselves to be better at communicating through ICT than we actually are (Kruger, Epley, Parker, & Ng, 2005). Furthermore, the norms regarding appropriate behavior when using ICT are not always as explicit to workers as in face-to-face situations (Park, Fritz, & Jex, 2015).

Cyber incivility refers to rude or uncivil behaviors and comments transmitted through email or text that are interpreted by the recipient as harmful (Giumetti, McKibben, Hatfield, Schroeder, & Kowalski, 2012; Park et al., 2015). As stated earlier in the chapter, the prevalence of workplace incivility is high and the transition to email by most organizations compounds a problem that already frequently occurs. Park et al. (2015) found 36% of workers received at least one email they perceived to be rude each day, while 91% of the respondents in Lim and Teo's (2009) study stated they received uncivil emails from their supervisor. Like workplace incivility, intent to harm is not a necessary requirement of cyber incivility, as many people are unaware that the emails they send appear to others as rude or hostile. Furthermore, some email and texting behaviors that are considered uncivil by recipients are not behaviors that the actor would consider rude or uncivil. Lim and Teo (2009) categorize cyber incivility behaviors into active and passive behaviors, with active behaviors being more directly offensive. Active behaviors include saying hurtful things to others, being condescending, making derogatory remarks, and using email to say negative things that would not be said if in a face-to-face situation. Passive behaviors include using email to schedule or cancel a meeting on short notice, not acknowledging an email was received when acknowledgment is requested, not responding to emails, and using email to communicate when face-to-face communication is considered necessary. Passive email behaviors can be particularly harmful to workers because the recipient often lacks the opportunity to get clarification or feedback from the sender (Lim & Teo, 2009), while also having the ability to ruminate about the email sitting in their inbox (Park et al., 2015).

The effects of cyber incivility behaviors are similar whether they are active or passive in a particular situation, as they both act as a stressor to workers. Consistent with the extant literature on general workplace incivility, the potential negative outcomes of cyber incivility include lower job satisfaction and organizational commitment (Lim & Teo, 2009), higher rates of burnout and withdrawal CWB such as absenteeism and turnover intentions (Giumetti et al., 2012), and an increase in state negative affect (Giumetti et al., 2013). The classification of cyber incivility as a stressor has led to Conservation of Resources (COR) theory being the dominant framework for studying the construct (Giumetti et al., 2013; Giumetti et al., 2012; Park et al., 2015). According to COR theory, resources are "those objects, personal characteristics, conditions, or energies that are valued by the individual" (Hobfoll, 1989, p. 516). People strive to maintain their maximum allotment of resources, and the loss or threat of loss of resources can be a stressor. In a direct test of COR theory as a framework to study cyber incivility, Giumetti et al. (2013) found individuals who interacted with an uncivil supervisor reported lower mental, emotional, and social energy after their interactions, and also had lower task performance than those who interacted with a supportive supervisor through email. Furthermore, participants who interacted with supportive supervisors had higher levels of social energy, resulting in more engagement in their tasks.

In addition to mental and emotional resources, cyber incivility can also affect the physical wellbeing of workers. Individuals who have been the recipient of rude emails throughout a work day are likely to suffer from negative physical symptoms such as headache, upset stomach, and fatigue (Park et al., 2015), impacting both the individual and rising health costs for organizations (Lim & Teo, 2009). The strain that cyber incivility places on workers highlights the need for employees to be able to replenish their resources and be productive and healthy workers. Two resources that Park et al. (2015) found can lower the resource-depleting effects of cyber incivility are job control and psychological detachment from work. Job control refers to the ability for an employee to have autonomy and latitude in how they accomplish their tasks at work (Karasek,

1979). Workers high in control of how their tasks were performed showed no relationship between cyber incivility and distress in the workplace, whereas those low in control were affectively and physically distressed at the end of their work day. The ability to psychologically detach from work at home is important for workers to overcome the distress they feel at the end of their work day and be able to replenish their resources for the next day (Park et al., 2015). However, technology has negatively impacted the ability for workers to detach. Receiving emails from supervisors and text messages from coworkers is now commonplace in workers' off-hours, and teleworkers who work from home may also lack the physical detachment from work that those who go to the office experience when they leave work premises. We agree with Park et al. (2015) that those who are subject to cyber incivility during their work day should be cognizant that detachment from work is especially necessary during their off-time immediately following.

Workplace Cyberbullying

As ICT devices and social media platforms became popular, there has been a rise in empirical research studying cyberbullying; however, most of the research in this domain has been conducted with the purpose of studying this phenomenon in adolescents and an educational context (Li, 2006; Smith et al., 2008; Tokunaga, 2010). Perhaps it is unsurprising that the beginnings of cyberbullying research have focused on teenagers and school settings, since nowadays nearly all students are digital natives (i.e. those who have only been alive in the Internet era) and younger generations are quick to adopt the newest social media platforms where much of the cyberbullying activity occurs. The extant literature in this field finds many negative outcomes associated with cyberbullying, including depression, anxiety, trouble sleeping, substance abuse, lower self-esteem, and even suicide (Kowalski, Giumetti, Schroeder, & Lattanner, 2014; Tokunaga, 2010; Vranjes, Baillien, Vandebosch, Erreygers, & De Witte, 2017). Further contributing to making the effects of cyberbullying salient to both researchers and the public is the attention given to the topic by the mainstream media that reported on several cases of young adults being cyberbullied that ended in suicide (nobullying.com, 2017). What might be considered surprising is that the transition to examining the effects of cyberbullying in the workplace has been much slower than its educational counterpart (Vranjes et al., 2017). Workplace cyberbullying can be defined as "a situation over time, an individual is repeatedly subjected to perceived negative acts through technology (e.g., phone, email, web sites, and social media) which are related to their work context" (Farley, Coyne, Axtell, & Sprigg, 2016, p. 295). Similar to workplace bullying that occurs in face-to-face contexts, simply receiving one rude email from a coworker does not constitute cyberbullying, but rather a pattern of harassing behavior targeted toward an individual represents cyberbullying.

The few studies that have examined how widespread the problem of cyberbullying is in organizational settings have used Leymann's (1996) operationalization of bullying (negative behavior directed at an individual at least weekly over a period of at least six months) to study the prevalence of the phenomenon and found between 10 and 18% of employees are targets of workplace cyberbullying (Coyne et al., 2017; Privitera & Campbell, 2009). The negative outcomes individuals suffer from being cyberbullied include higher turnover intentions (Baruch, 2005), and lower psychological wellbeing and job satisfaction (Coyne et al., 2017), with the link between cyberbullying behaviors and job satisfaction being stronger for those bullied in a cyber context than a face-to-face situation. This stronger relationship between cyberbullying and an organizational-related construct is a particularly relevant finding because there are many factors that can contribute to empirical differences between workplace cyberbullying and face-to-face bullying. One of these differentiating factors is the ability for the perpetrator to remain anonymous and invisible to the target (Coyne et al., 2017; Snyman & Loh, 2015). It is probably quite apparent to someone who was going to commit cyberbullying acts that their work email address or mobile phone number used to bully a coworker could be easily tracked by information technology monitoring or examining personnel records. However, actors have many ways to conceal their identity using ICT devices.

In a qualitative study conducted by D'Cruz and Noronha (2013), one participant spoke of someone who used mobile SIM cards to harass her fiancé, also using nonwork computer systems and impersonating others on Facebook to continue their cyberbullying. Another individual (and her colleagues) was subject to bullying on a social networking site by several of her subordinates after they were laid off by their employer. The anonymity that technology provides further complicates matters for those who are bullied by contributing to a feeling of helplessness and an inability to defend themselves because the identity of their attacker can be unknown. Furthermore, the power imbalance (i.e. abusive supervisor bullying a subordinate) that is typical in workplace bullying situations is no longer a prerequisite when the attacker can hide behind a false online persona.

Another factor unique to cyberbullying is the ability for the attacker to humiliate or harass the victim in a public manner that increases the number of people who can witness the acts (Coyne et al., 2017; Snyman & Loh, 2015). For example, an attacker could email large numbers of coworkers simultaneously, or could post harassing words, pictures, or videos to a social networking platform where the public could not only see the harassment, but also comment or participate in the attack on the victim. The wider potential audience of witnesses to bullying tactics can amplify the negative effects on the target, contributing to a theme recurrent in the nascent workplace cyberbullying literature: a feeling of pervasiveness and a lack of boundaries between work and nonwork situations that leads to individuals feeling as there is no escape from the bullying and it is salient in their lives at all times (Coyne et al., 2017; D'Cruz & Noronha, 2013; Snyman & Loh, 2015).

As stated before, the workplace cyberbullying research domain is in its infancy, and while individual and organizational outcomes have recently begun to be explored, the antecedents of workplace cyberbullying are even less researched. Consistent with previous CWB research, Vranjes et al. (2017) propose a theoretical model based on the stressor–strain model and Affective Events Theory (Weiss & Cropanzano, 1996) to understand what leads people to commit cyberbullying behaviors. The Vranjes et al. (2017) model explicates that workplace stressors (e.g., role conflict, interpersonal conflict, organizational climate) lead to emotions such as anger in the perpetrator or fear and sadness in the target, subsequently leading to cyberbullying victimization and perpetration through emotion regulation suppression.

Insider Threat and Cybersecurity Behaviors

The cases of Edward Snowden and Chelsea Manning brought the topic of insider attacks to the forefront of watercooler discussions in the early to mid-2010s. More recent cases such as that of Harold Thomas Martin III, arrested and subsequently indicted for stealing 50 terabytes of electronic data and boxes of paper documents from his employment as a contractor for the US National Security Agency (Chappell, 2017), and those like him are likely to continue the conversation for years to come. But while insider threats may be a more recent target of research for organizational psychologists, they are not a new phenomenon to information security specialists and have been acknowledged as a problem to the safety of an organization's data since the 1980s (Beeler, 1983; Chinchani, Iyer, Ngo, & Upadhyaya, 2005). An insider is anyone who is a current or former employee, contractor, or third party who has access to protected data, networks, and systems of an organization (Nurse et al., 2014), and insider threat can be defined as "an insider's action that puts at risk an organization's data, processes, or resources in a disruptive or unwelcome way" (Pfleeger, Predd, Hunker, & Bulford, 2010, p.170). As organizations regularly keep their data such as intellectual property and personnel records on networked servers, the opportunity for insider threat to occur in today's computerized world is ever-present, and there is a rich body of research devoted to modeling and predicting insider threats (Chinchani et al., 2005; Magklaras & Furnell, 2002; Nurse et al., 2014).

Malicious Insider Threats. Thus far the effort to model insider threat has been assisted by the CWB literature (Axelrad, Sticha, Brdiczka, & Shen, 2013; Greitzer, Kangas, Noonan, & Dalton, 2010; Nurse et al., 2014); however, there are several factors that have acted as hindrances to understanding the process that leads individuals to commit insider attacks. First, there are two distinct categories of attackers who differ in both motive and method of attack: those who are stealing data or committing fraudulent acts (thieves) and those who are attempting to sabotage the organization or specific individuals in the organization (saboteurs). Shaw (2006) found thieves to be motivated by money and greed, yet they were not necessarily technologically adept workers, but rather took advantage of their knowledge of business rules and regulations combined with their network access to steal from within the organization. Saboteurs are often disgruntled employees who are motivated by revenge. This group are often more technologically savvy than thieves and frequently attack the organization through remote access methods such as backdoors. Particularly relevant, saboteurs often appear to be undergoing significant stressful episodes in the workplace, including probation for behavioral issues or even termination. Further complicating the study of insider threat is the fact that most employees who have sufficient access to sabotage or steal from an organization have already gone through pre-employment screening measures and have obtained legitimate access to the organization's data and resources.

The operationalization of insider threat by many security researchers makes it difficult to draw a direct relationship to CWB and its literature. When examining the Pfleeger et al. (2010) definition used above, insider threat refers to "an insider's action," which includes both intentional and unintentional acts. The Pfleeger et al. (2010) definition is not alone in including unintentional acts as a part of insider threat, as this is quite common in insider threat research (e.g., Crossler et al., 2013; Nurse et al., 2014; Warkentin & Willison, 2009). Intentional acts in insider threat include those mentioned above (theft, fraud, sabotage), revenge against the organization or coworkers, and industrial or political espionage (Crossler et al., 2013). These behaviors are sometimes referred to as malicious acts and they are consistent with the operationalization of CWB (e.g., Gruys & Sackett, 2003; Spector et al. 2006) in that they are volitional acts committed against the organization or coworkers.

The personality and emotional predictors of intentional insider acts are similar to those found to be consistent across the CWB domain, including lack of self-control, anger and narcissism (Axelrad et al., 2013; Mehan, 2016). However, Shaw (2006) cautions against focusing solely on personality and trait predictors like these and others such as lack of social skills and self-entitlement. The evaluation and prediction of insider threat requires a more holistic view. The interrelated steps of Shaw's (2006) framework to study the critical factors leading up to an insider attack include the occurrence of a significant occupational or personal stressor in the six months leading up to the attack, negative emotional and behavioral reactions to that occupational stressor that can be exacerbated by personality and trait factors, the reactions being significant enough to draw attention from the organization in the form of formal action (e.g., discipline, counseling), and the formal action being unsuccessful in changing the behavioral direction of the employee. Shaw's (2006) framework is similar to the "hot" affective theories and models often employed in CWB research, such as the Stressor–Emotion model (Spector & Fox, 2005), where environmental factors in the workplace lead to negative emotions, which in turn lead to CWB.

Nonmalicious Insider Threats. Nonmalicious insider threat behaviors are those that unintentionally place an organization's data at risk by being lax in following safe data-handling practices. These can include cyberloafing on external websites using corporate computers, inadvertently posting confidential data onto social media websites, carelessly clicking on spear-phishing emails, forgetting to change passwords, and failing to log off or lock a workstation (Crossler et al., 2013; Warkentin & Willison, 2009). These behaviors most often occur because of human error (i.e., mistakes or accidents), negligence, lack of training, or lack of experience and are the most common type of insider threat (Nurse et al., 2014). That nonmalicious acts are more common than malicious acts, does not mean that the consequences are any less severe. An example that shows the possible magnitude of an attack resulting from nonmalicious insider threat behavior is the April 2015 hack of the Office of Personnel Management (OPM). As a result of the OPM attack, the personnel records of 21.5 million and the fingerprints of 5.6 million individuals were stolen. The hackers were able to obtain access to the data by using social engineering methods to infiltrate and install malware (i.e., malicious software) on OPM's internal network (Koerner, 2016).

Social engineering refers to "use of social disguises, cultural ploys, and psychological tricks to get computer users to assist hackers in their illegal intrusion or use of computer systems and networks" (Abraham & Chengalur-Smith, 2010, p. 183), and the methods used today are much more advanced than a simple email from a Nigerian prince requesting that you send personal information, banking information, or money as quickly as possible. Spear-phishing, a technique where individuals are personally targeted, is increasingly becoming the norm among hackers. It is becoming increasingly more difficult to avoid falling prey to social engineering methods, since much of the information used to bait users comes from publicly available information, especially in today's world where so many individuals have shared personal data on social media websites.

Given this, how can organizations minimize the human component of insider threat by reducing workers' behaviors that cause harm to the organization's data? Regardless of whether the behavior is malicious or unintentional, insider threat and social engineering awareness, training, and education should be mandatory for all employees and available to contractors and third-party vendors that have access to an organization's network. While we have already noted that unintentional acts would not be considered CWBs, that does not mean that the CWB literature cannot be helpful in understanding these behaviors. However, because unintentional insider threat occurs primarily from accidents, negligence, or a lack of training, perhaps the safety literature (e.g., safety training, safety climate, safety interventions) may be a more apt extant literature from which organizational psychologists can assist insider threat researchers. For example, Neal and Griffith (2002) provide evidence that safety climate leads to knowledge and skill motivation, which leads to both safety compliance and safety participation. Adapting this model of safety behaviors to a cybersecurity context could help researchers and organizations by providing a framework that assists companies in their efforts to ensure their employees are more cognizant of the impact their technology-related behavior can have on the organization.

Unethical Behavior

Though many of the CWBs and technology-related behaviors mentioned in this chapter would be considered unethical, unethical behavior in the workplace is not limited to CWB. While CWB focuses on behavior that violates organizational norms (Bennett & Robinson, 2000), unethical behavior encompasses behaviors that violate the social and moral norms of the larger community (Kaptein, 2008). Furthermore, CWB harms or is intended to harm the organization or its employees, and there is no such boundary condition regarding unethical behavior. In fact, at times it is quite the opposite. Some unethical behaviors have direct benefits for the organization, and this type of behavior has been referred to as unethical pro-organizational behavior (UPB; Umphress, Bingham, & Mitchell, 2010). Examples of UPB include an employee misrepresenting the truth to make an organization look better, exaggerating the truth to customers about an organization's products or services, and withholding negative information (Umphress et al., 2010). The organization benefiting from UPB aligns the construct more closely with organizational citizenship behavior than with CWB. The unfortunate side of UPB in the workplace is that, though the behaviors may have beneficial effects for the organization, they often can have deleterious effects on employees or prospective employees. Instead of broadly surveying the extant literature of unethical behavior in the workplace, the goal of this section is to examine some of the ethical issues surrounding two UPB domains affected by technology that can have positive outcomes for the organization, while possibly causing negative perceptions in workers or job applicants: workplace monitoring and social media screening/monitoring.

Workplace Monitoring

One obvious tactic that organizations can employ to minimize insider threat and the technology-related CWBs discussed in this chapter is to electronically monitor their employees. But as Dalal and Girab (2016) eloquently state, "just because firms *can* (in terms of technical ability and absence of legal restraints) electronically monitor vast quantities of employee behavior does not mean that they *should* do so without careful forethought" (p. 100). When considering technology-related CWB, electronic monitoring can certainly have positive aspects for both the organization and the worker. In the case of cyber bullying, as long as the perpetrator is not anonymously bullying the target (and sometimes even if they are, their identity can be discovered), there will be an electronic "paper trail" that can provide evidence to help prove to the organization or police that the bullying occurred. Electronic monitoring can be especially helpful for actors and targets of cyber incivility, with emails and responses available to help management deal with conflict and assisting with clarification of misinterpretations that may have occurred between employees when communicating through ICTs. Monitoring workplace Internet traffic has become commonplace (and necessary) as a means to defend the organization against insider threat and can also be used simultaneously to monitor cyberloafing. Twenty years ago, information technology departments could block all outbound Internet traffic to undesired websites and workers were unable to visit nonwork websites during work hours. IT departments can (and do) still do this, but workers can now circumvent this type of monitoring to cyberloaf by using their smartphone, which would require organizations to monitor through other methods such as video monitoring to combat this behavior.

An entire chapter could focus on privacy and legal issues surrounding electronic monitoring, but directly relevant to this chapter is the fact that monitoring affects workers by increasing stress and worsening job attitudes (Alge & Hansen, 2014). As previously mentioned, higher job stress and lower job satisfaction might lead to CWB, and these are the behaviors organizations and organizational psychologists are trying to remedy. The pursuit then becomes how to implement monitoring methods that maximize protection for the organization and employee, while minimizing CWB. A recent study by Glassman, Prosch, and Shao (2015) could offer insight into how to achieve the desired effects. Glassman et al. (2015) developed and examined the effectiveness of an Internet filtering and monitoring tool designed to combat cyberloafing. The tool they designed consisted of three modules: a blocking module, a confirmation module, and a quota module. The blocking module prohibited users from accessing blacklisted websites that were predetermined to be potentially harmful to the organization or counterproductive to work. The confirmation module prompted the user to confirm they were accessing websites for work-related purposes and they were then allowed access for five minutes before receiving another confirmation message. The quota module allowed users to visit nonwork-related websites in ten-minute increments, up to a total of 90 minutes before receiving a message that they had exceeded their daily web usage quota. While all three modules were positively related to appropriate use of Internet resources, the confirmation module was most effective. These findings and the concept of trust and control being important to employees are not new or revolutionary. But, we believe context is important, and the creation of a software program to study browsing habits and the effects of electronic monitoring is an ideal manner in which to research C-CWB.

Social Media Screening/Monitoring

The ubiquitous usage of social media in the past decade has led to increased monitoring of employees by organizations outside the workplace, and even of applicants to organizations. A 2017 CareerBuilder.com study of 2,300 hiring managers and human resource professionals found 70% of employers use social media screening when hiring candidates and 54% have decided to not hire an applicant based on their social media presence (Salm, 2017). Organizations are able to learn through social media screening whether potential employees have posted inappropriate photographs, discriminatory comments, or information about possible drug use or alcohol abuse. However, frequently applicants have negative reactions to organizations screening through social media. In a study design using a realistic hiring scenario, Stoughton, Thompson, and Meade (2015) found those who believed a future employer had used social media screening felt their privacy was invaded, which led to lower organizational attraction (i.e., they were less likely to want to work for that company). In a second study, Stoughton et al. (2015) found those who felt their privacy was invaded also had increased intentions to litigate.

Once employed, a common misconception among employees is that they can't, aren't or shouldn't be regulated by employers (Determann, 2012). However, the aforementioned CareerBuilder.com study reports that approximately half of organizations research current employees' social media presence, and 34% have found content that led to the employee being reprimanded or fired (Salm, 2017). According to the National Labor Relations Board (NLRB), an employee's social media comments are not protected if the employee is complaining about their workplace and the complaints are not in relation to group activity among employees (National Labor Relations Board, 2012). The NLRB also cautions organizations against social media policies that prohibit activity allowed by federal law.

Sometimes though, it is not even the employee's own social media posts that lead to negative consequences. The recent occurrence of identifying individuals on Twitter who took part in the Charlottesville "Unite the Right" rally, subsequently leading to the firing of some individuals from their jobs, supports the notion that sometimes behaviors committed by employees are lawful, yet deemed against societal norms and can lead to organizations terminating them. Off-duty deviance, defined as "behaviors committed by an employee outside the workplace or off-duty that are deviant by organizational and/or societal standards, jeopardize the employee's status within the organization, and threaten the interests and wellbeing of the organization and its stakeholders" (Lyons, Hoffman, Bommer, Kennedy, & Hetrick, 2016, p. 464), is an increasing concern for companies because of the swift nature of information sharing with social media.

It is beyond the scope of this chapter to settle any discussion on the pros and cons of social media monitoring, but we would like to highlight ethical concerns employees and organizations may have as a result of social media usage and monitoring. We would also like to note that the information an employer gleans from intruding into the personal life of its employees may lead to discriminatory practices against the employee and can threaten their privacy, dignity, and freedom (Sánchez Abril, Levin, & Del Riego, 2012), and these threats may lead to negative consequences for both the employee and the organization.

Recommendations for Employers and Organizations

The development of digital technology has created challenges for organizations in managing the behavior that employees engage in and receive from others. The widespread use of the Internet has facilitated many behaviors, both counterproductive and productive. Moving forward we need a better understanding of how technology affects employee behavior, and how we can best minimize detrimental effects. Organization management should develop policies and practices that can provide reasonable monitoring of employee behavior without producing the unintended negative consequences of privacy violation and erosion of trust. In large part this can involve the development of organizational climates that discourage potentially damaging behaviors.

Cyber-mistreatment, such as cyberbullying and cyber incivility, can be approached in much the same way as general bullying and incivility. Organizations should have policies that encourage respectful treatment among employees, and sanction extreme forms of abusive behavior such as bullying. Supervisors should provide support to those targeted, and take corrective actions with those who engage in the behavior. What is important is for there to be trust among supervisors and subordinates so that someone who is a target will feel safe in bringing the issue to his or her supervisor.

Cyberloafing is a complex issue that requires a nuanced response to separate behavior that can be a form of coping that may enhance an individual's ability to properly handle the stresses of a job, versus a withdrawal response by an individual who lacks motivation and is avoiding work. Organizations can develop policies that allow a reasonable amount of cyberloafing as long as it is not detrimental to productivity. One approach is to hold employees accountable for results and not for how they spend their time. Thus, an employee might find that a certain level of pacing is required to avoid excessive fatigue, and that might be accomplished with occasional cyber-breaks.

Insider cybersecurity threat is a complex problem because there are different reasons and mechanisms involved across people. Some cybersecurity should be dealt with as a crime, either theft or purposeful sabotage. Where sensitive data are concerned, systems to monitor access and prevent theft are necessary. Some level of employee monitoring of data is essential to track who accesses data and what is done with it. For nonmalicious threats, the proper handling of data should be considered a vital aspect of job performance, and employees should be held accountable for following proper safety protocols. As noted earlier, there are parallels with the employee accident/safety literature, where success has been achieved with the use of training, and the development of safety climate/culture (Colligan & Cohen, 2004; Wu, Chen, & Li, 2008; Zacharatos, Barling, & Iverson, 2005).

Conclusion

The goal of this chapter was to summarize the research areas of CWB and workplace mistreatment with attention to analogs of newer technology-related behaviors that are becoming more commonplace in today's technology-fueled workplace. We then provided a detailed literature review of newer C-CWB and the C-OHP topics of cyberbullying and cyber incivility. Next, we discussed how workplace monitoring of Internet traffic is becoming a necessity within organizations and social media monitoring is becoming increasingly more commonplace in the hiring, discipline, and firing processes in organizations. Therefore, we highlighted the need for organizations to consider the ethical and wellbeing implications associated with this increased monitoring. While the technology-driven CWB and workplace mistreatment domain is a burgeoning field, we believe the ongoing transition of the workplace (and home) to a technology-fueled world necessitates more attention by organizational psychologists and human resource professionals to these constructs, and we hope this chapter assists with the furthering of technology-related research in this area.

Acknowledgements

Preparation of this chapter was supported by the National Institute of Occupational Safety and Health (NIOSH) and the Sunshine Education and Research Center (Training Grant No. T72OH008438).

References

Abraham, S., & Chengalur-Smith, I. (2010). An overview of social engineering malware: Trends, tactics, and implications. *Technology in Society*, *32*(3), 183–196. https://doi.org/10.1016/j.techsoc.2010.07.001

Ajzen, I. (1985). From intentions to actions: A theory of planned behavior. In *Action control* (pp. 11–39). New York, NY: Springer.

Alge, B. J., & Hansen, S. D. (2014). *Workplace monitoring and surveillance research since "1984": A review and agenda*. In M. D. Coovert & L. F. Thompson (Eds.), *The psychology of workplace technology* (pp. 209–237). New York, NY: Routledge/Taylor & Francis Group.

Anandarajan, M., & Simmers, C. A. (2005). Developing human capital through personal web use in the workplace: Mapping employee perceptions. *Communications of the Association for Information Systems*, *15*(1), 776–791.

Andersson, L. M., & Pearson, C. M. (1999). Tit for tat? The spiraling effect of incivility in the workplace. *The Academy of Management Review, 24*(3), 452–471. doi: 10.2307/259136

Askew, K., Buckner, J. E., Taing, M. U., Ilie, A., Bauer, J. A., & Coovert, M. D. (2014). Explaining cyberloafing: The role of the theory of planned behavior. *Computers in Human Behavior*, *36*, 510–519. doi: 10.1016/j.chb.2014.04.006

Axelrad, E. T., Sticha, P. J., Brdiczka, O., & Shen, J. (2013). *A Bayesian network model for predicting insider threats*. Paper presented at the Security and Privacy Workshops (SPW), 2013 IEEE. San Francisco, CA.

Baruch, Y. (2005). Bullying on the net: Adverse behavior on e-mail and its impact. *Information & Management*, *42*, 361–371. doi: 10.1016/j.im.2004.02.001

Beeler, J. (1983). Insiders seen posing greater threat to DP security than outsiders. *ComputerWorld, 17*(37), 11–12.

Bennett, R. J., & Robinson, S. L. (2000). Development of a measure of workplace deviance. *Journal of Applied Psychology, 85*(3), 349–360. doi: 10.1037//0021-9010.85.3.349

Blanchard, A. L., & Henle, C. A. (2008). Correlates of different forms of cyberloafing: The role of norms and external locus of control. *Computers in Human Behavior, 24*(3), 1067–1084. doi: 10.1016/j.chb.2007.03.008

Challenger, Gray & Christmas (2016). Employers brace for March Madness. Retrieved from www.challengergray.com/press/press-releases/employers-brace-march-madness

Chappell, B. (2017, February 9) Ex-NSA contractor accused of taking classified information is indicted. Retrieved September 7, 2019, from www.npr.org/sections/thetwo-way/2017/02/09/514275544/ex-nsa-contractor-indicted-for-taking-classifed-information

Chinchani, R., Iyer, A., Ngo, H. Q., & Upadhyaya, S. (2005). Towards a theory of insider threat assessment. In *2005 International Conference on Dependable Systems and Networks, Proceedings* (pp. 108–117). Yokohama, Japan.

Colligan, M. J., & Cohen, A. (2004). The role of training in promoting workplace safety and health. In J. Barling, & M. R. Frone (Eds.), *The psychology of workplace safety* (pp. 223–248). Washington, DC: American Psychological Association.

Cortina, L. M., Kabat-Farr, D., Magley, V. J., & Nelson, K. (2017). Researching rudeness: The past, present, and future of the science of incivility. *Journal of Occupational Health Psychology, 22*(3), 299–313. doi: 10.1037/ocp0000089

Cortina, L. M., & Magley, V. J. (2003). Raising voice, risking retaliation: Events following interpersonal mistreatment in the workplace. *Journal of Occupational Health Psychology, 8*(4), 247–265. doi: 10.1037/1076-8998.8.4.247

Coyne, I., Farley, S., Axtell, C., Sprigg, C., Best, L., & Kwok, O. (2017). Understanding the relationship between experiencing workplace cyberbullying, employee mental strain and job satisfaction: A dysempowerment approach. *International Journal of Human Resource Management, 28*(7), 945–972. doi: 10.1080/09585192.2015.1116454

Crossler, R. E., Johnston, A. C., Lowry, P. B., Hu, Q., Warkentin, M., & Baskerville, R. (2013). Future directions for behavioral information security research. *Computers & Security, 32*, 90–101. doi: 10.1016/j.cose.2012.09.010

D'Cruz, P., & Noronha, E. (2013). Navigating the extended reach: Target experiences of cyberbullying at work. *Information and Organization, 23*(4), 324–343. doi: 10.1016/j.infoandorg.2013.09.001

Dalal, R. S., & Girab, A. (2016). Insider threat in cyber security: What the organizational psychology literature on counterproductive work behavior can and cannot (yet) tell us. In S. J. Zaccaro, R. S. Dalal, L. E. Tetrick, & J. A. Steinke (Eds.), *Psychosocial dynamics of cyber security*: New York, NY: Routledge, 122–140.

Determann, L. (2012). Social media privacy: A dozen myths and facts. *Stanford Technology Law Review, 7*, 1–14.

Einarsen, S. (2000). Harassment and bullying at work: A review of the Scandinavian approach. *Aggression and Violent Behavior, 5*(4), 379–401. doi: 10.1016/S1359-1789(98)00043-3

Einarsen, S., Hoel, H., & Notelaers, G. (2009). Measuring exposure to bullying and harassment at work: Validity, factor structure and psychometric properties of the Negative Acts Questionnaire – revised. *Work and Stress, 23*(1), 24–44. doi: 10.1080/02678370902815673

Farley, S., Coyne, I., Axtell, C., & Sprigg, C. (2016). Design, development and validation of a workplace cyberbullying measure, the WCM. *Work and Stress, 30*(4), 293–317. doi: 10.1080/02678373.2016.1255998

Fox, S., & Spector, P. E. (2010). Instrumental counterproductive work behavior and the theory of planned behavior: A "cold cognitive" approach to complement "hot affective" theories of CWB. In L. L. Neider & C. A. Schriesheim (Eds.), *Research in management. The "dark" side of management* (pp. 93–114). Charlotte, NC: IAP Information Age Publishing.

Giumetti, G. W., Hatfield, A. L., Scisco, J. L., Schroeder, A. N., Muth, E. R., & Kowalski, R. M. (2013). What a rude e-mail! Examining the differential effects of incivility versus support on mood, energy, engagement, and performance in an online context. *Journal of Occupational Health Psychology, 18*(3), 297–309. doi: 10.1037/a0032851

Giumetti, G. W., McKibben, E. S., Hatfield, A. L., Schroeder, A. N., & Kowalski, R. M. (2012). Cyber incivility @ work: The new age of interpersonal deviance. *Cyberpsychology Behavior and Social Networking, 15*(3), 148–154. doi: 10.1089/cyber.2011.0336

Glassman, J., Prosch, M., & Shao, B. B. M. (2015). To monitor or not to monitor: Effectiveness of a cyberloafing countermeasure. *Information & Management, 52*(2), 170–182. doi: 10.1016/j.im.2014.08.001

Greitzer, F. L., Kangas, L. J., Noonan, C. F., & Dalton, A. C. (2010). *Identifying at-risk employees: A behavioral model for predicting potential insider threats*. Arlington, VA: US Department of Energy,

Gruys, M. L., & Sackett, P. R. (2003). Investigating the dimensionality of counterproductive work behavior. *International Journal of Selection and Assessment, 11*(1), 30–42. doi: 10.1111/1468-2389.00224

Hershcovis, M. S. (2011). "Incivility, social undermining, bullying ... oh my!": A call to reconcile constructs within workplace aggression research. *Journal of Organizational Behavior, 32*(3), 499–519. doi: 10.1002/job.689

Hobfoll, S. E. (1989). Conservation of resources: A new attempt at conceptualizing stress. *The American Psychologist, 44*(3), 513–524. http://dx.doi.org/10.1037/0003-066X.44.3.513

Hoel, H., Sheehan, M. J., Cooper, C. L., & Einarsen, S. (2011). Organisational effects of workplace bullying. In S. Einarsen, H. Hoel, D. Zapf, & C. L. Cooper (Eds.), *Bullying and harassment in the workplace: Developments in theory, research, and practice* (pp. 129–148). Boca Raton, FL: CRC Press.

Jex, S. M., & Britt, T. W. (2014). *Organizational psychology: A scientist-practitioner approach* (3rd ed.). Hoboken, NJ: Wiley.

Kaptein, M. (2008). Developing a measure of unethical behavior in the workplace: A stakeholder perspective. *Journal of Management, 34*(5), 978–1008. doi: 10.1177/0149206308318614

Karasek, R. A., Jr. (1979). Job demands, job decision latitude, and mental strain: Implications for job redesign. *Administrative Science Quarterly, 24*(2), 285–308. doi: 10.2307/2392498

Koerner, B.L. (2016, Oct 23). Inside the cyberattack that shocked the US government. Retrieved September 7, 2019, from www.wired.com/2016/10/inside-cyberattack-shocked-us-government/

Kowalski, R. M., Giumetti, G. W., Schroeder, A. N., & Lattanner, M. R. (2014). Bullying in the digital age: A critical review and meta-analysis of cyberbullying research among youth. *Psychological Bulletin*, *140*(4), 1073–1137. doi: 10.1037/a0035618

Krajcevska, A., Pindek, S., & Spector, P. E. (2017). *Cyberloafing as an adaptive response to boredom*. Paper presented at the Southern Management Association 2017 Conference, Saint Pete Beach, FL.

Krischer, M. M., Penney, L. M., & Hunter, E. M. (2010). Can counterproductive work behaviors be productive? CWB as emotion-focused coping. *Journal of Occupational Health Psychology*, *15*(2), 154–166. doi: 10.1037/a0018349

Kruger, J., Epley, N., Parker, J., & Ng, Z.-W. (2005). Egocentrism over e-mail: can we communicate as well as we think? *Journal of Personality and Social Psychology*, *89*(6), 925–936. doi: 10.1037/0022-3514.89.6.925

Leymann, H. (1996). The content and development of mobbing at work. *European Journal of Work and Organizational Psychology*, *5*(2), 165–184. doi: 10.1080/13594329608414853

Li, Q. (2006). Cyberbullying in schools: A research of gender differences. *School Psychology International*, *27*(2), 157–170. doi: 10.1177/0143034306064547

Liberman, B., Seidman, G., McKenna, K. V. A., & Buffardi, L. E. (2011). Employee job attitudes and organizational characteristics as predictors of cyberloafing. *Computers in Human Behavior*, *27*(6), 2192–2199. doi: 10.1016/j.chb.2011.06.015

Lim, V. K. G. (2002). The IT way of loafing on the job: Cyberloafing, neutralizing and organizational justice. *Journal of Organizational Behavior*, *23*(5), 675–694. doi: 10.1002/job.161

Lim, V. K. G., & Chen, D. J. Q. (2012). Cyberloafing at the workplace: Gain or drain on work? *Behaviour & Information Technology*, *31*(4), 343–353. doi: 10.1080/01449290903353054

Lim, V. K. G., & Teo, T. S. H. (2005). Prevalence, perceived seriousness, justification and regulation of cyberloafing in Singapore – An exploratory study. *Information & Management*, *42*(8), 1081–1093. doi: 10.1016/j.im.2004.12.002

Lim, V. K. G., & Teo, T. S. H. (2009). Mind your E-manners: Impact of cyber incivility on employees' work attitude and behavior. *Information & Management*, *46*(8), 419–425. doi: 10.1016/j.im.2009.06.006

Lyons, B. D., Hoffman, B. J., Bommer, W. H., Kennedy, C. L., & Hetrick, A. L. (2016). Off-duty deviance: Organizational policies and evidence for two prevention strategies. *Journal of Applied Psychology*, *101*(4), 463–483.

Magklaras, G. B., & Furnell, S. M. (2002). Insider threat prediction tool: Evaluating the probability of IT misuse. *Computers & Security*, *21*(1), 62–73.

Mehan, J. E. (2016). *Insider threat: A guide to understanding, detecting, and defending against the enemy from within*: Ely, UK: IT Governance Publishing.

National Labor Relations Board (2012). The NLRB and social media. Retrieved September 9, 2019, from www.nlrb.gov/rights-we-protect/rights/nlrb-and-social-media

Neal, A., & Griffith, M. A. (2002). Safety climate and safety behaviour. *Australian Journal of Management*, *27*(Special Issue), 67–75.

Niedl, K. (1996). Mobbing and well-being: Economic and personnel development implications. *European Journal of Work and Organizational Psychology*, *5*(2), 239–249. doi: 10.1080/13594329608414857

nobullying.com. (2017). The top six unforgettable cyberbullying cases ever. Retrieved September 7, 2019, from https://nobullying.com/six-unforgettable-cyber-bullying-cases/

Nurse, J. R. C., Buckley, O., Legg, P. A., Goldsmith, M., Creese, S., Wright, G. R. T., & Whitty, M. (2014). *Understanding insider threat: A framework for characterising attacks*. Paper presented at the Security and Privacy Workshops (SPW), 2014 IEEE. San Jose, CA.

O'Neill, T. A., Hambley, L. A., & Bercovich, A. (2014). Prediction of cyberslacking when employees are working away from the office. *Computers in Human Behavior*, *34*, 291–298. doi: 10.1016/j.chb.2014.02.015

Park, Y., Fritz, C., & Jex, S. M. (2015). Daily cyber incivility and distress: The moderating roles of resources at work and home. *Journal of Management*. doi: 10.1177/0149206315576796

Pfleeger, S. L., Predd, J. B., Hunker, J., & Bulford, C. (2010). Insiders behaving badly: Addressing bad actors and their actions. *IEEE Transactions on Information Forensics and Security*, *5*(1), 169–179. doi: 10.1109/TIFS.2009.2039591

Porath, C., & Pearson, C. (2013). The price of incivility. *Harvard Business Review*, *91*(1/2), 114–121.

Privitera, C., & Campbell, M. A. (2009). Cyberbullying: The new face of workplace bullying? *Cyberpsychology & Behavior*, *12*(4), 395–400. doi: 10.1089/cpb.2009.0025

Purcell, K., & Rainie, L. (2014). Technology's impact on workers. Retrieved from www.pewinternet.org/2014/12/30/technologys-impact-on-workers/

Restubog, S. L. D., Garcia, P., Toledano, L. S., Amarnani, R. K., Tolentino, L. R., & Tang, R. L. (2011). Yielding to (cyber)-temptation: Exploring the buffering role of self-control in the relationship between organizational justice and cyberloafing behavior in the workplace. *Journal of Research in Personality*, *45*(2), 247–251. doi: 10.1016/j.jrp.2011.01.006

Rizzo, J. R., House, R. J., & Lirtzman, S. I. (1970). Role conflict and ambiguity in complex organizations. *Administrative Science Quarterly*, *15*(2), 150–163.

Salm, L. (2017). 70% of employers are snooping candidates' social media profiles. Retrieved from www.careerbuilder.com/advice/social-media-survey-2017

Sánchez Abril, P., Levin, A., & Del Riego, A. (2012). Blurred boundaries: Social media privacy and the twenty-first-century employee. *American Business Law Journal*, *49*(1), 63–124. doi: 10.1111/j.1744-1714.2011.01127.x

Schilpzand, P., de Pater, I. E., & Erez, A. (2016). Workplace incivility: A review of the literature and agenda for future research. *Journal of Organizational Behavior*, *37*, S57–S88. doi: 10.1002/job.1976

Shaw, E. D. (2006). The role of behavioral research and profiling in malicious cyber insider investigations. *Digital Investigation*, *3*(1), 20–31. https://doi.org/10.1016/j.diin.2006.01.006

Smith, P. K., Mahdavi, J., Carvalho, M., Fisher, S., Russell, S., & Tippett, N. (2008). Cyberbullying: Its nature and impact in secondary school pupils. *Journal of Child Psychology and Psychiatry*, *49*(4), 376–385. doi: 10.1111/j.1469-7610.2007.01846.x

Snyman, R., & Loh, J. M. I. (2015). Cyberbullying at work: The mediating role of optimism between cyberbullying and job outcomes. *Computers in Human Behavior, 53*, 161–168. doi: 10.1016/j.chb.2015.06.050

Spector, P. E., & Fox, S. (2005). The stressor–emotion model of counterproductive work behavior. In S. Fox, & P. E. Spector (Eds.), *Counterproductive work behavior: Investigations of actors and targets.* (pp. 151–174). Washington, DC: American Psychological Association.

Spector, P. E., Fox, S., Penney, L. M., Bruursema, K., Goh, A., & Kessler, S. (2006). The dimensionality of counterproductivity: Are all counterproductive behaviors created equal? *Journal of Vocational Behavior, 68*(3), 446–460. doi: 10.1016/j.jvb.2005.10.005

Stoughton, J. W., Thompson, L. F., & Meade, A. W. (2015). Examining applicant reactions to the use of social networking websites in pre-employment screening. *Journal of Business and Psychology, 30*(1), 73–88. doi: 10.1007/s10869-013-9333-6

Tepper, B. J. (2000). Consequences of abusive supervision. *Academy of Management Journal, 43*(2), 178–190. doi: 10.2307/1556375

Tokunaga, R. S. (2010). Following you home from school: A critical review and synthesis of research on cyberbullying victimization. *Computers in Human Behavior, 26*(3), 277–287. doi: 10.1016/j.chb.2009.11.014

Umphress, E. E., Bingham, J. B., & Mitchell, M. S. (2010). Unethical behavior in the name of the company: The moderating effect of organizational identification and positive reciprocity beliefs on unethical pro-organizational behavior. *Journal of Applied Psychology, 95*(4), 769–780. doi: 10.1037/a0019214

Van den Brande, W., Baillien, E., De Witte, H., Vander Elst, T., & Godderis, L. (2016). The role of work stressors, coping strategies and coping resources in the process of workplace bullying: A systematic review and development of a comprehensive model. *Aggression and Violent Behavior, 29*, 61–71. doi: 10.1016/j.avb.2016.06.004

Vranjes, I., Baillien, E., Vandebosch, H., Erreygers, S., & De Witte, H. (2017). The dark side of working online: Towards a definition and an Emotion Reaction model of workplace cyberbullying. *Computers in Human Behavior, 69*, 324–334. doi: 10.1016/j.chb.2016.12.055

Warkentin, M., & Willison, R. (2009). Behavioral and policy issues in information systems security: The insider threat. *European Journal of Information Systems, 18*(2), 101–105. doi: 10.1057/ejis.2009.12

Weiss, H. M., & Cropanzano, R. (1996). Affective events theory: A theoretical discussion of the structure, causes and consequences of affective experiences at work. *Research in Organizational Behavior, 18*, 1–74.

Wu, T. C., Chen, C. H., & Li, C. C. (2008). A correlation among safety leadership, safety climate and safety performance. *Journal of Loss Prevention in the Process Industries, 21*(3), 307–318. https://doi.org/10.1016/j.jlp.2007.11.001

Yang, L. Q., Caughlin, D. E., Gazica, M. W., Truxillo, D. M., & Spector, P. E. (2014). Workplace mistreatment climate and potential employee and organizational outcomes: A meta-analytic review from the target's perspective. *Journal of Occupational Health Psychology, 19*(3), 315–335. doi: 10.1037/a0036905

Zacharatos, A., Barling, J., & Iverson, R. D. (2005). High-performance work systems and occupational safety. *Journal of Applied Psychology*, *90*(1), 77–93. doi: 10.1037/0021-9010.90.1.77

Zakrzewski, C. (2016). The key to getting workers to stop wasting time online. Retrieved from www.wsj.com/articles/the-key-to-getting-workers-to-stop-wasting-time-online-1457921545

25 Implications of the Changing Nature of Work for the Employee–Organization Relationship

Mindy K. Shoss, Robert Eisenberger, Juseob Lee*, Blaine A. Lewis*, Dustin Maneethai*, Xueqi Wen*, Jia Yu*, and Jimmy Zheng*

As detailed throughout this volume, the past several decades have borne witness to substantial changes in (a) the economic, social, and political context surrounding work; (b) the nature of work itself; and (c) the characteristics of individuals employed in the labor force.

An altered employee–organization relationship (hereafter EOR) is one of the most oft-cited outcomes of these changes. For example, Rousseau and Wade-Benzoni (1995) argued that "present and likely future employment relationships reflect a fundamental shift in the nature of work" (p. 300). Similarly, Bidwell, Briscoe, Fernandez-Mateo, and Sterling (2013) surmised that "recent changes in US employment relationships have substantially redrawn the social contract between workers, employers, investors, and other stakeholders" (p. 97). More recently, Chernyak-hai and Rabenu (2018) questioned the contemporary relevance of social exchange–based theories of the EOR, such as organizational support and psychological contract theories.

The goal of this chapter is to consider how the changing nature of work has shaped, and will continue to shape, the EOR. First, we briefly detail key elements of the EOR as captured by the social exchange perspective, which has been the predominant theoretical perspective used to understand the EOR. Second, we discuss general trends in the EOR in light of questions about the extent to which workers' relationships with their organization can still be viewed as reciprocal, open-ended, and reflecting high involvement from both parties. Third, we discuss in greater depth six specific issues with implications for the EOR. The first three issues concern "arm's-length" employment contracts involving temporary and part-time workers, independent contractors, and tripartite employment relationships. The experiences of these workers have unfortunately gone relatively unaddressed in the organizational science literatures, arguably to the detriment of theory and practice (Bergman & Jean, 2015). The remaining sections explore in greater depth three trends linked to changing

---

* Authors contributed equally to this chapter

employment practices: job insecurity, job hopping, and income inequality. We orient our discussion towards examining what the data have to say about the state of the EOR in an effort to provide a data-driven analysis of these important questions. In cases where the data are thin, we highlight crucial avenues for future investigation.

The Employee–Organization Relationship: Key Constructs and Theories

The EOR, referring to employees' association with their work organization (Shore, Coyle-Shapiro, & Tetrick, 2012), has long been an important area of study in organization science. Organization theorists have argued that employees provide effort and loyalty in exchange for material and socioemotional rewards (e.g., Blau, 1964; Cropanzano & Mitchell 2005). The two major contemporary theoretical approaches to the EOR, perceived organizational support (Eisenberger, Huntington, Hutchison, & Sowa, 1986) and psychological contracts (Conway & Briner, 2005; Rousseau, 1995), are elaborations of social exchange theory. According to social exchange theory, individuals enter into relationships with other persons, groups, or organizations to maximize their material or socioemotional resources (Blau, 1964). Society promotes reciprocity as a norm to foster the strengthening of social relationships (Gouldner, 1960).

Considering the EOR, social exchange accounts hold that employees who perceive their organization has desirable resources are motivated toward voluntary actions that go beyond what is required, meanwhile observing whether these efforts are reciprocated by the organization. Correspondingly, managers, representing the organization, may provide promising employees with praise and choice assignments while attending to whether employees reciprocate with increased performance. As such reciprocation increases, employees develop increased trust that their investments in the organizaton will be borne out and attend more to long-term outcomes rather than short-term exchange (Shore, Tetrick, Lynch, & Barksdale, 2006). To the degree that employees possess the knowledge, skills, and abilities to enact performance valued by the organization, and the organization possesses the capability to supply resources desired by employees, strong social exchange relationships will be fostered.

Organizational support theory and psychological contract theory elaborate these basic propositions of social exchange theory. According to organizational support theory (Eisenberger & Stinglhamber, 2011; Kurtessis et al., 2017), employees form a general perception concerning the extent to which the organization values their contributions and cares about their wellbeing (perceived organizational support, or POS). POS meets socioemotional needs (e.g., approval, esteem, and affiliation) and provides evidence to employees that their increased efforts on behalf of the organization will be rewarded. Employees reciprocate POS with a greater affective commitment to the organization and efforts on the organization's behalf. POS is strengthened by favorable treatment received from the organization and its representatives, especially actions that appear motivated by a high regard for employees' welfare, as opposed to the organization's self-interest (Eisenberger, Cummings, Armeli, & Lynch, 1997). Further, the relationship between POS and affective commitment has recently been found to be stronger when employees believe the organization is competent in fulfilling its goals (Kim, Eisenberger, & Baik, 2016). Being positively evaluated by a more effective organization helps assure employees who have high POS that the organization can effectively meet their needs and goals. Qualitative and quantitative reviews of the literature have provided extensive support for these major tenets of organizational support theory (Eisenberger & Stinglhamber, 2011; Kurtessis et al., 2017).

The other primary social exchange approach to the EOR is psychological contract theory. Where organizational support theory emphasizes the favorableness of employees' work experiences as an antecedent of POS, psychological contract theory is concerned with the mutual obligations between employee and employer based on implicit or explicit promises (Schein, 1980). Rousseau (1995) looked at psychological contracts from the employee's viewpoint, and differentiated more economic, transactional contracts from longer-term, relational contracts that include the exchange of socioemotional resources. Tsui, Pearce, Porter, and Tripoli (1997) suggested that organizations with high investment strategies in employees would be more likely to cultivate long-term relational contracts. Shore and Tetrick (1994) argued that employees who sought a long-term relationship with their organization would be more likely than short-termers to seek out information regarding mutual obligations.

As previously noted, several popular and academic sources have pronounced the social exchange relationship between employees and the organization a relic of the past. Large-scale shifts in how employees and employers approach their relationship might suggest that social exchange–based accounts of the EOR, such as organizational support theory and psychological contract theory, are outdated or apply to only a small percentage of employees and employers. However, as we will see, the empirical evidence suggests these accounts continue to have considerable relevance for today's evolving workplace. We first discuss general trends in the EOR before turning to specific issues.

General Trends in the Employee–Organization Relationship

Table 25.1 presents key changes in employment practices that have occurred since the 1970s. This list is by no means exclusive, although we have sought to highlight those changes that are widely thought to be most symptomatic of an altered EOR. Most commentators view these trends as reflecting a fundamental shift away from a time when employer and employees desired relational psychological contracts and long-term mutual investment and commitment (Bidwell et al., 2013; Farber, 2008). Instead, such changes are thought

Table 25.1 *Key changes in employment practices since the 1970s*

1. Use of layoffs for strategic purposes to create "lean and mean" organizations
2. Emphasis on shareholder value, where "downsize and distribute" has increasingly replaced the "retain and reinvest" approach to organizational profits
3. Declining union participation and labor power
4. Career mobility increasingly occurring through external as opposed to internal labor markets
5. Increasing adoption of market-based retirement programs
6. Decline in organizational tenure
7. Job insecurity among groups of workers not typically insecure
8. Increased job hopping and emphasis on the protean/boundary-less career
9. Growth of nonstandard and "arm's-length" employment relationship (e.g., part-time, temporary, contingent workers)
10. Growing occurrence of tripartite employment relationships as employees are hired through intermediaries
11. Shift to performance-based incentive pay
12. Increasing pay inequality
13. Increased work–family benefits
14. Increased use of flexible work arrangements
15. Increased attention to diversity management practices
16. Increased emphasis on worker treatment (e.g., Forbes' Best Places to Work List)

Note. For reference, see Arthur (1994), Bidwell et al. (2013), Davis (2009), Dobbin & Kelly (2007), Farber (2008), Hall (1996), Hogler (Chapter 8, this volume), Jiang (Chapter 9, this volume), Kalleberg (2009); Keys & Danziger (2008), Matos, Galinsky, & Bond (2017).

to be indicative of both employees and employers abandoning the EOR in favor of more transactional and self-interested work arrangements. Note, however, that not all changes have been negative. Although much work remains to be done, increasingly greater attention has been paid to issues of work–family practices and to the fair and equitable treatment of employees (Bidwell et al., 2013).

We (Eisenberger, Rockstuhl, Shoss, Wen, & Dulebohn, 2019) recently conducted a large cross-temporal meta-analysis to investigate the question of whether the social exchange relationship between employees and employers has weakened over the past quarter-century. We focused on POS as one indicator of the EOR. We reasoned that if employees and employers have abandoned the social exchange relationship, we would observe (a) decreases in mean levels of POS over time, and (b) reductions in strength of the relationship between POS and its antecedents and outcomes, as indications of reduced willingness of employees to attribute favorable treatment to the beneficence of their employer and to reciprocate favorable treatment. Our results suggested that mean levels have slightly increased over time, albeit at levels only indicating average or moderate exchange quality. Given that the antecedent and consequent relationships have remained stable, we surmised that employees are willing to engage in relational social exchanges with their employers, and that current relationships, on average are of similar quality to the past.

While these findings suggest that workers and organizations have not on the whole abandoned the EOR, there is some evidence to suggest that organizations are doing better on some elements than others. Data from the General Social Survey (Smith, Davern, Freese, & Hout, 2018), a national cross-sectional survey of the American public, suggest that organizations today are providing more workers with several desirable inducements, especially regarding the social elements of the job. For example, 41% of 2016 respondents vs. 25.4% of 1989 respondents indicated that their job is useful in society, while 47.4% of 2016 respondents as compared with 28.8% of 1989 respondents said that social usefulness is a desirable quality of a job. On the more pessimistic side, however, organizations have not delivered on workers' desires for advancement opportunities and pay. Of 2016 respondents, 9.1% indicated that their job provides advancement opportunities as compared with 9% in 1986, despite 49.6% of 2016 respondents and 41.3% of 1989 respondents indicating that advancement opportunities are important. Similarly, 5.7% of 2016 respondents vs. 4.4% of 1989 respondents indicated that their job provides high pay, despite 29% of 2016 respondents and 24.7% of 1989 respondents indicating high pay is important. Interestingly, while there has been little change in the percentage of workers reporting job security (33.8% in 2016 vs. 28.6% in 1989), the percentage of people who view job security as important has increased dramatically from 54.5% in 1989 to 73.6% in 2016. As Cascio (Chapter 15, this volume) notes, to the extent that organizations can reduce uncertainty and provide opportunities for employees to advance and achieve higher pay, they may be rewarded with a more positive EOR on the part of employees.

Specific Issues/Challenges to the Employee–Organization Relationship

Social exchange accounts have provided plausible explanations of traditional EORs in which employees anticipate full-time employment for a substantial period. To the extent to which this reflects a majority of employees, the key tenets of the accounts seem to hold. Yet, because alternative work arrangements are increasing, it is important to examine the applicability of social exchange theory, particularly organizational support theory and psychological contract theory, to these work arrangements. Is POS an important resource for employees with alternative work arrangements, one for which they are willing to form strong exchange relationships with the organization? For employees with alternative work arrangements, has the nature of the psychological contract changed and, if so, how? The following sections address three categories of alternative work arrangements: temporary and part-time work, independent contractors, and tripartite employment relationships. We also discuss three challenges to the EOR, namely: job insecurity, job hopping, and income inequality.

Part-Time and Temporary Employees

Compared to permanent full-time employment, workers employed as temporary or part-time have limited temporal attachment to organizations (George & Chattopadhyay, 2017). In this respect, temporary employment focuses on the length of the employment contract, whereby workers are hired directly by the organization for a specific period of time. The length of this employment relationship is defined by fixed-term contracts that end on a predetermined date or on the completion of project or task (Kalleberg, 2000). Part-time employment concerns the length of working hours, whereby workers are employed in jobs with less than "normal" work hours (Thurman & Trah, 1990). The number of work hours that defines part-time work varies across countries but is usually considered as less than 30 or 35 hours per week (Van Bastelaer, Lemaître, & Marianna, 1997).

Evidence of Changes. The past several decades have seen a growth in temporary and part-time employment across labor markets worldwide. For instance, from 1980 to 2015, the Organisation for Economic Co-operation and Development (OECD) countries experienced an increase from 9.2 to 11.3% of temporary employment and an increase from 13.2 to 16.8% of part-time employment (OECD, 2018). A variety of factors have contributed to this increase. In response to global economic changes that have increased competition, uncertainty, and shareholder pressure for greater profits (Kalleberg, 2000), organizations have increasingly employed temporary and part-time workers because of the perceived benefits of scheduling flexibility, human capital allocation, and the cost savings associated with reduced worker wages and benefits (George & Chattopadhyay, 2017; Thurman & Trah, 1990). At the same time, advancements in communication and information systems have made it easier for organizations to employ temporary workers (Kalleberg, 2000). Alternatively, the changing demographic composition of the workforce, marked by an increase of women workers, older workers, and college students, has contributed to a greater demand for temporary and part-time employment (Kalleberg, 2000).

Implications. Some research suggests that the nature of the psychological contract of workers employed as temporary or part-time may differ from those employed in permanent full-time work. Individuals with ongoing and full-time employment are more likely to develop an EOR that is grounded in trust, reciprocity, and long-term commitment, which are all aspects of a relational psychological contract (De Cuyper & De Witte, 2007; Gakovic & Tetrick, 2003). In contrast, temporary contracts are organized around flexibility and a limited relationship with the organization (Van Dyne & Ang, 1998), in which monetizable exchanges (e.g., pay for attendance) are made over a specific period of time (Rousseau, 1990). Millward and Hopkins (1998) found that permanent (vs. temporary) workers scored higher on a measure of relational contract. In contrast, temporary (vs. permanent) workers scored higher on a measure of transactional contract. Additionally, full-time employees scored higher than part-time employees on a measure of relational contract. Taken together, this suggests that a shift from permanent full-time employment to one that is temporary and part-time may result in a workforce with psychological contracts that are on average less relational and more transactional in nature.

In contrast, the limited existing research seems to suggest that POS plays, at least, an equally important role in the social exchange relationships of part-time (vs. full-time) and temporary (vs. permanent) workers. For instance, Gakovic and Tetrick (2003) found that the positive relationships between POS and other social exchange variables (e.g., organizational commitment, fulfillment of obligations) did not differ across full-time and part-time workers. This suggests that regardless of work status (i.e., full-time, part-time), an employee who perceives that the organization values and cares about him/her will also have a socio-emotional relationship with that organization. Another study by Coyle-Shapiro and Kessler (2002) found that while temporary workers engaged in fewer organizational citizenship behaviors than permanent workers, the positive relationships between POS, employer inducements and organizational citizenship behavior were stronger for temporary as opposed to permanent workers. Their explanation for this unexpected finding is that due to the short-term nature of temporary contracts, temporary workers are less likely to expect a long-term relationship and thus will attribute greater importance to actual inducements instead of potential inducements that may appear in the future. Consequently, temporary workers may adopt a contingent view of the exchange relationship, in which their enactment of organizational citizenship behavior is contingent upon what they actually receive from the organization. In contrast, permanent workers may engage in organizational citizenship behavior independent of received inducements (Coyle-Shapiro & Kessler, 2002). Taken together, these findings suggest that POS may indeed play a key role in social exchange for employees in temporary and part-time work arrangements.

In sum, temporary and part-time work arrangements have increased. Although temporary and part-time workers still hold psychological contracts, their contracts appear to be, on average, less relational and more transactional in nature. However, POS appears to still play an important role in social exchange for temporary and part-time workers.

Independent Contractors

Independent contractors have been defined as self-employed individuals who sell their skills and services to an organization for a fixed term or through project completion (Connelly & Gallagher, 2006). In determining whether an individual is an employee or contractor, the US Internal Revenue Service (IRS) reviews various factors including whether or not the contractor earns a profit or suffers a loss, works for more than one organization at a time, invests in their own equipment and tools, and pays their own business expenses (Fragoso & Kleiner, 2005).

Evidence of Changes. The past decade has seen a rise in independent contractors. From 2005 to 2015, the proportion of independent contractors in the United States increased from 6.9 to 8.4% of the total workforce. This contrasts with the decade before which observed an increase from 6.3 to 6.9% from 1995 to 2005 (Katz & Krueger, 2016). One factor driving this increase is organizational attempts to build flexibility by maintaining a core group of permanent employees and rapidly expanding and contracting its contingent workforce, which includes temporary and part-time employees, tripartite employees, and independent contractors (Kalleberg, 2000). A second factor is the rise of the shared economy, in which individuals provide underutilized goods and services to others, often through online platforms (e.g., Uber, Airbnb; Hall & Krueger, 2016). In contrast to traditional organizational structures, the shared economy allows organizations to employ a small group of core employees and a large labor force of geographically dispersed independent contractors (Kalleberg, 2000).

Implications. Independent contractors have various reasons for seeking contract work, including increased flexibility in when and how they accomplish their work, the ability to choose the clients they work with, and as supplemental income (Connelly & Gallagher, 2006; Kalleberg, 2000). Therefore, unlike full-time employees and other contingent employment arrangements, such as temporary and seasonal workers, independent contractors may enter organizations with an exchange relationship outlined by the exchange of skills and services for economic reward that is strengthened with continued reciprocal exchange over time (Chen & Brudney, 2009).

The distinction between independent contractors and employees can be difficult from both a legal and contractor perspective (Connelly & Gallagher, 2006). While misclassification can occur for several reasons, the primary legal differentiator is the extent to which the organization exerts control over how the work is done (Kalleberg, 2000). For example, in the case of *Vizcaino III v. Microsoft*, the court ruled that contract workers were indeed employees of Microsoft, as contractors were given similar roles and responsibilities to those of employees, such as working in project teams with regular employees and having access to secure company files and resources (Kondrasuk, Reed, & Jurinski, 2001). As contractors perform similar roles and responsibilities to full-time permanent employees, their base of comparison shifts to those of regular employees. Thus, contractors may perceive an imbalance in the skills and services provided versus the rewards received from the organization, which may develop into deleterious attitudes and behaviors towards the organization (Connelly & Gallagher, 2006; Wilkin, 2013).

With respect to organizational commitment, independent contractors differ in comparison to permanent employees and other contingent work arrangements. Independent contractors often have multiple clients, and commitment towards each client often varies as relationships strengthen or weaken over time. If the formal relationship between the contractor and organization is long-term, individuals may become more embedded with organizational members, fulfilling socioemotional needs. However, independent contractors with short-term ties may be less committed toward client organizations, as the exchange relationship is based on transactional rather than relational exchanges (Gallagher & Parks, 2001; Rousseau & Wade-Benzoni, 1995). Independent contractors are also able to exercise a high level of volition, in which the contractor perceives a degree of choice in the terms of the relationship. While volition may not influence affective commitment towards the client organization, it may impact normative commitment, in which the contractor feels obligated to fulfill the responsibilities of the contract (Connelly & Gallagher, 2006).

In sum, the proportion of independent contractors in the workforce is rising. Contract work increases workforce flexibility and allows workers greater autonomy in their time and work. Therefore, the EOR is outlined as an exchange of skills and services for economic rewards, and if the relationship extends into the future, relational exchanges also occur, fulfilling socioemotional needs of the contractor and building commitment towards the organization.

Tripartite Employment Relationships

In an increasingly competitive and globalized economy, more and more organizations tend to focus on their core competencies and outsource peripheral work to temporary staffing agencies for the benefit of reducing cost and enhancing efficiency and flexibility. Agency workers refer to individuals who are recruited and paid by a staffing agency but are assigned by the agency to assume actual work responsibilities at the agency's client organization. In this type of work arrangement, we see a tripartite employment relationship: agency workers work for the client organization and under its supervision but remain the legal employees of the staffing agency (Claes, 2005; Liden, Wayne, Kraimer, & Sparrowe, 2003).

Evidence of Changes. From 1982 to 1998, the temporary staffing industry had a remarkable increase of 577% in the number of jobs provided, compared with the 41% increase in the number of jobs across all industries (GAO, 2000). This trend has continued. Katz and Krueger (2016) conducted the Contingent Worker Survey to monitor changes of contingency work in the United States from 2005 to 2015. They found a significant increase in the percentage of workers engaged in non-permanent jobs, among which the percentage of agency workers had the largest rise from 0.6% to 3.1% of the total workforce. Similarly, agency work has been recognized as an established feature in the labor markets of most European Union member countries and has doubled since the 1990s (CIETT, 2015).

Implications. Tripartite employment relationships involve two forms of EORs: the relationship between agency workers and their agency organization, and the relationship between agency workers and the agency's client organization. Accordingly, agency workers deal with two bosses simultaneously, making the discussions on their EORs more complex than for traditional workers (Claes, 2005; Liden et al., 2003).

In general, social exchange theory can still apply to this atypical employment relationship. Previous research has demonstrated a positive association between agency workers' POS and job satisfaction as well as organizational commitment toward the client organization (Liden et al., 2003). Psychological contract fulfillment has likewise shown similar patterns with job attitudes, wellbeing, and performance among temporary agency workers (Claes, 2005).

However, research suggests that social exchange theory may be less relevant for explaining the EOR of agency workers than of permanent workers. For example, De Cuyper, Notelaers, and De Witte (2009) found that the negative relationship between job insecurity and affective commitment was weaker among agency workers than among permanent workers because agency workers' relationships with the client organization are characterized as transactional and short-term. Both agency workers and the client organization have lower expectations for developing and maintaining high-quality long-term exchange relationships (De Cuyper et al., 2009).

While fewer studies have focused on the employment relationship between agency workers and the staffing agency, this relationship is also of importance. According to the limited research in this area, agency workers develop distinct organizational commitment toward different foci (agencies vs. client organizations). For instance, Liden and colleagues (2003) found that organization/agency procedural justice and POS led to commitment toward the client organization/agency respectively. They further investigated the spillover effect of agency workers' commitment toward the agency on their commitment toward the client organization. Surprisingly, they found a negative spillover effect: the more committed agency workers were to the agency, the less committed they were to the agency's client. They speculated that when agency workers are committed to their agencies, they are less likely to accept permanent jobs from client organizations (Liden et al., 2003). However, more research is needed.

In sum, recent decades have witnessed a remarkable increase in temporary agency jobs, which feature a tripartite employment relationship of agency workers, client organizations, and staffing agencies. While social exchange theory still applies, the relationships between agency workers and the client organizations are mostly transactional and short-term.

Job Insecurity

Recent changes characterized by declining employee tenure, increased organizational restructuring, layoffs, outsourcing, and use of contingent workers affect how individuals perceive the stability and continuity of their jobs.

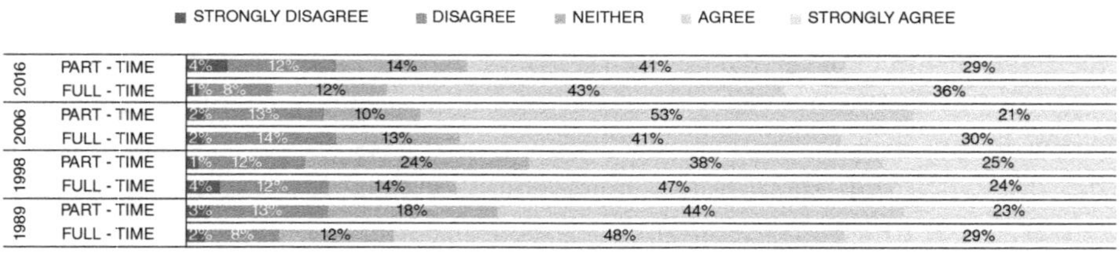

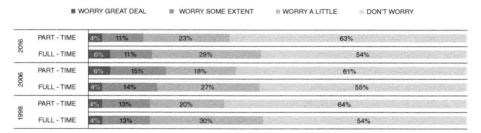

Figure 25.1 *Perceived job insecurity over time from responses to: "My job is secure."*
Note. Source: General Social Survey (United States). Ns = 808, 777, 945, and 857 for 1989, 1998, 2006, and 2016, respectively. Responses indicating higher job insecurity are located on the left

Figure 25.2 *Perceived job insecurity over time from responses to: "Do you worry about the possibility of losing your job?"*
Note. Source: General Social Survey (United States). Ns = 784, 951, and 855 for 1998, 2006, and 2016, respectively. Responses indicating higher job insecurity are located on the left

Defined as "perceived threat to the continuity and stability of employment as it is currently experienced" (Shoss, 2017, p. 1914), job insecurity is widely thought to be symptomatic of a changing EOR.

Evidence of Changes. Interestingly, despite some postulations of increasing job insecurity due to structural changes in the labor market (e.g., Gallie, Felstead, Green, & Inanc, 2017), there is less consistent evidence on a corresponding increase in overall *perceptions* of job insecurity in the past quarter century (Lübke & Erlinghagen, 2014). Figures 25.1 and 25.2 show perceived job insecurity among part-time and full-time employees in the United States based on data drawn from the General Social Survey. As can be seen from the figure, perceptions of the job insecurity do not necessarily increase uniformly over time (see also Weaver, 2015).

The invariability of perceived job insecurity despite time progress and associated changes in the labor market may be due to the nature of perceived job insecurity as an individual's subjective experience of his or her surroundings "in the eye of the beholder" (e.g., Sverke & Hellgren, 2002). Individuals appraise insecurity by making subjective comparisons around their surroundings that are characterized by proximity or contemporariness (Gallie et al., 2017; Walker &

Smith, 2002). That means, if one believes everyone else is slowly going through similar changes to how work is done (e.g., use of desktop computer or the Internet) or human resources practices (e.g., increasing use of independent contractors), the individual's perceived insecurity in comparison to others does not necessarily increase unless there are radical institutional influences that may disrupt the whole economic system such as an economic recession or a political turmoil. By the same token, the security paradox (Evers & Nowotny, 1987; Kaufmann, 2003; as cited in Lübke & Erlinghagen, 2014) suggests that individuals are adjusted to a certain level of security, so the subjective insecurity level becomes stable in *the long term* regardless of the fluctuating insecurity level *in the short term*.

However, given the accelerating pace of technological advancement, it is likely that the general job insecurity level may increase in the next few decades, especially in industries and job positions where tasks are more vulnerable to replacement by the nonhuman labor force. Although job insecurity is generally known to be more prevalent in low-skilled occupations (Keim et al., 2014), several recent examples signal that knowledge-based, highly skilled, and professional occupations are also prone to replacement by the nonhuman labor force. For example, increasing popularity of the use of tax-filing software decreases the demand for accountants, and artificial intelligence (e.g., Watson for Oncology from IBM) can now recommend medical treatments comparable to the quality of a professional medical team (Somashekhar, Sepúlveda, & Norden, 2017). Google's research project on artificial intelligence, *Magenta* (https://magenta.tensorflow.org/), suggests that artificial intelligence may soon be able to take over tasks that require divergent and creative thinking.

Implications. Regarding changes to the EOR, two questions can be asked: (a) "Is job security considered by employees as the employer's obligation in the psychological contract?" and (b) "Is job security under the organization's control?"

Job Security as the Employer's Obligation in the Psychological Contract. One important question on the effects of job insecurity in EOR is whether individuals consider job security as a promised term from the employing organization (e.g., Rousseau, 2001). Job insecurity is positively related to psychological contract breach (Vander Elst, De Cuyper, Baillien, Niesen, & De Witte, 2016), and psychological contract theory has been one of the dominant theories used to explain the negative consequences of job insecurity (Shoss, 2017). However, an individual's perception of job insecurity as the employer's obligation may vary depending on the individual's view of the EOR as transactional or relational. Employees with different contract types shape various psychological contracts (e.g., Coyle-Shapiro & Kessler, 2002; De Cuyper et al., 2008; Van Dyne & Ang, 1998), and as discussed previously in this chapter, part-time and temporary employees are less likely to view the nature of EOR as relational (Millward & Hopkins, 1998). Therefore, part-time and temporary employees are less likely to perceive job security as promised by the organization and to consider job insecurity as a psychological contract breach. To this point, De Cuyper and De Witte (2006) found that job insecurity is only detrimental to *permanent* employees' job satisfaction and organizational commitment. There are individual differences beyond contract type in the perception of EOR as well. Rousseau (1990) found a positive relationship between employee-perceived *employee*'s obligations for loyalty and intended duration of stay, and the employee-perceived *employer*'s obligation to provide job security. This suggests that the individual's perceptions of the nature of EOR as transactional or relational affects whether job insecurity is considered a psychological contract breach.

Organizational Control in Providing Job Security. Organizational support theory suggests that favorable job conditions that are perceived to be under the organization's control are more strongly associated with the individual's POS (Eisenberger et al., 1997). The literature on the psychological contract also suggests that contract breaches attributable to reasons outside of the organization's control will bring less negative consequences (Rousseau, 1995), which raises the question of whether job security is something over which organizations have control. Interestingly, Eisenberger et al.'s (1997) study found variability in perceptions of whether organizations have control over offering job security. Accordingly, massive layoffs or organizational restructuring resulting from external influences (e.g., merger or acquisition due to the economic downturn) are less likely to reduce employees' POS although they may significantly increase the employees' perceived job insecurity. Extenuating circumstances aside, in general, research finds that individuals perceive job security as an indication of POS (Kurtessis et al., 2017). Social exchange theorists assert that resources given by the other party are more appreciated by the recipients when such resources are highly valued and are given discretionarily by the donor (Blau, 1964; Cotterell, Eisenberger, & Speicher, 1992). Accordingly, providing job security to employees at a time of transition when employees feel insecure about their jobs may have greater effects on positive organizational outcomes. Supporting this hypothesis, a stronger relationship between POS and affective organizational commitment has been observed among those reporting higher (vs. lower) job insecurity (Lee & Peccei, 2007).

In summary, individuals consider job security as an indication of organizational support and failing to provide it as a sign of psychological contract breach. Negative consequences of job insecurity to organizations may vary based on whether employees consider the EOR as relational or transactional, job security is a part of the promised terms of employment, or job security is one of the job characteristics that employees believe the organization has control over.

Job Hopping

Frequent voluntary job transitions, otherwise known as job hopping, occur when employees attempt to escape a disliked work setting or advance their professional careers and paychecks (Lake, Highhouse, & Shrift, 2018). Several career orientation theories have been proposed to account for this phenomenon. First, employees are increasingly engaging in boundaryless careers that span across multiple organizational memberships and emphasize the pursuit of a seemingly infinite number of career opportunities to be successful (Arthur, 1994). Second, the protean career is one in which individuals self-direct their career paths in alignment with their core values (Hall, 1996). Workers with these two career orientations express an advancement motive: they are ambitious, tenacious, and possess a high internal locus of control (Lake et al., 2018). Finally, "hobo syndrome" (Ghiselli, 1974) describes those who move from organization to organization to discover new opportunities, avoid unfulfilling work environments, and who typically have a high openness to new experiences (Lake et al., 2018).

Evidence of Changes. Evidence from the US BLS suggests that in the private sector, average organizational tenure has gradually declined each successive decade from 1973 to 2006, particularly for men aged 40 and above (Farber, 2008). Farber (2008) found this decline in organizational tenure even when statistically controlling for race, Hispanic ethnicity, and education. However, these findings do not necessarily confirm employees have been job hopping more frequently. Perhaps average organizational tenure in the private sector has decreased due to a higher frequency of layoffs and discharges.

The BLS thus initiated the Jobs Openings and Labor Turnover Survey (JOLTS) December 2000 in order to acquire more profound insight into job openings, hires, and separations each month for a sample of 16,000 US organizations (Bureau of Labor Statistics, 2018a). Across both the private and public sectors, voluntary turnover (excluding retirement) has virtually mirrored the hiring rate. As hiring has increased, voluntary turnover has also risen and vice versa. This relationship was considerably strong in the private sector ($r = .91$) through June 2018 and moderately strong in the public sector ($r = .37$) through December 2010 (Bureau of Labor Statistics, 2018b). Interestingly, since 2010, layoffs and discharges have been relatively stable averaged across industries, yet voluntary turnover has been greater than layoffs and discharges, and this difference has been slowly increasing each year. It is essential to note that this increase in voluntary turnover did not result in higher unemployment, as the unemployment rate due to voluntary quitting has not markedly changed from 2000 to 2018, ranging from .4% to .7%, according to the Current Population Survey data (Bureau of Labor Statistics, 2018c). However, these data should be interpreted with caution, as aggregated voluntary turnover data do not account for the individual-level frequency of job hopping.

Implications. Despite numerous popular news articles claiming a recent upsurge in job hopping (e.g., Harrison & Morath, 2018), there are inadequate publicly available data to support any fluctuations. Some of the current measures available by the BLS, such as organizational tenure and voluntary turnover, only indirectly provide evidence concerning job hopping, but other possible explanations exist. For example, although voluntary turnover and hiring rates are highly correlated, this does not ensure that workers who quit were also able to secure jobs quickly; they could instead be replaced by other workers, unemployed, or no longer looking for work. Furthermore, these data do not track individual workers longitudinally, which is problematic because job hopping is a voluntary long-term employment tendency that can take many years to classify appropriately. Research attempts to explore this phenomenon also exhibit limitations since studies typically rely on self-report data of past work experiences that may be subject to cognitive inaccuracies and distortions (e.g., Lake et al., 2018; Woo, 2011).

There are a variety of driving forces that could cause individuals to job hop. March and Simon (1958) conceptualized one of the first and most influential models of turnover. According to their theory, an equilibrium must exist between an employee and organization's inputs and outputs in order to prevent the employee from leaving the organization. Employees consider both the internal and external job conditions before voluntarily leaving an organization. First, employees evaluate their *desirability of movement*. When short-term profitability takes precedence over the needs and welfare of employees, for example, organizational commitment, job satisfaction, and POS are diminished (Eisenberger & Stinglhamber, 2011). These factors, as well as a lack of trust in organizations' intentions, can increase voluntary turnover (Blau, 2007). The benefits of job hopping can also be particularly alluring: job hoppers in May 2018 received a 30% annual salary increase compared to workers who maintained consistent employment for the previous year (Harrison & Morath, 2018). Second, employees also assess their perceived *ease of movement*, which is affected by their age, family status, knowledge, skills, unemployment rate, and suitable external job openings (Maltarich, Nyberg, & Reilly, 2010). If perceived desirability and ease of movement are high, employees are likely to leave their organizations voluntarily.

Organizations that wish to retain job-hopping employees should focus on fulfilling the underlying motivations for job hopping, particularly in times of economic growth. For example, job hoppers with an advancement motive may desire periodic changes in job duties, greater promotion and training opportunities, more autonomy, better pay, and job security (Lake et al., 2018). These employees are typically ambitious, intrinsically motivated, and have a high need for growth, so the return on investment for potentially greater work performance may be worth the additional costs. Opportunities such as these demonstrate a sincere, high regard for employees, which may increase employees' POS and desire to remain committed to the organization. However, organizations should uphold implicit promises in order to forgo violating employees' psychological contracts for meaningful work experiences in exchange for their sustained hard work. Otherwise, they will be likely to quit once more (Rousseau, 1995).

In summary, workers appear to quit their jobs voluntarily when the economy is doing well and may be spending less time with a single employer. However, claims of individual-level job-hopping trends seem vastly overstated given the current evidence. Future research should attempt to more effectively measure job hopping in order to examine changes over time.

Income Inequality

Income inequality refers to the extent to which incomes are distributed unevenly within a certain entity (e.g., households, organizations, countries; Charles-Coll, 2011). The Occupy Wall Street movement and its slogan "We are the 99%" thrust the issue of income inequality into the public consciousness. Since then, the surging income discrepancies between the top 1% and the bottom 99% income earners have garnered greater awareness. Scholars of income inequality agree on two major trends: (1) inequality in wages, earnings, and total family incomes has grown remarkably since the 1980s and (2) income inequality today has reached the highest level of the past 40 years (McCall & Percheski, 2010).

Evidence of Changes. Over the period from 1993 to 2015, the incomes of the top 1% of workers grew by 94.5%, whereas the incomes of the bottom 99% grew only by 14% (Saez, 2016). The average real weekly wages of the top 10% earners rose from $1,479 in 1979 to $2,097 in 2017, whereas median and low–income workers had little or no growth in their weekly wages (Bureau of Labor Statistics, 2018d). In the workplace, the pay ratio of large company CEOs to typical worker has jumped from 42:1 in 1980 to 347:1 in 2016 (Bobb, 2016). The gap between CEOs' and workers' retirement benefits is even greater. At the end of 2013, the value of the top 100 CEOs' retirement funds was about $4.7 billion, while the ordinary workers with 401(k) plans only had an average balance of $18,443 (Anderson & Klinger, 2016). As the economic agents creating and distributing value, business organizations play a major role in economic inequalities (Bapuji, 2015). The widening gap between rich and poor, especially the disproportionate earnings of the top management within organizations, in turn, may redefine EORs.

Implications. Social comparison processes laid the basis for equity and distributive justice theories in explaining individuals' reactions to outcomes of resource distributions (Adams, 1965; Festinger, 1954). Social comparison theory holds that individuals evaluate their attitudes and anchor their judgments by comparing with similar others and contrasting to those whom they perceive as different (Baron & Pfeffer, 1994; Festinger, 1954). Income inequality makes the small number of upper-level managers with high incomes more salient, leading to an increased tendency of upward social comparison (Schor, 1998). Therefore, the tremendous difference between the wages of the upper management and most of the employees may contribute to employees' perception of unfairness in the distribution of resources (i.e., distributive injustice; Colquitt, 2001). In line with this view, previous studies found that hierarchical (i.e., dispersed) pay distribution within an organization could instill feelings of inequality among its employees (Bloom, 1999; Pfeffer, 1994). Reduced distributive justice, as one of the key predictors of POS, might reduce employees' inputs in EORs accordingly, leading to negative attitudinal and behavioral outcomes such as reduced affective commitment, in-role and extra-role performance, and increased turnover (Kurtessis et al., 2017).

Perceptions of being treated unfairly could reduce trust and reciprocity in reciprocal exchange (Adams, 1965; Blau, 1964; Cropanzano & Mitchell, 2005). As income disparities continue to grow, employees might question the worthiness of their investment in their relationships with the organization, and therefore dedicate less effort and commitment to EORs. Some early studies on income inequality provide support for this argument. Cowherd and Levine (1992) found that the pay difference between lower-level employees and upper-level managers was negatively related to product quality via employee commitment to upper-management goals, effort, and cooperation. The study by Pfeffer and Langton (1993) involving 60,000 faculty members from 303 colleges suggested that greater wage disparity within an academic department was associated with lower satisfaction and research productivity.

However, the potential problems associated with income inequality might make social exchange more salient in today's EORs than ever before, as social exchange stresses the importance of the symbolic values of resources exchanged over and beyond their economic values (Foa & Foa, 2012). In this case, organizations could counterbalance monetary inequality by providing more socioemotional rewards (Martin & Harder, 1994). Recently, realizing the significance of satisfying employees' socioemotional needs, many organizations have begun to provide employees with more favorable HR practices and job conditions including flexible work schedules and family-friendly practices. For instance, according to the 2016 National Study of Employers (Matos, Galinsky, & Bond, 2017), the percentage of employers allowing employees to return to work gradually after childbirth or adoption has increased from 73% in 2012 to 81% in 2016, and the percentage of employers offering employees the opportunities to work at home has changed from 33% in 2012 to 40% in 2016. Such favorable treatment, connoting the organization's sincere regard for and positive valuation of its employees, could enhance employees' POS and strengthen employees' relationships with the organizations (Eisenberger et al., 1986; Eisenberger & Stinglhamber, 2011).

In sum, the sharp growth in income inequality has the potential to reduce employees' perceptions of distributive justice and make them hesitant to invest effort and commitment in their relationships with the organization. Investing more socioemotional resources in EORs might help organizations to attenuate these negative effects, although more research is needed.

Conclusions

Taken together, the evidence suggests that there are likely those for whom the quality of the EOR is poor. However, it does not support the idea that employees and employers have abandoned the EOR or that it is no longer relevant to the majority of workers/organizations. Indeed, as illustrated throughout the chapter, social exchange models of the EOR provide useful frameworks to understand the variety of ways that employees relate to their employers. Thus, it may be more appropriate to claim that the substance of the EOR has changed, rather than that the EOR itself no longer exists. We call for researchers to continue to generate knowledge regarding the role of the EOR as workplace changes evolve.

References

Adams, J. S. (1965). Inequity in social exchange. *Advances in Experimental Social Psychology, 2*, 267–299.

Anderson, S., & Klinger, S. (2016, December 15). *As working families face rising retirement insecurity, CEOs enjoy platinum pensions*. Institute for Policy Studies. Retrieved from https://ips-dc.org/report-tale-two-retirements

Arthur, M. B. (1994). The boundaryless career: A new perspective for organizational inquiry. *Journal of Organizational Behavior, 15*(4), 295–306.

Auguste, B. (2018, July 5). *Skills and tomorrow's job report: The usual suspects*. Retrieved from www.forbes.com/sites/byronauguste/2018/07/05/skills-and-tomorrows-jobs-report-the-usual-suspects-warning-spoilers/#2cf3935e2af8

Bapuji, H. (2015). Individuals, interactions and institutions: How economic inequality affects organizations. *Human Relations, 68*(7), 1059–1083.

Baron, J. N., & Pfeffer, J. (1994). The social psychology of organizations and inequality. *Social Psychology Quarterly, 57*(3), 190–209.

Bergman, M. E., & Jean, V. A. (2015). Where have all the "workers" gone? A critical analysis of the unrepresentativeness of our samples relative to the labor market in the industrial–organizational psychology literature. *Industrial and Organizational Psychology, 9*, 84–113.

Bidwell, M., Briscoe, F., Fernandez-Mateo, I., & Sterling, A. (2013). The employment relationship and inequality: How and why changes in employment practices are reshaping rewards in organizations. *Academy of Management Annuals, 7*(1), 61–121.

Blau, G. (2007). Does a corresponding set of variables for explaining voluntary organizational turnover transfer to explaining voluntary occupational turnover? *Journal of Vocational Behavior, 70*(1), 135–148.

Blau, P. M. (1964). *Exchange and power in social life*. New York, NY: Wiley.

Bloom, M. (1999). The performance effects of pay dispersion on individuals and organizations. *Academy of Management Journal, 42*(1), 25–40.

Bobb, C. (2016, May 17). *CEOs paid 335 times average rank-and-file worker; Outsourcing results in even higher inequality*. The American Federation of Labor and Congress of Industrial Organizations. Retrieved from https://aflcio.org/2016/5/17/ceos-paid-335- times-average-rank-and-file-worker-outsourcing-results-even-higher

Bureau of Labor Statistics, US Department of Labor. (2018a). *Job openings and labor turnover – May 2018*. Retrieved from www.bls.gov/news.release/pdf/jolts.pdf

Bureau of Labor Statistics, US Department of Labor. (2018b). *Job openings and labor turnover survey (JOLTS)* [Database]. Retrieved from www.bls.gov/jlt/data.htm

Bureau of Labor Statistics, US Department of Labor. (2018c). *Labor force statistics from the Current Population Survey* [Database]. Retrieved from www.bls.gov/webapps/legacy/cpsatab11.htm

Bureau of Labor Statistics, US Department of Labor. (2018d). *Usual weekly earnings of wage and salary workers (quarter)*. Retrieved from www.bls.gov/cps/earnings.htm

Charles-Coll, J. A. (2011). Understanding income inequality: concept, causes and measurement. *International Journal of Economics and Management Sciences*, *1*(3), 17–28.

Chen, C. A., & Brudney, J. L. (2009). A cross-sector comparison of using nonstandard workers: Explaining use and impacts on the employment relationship. *Administration and Society*, *41*(3), 313–339.

Chernyak-Hai, L., & Rabenu, E. (2018). The new era workplace relationships: Is social exchange theory still relevant?. *Industrial and Organizational Psychology*, *11*, 456–481.

CIETT (2015). *"Economic report,"* International Confederation of Private Employment Services (based on data of 2013/2014)

Claes, R. (2005). Organization promises in the triangular psychological contract as perceived by temporary agency workers, agencies, and client organizations. *Employee Responsibilities and Rights Journal*, *17*(3), 131–142.

Colquitt, J. A. (2001). On the dimensionality of organizational justice: A construct validation of a measure. *Journal of Applied Psychology*, *86*(3), 386–400.

Connelly, C. E., & Gallagher, D. G. (2006). Independent and dependent contracting: Meaning and implications. *Human Resource Management Review*, *16*(2), 95–106.

Conway, N., & Briner, R. B. (2005). *Understanding psychological contracts at work: A critical evaluation of theory and research*. Oxford, UK: Oxford University Press.

Cotterell, N., Eisenberger, R., & Speicher, H. (1992). Inhibiting effects of reciprocation wariness on interpersonal relationships. *Journal of Personality and Social Psychology*, *62*(4), 658–668.

Cowherd, D. M., & Levine, D. I. (1992). Product quality and pay equity between lower-level employees and top management: An investigation of distributive justice theory. *Administrative Science Quarterly*, *37*(2), 302–320.

Coyle-Shapiro, J. A.-M. & Kessler, I. (2002). Contingent and non-contingent working in local government: Contrasting psychological contracts. *Public Administration*, *80*(1), 77–101.

Cropanzano, R., & Mitchell, M. S. (2005). Social exchange theory: An interdisciplinary review. *Journal of Management*, *31*(6), 874–900.

Davis, G. (2009). The rise and fall of finance and the end of the society of organizations. *The Academy of Management Perspectives*, *23*(3), 27–44.

De Cuyper, N., De Jong, J., De Witte, H., Isaksson, K., Rigotti, T., & Schalk, R. (2008). Literature review of theory and research on the psychological impact of temporary employment: Towards a conceptual model. *International Journal of Management Reviews*, *10*(1), 25–51.

De Cuyper, N., & De Witte, H. (2006). The impact of job insecurity and contract type on attitudes, well-being and behavioural reports: A psychological contract perspective. *Journal of Occupational and Organizational Psychology*, *79*(3), 395–409.

De Cuyper, N., & De Witte, H. (2007). Job insecurity in temporary versus permanent workers: Associations with attitudes, well-being, and behaviour. *Work & Stress*, *21*(1), 65–84.

De Cuyper, N., Notelaers, G., & De Witte, H. (2009). Job insecurity and employability in fixed-term contractors, agency workers, and permanent workers: Associations with job satisfaction and affective organizational commitment. *Journal of Occupational Health Psychology*, *14*(2), 193–205.

Dobbin, F., & Kelly, E. L. (2007). How to stop harassment: professional construction of legal compliance in organizations. *American Journal of Sociology*, *112*(4), 1203–1243.

Eisenberger, R., Cummings, J., Armeli, S., & Lynch, P. (1997). Perceived organizational support, discretionary treatment, and job satisfaction. *Journal of Applied Psychology*, *82*(5), 812–820.

Eisenberger, R., Huntington, R., Hutchison, S., & Sowa, D. (1986). Perceived organizational support. *Journal of Applied Psychology*, *71*(3), 500–507.

Eisenberger, R., Rockstuhl, T., Shoss, M.K., Wen, X., & Dulebohn, J. (2019). Is the employee–organization relationship dying or thriving? A temporal meta-analysis. *Journal of Applied Psychology*, *104*(8), 1036–1057.

Eisenberger, R., & Stinglhamber, F. (2011). *Perceived organizational support: Fostering enthusiastic and productive employees*. Washington, DC: American Psychological Association.

Farber, H. S. (2008). *Employment insecurity: The decline in worker–firm attachment in the United States* (Working Paper No. 530). Princeton, NJ: Princeton University Industrial Relations Section.

Festinger, L. (1954). A theory of social comparison processes. *Human Relations*, *7*(2), 117–140.

Foa, E. B., & Foa, U. G. (2012). Resource theory of social exchange. In *Handbook of social resource theory* (pp. 15–32). New York, NY: Springer.

Fragoso, J. L., & Kleiner, B. H. (2005). How to distinguish between independent contractors and employees. *Management Research News*, *28*(2), 136–149.

Gakovic, A., & Tetrick, L. E. (2003). Perceived organizational support and work status: A comparison of the employment relationships of part-time and full-time employees attending university classes. *Journal of Organizational Behavior*, *24*(5), 649–666.

Gallagher, D. G., & Parks, J. M. L. (2001). I pledge thee my troth ... contingently: Commitment and the contingent work relationship. *Human Resource Management Review*, *11*(3), 181–208.

Gallie, D., Felstead, A., Green, F., & Inanc, H. (2017). The hidden face of job insecurity. *Work, Employment and Society*, *31*(1), 36–53.

GAO (General Accounting Office) (2000, December 29). *Unemployment insurance: Role as safety net for low-wage workers is limited*. Washington, DC: US General Accounting Office.

George, E., & Chattopadhyay, P. (2017). *Understanding nonstandard work arrangements: Using research to inform practice*. SHRM-SIOP Science of HR Series. Retrieved from www.siop.org/siop-shrm/

Ghiselli, E. E. (1974). Some perspectives for industrial psychology. *American Psychologist*, *29*(2), 80–87.

Gouldner, A. W. (1960). The norm of reciprocity: A preliminary statement. *American Sociological Review*, *25*(2), 161–178.

Hall, D. T. (1996). Protean careers of the 21st century. *The Academy of Management Executive*, *10*(4), 8–16.

Hall, J. V, & Krueger, A. B. (2016). An analysis of the labor market for Uber's driver-partners in the United States. *Industrial and Labor Relations Review*, *71*(3), 705–732.

Harrison, D., & Morath, E. (2018, July 4). *In this economy, quitters are winning*. Wall Street Journal. Retrieved from www.wsj.com/articles/in-this-economy-quitters-are-winning-1530702001

Kalleberg, A. L. (2000). Nonstandard employment relations: Part-time, temporary and contract work. *Annual Review of Sociology*, *26*, 341–365.

Kalleberg, A. L. (2009). Precarious work, insecure workers: Employment relations in transition. *American Sociological Review*, *74*(1), 1–22.

Katz, L. F., & Krueger, A. B. (2016). *The rise and nature of alternative work arrangements in the United States, 1995–2015* (No. w22667). Cambridge, MA: National Bureau of Economic Research.

Keim, A. C., Landis, R. S., Pierce, C. A., & Earnest, D. R. (2014). Why do employees worry about their jobs? A meta-analytic review of predictors of job insecurity. *Journal of Occupational Health Psychology*, *19*(3), 269–290.

Keys, B. J., & Danziger, S. H. (2008). The risk of unemployment among disadvantaged and advantaged male workers, 1968–2003. In K. S. Newman (Ed.), *Laid off, laid low: Political and economic consequences of employment insecurity* (pp. 56–73). New York, NY: Columbia University Press.

Kim, K. Y., Eisenberger, R., & Baik, K. (2016). Perceived organizational support and affective organizational commitment: Moderating influence of perceived organizational competence. *Journal of Organizational Behavior*, *37*(4), 558–583.

Kondrasuk, J. N., Reed, L. J., & Jurinski, J. J. (2001). The dangers of misclassifying "employees": Microsoft litigation emphasizes distinctions between employees and nontraditional workers. *Employee Responsibilities and Rights Journal*, *13*(4), 165–173.

Kurtessis, J. N., Eisenberger, R., Ford, M. T., Buffardi, L. C., Stewart, K. A., & Adis, C. S. (2017). Perceived organizational support: A meta-analytic evaluation of organizational support theory. *Journal of Management*, *43*(6), 1854–1884.

Lake, C. J., Highhouse, S., & Shrift, A. G. (2018). Validation of the job-hopping motives scale. *Journal of Career Assessment*, *26*(3), 531–548.

Lee, J., & Peccei, R. (2007). Perceived organizational support and affective commitment: The mediating role of organization-based self-esteem in the context of job insecurity. *Journal of Organizational Behavior*, *28*(6), 661–685.

Liden, R. C., Wayne, S. J., Kraimer, M. L., & Sparrowe, R. T. (2003). The dual commitments of contingent workers: An examination of contingents' commitment to the agency and the organization. *Journal of Organizational Behavior*, *24*(5), 609–625.

Lübke, C., & Erlinghagen, M. (2014). Self-perceived job insecurity across Europe over time: Does changing context matter?. *Journal of European Social Policy*, *24*(4), 319–336.

Maltarich, M. A., Nyberg, A. J., & Reilly, G. J. (2010). A conceptual and empirical analysis of the cognitive ability–voluntary turnover relationship. *Journal of Applied Psychology, 95*(6), 1058–1070.

March, J. G., & Simon, H. A. (1958). *Organizations.* New York, NY: Wiley.

Martin, J., & Harder, J. W. (1994). Bread and roses: Justice and the distribution of financial and socioemotional rewards in organizations. *Social Justice Research, 7*(3), 241–264.

Matos, K., Galinsky, E., & Bond, J. T. (2017, March 8). *National Study of Employers.* The Society for Human Resource Management. Retrieved from www.shrm.org/hr-today/trends-and-forecasting/research-and-surveys/pages/national-study-of-employers.aspx

McCall, L., & Percheski, C. (2010). Income inequality: New trends and research directions. *Annual Review of Sociology, 36,* 329–347.

Millward, L. J., & Hopkins, L. J. (1998). Psychological contracts, organizational and job commitment. *Journal of Applied Social Psychology, 28*(16), 1530–1556.

OECD (Organisation for Economic Co-operation and Development)(2018). Part-time employment rate (indicator). doi: 10.1787/f2ad596c-en

Pfeffer, J. (1994). *Competitive advantage through people: Unleashing the power of the work force.* Boston, MA: Harvard Business School Press.

Pfeffer, J., & Langton, N. (1993). The effect of wage dispersion on satisfaction, productivity, and working collaboratively: Evidence from college and university faculty. *Administrative Science Quarterly, 38*(3), 382–407.

Rousseau, D. M. (1990). New hire perceptions of their own and their employer's obligations: A study of psychological contracts. *Journal of Organizational Behavior, 11*(5), 389–400.

Rousseau, D. M. (1995). *Psychological contracts in organizations: Understanding written and unwritten agreements.* Thousand Oaks, CA: Sage.

Rousseau, D. M. (2001). Schema, promise and mutuality: The building blocks of the psychological contract. *Journal of Occupational and Organizational Psychology, 74*(4), 511–541.

Rousseau, D. M., & Wade-Benzoni, K. A. (1995). Changing individual–organization attachments: A two-way street. In A. Howard (Ed.), *The Jossey-Bass social and behavioral science series: The changing nature of work* (pp. 290–321). San Francisco, CA: Jossey-Bass.

Saez, E. (2016, June 30). *Striking it richer: The evolution of top incomes in the United States.* Retrieved from https://eml.berkeley.edu/~saez/saez-UStopincomes-2015.pdf

Schein, E. H. (1980). *Organizational psychology.* Englewood Cliffs, NJ: Prentice Hall.

Schor, J. B. (1998). *The overspent American.* New York, NY: Basic Books.

Shore, L. M., Coyle-Shapiro, J. A., & Tetrick, L. E. (Eds.) (2012). *The employee–organization relationship: Applications for the 21st century.* New York, NY: Routledge.

Shore, L. M., & Tetrick, L. E. (1994). The psychological contract as an explanatory framework. In *Trends in organizational behavior* (pp. 91–109). Hoboken, NJ: John Wiley & Sons Ltd.

Shore, L. M., Tetrick, L. E., Lynch, P., & Barksdale, K. (2006). Social and economic exchange: Construct development and validation. *Journal of Applied Social Psychology, 36,* 837–867.

Shoss, M. K. (2017). Job insecurity: An integrative review and agenda for future research. *Journal of Management, 43*(6), 1911–1939.

Smith, T. W., Davern, M., Freese, J., & Hout, M. (2018). *General social surveys, 1972–2016* [Data file and code book]. Retrieved from http://gss.norc.org/get-the-data/spss

Somashekhar, S. P., Sepúlveda, M. J., & Norden, A. D. (2017). Double-blind concordance study of breast cancer treatment recommendations between multidisciplinary tumour board and an artificial intelligence advisor – Watson for Oncology. *Journal of Cancer Research & Therapeutics, 13*, pS100–S100.

Sverke, M., & Hellgren, J. (2002). The nature of job insecurity: Understanding employment uncertainty on the brink of a new millennium. *Applied Psychology: An International Review, 51*, 23–42.

Thurman J. E., & Trah G. (1990). Part-time work in international perspective. *International Labour Review, 129*, 23–40.

Tsui, A. S., Pearce, J. L., Porter, L. W., & Tripoli, A. M. (1997). Alternative approaches to the employee–organization relationship: Does investment in employees pay off? *Academy of Management Journal, 40*, 1089–1121.

Van Bastelaer, A., Lemaître, G., & Marianna, P. (1997). *The definition of part-time work for the purpose of international comparisons.* OECD Labour Market and Social Policy Occasional Papers no. 22. Paris: OECD.

Vander Elst, T., De Cuyper, N., Baillien, E., Niesen, W., & De Witte, H. (2016). Perceived control and psychological contract breach as explanations of the relationships between job insecurity, job strain and coping reactions: towards a theoretical integration. *Stress and Health, 32*, 100–116.

Van Dyne, L., and Ang, S. (1998), Organizational citizenship behavior of contingent workers in Singapore. *Academy of Management Journal, 41*, 692–703.

Walker, I. & Smith, H. J. (2002). *Relative deprivation: Specification, development, and integration.* Cambridge, UK: Cambridge University Press.

Weaver, C. N. (2015). *Worker's expectations about losing and replacing their jobs: 35 years of change (Monthly Labor Review).* Washington, DC: Bureau of Labor Statistics. Retrieved from www.bls.gov/opub/mlr/2015/article/workers-expectations-about-losing-and-replacing-their-jobs.htm

Wilkin, C. L. (2013). I can't get no job satisfaction: Meta-analysis comparing permanent and contingent workers. *Journal of Organizational Behavior, 34*, 47–64.

Woo, S. E. (2011). A study of Ghiselli's hobo syndrome. *Journal of Vocational Behavior, 79*, 461–469.

26 The Future of Work

Muriel Clauson

> Yes, excessive automation at Tesla was a mistake. To be precise, my mistake. Humans are underrated.
>
> Elon Musk, April, 2018

CRISPR-Cas-9, a gene-editing tool, can be used to engineer malaria-resistant mosquitoes (Dong et al., 2018). Machine learning–enabled image recognition can detect skin cancer better than a group of dermatologists (European Society for Medical Oncology, 2018). A hotel can be built by 3D printers (Grossman, 2017). Google's virtual assistant can speak in a nearly indiscernible way from humans while making phone calls (Vincent, 2018). As we live out a reality looking more and more akin to science fiction, many wonder what these changes mean for one of the hallmarks of our world today – work. The future of work is a topic that has grown rapidly in popularity over the past half-decade. Members of governments (e.g., Whitehouse – Office of the President, 2016), the popular press (e.g., Mims, 2017), corporations (e.g., Bryant, 2017), and academia (e.g., Frey & Osborne, 2017) have taken up the topic. Yet, there is a broad mix of predictions on what this future of work will look like, ranging from a potentially dystopian world of meager labor opportunities and robot overlords (see Cooper, 2018; Kottasova, 2016; Rotman, 2013) to a utopian world with work that is meaningful and a contributor to happiness (see Jenkins, 2018; Melendez, 2018; Wyman, 2018). Despite these differences, one constant among the many voices on this topic is that greater technological change is coming. Better understanding the nature, impact, and adaptation required of this change is an inherently multidisciplinary task. Technologists (see Frey & Osborne, 2017; Mitzner, Chen, Kemp, & Rogers, 2014), economists (see Acemoglu & Restrepo, 2017; Autor, 2013), social scientists (see Collins, 2018; Danaher, 2017; Weiss, 2013), and many others have contributed to this debate. Their early work indicates that future-of-work research is nascent: there is still much to be done, the future is uncertain, and we may have an active role in creating the future of work.

This chapter provides an overview of the current future-of-work landscape. This begins with a peek into how this topic has been approached in historical examples and what we can learn from this for our present inquiry. Secondly, the technological forces driving these changes will be explored, in addition to the factors that make this era of technological development unique. Next, studies exploring the potential for automation, which have dominated the future-of-work research landscape, will be explored. Finally, opportunities for research and applied involvement will be identified on this important topic.

Key Concepts to Describe the Future of Work

While the future of work is characterized by a wide array of multi-modal forces, much of the future-of-work research and broader interest is driven by changes brought on by technology (see Chapter 4, this volume, for a discussion of the influence of technology). This review will primarily focus on those technological changes and their impact. Paramount to this discussion is a common language with which to understand these novel phenomena. Below I summarize three key concepts commonly used when discussing the potential for technology to influence the future of work.

In present literature, the broad impact of technological advances has been captured by a variety of phenomena including technological unemployment (see Postel-Vinay, 2002), the fourth industrial revolution (see Schwab, 2017), and technological job disruptions (see Rotman, 2013). For the purposes of this review, the macro effects predicted to drive changes in work will be referred to as technological job disruptions, which can be described as the ability of technologies to alter the way work is attained, performed, and experienced in a substantial way. This term is more inclusive of perspectives than terms such as technological unemployment, as the potential for both negative and positive outcomes is afforded.

Two commonly discussed forms of technological job disruptions are: (1) automation and (2) augmentation. Automation refers to the replacement of the human worker by technology (Mason, 2016). This may manifest in an entire job category being replaced by technology – for example, autonomous vehicles potentially automating the transportation occupations in existence today. This may also manifest in lower-order ways, such as technology automating part of the check-in process at an airport (e.g., Otieno & Govender, 2018). Augmentation, on the other hand, refers to instances within which technologies operate as a support to the human worker (Manyika et al., 2017). An example would be a surgeon who is assisted in surgery by augmented reality guidance and stabilizing robotic arms (e.g., Singla et al., 2017). Both automation and augmentation are associated with technological job disruptions, yet their impact is very distinct. Simply put, automation is often considered more negative and augmentation more positive for workers.

Finally, it is important to note that the technologies being discussed are a special category of technologies that are associated with rapid change. There are several terms, which are essentially synonyms, that have been used to discuss this category of technologies. While advanced technologies (see Townsend, DeMarie, & Henrickson, 1998) or disruptive technologies (see Danneels, 2004) are terms often used in the literature when discussing this technological change, this review will use the term exponential technologies (Hagel et al., 2013; Kurzweil, 2005; Schaller, 1997). The term exponential technologies captures the exponential change associated with such technologies that is driving projected changes. Exponential technologies will be discussed in great detail later in the review, but they can be defined as technologies that consistently double in processing speed, power, or capability per unit of time, while their cost or barrier to use decreases (Ismail, Malone, & Van Geest, 2014; Kurzweil, 2005; Nagy, Farmer, Bui, & Trancik, 2013). Genomics, nanotechnology, 3-D printing, artificial intelligence, robotics, blockchain, and quantum computing are all examples of exponential technologies.

A History of the Future

> Nothing in life is to be feared, it is only to be understood. Now is the time to understand more, so that we may fear less.
>
> Marie Curie

Throughout the history of organized work, key stakeholders, including workers and policy makers, have expressed anxiety over potential technological job disruptions. Although some propose that technological change is functioning in a different, accelerated fashion today, it can be instructive to consider such concerns in a historical context. In the following sections, a few key instances of technological job disruption concerns are reviewed (see Mokyr, Vickers, & Ziebarth, 2015 for a comprehensive historical review).

Perhaps one of the most well-known instances of fears over technological job disruptions is the Luddite movement – a group of textile workers in nineteenth-century Europe who feared the rise of the textile manufacturing machines (Mokyr, 1992). Their fear of these technologies led them to organize protests and destroy some of the manufacturing equipment. This well-known labor group uprising is today often referred to as the Luddite Fallacy (e.g., Lorenz & Stephany, 2018), because the concerns of this group did not fully come to fruition – work still exists today, though the workers in question were negatively impacted (Thompson, 2015). Yet, examples of technological job disruption concerns stretch further back in the annals of history than the Luddites.

In the fourth century BCE, the earliest known writing on the topic of technological job disruptions appeared in Aristotle's text, *Politics*. In this writing, Aristotle refers to the potential that machines may become so advanced and useful that the need for human laborers would end (Meikle, 1997) – a prime example of automation concerns. His writing is not the only support for technological job disruption concerns in the ancient world. There is some evidence that the Ancient Greeks, Romans, Egyptians, and Chinese had periods of public works programs intended to curb the effects of ancient labor-saving technologies (Toutain, 2013). There are also historic examples of efforts undertaken to prevent technological job disruptions. In the 1400s, job disruption concerns arose in China with advances in shipping technology associated with the potential for broader trade relationships and less work for the land-based merchants (Finlay, 1991; Levathes, 2014). The shipping fleet at the time, known as the Treasure Fleet, was comprised of 3,500 ships – eight times larger than the entire United States navy fleet today. A century later, the entire fleet had been burned and destroyed at the urging of the merchant elite of the time.

Technological job disruption concerns have continued into more recent history. There are many examples of leading thinkers warning about automation, such as Keynes (1973) who predicted that the pace of job disruptions at the hand of technology would outpace the ability of workers to develop skills to keep up with the technology. Some salespersons in the 1920s in the United States, were concerned with what was often referred to as "robot salesmen" (Seagrave, 2012). Today, we know this technology as vending machines and it is hard to believe that anyone would have feared their ability to fully replace salespeople.

Past examples of technological job disruption concerns are often cited to support arguments that the future of work is probably not as dystopian as some futurists would have us believe. Those who hold this view, point to trends such as the capitalization effect, a phenomenon that has largely held true in the history of technological development, that new jobs are created faster than they are destroyed (Aghion & Howitt, 1994). This perspective is supported by the multitude of jobs that exist today that were perhaps inconceivable to past working populations. For example, 41% of the United States workforce was working in agriculture in 1900 (Autor, 2015; Dimitri et al., 2005) and today that number is at roughly 1.5% (Bureau of Labor Statistics, 2017). Today, over 80% of workers find themselves in the service economy (Bureau of Labor Statistics, 2017) – a likely unfathomable prospect in a time when nearly half of the population was needed to produce enough food to sustain a functioning society.

Additionally, technology experts have often overestimated the capabilities of technologies, and there are several practical constraints to applying new technologies in work contexts (Autor, 2015). Despite this, a key counterpoint is that if an organization can be more profitable applying a technology instead of a human worker the organization will likely do so (Rotman, 2013). The technological change we are facing today may be much different, or, at the very least, there is perhaps more that can be done to support workers as they deal with technological changes than has been done in the past. This rests upon an understanding of these technological changes and how they interplay with human work.

Drivers of Change

> Our intuition about the future is linear. But the reality of information technology is exponential, and that makes a profound difference.
>
> Ray Kurzweil

The future of work has emerged as an important topic, because some believe that the current technological change will create a situation where technologies are capable of completing many jobs in place of humans (see Frey & Osborne,

2013, 2017). However, skeptics about the rate of technological change may point out that the printer at their office rarely works. It is not uncommon to experience current technologies that are lackluster at best, so it can seem far-fetched to believe projections about fast-approaching and widespread technological job disruptions. This is why it is important to understand the nature of the technologies that are driving such predictions. Exponential technologies are projected to impact the world much differently than prior technological advances (Ismail et al., 2014; Kurzweil, 2005). Understanding what is driving this technological change is imperative to understand the change that the world may be facing.

Spotlight on Technology. As stated above, exponential technology refers to a type of technology that repeatedly doubles in processing speed or power over a relevant unit of time, while the cost or barrier to use decreases (Ismail et al., 2014; Nagy, Farmer, Bui, & Trancik, 2013). However, exponential technologies are a byproduct of other technological phenomena. Behind exponential technological change, there are two major drivers at play: Moore's Law and the digitization and growth of data.

Moore's Law epitomizes the ideas behind technological change. In the 1960s, Gordon Moore observed that the number of transistors per integrated circuit was doubling every 12 to 18 months, which means that the general computing capacity, or computing power, was doubling during this same timeframe (Moore, 1965). This doubling pace of computing capacity has continued beyond what Moore originally predicted (Kurzweil, 2004, 2005), and has largely continued into the present day. In layman's terms, this means that a single smartphone is more powerful than all of the computing power of the NASA program computers in 1969 (Ismail, et al., 2014; Kurzweil, 2005). This doubling of computing capacity is often referred to as exponential technological change, the basis of the term exponential technologies (Kurzweil, 2005; Schaller, 1997).

Exponential change is difficult to grasp as we are far more accustomed to thinking in terms of linear change (Kurzweil, 2014; Nagy, Farmer, Bui, & Trancik, 2013). To understand the difference, it is useful to think in terms of distance. Kurzweil (2005) illustrates exponential change by explaining that traveling 30 linear paces would result in traveling 30 meters, while traveling 30 exponential paces, doubling the length of every step after each step, would result in traveling over a billion meters, or 26 trips around the earth. If this pace of technological change continues, then it is possible that technological advances may alter the world of work much more rapidly than many will expect or be able to adapt to. While some argue that Moore's Law is slowing down (Theis & Wong, 2017) or stopping (Williams, 2017) (in terms of the number of transistors per integrated circuit) advances in nanotechnology and 3-D molecular computing – a new way of structuring the building blocks of computing at the level of atoms and molecules (less than 100 nanometers) to allow for greater performance – are positioned to continue the exponential increase of computing capacity (Oppitz & Tomsu, 2018).

However, this change in computing capacity alone is only one aspect of how technological advances are driving change in the world of work. The second force at play relates to the way in which these technologies learn and develop through information. Essentially, exponential technologies are information-enabled (Kurzweil, 2004, 2005). This means that their capabilities evolve in an iterative process through data inputs. The more data that is available, the more development can occur. Humanity is creating data at an exponential rate as well. According to the International Data Corp, humanity-generated data will reach 163 zettabytes (10^{21} bytes) by 2025 (Reinsel, Gantz, & Rydning, 2017).

With these two forces at play – exponential growth in computing capacity and a computer's ability to learn from the exponential increase in data – exponential technologies and their abilities are changing at a rate difficult to grasp, and potentially a rate difficult for workers to keep pace with. An understanding of the forces behind exponential technologies sheds light on why these technological innovations impact the world differently than technologies that came before them. While past technological job disruption concerns were sparked by novel technology inventions, these current changes associated with exponential technologies are not isolated inventions, but rather they are forces of iterative improvement and change. In fact, many of the exponential technologies are based in inventions from 20 years ago that now have the computing power and data to support them (Kurzweil, 2005). While there are many shortcomings of current exponential technologies (Chui, Manyika, & Miremadi, 2015), these technologies are on a trajectory of rapid iteration and improvement.

While all exponential technologies are poised to influence the future of work, a few are playing an especially important role. Artificial intelligence, robotics, and hyperconnectivity are the three technological trends most commonly associated with automation (or augmentation) in predictive labor studies (see Arntz et al., 2016; Bakhshi et al., 2017; Frey & Osborne, 2017). Artificial intelligence has been a huge focus for automation concerns, as this technology may pose a threat to functions previously thought to be chiefly human domains (Autor, 2013). For example, robotics have driven concern as they have already been used in manufacturing replacement, yet their capabilities with artificial intelligence advances led to the development of service robotics, with robots now capable of safely and effectively being leveraged in the care economy (Sharkey, 2008). Hyperconnectivity refers to the way that our various devices are connected, constantly and globally, and begin to touch every corner of our lives. Byproducts of this connected world, such as virtual labor markets, are projected to grow (Fredette et al., 2012).

There are other technological trends that are salient to the future-of-work issue as well. Blockchain, the quantified worker, and longevity advances are all poised to have a major impact. Blockchain, most commonly recognized as the basis of crypto-currencies today, is often touted as having the ability to alter organizational structures by decentralizing power, such as organizational leadership models (Sun, Yan, & Zhang, 2016). One example of how this could work is in decision-making contexts: blockchain allows for the removal of a third party, or centralized power, in decision-making processes because everyone in the system has access to the information, voting rights, and say in whether or not the decision was fair – at least in theory (Pilkington, 2016). For example, if there are three proposals for a housing development at a commercial real estate development firm, instead of leadership being presented with proposals and making a unilateral decision, all members in a blockchain system could collectively decide. The defining characteristic of blockchain is the removal of a middleman or third party (Pilkington, 2016), which may be an attractive premise in a changing labor market or in digitized employment models.

Additionally, the quantified self or worker – a term that encompasses the many ways technology allows employers to track employee performance, moods, attendance and make decisions based upon that data, with roots in Taylorism – is a domain ripe with ethical questions (see Moore & Robinson, 2016; O'Neill, 2017). Machine learning, digitization, and a more virtual workforce allow employers to gain abundant insight into their workers through data, and the implications of this are important to consider (O'Neill, 2017). For example, Amazon has recently been awarded two patents for a wristband technology that enables an employer to track employee movements and provide nudges when behaviors are deemed incorrect (Yeginsu, 2018). With the rise of technologies like sensors and artificial intelligence, employers will have a growing capability to monitor employees – it is important to consider what type of access and use of employee data is ethical. Finally, increased human longevity, a byproduct of medical technology innovations such as digital biology, will surely impact the way careers function across the lifespan in addition to driving a larger care economy (Dychtwald & Flower, 1989). For example, if humans are living longer lives, it may be important to reconsider the retirement age. All of these technological trends have the potential for immense impact, yet they remain small parts of a complex system of technological change.

While the technological forces at play have driven much of the future-of-work interest, these are not the only factors involved in job disruptions – globalization, urbanization, political uncertainty, and environmental changes all play a role as well (Bakhshi et al., 2017). In addition to considering the system of factors that align with technological change to alter work, it is important to consider other consequences of exponential technological change that may occur simultaneously with workforce changes. While exponential technologies such as artificial intelligence and robotics are anticipated to disrupt work, they are also anticipated to alleviate many other societal burdens such as access to low-cost and abundant food, water, and clean energy – some of the basic needs that workers earn a living to pay for (Diamandis & Kotler, 2012). Many of the concerns relating to technological job disruptions, specifically automation, are that this change may have major social (see Arntz et al.,

2016), economic (see Rotman, 2013), and worker wellbeing (see McAfee, 2013) implications. Exploring both the potentially positive and negative implications of exponential technologies can potentially help to navigate and prepare for the future of work. Foundational to the wide array of factors to consider, the majority of future-of-work research has focused on an important topic – the potential for technologies to alter job opportunities.

Understanding Current Trends and the Potential Future of Jobs

Prediction is very difficult, especially if it's about the future.

Nils Bohr

In the following section, two trends are reviewed that are suggestive that major labor changes are already happening. Next, the majority of future-of-work research has looked beyond current trends and explored the potential for exponential technological change to alter work in the future – these studies will be reviewed in great detail as they dominate the current future-of-work research landscape. Finally, potential economic impact and a consideration of uncertainty inherent in these future-oriented studies will be discussed.

Current Trends

While historical perspectives and recent labor replacement trends may suggest the future of work will remain largely the same as work today, there are some observations that point to the uniqueness of the present change. One such trend was identified by Brynjolfsson and McAfee (2011) who observed that productivity and median income were represented by tangential and nearly equal lines when graphed since the time of World War II, and in the year 2000 these lines began to diverge (with a continued increase in productivity and without that same increase in median income). This signals that productivity growth is not in parallel with the creation of jobs (Rotman, 2013). Brynjolfsson and McAfee (2011) declared this was a "great decoupling" of employment and general economic growth which they assert may largely be driven by exponential technologies.

A second differentiating trend relates to the domains in which technologies can be applied. One useful framework for understanding technology and task overlap, proposed by Autor, Levy, and Murnane (2003), is a four-cell typology delineating between cognitive and manual tasks in addition to routine and non-routine tasks. They applied this task model to study how computers altered job task demands by examining the procedural and rules-based logic of computers against job tasks. They argued that computerization has the potential to automate routine cognitive and manual tasks and augment (or complement) non-routine cognitive and manual tasks. Yet more recent analysis of this task model suggests a new trend: that the capabilities of technologies are growing and that now some nonroutine cognitive tasks can potentially be automated in addition to routine tasks (Acemoglu, & Autor, 2011; Brynjolfsson and McAfee, 2011; Frey & Osborne, 2017). While past automation was constrained to precise tasks such as some routine manufacturing processes, automation has begun replacing more service industry–oriented occupations, including bank tellers and travel agents (Rampell, 2015). These two trends set the stage for forward-looking research – the vast majority of early research in the future-of-work space does not look to current trends, rather predictive research exploring the potential for automation has become a key focus. Such research is looking beyond what we have seen so far and considering what work may look like as technologies continue to advance in the future.

Potential for Automation

Making predictions regarding technological job disruptions is a complicated endeavor that requires analyzing future potential based upon present labor and technology insights and a careful consideration of uncertainty. Cagnin, Havas, and Saritas (2013) point to the potential of future-oriented technology analysis (FTA) in understanding technological change and to support key decision-makers as they prepare for such change. FTA is a class of methods aimed at understanding complex, macro-level shifts as well as developing responses to these shifts. This involves foresight (what the potential challenges may be in the future), technology assessment (what is driving this change), and forecasting (what are the potential impacts and recommended preparations). FTA encompasses methods leveraging empirical insights and scientific methods in analyzing the past and present to consider future options (e.g., the future depends upon key decision points) or to make predictions about the future (e.g., there are specific preparations needed). The following studies can be thought of as FTA approaches, with each applying scientific methods to "an imaginative projection of current knowledge" (Cagnin, Havas, & Saritas, 2013, p. 380).

Occupation-Level Approaches. The most notable predictive labor study first gained attention with a headline-catching working paper (Frey & Osborne, 2013) followed by a peer-reviewed manuscript (Frey & Osborne, 2017). Frey and Osborne's work has been credited with sparking a global interest in the future-of-work topic (Arntz, Gregory, & Zierahn, 2016). Their study involved a novel methodology leveraging subject matter expertise and machine learning. They identified the probability of computerization for an occupation as low, medium, or high, based upon an examination of the relationship between O*Net variables (knowledge, skills, and abilities) and what technology subject–matter experts define as bottlenecks for computerization – areas where technologies currently require human intervention (Frey & Osborne, 2017). A comparison of the O*Net variables and current technology capability (identifying if there is a bottleneck or not) determine if a component of a job can potentially be replaced by a technology. An aggregate of these variables produces an occupation-level judgment regarding whether or not the job is at risk.

Ultimately, Frey and Osborne found that 47% of total US employment falls into the high risk category, with examples of high risk occupations including telemarketers and tax preparers. While no specific timeframe was specified, they explained that automation could potentially impact these occupations over the next two decades. In a follow-up opinion piece (Frey & Osborne, 2018), they asserted that the results of their study had frequently been miscited and they were careful to specify that they were not trying to predict job loss, rather they were purely noting the potential for automation. They argue that several key factors may alter the actual impact of technology on jobs, which their study intentionally did not account for. Follow-up studies, most often in the form of reports rather than peer-reviewed literature, have employed a similar method applied to labor data from other countries. This includes a study focused on the European workforce which found that 45–60% of jobs were at risk (Arntz et al., 2016; Bowles, 2014), a study focused on Germany which found 59% of jobs were at risk (Arntz et al., 2016; Brzeski & Burk, 2015), and a study focused on Finland which found that 35% of jobs were at risk (Arntz et al., 2016; Parajinen & Rouvinen, 2014) potentially within the next few decades.

Survey-based research from the World Economic Forum (2018) captured the beliefs of human-capital decision makers regarding automation potential and found that nearly 50% expect automation will lead to some form of reduction in their workforce by the year 2022. Yet they also found that there are many occupations where organizations anticipate a growing demand in that same timeframe including data scientists, software developers, ecommerce specialists, people and culture specialists, marketing professionals, and organizational development specialists. Based on their survey and analyses, they predict that job growth would offset a decline in jobs. Specifically, they estimate a reduction in 0.98 million jobs and a gain of 1.74 million jobs by the year 2022.

Task-Level Approaches. In addition to studies looking to predict occupation level automation, studies emerged exploring task or skill level automation. A working paper from Centre for European Economic Research (ZEW) scholars published with the Organisation for Economic Co-operation and Development (OECD), an organization of 34 democracies with market economies, argued that the way that predictive studies arrived at occupation-level findings could be improved upon (Arntz, Gregory, & Zierahn, 2016). They argued that entire jobs are not likely to be replaced as much as job tasks (e.g., augmentation) and that the occupation-based approach has serious upward bias toward automation conclusions. They conducted a study in a similar fashion to Frey and Osborne, yet they took what they referred to as a task-level approach, with the primary difference being that they collected individual level survey data on job tasks, to account for a lack of homogeneity in within-occupation job tasks (Autor & Handel, 2013), and they determined that an occupation was at risk when there was not a reasonable task-switching opportunity within the job, meaning that the underlying tasks of the job were each automatable. This primarily represents a difference in how the judgment of automation risk is decided while resting on similar predictive analyses.

Arntz, Gregory, and Zierahn (2016)argue that this is a superior approach as most occupations have some tasks that would be difficult to substitute in the foreseeable future and so the nature of occupations is likely to change, but not necessarily be fully automated. For example, they cite that while bookkeeping jobs face an automation risk of 98% in Frey and Osborne's study (2013, 2017), in the majority of instances this occupation cannot be completed without group work (a task with lower risk of automation) (Arntz et al., 2016). Thus, the role of bookkeepers may vary and be augmented by technology, rather than automated. Leveraging this approach, they found that 9% of jobs were at risk in OECD countries (including the United States) as they lacked sufficient task-switching potential; the timeframe for this prediction was again not specified. Additionally, they argued that low skill workers would likely bear the brunt of job automation as these individuals were less likely to hold jobs with a wide array of job tasks.

A series of reports from McKinsey Global Institute leveraged a similar task-level approach, finding that 45% of the work activities that workers are currently paid to perform could be automated by applying near-term technology capability (Chui, Manyika, Miremadi, 2015), yet full job automation could impact only 5% of occupations (Manyika, Chui, Madgaykar, & Lund, 2017). Additionally, a Pearson report explored the future demand for skills in the United States, among other analyses (Bakhshi, Downing, Osborne, & Schneider, 2017). The directional predictions regarding occupation change, based upon skill demand changes, found that 9.6% of the current United States workforce are in occupations that are likely to grow in overall workforce share and 18.7% are in occupations likely to fall in workforce share by the year 2030. See Table 26.1 for a summary of the discussed studies exploring the potential for automation.

Potential for Economic Impact

In addition to predictions regarding the impact of technology on the amount of viable occupations, researchers have leveraged economic modeling to assess the likely impact on wages. DeCanio (2016) presents that expansion in artificial intelligence skill sets is likely to be associated with increased measured inequality as this may produce a polarization of those who are automated by such technology or augmented by it. Additionally, Decanio suggests that this would lead to depressed wages over time, unless the returns of technological advances are broadly spread across the population more than currently predicted. In an exploration of potential economic impacts, Decker, Fischer, and Ott (2017) analyzed the potential of service robotics in relation to the current work

Table 26.1 *Potential for automation: summary of studies*

	Occupation-Level Approach	
Study	Approach	Automation Potential
Frey & Osborne (2013, 2017)	Leveraged machine learning and subject matter expertise to assess 702 detailed occupations as represented in O*Net. Delineated between high, medium, and low-risk occupations from the probability of computerization based upon an examination of the relationship between O*Net variables (knowledge, skills, and abilities) and what technology subject–matter experts define as bottlenecks for computerization – areas where technologies currently require human intervention. Most studies considering the potential for automation draw upon their method.	47% of occupations (United States)
Bowles (2014)	Applied a similar methodology as Frey and Osborne (2013, 2017) to European employment data.	45–60% of occupations across Europe depending upon region; averaging 54% (Europe)
Brzeski & Burk (2015)	Applied a similar methodology as Frey and Osborne (2013; 2017) to German employment data.	59% of occupations (Germany)
Pajarinen & Rouvinen (2014)	Applied a similar methodology as Frey and Osborne (2013; 2017) to Finnish employment data.	35.7% of occupations (Finland)
World Economic Forum (2018)	Surveyed human-capital decision makers within companies – from companies representing over 15 million workers in total – to understand their perceptions of the impact of technology on the jobs within their organizations.	Experts predicting workforce reduction by 2022: Nearly 50% Reduction in jobs: 0.98 million Increase in jobs: 1.74 million

	Task-Level Approach	
Study	Approach	Potential for Automation
Arntz, Gregory, & Zierahn (2016)	Applied a similar methodology as Frey and Osborne (2013, 2017), yet considered task-level automation potential and only deemed an occupation as at risk for automation if analyses revealed a lack of reasonable task-switching opportunity within the job. Additionally, they collected individual-level survey data on job tasks to capture within occupation variance.	9% of occupations (OECD countries) 9% of occupations (United States)

(*cont.*)

Task-Level Approach		
Study	Approach	Potential for Automation
Chui, Manyika, & Miremadi, (2015)	Analyzed near-term technology potential relative to work activities that workers are currently paid to perform.	45% of work activities
Manyika, Chui, Madgavkar, & Lund (2017)	Analyzed near-term technology potential relative to work activities that workers are currently paid to perform. Extended these findings to project occupation level automation.	Full automation: 5% of occupations Partial automation: All occupations
Bakhshi, Downing, Osborne, & Schneider (2017)	Combined technology subject–matter experts, machine learning and trend analyses to predict the demand for skills. Automation potential was measured through directional predictions regarding occupation change and identification of the knowledge, skills, and abilities that are likely to experience growth and decline.	Workers in occupations with decrease in workforce share: 18.7% Workers in occupations with increase in workforce share: 9.6%

processes of humans. They argue that the capabilities of robotics are likely to replace services currently performed by humans, yet argue generally valid conclusions regarding the impact this has on the labor economy cannot be drawn at this time with the current level of uncertainty.

Additionally, a study leveraging economic modeling from Acemoglu and Restrepo (2017) compared robotic labor impact in relation to human labor leveraging historical robotic labor adoption data and found that robots may reduce employment and wages. Controlling for other labor reduction factors, they estimated that for every additional robot per 1,000 workers there is likely to be a 0.18 to 0.34% reduction in employment relative to the population and a 0.25 to 0.5% reduction in wages if historical trends continue. They also found that the distribution of such wage decreases disproportionately impacts certain occupational sectors, such as routine manual and transport occupations. These estimates are based upon limited robotic adoption in the past, yet evaluating the impact of one additional robot per 1,000 workers allows for projections into a future with wider robotic labor adoption. Yet these researchers argue that net job loss and resulting wage effects, ultimately, are dependent upon the supply of new job opportunities and this element is difficult to capture (Acemoglu & Restrepo 2017; Gregory et al. 2016).

Uncertainty in Prediction

An important note captured in several of the potential-for-automation and economic impact studies discussed above is that jobs being deemed at risk does not necessarily equate to employment losses (Arntz et al., 2016; Bakhshi et al.,

2017; Chui et al., 2015; Frey & Osborne, 2017). There are numerous factors that will influence actual technological adoption such as economic, legal, and societal hurdles. Even if adoption of technologies is widespread, workers can also adjust – whether that is accomplished through task-switching or learning new skills. Additionally, it may be easier to identify facets of current jobs that are susceptible to automation than it is to imagine what new jobs technology may help to create.

In a conceptual paper, Autor (2015) – originator of the task model discussed above (Autor et al., 2003) – discusses why understanding technology's impact on jobs requires thinking about more than just substitution. Autor argues that it is important to consider the range of tasks involved in jobs and the complementary role that humans can play alongside technology. The interplay between work and exponential technologies is certainly complex. Early predictive studies exploring the potential for automation have played an important role in shaping interest in the topic, yet there are still immense opportunities to explore this area further.

Taken together, these various studies attempt to accomplish two things: predict how technology will change the workforce and identify important points of intervention to ensure positive outcomes for workers throughout this transition. With regard to what the future holds for the workforce, we are left with a wide variety of predictions that make it difficult to ascertain the actual impact technologies will have. With regard to interventions, many of these studies mention key decision points – technology adoption decisions, worker adaptations, policy decisions, economic factors, etc. – that can alter the ultimate impact of technologies on work. Such decision points and interventions are poised to be a focus of future-of-work research and practice moving forward.

Preparing for the Future of Work

> The future is already here, just not evenly distributed.
>
> William Gibson

Key Areas for Future-of-Work Intervention

With the backdrop of uncertainty, it may be important to work on preemptive improvements that can be made in the work domain – how it is done, how we train for it, and even what it is. While there are many proposed solutions and interventions, the following presents a few specific domains of interest relating to preparing for the future of work.

Alternative Work Arrangements. A key area of interest revolves around non-traditional work arrangements. The growth of nontraditional work can be thought of as the gig economy, defined as the trend toward technology-based platforms for work arrangements (Brawley, 2017; Kuhn, 2016). In 2015, it was estimated that over 15.8% of the workforce engaged in some form of alternative employment, an increase from 10.7% in 2005 (Katz & Krueger, 2016). More recent estimates are that the gig economy will grow to 43% of the workforce by 2020 (Gillespie, 2017). This has led some to claim that today's organizational structures and our current conceptualization of work may alter dramatically or cease to exist (see Chernyak-Hai & Rabenu, 2018; Morrison, 2017; Sundararajan, 2016). A driver of this growth has been platforms such as Uber which allow individuals to become contract workers seamlessly through digitized employment platforms.

A defining feature of such platforms is that workers are not assigned work, rather workers choose what work tasks they will engage in and when (Mrass, Peters, & Leimeister, 2016). Examples of such platforms include crowdsourced employment platforms (like Amazon's Mechanical Turk), ridesharing services (such as Uber), and on-demand employment platforms (such as Upwork). More research is needed to understand how a widespread gig economy functions, and the impact on workers when they are forced into such arrangements by economic necessity rather than personal preference. Bergman and Jean (2016) argue that contract workers are an understudied group who are growing in prevalence, thus such research is needed. There is much to learn on how workers can be helped in navigating an ever-changing career landscape, one in which they may not place the same reliance on a traditional employer as they once did.

The Future of Skills. Additionally, it is important to consider the skills that will be increasingly relevant in the future and hold up against automation. The pursuit of future skill understanding may even prove to be more important than occupational predictions: the jobs of the future are difficult to predict, but an understanding of the skills that can be applied in tandem alongside technologies is perhaps more attainable. Some experts argue that this adaptive approach is better than a predictive one as humans can exercise creativity and inventiveness to adapt to a new world of work (Eichhorst, 2015).

Recently, there has been a high demand for, and oftentimes a shortage of, STEM (science, technology, engineering, and math) talent (Society for Human Resource Management, 2016). According to a survey completed by the Society for Human Resource Management, nearly three out of four respondents working in a human resources role reported having difficulty filling positions related to engineering and other STEM disciplines. Respondents also noted that there is a challenge finding applicants with appropriate technical, critical thinking, and leadership skills. These results mirror what several reports on the future of work have cited as key skills relevant for the future of work. Reports from McKinsey, the World Economic Forum, and Pew Research all indicate that technical knowledge in STEM disciplines, critical thinking, and leadership skills are important skills in the context of the future of work, particularly in contrast to the growing capabilities of technologies (Chui et al., 2015; Rainie & Anderson, 2017; World Economic Forum, 2016).

Twenty-first-century skills is a term often used to refer to the category of skills that are considered both important today and likely to emerge in importance with technological development (Su, Golobovich, & Robins, 2015). Neubert, Mainert, Kretzschmar, and Greiff (2015) asserted that twenty-first-century skills are the skills needed to perform interactive and nonroutine tasks – the tasks least automatable by technological advances and salient to an increasingly complex world of work. However, there is some confusion regarding what falls into the domain of twenty-first-century skills. Some argue that twenty-first-century skills are ill-defined and that a standard framework is needed to organize such constructs (Su, Golobovich, & Robins, 2015), while others argue that existing approaches, such as competency modeling, already allow us to capture and create a framework to represent the twenty-first-century skill clusters (Sliter, 2015).

Despite some debate around the framework of twenty-first-century skills, there are insights into which skills, or skill clusters, are most salient in an increasingly digitized working world. Neubert and coauthors (2015) specifically call out complex problem solving – solving novel, ill-defined problems in real-life settings – and collaborative problem solving – effectively engaging with others to solve a problem – as skills that will become a more important component of human work. Relatedly, Riggio and Saggi (2015), argue for the importance of "soft skills" in a future context – though they are quick to admit that the term is not ideal. Specifically, they point to the importance of interaction skills as the basis of collaborative problem solving (referencing the work of Neubert et al., 2015). They assert that interpersonal communication, influence, persuasion, intrapersonal skills, and ethics are particularly salient interaction skills in a future context. Additional research is needed to identify the full range of skills most relevant in the future and some researchers have called for the development of a taxonomy of twenty-first-century skills (Morelli, Illingworth, & Handler, 2015; Su et al., 2015).

A key implication of identifying important skills of the future is that organizations and educational institutions can focus on providing training to help employees and students gain skills that will be increasingly in demand. Yet, the value of these predictions is predicated on the ability of these institutions to adequately prepare people for the skills of the future. In a study conducted in a partnership between the Pew Research Center and Elon University's Imagining the Internet Center, they found that 70% of the experts surveyed believed that learning offerings would evolve with the exponential technological trends (Rainie & Anderson, 2017). While this paints an optimistic picture, of the 30% who reported that they did not believe learning would evolve, the majority believed that this would not happen because the pace of technological change would be too rapid. This is important both so that education can begin a shift toward teaching these skills and organizations can begin the process of up-skilling their employees by offering on-the-job training of skills that will be critical in the future (Brynjolfsson and McAfee, 2011). A critical step for future research will be to examine the methods of training that facilitate the greatest transfer of skills that will be in demand in the future, specifically when new skills need to be acquired rapidly, in a context of exponential technological change.

Universal Basic Income. Additionally, universal basic income has been a core focus for those who believe intervention is necessary in light of potential technological job disruption. Universal basic income is sometimes also referred to as generalized basic income or minimum earned income. Universal basic income is essentially unconditional income that every member of an economy is entitled to receive (Woodbury, 2017). Universal basic income is often touted as a component of the future of work, based on the idea that many workers will not be able to keep pace with the changes of exponential technologies and those workers will not have work as a regular source of income. In order to help individuals meet their basic needs, some have touted providing an unconditional income. Though interest in universal basic income has been reawakened with technological advances, the notion is not a new one. Proposals of a universal basic income have been around since at least the 1700s (Caputo, 2012).

Although no municipality has ever fully adopted a universal basic income there have been some recent examples of experiments around this idea (Peter, 2018). For instance, a joint effort by a not-for-profit and a group of technology start-up investors was announced in support of a universal basic income experiment in the city of Oakland, California (Kotecki, 2018; Pender, 2017). Additionally, the city of Stockton, California, announced plans to begin a program for low-income families (Bronklow, 2018; Goodman, 2018). However, some early trials have not lasted long. For example, Ontario, Canada, suspended their basic income pilot two years early after a change in provincial political leadership (Frazee, 2018) and Finland's basic income program ended abruptly after political leadership chose to divert additional funds elsewhere (Peter, 2018).

Universal basic income is certainly a controversial idea. A chief source of controversy is whether it will even be needed. That is, will exponential technologies effectively automate so many occupations that a significant proportion of the populace will be unable to find work? In addition, universal basic income is clearly expensive. Thus, it is unclear how governments will be able to pay for such an expenditure. On the other hand, some project technological advances will reduce the costs of food, water, shelter, and energy to make a universal basic income more feasible (Kurzweil, 2004, 2005). Universal basic income remains an area of immense uncertainty, with a premise largely dependent upon a world where work is less secure than it is today.

Education Reform. Another area where many future-of-work preemptive efforts have been focused is around education. A recent report from the National Academy of Sciences pointed out that education would need to be adapted for the future of work, yet remarked that creating new technology–enabled tools for rapidly adapting education is made easier by technological advances (National Academies of Sciences, Engineering, and Medicine, 2017). Examples of such adaptations include altering the delivery methods of education by incorporating advanced technology like virtual reality, altering the core subjects that students are trained in, such as a focus on soft skills, and individualizing content to specific student progress through adaptive education software. Some argue that technological advances will dramatically improve education by allowing for more continuity in education quality and more personalized learning experiences enabled by artificial intelligence (Sharples, 2000; Bingham, Pane, Steiner, & Hamilton, 2018).

Additionally, some argue that innovations must go beyond just the source or means of education, but also extend into the basic ideas held around the competencies needed for employability – meaning what an individual needs to learn in school in order to gain employment later on. For example, Oliver (2015, p. 59) proposed that employability in the future may mean "that students and graduates can discern, acquire, adapt and continually enhance the skills, understandings and personal attributes that make them more likely to find and create meaningful paid and unpaid work that benefits themselves, the workforce, the community and the economy." Essentially, the ability to be a lifelong learner is likely a key success factor of the future in order to be employable in the job market (Oliver, 2015; Quendler & Lamb, 2016). This idea of preparing students to be lifelong learners stems from the idea that the future of work is so uncertain that we need to be prepared for constant change in the knowledge and skills that we apply at work (De Fruyt, Willie, & John, 2015). While there are early efforts in reimagining education systems, including a focus on soft skills and an emphasis on learning by doing (see World Economic Forum, 2016), there is still much work to be done to ensure education efforts prepare students for the future of work.

Research Directions

While the working world grinds on alongside exponential technological advances, scholars stand positioned for a pivotal role in shaping our understanding and interventions around the future of work. Though there are numerous research directions of interest relating to the future of work, a few areas of particular interest are outlined here.

Potential for Automation Studies. Paramount to future research is an extension and refinement of the predictive studies exploring the potential for automation explored earlier. One of the primary criticisms of such studies relates to the level of analysis, typically a focus on entire occupations, being far too broad to meaningfully indicate the real likelihood of automation – potentially resulting in confusing augmentation effects with automation effects (Arntz et al., 2016). While the majority of predictive studies today focus on an occupational level of analysis, it is important to consider that: (1) a focus on skills or tasks is likely superior to occupations as the jobs of the future may look much different than they do today, and (2) more granular analysis (skills or tasks instead of full occupation categories) may protect from overestimates of automation potential and shed light on the augmenting role of technology. With respect to the jobs-of-the-future argument, this stems from the idea that many of the occupations that we have today are not reminiscent of jobs that came before (i.e., computer programming jobs) and that this trend is likely to continue.

The wider concern, that the occupation level of analysis overestimates the impact of automation, relates to the idea that taking an overly broad perspective of an occupation and overlaying technology capabilities often misses the nuance of what that work role entails and how vital a human worker is in that role. An additional consideration salient to further work in this area is clarity around the timeframe in question and the implications of that timeframe. While Frey and Osborne (2017) did not specify a timeframe (though they did mention that potential changes could occur within 10–20 years) and the majority of similar studies followed suit, there are many timescales that can be analyzed. There are also many opportunities to consider the differing societal implications at varying timescales.

Job and Task Analysis. Predictive studies in the future-of-work space depend upon labor data that is robust and representative of the work experience. The more that the process behind capturing the building blocks of work are explored, the higher quality predictions and related research are likely to be. Fortunately, job and task analysis are ripe for their own technological disruption. Machine learning is a promising tool which may radically improve our ability to perform job and task analysis more efficiently. Additionally, there is more that can be done to perform job and task analysis efforts in a multi-disciplinary fashion that simultaneously considers the impact of exponential technologies and the future resiliency of the components of a job or task. Additionally, there is related work to be completed regarding the skills of the future. While there have been preliminary studies pursuing these insights, there is much more to be done in order to understand the skills most likely to remain or become important alongside technology.

Labor Participation. Another important area of research relates to the disproportionate impact of technological job disruptions. While automation is projected to impact those in lower-income occupations and with low educational attainment the hardest (Frey & Osborne, 2017), it is important to consider the related stratification implications. An analysis of automatable tasks found that work associated with the bottom 10% of earners, and workers with a high school diploma or less, was the most highly automatable in the near term (Arntz et al., 2016). While the future of work holds potential to be positive, it is important to consider how those positive outcomes are likely to be distributed.

Ethics of Exponentials. Another important area involves the general ethics of exponential technologies such as artificial intelligence. Many scholars have noted that artificial intelligence, and other exponential technologies, have the potential to bring major benefits to society in addition to serious dangers (Russell, Dewey, & Tegmark, 2015). For example, early work on the ethics of job automation has focused on distributive justice – how will efficiency gains from automation be distributed? – and personal fulfillment – if one doesn't need to work then what do they do with their life? (Danaher, 2017). Additional areas of inquiry have focused on matters of data security and privacy (see Li & Zhang, 2017) – specifically, how personal data is used and shared in artificial intelligence applications, particularly in the workplace. The ethics of using such technologies is an emerging area of research that is sure to be a trademark of this literature moving forward. Perhaps this is the most important domain for multidisciplinary involvement from ethicists, technologists, psychologists, policy makers, and others, as a digitized world of work means a highly connected world and that we are all touched by these technologies.

The Meaning of Work. Finally, while the future remains uncertain, some believe that we are moving toward a post-work world. Whether one shares this view or not, there are numerous research inquiries that can prepare us to cope with this outcome, yet also shed light on matters salient today in an active world of work. Universal basic income is often touted as a future-of-work solution (Woodbury, 2017), yet this is primarily a response to economic impacts. It is important to understand what other impacts of automation are important to prepare for, such as the dignity and wellbeing of workers, in addition to meaningful and purposeful activities. There is a robust research stream pertaining to job insecurity (see Cheng & Chan, 2008; Keim, Landis, Pierce, & Earnest, 2014) yet there is still an opportunity to explore additional questions specific to job insecurity driven by automation.

Fortunately, better understanding such domains is pursuant to our increased understanding of what elements of work are important today. In a conceptual essay, Weiss (2013) argues that technological changes may alter the human experience and urges researchers to take a person-centric viewpoint (Weiss & Rupp, 2011) to consider these changes to further understand the role of work in the human experience. The future-of-work research domain is only in its advent and there are numerous areas of inquiry to be explored to help us better understand and prepare for changes in work.

Conclusion: The Future of Work

Even while we begin to better understand the changes brought on by technology, the future of work is inherently uncertain. With this uncertainty, it may be tempting to ignore the topic in scientific inquiry or save it for another day. Yet, much of what is most important to understand relating to the future of work also sparks a greater understanding of work today. While the future of work is discussed and explored, there is a great opportunity to make work better for today's, as well as tomorrow's, workers. Exponential technologies are, first and foremost, tools. Perhaps those tools can be leveraged for improvement, both in work science and work itself.

As presented in this chapter, the future of work is an important topic of this time. While this is not the first time the topic has garnered attention, perhaps there are reasons that it is especially important in the current context of technological change. Today, researchers are focused on making a variety of predictions about the future of work, but there is extensive work still to be done to understand these changes and their impact. Looking closely at technological trends, it is evident that technological change is coming, solutions are being proposed and implemented, and researchers have an influential voice on this topic. Perhaps the task is not to predict the future of work, but to create it.

References

Acemoglu, D., & Autor, D. (2011). Skills, tasks and technologies: Implications for employment and earnings. *Handbook of Labor Economics, 4*, 1043–1171.

Acemoglu, D., & Restrepo, P. (2017). Robots and jobs: Evidence from US labor markets. *National Bureau of Economic Research Working Paper*. Retrieved from www.sipotra.it/wp-content/uploads/2017/04/Robots-and-Jobs-Evidence-from-US-Labor-Markets.pdf

Aghion, P., andHowitt, P. (1994). Growth and unemployment. *Review of Economic Studies, 61*, 477–494.

Arntz, M., Gregory, T. and Zierahn, U. (2016), The Risk of automation for jobs in OECD countries: A comparative analysis. *OECD Social, Employment and Migration Working Papers*, No. 189. Paris: OECD Publishing. Retrieved from http://dx.doi.org/10.1787/5jlz9h56dvq7-en

Autor, D. H. (2013). The 'task approach' to labor markets: An overview. *Journal for Labour Market Research, 46*, 185–199.

Autor, D. H. (2015). Why are there still so many jobs? The history and future of workplace automation. *Journal of Economic Perspectives, 29*, 3–30.

Autor, D. H., & Handel, M. J. (2013). Putting tasks to the test: Human capital, job tasks, and wages. *Journal of Labor Economics, 31*, 59–96.

Autor, D. H., Levy, F., & Murnane, R. J. (2003). The skill content of recent technological change: An empirical exploration. *Quarterly Journal of Economics, 118*, 1279–1333.

Bakhshi, H., Downing, J., Osborne, M., & Schneider, P. (2017). The future of skills: employment in 2030. Retrieved from https://futureskills.pearson.com/research/assets/pdfs/technical-report.pdf

Bergman, M. E., & Jean, V. A. (2016). Where have all the "workers" gone? A critical analysis of the unrepresentativeness of our samples relative to the labor market in the industrial–organizational psychology literature. *Industrial and Organizational Psychology: Perspectives on Science and Practice, 9*, 84–113.

Bingham, A. J., Pane, J. F., Steiner, E. D., & Hamilton, L. S. (2018). Ahead of the curve: Implementation challenges in personalized learning school models. *Educational Policy, 32*, 454–489.

Bowles, J. (2014), The computerization of European jobs, Bruegel Technical Report. Retrieved from http://bruegel.org/2014/07/the-computerisation-of-european-jobs/ http://bruegel.org/2014/07/chart-of-the-week-54-of-eu-jobs-at-risk-of-computerisation/

Brawley, A. M. (2017). The big, gig picture: We can't assume the same constructs matter. *Industrial and Organizational Psychology: Perspectives on Science and Practice, 10*, 687–696.

Bronklow, A. (2018, February). Stockton rolls out universal income experiment. Retrieved from https://sf.curbed.com/2018/2/1/16959714/stockton-universal-income-economy-families

Bryant, D. (2017). Protecting the future of work. *The Aspen Institute*. Retrieved from www.aspeninstitute.org/blog-posts/protecting-future-work/

Brynjolfsson, E., and McAfee, A. (2011). *Race against the machines : How the digital revolution is accelerating innovation, driving productivity, and irreversibly transforming employment and the economy*. Lexington, MA: Digital Frontier Press.

Brzeski, C. & Burk I. (2015). Die Roboter kommen. Folgen der Automatisierung für den deutschen Arbeitsmarkt [The robots come. Consequences of automation for the German labour market]. *ING DiBa Economic Research*. Retrieved from https://ingwb.de/media/1398074/ing-diba-economic-research-die-roboter-kommen.pdf

Bureau of Labor Statistics (2017). Employment by major industry sector. Retrieved from www.bls.gov/emp/tables/employment-by-major-industry-sector.htm

Cagnin, C., Havas, A., & Saritas, O. (2013). Future-oriented technology analysis: Its potential to address disruptive transformations. *Technological Forecasting and Social Change, 80*, 379–385.

Caputo, R. (Ed.) (2012). *Basic income guarantee and politics: International experiences and perspectives on the viability of income guarantee*. New York, NY: Springer.

Cheng, G. H. L., & Chan, D. K. S. (2008). Who suffers more from job insecurity? A meta-analytic review. *Applied Psychology, 57*, 272–303.

Chernyak-Hai, L., & Rabenu, E. (2018). The new era workplace relationships: Is social exchange theory still relevant?. *Industrial and Organizational Psychology, 11*, 456–481.

Chui, M., Manyika, J., & Miremadi, M. (2015, November). Four fundamentals of workplace automation. *McKinsey Quarterly, 29*, 1–9. Retrieved from www.mckinsey.com/business-functions/digital-mckinsey/our-insights/four-fundamentals-of-workplace-automation

Collins, H. M. (2018). Expert systems, artificial intelligence and the behavioral co-ordinates of skill. In *The question of artificial intelligence*. New York, NY: Routledge, 258–281.

Cooper, Y. (2018, August). Automation could destroy millions of jobs. We have to deal with it now. Retrieved from www.theguardian.com/commentisfree/2018/aug/06/automation-destroy-millions-jobs-change

Danaher, J. (2017). Will life be worth living in a world without work? Technological unemployment and the meaning of life. *Science and Engineering Ethics, 23*, 41–64.

Danneels, E. (2004). Disruptive technology reconsidered: A critique and research agenda. *Journal of Product Innovation Management, 21*, 246–258.

De Fruyt, F., Wille, B., & John, O. P. (2015). Employability in the 21st century: Complex (interactive) problem solving and other essential skills. *Industrial and Organizational Psychology, 8*, 276–281.

DeCanio, S. J. (2016). Robots and humans: complements or substitutes?. *Journal of Macroeconomics, 49*, 280–291.

Decker, M., Fischer, M., & Ott, I. (2017). Service robotics and human labor: A first technology assessment of substitution and cooperation. *Robotics and Autonomous Systems, 87*, 348–354.

Diamandis, P. H., & Kotler, S. (2012). *Abundance: The future is better than you think*. New York, NY: Simon and Schuster.

Dimitri, C., Effland, A. B., Conklin, N. C., & Dimitri, C. (2005). *The 20th century transformation of US agriculture and farm policy, 3*. Washington, DC: US Department of Agriculture, Economic Research Service.

Dong, Y., Simões, M. L., Marois, E., Dimopoulos, G. (2018). CRISPR/Cas9 -mediated gene knockout of Anopheles gambiae FREP1 suppresses malaria parasite infection. *PLOS Pathogens, 14*. Retrieved from e1006898 DOI: 10.1371/journal.ppat.1006898

Dychtwald, K., & Flower, J. (1989). *Age wave*. New York, NY: JP Tarcher.

Eichhorst, W. (2015). Do we have to be afraid of the future world of work?, *IZA Policy Paper*, No. 102, Institute for the Study of Labor (IZA), Bonn.

European Society for Medical Oncology. (2018, May) Man against machine: AI is better than dermatologists at diagnosing skin cancer. *ScienceDaily*. Retrieved from www.sciencedaily.com/releases/2018/05/180528190839.htm.

Finlay, R. (1991). The treasure-ships of Zheng He: Chinese maritime imperialism in the Age of Discovery. *Terrae Incognitae, 23*, 1–12.

Frazee, G. (2018, August). Ontario is canceling its basic income experiment. Retrieved from www.pbs.org/newshour/economy/making-sense/ontario-is-canceling-its-basic-income-experiment

Fredette, J., Marom, R., Steiner, K., & Witters, L. (2012). The promise and peril of hyperconnectivity for organizations and societies. *The global information technology report* (pp. 113–119). World Economic Forum. Retrieved from https://core.ac.uk/download/pdf/30679485.pdf#page=139

Frey, C. B., & Osborne, M. (2013). The future of employment. How susceptible are jobs to computerization? (Working paper.) Retrieved from www.oxfordmartin.ox.ac.uk/downloads/academic/The_Future_of_Employment.pdf

Frey, C. B., & Osborne, M. A. (2017). The future of employment: how susceptible are jobs to computerization?. *Technological Forecasting and Social Change, 114*, 254–280.

Frey, C. B., & Osborne, M. (2018). Automation and the future of work – understanding the numbers. (Working paper.) *Oxford Martin School*. Retrieved from www.oxfordmartin.ox.ac.uk/opinion/view/404

Gillespie, P. (2017). Intuit: Gig economy is 34% of US workforce. *CNN Money*. Retrieved from http://money.cnn.com/2017/05/24/news/economy/gig-economy-intuit/

Goodman, P. (2018, May). Free cash to fight income inequality? California city is first in US to try. Retrieved from www.nytimes.com/2018/05/30/business/stockton-basic-income.html

Gregory, T., Salomons, A., and Zierahn, U. (2016). Racing with or against the machine? Evidence from Europe. *ZEW Discussion Paper* No. 16. Retrieved from http://ftp.zew.de/pub/zew-docs/dp/dp16053.pdf

Grossman, D. (2017). This giant 3D printer could build you a house today. *Popular Mechanics*. Retrieved from www.popularmechanics.com/technology/infrastructure/a26252/3d-printer-build-house-mit/

Hagel, J., Brown, J. S., Samoylova, T., & Lui, M. (2013). From exponential technologies to exponential innovation. Deloitte Center for the Edge, San Jose, California. Retrieved from www2.deloitte.com/content/dam/Deloitte/es/Documents/sector publico/Deloitte_ES_Sector-Publico_From-exponentialtechnologies-to-exponential-innovation. pdf.

Ismail, S., Malone, M. S., & Van Geest, Y. (2014). *Exponential organizations. Why new organizations are ten times better, faster, and cheaper than yours (and what to do about it)*. New York, NY: Diversion Books.

Jenkins, S. (2018, August). Worrying about robots stealing our jobs? How silly. Retrieved from www.theguardian.com/commentisfree/2018/aug/20/robots-stealing-jobs-digital-age

Katz, L. F., & Krueger, A. B. (2016). *The rise and nature of alternative work arrangements in the United States, 1995–2015*. National Bureau of Economic Research. Retrieved from www.nber.org/papers/w22667

Keim, A. C., Landis, R. S., Pierce, C. A., & Earnest, D. R. (2014). Why do employees worry about their jobs? A meta-analytic review of predictors of job insecurity. *Journal of Occupational Health Psychology, 19*, 269–290.

Keynes, J. M. (1973). The monetary theory of production (1933). In *The Collected Writings of John Maynard Keynes* (vol. 13, pp. 408–411). London: Macmillan.

Kotecki, P. (2018, August). An ambitious basic income experiment started by a major Silicon Valley tech accelerator has been delayed. Retrieved from www.businessinsider.com/basic-income-experiment-started-by-y-combinator-delayed-until-2019-2018-8

Kottasova, I. (2016, January). Smart robots could soon steal your job. Retrieved from https://money.cnn.com/2016/01/15/news/economy/smart-robots-stealing-jobs-davos/index.html

Kuhn, K. M. (2016). The rise of the "Gig Economy" and implications for understanding work and workers. *Industrial and Organizational Psychology, 9*, 157–162.

Kurzweil, R. (2004). The law of accelerating returns. In *Alan Turing: Life and legacy of a great thinker*. Berlin–Heidelberg: Springer, 381–416.

Kurzweil, R. (2005). *The singularity is near: When humans transcend biology*. Harmondsworth: Penguin.

Kurzweil, R. (2014). *The singularity is near*. In R. L. Sandler (Ed.), *Ethics and emerging technologies* (pp. 393–406). London: Palgrave Macmillan.

Levathes, L. (2014). *When China ruled the seas: The treasure fleet of the dragon throne, 1405–1433*. New York, NY: Oxford University Press.

Li, X., & Zhang, T. (2017, April). An exploration on artificial intelligence application: From security, privacy and ethic perspective. In *Cloud Computing and Big Data Analysis (ICCCBDA), 2017 Institute of Electrical and Electronics Engineers 2nd International Conference*, 416–420.

Lorenz, H., & Stephany, F. (2018). *Back to the future: Changing job profiles in the digital age, 13*. Agenda Austria Working Paper. Retrieved from www.econstor.eu/bitstream/10419/175270/1/1013982509.pdf

Manyika, J., Chui, M., Madgavkar, A., & Lund, S. (2017). Technology, jobs, and the future of work. *McKinsey Global Institute*. Retrieved from www.mckinsey.com/featured- insights/employment-and-growth/technology-jobs-and-the-future-of-work

Manyika, J., Chui, M., Miremadi, M., Bughin, J., George, K., Willmott, P., & Dewhurst, M. (2017, January). *A future that works: Automation, employment, and productivity*. Retrieved from www.mckinsey.com/global-themes/digital-disruption/harnessing-automation-for-a-future-that-works

Mason, P. (2016, February). Automation may mean a post-work society but we shouldn't be afraid. Retrieved from www.theguardian.com/sustainable-business/2016/feb/17/automation-may-mean-a-post-work-society-but-we-shouldnt-be-afraid

McAfee, A. (2013). *Andrew McAfee: What will future jobs look like?* [Video file]. Retrieved from www.ted.com/talks/andrew_mcafee_what_will_future_jobs_look_like/up-next

Meikle, S. (1997). Aristotle's economic thought. *OUP Catalogue*. Oxford University Press, number 9780198152255. https://ideas.repec.org/b/oxp/obooks/9780198152255.html

Melendez, C. (2018, August). AI: Creating a paradigm shift in how we work. Retrieved from www.forbes.com/sites/forbestechcouncil/2018/08/01/ai-creating-a-paradigm-shift- in-how-we-work/#10002b1f2d62

Mims, C. (2017, January). Technology versus the middle class. *Wall Street Journal*. Retrieved from www.wsj.com/articles/technology-vs-the-middle-class- 1485107698

Mitzner, T. L., Chen, T. L., Kemp, C. C., & Rogers, W. A. (2014). Identifying the potential for robotics to assist older adults in different living environments. *International Journal of Social Robotics, 6*, 213–227.

Mokyr, J. (1992). Technological inertia in economic history. *Journal of Economic History, 52*, 325–338.

Mokyr, J., Vickers, C., & Ziebarth, N. L. (2015). The history of technological anxiety and the future of economic growth: Is this time different? *Journal of Economic Perspectives, 29*, 31–50.

Moore, G. E. (1965). Moore's Law, "Cramming more components onto integrated circuits." *Electronics Magazine, 38*, 114–117.

Moore, P., & Robinson, A. (2016). The quantified self: What counts in the neoliberal workplace. *New Media & Society, 18*, 2774–2792.

Morelli, N., Illingworth, A. J., & Handler, C. (2015). Questions about IO psychology's future. *Industrial and Organizational Psychology: Perspectives on Science and Practice, 8*, 269–276.

Morrison, M. (2017, April). SIOP shaken & stirred: What if work becomes optional in the future? Presented at the 32nd Annual Conference of the Society of Industrial and Organizational Psychology, Orlando, FL.

Mrass, V.; Peters, C. & Leimeister, J. M. (2016). New work organization through crowdworking platforms – a case study. In: Zukunftsprojekt Arbeitswelt 4.0, Stuttgart, Germany.

Nagy, B., Farmer, J. D., Bui, Q. M., & Trancik, J. E. (2013). Statistical basis for predicting technological progress. *PLOS ONE, 8*, e52669. Retrieved from https://journals.plos.org/plosone/article?id=10.1371/journal.pone.0052669

National Academies of Sciences, Engineering, and Medicine. (2017). *Information technology and the US workforce: Where are we and where do we go from here?* Washington, DC: The National Academies Press. doi:10.17226/24649

Neubert, J. C., Mainert, J., Kretzschmar, A., & Greiff, S. (2015). The assessment of 21st century skills in industrial and organizational psychology: Complex and collaborative problem solving. *Industrial and Organizational Psychology, 8*, 238–268.

Oliver, B. (2015). Redefining graduate employability and work-integrated learning: Proposals for effective higher education in disrupted economies. *Journal of Teaching and Learning for Graduate Employability, 6*, 56–65.

O'Neill, C. (2017). Taylorism, the European science of work, and the quantified self at work. *Science, Technology, & Human Values, 42*, 600–621.

Oppitz, M., & Tomsu, P. (2018). New paradigms and big disruptive things. In *Inventing the cloud century* (pp. 547–596). Cham: Springer.

Otieno, P. S., & Govender, K. (2018). Managing airport service quality: the impact of self- service technologies. *Investment Management and Financial Innovations, 13*. Retrieved from doi:10.21511/imfi.13(3- 2).2016.11

Pajarinen, M. & Rouvinen P. (2014), "Computerization threatens one third of Finnish employment. *Research Institute of the Finnish Economy (ETLA) Brief, 22*, 1–6. Retrieved from www.researchgate.net/profile/Mika_Pajarinen/publication/ 27172 4486_Computerization_Threatens_One_Third_of_Finnish_Employ ment/links/54d08b8f0cf298d65667070b/Computerization-Threatens-One-Third-of-Finnish-Employment.pdf

Pender, K., (2017, September). Oakland group plans to launch nation's biggest basic-income research project. *San Francisco Chronicle*. Retrieved from www.sfchronicle.com/business/networth/article/Oakland-group-plans-to-launch-nation-s-biggest-12219073.php

Peter, L. (2018). No plans to expand Finland basic income trial. *BBC News*. Retrieved from www.bbc.com/news/world-europe-43866700

Pilkington, M. (2016). Blockchain technology: principles and applications. In F. X. Olleros & M. Zhegu (Eds.), *Research handbook on digital transformations* (pp. 225–253). Cheltenham, UK: Edward Elgar Publishing.

Postel-Vinay, F. (2002). The dynamics of technological unemployment. *International Economic Review, 43*, 737–760.

Quendler, E., & Lamb, M. (2016). Learning as a lifelong process – meeting the challenges of the changing employability landscape: competences, skills and knowledge for sustainable development. *International Journal of Continuing Engineering Education and Life Long Learning, 26,* 273–293.

Rainie, L., & Anderson, J. (2017). The future of jobs and jobs training. *Pew Research Center.* Retrieved from www.pewinternet.org/2017/05/03/the-future-of-jobs-and-jobs-training/

Rampell, C. (2015). The robots aren't threatening your job. *Washington Post.* Retrieved from www.washingtonpost.com/opinions/dont-fear-the-robots/2015/04/09/e7ea1316-def3-11e4-a1b2ed88bc190d2_story.html?noredirect=on&utm_term=.7ac743eded3c

Reinsel, D., Gantz, J., & Rydning, J. (2017, April). Data age 2025: The evolution of data to life-critical. Don't focus on big data; focus on the data that's big. *IDC, Seagate.* Retrieved from https://assets.ey.com/content/dam/ey-sites/ey-com/en_gl/topics/workforce/Seagate-WP-DataAge2025-March-2017.pdf

Riggio, R. E., & Saggi, K. (2015). Incorporating "soft skills" into the collaborative problem-solving equation. *Industrial and Organizational Psychology, 8,* 281–284.

Rotman, D. (2013, June). How technology is destroying jobs. *Technology Review, 16,* 28–35. Retrieved from www.technologyreview.com/s/515926/how-technology-is-destroying-jobs/

Russell, S., Dewey, D., & Tegmark, M. (2015). Research priorities for robust and beneficial artificial intelligence. *Ai Magazine, 36,* 105–114.

Schaller, R. R. (1997). Moore's law: past, present and future. *IEEE Spectrum, 34,* 52–59.

Schwab, K. (2017). *The fourth industrial revolution.* New York, NY: Crown Business.

Seagrave, K. (2012). *Vending machines: An American social history.* Jefferson, NC: McFarland & Company, Inc.

Sharkey, N. (2008). The ethical frontiers of robotics. *Science, 322,* 1800–1801.

Sharples, M. (2000). The design of personal mobile technologies for lifelong learning. *Computers & Education, 34,* 177–193.

Singla, R., Edgcumbe, P., Pratt, P., Nguan, C., & Rohling, R. (2017) Intra-operative ultrasound-based augmented reality guidance for laparoscopic surgery. *Healthcare Technology Letters, 4,* 204–209.

Sliter, K. A. (2015). Assessing 21st century skills: Competency modeling to the rescue. *Industrial and Organizational Psychology, 8,* 284–289.

Society for Human Resource Management (SHRM). (2016). The new talent landscape: Recruiting difficulty and skills shortages. Retrieved from www.shrm.org/hr-today/trends-and-forecasting/research-and surveys/Documents/SHRM%20New%20Talent%20Landscape%20Recruiting%20Difficulty%20Skills.pdf

Su, R., Golubovich, J., & Robbins, S. B. (2015). Bridging science and practice: Toward a standard, evidence-based framework of 21st century skills. *Industrial and Organizational Psychology, 8,* 289–294.

Sun, J., Yan, J., & Zhang, K. Z. (2016). Blockchain-based sharing services: What blockchain technology can contribute to smart cities. *Financial Innovation, 2,* 26. https://doi.org/10.1186/s40854-016-0040-y

Sundararajan, A. (2016). *The sharing economy: The end of employment and the rise of crowd-based capitalism.* Cambridge, MA: The MIT Press.

Theis, T. N., & Wong, H. S. P. (2017). The end of Moore's Law: A new beginning for information technology. *Computing in Science & Engineering, 19,* 41–50.

Thompson, D. (2015). A world without work. *The Atlantic, 316,* 50–61.

Toutain, J. (2013). *The economic life of the ancient world.* New York, NY: Routledge.

Townsend, A. M., DeMarie, S. M., & Hendrickson, A. R. (1998). Virtual teams: Technology and the workplace of the future. *The Academy of Management Executive, 12,* 17–29.

Vincent, J. (2018, May). Google's AI sounds like a human on the phone, should we be worried? *The Verge.* Retrieved from www.theverge.com/2018/5/9/17334658/google-ai-phone-call-assistant-duplex-ethical-social-implications

Weiss, H. M. (2013). Working as human nature. In J. K. Ford, J. R. Hollenbeck, & A. M. Ryan (Eds.), *The nature of work: Advances in psychological theory, methods, and practice* (pp. 35–47). Washington, DC: American Psychological Association.

Weiss, H. M., & Rupp, D. E. (2011). Experiencing work: An essay on a person-centric work psychology. *Industrial and Organizational Psychology, 4,* 83–97.

Whitehouse – Office of the President (2016). Artificial intelligence, automation, and the economy. *Executive Office of the President.* Retrieved from https://obamawhitehouse. archives. gov/sites/whitehouse. gov/files/documents/Artificial-Intelligence-Automation-Economy. PDF.

Williams, R. S. (2017). What's next? The end of Moore's law. *Computing in Science & Engineering, 19,* 7–13.

Woodbury, S. A. (2017). *Universal basic income. The American middle class: An economic encyclopedia of progress and poverty [2 volumes].* Santa Barbara, CA: Greenwood.

World Economic Forum. (2016). New vision for education: Fostering social and emotional learning through technology. Geneva, Switzerland: World Economic Forum. Retrieved from www3.weforum.org/docs/WEF_New_Vision_for_Education.pdf

World Economic Forum. (2018). The Future of Jobs Report. Geneva, Switzerland: World Economic Forum. Retrieved from www3.weforum.org/docs/wef_future_of_jobs_2018.pdf

Wyman, N. (2018, June). Fear not the job-stealing robots. *Forbes.* Retrieved from www.forbes.com/sites/nicholaswyman/2018/06/13/fear-not-the-job-stealing-robots/#34295d595f5a

Yeginsu, C. (2018, February). If workers slack off this wristband will know. And Amazon has a patent for it. *New York Times.* Retrieved from www.nytimes.com/2018/02/01/technology/amazon-wristband-tracking- privacy.html

27 Sustainability as a Driver of Organizational Change

Lori Foster[*] and Telma Viale

An enabled, properly regulated, responsible and profitable private sector is critical for employment, living wages, growth, and revenues for public programmes. Transforming business models for creating shared value is vital for growing inclusive and sustainable economies.

(United Nations, 2014, p. 22)
Ban Ki-moon, Eighth Secretary-General
of the United Nations

Sustainability as a Driver of Organizational Change

A key factor that differentiates the United Nations Sustainable Development Goals (SDGs) from their predecessor, the Millennium Development Goals (MDGs), is the active engagement of the private sector in their accomplishment. In fact, SDG 17 explicitly focuses on "Partnerships for the Goals," which includes public–private partnerships and other corporate initiatives. Within the UN framework, efforts such as the United Nations Global Compact and the United Nations Development Programme (UNDP)'s Istanbul International Center for the Private Sector in Development support private sector involvement in poverty reduction and development. Outside of the UN system, companies have been implementing their own initiatives – sometimes with the support of other companies – that take corporate social responsibility to a new level. Examples include initiatives aimed at protecting the environment, such as efforts toward water stewardship and actions to become climate positive. However, the SDGs are not solely about the environment. They also involve social aims, such as poverty reduction, gender equality, lifelong learning, and access to decent work. There are tremendous opportunities for companies to play a role there too, through human-centered policies, programs, practices, and initiatives and through core missions aimed at social impact. This raises questions about organizations' readiness and capacity to execute on such initiatives, and how insights from behavioral sciences can be applied to facilitate such readiness and capacity, creating sustainable ways for the private sector to benefit from "doing good," while making a meaningful contribution to development.

---

[*] The first author has affiliations with two of the organizations highlighted in this chapter: UNICEF and pymetrics.

What Is Sustainable Development?

Many readers are familiar with the concept of development, particularly as it is used to categorize countries around the world. One simplistic classification is reflected by the common distinction between the "developed" and "developing" worlds. Other classifications divide this further into, for example, developing economies, economies in transition, and developed economies (United Nations, 2018). Historically, such classifications have been based largely on financial indices such as Gross National Income (GNI) or Gross Domestic Product (GDP). However, there is a growing recognition that economic growth and productivity alone are insufficient.

According to World Bank statistics, the world economy by nominal GDP- more than doubled in size in recent years, from US$33.57 trillion in 2000 to US$80.68 trillion in 2017 (World Bank Group, 2018). But alongside booms of global economic growth, the spread of globalization, the exponential growth of technology, and the dissemination of the Internet which connects people around the world, dystopian views of the future have emerged. They stem from harsh realities that have coincided with economics gains: the increased inequality within and among nations, the persistent social gap widened by poor education and gender inequality, the rise of wars and terrorism, environmental degradation, plastic pollution in the oceans, deforestation, overfishing, climate change, natural disasters, the increasing concern around health hazards, uncontrolled industrialization, air pollution, food and water security, massive migrations, and a world population crowded in developing countries. In short, there has been a growing recognition that financial indices alone provide an incomplete picture of where a country is at, where our world is headed in terms of development, as well as the sustainability of global progress. Nearly three decades ago, this recognition formed the basis of the UNDP's Human Development Index, established in 1990, which takes into account human or social indicators – namely health and education – alongside material well-being, when determining a country's level of development (Herrero, Martínez, & Villar, 2018).

Leading into the year 2015, the international community had an opportunity to once again reflect on the question, "What is development?" Far more than an academic exercise, the answer to this question would form the basis of Agenda 2030, otherwise known as the Sustainable Development Goals (SDGs), which countries around the world would commit to achieve. In a sense, the days leading up to Agenda 2030 started by changing the question from *What is development?* to *What is sustainable development?* In other words, discussions focused on how countries around the world can achieve progress that will persist over time, rather than focusing on short-term gains at odds with longer-term wellbeing. The interplay among economic, social, and environmental factors is central to today's conceptualization of sustainable development. Consider, for example, a country producing in a way that depletes natural resources. Such productivity cannot be sustained once those natural resources are gone. Or, imagine a country where rising GDP coincides with rising levels of inequality. Such inequality can trigger social unrest, which negatively impacts a country's capacity to function and produce. Of course, sustainable development also requires sound financial management, in part to ensure that countries have the continued financial resources to make the investments necessary to achieve longer-term aims (Mazzucato, 2011; United Nations, 2018).

Sharafat and Lehr (2017) offer a "business case" of sorts for paying attention to social wellbeing, noting that "the very basis upon which economic growth can be achieved will be under threat unless inequality is also addressed" (p. 53). Citing work by the Organisation for Economic Co-operation and Development (OECD, 2015), these authors maintain that rising inequality creates social and political tensions that drain the economy, reduce GDP, and prevent people from realizing their economic potential. Another perspective is that equality and wellbeing should be primary objectives in and of themselves. In other words, one could argue that economic prosperity should be a means for achieving social and environmental wellbeing, rather than social and environmental wellbeing being a pathway to economic prosperity. Regardless of which perspective one takes, sustainable development requires attention to all three factors: social, environmental, and economic wellbeing. These three factors align quite clearly with the triple bottom line concept in the private sector which emphasizes a focus on people, planet and profit by attending to social, environmental, and financial performance (Swanson & Orlitzky, 2018).

In September of 2015, the nations of the world adopted 17 Sustainable Development Goals (SDGs), shown in Table 27.1, which effectively operationalize the pathway to enduring progress. The 2030 Agenda for Sustainable Development and its 17 SDGs, also known as the Global Goals, take social, environmental, and economic factors into account, providing the world with a timely and unique opportunity to be coherent in efforts to meet the urgent need of achieving a better future for all. It is the most ambitious and complex development framework ever adopted, by 193 nations "resolved to free the human race from the tyranny of poverty and want and to heal and secure our planet" (United Nations General Assembly, 2015, p. 1). Meant to guide the global development agenda for 15 years, these goals run from 2015 to 2030. Each SDG includes sub-goals known as targets, which further specify the aspiration at hand. For example, SDG 8 on Decent Work and Economic Growth has 12 targets, including:

- Target 8.5: *By 2030, achieve full and productive employment and decent work for all women and men, including for young people and persons with disabilities, and equal pay for work of equal value.*
- Target 8.6: *By 2020, substantially reduce the proportion of youth not in employment, education or training.*
- Target 8.8: *Protect labour rights and promote safe and secure working environments for all workers, including migrant workers, in particular women migrants, and those in precarious employment.* (United Nations General Assembly, 2015, pp. 19–20).

Table 27.1 *The United Nations Sustainable Development Goals*

Goal #	Title[a]	Goal[b]
1	No Poverty	End poverty in all its forms everywhere.
2	Zero Hunger	End hunger, achieve food security and improved nutrition and promote sustainable agriculture.
3	Good Health and Well-Being	Ensure healthy lives and promote well-being for all at all ages.
4	Quality Education	Ensure inclusive and equitable quality education and promote lifelong learning opportunities for all.
5	Gender Equality	Achieve gender equality and empower all women and girls.
6	Clean Water and Sanitation	Ensure availability and sustainable management of water and sanitation for all.
7	Affordable and Clean Energy	Ensure access to affordable, reliable, sustainable and modern energy for all.
8	Decent Work and Economic Growth	Promote sustained, inclusive and sustainable economic growth, full and productive employment and decent work for all.
9	Industry, Innovation, and Infrastructure	Build resilient infrastructure, promote inclusive and sustainable industrialization and foster innovation.
10	Reduced Inequalities	Reduce inequality within and among countries.
11	Sustainable Cities and Communities	Make cities and human settlements inclusive, safe, resilient and sustainable.
12	Responsible Consumption and Production	Ensure sustainable consumption and production patterns.
13	Climate Action	Take urgent action to combat climate change and its impacts.
14	Life Below Water	Conserve and sustainably use the oceans, seas and marine resources for sustainable development.
15	Life on Land	Protect, restore and promote sustainable use of terrestrial ecosystems, sustainably manage forests, combat desertification, and halt and reverse land degradation and halt biodiversity loss.
16	Peace, Justice and Strong Institutions	Promote peaceful and inclusive societies for sustainable development, provide access to justice for all and build effective, accountable and inclusive institutions at all levels.
17	Partnerships for the Goals	Strengthen the means of implementation and revitalize the Global Partnership for Sustainable Development.

[a] From United Nations Department of Economic and Social Affairs (2018). *Sustainable development knowledge platform*. Retrieved from https://sustainabledevelopment.un.org/topics/sustainabledevelopmentgoals
[b] From United Nations General Assembly (2015). Transforming our world: The 2030 agenda for sustainable development.

Goal 17, "Partnerships for the Goals," is last but certainly not least in the list of SDGs. Its 17th target is particularly notable, articulating the aim to "Encourage and promote effective public, public–private and civil society partnerships, building on the experience and resourcing strategies of partnerships" (United Nations General Assembly, 2015, p. 27). In short, accomplishing sustainable development requires a variety of different actors to work together for collective impact (Kania & Kramer, 2011). Government, civil society, academia, faith communities, and numerous other actors all have a role to play. The private sector is an especially important "other actor." While pointing to the important role of governments in setting the policy framework within which the private sector will operate, Evans (2015) states that "most of the heavy lifting on the post-2015 agenda will need to be done by the private sector" (p. 60).

Discussions of the changing nature of work would thus be incomplete without a consideration of the changing role of the private sector in sustainable development, which affects what companies are working toward and how they are accomplishing their aims, with implications for work, workers, and working. Accordingly, this chapter considers and illustrates how the private sector can contribute to sustainable development. As will be demonstrated, opportunities for impact include and extend beyond traditional forms of Corporate Social Responsibility (CSR). Enabling companies to embed people-friendly, planet-sensitive policies and practices in ways that are good for business can propel the positive transformation needed to achieve the SDGs. This leads to questions of how to create such enabling environments. Answers require a keen understanding not only of businesses, but of the people that lead, comprise, and support them. As such, the behavioral and organizational sciences are key to facilitating the kinds of private sector contributions necessary to accomplish the SDGs.

The remainder of this chapter is organized into six sections. First, we begin with a brief consideration of CSR, including some of its historical underpinnings. Second, examples are provided of the private sector's engagement with the SDGs. Third, a critique of the private sector's role in sustainable development is offered alongside the proposition that prominent concerns may be addressed by solutions that align people, planet, and profit motives. Fourth, examples are provided which describe (a) companies and (b) global partnerships that facilitate such alignment. Fifth, we speculate on how embedding sustainability into organizational functioning will challenge leaders and change the nature of work requirements in the days to come. The sixth and final section details ways in which behavioral science can support the private sector's contributions to sustainable development.

CSR: Coming a Long Way, with More Ground Yet to Cover

A brief look at the past informs the way forward as companies and policy makers consider the immense opportunities and responsibilities for the private sector to contribute to sustainable development in the years to come. Well into the past, we can trace evidence of concern over corporate actions, including during eras in which there were relatively few regulations guiding the manner in which companies treated society, even their own employees. Consider, for example, the unsafe factory conditions in which US labor rights activist Clara Lemlich Shavelson and her contemporaries worked in the early 1900s. Such poor conditions led to labor movements aimed at putting pressure on policy makers and business owners to ensure and adopt more humane workplace practices.[1]

Meanwhile, there has long been a notion that companies' responsibility to people and society extends beyond their employees and transcends their legal and regulatory requirements. Back in the day, when the dominance of corporations was not occupying center stage, the concept of CSR was often conceptualized as a matter for men and for business. In the early writings of the 1950s, CSR was more often referred to as Social Responsibilities (SR), and it was in the context of businessmen that the issue was addressed. The title of the landmark book of Howard R. Bowen (1953), *Social Responsibilities of the Businessman*, supports this reflection. Bowen, considered by some as the "Father of Corporate and Social Responsibility" (Carroll, 1999), wrote the first comprehensive discussion of business ethics and the way that business behaves towards society. Bowen based his work on the belief that the largest businesses are centers of power and decision making and their actions touch the lives of citizens at many points. He argued that while social responsibility is not the magic cure, it contains an important truth that must guide business in the future.

The discussion and literature of CSR truly gained momentum during the 1950s, with a primary focus on "doing good deeds" for society. In the 1960s, key events, people, and ideas that triggered social changes were the center of attention for CSR. From the 1970s to the 1980s, the evolution was towards a stronger intersection between the concerns of business and social interests, with corporations becoming more responsive to their stakeholders. Around the 1990s "the idea" of CSR became almost globally approved, and it paved the path that led to the Millennium, where CSR became a key strategic element for corporations (Moura-Leite & Padgett, 2011). Within five decades, CSR went from doing "good deeds" to being a strategic building block in the corporate world.

Today, we are said to be "entering an era in which the most powerful law is not that of sovereignty but that of supply and demand" (Khanna, 2016, p. 54). The private sector has become increasingly influential and rich, with single companies now possessing financial resources exceeding the GDPs of two-thirds of the countries in our world (Khanna, 2016). CSR persists, and its research base has grown. However, the literature on CSR is notably fragmented, in part because scholars study CSR through different disciplinary and conceptual lenses, and at different levels of analysis (Aguinis & Glavas, 2012; Opoku-Dakwa, Chen, & Rupp, 2018). Definitions of CSR also vary in fundamental ways, raising questions about whether everyone is referring to quite

---

[1] Incidentally, Clara Lemlich Shavelson's story appeared in the *New York Times* in August of 2018, many years after her labor activism and decades after her unpublicized death, amid a growing awareness that since 1851, obituaries in newspapers like the *New York Times* have been dominated by white men (Greenberg, 2018).

the same thing when they use the term. Some scholars (e.g., Rupp, Shao, Skarlicki, Paddock, Kim, & Nadisic, 2018) define CSR as "actions on the part of the firm that appear to advance, or acquiesce in the promotion of some social good, beyond the immediate interests of the firm and its shareholders and beyond that which is required by law" (Waldman, Siegel, & Javidan, 2006, p. 1703). Others (e.g., Aguinis & Glavas, 2012, 2013) define CSR differently, as "context-specific organizational actions and policies that take into account stakeholders' expectations and the triple bottom line of economic, social and environmental performance" (Aguinis, 2011, p. 858). Whereas the first of these two definitions emphasizes actions beyond the company's own interests, the second does not. Rather, the second definition highlights the financial bottom line and stakeholders' expectations alongside the promotion of social and environmental good.

Theories of CSR abound, including those which differentiate CSR motivated by altruistic values from CSR that occurs for more instrumental purposes, motivated by a financial cost–benefit analysis. Garriga and Melé (2004) divide CSR approaches and theories into four types: instrumental, political, integrative, and ethical theories, which focus on profits, political performance, social demands, and ethical values, respectively. In instrumental CSR theories, companies are viewed as an instrument for wealth creation, and CSR is a means to an economic end. Political theories look at the responsible use of corporate power in society and politics. With integrative theories, the focus is on companies' satisfaction of social demands. These theories are labeled "integrative" not because they combine other theories together, but rather because they concentrate on how corporate management should integrate social demands into the way businesses operate, given that businesses depend on society for their existence and growth. Finally, ethical theories examine companies' ethical responsibilities to society (Garriga & Melé, 2004).

Practically, consideration is also given to whether CSR initiatives are internally or externally directed, the proximity of stakeholders benefiting from CSR initiatives, and the degree to which CSR activities are integrated or embedded into a company's core functions, regardless of whether they are motivated by humanitarian values or financial calculations. Internal CSR focuses on employee wellbeing whereas external CSR concentrates on beneficiaries outside of the company in question (Brammer, Millington, & Rayton, 2007; Jones & Rupp, 2018). Proximal stakeholders of internal and external CSR include employees who benefit from internal CSR initiatives as well as customers, employees' families, and the local community where a company conducts business; distal stakeholders are communities and organizations with whom a company conducting CSR has only indirect or tangential contact (Glösenberg, Carr, & Foster, in press). With respect to CSR's integration, Aguinis and Glavas (2013) usefully differentiate between embedded and peripheral CSR – a distinction we believe to be quite important if the private sector is to become a true partner in sustainable development. Relying on the company's core competencies, embedded CSR integrates CSR within a firm's operations, routines, and strategy. In contrast, peripheral CSR, as its name suggests, encompasses initiatives that are not integrated in such a manner.

Many of the activities traditionally thought of as CSR are peripheral. For example, a technology company that engages in philanthropy by donating money to a children's hospital, or an investment firm that incentivizes employees to volunteer to cook and serve meals at a local soup kitchen established to feed homeless people is typically engaging in peripheral CSR. Glösenberg et al. (in press) note the potential for such CSR activities to unintentionally harm beneficiaries, such as when volunteer labor, for example, suppresses wages or reduces paid employment opportunities for local workers in a lower-income region of the world. Asserting that good intentions are not enough, Glösenberg et al. urge companies engaging in CSR to know, understand, and adhere to best practice principles in the delivery of humanitarian aid.

The contrast between peripheral and embedded CSR is notable. Aguinis and Glavey (2014) offer examples to illustrate embedded CSR, including efforts by GE, whose products generate 25% of the world's daily electricity, to conceptualize and build solutions to environmental problems in a manner that supports the company's economic growth. The authors favor embedded CSR, pointing out a number of advantages of embedded over peripheral CSR, including the potential for embedded CSR to help managers bypass conflicts of interest – that is, the often counterproductive tension between serving the financial interests of the firm and those of society.

There is an interesting parallel between (a) the shift from peripheral (e.g., philanthropy, volunteerism) to embedded (i.e., integrated) CSR and (b) the transition from the MDGs, which guided global development efforts from 2000 to 2015, to the SDGs driving today's development agenda. As the UK's Institute of Development Studies (IDS) puts it, "The world has changed significantly since the MDGs were created in 2000. Notions of developed and developing have changed. International development is less about the transfer of aid from rich to poor countries and more about progressive change for everyone, everywhere" (IDS, 2017, p. 1). Accordingly, with the SDGs, all countries – not only those labeled as "developing" – are responsible for working toward and reporting on goal progress (Scheyvens, Banks, & Hughes, 2016). In effect, compared to the MDGs, the SDGs are less focused on the notion of "rich countries helping poor countries," and more universally focused on how global partnerships can support sustainable development worldwide. Similarly, CSR is moving from philanthropy to the integration of people-, planet- and profit-centered programs and policies into companies' core operations, routines, and strategies. As noted, we view this shift as essential to the private sector's participation as a partner in sustainable development.

From Philanthropy to Integrated Sustainability: Examples

Since the approval of the global goals, major corporations have redesigned their CSR platforms to reflect their engagement, explicitly supporting goals related to the core of their business. Whether the intention of companies is to rethink their value chain to integrate sustainability in their business model, give back to society, or go as far as replenishing the environmental resources central to their businesses, companies are increasingly relying on partnerships to scale impact towards sustainability. Consider, for example, Uniliever, a company that sells food, beverages, cleaning agents, and personal care products such as soap around the world. At the core of its business is the Unilever Sustainable Living Plan (Jack, 2015). The Unilever Sustainable Living Plan is Unilever's blueprint for growing (profit) in environmentally sustainable ways (planet) with a positive social impact (people). Encompassed in the Unilever Sustainable Living Plan is Unilever's commitment to work with others (partnerships) to focus specifically on those areas where it "can drive the biggest change and support the UN Sustainable Development Goals" (Unilever, 2018a). The Unilever Sustainable Living Plan includes three overarching goals, as follows:

- Improve health and wellbeing for more than 1 billion: By 2020 Unilever commits to helping more than a billion people across the globe take action to improve their health and wellbeing. Sub-goals relate to health and hygiene and improving nutrition.
- Reducing environmental impact by half: By 2030, Unilever commits to halving the environmental footprint of the making and use of their products while growing their business. Sub-goals relate to greenhouse gases, water use, waste and packaging, and sustainable sourcing.
- Enhancing livelihoods for millions: By 2020, Unilever commits to enhancing the livelihoods of millions of people as they grow their business. Sub-goals relate to fairness in the workplace, opportunities for women, and inclusive business (Unilever, 2018a).

Unilever explicitly links each of the preceding goals and sub-goals to specific SDGs. For example, the fairness in the workplace sub-goal indicated above is connected to SDG 3 (Good Health and Well-being), SDG 8 (Decent Work and Economic Growth), and SDG 10 (Reduced Inequalities). Unilever further notes that "Underpinning the achievement of these goals is SDG 17 (Partnerships for the Goals)" (Unilever, 2018b). Where possible, Unilever has its goal performance independently evaluated by outside entities such as PricewaterhouseCoopers LLP (PwC), DNV GL, and KPMG LLP (Unilever, 2018c), thereby embedding objectivity into the process. Accountability is emphasized through publicly displayed color-coded icons that indicate whether each goal has been achieved (blue dot with a checkmark), is on track for achievement (green dot), or is not on track (red dot).

A full account of the Unilever Sustainable Living Plan is beyond the scope of this chapter, but a glance at one component – opportunities for women – clearly demonstrates how the private sector's contributions to sustainable development can move beyond older, more traditional, conceptualizations of CSR. In the case of the Unilever Sustainable Living Plan, promoting opportunities for women begins with progressive policies and programs in the company's own workplace and supply chain operation. This includes programs that increase fairness in hiring, agile working arrangements, mentoring and networking opportunities for women, opportunities for personal and professional growth, access to role models and mentors, leadership development, paternity and maternity support, access to breastfeeding and daycare facilities at work, and careful attention to fairness in pay and living wages (Adrian Hodges Advisory, 2017). In addition, Unilever pays attention to workers and workplace practices in its supply chain. For example, like many companies, Unilever relies on people tending small farms across the world to supply the materials needed to make its products. To be effective and empowered, smallholder farmers need not only traditional agricultural skills, but also skills in business, finance, nutrition, hygiene, and sanitation. Women often lack access to training in these areas, putting them at a disadvantage when it comes to farming practices, performance, opportunities, and success. Partnering with other organizations, Unilever has put programs in place to help provide training and development opportunities to close this skills gap (Unilever, 2018d).

Unilever is by no means alone in its endeavors to grow and prosper in people-centered, planet-sensitive ways. Many companies, large and small, across a range of different sectors, are rethinking the way they do business and figuring out how to grow in sustainable ways that align with the SDGs. Table 27.2 shows but a few examples from the transportation sector. Table 27.2 is an excerpt from an SDG Industry Matrix developed by the United Nations Global Compact, in collaboration with KPMG (United Nations Global Compact & KPMG, 2015), which showcases industry-specific examples and ideas for corporate actions to collectively address the 17 SDGs. The sectors covered, inter alia, include construction and materials, aerospace and defense, industrial engineering, industrial transportation, automobiles and parts, beverages, food producers, healthcare equipment and services, pharmaceuticals and biotechnology, and financial services. Around the transportation sector alone, over 20 multi-stakeholder partnerships and global collaborative platforms are recorded by the UN Global Compact, in addition to various international associations and alliances. As can be seen, the private sector's contributions to sustainable development are expansive. Even holding the sector constant, companies' initiatives span the globe and cover a range of SDGs.

Criticisms

The notion of including the private sector as a strategic partner in sustainable development has generated a great deal of enthusiasm. However, some have argued that this enthusiasm is too often going unchecked. Scheyvens et al. (2016) point out that while there is no shortage of blogs by business consultants and sustainability experts extolling the virtues of private sector engagement with the SDGs, a balanced view is lacking, with very little academic work addressing the private sector's limitations as a partner in

Table 27.2 *Corporate action on the SDGs: examples from the transportation sector*[a]

Goal #	Title	Example
1	No Poverty	• Renault, a French car manufacturer, launched a social enterprise to help remove the mobility obstacles preventing low-income job seekers from accessing employment. Through a program called "Solidarity Garage," Renault, in partnership with welfare and employment agencies, facilitates transport of vulnerable populations and enables them to use and maintain their vehicles optimally. The garages provide affordable maintenance and cheaper cars.
2	Zero Hunger	• Pirelli & C. SpA has developed a partnership with its Supplier Kirana Megatara, one of the major rubber processors in Indonesia, to support natural rubber farmers (second-tier in Pirelli's supply chain) through quality training aimed at enhancing rubber tree productivity as a base to not only enhance farmers' earnings, but also to prevent deforestation risks linked to low productivity. Moreover, the program involves the distribution of scholarships to support education for the farmers' children. Today, around 6,000 farmers are involved in the program. • CSX, an international transport company, together with a nonprofit organization helps local farmers improve food delivery services in order to increase access to fresh and healthy foods to low-income families and individuals in the United States.
4	Quality Education	• Volvo Group, together with the US Agency for International Development and the Swedish International Development Cooperation Agency, entered into a partnership to provide vocational training schools for 4,500 young people in ten countries between 2013 and 2018, primarily in Africa and South-East Asia. This initiative supports Volvo Group's planned geographic expansion and it addresses the challenge of existing educational systems which do not develop the skills that are needed by the industry. The first schools have been launched in Ethiopia, Morocco, and Zambia including a training school in Settat (Morocco) to develop mechanical skills which can be directly applied in the heavy-equipment industry.
5	Gender Equality	• Lufthansa, Germany's air carrier, works towards increasing the representation of women pilots by challenging perceptions that it is a male role. In cooperation with Hamburg Aviation, the company organizes a series of outreach events including the Women in Aviation exhibition which showcases the

Table 27.2 (*cont.*)

Goal #	Title	Example
		professional careers of women in aviation. Lufthansa also offers family-friendly policies such as part-time opportunities to support work/life balance. • Transnet, a large transport company in South Africa, launched an enterprise development program in partnership with a global car manufacturer to empower female entrepreneurs in the engineering sector. The program enhances women's engineering skills so they can perform repairs and maintenance, equipment supply, plumbing and installation for Transnet and other companies.
7	Affordable and Clean Energy	• Airbus Group is supporting the development of sustainable fuels made from biomass feedstock that, through their lifecycle, emit less CO_2 than conventional fossil fuels. The Group has been working with a broad range of partners – universities, farmers, airlines, refineries and standard-setting organizations – to act as an agent of change, helping to develop value chains that produce 'drop-in' sustainable fuels that today's aircraft can burn without modification. Airbus aims to be a catalyst, sparking the search for production of affordable sustainable fuels, in sufficient commercial quantities to help the aviation industry reach its goals for minimizing greenhouse gas emissions. Airbus currently has development partnerships in place in Spain, Qatar, Brazil, Australia, Malaysia and China.
8	Decent Work and Economic Growth	• Royal Caribbean Cruises Ltd., in partnership with the Pan-American Development Foundation, supports the development of local artisans' businesses. Throughout the Caribbean and Latin America, this partnership helps artisans become third-party certified as sustainable vendors. Royal Caribbean Cruises invites the artisans to market their products to customers on their cruise ships, which also enhances the customer experience.
10	Reduced Inequalities	• Ford launched its supplier diversity development program in 1978 with the goals of supporting minority and women owned businesses, creating business opportunities for diverse suppliers to grow into profitable enterprises, and further strengthening the Ford supplier network to reflect the company's workforce and customer base. Ford's diverse suppliers play an important role in the company's revitalized and expanding portfolio of high-quality, safe, fuel-efficient products equipped with smart technologies. In 2015, Ford purchased goods and services worth:

Table 27.2 (*cont.*)

Goal #	Title	Example
		US$8.2 billion from minority-owned suppliers, US$1.1 billion from veteran-owned companies and US$2.3 billion from women-owned businesses.
11	Sustainable Cities and Communities	• FedEx, a global logistics company, embarked on a project with EMBARQ (a think tank) to identify sustainable public transport solutions in cities in Mexico, Brazil, and India. The three-year project reached out to over 1,600 transport officials and drivers, contributing to a reduction of 20,000 tons of carbon dioxide emissions. In addition, the program helped urban transport operators provide enhanced and more efficient services. • Accell Group, a bicycle manufacturer, introduced an electrically-assisted bicycle to facilitate the mobility of people with physical limitations and to enable people to cover long distances by bicycle.
12	Responsible Consumption and Production	• Michelin is collaborating with UPS, Route Monkey, Total and Nestlé on WBCSD's Road Freight Lab. The Lab explores the untapped and unmapped potential for emissions reduction through optimization and collaboration between road freight transport companies. (Meeting the climate challenge requires a 48% decrease in absolute emissions from freight by 2050, based on 2010 levels, whilst meeting a predicted four-fold increase in demand.) In the first phase, the Lab aims to design an information and technology platform that enables small and medium-sized enterprises to share data and assets in order to increase asset efficiency and usage. In the second phase, the Lab will bring together companies, government and customers in two locations to demonstrate the developed inter- and intra-city road freight solutions. This collaboration also aims to raise awareness among policy-makers of the potential of these solutions.
16	Peace, Justice and Strong Institutions	• Shipping Corporation of India Ltd. adopted the Integrity Pact Programme for the company's major public procurements. The Integrity Pact was designed and launched by Transparency International (a non-governmental organisation) in the 1990s with the primary objective of helping governments, businesses, and civil society to fight corruption in public contracting. The Integrity Pact is an agreement between prospective vendors/bidders and the buyer, committing the persons/officials of both parties to not exercise any corrupt influence over any aspect of the contract.

[a]Replicated from United Nations Global Compact and KPMG (2015). *SDG industry matrix: Transportation.* Retrieved from www.unglobalcompact.org/library/3111

sustainable development. While they acknowledge that examples abound of companies partnering with governments and nonprofit organizations to deliver on development goals, they note that there are risks to putting companies at the heart of the sustainable development agenda. Scheyvens et al. describe six interrelated criticisms pertaining to the private sector as a partner in accomplishing the SDGs. These six concerns are briefly summarized as follows:

1. *Dominance of a Neoliberal Agenda.* According to this view, promoting the private sector's role in development entrenches neoliberalism. Neoliberalism is "an economic and political ideology that aims to subject social and ecological affairs to capitalist market dynamics" (Kumi, Arhin, & Yeboah, 2014, p. 541). Scheyvens et al. maintain that neoliberal mechanisms have historically led to social inequalities, heightening the power imbalance between developing and capitalist countries. According to this view, neoliberalism effectively calls for a reliance on the mechanisms responsible for inequalities to solve the very problems they created in the first place and continue to exacerbate. Putting companies at the heart of the sustainable development agenda risks affording the private sector undue influence in policy making, giving it an opportunity to put corporate capital at the forefront, at the expense of the citizenry.
2. *Structural Causes of Poverty Are Not Addressed.* Proponents of this view argue that with neoliberal solutions to achieving the SDGs, development winds up being dominated by powerful corporations, financial institutions, and local elites. This does little to challenge structural causes of poverty such as illicit financial flows, debt, unfair trade rules, and corporate power.
3. *Problems with "Partnership."* This criticism notes that the rhetoric of partnerships conceals tensions and conflicts of interest, noting that true partnerships are difficult when there are competing goals, values, and ways of operating. Scheyvens et al. (2016) further note that some may be unwilling to accept the notion of a partnership with businesses unless and until the private sector is held accountable for their contributions toward environmental degradation and poverty. Partnerships require trust, and a lack of trust can impede effective partnerships if the prevailing view is that the private sector has not acknowledged and made amends for past damages it has inflicted.
4. *Short-Term and Flexible Business Models.* This criticism revolves around what is perceived to be a fundamental mismatch between business, which strives to reach short-term financial goals, and sustainable development, which requires taking the long view, including near-term sacrifices in favor of longer-terms gains, such as preserving the planet for future generations.
5. *Inability to Move beyond the Business Case.* This criticism takes issue with the private sector's motivation for sustainable development. Scheyvens et al. (2016) argue that big companies are only interested in sustainable development because it has implications for their business, such as helping them maintain a competitive position, helping to avoid supply disruptions, and helping to build customer loyalty.

6. *Lack of Coherence within and among Private Sector Actors' Approaches.* This criticism rests on the assumption that most companies will focus primarily on making a profit, leading to decisions that undermine social and environmental initiatives, which get sidelined when profit is threatened. This focus on the bottom line, Scheyvens et al. (2016) argue, can also prevent effective partnerships with other companies, governments, or civil society, particularly if such partnerships threaten the company's near-term financial interests.

Taken together, a number of Scheyvens et al.'s (2016) criticisms pertain to the problems that arise when companies' financial interests are at odds with what is best for people and the environment. One response is to reduce the emphasis and reliance on the private sector as we work toward sustainable development. Another is to figure out ways to make socially and environmentally responsible decisions easier and more lucrative than their alternatives. The next section illustrates how entities ranging from start-ups to intergovernmental organizations to academia are partnering to design and deliver innovative solutions that enable companies to contribute to sustainable development in ways that are good for business.

Making "Good" Business Good for Business

Support for the businesses' engagement in sustainable development is growing and can take vastly different forms. A number of purposefully different examples follow. These examples are by no means exhaustive, but they do illustrate a variety of ways in which new and emerging companies and global collaborations can facilitate the private sector's efforts to grow in sustainable ways.

Start-Ups Supporting Sustainable Growth

For starters, a wide range of companies now provide products and services that help other companies operate sustainably. Consider, for example, three different organizations established over the past ten years: Modern Species, pymetrics, and Madeira Global. The first, Modern Species, is an entity that provides "strategic branding and responsible graphic design for forward-thinking organic and natural products companies" (Modern Species, 2018a). Modern Species, which itself adheres to sustainable business principles and practices, seeks to help socially responsible companies gain market share by designing high-quality branding materials such as brochures and websites for use in advertising, marketing, and other communications. As stated by Modern Species, "Design can catapult a company to massive success which is why we only offer our services to those companies who want to benefit the world socially or environmentally" (Modern Species, 2018b). Modern Species' clients span industries including, for example, cosmetics (Aveda), banking (Heartland Credit Union cooperative), and animal feed (Scratch and Peck).

Other organizations support the private sector's role in development in a very different way – namely, by helping companies improve the effectiveness and fairness of their hiring. This can reduce inequalities and improve access to employment opportunity, including for groups traditionally disadvantaged by hiring techniques such as resume screening, which is common practice (Piotrowski & Armstrong, 2006) and shown to be biased against groups such as women and minorities (Bertrand & Mullainathan, 2004; Derous, Ryan, & Nguyen, 2012; Hausman, 2012). A start-up called Textio, for instance, uses artificial intelligence (AI) in an effort to improve recruitment by making the wording of job descriptions more relatable to historically underrepresented candidates (Hire education, 2018). Other organizations are using technology to enhance the manner in which job candidates are sourced and assessed (Scott, Bartram, & Reynolds, 2018). New platforms have emerged in recent years, which allow employers to quickly identify precisely matched candidates from large talent pools, thereby offering diversity and efficiency in hiring (Brodock & Massam, 2016). In this vein, our second feature example, a start-up called pymetrics, has a particular approach to assessment that incorporates elements of gamification and AI (Hawkes, Cek, & Handler, 2018). In brief, companies that use the pymetrics system begin by asking high-performing incumbents to play pymetrics games, which are a series of computer exercises rooted in cognitive neuroscience. The decisions incumbents make while playing the games are measured at a detailed level, revealing their standing on a range of traits such as concentration under pressure, attitudes toward risk, and short-term memory. pymetrics then uses machine learning to build custom algorithms or models representing the trait profile that distinguishes successful incumbents. An iterative algorithm-auditing process ensures that finalized algorithms do not favor people from any particular demographic group. Once this is complete, job candidates for the position in question are asked to play pymetrics games. Their game play data are analyzed to determine the degree to which each candidate matches the trait profile of successful incumbents. Those who are rejected are given the opportunity to match to other opportunities across other client companies using pymetrics, thereby increasing the chances that candidates will find a suitable job (pymetrics, 2018; Roose, 2017). The introduction of such objective measures at early stages of the hiring process is meant to help candidates advance to the next stage of the hiring process based on initial fit indices, rather than sex, ethnicity, age, and other biases that have been shown to influence decision makers at early stages of employment selection. This approach demonstrates one way to support companies that wish to reduce the inequalities in the workplace born out of unfair hiring and promotion practices. A variety of large organizations have started using pymetrics for hiring, including Unilever, Accenture, LinkedIn, Tesla, and DBS.

Modern Species and pymetrics illustrate the emergence of start-ups that are helping to make environmentally and socially responsible actions profitable for businesses. Our third example, Madeira Global, follows suit, but in a different manner, by helping to make people-centered, planet-sensitive businesses more attractive to investors. This chapter has alluded to businesses' social and environmental "footprint" – that is, the impact a company has on people and the planet. In a similar way, there is value in thinking about an *investor's* social and environmental footprint. Investors, after all, have options. For example, they can provide capital to companies that pay their employees living wages and use energy-efficient equipment and biodegradable materials and products. Or, they can fund companies that violate fair labor standards and use materials that pollute the environment. Holding investors accountable for the footprint being left behind by the companies they invest in can put positive pressure on investors to support socially and environmentally responsible entities, thus giving people-centered and planet-sensitive businesses a competitive advantage when it comes to attracting investment capital. All of this requires, however, a way to measure the environmental (E), social (S), and governance (G) activities of the companies in an investment portfolio, and score the portfolio accordingly. ESG scorecards provide a complement to financial reporting – a complement of notable importance to impact investors and stakeholders who value social as well as financial returns. Such information is also important to profit-minded individuals and investors who understand poor ESG performance to be a business risk. Madeira Global works directly in this space. Madeira Global is an advisory and analytics firm that helps asset managers make more informed investment decisions. Madeira Global's clients include private funds, holding companies, family foundations, and institutional investors. Using research and analytics, Madeira Global independently evaluates the nonfinancial performance of their clients' new and existing investment portfolios. In other words, they help investors understand how well the entities they support are performing with respect to environmental, social, and good governance indices. Increasing the transparency of the ESG "footprint" of an investment portfolio enables stakeholders and others to hold asset managers accountable for investing responsibly, in entities that align with the SDGs, which are prominently displayed on Madeira Global's website (Madeira Global, 2018).

International Platforms and Alliances Supporting Sustainable Growth

All three of the examples above illustrate the emergence of businesses that profit by supporting other companies' efforts to grow in sustainable ways. Outside of the private sector, efforts to bolster the private sector's role in development also abound. Selected examples, described next, include: the United Nations Global Compact; other UN initiatives such as the Istanbul International Center for the Private Sector in Development; and the Global Organizational Learning and Development Network (GOLDEN), a community of scholars spanning many different countries.

Over the years, the United Nations has evolved to better support the private sector's contributions to sustainable prosperity. The United Nations Global

Compact is a case in point. The UN Global Compact is an initiative designed to encourage companies around the world to adopt and report on socially responsible, sustainable practices. Businesses can sign up to become members of the Global Compact, which means committing to ten principles pertaining to human rights, labor, the environment, and anti-corruption. To date, more than 8,000 companies, in addition to thousands of nonbusiness members including graduate programs training doctoral students in industrial–organizational (I-O) psychology (Mallory et al., 2015), have signed up for the Global Compact, which has been dubbed "the world's largest global corporate sustainability initiative" (United Nations Global Compact, 2018a). Members of the Global Compact voluntarily pledge to:

- Operate responsibly, in alignment with the Global Compact's ten sustainability principles;
- Take actions that support the society around them;
- Commit to the effort from their organization's highest level, pushing sustainability deep into the organization's metaphorical DNA;
- Report annually on ongoing efforts;
- Engage locally where the organization has a presence (United Nations Global Compact, 2018b).

The UN Global Compact supports the private sector's contributions to sustainable development in a variety of ways. For example, the Global Compact has developed a toolkit to help businesses take action on the SDGs (United Nations Global Compact, 2018c). It also organizes and publicizes companies' sustainability efforts. For example, Table 26.2 is part of a larger compilation developed jointly by the UN Global Compact and KPMG. Such compilations serve to illustrate how various businesses have operationalized the admittedly broad charge to contribute to the SDGs. Publicizing such efforts can show companies that have not fully engaged with the SDGs the energy being exerted by others in their sector. This can serve as a form of "social proof," communicating a positive norm around SDG engagement while also giving others ideas for implementing sustainable strategies.

The UNDP's Istanbul International Center for the Private Sector in Development (IICPSD) is another noteworthy initiative. The IICPSD maintains that the private sector and foundations have tremendous potential as transformative partners to help accelerate progress toward sustainable development. IICPSD efforts therefore aim to support such potential. Support is provided in a variety of ways, such as through research, the creation of evidence-based policy options, advocacy for inclusive business, facilitating public–private dialogue, and brokering partnerships. The IICPSD focuses on four thematic areas (United Nations Development Programme, 2017a):

(a) Inclusive Business. People living in poverty and those with low incomes can be included in companies' value chains on the supply side as producers, entrepreneurs, and employees as well as on the demand side as consumers and clients. Under the right circumstances, such arrangements are advantageous to both the private sector and traditionally disadvantaged populations. The IICPSD conducts research on inclusive business models, supports governments in creating policies to enable inclusive business practices, and works to advance regional value chains. For example, the IICPSD has worked in Afghanistan, Kyrgyzstan, and Tajikistan to improve job and livelihood opportunities by increasing exports of agricultural products (United Nations Development Programme, 2017b).

(b) Private Sector Engagement in Skills Development. Companies need a skilled labor force to produce, grow, and compete. Meanwhile, skills development opportunities can be economically and psychologically empowering, including for vulnerable people from disadvantaged backgrounds. There are barriers to skills development in formal educational settings and beyond, which the private sector can help overcome, to everyone's benefit. The IICPSD conducts research on inclusive business approaches to skills design and delivery, draws insights from field-tested models, and produces guidelines and toolkits to support the private sector's engagement in skills generation (United Nations Development Programme, 2017c).

(c) Impact Investing. The IICPSD also focuses on supporting impact investing, which seeks both social and financial returns and occurs across asset classes including private equity and venture capital, as well as debt (United Nations Development Programme, 2017d). There is growing interest in investing in assets that make a positive contribution to sustainable development (Simon & Barmeier, 2010). However, more work is needed to better understand how to achieve commercial returns and social impact without tradeoffs (Gregory, 2016) and to help investors find good, scalable investment opportunities. The IICPSD works in this space. For example, the IICPSD recently launched a platform to connect Islamic impact investors and public or private funds with impact enterprises.

(d) Resilience and Crisis Response. The IICPSD engages the private sector in disaster risk reduction, crisis preparedness, response, and recovery efforts. In addition, there is a focus on helping communities as well as micro, small, and medium-sized enterprises (MSMEs) become more resilient. Example projects include facilitating private sector involvement in mobile money transfer systems to support post-disaster housing reconstruction, and a collaboration with Deutsche Post DHL, leveraging DHL's core capabilities, to train airport staff to better respond to crises such as natural disasters. This is important in part because an airport's capacity to respond during crisis situations has implications for the delivery of emergency aid (United Nations Development Programme, 2017e).

The IICPSD and the UN Global Compact are nowhere near the only relevant UN efforts underway. For instance, UNICEF in the country of

Jordan is working with the private sector and other entities to help combat high levels of unemployment among young adults. Public–private partnerships include training programs to teach life skills such as problem solving and communication, opportunities for youth to volunteer in companies to gain work experience and incentives, vocational training, and job mentoring (Arar, 2018; UNICEF, 2017). Meanwhile, through its One Planet Network, the UN Environment Programme works with the private sector to determine methods for environmentally friendly growth, such as through innovative business models that embed circularity into company systems (United Nations Environment Programme, 2018). In effect, a "circular economy" turns goods or products at the end of their service life into resources for future goods and products. Such efforts to close the loop in industrial ecosystems help minimize waste and contribute to sustainable production patterns (Stahel, 2016).

In short, there are a number of UN initiatives to stimulate and support private sector engagement in the SDGs. However, it is important to emphasize that there are many equally notable efforts emanating from outside of the UN system, which are also designed to support the private sector's role in sustainable development. Our final example in this section highlights one such initiative: the Global Organizational Learning and Development Network (GOLDEN). GOLDEN is a global community of scholars spanning 60 universities, 22 countries, and a variety of disciplines including the management, social, environmental, and cognitive neurosciences. Through engaged scholarship, the GOLDEN community collaborates with companies to design and execute field experiments to help firms uncover strategically relevant solutions to sustainability challenges. Through multimethod designs, GOLDEN also studies how companies evolve into sustainable enterprises. For examples, researchers in the GOLDEN network conduct studies to pinpoint factors that facilitate or hinder the integration of sustainability through a company's entire business model. GOLDEN has developed a global database of more than 37,000 corporate sustainability change initiatives around the world and across industries, developed through systematically coding corporate sustainability and annual reports. This enables researchers to begin assessing the impact of change initiatives, and it also facilitates comparisons of companies within and across industries. GOLDEN works with national and international organizations through its Sustainable Enterprise Model Innovations Labs to support governments' and companies' efforts to engage the private sector in development. GOLDEN members have also been involved in the development and deployment of a Massive Open Online Course (MOOC), provided through Coursera, on the topic of Corporate Sustainability (GOLDEN, 2018). This MOOC allows students to learn from thought leaders about whether and how companies can contribute to the accomplishment of the SDGs while generating business opportunities and value for their stakeholders (GOLDEN, 2015).

Embedding Sustainability: Workforce Implications

Shifting from peripheral to embedded CSR affects all employees because embedded CSR integrates sustainability into every aspect of a company, from strategy to routines to operations (Aguinis & Glavas, 2013). Such a transition changes the nature of work, requiring new ways of organizing and working across the organization – new ways, which call for new skills. A better understanding of these changes at an individual level of analysis is imperative. Indeed, following an extensive review of the CSR literature, the most important knowledge gap identified by Aguinis and Glavas (2012) pertained to the need to better understand individual-level issues because, at the end of the day, it is individuals in organizations who actually strategize, decide, and execute on plans and strategies (Aguinis, 2011; Aguinis & Glavas, 2013). There remains a particular need for research at the individual level of analysis that pinpoints the changing skill and process requirements prompted by the private sector's strategic involvement in sustainable development. Next, we speculate on a few of the ways in which people and roles at varying levels of the organizational hierarchy may need to change in order to support the partnerships required for sustainable growth.

Leadership Challenges

Philanthropy projects overseen by a CSR department can coexist with "business as usual." However, in order for the private sector to become true partners in sustainable development, sustainability cannot be relegated to a CSR department. Rather, sustainability must drive organizational change. Embedding sustainability will challenge leaders to adapt and rethink their strategies. Partnerships for sustainability are the *sine qua non* for collaboration, requiring leaders to pinpoint intersections, identify tradeoffs, and empower teams to deal with the complexity brought in by such a wide range of crosscutting priorities. For this, C-suite executives have an opportunity to play a life-changing role, affecting people and the manner in which they relate to each other. Firmly and courageously, they must deal with a few "elephants in the room" – those game changers everyone talks about, but where action is yet to be seen. Failure to do so threatens the organization's capacity for sustainable growth. Eweje and Bathurst (2017) identify ineffective leadership as a key reason why organizations' CSR initiatives fail. When CSR moves from a peripheral to an embedded position in the organization, failure can have even greater consequences.

Identifying pathways to sustainable growth is admittedly a complex charge, as changes at one level of the organization have second and third order effects on other aspects of the business. The SDGs are also complex. In one Sustainable Development Goal alone, many other goals are closely interrelated. For instance, to achieve quality education (SDG 4), one needs to understand with some level of depth its interdependence with poverty, hunger, good health and wellbeing, gender equality, clean water and sanitation, decent work and economic growth, reduced inequalities, peace, justice, building strong institutions, as well as strong partnerships for the goals. To go beyond the surface and "best guessing," companies must humbly accept that building a strategic and nuanced mindset for sustainability is a challenge for their talent management architectures. For decades, C-suite executives have prided themselves on workforces with a high concentration of specialized skills and knowledge in diverse areas core to their business. With sustainability, a number of new knowledge bases may need to be mastered and visualized, requiring leadership to quickly get up to speed on new content areas quite unlike those of the past.

Balancing Expert and Multidisciplinary Perspectives

At the people level, the new issues that need depth are specific and complex; hence, companies must continue to rely on their experts. But to drive the change needed for sustainable growth, expert minds will likely need to understand not only their own specialties, but also how their specialty connects to the bigger picture. This includes understanding key interrelationships among priorities, which requires agility and perhaps the willingness and ability to "exchange glasses" with other specialists to gain fluency in others' professional language and deep familiarity with others' perspectives. In a sense, companies' success in achieving sustainability will require a growth mindset (Ehrlinger, Mitchum, & Dweck, 2016; O'Keefe, Dweck, & Walton, 2018) that enables "humble learners" to venture into new areas of knowledge – a journey of upskilling and cross-skilling, balancing the tension between high level expertise and a multidisciplinary understanding.

Teamwork, Coordination, and Managing Ambiguities

High specialization, accountable for great innovations, has also given rise to the paradox of silos, creating one of the more difficult management tests of our times: that of breaking the silo mentality. Corporations seek highly specialized talent, striving to bring in the stars. However, fully leveraging that talent in today's age of partnerships requires innovative ways of simultaneously developing individual inputs and coordinating experts, through constant teamwork, and collaboration towards common goals. For the leadership, partnerships towards the common good require the ability to engage leading soloists or prima donnas, and with exceptional competence, convince the "stars" to dive into diverse and often competing fields. This is a significant leadership challenge as companies move toward sustainable growth models. It is likely to require modeling collaboration, rallying high-level experts around key priorities, skillfully coordinating action and results across multidisciplinary teams, all while gaining commitment from strategic partners. The risk of not achieving high-level collaboration is gridlock or poor execution. The constant challenge for leadership will be to engage high-level thinking and action across disciplines, while balancing the tension between independent thinking and the collaborative mindset.

Of course, the preceding challenges do not belong to leadership alone. It takes a metaphorical village to transform a silo mentality into a Renaissance soul. Increasingly, individuals may need to engage themselves in experiences outside their comfort zones, develop a growth mindset, be "humble learners," and remain curious. The Renaissance creative genius Leonardo da Vinci was a disciple of experience and experiment, had a freethinking attitude, and was self-taught (Isaacson, 2017). During the Renaissance period, the management of ambiguities was the hallmark of life. Today, the capacity to manage ambiguities could indeed prove essential to advance the conflicting legislation and interests that exist around sustainability. The culture to foster sustainability partnerships will likely require a way of work that encourages passion around "new stuff," applauds diverse pursuits, and creates an ongoing outside-in perspective. People with zealous minds and high-level interpersonal skills are well positioned to be the champions of integration, balancing the tension between experts and multi-potentialities.

The Role of Behavioral Science

Embedded CSR integrates sustainability into a company's strategy, routines, and operations, with implications for all aspects of the organization, including but not limited to finance, accounting, human resources, marketing, operations, sales, and strategy (Aguinis & Glavas, 2013). Accordingly, insights from scholars and practitioners with expertise spanning a wide variety of disciplines are needed to achieve the planet-sensitive, people-centered, profitable private sector envisioned by the SDGs. As suggested above, partnerships among such experts will also be important. For example, there is little doubt that the development of environmentally sound technologies and innovations will be key to helping the private sector produce in ways that are both environmentally sustainable and profitable. However, the type of expertise needed to develop green technologies is very different from the knowledge and skill set needed to promote its transfer, dissemination, adoption, and diffusion.

Business experts, behavioral scientists, technologists, and those working at the intersection of these worlds have an important role to play. For example, through the use of technology acceptance theories such as the Technology Acceptance Model (TAM; Davis, 1989; Verma & Sinha, 2016) and the Unified Theory of Acceptance and Use of Technology (UTAUT; Venkatesh, Morris, Davis, & Davis, 2003), experts in management information systems can help guide and encourage the adoption and integration of environmentally friendly technologies in corporate settings as such innovations emerge. There is also a clear need for contributions from people with expertise in fields such as finance and economics. For instance, acknowledging that impact investing is not always as profitable as asset managers and investors might hope, economists have begun to use their expertise to develop approaches to de-risking impact investing in order to make it more commercially viable (Gregory, 2016).

In a similar vein, insights from the behavioral sciences can be used to help organizations reduce the risks and realize the benefits of sustainable business. We elaborate below. In doing so, we do not mean to suggest that behavioral science alone is the answer to the challenges that lie ahead. However, we do believe it is an important piece of the puzzle. The following pages illustrate ways in which social, behavioral, and organizational sciences can contribute alongside other necessary mechanisms (e.g., appropriate regulations) and forms of expertise (e.g., innovations in green technologies and investment strategies).

Behavioral Insights

Many readers are familiar with Kerr's (1995) classic *Academy of Management Executive* article titled "On the folly of rewarding A while hoping for B." Whether at the level of the organization, its leaders, teams, employees, or customers, it may indeed be folly to hope for private sector behaviors that support the SDGs while decisions, actions, and short-term results at odds with the SDGs are being directly or indirectly rewarded. Behavioral scientists can contribute to a more rounded understanding of human motivation (e.g., Deci, Olafsen & Ryan, 2017), which can help organizations design systems that intrinsically or extrinsically reward and reinforce SDG-friendly behaviors.

One way is through the very design of new organizations at their inception. Behavioral scientists understand, for example, human motivation at a fundamental level that can be useful when thinking about how to structure a business in ways that incentivize desired behaviors. The insurance company Lemonade is a case in point. Lemonade sells renter's and homeowner's insurance. This is an industry often plagued by conflicts of interest leading to organizational and consumer behaviors that are very much at odds with the kinds of aspirations outlined in the SDGs. Typically, by denying or reducing customers' claims, insurance companies gain more money in profit at the end of the year. Meanwhile, by artificially inflating claims (for example, exaggerating the value of an item stolen from one's apartment), the customer normally has more to gain. Such exaggeration may be further motivated by an expectation that the insurance company will pay out less than what is requested. In short, there is arguably folly in hoping for "B" (fair and honest behavior on the part of insurance companies and customers) while just the opposite "A" is being rewarded. An important question, which is not unique to the insurance industry, is: Does it have to be this way, even if it has seemingly always been this way? The emergence and success of an insurance company called Lemonade suggests the answer to this question is "no." Early in its formation, Lemonade appointed psychology and behavioral economics professor Dan Ariely as its chief behavioral officer. Aiming to shake up the insurance industry (Ryan, 2017), Lemonade is structured in a way that inherently avoids the conflicts of interest described above and supports behaviors consistent with the SDGs.

Lemonade keeps a fixed percentage of all premiums, which goes toward running the business and making a profit. The rest of the money received in premiums is set aside to pay claims. Surplus premiums remaining at the end of the year do not get returned to Lemonade. Instead, they go to a charity of the customer's choosing. Using behavioral science, Lemonade also includes steps to encourage honesty on the part of the customer. For example, customers making claims sign an honesty pledge and submit a video of themselves, explaining what happened. This not only primes identity and self-awareness in a manner meant to help ward off dishonesty during the claims process, it also enables the company to run a number of AI-driven anti-fraud algorithms on the claim, which often leads to payment of the claim within three seconds (Harris, 2017; Lemonade, 2018).

What are the circumstances under which business owners, investors, leaders, employees, and customers will and will not choose to behave in ways that support the SDGs? The science of judgment and decision making is embedded into Lemonade's design, and can be more strategically leveraged in other ways to develop interventions that encourage sustainable decisions and behaviors (Shankar & Foster, 2016). The field of behavioral economics has a growing track record of applying such insights to "nudge" a wide variety of choices related to health, financial wellbeing, education and training, workforce development, and the environment (Thaler & Sunstein, 2008). Behavioral nudges can involve a range of different interventions including but not limited to the strategic use of social norms, simplification, increases in ease and convenience, disclosure, warnings, pre-commitment strategies, reminders, implementation intentions, and default rules (Sunstein, 2014). Consider, for example the cost to the environment and the company's financial bottom line when hotels launder guests' towels on a daily basis. Hotel chains have successfully used messaging applying descriptive social norms (e.g., "the majority of guests in this room reuse their towels") to increase customers' willingness to reuse their towels rather than having them laundered daily (Goldstein, Cialdini, & Griskevicius, 2008). Organizations have used behavioral insights to nudge employees as well. For example, employee obesity negatively affects workers' health and can be costly to employers due to losses in productivity and absences stemming from related illnesses (van der Starre, Coffeng, Hendriksen, van Mechelen, & Boot, 2013). Behavioral insights have been used to increase exercise and promote weight loss among office workers (Organisation for Economic Co-operation and Development, 2017). Other examples have targeted the environmental and financial costs of paper usage through interventions that nudge employees to print on both sides of each sheet of paper instead of choosing single-sided printing (SBST, 2015). A particularly powerful "nudge" pertains to the strategic use of green default rules. Whether the choice in question pertains to double-sided printing, where to set a thermostat at work, or how much to save for retirement, the power of inertia is such that people often stick with default settings even when given the power to change them (Thaler & Sunstein, 2008). Indeed, Sunstein and Reisch (2014) argue that "green default rules may be a more effective tool for altering outcomes than large economic incentives" (p. 127).

The power of defaults relates to a fundamental tenet in the field of behavioral economics: a key to changing behavior is to make the desired course of action the easiest course of action. This can involve making the desired behavior easier or more convenient by removing small "frictions" or impediments (Madrian, 2014). This can also be accomplished by adding impediments to discourage the less desirable course of action. In the context of corporate partnerships for the SDGs, we might think more strategically about how to further apply the "choice architecture" concept frequently utilized in behavioral economics on a larger scale, designing business models and environments in which the more (less) socially and environmentally responsible course of action is both easier (harder) and more (less) profitable for individuals and organizations. There is also value in thinking about how to use behavioral economics to influence upstream decisions made by infrastructure designers – for example, those designing company office buildings – to help them overcome barriers to the selection of more sustainable building design options (National Science Foundation, 2016).

Organizational Sciences

Insights from I-O psychology and related fields such as organizational behavior (OB) and human resource management (HRM) can also be particularly useful moving forward, especially in relation to people-centered SDGs. As Aguinis and Glavas (2013) point out, "By focusing on the role of individuals (i.e., consumers, managers), knowledge originating in fields that address microlevel issues such as I-O psychology, OB, and HRM can help explain when and why CSR leads to specific outcomes" (p. 326). Such explanations are critical to sustainable growth.

I-O psychology and related fields are quite clearly suited to maximizing internal CSR efforts, which focus on employee wellbeing. Already, there are mature research literatures on relevant topics, including employee engagement, work–family balance, occupational health and safety, diversity and inclusion, organizational justice, and behavioral ethics, to name a few examples (Jones & Rupp, 2018). Beyond enhancing the wellbeing of a company's own employees, there is also an opportunity for the organizational sciences to contribute to corporate SDG partnerships that are more external in nature. Recall, for example, the previous description of a company partnering to provide meaningful training and development opportunities to empower female smallholder farmers in the supply chain. Theories, methods, insights, and evidence-based best practices from I-O psychology and related disciplines can help maximize the success of such initiatives.

Whether the focus is on internal CSR, external CSR, or partnerships for the goals that do not fit neatly into a single category, insights from the organizational sciences can support environmental and social policies, programs, and solutions that enable sustainable growth. Ones, Dilchert, Wiernik, and Klein (2018) point to relevant scholarship (e.g., Chen, 2008) demonstrating the competitive advantage that can be gained through environmental sustainability, in part due to reputational enhancements. With respect to reputation, customers and investors are not the only stakeholders that matter. Applicants' and employees' perceptions matter too and can be positively affected by knowledge that an employer prioritizes CSR.

Consider, for instance, the topic of employee engagement, defined as "a positive, fulfilling, work-related state of mind that is characterized by vigor, dedication, and absorption" (Schaufeli, Salanova, Gonzalez-Roma, & Bakker, 2002, p. 74). Employee engagement is a good example of an opportunity for alignment between people and profit motives. Employees are happier and healthier when they derive meaning from their work (Kinjerski & Skrypnek, 2008; Rupp et al., 2018). In addition, employees perform better and customers are more loyal when employees are engaged at work (Salanova, Agut, & Peiro, 2005), which is good for the financial bottom line. I-O psychology research and practice can help guide efforts to understand and bolster employee engagement and its positive effects. For example, Rupp et al. (2018) introduced self-determination theory to the micro-CSR literature to help explain when employees do and do not derive engagement from their employers' CSR activities. Results show that both individual and contextual factors place boundary conditions on the demonstrated link between CSR perceptions and work engagement, thus pointing to circumstances under which employers' CSR efforts are most likely to boost engagement. It is important to point out that Rupp et al.'s (2018) study adopted Waldman et al.'s (2006) conceptualization of CSR, which includes peripheral CSR. In particular, CSR perceptions were assessed with a discretionary citizenship measuring asking employees to report the degree to which they perceive their organization to be involved in activities such as corporate philanthropy, community partnerships, and green initiatives (Rupp et al., 2018). This type of CSR differs from the kinds of embedded sustainable growth partnerships central to this chapter and the SDGs. A challenge moving forward will be to understand the degree to which research findings on peripheral CSR generalize to companies that have embedded sustainable growth into their core operations, routines, and strategy.

In addition to bringing research and theory to bear on questions of how to best achieve people-friendly, planet sensitive corporate growth, the organizational sciences also have a number of evidence-based best practices to offer both large corporations and smaller companies such as the start-ups described previously, which support larger organizations' capacity for sustainable growth. Areas where I-O psychology practice principles and techniques can support people-friendly prosperity in the private sector include but are not limited to:

- Staffing decision making (Zedeck, 2011). Following the Society for Industrial and Organizational Psychology's "Principles for the Validation and Use of Personnel Selection Procedures" (SIOP, 2003) helps organizations use scientific methods to select candidates for jobs. This not only improves productivity, it also focuses hiring managers' attention and selection decisions on job-relevant factors, rather than factors such as ethnicity, sex, social class, age, disability status, and other characteristics that lead to or perpetuate the kinds of inequalities that goals such as SDGs 5, 8, and 10 mean to combat. Aguinis (2011) describes test score banding as another way in which organizations can simultaneously achieve economic and social interests when making hiring decisions.

- Training design and evaluation (Brown & Sitzmann, 2011). Psychological expertise in training design and evaluation can contribute to lifelong learning and growth opportunities in the workplace, which can benefit employees and employers alike. Employees stand to benefit from a sense of mastery and competence gained through training, and employers can benefit from increases in productivity stemming from a more highly skilled workforce. Proper training evaluation can also help ensure money, time, and psychological resources are not wasted on ineffective or counterproductive instructional programs. At a more macro level, effective training improves the quality of a country's labor force, which is an important determinant of national economic growth (Aguinis & Kraiger, 2009).

- Performance measurement and management (DeNisi & Sonesh, 2011; Wildman, Bedwell, Salas, & Smith-Jentsch, 2011). Sound scientific principles can improve the accuracy of performance measurement, which encourages personnel decisions such as promotions that are based on merit rather than irrelevant demographic cues known to contribute to the marginalization of vulnerable populations. Valid performance measurement also supports effective performance management, which helps people develop in ways that are personally and organizationally meaningful. Aguinis (2011) maps out a multistep process, from an I-O psychology perspective, to help organizations transitioning to strategies that embed sustainability. The process includes elements of employee training as well as efforts to measure and reward work processes and performance that align with sustainable priorities and initiatives.

- Leadership (Barling, Christie, & Hoption, 2011). A number of leadership challenges inherent in the transition to embedding sustainability were discussed previously. Best practices in leadership development can help organizations identify and develop leaders with the knowledge, skills, abilities, attitudes, values, and other characteristics needed to align and contribute to people, planet, and profit motives. Strategic applications of executive coaching (Peterson, 2011) could also be a useful component of a larger talent management strategy in organizations transitioning to embedded CSR.

- Organizational survey design and analysis (Kraut, 2006). Organizational surveys are an important channel through which the voices (ideas, feedback) of employees, customers, and other external stakeholders (e.g., community members) can be heard. As organizations embed sustainability into their operations and routines, survey data can help leaders understand when things

are going well, when and how to make changes, and when to stay the course. Well-designed surveys provide high-quality data that organizations can act on in the pursuit of a triple bottom line. Kumi et al. (2014) express concern that "poor people will struggle to make their views, thoughts and concerns heard in a neoliberal world" (p. 550). Coupled with the transparency afforded by the Internet, carefully constructed surveys can give a voice to stakeholders external to organizations, including community members living in poverty, which could create a greater sense of accountability on the part of organizational leaders. Such surveys do not necessarily need to be sponsored by companies themselves. Consider, for example, contemporary systems like the platform provided by Glassdoor, Inc. Glassdoor allows job candidates, employees, and former employees to candidly rate and comment on their experiences with companies and their management. In efforts to promote greater workplace transparency, Glassdoor enables people familiar with companies to submit company reviews, salary information, CEO approval ratings, and other such input. At the time of this writing, the Glassdoor platform includes ratings, insights, and reviews for 770,000 companies spanning more than 190 countries (Dow Jones Institutional News, 2018). Similar platforms could be built to allow other stakeholders affected by corporate actions to comment in an organized manner. Such platforms would benefit from expertise in survey design and analysis.
- Teamwork (Cannon-Bowers & Bowers, 2011). Best practices for forming, training, developing, and evaluating virtual and collocated teams can facilitate new intra- and inter-organizational collaborations needed as and after companies embed CSR. To the extent that partnerships for the goals (SDG 17) entail interdependencies, the science of teamwork can prove useful.

In short, insights from the organizational sciences can support corporate efforts to succeed in ways that are simultaneously people friendly, planet sensitive, and profitable. Already, we have seen the inclusion of I-O psychologists in global initiatives ranging from the United Nations Global Compact (Carr, 2010) to the Istanbul International Center for the Private Sector in Development's foundational report on Barriers and Opportunities at the Base of the Pyramid (Bhawuk, Carr, Gloss, & Foster Thompson, 2014). Notably, using I-O psychology in such ways is consistent with trends toward humanitarian work psychology (HWP), which is defined as "the synthesis of I-O psychology with deliberate and organized efforts to enhance human welfare" (Gloss & Foster Thompson, 2013, p. 353).

Conclusion

Today's changes in the nature of work are accompanied by the private sector's advances in sustainable development. But in light of the pressing 2030 global agenda, social media's capacity to empower individual voices, and civil society's activism to hold key players accountable for the needed transformations, new legislation and shifts in patterns of consumption may ultimately define the positioning of sustainable development in the private sector and be the conscientious drivers of change. While the private sector is by no means a silver bullet for achieving sustainable development in the world, companies arguably bear an ethical responsibility to make the world a better place for all, and more than ever are strategically positioned to significantly contribute to the broader effort of embedding sustainability into what they do and how they do it.

References

Adrian Hodges Advisory (2017). *Opportunities for women: Challenging harmful social norms and gender stereotypes to unlock women's potential.* Retrieved from www.unilever.com/Images/unilever-opportunities-for-women_tcm244-500987_en.pdf

Aguinis, H. (2011). Organizational responsibility: Doing good and doing well. In S. Zedeck (Ed.), *APA handbook of industrial and organizational psychology, volume 3: Maintaining, expanding, and contracting the organization* (pp. 855–879). Washington, DC: American Psychological Association.

Aguinis, H., & Glavas, A. (2012). What we know and don't know about corporate social responsibility: A review and research agenda. *Journal of Management, 38*, 932–968.

Aguinis, H., & Glavas, A. (2013). Embedded versus peripheral corporate social responsibility: Psychological foundations. *Industrial and Organizational Psychology, 6*, 314–332.

Aguinis, H., & Kraiger, K. (2009). Benefits of training and development for individuals and teams, organizations, and society. *Annual Review of Psychology, 60*, 451–474.

Arar, S. (2018, February 14). UNICEF's youth engagement pathway vision launched. *The Jordan Times.* Retrieved from www.jordantimes.com/news/local/unicef%E2%80%99s-youth-engagement-pathway-vision-launched

Barling, J., Christie, A., & Hoption, C. (2011). Performance measurement at work: A multilevel perspective. In S. Zedeck (Ed.), *APA handbook of industrial and organizational psychology, volume 1: Building and developing the organization* (pp. 183–240). Washington, DC: American Psychological Association.

Bertrand, M., & Mullainathan, S. (2004). Are Emily and Greg more employable than Lakisha and Jamal? A field experiment on labor market discrimination. *American Economic Review, 94*, 991–1013.

Bhawuk, D. P. S., Carr, S. C., Gloss, A. E., & Foster Thompson, L. (2014). Poverty reduction through positive work cycles: Exploring the role of information about work, culture and diversity, and organizational justice. In S. Al-Atiqi (Ed.), *Barriers to and opportunities for poverty reduction: Prospects for private-sector led interventions* (Background paper to the United Nations Development Programme 2014 foundational report, *The role of the private sector in inclusive development: Barriers and opportunities at the base of the pyramid*). Istanbul, Turkey: United Nations Development Programme.

Bowen, H. R. (1953). *Social responsibilities of the businessman.* New York, NY: Harper.

Brammer, S., Millington, A., & Rayton, B. (2007). The contribution of corporate social responsibility to organizational commitment. *International Journal of Human Resource Management, 18*, 1701–1719.

Brodock, K., & Massam, G. (2016). How and why to hire a diverse workforce: What you need to know. *Strategic HR Review, 15*(5), 208–213.

Brown, K.G., & Sitzmann, T. (2011). Training and employee development for improved performance. In S. Zedeck (Ed.), *APA handbook of industrial and organizational psychology, volume 2: Selecting and developing members for the organization* (pp. 469–503). Washington, DC: American Psychological Association.

Cannon-Bowers, J. A., & Bowers, C. (2011). Team development and functioning. In S. Zedeck (Ed.), *APA handbook of industrial and organizational psychology, volume 1: Building and developing the organization* (pp. 597–650). Washington, DC: American Psychological Association.

Carr, S. C. (2010). Corporate social responsibility has gone global: The UN Global Compact. *The Industrial–Organizational Psychologist, 48*(2), 99–102.

Carroll, A. B. (1999). Corporate social responsibility: Evolution of a definitional construct. *Business and Society, 38*, 268–295.

Chen, Y. (2008). The positive effect of green intellectual capital on competitive advantages of firms. *Journal of Business Ethics, 77*, 271–286.

Davis, F. D. (1989). Perceived usefulness, perceived ease of use, and user acceptance of information technology. *MIS Quarterly, 13*, 319–340.

Deci, E. L., Olafsen, A. H., & Ryan, R. M. (2017). Self-determination theory in work organizations: The state of science. *Annual Review of Organizational Psychology and Organizational Behavior, 4*, 19–43.

DeNisi, A. S., & Sonesh, S. (2011). The appraisal and management of performance at work. In S. Zedeck (Ed.), *APA handbook of industrial and organizational psychology, volume 2: Selecting and developing members for the organization* (pp. 255–279). Washington, DC: American Psychological Association.

Derous, E., Ryan, A. M., & Nguyen, H. D. (2012). Multiple categorization in resume screening: Examining effects on hiring discrimination against Arab applicants in field and lab setting. *Journal of Organizational Behavior, 33*, 544–570.

Dow Jones Institutional News (2018, May 8). *Glassdoor to be acquired by recruit holdings for $1.2 billion*. New York, NY: Dow Jones & Company Inc.

Ehrlinger, J., Mitchum, A. L., & Dweck, C. S. (2016). Understanding overconfidence: Theories of intelligence, preferential attention, and distorted self-assessment. *Journal of Experimental Social Psychology, 63*, 94–100.

Evans, A. (2015). Private sector partnerships for sustainable development. In *Development co-operation report 2015: Making partnerships effective coalitions for action* (pp. 59–65). Paris, France: OECD Publishing.

Eweje, G., & Bathurst, R. J. (2017). Introduction: Leading for corporate social responsibility and sustainability. In G. Eweje & R. J. Bathurst (Eds.), *CSR, sustainability, and leadership*. New York, NY: Routledge.

Garriga, E., & Melé, D. (2004). Corporate social responsibility theories: Mapping the territory. *Journal of Business Ethics, 53*, 51–71.

Glösenberg, A., Carr, S. C., & Foster, L. L. (in press). A psychological lens on evaluating the social impact of corporate social responsibility. In A. McWilliams, D. E. Rupp, D. S. Siegel, G. K. Stahl, & D. A. Waldman (Eds.), *The Oxford handbook of corporate social responsibility*.

Gloss, A. E., & Foster Thompson, L. (2013). I-O psychology without borders: The emergence of humanitarian work psychology. In J. B. Olson-Buchanan, L. K. Bryan, & L. F. Thompson (Eds.), *Using I-O psychology for the greater good: Helping those who help others* (pp. 353–393). New York, NY: Routledge Academic.

GOLDEN (Global Organizational Learning and Development Network) (2015, November 12). *GOLDEN for sustainability: An introduction.* Retrieved from www.slideshare.net/secret/qSADoWKfaBKdot

GOLDEN (2018, April 6). *MOOC on corporate sustainability launched with Bocconi.* Retrieved from http://goldenforsustainability.com/golden-events/4229/

Goldstein, N. T., Cialdini, R. B., & Griskevicius, V. (2008). A room with a viewpoint: Using social norms to motivate environmental conservation in hotels. *Journal of Consumer Research, 35,* 472–482.

Greenberg, Z. (2018, August 1). Overlooked no more: Clara Lemlich Shavelson, crusading leader of labor rights. *New York Times.* Retrieved from www.nytimes.com/2018/08/01/obituaries/overlooked-clara-lemlich-shavelson.html

Gregory, N. (2016). De-risking impact investing. *World Economics, 17,* 143–158.

Harris, A. (2017, March 17). Lemonade is using behavioral science to onboard customers and keep them honest. *Fast Company.* Retrieved from www.fastcompany.com/3068506/lemonade-is-using-behavioral-science-to-onboard-customers-and-keep-them-honest

Hausman, D. (2012). How Congress could reduce job discrimination by promoting anonymous hiring. *Stanford Law Review, 64,* 1343–1369.

Hawkes, B., Cek, I., & Handler, C. (2018). The gamification of employee selection tools: An exploration of viability, utility, and future directions. In J. C. Scott, D. Bartram, & D. H. Reynolds (Eds.), *Next generation technology-enhanced assessment: Global perspectives on occupational and workplace testing.* Cambridge, UK: Cambridge University Press.

Herrero, C., Martínez, R., & Villar, A. (2018). Population structure and the human development index. *Social Indicators Research,* 1–33. Retrieved from https://doi.org/10.1007/s11205-018-1852-0

Hire education (2018, March 31). AI is changing the way firms screen, hire and manage their talent. *The Economist, 426*(9085), 7S–9S.

IDS (Institute of Development Studies) (2017). *Sustainable development goals.* Retrieved from www.ids.ac.uk/idsresearch/sustainable-development-goals

Isaacson, W. (2017). *Leonardo da Vinci.* New York, NY: Simon & Schuster.

Jack, L. (2015, October 2). Why Unilever is betting big on sustainability. *Fast Company.* Retrieved from www.fastcompany.com/3051498/why-unilever-is-betting-big-on-sustainability

Jones, D. A., & Rupp, D. E. (2018). Social responsibility in and of organizations: The psychology of corporate social responsibility among organizational members. In D. S. Ones, N. Anderson, C. Viswesvaran, & H. K. Sinangil (Eds.), *The SAGE handbook of industrial, work & organizational psychology* (pp. 333–348). London: SAGE Publications Ltd.

Kania, J., & Kramer, M. (2011). Collective impact. *Stanford Social Innovation Review,* Winter, 36–41.

Kerr, S. (1995). On the folly of rewarding A, while hoping for B. *Academy of Management Executive, 9,* 7–14.

Khanna, P. (2016, March/April). Rise of the Titans. *Foreign Policy, 217,* 50–55.

Kinjerski, V., & Skrypnek, B. J. (2008). Four paths to spirit at work: Journeys of personal meaning, fulfillment, well-being, and transcendence through work. *The Career Development Quarterly, 56*, 319–329.

Kraut, A. (2006). *Getting action from organizational surveys: New concepts, technologies and applications.* San Francisco, CA: Jossey-Bass.

Kumi, E., Arhin, A. A., & Yeboah, T. (2014). Can post-2015 sustainable development goals survive neoliberalism? A critical examination of the sustainable development–neoliberalism nexus in developing countries. *Environment, Development and Sustainability, 16*, 539–554.

Lemonade (2018). *The secret behind Lemonade's claims.* Retrieved from www.lemonade.com/claims

Madeira Global (2018). *Madeira Global: What we do.* Retrieved from www.madeiraglobal.com/what-we-do.

Madrian, B. C. (2014). Applying insights from behavioral economics to policy design. *Annual Review of Economics, 6*, 663–688.

Mallory, D., Rupp, D. E., Scott, J. C., Saari, L., Foster Thompson, L., Osicki, M., & E. Sall (2015). Attention all I-O programs: It's time to join the United Nations Global Compact. *The Industrial–Organizational Psychologist, 52*(4), 135–136.

Mazzucato, M. (2011). The entrepreneurial state. *Soundings, 49*, 131–142.

Modern Species (2018a). *We help brands evolve.* Retrieved from https://modernspecies.com/

Modern Species (2018b). *Ethos: The new world of business.* Retrieved from https://modernspecies.com/ethos.

Moura-Leite, R. C., & Padgett, R. C. (2011). Historical background of corporate social responsibility. *Social Responsibility Journal, 7*, 528–539.

National Science Foundation (2016). Intentional defaults for more sustainable infrastructure: Studying interventions to alleviate biases in upstream, multi-stakeholder decisions. *Award Abstract #1531041.* Retrieved from www.nsf.gov/awardsearch/showAward?AWD_ID=1531041

O'Keefe, P. A., Dweck, C. S., & Walton, G. M. (2018). Implicit theories of interest: Finding your passion or developing it? *Psychological Science, 29(10)*, 1653–1664.

Ones, D. S., Dilchert, S., Wiernik, B. M., & Klein, R. M. (2018). Environmental sustainability at work. In D. S. Ones, N. Anderson, C. Viswesvaran, & H. K. Sinangil (Eds.), *The SAGE handbook of industrial, work & organizational psychology* (pp. 351–373). London: SAGE Publications Ltd.

Opoku-Dakwa, A., Chen, C. C., & Rupp, D. E. (2018). CSR initiative characteristics and employee engagement: An impact-based perspective. *Journal of Organizational Behavior, 39*, 580–593.

Organisation for Economic Co-operation and Development (2015). *In it together: Why less inequality benefits all.* Paris, France: OECD Publishing.

Organisation for Economic Co-operation and Development (2017). *Behavioural insights and public policy: Lessons from around the world.* Paris, France: OECD Publishing.

Peterson, D. B. (2011). Executive coaching: A critical review and recommendations for advancing the practice. In S. Zedeck (Ed.), *APA handbook of industrial and organizational psychology, volume 2: Selecting and developing members for the organization* (pp. 527–566). Washington, DC: American Psychological Association.

Piotrowski, C., & Armstrong, T. (2006). Current recruitment and selection practices: A national survey of Fortune 1000 firms. *North American Journal of Psychology, 8*, 489–496.

pymetrics (2018). *Matching talent to opportunity, bias free.* Retrieved from www.pymetrics.com/employers/

Roose, K. (2017, December 28). Tech also did some good things in 2017. *New York Times*, p. B1.

Rupp, D. E., Shao, R., Skarlicki, D. P., Paddock, E. L., Kim, T., & Nadisic, T. (2018). Corporate social responsibility and employee engagement: The moderating role of CSR-specific relative autonomy and individualism. *Journal of Organizational Behavior, 39*, 559–579.

Ryan, K. J. (2017, June 13). An insurance company that homeowners actually might love. *Inc.* Retrieved from www.inc.com/kevin-j-ryan/insurance-startup-lemonade-california-90-percent-of-americans.html

Salanova, M., Agut, S., & Peiro, J. M. (2005). Linking organizational resources and work engagement to employee performance and customer loyalty: The mediation of service climate. *Journal of Applied Psychology, 90*, 1217–1227.

SBST (2015). *Social and Behavioral Science Team Annual Report. National Science and Technology Council*, Executive Office of the President, Washington DC. Retrieved from https://sbst.gov/download/2015%20SBST%20Annual%20Report.pdf

Schaufeli, W. B., Salanova, M., Gonzalez-Roma, V., & Bakker, A. B. (2002). The measurement of engagement and burnout: A two sample confirmatory factor analytic approach. *Journal of Happiness Studies, 3*, 71–92.

Scheyvens, R., Banks, G., & Hughes, E. (2016). The private sector and the SDGs: The need to move beyond "business as usual." *Sustainable Development, 24*, 371–382.

Scott, J. C., Bartram, D., & Reynolds, D. H. (Eds.) (2018). *Next generation technology-enhanced assessment: Global perspectives on occupational and workplace testing.* Cambridge, UK: Cambridge University Press.

Shankar, M. U., & Foster, L. L. (2016). *Behavioural insights at the United Nations: Achieving agenda 2030.* New York, NY: United Nations Development Programme. Retrieved from www.undp.org/content/undp/en/home/librarypage/development-impact/behavioural-insights-at-the-united-nations-achieving-agenda-203/

Sharafat, A. R., & Lehr, W. H. (2017). ICT4SDGs: ICT-centric economic growth, innovation and job creation. *International Telecommunication Union.* Retrieved from www.itu.int/dms_pub/itu-d/opb/gen/D-GEN-ICT_SDGS.01-2017-PDF-E.pdf

Simon, J., & Barmeier, J. (2010). *More than money: Impact investing for development.* Washington, DC: Center for Global Development.

SIOP (2003). *Principles for the validation and use of personnel selection procedures* (4th ed.). Bowling Green, OH: Society for Industrial and Organizational Psychology. Retrieved from www.siop.org/_principles/principles.pdf

Stahel, W. R. (2016). Circular economy. *Nature, 531*, 435–438.

Sunstein, C. R. (2014). Nudging: A very short guide. *Journal of Consumer Policy, 37*, 583–588.

Sunstein, C. R., & Reisch, L. A. (2014). Automatically green: Behavioral economics and environmental protection. *Harvard Law Review, 38*, 127–158.

Swanson, D. L., & Orlitzky, M. (2018). Leading the triple bottom line: A corporate social responsibility approach. In D. S. Ones, N. Anderson, C. Viswesvaran, & H. K. Sinangil (Eds.), *The SAGE handbook of industrial, work & organizational psychology* (pp. 313–330). London: SAGE Publications Ltd.

Thaler, R. H., & Sunstein, C. R. (2008). *Nudge: Improving decisions about health, wealth, and happiness.* New Haven, CT: Yale University Press.

UNICEF (2017, October 12). *UNICEF and private sector companies in Jordan discuss youth empowerment strategies for employment.* Retrieved from www.unicef.org/jordan/media_12273.html

Unilever (2018a). *Sustainable living.* Retrieved from www.unilever.co.uk/sustainable-living/

Unilever (2018b). *Fairness in the workplace.* Retrieved from www.unilever.co.uk/sustainable-living/the-unilever-sustainable-living-plan/fairness-in-the-workplace/

Unilever (2018c). *Independent assurance.* Retrieved from www.unilever.com/sustainable-living/our-approach-to-reporting/independent-assurance/

Unilever (2018d). *Opportunities for women.* Retrieved from www.unilever.com/sustainable-living/enhancing-livelihoods/opportunities-for-women/enhancing-womens-access-to-training-skills/

United Nations (2014). *The road to dignity by 2030: Ending poverty, transforming all lives and protecting the planet. Synthesis Report of the Secretary-General on the Post-2015 Agenda.* Retrieved from www.un.org/disabilities/documents/reports/SG_Synthesis_Report_Road_to_Dignity_by_2030.pdf

United Nations (2018). *World economic situation and prospects 2018.* New York: United Nations. Retrieved from www.un.org/development/desa/dpad/wp-content/uploads/sites/45/publication/WESP2018_Full_Web-1.pdf

United Nations Department of Economic and Social Affairs (2018). *Sustainable development knowledge platform.* Retrieved from https://sustainabledevelopment.un.org/topics/sustainabledevelopmentgoals

United Nations Development Programme (2017a). *Istanbul International Center for the Private Sector in Development (IICPSD): Progress report.* Retrieved from www.iicpsd.undp.org/content/dam/istanbul/IICPSD/UNDP%20IICPSD%20Progress%20Report%202017.pdf

United Nations Development Programme (2017b). *Istanbul International Center for the Private Sector in Development: Inclusive business overview.* Retrieved from www.iicpsd.undp.org/content/istanbul/en/home/our-work/inclusive-business-models/overview.html

United Nations Development Programme (2017c). *Istanbul International Center for the Private Sector in Development: Skills development overview.* Retrieved from www.iicpsd.undp.org/content/istanbul/en/home/our-work/private-sector-role-skills-development/overview.html

United Nations Development Programme (2017d). *Istanbul International Center for the Private Sector in Development: Impact investment overview.* Retrieved from www.iicpsd.undp.org/content/istanbul/en/home/our-work/impact-investment/overview.html

United Nations Development Programme (2017e). *Istanbul International Center for the Private Sector in Development: Resilience and crisis response overview.* Retrieved from www.iicpsd.undp.org/content/istanbul/en/home/our-work/resilience-and-crisis-response/overview.html

United Nations Environment Programme (2018, March 20). *Secretariat update on sustainable consumption and production.* Retrieved from https://wedocs.unep.org/bitstream/handle/20.500.11822/25178/Sustainable%20consumption%20and%20production%20-%20Update.pdf?sequence=26&isAllowed=y

United Nations General Assembly (2015). *Transforming our world: The 2030 agenda for sustainable development,* A/RES/70/1. Retrieved from www.un.org/ga/search/view_doc.asp?symbol=A/RES/70/1&Lang=E

United Nations Global Compact (2018a). *What's the commitment?* Retrieved from www.unglobalcompact.org/participation/join/commitment

United Nations Global Compact (2018b). *The ten principles of the UN Global Compact.* Retrieved from www.unglobalcompact.org/what-is-gc/mission/principles

United Nations Global Compact (2018c). *How the UN Global Compact helps.* Retrieved from www.unglobalcompact.org/sdgs/about

United Nations Global Compact and KPMG (2015). *SDG industry matrix: Transportation.* Retrieved from www.unglobalcompact.org/library/3111

van der Starre, R. E., Coffeng, J. K., Hendriksen, I. J. M., van Mechelen, W., & Boot, C. R. L. (2013). Associations between overweight, obesity, health measures and need for recovery in office employees: A cross-sectional analysis. *BMC Public Health, 13,* 1207–1214.

Venkatesh, V., Morris, M. G., Davis, G. B., & Davis, F. D. (2003). User acceptance of information technology: Toward a unified view. *MIS Quarterly, 27,* 425–478.

Verma, P., & Sinha, N. (2016). Technology acceptance model revisited for mobile based agriculture extension services in India. *Management Research and Practice, 8* (4), 29–38.

Waldman, D. A., Siegel, D., & Javidan, M. (2006). Components of CEO transformational leadership and corporate social responsibility. *Journal of Management Studies, 43,* 1703–1725.

Wildman, J. L., Bedwell, W. L., Salsa, E., & Smith-Jentsch, K. A. (2011). Performance measurement at work: A multilevel perspective. In S. Zedeck (Ed.), *APA handbook of industrial and organizational psychology, volume 1: Building and developing the organization* (pp. 303–341). Washington, DC: American Psychological Association.

World Bank Group (2018). *World Bank data: GDP.* Retrieved from https://data.worldbank.org/indicator/ny.gdp.mktp.cd

Zedeck, S. (Ed.). (2011). *APA handbook of industrial and organizational psychology, volume 2: Selecting and developing members for the organization.* Washington, DC: American Psychological Association.

Index

aerospace engineering, 120
Affective Events Theory, 518
Affordable Care Act, 500
AFL-CIO, 176, 179
African Americans, 142, 151, 156, 240, 252, 332, 389
age and changing attitude, 29
Age Discrimination in Employment Act (1967), 27, 157
age-friendly work climates, 22
age management. *See* aging workforce, management of
aging workforce, 21, 387, 426, 428–429, 431, 433
 cultural values, 437
 management of, 432, 434, 436, 438
agriculture, as major employer, 47
Airbnb, 282
Alito, Samuel, 182
Amazon, 76, 416, 512, 561, 569
Amazon Prime Now, 159
American Community Survey, 134–136, 140, 143, 153
American Express, 276, 394
American Industrial Revolution, 364
American Innovation and Competitiveness Act (2010, 2016), 108
Americans with Disabilities Act (1990), 27, 77, 87, 157, 304
Anglo-Saxon firms, 223
Apache helicopter pilots, 415
Apple campus, 186
applicant-tracking software (ATS), 330
Argentina, 111, 122
Ariely, Dan, 606
Aristotle, 557
artificial intelligence (AI), 84–86, 101, 115, 320, 390, 470, 543, 557, 560–561, 572, 574, 598
 cars, 85
 education industry, 85
 enviroment, 89
 general, 90, 92
 medical industry, 85
 military applications, 85
 narrow, 90
ASEAN, 215

Asia, 110, 116, 125
Asian Americans, 142, 144
Asia-Pacific, 395
assistive tools, 77
AT&T, 88, 250
Attraction–Selection–Attrition model, 12
at-will employment, 473
augmentation, 556
Austin, 118
authentic leadership theory, 395
autism spectrum disorder (ASD), 84
automation, 49, 52, 55, 91, 133, 149, 318, 370, 471, 556, 558, 563, 567, 571, 573
 barriers to, 52, 54–55, 60–61
 education and, 150
 occupational level of analysis, 573
 studies, 572–573
automotive engineering, 120
autonomous learning, 429
autonomy, 325, 476

Baby Boomer generation, 242, 246, 248, 261, 263, 269, 387, 472, 477
Bangladesh, 230
Barbados, 121
Bayer Healthcare, 394
behaviors
 change-oriented, 384
 external-focused, 384
 relations-oriented, 384, 386
 task-oriented, 384, 386
Belgium, 119, 353
benefits, 473, 489
big data, 81, 271, 322–324, 390
 employment decisions, 167–169
 HR applications, 323–324
 risks, 323
Big Five personality traits, 267
Bill and Melinda Gates Foundation, 75
Bisignano, Frank, 204
bitcoins, as payment, 107
Blockbuster, 93
blockchain, 103, 557, 560–561
blue-collar work, 134
Brazil, 111, 119–120, 122, 125

Brexit, 123–124
British Commonwealth, 121, 123
Broadcom, 204
Buddhism, 247
Budweiser, 185
bullying, 510
bureaucratic organization
 characteristics of, 218
bureaucratic organizations, 217
burnout, 392, 457–458, 492
Bush administration, 164
business services, 103–104
Byrd, Robert, 177

Caesar's Casino, 324
California, 571
California Employment Development Department, 159
California Fair Pay Act (CFPA 2016), 165
Canada, 119, 330, 571
captive governance, 223
CareerBuilder.com, 331, 522–523
CareerCast.com, 393
career development, research on, 428–429
Caribbean, 121
Carney, John, 250
Carter, Jimmy, 177
Castlight Healthcare, 324
Caveon Security Insights, 306
cell phones, *See* smartphones
Center for Organizational Excellence's Psychologically Healthy Workplace Award (PHWA), 500
CEO-to-worker pay ratio, 193
Changing Nature of Work, The (Howard), 50
Charlottesville "Unite the Right" rally, 523
Cheney, Dick, 180
chief executive officers (CEOs), 388, 547
 compensation, 192, 196–197
 sources of value, 199
Chile, 111
China, 109, 111–112, 115–116, 118, 120, 124–125, 195, 202, 246, 284, 328, 346, 557
Christians, 247
Chrysler, 394
City Bank, 394
Civil Rights Act (1964), 27, 87, 156, 163, 249
Clinton administration, 179–180, 197
Clinton, Hillary, 181
"clopening," 474
clothing firms, 223
coaching, 353–354
Coalition of State Governments, 250
co-bots, 416
coerced labor, 49
college enrollment, 239
Columbia, 122

communication, 480
Compatible Time-Sharing System (CTSS), 71
compensation
 board of directors, 203
 CEOs, 196–197, 203
 effects of, 198
 employee relations, 200
 interpersonal interactions, 200
 investor-style effects, 202
 nonperformance-based, 197
 performance-based, 197
 shareholders, 203
 taxation of CEOs, 203
 vertical pay dispersion, 199–201
competencies, 325
 analytical competition competency, 302, 304
 core, 110, 117
 future work, 299–300
 social media pages, 311
 talent, 110
competency modeling, 307
 definition, 298
computerization, 149, *See also* automation
 history of, 70
 mid-level jobs, 134
computerized systems and demands on skills, 44
Conservation of Resources (COR) theory, 515
Continuous Quality Improvement, 498
contract work, 540
core self-evaluation (CSE), 305
corporate profits, 196
Corporate Social Responsibility (CSR), 587–599, 603
 external and internal stakeholders, 589
 partnerships, 603
corporations
 collaboration with start-ups, 219
Costa Rica, 119, 122
Costco, 203
Counterproductive Work Behaviors (CWB), 509–520
 definition of, 510
countries and cities
 ranking of, 104–105
Coursera, 602
coworking, 274, 283–286
 challenges, 285–286
 growth, 284
creative destruction, 320, 471
CRISPR, 555
cross-sectional data analysis, 8–9
cross-temporal meta-analysis (CTMA), 9–10
crowdsourcing, 78, 412–413
crowdwork, 57
customized HR policies, 25
 legal issues, 24–28
cyberattacks, 79
 education sector, 79

cyberbullying, 516–518, 521, 524
    anonymity, 517
cyber incivility, 514–516
cyberloafing, 88, 511–514, 519, 522, 524
    job satisfaction, 513
cybersecurity, 107, 518–520, 524
    saboteurs, 519
cyclical model of generations, 264
Czech Republic, 120

Dallas, 118
data journalism, 304, 310
da Vinci, Leonardo, 605
defined benefit, 194
defined contribution, 194
Deloitte, 308, 341
Department of Justice's (DOJ) Civil Right Division, 157
Deutsche Post DHL, 601
developmental systems theory, 427
Diane B. Allen Equal Pay Act (2018), 165
dice.com, 331
Dirksen, Everett, 176
Dominican Republic, 111, 122
dual labor market theory, 133

earbud coaching, 75
earnings polarization, 149, *See also* income inequality
    men, 147
    women, 147
Eastern Europe, 110, 112, 117, 122–123, 125
Eastman Kodak, 186
Ebay, 512
Ecole National d'Administration, 116
education
    earnings, 251
    reform, 572
    relative attainment, 139
    systems
        US, 107
        world, 108
Egypt, 120
electronic performance monitoring (EPM), 80
email, 514–516
EMC Corp., 323
emotional intelligence (EI), 304
emotion regulation processes, 430
empathy, 304
employee compensation
    employment status, 196
employee-driven innovation programs, 281
employee engagement, 447
    definition, 609
Employee Free Choice Act (EFCA), 180
employee health, 489
employee retention, 494
encryption, 79–80, 91

engineers
    transactional, 120
enterprise resource planning (ERP), 113
environmental (E), social (S), and governance (G) (ESG) scorecards, 599
episodic memory, 432
equal employment opportunity, 162
Equal Employment Opportunity Commission (EEOC), 157, 163, 167, 369, 389
Equal Pay Act (1963), 157, 165
Equal Pay Act (2018), 165
Equal Pay Opportunity Act (2018), 165
equal work, 165
equity theory, 201
equivalized household incomes, 136
Ernst & Young, 250
Esposito, Lauren, 184
Estonia, 111, 117
ethical-based theories, 395
Europe, 124, 395
    high tech, 119
European Union, 56, 114, 123, 215
    temporary staffing agencies, 540
Evans, Oliver, 70
Every Student Succeeds Act (2015), 109
exit interviews, 334
expatriate career assignment, 470
experienced workers
    downsides, 76
exponential technologies, 556, 559, 570, 574–575

Facebook, 321, 330, 333
Fair Labor Standards Act (FLSA 1938), 155–156, 158–159, 161
family, 468–469
Federal Aviation Administration, 177
Federal Civil Service Reform Act (1978), 178
FedEx, 199–200
Feedback Environment Scale, 352
feedback orientation
    and age, 432
Fiat, 394
film industry, 228
Fink, Gary, 177
Finland, 111, 117, 119, 571
Finnish youth, 428
firms
    small and medium-sized, 220
First Data, 204
first job assignment, 333
flexibility, 475–478, 489, 491, 494–496, 540
flexible leadership theory, 385
flexible working arrangements (FWAs), 495
flexpatriation, 470
flexspace, 275
flextime, 279–281, 480, 495
forced distribution rating systems (FDRS), 350

Ford, Gerald, 177
Fortune 500 companies, 5, 238, 249, 329, 350, 388
Fortune 1,000 companies, 250
France, 119
freelancers, 282, 286
Friedman, Tom, 326, 395
future-oriented technology analysis (FTA), 563

gamification and learning, 82–83
garment industry, 230
gender and sexual minorities
    companies and nondiscrimination policies, 249
    lack of protection, 249
general AI, 90, 92
general mental ability (GMA), 301–305, 309
General Motors, 173, 176
General Social Survey, 270, 536, 542
generational differences, 20–22, 328, 425, 434
    age effects, 262
    as good business practice, 24
    big data, 271
    birth cohort, 265
    business practices, 29–31
    capitalize on generational stregnths, 31–33
    changes in personality, 267
    conflict and, 26
    culture, 34
    economic models, 265
    goals, 29
    immigration, 269
    job satisfaction, 456
    legality of making employment decisions based on, 24
    lifespan developmental perspective, 32, 426–437
    life stage, 387–388
    no change model, 265
    occupational commitment, 454
    personality, 268–269
    regarding organizations, 268
    rising extrinsic individualism model, 264
    self-expressive liberation model, 265
    skepticism, 21, 34, 261, 434
    social constructionism perspective, 425
    validity, 24
generational strengths, capitalizing on, 26
generations
    defining, 261
Generation X, 261, 264, 269, 387, 472
Generation Y, 472
Generation Z, 262
genomics, 557
Germany, 119, 223, 435
gig economy, 56–57, 59, 158–159, 282, 297, 393–394, 413, 469, 480, 493, 568
GI Generation, 264
gig project management, 302

glass ceiling, 239
Glassdoor.com, 167, 297, 309–310, 331, 611
Global Compact (United Nations), 583, 592, 599, 611
global financial crisis. *See* Great Recession
globalization, 101–102, 194, 222, 325–327, 368, 394, 584
    cross-cultural training, 369
    labor markets, 326
    leadership behaviors, 386
    recruitment, 331
Global Organizational Learning and Development Network (GOLDEN), 599, 602
global services economy, 103
global workforce
    cultural diversity, 112
    demographic diversity, 112
goal-oriented system, 29
Goel, Ashok, 85
Google, 90, 281, 323, 394, 413, 543, 555
    Hangouts, 391
    Maps, 413
    News, 413
Gorsuch, Niel, 182
Go to Meeting, 391
GPS and employees, 81
Great Depression, 435
Great Recession, 145, 251, 265, 267, 282
Greenhouse, 330
guanxi, 46
Guatemala, 122

Haier, 281
healthcare
    industry, 78, 89
    insurance coverage, 194, 197
Hierarchical Age–Period–Cohort model (HAPC), 9, 263
hierarchies, 371, 451–452, 454–455
high sales tournament reward dispersion, 201
high-skilled workers, 214, 369
high-tech jobs, 103
high technology, 120
Hinduism, 247
Hispanics, 142–144, 150, 240, 246, 252, 327, 389, 545
history-based cohorts, 32
H1B visas, 107
Hong Kong, 119
household tasks, 449
HR policies
    legal issues, 24–28
HR systems, 307
Human Development Index, 584
humanitarian work psychology (HWP), 611
Human Resource Information Systems (HRIS), 324–325, 331

human resource management (HRM), 608
Hungary, 117

IBM, 109
   ACE, 352
   Kenexa BrassRing, 330
   Watson, 330
iCliniq, 80
Idealist.com, 331
iGen, 270
immersion, 82
immigration, 241, 246–247, 269, 327, 470
Immigration and Nationality Services Act, 247
Incline Village, 118
income
   decline in, 145
income inequality, 147, 547–548, 585
   causes, 194–195
   performance vs tenure, 195
   ramifications, 192
Indeed.com, 309, 331
independent contractors, 158, 196, 199, 228, 538–540
India, 109, 111–113, 116, 118, 120–125, 246, 425
Indian diaspora, 117, 123
individual differences
   influences on, 435–436
individualism, 268
Individuals with Disabilities (IWDs), 324
   diminished expectations, 250
   labor participation rates, 249
information and communication technologies (ICT), 509
information technology (IT), 45, 117–119
innovation, 393
Institute of Technology – Bombay, 116
Intendis, 394
Internal Revenue Code, 197
Internal Revenue Service (IRS), 538
international assignment, 475
international careers, 476
international work assignments, 470
Internet (at work), 514
Internet of Things, 81
   education industry, 82
   environment, 89
interpersonal interactions, 88
Interpersonal Reactivity Index, 304
interpersonal skills, 451
intersectionality theory, 252
intraindividual plasticity, 433
I-O psychology, 4–5, 160, 274, 298, 608–610
IPUMS, 135–136, 140, 143, 153
Ireland, 121
   Silicon Bog, 119
IRS, 159
Israel, 120, 125

Istanbul International Center for the Private Sector in Development (IICPSD), 583–601, 611

Jamaica, 121
Japan, 48, 119, 122
JD Edwards, 276
job complexity, 433
   cognitive function, and, 433
job crafting, 44, 433
   older workers, 442
Job Demands–Resources model (JD-R), 491–492
job hopping, 113, 374–375, 544–547
job insecurity, 455–456, 541–544
job satisfaction, 455–456, 472, 517
   cyberloafing, 513
Jobs Openings and Labor Turnover Survey (JOLTS), 545
Jobster, 321
job switching, 113
Johnson, Lyndon, 176, 247
Jordan, 602

Keynes, Maynard, 558
knowledge clusters, 104, 109, 112, 120
knowledge, skills, abilities, and other characteristics (KSAOs), 297
knowledge, skills, and abilities (KSAs), 307, 365, 431, 450–451
   innovation, 370
   training, 365–367
knowledge transfer, 302
knowledge workers, 101, 274, 393, 450, 471, 476
   hiring time, 297
Koch Foods poultry plant, 200
Korea, 118
Kurzweil, Ray, 90

labor
   deregulation of, 46
   force, *See* workforce
   participation, 573–574
   saving technologies, 557
Labor Law Revision Bill (1978), 177
Labor's Rehabilitation Act (2014), 250
Las Vegas shooting, 408–410
Latin America, 110
layoffs, 194, 452, 454
leadership, 610
   behaviors, 278, 304, 383–386, 397–398, 400
   conceptual skills, 396–397
   distinguishing leaders, 395
   extraversion, 396
   followers, 398
   integrative perspective, 429
   interpersonal skills, 396–397

leadership (cont.)
    lifelong perspective, 429–430
    openness, 396
    shared or distributed forms, 414
    task-oriented behaviors, 398
    teams managed by team members, 414–415
    technical skills, 396
    training, 374
leading generations differently, 25
lean production, 498–499
learning workers, 101
Lee Kwan Yu, 112
Lee Valley Tools, 203
Lemonade, 606–607
Lewis, John L., 175
lifespan perspective, 33, 435
    history of, 426
    socioemotional selectivity, 430
Lilly Ledbetter Fair Pay Act (2009), 164
LinkedIn, 167, 321, 323–324, 329, 331
LinkUp.com, 331
logistics, 111
logistics industry, 228
London, City of, 123
longitudinal diary study, 399
longitudinal field experiment, 399
Looking Backward: 1889–2000 (Bellamy), 186
Lost Generation, 264
lower agreeableness, 435
low-skilled workers, 214
loyalty, 55
Luddite movement, 557
Lycos Europe, 394
Lydenherg, Domini & Co. Company Profiles, 200
Lyft, 159
Lynch, Loretta, 254

machine learning, 573
Madeira Global, 599
Magenta, 543
Malaysia, 119
Malta, 111
managerial power theory, 198–201
manned–unmanned teams (MUM-Ts), 415–416
Manning, Chelsea, 518
Mansfield, Mike, 176
March Madness, 511
market- or market-like mechanisms
    penetration of workplace, 219
Martin, Harold Thomas, 518
Marx, Karl, 133
Maryland Equal Pay for Equal Work Act (2016), 165
Massachusetts Institute of Technology, 116
Massive Open Online Courses (MOOCs), 106, 371, 373, 602

mathematics, 116
Mauritius, 111
Mayer, Marissa, 391
McDonald's, 184
Meany, George, 176
Mechanical Turk, 569
Mexico, 122, 246
Microbe Invader, 83
Microsoft, 109, 539
Millennials, 21, 35, 248, 261–262, 264, 267–270, 373, 387, 473, 477
Millennium Development Goals (MDGs), 583
Miller Analogies Test, 303
Miller, George, 180
minimum wage, 156, 158
minorities, 332, 389, 455, *See also* African Americans; Asians; Hispanics
Modern Species, 597–598
modular governance, 222–223
monitoring
    tool, 522
    workplace, 521–522
Monster.com, 331
Moore's Law, 72, 75, 91, 559
Morgan, J. P., 202
multinational corporations, 326, 345, 354
multiple-linkage model, 385
multiteam systems, 408–409
Musk, Elon, 92
Muslims, 247

nanotechnology, 89–90, 124, 557
narrow AI, 90
NASA, 559
National Collegiate Athletic Association (NCAA), 511
National Labor Relations Act (Wagner 1935), 164, 174
National Labor Relations Board, 183–184
National Right to Work Legal Defense Foundation (2016), 182
nature of work changes
    skepticism, 43
naval engineering, 120
Netherlands, 119
network governance
    allocating, 224
    evaluating, 224
    regulating, 224
    selecting network participants, 224
network management perspective, 224
Neuberg, Brad, 283
neuroticism, 435
Nevada, 118, 408–410
New York Achieves Fair Pay (2016), 165
New York City, 124
New Zealanders, 353
Nicaragua, 122

Index

NIOSH concept, 490–491, 501
Nixon, Richard, 176
No Child Left Behind Act (2001), 109
non-employee workers, 158
nonfarm workforce, 47
nonperformance-based compensation, 197
Northrop Grumman, 250
Norway, 120

O*Net variables, 563, 566
Obama administration, 164, 180–181
Obama, Barack, 180
occupational health, 276
Occupational Health Psychology (OHP), 490–492
occupational injuries, 489
Occupy Wall Street movement, 547
Office of Federal Contracts Compliance Programs (OFCCP), 157, 164
Office of Personnel Management (OPM), 520
offshore manufacturing, 103
off the clock
　liability issues, 161
　remote employees, 161
older workers, 269, 430, 438, 472
　job crafting, 442
　training, 369, 373
One Planet Network, 602
online assessments, 309
online job sites, 331, *See also* Glassdoor.com; Indeed.com; LinkedIn
OpenAI, 92
open source, 78
opportunities for advancement, 481
Oregon Equal Pay Act (2017), 165
O'Reilly, Tim, 92
organizational behavior (OB), 608
organizational commitment (OC), 453–454
organizational justice, 455
organizational pay dispersion, 193
organizational support theory, 533–534
organizational survey design, 610
Otto (unmanned tractor trailer), 185
outsourcing, 110, 122, 220–222, 229, 327
　engineering, 120
　IT, 118

Panama, 122
P&G, 281
partial organization, 228–229
part-time employment, 58, 481, 495
　definition, 537
pay-for-performance, 194
pay gap, 389
perceived organizational support (POS), 453, 533, 535–536, 538, 544, 546, 548
performance appraisal (PA), 341

performance management (PM)
　coaching, 342
　contract workers, 355
　definition, 340
　employee participation, 351–352
　feedback environment, 352
　feedback orientation, 353–354
　globalization, 353
　individuals, 343
　inputs, 343, 345, 348
　national culture, 346
　nonprofit sector, 347
　organizational culture, 347
　organizational needs, 340
　outputs, 344
　performance appraisal (PA), 341
　private organizations, 346
　processes, 343, 349–353
　rating sources, 351
　strategy, 348
　systems-based model, 343
　tasks, 343
　team-based approaches, 350
　unions, 347
performance-based compensation, 197
performance ratings, 342
personality development, models of, 435
personalizable tools, 76
person–environment fit, 431, 433, 435
Philippines, 121
physical injury prevention, 490
planned behavior (TPB), theory of, 512
Plato, 202
Poland, 120
pop musicians, 428
portfolio workers, 228
post-bureaucratic organizations, 215, 217–220
　characteristics of, 218
post-industrial economy, 47
Postmates, 159
Premier, US healthcare alliance network, 72
prisoner's dilemma game, 199
privacy rights, 168
production line, continuous, 70
Professional Air Traffic Controllers Organization (PATCO), 177
Program for International Student Assessment, 105
Programme for the International Assessment of Adult competencies, 52
project-based organizations (PBOs), 219, 226–227
project-based work, 281
　horizontal authority, 227
project-citizenship behavior, 227
project network (PNW), 226
project-supported organizations (PSOs), 226–227

protean career orientation (PCO), 478
Protestant Relational Ideology, 46
psychological contracts, 454, 538, 544
    theory, 534
psychological disorder prevention, 491
psychological health promotion, 491
Puerto Rico Equal Pay Act (2017), 165
pymetrics, 598
Python (software), 167

quality of life, 113, 116
quantum computing, 557

Reagan administration, 177–178
Reagan, Ronald, 187
realistic job previews (RJPs), 333
real simple syndication (RSS), 331
real-time locating systems (RTLS), 81
recruitment
    globalization, 331
Reddit, 512
relatedness, 325
relational governance, 222–223
relative deprivation theory, 201
religious conflict, prevention, 248
remote work, 88, 275–279, 318, 390–392, 474, 477, 479
    downsides, 283, 391
    15-hour mark, 279
    lack of face time, 278
    loyalty, 278
Research Triangle, North Carolina, 118
results-only work environment (ROWE), 280
retention, 277, 309, 332–334
Reuther, Walter, 176
right-to-work laws, 173, 176
robotics, 557
Rometty, Ginny, 320
Roosevelt, Franklin D., 173
Russia, 117, 120, 123

school-to-work transitions, 435
Seattle–Portland, 118
selection tests, 309
    face validity, 310
    litigation, 310
self-determination theory, 325
self-driving car, 91
self-employed workers, 59
self-esteem, 435
self-management skills, 451
Senior Citizens Freedom to Work Act, 243
sensemaking prediction, 302
Sermo, 78
servant leadership theory, 395
service jobs
    service-oriented careers, 239

shareholders, 196–197, 203, 319, 469
    executive compensation, 203
    returns, 196
    value movement, 195
Shavelson, Clara Lemlich, 588
Silent Generation, 270
Silicon Valley, 107, 109, 118
SimplyHired.com, 331
simSchool, 83
Singapore, 119–120, 125
situational judgment tests (SJTs), 302–303, 305
Skype, 391
sleepiness, 495
smart glasses, 76
Smart Micromanipulation Aided Robotic-surgical Tool (SMART), 77
smartphones, 75, 81, 262, 496, 498, 513–514, 522, 559
SmartRecruiters, 330
smartwatches, 76
Snowden, Edward, 518
social engineering, 520
social entrepreneurship, 304
social exchange theory, 533
social insurance, 473
social media
    changes in work, 321–322
    content and employee screening, 311
    employee uses, 321
    recruitment, 329–330
    risks, 322
Social Responsibilities (SR). *See* Corporate Social Responsibilities (CSR)
Social Security, 243
Society for Human Resource Management, 184
soft skills, 308, 371
software-as-a-service (SAAS) systems, 324
South Africa, 111, 120
South Korea, 120
Spain, 119
spiritual leadership theory, 395
staffing decision making, 609
Starbucks, 250
start-ups, 107
STEM (science, technology, engineering, and math), 569–570
stress, 456–457, 471, 473–476, 480, 489, 496, 516, *See also* burnout
supplemental work, 448
Survey of Income and Program Participation (SIPP), 144
Sustainable Development Goals (SDGs), 590, 606
    criticism of private sector as strategic partner, 592–597, *See also* Corporate Social Responsibilities (CSR)
Sustainable Enterprise Model Innovations Labs, 602

Sweden, 48
Switzerland, 117

Taft–Hartley Act (1935, 1947), 173, 175–176
Taiwan, 119–120
talent
  clusters, 109
  competencies, 110
  scalability, 110
Tan, Hock, 204
Taskrabbit, 493
tasks, duties, and responsibilities (TDRs), 298
Teach for America, 75
TeachLivE™, 84
team cognition, 417
teamwork, 374, 451–452, 604, 611
  balancing human robot relations, 417
  behavioral processes, 406
  composition, 410
  importance of, 406–407
  managing, 408, 411, 414–415, 417–418
  multiteam membership, 410
  skills, 371
  socialization processes, 411
  standardization, 411
  stress perceptions, 457
technology
  creative destruction, 320
  displacement of jobs, 44
  downsides, 392
  effects on employees, 447
  managing team, 417–418
  work–life balance, 448
Technology Acceptance Model (TAM), 86, 605
technostress, 497
telemedicine, 78
telepressure, 497
television industry, 228
telework, 480
teleworkers, 276–279, 474, 479, 513
temporary employment, 226, 228, 537, *See also* part-time employment
temporary organizations, 225–228
temporary staffing agency, 58, 194, 228, 540
Textio, 598
Thailand, 120
TheJobCrowd.com, 331
theory of planned behavior (TPB), 512
3-D printing, 557
3M, 281
Title VIIII. *See* Civil Rights Act (CRA 1964)
Tokyo, 124
Total Quality Management (TQM), 341, 498
Total Worker Health, 501–502
tournament theory, 201
Toyota Production System, 498

training, 399, 570–571, 592, 610
  effective learning, 366
  gamification, 372
  KSAs, 365–367
  microlearning, 372
  MOOCs, 371
  motivation, 366
  older workers, 369, 373
  retraining low-skilled workers, 369
  technology, 372
Treasure Fleet, 558
Truman administration, 175
Truman, Harry, 175
Trump administration, 174, 181–185
Trump, Donald, 187
turnover, 517
24/7 work, 276

Uber, 159, 185, 282, 413, 475, 493, 569
uberization. *See* gig economy
UN Environment Programme, 602
unethical pro-organizational behavior (UPB), 521
UN Global Compact (United Nations), 601
UNICEF, 601
Unified Theory of Acceptance and Use of Technology (UTAUT), 605
Uniform Guidelines on Employee Selection Procedures, 168, 310
Unilever
  Sustainable Living Plan, 591–592
unions, 48
  American politics, 174–179
  auto sector, 173
  decline of, 174, 187, 195
  membership, 173, 187, 195
United Auto Workers (UAW), 173, 176
United Kingdom, 121
  pay gap, 166
  Silicon Corridor, 119
  Silicon Fen, 119
  Silicon Glen, 119
United States, 121, 124–125, 132, 155–168, 214, 328, 330, 369, 395, 425, 435, 451, 476, 489, 539–540, 542, 558
  Army, 415
  Bureau of Labor Statistics (BLS), 237
  changing demographics and generational chamge, 268
  Department of Justice, 157
  Department of Labor, 57, 156, 159
  economic inequality, 133
  economy, 49, 131
  education institutions, 118
  employment, 46
  future demnd for skills, 565

United States (cont.)
  higher education institutions, 107
  immigration policy, 107–108
  knowledge base, 107–109
  manufacturing, 195
  middle class, 251
  Supreme Court, 175
  training programs, 365
  workforce, 47, 237–254
  workplace
    changes in, 51–55
universal basic income, 571, 574
UN Sustainable Development Goals (SDGs), 583–587
Upwork, 569
Uruguay, 122

Valve (video game company), 282
vertical pay dispersion, 201, 203
video-based interviews, 309
Vietnam, 116
virtual reality (VR), 83–84
vocational
  interests, 302, 304, 436
Volkswagen, 498
Volvo, 48

wages. *See* income inequality
wage stagnation, 192, 198, 203
  effects of, 201
  government policy, 192
Wal-Mart, 324
Watson (IBM), 85
wellness programs, 500–501
Wells Fargo, 308
Wellworks-2 program, 501
Western Europe, 117, 214
white collar work, 134
Wipro Technologies, 109
women in the workforce, 47, 136, 139, 145, 156, 196, 244, 252, 328, 332, 353, 388, 449, 467
  American, 238–239
  education level, 141–142
  increasing participation, 238
  lack of ladder, 186
  pay equity, 162–167
  pay gap, 238–239
  polarization of wages, 147
  service-oriented careers, 239
  training, 592
women in the workplace
  access for, 113–115
Wonderlic test, 303
work at home, 78, 92, 276–279, 476, *See also* remote work
work-based projects
  employment, 226

worker demands
  autonomy, 274
  flexibility, 275
worker education levels
  BA, 139
  graduate degree, 141
  some college, 141
  without a high school degree (LTHS), 139–143
workforce, 332, *See also* aging workforce, management of; women in the workforce
  age, 242–243, 327–328, 387, 425
  aging, 242–243
  American Indian/Alaska Native, 241
  Asians, 240, 246
  Black/African Americans, 240, 332, 389
  Black and Hispanic women, 252
  Black immigration, 246
  children and marriage, 244–245
  decrease in employee tenure, 195
  discrimination, 156–157
  diversity, 253, 327–328, 388–389, 395, 448
  education, 242, 451
    earnings, 251
  gender, 238–239
  globalization, 101
  higher education levels, 251
  Hispanics, 240, 389
  hollowing out by ethnic group, 142–144
  immigration, 246–247
  increase in negative perceptions, 459
  intersectionality, 252
  men and education, 252
  mental abilities of older workers, 431
  motivation, 427
  multiracial individuals, 245–246
  Native Hawaiian/other Pacific Islander, 241
  non-Hispanic white, 241
  occupational change, 145, 449–450
  older workers, 430, 438
  participation, 14, 237
  participation rates
    by race, 241
    economic class and, 251
    women, 239
  race, 240–241, 389
  racial differentials, 150
  religious minorities, 247–248
  self-employed, 158
  talent gap, 327
  United States, 237–254, 327, 558
  White immigrants, 246
  women, 467
work–life balance, 392, 474–475, 478–480
  conflict, 468
  enrichment, 468

work–nonwork decisions, 478–481
work outcomes, 437
　issues that effect, 434
workplace
　monitoring, 521–522
　technologies
　　going green, 89
　　history of, 70–86
　　miniaturization, 75
　work space, 573
world cities, ranking of, 105
world economy, 584

World Is Flat, The (Friedman), 394

Xiaomi Corp, 202

Yahoo, 391
Yammer, 321
YouTube, 321, 512
　performers, 55

zero hours contracts, 57
Zooniverse, 412–413
Zynga, 323

Lightning Source UK Ltd.
Milton Keynes UK
UKHW050251300820
369051UK00008B/25

9 781108 417631